Religious Rites of War beyond the Medieval West

Volume 1

Explorations in Medieval Culture

General Editor

Larissa Tracy (*Longwood University*)

Editorial Board

Tina Boyer (*Wake Forest University*)
Emma Campbell (*University of Warwick*)
Kelly DeVries (*Loyola Maryland*)
David F. Johnson (*Florida State University*)
Asa Simon Mittman (*CSU, Chico*)
Thea Tomaini (*USC, Los Angeles*)
Wendy Turner (*Augusta University*)
David Wacks (*University of Oregon*)
Renée Ward (*University of Lincoln*)

VOLUME 24/1

The titles published in this series are listed at *brill.com/emc*

Religious Rites of War beyond the Medieval West

Volume 1
Northern Europe and the Baltic

Edited by

Radosław Kotecki
Jacek Maciejewski
Gregory Leighton

BRILL

LEIDEN | BOSTON

Cover illustration: St. Olav altar frontal. Section one / first scene. King Olav of Norway makes a generous money offering to the clergyman while marching to war against the pagans. Trondheim, Nidaros Cathedral(?), ca. 1300. Now in Archbishop's Palace Museum in Trondheim. With kind permission of © Daniela Pawel, The Restoration Workshop of Nidaros Cathedral.

Library of Congress Cataloging-in-Publication Data

Names: Kotecki, Radosław, editor. | Maciejewski, Jacek, editor. | Leighton, Gregory, editor.
Title: Religious rites of war beyond the medieval West / edited by Radosław Kotecki, Jacek Maciejewski, Gregory Leighton.
Description: Leiden ; Boston : Brill, [2023] | Series: Explorations in medieval culture, 2352-0299 ; volume 24 | Includes bibliographical references and index. |
Contents: Volume 1. Northern Europe and the Baltic—Volume 2. Central and Eastern Europe.
Identifiers: LCCN 2023036478 (print) | LCCN 2023036479 (ebook) |
   ISBN 9789004683426 (set ; hardback) | ISBN 9789004683402 (v. 1 ; hardback) |
   ISBN 9789004683419 (v. 2 ; hardback) | ISBN 9789004686366 (v. 1 ; ebook) |
   ISBN 9789004686373 (v. 2 ; ebook)
Subjects: LCSH: Military history, Medieval. | War—Religious aspects—Christianity. | Christianity and politics—Europe—History—To 1500. | Church and state--Europe—History—To 1500. | Church history—Middle Ages, 600–1500. | Europe—History, Military.
Classification: LCC D128 .R45 2023 (print) | LCC D128 (ebook) |
   DDC 355.009/02—dc23/ENG/20230831
LC record available at https://lccn.loc.gov/2023036478
LC ebook record available at https://lccn.loc.gov/2023036479

Typeface for the Latin, Greek, and Cyrillic scripts: "Brill". See and download: brill.com/brill-typeface.

ISSN 2352-0299
ISBN 978-90-04-68342-6 (set)
ISBN 978-90-04-68340-2 (hardback, vol. 1)
ISBN 978-90-04-68636-6 (e-book, vol. 1)
ISBN 978-90-04-68341-9 (hardback, vol. 2)
ISBN 978-90-04-68637-3 (e-book, vol. 2)
DOI 10.1163/9789004686366

Copyright 2023 by Koninklijke Brill NV, Leiden, The Netherlands.
Koninklijke Brill NV incorporates the imprints Brill, Brill Nijhoff, Brill Schöningh, Brill Fink, Brill mentis, Brill Wageningen Academic, Vandenhoeck & Ruprecht, Böhlau and V&R unipress.
All rights reserved. No part of this publication may be reproduced, translated, stored in a retrieval system, or transmitted in any form or by any means, electronic, mechanical, photocopying, recording or otherwise, without prior written permission from the publisher. Requests for re-use and/or translations must be addressed to Koninklijke Brill NV via brill.com or copyright.com.

This book is printed on acid-free paper and produced in a sustainable manner.

Contents

List of Figures and Maps   VII
List of Abbreviations   IX
Notes on Contributors   XII

Introduction

1 Religious Rites of War beyond the Medieval West: An Introduction   3
 Gregory Leighton

2 Fighting on a Prayer: Liturgical and Physical Engagement of Sacralized Warfighting in High Medieval Latin Christendom, ca. 1000–1250   30
 Kyle C. Lincoln

Northern Europe and the Baltic

3 Battle Psalms and War Liturgy in the Medieval Gaelic World and Its Neighbors before 1200   71
 Jesse Patrick Harrington

4 Religious Rites and Integrated Warfare in Civil War Era Norway (1130–1240)   117
 Max Naderer

5 Religiosity and Religious Rituals in the Battle of Bannockburn, 1314   153
 Robert Bubczyk

6 Invocations by Knights for Supernatural Aid in the Sources of the Baltic Crusades, Medieval Poland and the *Chansons* of the Crusades   189
 Sini Kangas

7 Rituals of War as Religious Markers during the Early Crusades in Livonia and Estonia in the Light of Henry's *Chronicon Livoniae*   231
 Carsten Selch Jensen

8 "Devotis oracionibus plusquam gladiis": Rituals and Sacralization of
Warfare in the Teutonic Order's Prussian Lands   260
   Gregory Leighton

Index   297

Figures and Maps

Figures

2.1 The Abbey of Santa María la Real de Las Huelgas in Burgos, Spain. A mural depicting the Battle of Las Navas de Tolosa (1212) by Pedro Ruiz de Camargo, ca. 1600. Christian army is led by the Canon Domingo Pascual with an archiepiscopal cross, Archbishop Rodrigo Jiménez de Rada of Toledo advises the King Alfonso VIII of Castile from the second line of the battle. Two Christian banners are prominently displayed, a banner with the image of the Blessed Virgin Mary, patroness of Toledo and all of Spain, and one depicting Christ on the Cross   38

2.2a–b The Abbey of Santa María de Huerta, Spain. Murals above the tomb of Archbishop Rodrigo Jiménez de Rada of Toledo by Bartolomé Matarana (ca. 1580) depicting scenes from the Battle of Las Navas de Tolosa (1212). a) field mass celebrated by Archbishop Rodrigo for the Christian army before the battle; b) the battle scene: Domingo Pascual with an archiepiscopal cross in the first line is followed by Archbishop Rodrigo and King Alfonso VIII of Castile. Toledan banner with the image of the Blessed Virgin Mary is visible in the background   39

3.1 The portable reliquary shrine of *An Cathach* ("The Battler"), an early medieval psalter and one of many relics traditionally associated with the sixth-century abbot and "warrior saint" Columba. This psalter is by far the most celebrated of the relic-standards known to have been used in war in the Gaelic world. National Museum of Ireland   90

3.2 The Monymusk Reliquary, an eighth-century reliquary made of wood covered in bronze and silver plates with enameled bronze mounts, possibly similar to other reliquaries carried on campaigns in the medieval Gaelic world. This reliquary was formerly identified with the *Brecbennach*, though there is little to substantiate the conjecture. National Museum of Scotland   92

3.3 The Cross of Cong, an Irish ornamented processional cross crafted ca. 1123 for Tairdelbach Ua Conchobair, king of Connacht (r. 1106–1156), to contain a relic of the True Cross. Front view. National Museum of Ireland   95

3.4 The Cross of Cong close up. Back view. A piece of the wood inside is believed to be a relic of the True Cross. National Museum of Ireland   96

6.1 Blessed Czesław defending Wrocław from Mongols in 1241. Copperplate print from Dominicus Frydrychowicz's *S. Hyacinthvs Odrovasivs* … (Cracow: Typis Universitatis, 1688), 194   211

8.1a–b Reliquary of Tilo of Lorich, probably taken as booty by the Polish king Władysław Jagiełło after the Battle of Grunwald/Tannenberg (1410) and given to Gniezno Cathedral   273

Maps

0.1   Map of Northern Europe and the Baltic depicting major locations appearing in the volume   XVI

Abbreviations

Titles of series and journals without further explanation

APH	*Acta Poloniae Historica.*
BF	Beihefte der Francia.
CB	Crossing boundaries: Turku medieval and early modern studies.
CCCM	Corpus Christianorum. Continuatio Mediaevalis, 301 vols. (Turnhout: Brepols, 1966–).
CEMT	Central European medieval texts.
ChH	*Church History.*
CHR	*Catholic Historical Review.*
Commentaria	Commentaria: Sacred texts and their commentaries. Jewish, Christian and Islamic
CSML	Cambridge studies in medieval life and thought.
CTT	Crusade texts in translation.
DHIW	Deutsches Historisches Institut Warschau. Quellen und Studien.
Dusburg, *Chron. Pr.*	*"Chronicon terre Prussie" von Peter von Dusburg*, ed. Max Töppen, SrP 1 (Leipzig: Hirzel, 1861), 3–219.
ECEE	East Central and Eastern Europe in the Middle Ages, 450–1450.
EMC	Explorations in medieval culture.
FKG	Forschungen zur Kirchen- und Geistegeschichte.
FQKK	Forschungen und Quellen zur Kirchen- und Kulturgeschichte Ostdeutschlands.
FS	*Frühmittelalterliche Studien.*
Gallus, *Gesta*	Gallus Anonymus, *Gesta principum Polonorum*, ed., trans., and ann. Paul W. Knoll and Frank Schaer, CEMT 3 (Budapest and New York: Central European University Press, 2003).
Henry, *Chron. Liv.*	Henry of Livonia, *Chronicon Livoniae*, ed. Leonid Arbusow and Albert Bauer, MGH SS rer. Germ. 31 (Hannover: Hahn, 1955).
HSJ	*Haskins Society Journal.*
HT	*Historisk Tidsskrift* (Norway).
IR	*Innes Review.*
JEH	*Journal of Ecclesiastical History.*

Jeroschin, *Di Kronike*	Nicolaus von Jeroschin, *Di Kronike von Pruzinlant des Nicolaus v. Jeroschin*, ed. Ernst Strehlke, SrP 1 (Leipzig: Hirzel, 1861), 303–624.
JMH	*Journal of Medieval History*.
JMIS	*Journal of Medieval Iberian Studies*.
JMMH	*Journal of Medieval Military History*.
JRSAI	*Journal of the Royal Society of Antiquaries of Ireland*.
KG	*Krieg in der Geschichte*.
KH	*Kwartalnik Historyczny*.
MCS	Medieval Church studies.
MEMI	The medieval and early modern Iberian world.
MGH	Monumenta Germaniae Historica.
MGH SS	MGH Scriptores (in folio), 39 vols. (Hannover and Leipzig: Hahn and Hiersemann, 1826–2009).
MGH SS rer. Germ.	MGH Scriptores rerum Germanicarum in usum scholarum separatim editi, 81 vols. (Berlin, Hannover, Leipzig, and Wiesbaden: Hahn, Weidmann, and Harrassowitz, 1846–).
MMED	The medieval Mediterranean: peoples, economies and cultures, 400–1500.
MPH NS	Monumenta Poloniae Historiaca. Nova series, 16 vols. (Cracow and Warsaw: Polska Akademia Umiejętności and Państwowe Wydawnictwo Naukowe, 1946–).
MTCN	Medieval texts and cultures of Northern Europe.
OFCC	The Old French crusade cycle.
OFVK	Otto-von-Freising-Vorlesungen der Katholischen Universität Eichstätt.
OM	Ordines Militares.
Outremer	Outremer: Studies in the Crusades and the Latin East.
PH	*Przegląd Historyczny*.
PL	Patrologiae cursus completus. Series Latina, ed. Jacques-Paul Migne, 221 vols. (Paris: Vrayet and Apud Editorem J.-P. Migne, 1841–1864).
QMAN	*Quaestiones Medii Aevi Novae*.
QSBG	Quellen und Studien zur baltischen Geschichte.
QSGD	Quellen und Studien zur Geschichte des Deutschen Ordens.
RHC HO	Recueil des Historiens des Croisades. Historiens Occidentaux, 5 vols. (Paris: Imprimerie Impériale, 1844–1895).
RHE	*Revue d'Histoire Ecclésiastique*.
RSC	*Rivista di storia del cristianesimo*.
RSS	*Religion, State and Society*.

SBS	Sacra bella septentrionalia.
SCelH	Studies in Celtic history.
SCH	*Studies in Church History.*
Sermo	Sermo: Studies on patristic, medieval, and Reformation sermons and preaching.
SHKK	Schriften des Historischen Kollegs. Kolloquien.
SMEM	Studies in medieval and early modern culture.
SrP	Scriptores rerum Prussicarum, ed. Theodor Hirsch, Max Töppen, and Ernst Strehlke, 5 vols. (Leipzig: Hirzel, 1861–1874).
Statuten	*Die Statuten des Deutschen Ordens nach den ältesten Handschriften*, ed. Max Perlbach (Halle: Niemeyer, 1890).
TKH OL PAN	*Teka Komisji Historycznej. Oddział Lubelski PAN.*
TMS	Transcultural medieval studies.
TNW	The Northern world.
VF	Vorträge und Forschungen.
VKSM	Veröffentlichungen aus dem Kirchenhistorischen Seminar München.
Wigand, *Cron. Prut.*	Wigand von Marburg, *Nowa kronika Pruska*, ed. Sławomir Zonenberg and Krzysztof Kwiatkowski (Toruń: Towarzystwo Naukowe w Toruniu, 2017).
ZfO	*Zeitschrift für Ostmitteleuropa-Forschung.*
ZH	*Zapiski Historyczne.*

Notes on Contributors

Robert Bubczyk | ORCID: 0000-0002-6592-5464
is Associate Professor of Medieval History in the Institute for Cultural Studies at Maria Curie-Skłodowska University (Lublin/Poland). He specializes in the cultural history of medieval elites. He is the author of three academic books, including the monograph, *Gry na szachownicy w kulturze dworskiej i rycerskiej średniowiecznej Anglii na tle europejskim* [Board games in the courtly and chivalric culture of medieval England in the European context] (Wydawnictwo Uniwersytetu Marii Curie-Skłodowskiej w Lublinie, 2009), where he investigates the role chess and other board games played in social and cultural life in medieval England and other European countries. Robert Bubczyk is also the author of over eighty other works, including chapters in monographs, articles and reviews, published in Polish and in English. In his works, Robert Bubczyk mainly focuses on various social and cultural aspects of leisure and entertainment of the representatives of medieval political and social elites, comprising the aristocracy and clergy. Robert Bubczyk is also interested in the lives of medieval secular clerics, their careers at aristocratic courts, views, travels and ethnographic observations which they included in their works. He has published several articles on different topics (e.g. criticism of worldly pleasures, curiosity of the medieval clerk, the other and otherness) discussed in the oeuvres by Henry of Huntingdon, Walter Map, and Gerald of Wales—twelfth-century clergymen, intellectuals and authors who served the Plantagenet dynasty in England. Among his recent articles are the following: "'Ludus inhonestus et illicitus?': Chess, Games, and the Church in Medieval Europe," in *Games and Gaming in Medieval Literature*, ed. Serina Patterson (Palgrave Macmillan, 2015), 23–43; "Values and Virtues: Church Life and Courtly Culture," in *Writing History in Medieval Poland: Bishop Vincentius of Cracow and the "Chronica Polonorum,"* ed. Darius von Güttner-Sporzyński, Cursor mundi 28 (Brepols, 2017), 221–42; "Sports and Games," in *A Cultural History of Leisure in the Medieval Age*, ed. Paul Milliman (Bloomsbury, forthc. 2023). Robert Bubczyk's current project entails stereotypical perceptions of the Welsh by English authors in the eleventh-thirteenth centuries.

Jesse Patrick Harrington | ORCID: 0000-0002-2766-5550
is Government of Ireland Postdoctoral Research Fellow (2021–2023), with the Irish National Institute for Historical Research and the School of History, University College Cork. He was previously based at the University of Cambridge, where he trained at the Faculty of History and the Department of Anglo-Saxon,

Norse, and Celtic, and where he earned his doctorate in History. He is a specialist in the literary and religious cultures of medieval Britain, France, Ireland, and the Mediterranean, with an emphasis on the hagiographical, historical, and homiletic writing of the tenth to thirteenth centuries, and a key interest in the classical and homiletic frameworks of medieval battle orations. His current project concerns the life, career, and afterlife of St. Lorcán Ua Tuathail, archbishop, legate, and peacemaker of the 1169 English invasion of Ireland. His recent research in medieval religious culture, history, and literature has been awarded the Griffiths Roman Prize (2018), the Irish Conference of Medievalists' Four Courts Press Donnchadh Ó Corráin Prize (2019), the Haskins Society's Dennis Bethell Prize (2020), the Scottish Society for Northern Studies' Magnus Magnusson Prize (2021), and Northern History's Gordon Forster Prize (2022).

Carsten Selch Jensen | ORCID: 0000-0002-1778-3078
is Professor in Church History and Dean at the Faculty of Theology, University of Copenhagen, Denmark. In his research, he has mainly focused on medieval history, especially the history and historiography of the Baltic Crusades. He has published many works on various aspects of the processes of Christianization and Crusading in the Baltic Region. The most recent of these include: *Fighting for the Faith—The Many Crusades*, ed. Kurt Villads Jensen, Carsten Selch Jensen and Janus Møller Jensen, Scripta minora 27 (Sällskapet Runica et Mediævalia, 2018); "The Lord's Vineyard: Henry of Livonia and the Danish conquest of Estonia," in *Denmark and Estonia 1219–2019. Studien zur Geschichte der Ostseeregion*, vol. 1, ed. Jens E. Olesen (Universität Greifswald, 2019) and "The Early Church of Livonia, 1186–c. 1255," in *Die Kirche im Mittelalterlichen Livland*, ed. Radosław Biskup, Johannes Götz, and Andrzej Radzimiński (Wydawnictwo Uniwersytetu Mikołaja Kopernika w Toruniu, 2019); "Religion and War in Saxo Grammaticus's 'Gesta Danorum': The Examples of Bishop Absalon and King Valdemar I," in *Christianity and War in Medieval East Central Europe and Scandinavia*, ed. Radosław Kotecki, Carsten Selch Jensen and Stephen Bennett (ARC Humanities, 2021), 189–206. Professor Jensen also has a forthcoming book *Through Words, not Weapons: Theology and History Writing in the Chronicle of Henry of Livonia (ca.1227)* (Brepols).

Sini Kangas | ORCID: 0000-0001-8630-8038
is Researcher at the Faculty of Social Sciences, Tampere University, Finland. Her work focuses on medieval ideological warfare and violence, the crusades, in addition to the history of childhood. Her recent publications include: "The Image of Warrior Bishops in the Northern Tradition of the Crusades," in *Christianity and War in Medieval East-Central Europe and Scandinavia: The*

Church at War, Religion in War, and Perceptions of War, ed. Radosław Kotecki, Carsten Selch Jensen, and Stephen Bennett (ARC Humanities, 2021), 57–73; "Scripture, Hierarchy, and Social Control: [The] Uses of the Bible in the Twelfth- and Thirteenth-Century Chronicles and Chansons of the Crusades," in *Transcultural Approaches to the Bible: Exegesis and Historical Writing in the Medieval Worlds*, ed. Matthias M. Tischler and Patrick S. Marschner, TMS 1 (Brepols, 2021), 109–44; "Slaughter of the Innocents and Depiction of Children in the Twelfth-Century Sources of the Crusades," in *The Uses of the Bible in Crusading Sources*, ed. Elizabeth Lapina and Nicholas Morton, Commentaria 7 (Brill, 2017), 74–101; and the monograph *Authorities in the Middle Ages: Influence, Legitimacy, and Power in Medieval Society* (De Gruyter, 2013), edited in collaboration with Mia Korpiola and Tuija Ainonen.

Gregory Leighton | ORCID: 0000-0002-4203-2313 was awarded his PhD in History from Cardiff University in April of 2019 and now he is NAWA-Ulam Postdoctoral Fellow in the Institute of History at Nicolaus Copernicus University in Toruń, Poland. His research interests are the Teutonic Order in the Baltic region, specifically Prussia. The relationship between crusading and landscape form his primary topics of specialty, in addition to concepts of the Teutonic Order's self-image, and its reception by the Order's supporters from the thirteenth to the fifteenth century. In 2022, Dr. Leighton published his first monograph, *Ideology and Holy Landscape in the Baltic Crusades* (ARC Humanities), which is based on the research for his PhD thesis. Besides, he has published in leading journals on the history of the Teutonic Order and crusading in Prussia. These include: "Did the Teutonic Order Create a Sacred Landscape in Thirteenth-Century Prussia?" *JMH* 44 (2018): 457–483; a collaborative article with Prof. Florin Curta (University of Florida), "Teutonic Hierotopy: St Christopher at Lochstedt," *Ephemeris Napociensis* 29 (2019): 127–164; "'Reysa in laudem Dei et virginis Marie contra paganos': The Experience of Crusading in Prussia during the Thirteenth and Fourteenth Centuries," *ZfO* 69 (2020): 1–25; "The Relics of St Barbara at Althaus Kulm: History, Patronages, and Insight into the Teutonic Order and the Christian Population in Prussia (Thirteenth–Fifteenth Centuries)," *ZH* 85 (2020): 5–50; "Military Order Castles in the Holy Land and Prussia: A Case for Cultural History," in *The Templars, the Hospitallers, and the Crusades: Essays in Homage to Alan J. Forey*, ed. Helen J. Nicholson and Jochen Burgtorf (Routledge, 2020), 167–82. He is currently on the editorial board of *Ordines Militares* (based at Nicolaus Copernicus University in Toruń, Poland), and is a contributor to the project headed by the Malbork Castle Museum, The Beautiful Style in Prussia: Stone Sculpture from 1380–1400. Visual culture, the roles of women in medieval Prussia, and pilgrimage are also topics of interest.

Kyle C. Lincoln | ORCID: 0000-0002-7473-6622
is Assistant Professor of Pre-Modern European History and Interdisciplinary Humanities at Southeastern Oklahoma State University. He co-edited *King Alfonso VIII: Government, Family, and War* (Fordham University Press, 2019), and has a forthcoming monograph, *A Constellation of Authority: Castilian Bishops and the Secular Church during the Reign of Alfonso VIII of Castile, c.1150–1225*, with Pennsylvania State University Press. His 2021 textbook co-authored with John Giebfried, *Remaking the Medieval World: The Fourth Crusade, 1204*, won several prizes and he is also currently revising two medieval studies textbook projects for the Reacting to the Past Consortium, on the Investiture Contest and the Conquest of Granada in 1492. His articles have appeared in the *Journal of Medieval History, Zeitschrift der Savigny-Stiftung für Rechtsgeschichte: Kanonistische Abteilung*, the *Journal of Medieval Iberian Studies, eHumanista, Crusades*, the *Bulletin of Medieval Canon Law*, and the *Revista Chilena de Estudios Medievales*, as well as in several edited volumes. His most recent works include: "About Three Clerics and Towards a 'History from the Middle' for Medieval Castile: Miguel de San Nicolás of Toledo, Gíl of Cuenca, and Lanfranco di Palacio of Palencia," *Journal of Religious History* 46.1 (2022): 220–42; "'Because of Incest Which One of the Two of Them Committed': A Letter About Two Third Crusade Participants form the Archivo Catedralicio de Toledo," *Crusades* 20 (2021): 121–29; "'In exercitu loco eius pontificalia exercet': Warrior Clerics in the Era of Fernando III," in *The Sword and the Cross: Castile-León in the Era of Fernando III*, ed. Edward L. Holt and Teresa Witcombe MEMI 77 (Leiden and Boston MA: Brill, 2020), 85–104; "Riots, Reluctance, and Reformers: The Church in the Kingdom of Castile and the IV Lateran Council," *JMIS* 103.1 (2020): 1–18.

Max Naderer | ORCID: 0000-0002-5824-1494
was awarded his PhD in History from the University in Oslo in October 2020. His research interests include the perception and legitimacy of violence, political culture as well as notions of masculinity and honor among elite men in high medieval Norway and Denmark. He is currently preparing a monograph based on his doctoral thesis, *Exploring the Perception and Legitimacy of Violence in the 'Civil War' Period in Norway and Denmark, c.1130–1240*, which is planned to be published with Brill (The Northern world series). His recent publication dealt with kingship ideology, emotions of power, and the use of violence, "Den fryktede kongen i Norges 'borgerkrigstid'" [The feared king in Norway's "civil war era"], *Collegium Medievale* 32.2 (2019): 235–52. In a future postdoctoral project, he will be looking at connections between the perception and assignment of humanity and practices of violence in a comparative approach.

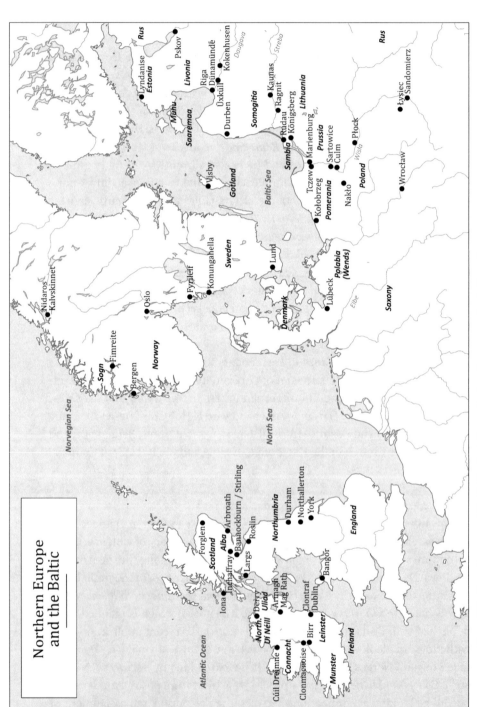

MAP 0.1   Map of Northern Europe and the Baltic depicting major locations appearing in the volume

Introduction

∴

CHAPTER 1

Religious Rites of War beyond the Medieval West: An Introduction

Gregory Leighton

It took the blessing Russia's invasion of Ukraine in February 2022 by Kirill, Patriarch of Moscow, to remind the world that the link between religion and warfare is not something to be relegated to the past. Framing the conflict as a "metaphysical" as opposed to a physical struggle, he provided a link between Eastern Europe and the West, where political struggles at local and international levels take on highly religious tones and symbolisms. Therefore, historians and scholars of the humanities find themselves increasingly at the center of this development. Their role in explaining and contextualizing these phenomena, their meanings, and their contexts to the broader public has only increased in a world where such phenomena play equally important roles as their physical performance does.

This two-volume collection, in many ways, offers a response to this increased need. It brings together sixteen contributions to explore the intersection between religious rites and armed conflict in the Middle Ages. Specifically, it focuses on the regions of Northern and Eastern Europe, areas that tend to remain regional in terms of scholarly output and, until recently, peripheral in Anglophone scholarship. Its geographical scope encompasses Scotland, the Eastern and Southern Baltic to the Kingdom of Hungary, Bohemia, and Rus. The collection of English-language publications on the medieval history of these areas has experienced a significant boom, thus increasing the internationalization of their histories among scholars of the Middle Ages and Early Modern Period. The crusades in the Baltic region (which spanned from 1198 to 1503) in particular has been a field in which various monographs and collections of studies have appeared in the last two decades, but so have other studies concerning the spread of the idea of holy war and crusade into these regions before the early thirteenth century.[1] Moreover, comparative studies

---

[1] One can mention, e.g., Jason T. Roche and Janus M. Jensen, ed., *The Second Crusade: Holy War on the Periphery of Latin Christendom*, Outremer 2 (Turnhout: Brepols, 2015); Torben Kjersgaard Nielsen and Iben Fonnesberg-Schmidt, ed., *Crusading on the Edge: Ideas and Practice of Crusading in Iberia and the Baltic Region, 1100–1500*, Outremer 4 (Turnhout: Brepols,

across regions and boundaries have started to appear, especially relevant in terms of how societies not only conduct warfare but also the ways in which they rationalize it and sacralize it. And yet, a book partially concerning the treatment of religious *rituals* and their relationship to warfare on the northern and eastern frontiers of Europe in the Middle Ages has yet to be produced.[2] This brief introduction will therefore outline the historiography surrounding religious rites in times of war in general, before moving to its treatment in the regions under study (which have, until recently, tended to operate in isolation, especially for the later medieval period). It will conclude with an overview of the contents of this book.

1 Historiographical Approaches

Scholarship generally agrees that the relationship between religious rituals and warfare in the Middle Ages dates back to the very beginning of the period, but with exceptions, in a more pronounced form, began to appear only during the ninth century. Important light has already been shed on this matter by Albert M. Königer, whose short book is somewhat forgotten today,[3] and then, especially by Michael McCormick's seminal work, *Eternal Victory*. McCormick, among others, has written extensively on liturgies of war, the function of prayers for rulers, for victory, for bringing peace, and their developments during the age of the Carolingians and beyond.[4] Prayers performed on the home

---

2016); Carsten Selch Jensen, Janus Møller Jensen, and Kurt Villads Jensen, ed., *Fighting for the Faith: The Many Crusades*, Scripta minora 27 (Stockholm: Runica et mediævalia, 2018); Paul Srodecki and Norbert Kersken, ed., *The Expansion of the Faith: Crusading on the Frontiers of Latin Christendom in the High Middle Ages*, Outremer 14 (Turnhout: Brepols, 2022); Paul Srodecki and Norbert Kersken, ed., *Defending the Faith: Crusading on the Frontiers of Latin Christendom in the Late Middle Ages* (Turnhout: Brepols, forthc. 2024).

2 Radosław Kotecki, Carsten Selch Jensen, and Stephen Bennett, ed., *Christianity and War in Medieval East Central Europe and Scandinavia* (Leeds: ARC Humanities Press, 2021), esp. chapters by Jacek Maciejewski, Dušan Zupka, Radosław Kotecki, Carsten Selch Jensen, and Bjørn Bandlien.

3 Albert M. Königer, *Die Militärseelsorge der Karolingerzeit. Ihr Recht und ihre Praxis*, VKSM 4.7 (Munich: Lentner, 1918).

4 Michael McCormick, "The Liturgy of War in the Early Middle Ages: Crisis, Litanies, and the Carolingian Monarchy," *Viator* 15 (1984): 1–23; idem, "Liturgie et guerre des Carolingiens à la première croisade," in *"Militia Christi" e crociata nei secoli XI–XIII*, Miscellanea del Centro di studi medioevali 13 (Milan: Vita e pensiero, 1992), 209–40; idem, *Eternal Victory: Triumphal Rulership in Late Antiquity, Byzantium and the Early Medieval West* (Cambridge: Cambridge University Press, 1990), 342–43, for liturgical celebrations of war, victory, and security during the Merovingian age. For an example of this type of mass, see Carl Erdmann, "Heidenkrieg

front, that is, for the victory of the army, the security of the kingdom, and the bringing of peace, were all reflections of the belief that victory in battle was dependent upon observing specific religious rituals.[5] Moreover, they served to involve those who were not on the frontline in the act of obtaining victory from Heaven. This reflected what McCormick calls "the new military spirituality" that emerged during the last decades of the ninth century.[6]

McCormick's works are a kind of *lapis primarius* for the plenty of new research on the sacralization and ritualization of war in early and high medieval western Europe and Byzantium. A special place among them is held by David S. Bachrach's 2004 book *Religion and the Conduct of War, c. 300–1215*, which is the most comprehensive study to date on the relationship between warfare and religion. Indeed, in this book and several other minor works Bachrach confirms that this phenomenon was not only relegated to the cathedrals, monasteries, and churches of medieval European monarchies. His valuable studies show, among other things, the presence of priests in armies and that religious rites were also key in times of battle. Priests were present in those armies not only to perform military service but also to perform confession for combatants before battle, in addition to absolution for those who had killed men in war.[7] Moreover, Bachrach points to "traditional duties of inspiring men to bravery" and ensuring that they behave properly in battle.[8] While Bachrach offers a comprehensive discussion of the changing nature of military devotion and simultaneously emphasizes an undercurrent of continuity in different regions, all his works touch only Western Europe, in the east without going beyond the Ottonian, Salian, and Staufen empires, and the north beyond the Norman rule in the British Isles.

Although many studies focus on the Carolingian and Ottonian periods, they do nonetheless begin to touch upon the geographical areas under study in this book. For instance, some of the earliest examples of the *missa contra paganos* in the liturgical texts of these eras are connected with campaigns against the

---

    in der Liturgie u. Kaiserkrönung Ottos I.," in *Heidenmission und Kreuzzugsgedanke in der Deutschen Ostpolitik des Mittelalters*, ed. Helmut Beumann, Wege der Forschungen 7 (Darmstadt: Wissenschaftliches Buchgesellschaft, 1963), 47–64 at 62, prayers for when the Emperor was fighting the pagans: "Idem etiam ex hoste reportare tribuat gaudia pacis et pro istiusmodi laboribus regnare vos faciat in aeternum cum sanctis."

5 McCormick, "Liturgy of War," 9.
6 McCormick, *Eternal Victory*, 348.
7 David S. Bachrach, *Religion and the Conduct of War, c. 300–1215* (Woodbridge: Boydell Press, 2003). Among other Bachrach's works, see esp., "Military Chaplains and the Religion of War in Ottonian Germany, 919–1024," *RSS* 39.1 (2011): 13–31.
8 Bachrach, "Military Chaplains," 14.

Avars, Magyars, and Slavs.[9] The work of Carl Erdmann, namely his groundbreaking *Entstehung des Kreuzzugsgedanken*, served as the impetus from which research on war liturgies and rituals were studied from a broader chronological scope.[10] Erdmann's analysis of the so-called *Kaisersagen*, in addition to the blessing rituals of banners carried in war, served to highlight the value of the *longue durée* approach to studying the relations between society, religion, and war in the Middle Ages.[11] The impact of this work can be seen in the publications of M. Cecilia Gaposchkin, with her excellent *Invisible Weapons* at the forefront. From the commemorative liturgies and rituals that developed as a product of war, such as the conquest of Jerusalem in 1099, the impact of pre-battle religious rites on the creation of communal identities among crusaders, and the importance of war liturgies and rituals in the development of crusading ideology from the eleventh century and into the fifteenth, her work perhaps best exemplifies the considerable pathways for future research into the intersection between medieval warfare, religion, and rituals.[12]

2   Rites of War on the Borders: Northern and Eastern Europe

Northern and Eastern Europe have their own body of research devoted to the phenomena of sacralization and ritualization of war in the Middle Ages. It tends to be poorly known outside of local scholarship and is generally thinly rooted in the international (mainly English-language) studies discussed above. It is, however, worth at least a cursory review here because of the potential it may hold for researchers dealing with religious-martial rituals in various sections of the medieval world.

As for research concerning religious-martial rituals in Northern Europe, the study of Anglo-Norman England is the obvious exception, naturally, due to the integration within the international scholarship. Particularly much

---

9   Ibid., 19.
10 Carl Erdmann, *Die Entstehung des Kreuzzugsgedanken*, FKG 6 (Stuttgart: Kohlhammer, 1935), 77–78.
11 Ibid., 276–83 (*Kaisersagen*), and 326–35 (blessing rituals).
12 M. Cecilia Gaposchkin, *Invisible Weapons: Liturgy and the Making of Crusade Ideology* (Ithaca NY: Cornell University Press, 2017), at 226–54 for the role of crusade liturgies in the context of the Ottoman threat in the fifteenth century. *For Gaposchkin's other works, see esp.*, see esp. "From Pilgrimage to Crusade: The Liturgy of Departure, 1095–1300," *Speculum* 88.1 (2013): 44–91; "The Echoes of Victory: Liturgical and Para-Liturgical Commemorations of the Capture of Jerusalem in the West," *JMH* 40.3 (2014): 237–59; "The Pre-Battle Processions of the First Crusade and the Creation of Militant Christian 'communitas,'" *Material Religion* 14.4 (2018): 454–68.

attention has been paid to issues related to William the Conqueror's conquest of England and subsequent warfare aimed at stabilizing Norman power, up to the Battle of the Standard fought at Northallerton against the Scots in 1138. Anglo-Norman England was also included by David Bachrach in his reflections on the relationship between religion and war, showing the local situation in the broader Continental context.[13] However, the situation is already slightly different when it comes to later times. For example, the religious elements in the wars of thirteenth-century English kings against the Scots, so widely represented in the sources, have received attention only recently.[14] As in recent studies on England, the increase in interest in the religious aspects of warfare in late medieval Scotland may be recently noted in the works of the irreverent Michael Penman. The study of the rituals used by both sides in these wars is a rewarding example showing the transformations taking place under the influence of the developing chivalric culture and the crusading ideology formalized in the thirteenth century.[15] As such, it deserves wider attention from scholars from various research circles.

Compared to England proper, research on the use of religious-martial rituals in the Gaelic domains and later in Ireland and Scotland is much more modest. However, it is worth noting that Anthony T. Lucas, Thomas O. Clancy and, more recently, Alan Thacker have analyzed the phenomenon of the use of relics of native saints in warfare in the early Middle Ages.[16] Due to the

---

13   Bachrach, *Religion*, 152–64.
14   David S. Bachrach, "The 'Ecclesia Anglicana' Goes to War: Prayers, Propaganda, and Conquest during the Reign of Edward I of England, 1272–1307," *Albion* 36.3 (2004): 393–406; Richard Sharpe, "Banners of the Northern Saints," in *Saints of North-East England, 600–1500*, ed. Margaret Coombe, Anne Mouron, and Christiania Whitehead, MCS 39 (Turnhout: Brepols, 2017), 245–303.
15   Michael A. Penman, "Christian Days and Knights: The Religious Devotions and Court of David II of Scotland, 1329–71," *Historical Research* 75.189 (2002): 249–72; idem, "Faith in War: The Religious Experience of Scottish Soldiery, c.1100–c.1500," *JMH* 37.3 (2011): 295–303; idem, "'Sacred Food for the Soul': In Search of the Devotions to Saints of Robert Bruce, King of Scotland, 1306–1329," *Speculum* 88.4 (2013): 1035–62. See also Iain M. MacInnes, *Scotland's Second War of Independence, 1332–1357* (Woodbridge: Boydell Press, 2016), 223–29.
16   Anthony T. Lucas, "The Social Role of Relics and Reliquaries in Ancient Ireland," *JRSAI* 116 (1986): 5–37, esp. at 17–27; Thomas O. Clancy, "Columba, Adomnan and the Cult of Saints in Scotland," in *"Spes Scotorum," Hope of Scots: Saint Columba, Iona and Scotland*, ed. Dauvit Broun and Thomas O. Clancy (Edinburgh: T&T Clark, 1999), 3–33; Alan T. Thacker, "The Church and Warfare: The Religious and Cultural Background to the Hoard," in *The Staffordshire Hoard: An Anglo-Saxon Treasure*, ed. Chris Fern, Tania M. Dickinson, and Leslie Webster, Research report of the Society of Antiquaries of London 80 (London: Society of Antiquaries of London, 2019), 293–99.

uniqueness of Gaelic sources, their research seems relevant to all researchers seeking ancient, pre-Crusade, traditions of sacralization and ritualization of war on the European continent.

Concerning the northern and eastern frontiers of Europe, scholarship appears to draw on the impact of the crusading movement and ideas related to the sacralization of warfare. Indeed, the Christianization of Livonia and Prussia, a process that spans the twelfth century to the fourteenth, is a direct product of the crusading idea. Livonia has received considerable attention from Scandinavian scholars, with prime examples being the work of Carsten Selch Jensen,[17] Torben Kjersgaard Nielsen,[18] and Kurt Villads Jensen.[19] Their work considers the rich variety of information preserved in the thirteenth-century chronicle of Henry of Livonia and the ways in which war transformed societies and landscapes.[20] For Prussia, examinations of war rituals and their development have not been subject to much research until very recently.[21] This is quite surprising, for most of the historical texts for the region's history were produced by priests in the Teutonic Order, men who had a religious education and were bound to motivate brothers to engage in combat.[22] Indeed, one should also consider the complex mix between crusading activity and chivalric goals in this region, exemplified in the role played by the "table of honor": an object meant to commemorate knightly prowess while fighting "the enemies of the faith."[23] Key works remain Jarosław Wenta's consideration of

---

17   Carsten Selch Jensen, "History Made Sacred: Martyrdom and the Making of a Sanctified Beginning in Early Thirteenth-Century Livonia," in *Saints and Sainthood around the Baltic Sea: Identity, Literacy, and Communication in the Middle Ages*, ed. Carsten Selch Jensen, Tracey Renée Sands, and Nils Holger Petersen, SMEM 54 (Kalamazoo MI: Medieval Institute Publications, 2018), 145–73.

18   Torben Kjersgaard Nielsen, "The Making of New Cultural Landscapes in the Medieval Baltic," in *Medieval Christianity in the North: New Studies*, ed. Kirsti Salonen, Kurt Villads Jensen, and Torstein Jørgensen, Acta Scandinavica 1 (Turnhout: Brepols, 2013), 121–53 at 138–40.

19   Kurt Villads Jensen, "Martyrs, Total War, and Heavenly Horses: Scandinavia as Centre and Periphery in the Expansion of Medieval Christendom," in *Medieval Christianity in the North*, 89–120.

20   Also see the work of Alan V. Murray, "The Sword Brothers at War: Observations on the Military Activity of the Knighthood of Christ in the Conquest of Livonia and Estonia (1203–1227)," *OM* 18 (2013): 27–38.

21   E.g., Antoni R. Chodyński, "The Preparations for War Expeditions to Lithuania and Samogitia According to the Chronicle by Wigand of Marburg," *Fasciculi Archaeologicae Historicae* 15 (2002): 39–46, a superb study of military operations as reflected in the chronicle of Wigand von Marburg, though silent on the *religious* preparations for war.

22   See the chapter of Gregory Leighton in this collection (vol. 1, chap. 8).

23   The most comprehensive treatment remains that of Werner Paravicini, *Die Preußenreisen des europäischen Adels*, 2 vols., BF 17.1–2 (Sigmaringen: Thorbecke, 1989–1995), 1:316–33.

"a liturgy for the war against pagans" in Prussia,[24] in addition to the work of Annette Löffler on the Order's liturgy in general.[25] One should also consult the work of Krzysztof Kwiatkowski on the corporate (and religious) mentality of the Teutonic Order (which was expressed through rituals performed in times of war),[26] and Gregory Leighton on the function of relics on and off the battlefield.[27] In any case, the papers in this collection concerning the Baltic region demonstrate that there remain considerable research avenues, geographically and chronologically, concerning the intersection between warfare, ritual, violence, and the ways in which contemporaries used them and communicated them.

Against this backdrop of research in mainstream Medieval Studies, scholarship on the hinterland of Eastern and Northern Europe is less advanced and not readily undertaken outside of specialist circles. It is curious because the sources, however less numerous than those for the core regions of the Latin West, are not at all as scarce as they might seem. Especially when employing a broader chronological spectrum, one can find a vast amount of source material that, with proper insight, turns out to be very rich in cultural content. It is hard not to see here a symptom of the barrier within Medieval Studies. This barrier has a two-sided dimension. On the one hand, Western scholars dealing

---

Also see Axel Ehlers, "The Crusade of the Teutonic Knights against Lithuania Reconsidered," in *Crusade and Conversion on the Baltic Frontier, 1100–1550*, ed. Alan V. Murray (Aldershot and Burlington VT: Ashgate, 2001), 21–44 for the overview of complexities of the *Reisen* as chivalric crusades.

24 Jarosław Wenta, *Studien über die Ordensgeschichtsschreibung am Beispiel Preußens*, Subsidia historiographica 2 (Toruń: Wydawnictwo Naukowe Uniwersytetu Mikołaja Kopernika, 2000), at 158–68.

25 Annette Löffler, "Die Rolle der Liturgie im Ordenskonvent. Norm und Wirklichkeit," in *Das Leben im Ordenshaus*, ed. Juhan Kreem, QSGD 81 (Weimar: VDG, 2019), 1–20 at 11.

26 Krzysztof Kwiatkowski, "Prolog und Epilog 'temporis sanctis'. Die Belagerung Kauens 1362 in der Beschreibung Wigands von Marburg," *ZfO* 57.2 (2008): 238–54 at 250–53; idem, "'Christ ist erstanden …' and Christians Win! Liturgy and the Sacralization of Armed Fight against the Pagans as Determinants of the Identity of the Members of the Teutonic Order in Prussia," in *Sacred Space in the State of the Teutonic Order in Prussia*, ed. Jarosław Wenta and Magdalena Kopczyńska, SBS 2 (Toruń: Wydawnictwo Naukowe Uniwersytetu Mikołaja Kopernika, 2013), 101–29; idem, *Zakon niemiecki jako "corporatio militaris." Część 1: Korporacja i krąg przynależących do niej. Kulturowe i społeczne podstawy działalności militarnej zakonu w Prusach (do początku XV wieku)*, Dzieje zakonu niemieckiego 1 (Toruń: Wydawnictwo Naukowe Uniwersytetu Mikołaja Kopernika, 2012), 88.

27 Gregory Leighton, "'Reysa in laudem Dei et virginis Marie contra paganos': The Experience of Crusading in Prussia during the Thirteenth and Fourteenth Centuries," *ZfO* 69.1 (2020): 1–25 at 5–16; idem, "The Relics of St Barbara at Althaus Kulm: History, Patronages, and Insight into the Teutonic Order and Christian Population in Prussia (Thirteenth–Fifteenth Centuries)," *ZH* 85.1 (2020): 5–50 at 22–31.

with the relationship between religion and war only to a very small extent go beyond the so-called medieval West.

This approach avoids the vast areas of Ireland, Scotland, Scandinavia, countries of Central Europe, and of the area of the former Kievan Rus (today Belarus, Russia, Ukraine), as well as the Baltic and Grand Duchy of Lithuania. On the other hand, local northern and eastern European scholarly circles are insufficiently versed in the rich literature produced by Western scholars dealing with the sacralization and ritualization of war. As such, the lack of greater awareness for this scholarship results in only a sporadic pursuit of the topic. Most often it is simply limited to listing a certain catalog of references found in the source material and their rather superficial interpretation. Local scholarship on the topic of Christian war rituals thus presents a rather paltry picture, although it is worth noting a few works that deserve wider attention. Arnved Nedkvitne, in his book on beliefs of laypeople in early and high medieval northern society, drew attention to the accounts in saga literature about various religious performances related to the conduct of war. These range from granting of communion to soldiers before battles, performance of penance by soldiers and priests before combat, in addition to the observance of prayers, chants, and vows in times of war, showing that in the twelfth–thirteenth centuries, religious practices related to war found a fairly receptive audience in Northern society.[28]

The rich body of sources for Rus have so far been used minimally.[29] So far, the most valuable work striving for a broader view of the relationship between the religion of war in Rus is the work by Irina Moroz, which can be considered a good starting point for more in-depth studies on the ritualization of war.[30] The latter task has been undertaken only very recently by Alexandra Vukovich in her doctoral thesis on the ritualization of political life in Kievan Rus in the tenth–twelfth centuries. She observed, for example, the tradition of celebrating war departures by giving them a sacred character in a manner

---

28 Arnved Nedkvitne, *Lay Belief in Norse Society 1000–1350* (Copenhagen: Museum Tusculanum Press, 2009), 103–4, 124–28, 183.

29 Alexandr Musin's book, fundamental to the issue of the relationship between religion and war in Old Rus, although it touches on many important issues, has been dominated by an archaeological perspective. Aleksandr E. Musin, *"Milites Christi" Drevnej Rusi. Voinskaja kultura russkogo Srednevekovja v kontekste religioznogo mentaliteta*, Militaria Antiqua 8 (St. Petersburg: Peterburgskoe Vostokovedenie, 2005). The issue of clergy participating in war campaigns has been also addressed in Artem Yu. Grachev, "K voprosu o roli i meste duhovenstva v voennoj organizacii Drevnej Rusi," *Pskovskij voenno-istoricheskij vestnik* 94 (2015): 43–47.

30 Irina Moroz, "The Idea of Holy War in the Orthodox World (On Russian Chronicles from the Twelfth–Sixteenth Century)," *QMAN* 4 (1999): 45–67.

reminiscent of the practice of *profectio bellica*. Vukovich's research brings hope for a new quality in the study and problem of the liturgization of war in the early period of the Rurikids' rule also because she is aware of the influence of Byzantine culture on the Rusian realities.[31] It is important that not only in the study of Rus but also Eastern and Northern Europe, more consideration should be given to the possible influence of Byzantine customs.[32] It is, more-

---

31   Alexandra Vukovich, "The Ritualisation of Political Power in Early Rus' (10th–12th Centuries)" (PhD thesis, University of Cambridge, 2015); eadem, "Victory and Defeat Liturgified: The Symbolic World of Martial Ritual in Early Rus," in *Victors and Vanquished: Cultures of War in the Northern and Mediterranean Worlds. Byzantium and European Cultures of War*, ed. Johannes Pahlitzsch and Jörg Rogge, Byzanz und die euromediterranen Kriegskulturen 1 (Mainz: Mainz University Press, forthc. 2023). As for the thirteenth century, Mari Isoaho and Dariusz Dąbrowski have studied religious practices used in connection with war. Mari Isoaho, *The Image of Aleksandr Nevskiy in Medieval Russia: Warrior and Saint*, TNW 21 (Leiden and Boston MA: Brill, 2006), esp. Part II; Dariusz Dąbrowski, "Religijność króla Daniela Romanowicza," *Knâža doba. Ìstorìâ ì kul'tura* 9(9) (2015): 79–90; idem, *Król Rusi Daniel Romanowicz. O ruskiej rodzinie książęcej, społeczeństwie i kulturze w XIII w*. Monografie pracowni badań nad dziejami Rusi Uniwersytetu Kazimierza Wielkiego w Bydgoszczy 4 (Cracow: Avalon, 2016), 282–86.

32   In last two decades significant progress has been made in research not only on the understanding of the idea of holy war, but also on the issue of ritualization of military action in Byzantium. See esp. Nancy Sevcenko, "The Limburg Staurothek and Its Relics," in *Thymíama. Stē mnémē tēs Laskarínas Mpoúra* (Athenes: Mouseío Mpenákē, 1994), 289–94; Sophia Mergiali-Sahas, "Byzantine Emperors and Holy Relics: Use, and Misuse, of Sanctity and Authority," *Jahrbuch der Österreichischen Byzantinistik* no. 51 (2001): 41–60; Holger A. Klein, "Sacred Relics and Imperial Ceremonies at the Great Palace of Constantinople," in *Visualisierungen von Herrschaft. Frühmittelalterliche Residenzen Gestalt und Zeremoniell*, ed. Franz A. Bauer, Byzas 5 (Istanbul: Ege Yayınları, 2006), 79–99; Robert S. Nelson, "'And So, With the Help of God': The Byzantine Art of War in the Tenth Century," *Dumbarton Oaks Papers* 65–66 (2011): 169–92; Denis F. Sullivan, "Siege Warfare, Nikephoros II Phokas, Relics and Personal Piety," in *Byzantine Religious Culture: Studies in Honor of Alice-Mary Talbot*, ed. Alice-Mary M. Talbot and Denis F. Sullivan, MMED 92 (Leiden and Boston MA: Brill, 2012), 395–409; Anthony Kaldellis, "The Military Use of the Icon of the Theotokos and its Moral Logic in the Historians of the Ninth–Twelfth Centuries," *Estudios Bizantinos* 1 (2013): 56–75; Abdel-Aziz Ramadan, "The Role of Super Natural Powers in Arab-Byzantine Warfare as Reflected by Popular Imagination," *Journal of Medieval and Islamic History* 9.9 (2015): 3–38; Bernard Flusin, "Le culte de la Croix au palais de Constantinople d'après le 'Livre des cérémonies,'" in *The Church of the Holy Cross of Ałt'amar*, ed. Zaroui Pogossian and Edda Vardanyan, Armenian texts and studies 3 (Leiden and Boston MA: Brill, 2019), 100–25; Holger A. Klein, "Objektkultur und Kultobjekte im kaiserlich-byzantinischen Prozessionswesen," in *"Palatium sacrum"—Sakralität am Hof des Mittelalters. Orte, Dinge, Rituale*, ed. Manfred Luchterhandt and Hedwig Röckelein (Regensburg: Schnell & Steiner, 2021), 77–100; Joaquin Serrano del Pozo, "Relics, Images, and Christian Apotropaic Devices in the Roman-Persian Wars (4th–7th Centuries)," *Eikón Imago* 11 (2022): 57–69.

over, rather disturbing to see how the study of the Eastern Empire and the study of Latin Europe are separated from each other. While McCormick was still aware of the necessity of making parallel investigations, later scholars have already abandoned such a perspective. It seems appropriate to return to it now, and a convenient field for such studies seems to be the space of Europe lying between these great centers of Christianity as an area of penetration of influences coming from East and West.

Czech and Hungarian scholars have so far paid even less attention to religious war rituals. Exceptions include László Veszprémy, who is the author of an important article on weeping rulers before or during military clashes.[33] As far as Bohemia is concerned, the figure of St. Wenceslas as the military protector of the Bohemian community has received the bulk of scholarly attention, but this largely ignores the ritual aspect of the relationship between the people and the victory-giving saint.[34] This trend of prioritizing research of patron saints over the rituals in which their aid was secured is by no means a Czech peculiarity.[35] A more distinct change in the desired direction can be noted only

---

33 László Veszprémy, "A pityergő Árpádtól a könnyező Szent Lászlóig. A könnyekre fakadó hadvezér a Névtelen Gesztája 39. és a Krónikaszerkesztés 121., 137. Fejezetében," *Acta Historica (Szeged)* 138 (2015): 17–32, rprt. in idem, *Történetírás és történetírók az Árpád-kori Magyarországon (XI–XIII. század közepe)*, Rerum Fides 2 (Budapest: Line Design, 2019), 119–28.

34 Here the exception is a brief essay by Marie Bláhová, "Vidění kanovníka Víta—zjitřené emoce nebo promyšlená inscenace?" in *"Fontes ipsi sitiunt." Sborník prací k sedmdesátinám archiváře a historika Eduarda Mikuška*, ed. Petr Kopička (Litoměřice and Prague: Scriptorium, 2016), 35–41.

35 Among the vast literature on patron saints and saintly aid in wartime need, see, e.g., Vasile Draguț, "La légende du 'Héros de frontière' dans la peinture médiévale de Transylvanie," *Revue Roumaine de l'Histoire de l'Art, S. Beaux-Arts* 11 (1974): 11–40; František Graus, "Der Heilige als Schlachtenhelfer—Zur Nationalisierung einer Wundererzählung in der mittelalterlichen Chronistik," in *Festschrift für Helmut Beumann zum 65. Geburtstag*, ed. Kurt-Ulrich Jäschke and Reinhard Wenskus (Sigmaringen: Thorbecke, 1977), 330–48; Helen Y. Prochazka, "Warrior Idols or Idle Warriors? On the Cult of Saints Boris and Gleb as Reflected in the Old Russian Military Accounts," *Slavonic and East European Review* 65.4 (1987): 505–16; Marian Dygo, "The Political Role of the Cult of the Virgin Mary in Teutonic Prussia in the Fourteenth and Fifteenth Centuries," *JMH* 15.1 (1989): 63–80; Aleksander Gieysztor, "Politische Heilige im hochmittelalterlichen Polen und Böhmen," in *Politik und Heiligenverehrung im Hochmittelalter*, ed. Jürgen Petersohn, VF 42 (Sigmaringen: Thorbecke, 1994), 325–41; Agata Siwczyńska, "Interwencje i działania świętych w najstarszych kronikach polskich i czeskich," *Historia* 3.4 (1995–1996): 7–44; Christopher Holdsworth, "'An Airier Aristocracy': The Saints at War," *Transactions of the Royal Historical Society* 6 (1996): 103–22; Kent G. Hare, "Apparitions and War in Anglo-Saxon England," in *The Circle of War in the Middle Ages: Essays on Medieval Military and Naval History*, ed. Donald J. Kagay and L.J.A. Villalon (Woodbridge: Boydell Press, 1999), 75–86; Marcin R. Pauk, "Święci patroni a średniowieczne wspólnoty polityczne w Europie

recently with Dušan Zupka's research, which emphasizes that the Christian religionization of war is a process that progressed in Bohemia and Hungary starting from the early phases of the Middle Ages (tenth–eleventh century) and that a whole range of religious practices calculated to gain the supernatural support in military struggle or danger underpinned this process.[36] Zupka's research is also a good example of how Central European sources present a slightly different situation compared to the world of the Baltic/Northern crusades with respect to scholarly investigations, namely in that research tends to

---

Środkowej," in *Sacrum. Obraz i funkcja w społeczeństwie średniowiecznym*, ed. Aneta Pieniądz-Skrzypczak and Jerzy Pysiak, Aquila volans 1 (Warsaw: Wydawnictwa Uniwersytetu Warszawskiego, 2005), 237–60; Norbert Kersken, "God and the Saints in Medieval Polish Historiography," in *The Making of Christian Myths in the Periphery of Latin Christendom (c. 1000–1300)*, ed. Lars B. Mortensen (Copenhagen: Museum Tusculanum Press, 2006), 153–94; Ivan Gerát, *Svätí bojovníci v stredoveku. Úvahy o obrazových legendách sv. Juraj a sv. Ladislava na Slovensku* (Bratislava: VEDA, 2011); John R.E. Bliese, "Saint Cuthbert and War," *JMH* 24.3 (2012): 215–41; Enikő Csukovits, "Les saints libérateurs des Turcs en Hongrie à la fin du Moyen Âge," in *Les saints et leur culte en Europe centrale au Moyen Âge*, ed. Marie-Madeleine de Cevins and Olivier Marin, Hagiologia 13 (Turnhout: Brepols, 2017), 109–21; Kurt Villads Jensen, "Saints at War in the Baltic Region," in *Saints and Sainthood*, 251–71; Monika Juzepczuk, "Kult świętych a zwycięstwa militarne pierwszych Piastów (od X do początków XIII w.)," *Saeculum Christianum* 25.1 (2018): 63–76; Tomasz Tarczyński, "The King and the Saint against the Scots: The Shaping of English National Identity in the 12th Century Narrative of King Athelstan's Victory over His Northern Neighbours," in *Imagined Communities: Constructing Collective Identities in Medieval Europe*, ed. Andrzej Pleszczyński et al., EMC 8 (Leiden and Boston MA: Brill, 2018), 85–102; Stefan Samerski, "Zwischen Waffengang und 'caritas'. Der Deutsche Orden und seine Heiligen im Mittelalter und in der Frühneuzeit," in *Die Militarisierung der Heiligen in Vormoderne und Moderne*, ed. Liliya Berezhnaya, Historische Forschungen 122 (Berlin: Duncker & Humblot, 2020), 127–42.

36 Dušan Zupka, "Náboženské rituály vojny a vytváranie kresťanskej identity v stredovekej strednej Európe 12. storočia," *Historický Časopis* 68.4 (2020): 577–90; idem, "Religious Rituals of War in Medieval Hungary Under the Árpád Dynasty," in *Christianity and War*, 141–57; idem, "Political, Religious and Social Framework of Religious Warfare and Its Influences on Rulership in Medieval East Central Europe," in *Rulership in Medieval East Central Europe: Power, Rituals and Legitimacy in Bohemia, Hungary and Poland*, ed. Grischa Vercamer and Dušan Zupka, ECEE 78 (Leiden and Boston MA: Brill, 2021), 135–59; idem, "Ritual Representation of Power in Medieval East Central European Rulership, Sacrality and Warfare (Hungary, Bohemia, Poland, 10th–14th Century)," in *Continuation or Change? Borders and Frontiers in Late Antiquity and Medieval Europe: Landscape of Power Network, Military Organisation and Commerce*, ed. Gregory Leighton, Piotr Pranke, and Łukasz Różycki (Abingdon and New York: Routledge, 2023), 103–22. Zupka is also the author of a book synthesizing the relationship between religion and war in East Central Europe (focused mostly on Hungary and Bohemia) at the level of ideology and practice. Dušan Zupka, *Meč a kríž. Vojna a náboženstvo v stredovekej strednej Európe (10.–12. storočie)* (Bratislava: VEDA, 2020).

focus on how rituals reflected and symbolized relationships between rulers or ecclesiastical officials. This is an important matter and one that will require a more thorough investigation in the future. And yet, the studies in this collection show that the sphere of religious ritual connected to war also drew from older traditions of the sacralization of warfare. This phenomenon perhaps can be derived from the late antique and the early medieval immersion of war in religious imagery, particularly clear in the example of the imperial ideology of war and the notion of "Elect Nation."[37]

In contrast to the above, Polish researchers have so far had the most to say about war rituals and the sacralization of combat. A characteristic feature of the older studies was the focus on the role of military chaplains, and an overly schematic view of the role of religious practices in institutional terms and through the prism of such concepts as "church pastoral care" or "military chaplaincy." However, it is highly symptomatic that, in these works, both terms take on the meaning they had in the context of twentieth-century military organization. Among the researchers to whom we are indebted for studies devoted to these matters, one should mention above all Jan Manthey, Jerzy Sójka, and Jan Ptak.[38] It is worth emphasizing that the latter scholar returned

---

37 For a better understanding of this perspective, the recent work of Prof. Goetz is particularly important. Hans-Werner Goetz "'Glaubenskriege?' Die Kriege der Christen gegen Andersgläubige in der früh- und hochmittelalterlichen Wahrnehmung," *FS* 53.1 (2019): 67–114. Also see Boris Gübele, *"Deus vult, Deus vult." Der christliche heilige Krieg im Früh- und Hochmittelalter*, Mittelalter-Forschungen 54 (Ostfildern: Thorbecke, 2018), however with important reservations in Goetz, "'Glaubenskriege?'" 113–14. For the close link between war and idea of "Elect Nation" in the early Middle Ages, see esp. Mary Garrison, "The Franks as the New Israel? Education for an Identity from Pippin to Charlemagne," in *The Uses of the Past in Early Medieval Europe*, ed. Yitzhak Hen and Matthew Innes (Cambridge: Cambridge University Press, 2000), 114–61; Zbigniew Dalewski, "A New Chosen People? Gallus Anonymus's Narrative about Poland and Its Rulers," in *Historical Narratives and Christian Identity on a European Periphery: Early History Writing in Northern, East-Central, and Eastern Europe (c. 1070–1200)*, ed. Ildar H. Garipzanov, MTCN 26 (Turnhout: Brepols, 2011), 145–66; Shay Eshel, *The Concept of the Elect Nation in Byzantium*, MMED 113 (Leiden and Boston MA: Brill, 2018), chap. 6; Gerda Heydemann, "The People of God and the Law: Biblical Models in Carolingian Legislation," *Speculum* 95.1 (2020): 89–131; Patrick S. Marschner, *Das neue Volk Gottes in Hispanien. Die Bibel in der christlich-iberischen Historiographie vom 8. bis zum 12. Jahrhundert*, Geschichte und Kultur der Iberischen Welt 19 (Münster, Berlin, Vienna, and Zürich: LIT Verlag, 2023).

38 Jan Manthey, "Średniowieczne duszpasterstwo wojskowe," *Duszpasterz Polski Zagranicą* 9.3(36) (1958): 259–77; Sójka Jerzy, "Posługi duszpasterskie przy wojskach polskich w wiekach średnich," in *Studia z dziejów feudalizmu*, ed. Stanisław M. Zajączkowski (Łódź: Wydawnictwo Uniwersytetu Łódzkiego, 1994), 93–105; Jan Ptak, "Duszpasterstwo rycerstwa polskiego w epoce Piastów i Jagiellonów," in *Historia duszpasterstwa wojskowego na ziemiach polskich*, ed. Jan Ziółek (Lublin: Towarzystwo Naukowe KUL, 2004), 83–108.

to this issue relatively recently, in an article devoted to religious preparations for armed struggle in medieval Poland.[39] Ptak's article deserves special attention here because, on the one hand, it departs from the schemes typical of older historiography, while at the same time attempting to present the problem comprehensively, considering changes over time. It cannot be ignored, however, that the author did not try to confront the image he was creating within the broader scholarship.

In recent years, a significant intensification of research on religious practices accompanying or carried out in connection with warfare in medieval Poland can be observed. Perhaps one of the most fruitful fields in terms of recent historiography on religious rituals and warfare can be seen in the work of Radosław Kotecki, particularly in his considerations of the relationship between clergy and warfare in Poland during the twelfth century. Another important theme of Kotecki's research concerns the ritual of the march to battle, which consisted of the army following a sacred emblem (relics, cross, holy spear) resting in the hands of a clerical "standard-bearer." This figure served as a liaison between the temporal and the supernatural domains.[40] As such, his work highlights the parallels between Poland, East Central Europe, Rus, the West, and Byzantium, demonstrating the considerable potential for future avenues of "de-regionalization" of research.[41] Jacek Maciejewski is another scholar who connected these phenomena extensively in his works, demonstrating the power of rituals and their relation to sacralizing warfare over time. Together with Kotecki and in his separate works, he shows, above all, the importance that Polish bishops played in achieving such an effect. In doing so, Maciejewski shows how such practices changed over time as the social and cultural role

---

39 Jan Ptak, "Zanim wyruszyli na wroga ... Religijne przygotowanie do walki zbrojnej w średniowiecznej Polsce," *TKH OL PAN* 11 (2014): 20–45.

40 Kotecki is currently preparing a book on the "standard-bearers" and "signs of victory" (*signa victricia*) in Central and Eastern European historical writing that will be also a study on sacralization and ritualization of war, entitled *"Signiferi." Narracje o "chorążych" i znakach zwycięstwa w środkowo- i wschodnio-europejskim piśmiennictwie historycznym. Studium z problematyki sakralizacji i rytualizacji wojny w średniowieczu.*

41 Radosław Kotecki, "With the Sword of Prayer, or How the Medieval Bishop Should Fight," *QMAN* 21 (2016): 341–69; idem, "Aleksander z Malonne—'persona mixta'. Wojowniczy biskup na krańcach chrześcijańskiego świata i jego kronikarski portret," *Studia Źródłoznawcze* 55 (2017): 51–78; idem "Pious Rulers, Princely Clerics, and Angels of Light: Imperial Holy War Imagery in Twelfth-Century Poland and Rus'," in *Christianity and War*, 159–88.

of the episcopate of Gniezno ecclesiastical province changed from the early twelfth to the late fifteenth century.[42]

Paweł Figurski has recently raised important issues in his work on prayers in high medieval Polish liturgical sources. These can be interpreted in the context of the sacralization of the Piast wars. This is primarily about the formulas of the benediction of weapons present in pontificals, which so far have been interpreted mainly in the context of the inauguration of the princely power. Referring to the wider scholarship on medieval liturgy, including especially the war liturgy, he showed the proper meaning of these prayers as means used by bishops participating in the Piast military campaigns or celebrating the rites of departure for war.[43] Moreover, Figurski has recently found a manuscript from the twelfth century (Biblioteka Kapitulna we Wrocławiu, MS 148) that could have been used by the bishops of Wrocław which contains prayers for blessing weapons and its examination let him formulate highly interesting conclusions and hypotheses regarding the possible use of the in Piast warfare against pagans.[44]

Figurski's research provides something very important for the issues taken up in this book. It cannot be ignored that there is still much work to be done in this area, especially when it comes to Northern and Eastern Europe. While the issue of the military liturgy in the West has long been an important subject of research by many scholars who followed Michael McCormick, in the regions

---

42 Radosław Kotecki and Jacek Maciejewski, "Writing Episcopal Courage in Twelfth-Century Poland: Gallus Anonymous and Master Vincentius," in *Episcopal Power and Personality in Medieval Europe, 900–1480*, ed. Peter Coss et al., MCS 42 (Turnhout: Brepols, 2020), 35–61; iidem, "Ideas of Episcopal Power, Legal Norms and Military Activity of the Polish Episcopate between the Twelfth- and Fourteenth Centuries," *KH* 127.Eng.-Language Edition 4 (2020): 5–46; Jacek Maciejewski, "A Bishop Defends His City, or Master Vincentius's Troubles with the Military Activity of His Superior," in *Between Sword and Prayer: Warfare and Medieval Clergy in Cultural Perspective*, ed. Radosław Kotecki, Jacek Maciejewski, and John S. Ott, EMC 3 (Leiden and Boston MA: Brill, 2018), 341–368; idem, "Memory of the 'Warrior-Bishops' of Płock in the Writings of Jan Długosz," in *Christianity and War*, 75–96.

43 Paweł Figurski, "Liturgiczne początki 'Polonii'. Lokalna adaptacja chrześcijańskiego kultu a tworzenie 'polskiej' tożsamości politycznej w X–XI w.," in *Oryginalność czy wtórność? Studia poświęcone polskiej kulturze politycznej i religijnej (X–XIII wiek)*, ed. Roman Michałowski and Grzegorz Pac (Warsaw: Wydawnictwa Uniwersytetu Warszawskiego, 2020), 725–96 at 790–93.

44 Figurski announces the edition and detailed study of the manuscript. So far, see esp. Paweł Figurski, "Beyond the 'Monarchical Church' Model: Liturgy, Manuscripts, and Bishops in the Kingdom of Poland. Case Studies from the Eleventh and Twelfth Centuries," in *Die "Episkopalisierung der Kirche" im europäischen Vergleich*, ed. Hedwig Röckelein and Andreas Bihrer, Studien zur Germania Sacra. Neue Folge 13 (Berlin and Boston MA: De Gruyter, 2022), 361–404 at 399–402.

of interest of this book this research is neglected.[45] For example, a large accumulation of wartime prayers is witnessed in surviving Hungarian manuscripts; however, they are so far poorly studied.[46]

Another distinguishing feature of Polish historiography is a large number of works treating the subject of pagan war rituals or the borderline between pagan (nativist) and Christian mentality. However, the weight of these works varies, which is related to the insufficient sensitivity of scholars to the influence of unorthodox (from today's point of view) Christian practices based on biblical or even ancient models. Such an approach is particularly characteristic of researchers interested in Slavic religions and the archaeology of cult sites, who are largely unfamiliar with Christian rituals and ceremonies.[47] On the other extreme, there are important works of scholars focusing attention on the presented world of the text as a research issue. These are the works of, first of all, Jacek Banaszkiewicz and Paweł Żmudzki.[48] Even if they do not

---

45   Beyond widely known works of McCormick, Bachrach, and Gaposchkin other relevant studies to the topic of war liturgy include, e.g.: Bernabé Cabañero Subiza and Fernando Galtier Martí, "'Tuis exercitibus crux Christi semper adsistat'. El relieve real prerrománico de Luesia," *Artigrama* 3 (1986): 11–28; Carlos Laliena Corbera, "Rituales litúrgicos y poder real en el siglo XI," *Aragón en la Edad Media* 16 (2000): 467–76; Alexander Pierre Bronisch, *Reconquista y guerra santa. La concepción de la guerra en la España cristiana desde los visigodos hasta comienzos del siglo XII*, Monográfica. Biblioteca de humanidades. Chronica nova estudios históricos 99 (Granada: Universidad de Granada, 2006); Walter Pohl, "Liturgie di guerra nei regni altomedievali," *RSC* 5 (2008): 29–44; Andreas Heinz, "'Waffensegen' und Friedensgebet. Zur politischen Dimension der Liturgie," in *Lebendiges Erbe: Beiträge zur abendländischen Liturgie- und Frömmigkeitsgeschichte*, Pietas liturgica. Studia 21 (Tübingen and Basel: Francke, 2010), 221–41; Jürgen Bärsch, "'Pax Domini' und 'Depressio inimicorum.' Skizzen zu Krieg und Frieden im Spiegel der abendländischen Liturgie in Spätantike und Mittelalter," in *Friedensethik im frühen Mittelalter. Theologie zwischen Kritik und Legitimation von Gewalt*, ed. Gerhard Beestermöller, Studien zur Friedensethik 46 (Münster: Aschendorff, 2014), 53–84.

46   *Esztergom Benedictional* (*Benedictionale Strigoniense*), dated between 1075–1092 (*In tempore belli*), *Pontifical of Bishop Hartvik of Győr* (*Agenda pontificalis*), written probably between 1090 and 1095 (*Ordo in tempore belli*), or *Codex Pray* compiled ca. 1200 (*Missa pro rege tempore belli*).

47   See, e.g., Andrzej Kuczkowski, "Magiczno-religijne elementy sztuki wojennej u Słowian Zachodnich wczesnego średniowiecza," *Acta Militaria Mediaevalia* 5 (2009): 7–19.

48   Jacek Banaszkiewicz, "Włócznia i chorągiew. O rycie otwierania bitwy w związku z cudem kampanii nakielskiej Bolesława Krzywoustego (Kadłubek, III,14)," *KH* 94.4 (1987): 3–24; idem, "Bolesław i Peredsława. Uwagi o uroczystości stanowienia władcy w związku z wejściem Chrobrego do Kijowa," *KH* 97.3–4 (1990): 3–35; idem, "Potrójne zwycięstwo Mazowszan nad Pomorzanami—Gall II,49—czyli historyk między 'rzeczywistością prawdziwą' a schematem porządkującym," in *Kultura średniowieczna i staropolska. Studia ofiarowane Aleksandrowi Gieysztorowi w pięćdziesięciolecie pracy naukowej*, ed. Danuta Gawinowa (Warsaw: Państwowe Wydawnictwo Naukowe, 1991), 305–13; idem, "Nadzy

always directly touch on the issues of rituals and religious customs but focus more on the relationship of the community/body politic/army/rulers with the divine, they are extremely important for understanding the part of the medieval mentality that was responsible for resorting to ritual actions aimed at achieving victory.

What is clear is that, in the historiography of local research communities, there are several works on the issues addressed in this collection. However, the works listed here are mostly minor contributions, which can be considered at most as starting points for further in-depth analysis. It is only in recent years that a change in this situation can be observed, which means, however, that we are only at the beginning of the pathway. The path is a narrow and poorly trodden one, and in places disappears among the bushes, but even more intriguing and worth exploration. The task of this collection of chapters is to blaze a bit of a trail and lay the groundwork for more methodologically advanced research that will hopefully come in the future.

3 Chapter Outline

The first volume of this book focuses on Northern Europe and the Baltic. Comprised of eight chapters, it begins with an outline of the theoretical framework that shapes the contents of the book, written by Kyle Lincoln. His chapter examines the main innovations in scholarly research with respect to the role played by the liturgy and the interventions of saints in combat. While

---

wojownicy'—o średniowiecznych pogłosach dawnego rytu wojskowego," in *Człowiek, sacrum, środowisko. Miejsca kultu we wczesnym średniowieczu*, ed. Sławomir Moździoch, Spotkania Bytomskie 4 (Wrocław: Werk, 2000), 11–25; idem, "Czym była i jak została zniszczona chorągiew Świętowita? (Saxo Grammaticus, 'Gesta Danorum', XIV, 39)," in *Heraldyka i okolice*, ed. Andrzej Rachuba, Sławomir Górzyński, and Halina Manikowska (Warsaw: DiG, 2002), 57–70; Paweł Żmudzki, "Opisy bitew ukazujące wojowników gotowych przyjąć swój los (przykłady słowiańskie XI–XIII w.)," in *Sacrum. Obraz i funkcja*, 151–75; idem, *Władca i wojownicy. Narracje o wodzach, drużynie i wojnach w najdawniejszej historiografii Polski i Rusi* (Wrocław: Wydawnictwo Uniwersytetu Wrocławskiego, 2009); idem, "Psy Jaćwingów. Dlaczego Marcin Kromer zinterpretował rocznikarską zapiskę o zwycięstwie Leszka Czarnego inaczej niż Jan Długosz," in *"Historia narrat." Studia mediewistyczne ofiarowane profesorowi Jackowi Banaszkiewiczowi*, ed. Andrzej Pleszczyński et al. (Lublin: Wydawnictwo Uniwersytetu Marii Curie-Skłodowskiej, 2012), 75–94; idem, "Las Solec i Las Birnamski: Nadnaturalna pomoc dla Bolesława Pobożnego w walce z Kazimierzem Konradowicem ('Rocznik kapituły poznańskiej', 1259 rok)," in *"Homini, qui in honore fuit." Księga pamiątkowa poświęcona śp. profesorowi Grzegorzowi Białuńskiemu*, ed. Alicja Dobrosielska, Aleksander Pluskowski, and Seweryn Szczepański (Olsztyn: Towarzystwo Naukowe Pruthenia, 2020), 429–44.

not exclusively focused on the regions under study and focusing on the eleventh to the thirteenth centuries, Lincoln's contribution situates the study of religion and warfare in the Middle Ages within a broader context. In this way, it outlines the horizon of comparative research for the topics taken up in the book.

The volume then proceeds to discuss the functions of rituals in times of war in Northern Europe and the Baltic. Jesse Harrington's chapter begins this volume with consideration of the presence of war liturgy and religious rites in the Gaelic world and its surrounding areas before 1200. Although this is an area that remains on the periphery when it comes to religious rites in times of war, Harrington's piece demonstrates the rich and diverse traditions in this part of Christendom concerning the performance of the Psalter, fasting, and processions of relics and "battle talismans." Harrington succeeds in showing us how, as in other parts of the medieval world, these performances served to boost morale on the Gaelic frontier.

Religious rituals and "integrated warfare" in twelfth-century Norway form the subject of Max Naderer's contribution. Drawing on a variety of sources, especially sagas, Naderer presents the first systematic attempt to consider religious rituals and spiritual weapons in this region. In doing so, he highlights, among other things, the impact of crusading ideology on military culture in Norway while also addressing the use of relics, prayers, kissing churches, and excommunication. Naderer convincingly argues how these phenomena shaped the experience of war on the northern peripheries of the Christian world as they did in other, more—studied regions of the medieval world, highlighting the continuity between seemingly disparate regions. Moving west from Scandinavia, Robert Bubczyk's chapter takes us to Scotland, analyzing the Battle of Bannockburn (23–24 June, 1314) in the context of religious rites performed by participants on both sides. In doing so, he offers a better understanding of medieval notions of piety, especially how these notions can be read from narrative depictions of the battle over time. Bubczyk demonstrates that religiosity significantly affected the actions of the participants in the battle, a facet that has remained in the background with respect to the multitude of research carried out on the battle.

Sini Kangas' chapter marks the first of this book's contributions focused on the Baltic Region. Taking a comparative approach utilizing chronicles of the Teutonic Order in Livonia and Prussia, in addition to the *chansons de gestes* produced during the crusades to the Holy Land, her chapter shows the importance of rituals performed in times of war by individuals (such as knights). As such, the chapter investigates not so much the role of clergy in supervising and regulating religious rituals in times of war, but rather the extent to which lay piety among individuals can be observed in these texts. From here, Carsten Selch Jensen provides a novel approach to reading one of the most important narrative sources for the conquest of the eastern Baltic: the thirteenth-century chronicle of Henry, a priest to the non-Christian peoples of Livonia. Addressing the performance of rituals in times of war as "religious markers," Jensen demonstrates that the performance of religious rituals not just by Christians in the chronicle, but also pagans, form a significant component to the text's narrative structure (which was ultimately to place Livonia, and crusading there, within a providential history). Gregory Leighton's paper continues this thread, taking us south to the land of Prussia and analyzing the campaigns of the Teutonic Order. Drawing on a wide variety of texts, including letters, church inventories, and liturgical sources, Leighton's paper highlights how religious rituals in times of war played not only a significant role in the Christianization process on the southern Baltic periphery but also the ways in which they impacted the perception of space and landscape there.

Bibliography

Bachrach, David S. "Military Chaplains and the Religion of War in Ottonian Germany, 919–1024." *RSS* 39.1 (2011): 13–31.

Bachrach, David S. "The 'Ecclesia Anglicana' Goes to War: Prayers, Propaganda, and Conquest during the Reign of Edward I of England, 1272–1307." *Albion* 36.3 (2004): 393–406.

Bachrach, David S. *Religion and the Conduct of War, c. 300–1215*. Woodbridge: Boydell Press, 2003.

Banaszkiewicz, Jacek. "Bolesław i Peredsława. Uwagi o uroczystości stanowienia władcy w związku z wejściem Chrobrego do Kijowa." *KH* 97.3–4 (1990): 3–35.

Banaszkiewicz, Jacek. "Czym była i jak została zniszczona chorągiew Świętowita? (Saxo Grammaticus, 'Gesta Danorum', XIV, 39)." In *Heraldyka i okolice*. Edited by Andrzej Rachuba, Sławomir Górzyński, and Halina Manikowska, 57–70. Warsaw: DiG, 2002.

Banaszkiewicz, Jacek. "'Nadzy wojownicy'—o średniowiecznych pogłosach dawnego rytu wojskowego." In *Człowiek, sacrum, środowisko. Miejsca kultu we wczesnym średniowieczu*. Edited by Sławomir Moździoch, 11–25. Spotkania Bytomskie 4. Wrocław: Werk, 2000.

Banaszkiewicz, Jacek. "Potrójne zwycięstwo Mazowszan nad Pomorzanami—Gall II,49—czyli historyk między 'rzeczywistością prawdziwą' a schematem porządkującym." In *Kultura średniowieczna i staropolska. Studia ofiarowane Aleksandrowi*

Gieysztorowi w pięćdziesięciolecie pracy naukowej. Edited by Danuta Gawinowa, 305–13. Warsaw: Państwowe Wydawnictwo Naukowe, 1991.

Banaszkiewicz, Jacek. "Włócznia i chorągiew. O rycie otwierania bitwy w związku z cudem kampanii nakielskiej Bolesława Krzywoustego (Kadłubek, III,14)." *KH* 94.4 (1987): 3–24.

Bärsch, Jürgen. "'Pax Domini' und 'Depressio inimicorum. Skizzen zu Krieg und Frieden im Spiegel der abendländischen Liturgie in Spätantike und Mittelalter." In *Friedensethik im frühen Mittelalter. Theologie zwischen Kritik und Legitimation von Gewalt.* Edited by Gerhard Beestermöller, 53–84. Studien zur Friedensethik 46. Münster: Aschendorff, 2014.

Bláhová, Marie. "Vidění kanovníka Víta—zjitřené emoce nebo promyšlená inscenace?" In *"Fontes ipsi sitiunt." Sborník prací k sedmdesátinám archiváře a historika Eduarda Mikuška.* Edited by Petr Kopička, 35–41. Litoměřice and Prague: Scriptorium, 2016.

Bliese, John R.E. "Saint Cuthbert and War." *JMH* 24.3 (2012): 215–41.

Bronisch, Alexander Pierre. *Reconquista y guerra santa. La concepción de la guerra en la España cristiana desde los visigodos hasta comienzos del siglo XII.* Monográfica. Biblioteca de humanidades. Chronica nova estudios históricos 99. Granada: Universidad de Granada, 2006.

Chodyński, Antoni R. "The Preparations for War Expeditions to Lithuania and Samogitia According to the Chronicle by Wigand of Marburg." *Fasciculi Archaeologicae Historicae* 15 (2002): 39–46.

Clancy, Thomas O. "Columba, Adomnan and the Cult of Saints in Scotland." In *"Spes Scotorum," Hope of Scots: Saint Columba, Iona and Scotland.* Edited by Dauvit Broun and Thomas O. Clancy, 3–33. Edinburgh: T&T Clark, 1999.

Corbera, Carlos Laliena. "Rituales litúrgicos y poder real en el siglo XI." *Aragón en la Edad Media* 16 (2000): 467–76.

Csukovits, Enikő. "Les saints libérateurs des Turcs en Hongrie à la fin du Moyen Âge." In *Les saints et leur culte en Europe centrale au Moyen Âge.* Edited by Marie-Madeleine de Cevins and Olivier Marin, 109–21. Hagiologia 13. Turnhout: Brepols, 2017.

Dąbrowski, Dariusz. "Religijność króla Daniela Romanowicza." *Knâža doba. Ìstorìâ ì kul'tura* 9(9) (2015): 79–90.

Dąbrowski, Dariusz. *Król Rusi Daniel Romanowicz. O ruskiej rodzinie książęcej, społeczeństwie i kulturze w XIII w.* Monografie pracowni badań nad dziejami Rusi Uniwersytetu Kazimierza Wielkiego w Bydgoszczy 4. Cracow: Avalon, 2016.

Dalewski, Zbigniew. "A New Chosen People? Gallus Anonymus's Narrative about Poland and Its Rulers." In *Historical Narratives and Christian Identity on a European Periphery: Early History Writing in Northern, East-Central, and Eastern Europe (c. 1070–1200).* Edited by Ildar H. Garipzanov, 145–66. MTCN 26. Turnhout: Brepols, 2011.

Draguţ, Vasile. "La légende du 'Héros de frontière' dans la peinture médiévale de Transylvanie." *Revue Roumaine de l'Histoire de l'Art, S. Beaux-Arts* 11 (1974): 11–40.

Dygo, Marian. "The Political Role of the Cult of the Virgin Mary in Teutonic Prussia in the Fourteenth and Fifteenth Centuries." *JMH* 15.1 (1989): 63–80.

Ehlers, Axel. "The Crusade of the Teutonic Knights against Lithuania Reconsidered." In *Crusade and Conversion on the Baltic Frontier, 1100–1550*. Edited by Alan V. Murray, 21–44. Aldershot and Burlington VT: Ashgate, 2001.

Erdmann, Carl. *Die Entstehung des Kreuzzugsgedanken*. FKG 6. Stuttgart: Kohlhammer, 1935.

Erdmann, Carl. "Heidenkrieg in der Liturgie u. Kaiserkrönung Ottos I." In *Heidenmission und Kreuzzugsgedanke in der Deutschen Ostpolitik des Mittelalters*. Edited by Helmut Beumann, 47–64. Wege der Forschungen 7. Darmstadt: Wissenschaftliches Buchgesellschaft, 1963.

Eshel, Shay. *The Concept of the Elect Nation in Byzantium*. MMED 113. Leiden and Boston MA: Brill, 2018.

Figurski, Paweł. "Beyond the 'Monarchical Church' Model: Liturgy, Manuscripts, and Bishops in the Kingdom of Poland. Case Studies from the Eleventh and Twelfth Centuries." In *Die "Episkopalisierung der Kirche" im europäischen Vergleich*. Edited by Hedwig Röckelein and Andreas Bihrer, 361–404. Studien zur Germania Sacra. Neue Folge 13. Berlin and Boston MA: De Gruyter, 2022.

Figurski, Paweł. "Liturgiczne początki 'Polonii'. Lokalna adaptacja chrześcijańskiego kultu a tworzenie 'polskiej' tożsamości politycznej w X–XI w." In *Oryginalność czy wtórność? Studia poświęcone polskiej kulturze politycznej i religijnej (X–XIII wiek)*. Edited by Roman Michałowski and Grzegorz Pac, 725–96. Warsaw: Wydawnictwa Uniwersytetu Warszawskiego, 2020.

Flusin, Bernard. "Le culte de la Croix au palais de Constantinople d'après le 'Livre des cérémonies.'" In *The Church of the Holy Cross of Ałt'amar*. Edited by Zaroui Pogossian and Edda Vardanyan, 100–25. Armenian texts and studies 3. Leiden and Boston MA: Brill, 2019.

Gaposchkin, M. Cecilia. "The Echoes of Victory: Liturgical and Para-Liturgical Commemorations of the Capture of Jerusalem in the West." *JMH* 40.3 (2014): 237–59.

Gaposchkin, M. Cecilia. "From Pilgrimage to Crusade: The Liturgy of Departure, 1095–1300." *Speculum* 88.1 (2013): 44–91.

Gaposchkin, M. Cecilia. *Invisible Weapons: Liturgy and the Making of Crusade Ideology*. Ithaca NY: Cornell University Press, 2017.

Gaposchkin, M. Cecilia. "The Pre-Battle Processions of the First Crusade and the Creation of Militant Christian 'communitas.'" *Material Religion* 14.4 (2018): 454–68.

Garrison, Mary. "The Franks as the New Israel? Education for an Identity from Pippin to Charlemagne." In *The Uses of the Past in Early Medieval Europe*. Edited by Yitzhak Hen and Matthew Innes, 114–61. Cambridge: Cambridge University Press, 2000.

Gerát, Ivan. *Svätí bojovníci v stredoveku. Úvahy o obrazových legendách sv. Juraj a sv. Ladislava na Slovensku*. Bratislava: VEDA, 2011.

Gieysztor, Aleksander. "Politische Heilige im hochmittelalterlichen Polen und Böhmen." In *Politik und Heiligenverehrung im Hochmittelalter*. Edited by Jürgen Petersohn, 325–41. VF 42. Sigmaringen: Thorbecke, 1994.

Goetz, Hans-Werner. "'Glaubenskriege?' Die Kriege der Christen gegen Andersgläubige in der früh- und hochmittelalterlichen Wahrnehmung." FS 53.1 (2019): 67–114.

Grachev, Artem Yu. "K voprosu o roli i meste duhovenstva v voennoj organizacii Drevnej Rusi." *Pskovskij voenno-istoricheskij vestnik* 94 (2015): 43–47.

Graus, František. "Der Heilige als Schlachtenhelfer—Zur Nationalisierung einer Wundererzählung in der mittelalterlichen Chronistik." In *Festschrift für Helmut Beumann zum 65. Geburtstag*. Edited by Kurt-Ulrich Jäschke und Reinhard Wenskus, 330–48. Sigmaringen: Thorbecke, 1977.

Gübele, Boris. *"Deus vult, Deus vult." Der christliche heilige Krieg im Früh- und Hochmittelalter*. Mittelalter-Forschungen 54. Ostfildern: Thorbecke, 2018.

Hare, Kent G. "Apparitions and War in Anglo-Saxon England." In *The Circle of War in the Middle Ages: Essays on Medieval Military and Naval History*. Edited by Donald J. Kagay and L.J.A. Villalon, 75–86. Woodbridge: Boydell Press, 1999.

Heinz, Andreas. "'Waffensegen' und Friedensgebet. Zur politischen Dimension der Liturgie." In *Lebendiges Erbe: Beiträge zur abendländischen Liturgie- und Frömmigkeitsgeschichte*, 221–41. Pietas liturgica. Studia 21. Tübingen and Basel: Francke, 2010.

Heydemann, Gerda. "The People of God and the Law: Biblical Models in Carolingian Legislation." *Speculum* 95.1 (2020): 89–131.

Holdsworth, Christopher. "'An Airier Aristocracy': The Saints at War." *Transactions of the Royal Historical Society* 6 (1996): 103–22.

Isoaho, Mari. *The Image of Aleksandr Nevskiy in Medieval Russia: Warrior and Saint*. TNW 21. Leiden and Boston MA: Brill, 2006.

Jensen, Carsten Selch. "History Made Sacred: Martyrdom and the Making of a Sanctified Beginning in Early Thirteenth-Century Livonia." In *Saints and Sainthood around the Baltic Sea: Identity, Literacy, and Communication in the Middle Ages*. Edited by Carsten Selch Jensen, Tracey Renée Sands, and Nils Holger Petersen, 145–73. SMEM 54. Kalamzoo MI: Medieval Institute Publications, 2018.

Jensen, Carsten Selch, and Janus Møller Jensen, and Kurt Villads Jensen, ed. *Fighting for the Faith: The Many Crusades*. Scripta minora 27. Stockholm: Runica et mediævalia, 2018.

Jensen, Kurt Villads. "Martyrs, Total War, and Heavenly Horses: Scandinavia as Centre and Periphery in the Expansion of Medieval Christendom." In *Medieval Christianity in the North: New Studies.* Edited by Kirsti Salonen, Kurt Villads Jensen, and Torstein Jørgensen, 89–120. Acta Scandinavica 1. Turnhout: Brepols, 2013.

Jensen, Kurt Villads. "Saints at War in the Baltic Region." In *Saints and Sainthood around the Baltic Sea: Identity, Literacy, and Communication in the Middle Ages.* Edited by Carsten Selch Jensen et al., 251–71. SMEM 54. Kalamazoo MI: Medieval Institute Publications, 2018.

Jerzy, Sójka. "Posługi duszpasterskie przy wojskach polskich w wiekach średnich." In *Studia z dziejów feudalizmu.* Edited by Stanisław M. Zajączkowski, 93–105. Łódź: Wydawnictwo Uniwersytetu Łódzkiego, 1994.

Juzepczuk, Monika. "Kult świętych a zwycięstwa militarne pierwszych Piastów (od X do początków XIII w.)." *Saeculum Christianum* 25.1 (2018): 63–76.

Kaldellis, Anthony. "The Military Use of the Icon of the Theotokos and its Moral Logic in the Historians of the Ninth–Twelfth Centuries." *Estudios Bizantinos* 1 (2013): 56–75.

Kersken, Norbert. "God and the Saints in Medieval Polish Historiography." In *The Making of Christian Myths in the Periphery of Latin Christendom (c. 1000–1300).* Edited by Lars B. Mortensen, 153–94. Copenhagen: Museum Tusculanum Press, 2006.

Klein, Holger A. "Objektkultur und Kultobjekte im kaiserlich-byzantinischen Prozessionswesen." In *"Palatium sacrum"—Sakralität am Hof des Mittelalters. Orte, Dinge, Rituale.* Edited by Manfred Luchterhandt and Hedwig Röckelein, 77–100. Regensburg: Schnell & Steiner, 2021.

Klein, Holger A. "Sacred Relics and Imperial Ceremonies at the Great Palace of Constantinople." In *Visualisierungen von Herrschaft. Frühmittelalterliche Residenzen Gestalt und Zeremoniell.* Edited by Franz A. Bauer, 79–99. Byzas 5. Istanbul: Ege Yayınları, 2006.

Königer, Albert M. *Die Militärseelsorge der Karolingerzeit. Ihr Recht und ihre Praxis.* VKSM 4.7. Munich: Lentner, 1918.

Kotecki, Radosław. "Aleksander z Malonne—'persona mixta'. Wojowniczy biskup na krańcach chrześcijańskiego świata i jego kronikarski portret." *Studia Źródłoznawcze* 55 (2017): 51–78.

Kotecki, Radosław. "Pious Rulers, Princely Clerics, and Angels of Light: Imperial Holy War Imagery in Twelfth-Century Poland and Rus'." In *Christianity and War in Medieval East Central Europe and Scandinavia.* Edited by Radosław Kotecki, Carsten Selch Jensen, and Stephen Bennett, 159–88. Leeds: ARC Humanities Press, 2021.

Kotecki, Radosław. "With the Sword of Prayer, or How the Medieval Bishop Should Fight." *QMAN* 21 (2016): 341–69.

Kotecki, Radosław, and Jacek Maciejewski. "Ideas of Episcopal Power, Legal Norms and Military Activity of the Polish Episcopate between the Twelfth- and Fourteenth Centuries." *KH* 127.Eng.-Language Edition 4 (2020): 5–46.

Kotecki, Radosław, and Jacek Maciejewski. "Writing Episcopal Courage in Twelfth-Century Poland: Gallus Anonymous and Master Vincentius." In *Episcopal Power and Personality in Medieval Europe, 900–1480*. Peter Coss et al., 35–61. MCS 42. Turnhout: Brepols, 2020.

Kotecki, Radosław, Carsten Selch Jensen, and Stephen Bennett, ed. *Christianity and War in Medieval East Central Europe and Scandinavia*. Leeds: ARC Humanities Press, 2021.

Kuczkowski, Andrzej. "Magiczno-religijne elementy sztuki wojennej u Słowian Zachodnich wczesnego średniowiecza." *Acta Militaria Mediaevalia* 5 (2009): 7–19.

Kwiatkowski, Krzysztof. "'Christ ist erstanden ...' and Christians Win! Liturgy and the Sacralization of Armed Fight against the Pagans as Determinants of the Identity of the Members of the Teutonic Order in Prussia." In *Sacred Space in the State of the Teutonic Order in Prussia*. Edited by Jarosław Wenta and Magdalena Kopczyńska, 101–29. SBS 2. Toruń: Wydawnictwo Naukowe Uniwersytetu Mikołaja Kopernika, 2013.

Kwiatkowski, Krzysztof. "Prolog und Epilog 'temporis sancti'. Die Belagerung Kauens 1362 in der Beschreibung Wigands von Marburg." *ZfO* 57.2 (2008): 238–54.

Kwiatkowski, Krzysztof. *Zakon niemiecki jako "corporatio militaris." Część 1: Korporacja i krąg przynależących do niej. Kulturowe i społeczne podstawy działalności militarnej zakonu w Prusach (do początku XV wieku)*. Dzieje zakonu niemieckiego 1. Toruń: Wydawnictwo Naukowe Uniwersytetu Mikołaja Kopernika, 2012.

Leighton, Gregory. "The Relics of St Barbara at Althaus Kulm: History, Patronages, and Insight into the Teutonic Order and Christian Population in Prussia (Thirteenth-Fifteenth Centuries)." *ZH* 85.1 (2020): 5–50.

Leighton, Gregory. "'Reysa in laudem Dei et virginis Marie contra paganos': The Experience of Crusading in Prussia during the Thirteenth and Fourteenth Centuries." *ZfO* 69.1 (2020): 1–25.

Löffler, Annette. "Die Rolle der Liturgie im Ordenskonvent. Norm und Wirklichkeit." In *Das Leben im Ordenshaus*. Edited by Juhan Kreem, 1–20. QSGD 81. Weimar: VDG, 2019.

Lucas, Anthony T. "The Social Role of Relics and Reliquaries in Ancient Ireland." *JRSAI* 116 (1986): 5–37.

Maciejewski, Jacek. "A Bishop Defends His City, or Master Vincentius's Troubles with the Military Activity of His Superior." In *Between Sword and Prayer: Warfare and Medieval Clergy in Cultural Perspective*. Edited by Radosław Kotecki, Jacek Maciejewski, and John S. Ott, 341–68. EMC 3. Leiden and Boston MA: Brill, 2018.

Maciejewski, Jacek. "Memory of the 'Warrior-Bishops' of Płock in the Writings of Jan Długosz." In *Christianity and War in Medieval East Central Europe and Scandinavia*. Edited by Radosław Kotecki, Carsten Selch Jensen, and Stephen Bennett, 75–96. Leeds: ARC Humanities Press, 2021.

MacInnes, Iain M. *Scotland's Second War of Independence, 1332–1357*. Woodbridge: Boydell Press, 2016.

Manthey, Jan. "Średniowieczne duszpasterstwo wojskowe." *Duszpasterz Polski Zagranicą* 9.3(36) (1958): 259–77.

Marschner, Patrick S. *Das neue Volk Gottes in Hispanien. Die Bibel in der christlich-iberischen Historiographie vom 8. bis zum 12. Jahrhundert*. Geschichte und Kultur der Iberischen Welt 19. Münster, Berlin, Vienna, Zürich: LIT Verlag, 2023.

McCormick, Michael. *Eternal Victory: Triumphal Rulership in Late Antiquity, Byzantium and the Early Medieval West*. Cambridge: Cambridge University Press, 1990.

McCormick, Michael. "Liturgie et guerre des Carolingiens à la première croisade." In *"Militia Christi" e crociata nei secoli XI–XIII*, 209–40. Miscellanea del Centro di studi medioevali 13. Milan: Vita e pensiero, 1992.

McCormick, Michael. "The Liturgy of War in the Early Middle Ages: Crisis, Litanies, and the Carolingian Monarchy." *Viator* 15 (1984): 1–23.

Mergiali-Sahas, Sophia. "Byzantine Emperors and Holy Relics: Use, and Misuse, of Sanctity and Authority." *Jahrbuch der Österreichischen Byzantinistik* no. 51 (2001): 41–60.

Moroz, Irina. "The Idea of Holy War in the Orthodox World (On Russian Chronicles from the Twelfth-Sixteenth Century)." *QMAN* 4 (1999): 45–67.

Murray, Alan V. "The Sword Brothers at War: Observations on the Military Activity of the Knighthood of Christ in the Conquest of Livonia and Estonia (1203–1227)." *OM* 18 (2013): 27–38.

Musin, Aleksandr E. *"Milites Christi" Drevnej Rusi. Voinskaja kultura russkogo Srednevekovja v kontekste religioznogo mentaliteta*. Militaria Antiqua 8. St. Petersburg: Peterburgskoe Vostokovedenie, 2005.

Nedkvitne, Arnved. *Lay Belief in Norse Society 1000–1350*. Copenhagen: Museum Tusculanum Press, 2009.

Nelson, Robert S. "'And So, With the Help of God': The Byzantine Art of War in the Tenth Century." *Dumbarton Oaks Papers* 65–66 (2011): 169–92.

Nielsen, Torben Kjersgaard. "The Making of New Cultural Landscapes in the Medieval Baltic." In *Medieval Christianity in the North: New Studies*. Edited by Kirsti Salonen, Kurt Villads Jensen, and Torstein Jørgensen, 121–53. Acta Scandinavica 1. Turnhout: Brepols, 2013.

Nielsen, Torben Kjersgaard, and Iben Fonnesberg-Schmidt, ed. *Crusading on the Edge: Ideas and Practice of Crusading in Iberia and the Baltic Region, 1100–1500*. Outremer 4. Turnhout: Brepols, 2016.

Paravcini, Werner. *Die Preußenreisen des europäischen Adels.* 2 vols. BF 17.1–2. Sigmaringen: Thorbecke, 1989–1995.

Pauk, Marcin R. "Święci patroni a średniowieczne wspólnoty polityczne w Europie Środkowej." In *Sacrum. Obraz i funkcja w społeczeństwie średniowiecznym.* Edited by Aneta Pieniądz-Skrzypczak and Jerzy Pysiak, 237–60. Aquila volans 1. Warsaw: Wydawnictwa Uniwersytetu Warszawskiego, 2005.

Penman, Michael A. "Christian Days and Knights: The Religious Devotions and Court of David II of Scotland, 1329–71." *Historical Research* 75.189 (2002): 249–72.

Penman, Michael A. "Faith in War: The Religious Experience of Scottish Soldiery, c.1100–c.1500." *JMH* 37.3 (2011): 295–303.

Penman, Michael A. "'Sacred Food for the Soul': In Search of the Devotions to Saints of Robert Bruce, King of Scotland, 1306–1329." *Speculum* 88.4 (2013): 1035–62.

Pohl, Walter. "Liturgie di guerra nei regni altomedievali." *RSC* 5 (2008): 29–44.

Prochazka, Helen Y. "Warrior Idols or Idle Warriors? On the Cult of Saints Boris and Gleb as Reflected in the Old Russian Military Accounts." *Slavonic and East European Review* 65.4 (1987): 505–16.

Ptak, Jan. "Duszpasterstwo rycerstwa polskiego w epoce Piastów i Jagiellonów." In *Historia duszpasterstwa wojskowego na ziemiach polskich.* Edited by Jan Ziółek, 83–108. Lublin: Towarzystwo Naukowe KUL, 2004.

Ptak, Jan. "Zanim wyruszyli na wroga … Religijne przygotowanie do walki zbrojnej w średniowiecznej Polsce." *TKH OL PAN* 11 (2014): 20–45.

Ramadan, Abdel-Aziz. "The Role of Super Natural Powers in Arab-Byzantine Warfare as Reflected by Popular Imagination." *Journal of Medieval and Islamic History* 9.9 (2015): 3–38.

Roche, Jason T., and Janus M. Jensen, ed. *The Second Crusade: Holy War on the Periphery of Latin Christendom.* Outremer 2. Turnhout: Brepols, 2015.

Samerski, Stefan. "Zwischen Waffengang und 'caritas'. Der Deutsche Orden und seine Heiligen im Mittelalter und in der Frühneuzeit." In *Die Militarisierung der Heiligen in Vormoderne und Moderne.* Edited by Liliya Berezhnaya, 127–42. Historische Forschungen 122. Berlin: Duncker & Humblot, 2020.

Serrano del Pozo, Joaquin. "Relics, Images, and Christian Apotropaic Devices in the Roman-Persian Wars (4th–7th Centuries)." *Eikón Imago* 11 (2022): 57–69.

Sevcenko, Nancy. "The Limburg Staurothek and Its Relics." In *Thymíama. Stē mnémē tēs Laskarínas Mpoúra*, 289–94. Athenes: Mouseío Mpenákē, 1994.

Sharpe, Richard. "Banners of the Northern Saints." In *Saints of North-East England, 600–1500.* Edited by Margaret Coombe, Anne Mouron, and Christiania Whitehead, 245–303. MCS 39. Turnhout: Brepols, 2017.

Siwczyńska, Agata. "Interwencje i działania świętych w najstarszych kronikach polskich i czeskich." *Historia* 3.4 (1995–1996): 7–44.

Srodecki, Paul, and Norbert Kersken, ed. *Defending the Faith: Crusading on the Frontiers of Latin Christendom in the Late Middle Ages*. Turnhout: Brepols, forthc. 2024.

Srodecki, Paul, and Norbert Kersken, ed. *The Expansion of the Faith: Crusading on the Frontiers of Latin Christendom in the High Middle Ages*. Outremer 14. Turnhout: Brepols, 2022.

Subiza, Bernabé Cabañero, and Fernando Galtier Martí. "'Tuis exercitibus crux Christi semper adsistat'. El relieve real prerrománico de Luesia." *Artigrama* 3 (1986): 11–28.

Sullivan, Denis F. "Siege Warfare, Nikephoros II Phokas, Relics and Personal Piety." In *Byzantine Religious Culture: Studies in Honor of Alice-Mary Talbot*. Edited by Alice-Mary M. Talbot and Denis F. Sullivan, 395–409. MMED 92. Leiden and Boston MA: Brill, 2012.

Tarczyński, Tomasz. "The King and the Saint against the Scots: The Shaping of English National Identity in the 12th Century Narrative of King Athelstan's Victory over His Northern Neighbours." In *Imagined Communities: Constructing Collective Identities in Medieval Europe*. Edited by Andrzej Pleszczyński et al., 85–102. EMC 8. Leiden and Boston MA: Brill, 2018.

Thacker, Alan T. "The Church and Warfare: The Religious and Cultural Background to the Hoard." In *The Staffordshire Hoard: An Anglo-Saxon Treasure*. Edited by Chris Fern, Tania M. Dickinson, and Leslie Webster, 293–99. Research report of the Society of Antiquaries of London 80. London: Society of Antiquaries of London, 2019.

Veszprémy, László. "A pityergő Árpádtól a könnyező Szent Lászlóig. A könnyekre fakadó hadvezér a Névtelen Gesztája 39. és a Krónikaszerkesztés 121., 137. Fejezetében." *Acta Historica (Szeged)* 138 (2015): 17–32. Rprt. in idem, *Történetírás és történetírók az Árpád-kori Magyarországon (XI–XIII. század közepe)*, 119–28. Rerum Fides 2. Budapest: Line Design, 2019.

Vukovich, Alexandra. "The Ritualisation of Political Power in Early Rus' (10th–12th Centuries)." PhD thesis, University of Cambridge, 2015.

Vukovich, Alexandra. "Victory and Defeat Liturgified: The Symbolic World of Martial Ritual in Early Rus." In *Victors and Vanquished: Cultures of War in the Northern and Mediterranean Worlds*. Edited by Johannes Pahlitzsch and Jörg Rogge. Byzanz und die euromediterranen Kriegskulturen 1. Mainz: Mainz University Press, forthc. 2023.

Wenta, Jarosław. *Studien über die Ordensgeschichtsschreibung am Beispiel Preußens*. Subsidia historiographica 2. Toruń: Wydawnictwo Naukowe Uniwersytetu Mikołaja Kopernika, 2000.

Zupka, Dušan. *Meč a kríž. Vojna a náboženstvo v stredovekej strednej Európe (10.–12. storočie)*. Bratislava: VEDA, 2020.

Zupka, Dušan. "Náboženské rituály vojny a vytváranie kresťanskej identity v stredovekej strednej Európe 12. storočia." *Historický Časopis* 68.4 (2020): 577–90.

Zupka, Dušan. "Political, Religious and Social Framework of Religious Warfare and Its Influences on Rulership in Medieval East Central Europe." In *Rulership in Medieval*

East Central Europe: Power, Rituals and Legitimacy in Bohemia, Hungary and Poland. Edited by Grischa Vercamer and Dušan Zupka, 135–59. ECEE 78. Leiden and Boston MA: Brill, 2021.

Zupka, Dušan. "Religious Rituals of War in Medieval Hungary Under the Árpád Dynasty." In *Christianity and War in Medieval East Central Europe and Scandinavia*. Edited by Radosław Kotecki, Carsten Selch Jensen, and Stephen Bennett, 141–57. Leeds: ARC Humanities Press, 2021.

Zupka, Dušan. "Ritual Representation of Power in Medieval East Central European Rulership, Sacrality and Warfare (Hungary, Bohemia, Poland, 10th–14th Century)." In *Continuation or Change? Borders and Frontiers in Late Antiquity and Medieval Europe: Landscape of Power Network, Military Organisation and Commerce*. Edited by Gregory Leighton, Piotr Pranke, and Łukasz Różycki, 103–22. Abingdon and New York: Routledge, 2023.

Żmudzki, Paweł. "Las Solec i Las Birnamski: Nadnaturalna pomoc dla Bolesława Pobożnego w walce z Kazimierzem Konradowicem ('Rocznik kapituły poznańskiej', 1259 rok)." In *"Homini, qui in honore fuit." Księga pamiątkowa poświęcona śp. profesorowi Grzegorzowi Białuńskiemu*. Edited by Alicja Dobrosielska, Aleksander Pluskowski, and Seweryn Szczepański, 429–44. Olsztyn: Towarzystwo Naukowe Pruthenia, 2020.

Żmudzki, Paweł. "Opisy bitew ukazujące wojowników gotowych przyjąć swój los (przykłady słowiańskie XI–XIII w.)." In *Sacrum. Obraz i funkcja w społeczeństwie średniowiecznym*. Edited by Aneta Pieniądz-Skrzypczak and Jerzy Pysiak, 151–75. Aquila volans 1. Warsaw: Wydawnictwa Uniwersytetu Warszawskiego, 2005.

Żmudzki, Paweł. "Psy Jaćwingów. Dlaczego Marcin Kromer zinterpretował rocznikarską zapiskę o zwycięstwie Leszka Czarnego inaczej niż Jan Długosz." In *"Historia narrat." Studia mediewistyczne ofiarowane profesorowi Jackowi Banaszkiewiczowi*. Edited by Andrzej Pleszczyński et al., 75–94. Lublin: Wydawnictwo Uniwersytetu Marii Curie-Skłodowskiej, 2012.

Żmudzki, Paweł. *Władca i wojownicy. Narracje o wodzach, drużynie i wojnach w najdawniejszej historiografii Polski i Rusi*. Wrocław: Wydawnictwo Uniwersytetu Wrocławskiego, 2009.

CHAPTER 2

Fighting on a Prayer: Liturgical and Physical Engagement of Sacralized Warfighting in High Medieval Latin Christendom, ca. 1000–1250

Kyle C. Lincoln

In the popular historiography of high medieval Latin Christendom, the myth of the "three orders"—*bellatores, oratores,* and *laboratores*—remains persistent because, although being a too-simplified version of the differences between vocations in the medieval world, it retains a modicum of truth on which more sophisticated analyzes can rely and then be revised.[1] Professional historians, of course, are no longer bounded by structuralist assumptions of enduring forms of organization, but the pedagogical utility of the "three orders" nevertheless makes it a conversation point with which much fruitful discussion might begin.[2] The overlap between these spheres of social organization is frequent and well-attested: prelates and nobles were often from the same families, as the examples of the Barbarossa and Otto of Friesing iconically demonstrate.[3] Yet, it is only recently that increased scholarly attention has been brought

---

1 The classic historiographical formulation is, of course, Duby's and has come under reasonable criticism since its promulgation but its resonance is still tangible in some of the lines drawn between spheres of dominance in the medieval world: Georges Duby, *The Three Orders: Feudal Society Imagined,* trans. Arthur Goldhammer, (Chicago: University of Chicago Press, 1980); Robert Ian Moore, "George Duby's Eleventh Century," *History* 69.225 (1984): 36–49. The lasting impact of Duby's formulation can be found widely, but, for the sake of example, see the first three (or four, depending on one's ambition and willingness to expand the boundaries of inquiry) of the collection edited by Le Goff: Jacque le Goff, ed., *The Medieval World,* trans. Lydia G. Cochrane (New York: Collins and Brown, 1990), 37–180.
2 North American textbooks, in particular, love repeating the formula. For the sake of example, see Barbara Rosenwein, *A Short History of the Middle Ages,* 5th ed. (Toronto: University of Toronto Press, 2018); Michael Burger, *The Shaping of Western Civilization* (Toronto: University of Toronto Press, 2003).
3 Otto of Friesing, *The Deeds of Frederick Barbarossa,* trans., ann. and intro. Charles Christopher Mierow, Records of civilization 49 (New York: Columbia University Press, 1953). For an exploration of Otto's authorial intentions and how they shaped what information was curated, how that was shaped by his background, and how it was transmitted in his historical writing: Romedio Schmitz-Esser, "The Bishop and the Emperor: Tracing Narrative Intent in Otto of Frtiesing's 'Gesta Frederici,'" *Medieval Chronicle* 9 (2014): 297–324.

to areas where those family units had mutual interests: in the unification of Gelasius's "Two Swords" in the practice of fighting a just war.

This chapter will provide much of the theoretical groundwork for the studies that follow in this collection by examining, at a wide angle, the main recent innovations in scholarly research into the practices of liturgical and hagiographical intervention in combat. It will also explore the recruitment of armsbearing laity in the sacralized context of crusade preaching and enrollment in the military orders. In doing so, it presents one set of intersecting inquiries that help uncover the cultural understandings of both religious and military-historical topics, complexifying but (it is hoped) not occluding either from scholarly view. Because the latter studies of this collection have their own, narrower, background section, the goal of this chapter will be to offer a kind of introductory reading of much of the important scholarship that provides crucial points of comparative data for deeper study in the pages that follow. Even with the narrow chronology offered here, these elements show that, by the high medieval period, Latin Christendom was already suffused with the thematic elements that comprise much of the body of this collection. Where the material that precedes the two centuries under survey here is under scholarly scrutiny in other chapters, they should be understood as laying out those very foundational elements on which so much of the later centuries' material depends.

1   Liturgical and Hagiographical Intervention in Warfighting: Expanding the Ambit of Spiritual Warfare

The first section of this chapter examines the historiographical work that underlines so much of our understanding of how spiritual intervention functioned in high medieval Latin Christendom. In the liturgy to support military actions, the clergy sought divine protection and intervention in the progress of warfighting; hagiographical accounts provided proofs for their audience of the impact of that liturgical intercession. Taken together, they represent calls for and responses to requests for divine assistance. A comprehensive examination of all scholarship on the subject would run too long and provide diminishing returns, but a review of recent and impactful work on these linked topics helps outline the importance of spiritual warfare in the period.

1.1   *Liturgical Traces*
The study of liturgy has received considerable attention, as scholars continue to unfold the variety of ways in which both the charters that comprise

the records of the medieval past and the rituals of the divine offices were acts of performance. Where charters give us the direct evidence in many cases of the fighting of wars and provisioning of armies, liturgical evidence uncovers the ways in which holy authority certified these efforts and its power supported their engagement with an enemy. In this section, I wish to highlight both studies of local liturgical intercession for kings and local leaders, as well as those studies that attest to liturgical influences on the ways that these campaigns were contextualized in the wider discourse on the progress of the wars in question.

In the Iberian Peninsula, the work done on liturgical intercession for the campaigns against al-Andalus has received considerable and fruitful attention. Martín Alvira Cabrer has shown that the Las Navas campaign was a major focal point for both liturgical commemoration (after the fact) as well as liturgical support in the form of processions in Rome and even in the process of the Battle of Las Navas itself.[4] Alvira has even recovered an early version of the liturgical commemoration of the battle, preserved at the royal necropolis of Las Huelgas of Burgos.[5] Similarly, Holt has shown that the *missa pro rege* formulae common in both the County of Barcelona and in Castile present considerable evidence of the interpolation of popular crusade liturgical forms.[6] The example of the conquest of Santarem in 1147 presented a similar point of commemoration of that city's conquest by Afonso Henriques, as Nascimiento has shown, and the preservation of other accounts from Cistercian propagandists, as Wilson has noted, makes a clear case for connecting both the popularization of these conquests and their likely solemnification in liturgical settings as sacralized violence.[7] Oliveira, too, has shown that much of the historical memory of the

---

4 Martín Alvira Cabrer, *Las Navas de Tolosa 1212. Idea, liturgía y memoria de la batalla* (Madrid: Sílex, 2013), 127–76.

5 Martín Alvira Cabrer, "El 'Triunfo de la Santa Cruz' en los 'flores sanctorum'. Pervivencia en castellano de un texto latino medieval," *e-Spania* 26 (2017): doi.org/10.4000/e-spania.26450; idem, "Conmemorando la victoria. La 'Fiesta del Triunfo de la Santa Cruz,'" in *Memoria y fuentes de la guerra santa peninsular (siglos X–XV)*, ed. Carlos de Ayala Martínez, Francisco García Fitz, and J. Santiago Palacios Ontalva (Madrid: Trea, 2021), 435–62.

6 Edward L. Holt, "Crusading Memory in the Templar Liturgy of Barcelona," *Crusades* 18 (2019): 217–30; idem, "'Laudes regiae': Liturgy and Royal Power in Thirteenth-Century Castile-León," in *The Sword and the Cross: Castile-León in the Era of Fernando III*, ed. Edward L. Holt and Teresa Witcombe, MEMI 77 (Leiden and Boston MA: Brill, 2020), 140–64.

7 Aires A. Nascimiento, "O Júbilo da Vitória. Celebraçâo da Tomado de Santarém aos Mouros (A.D. 1147)," in *Actes del X Congrés Internacional de L'Associació Hispànica de Literatura Medieval*, ed. Rafael Alemany, Josep Lluís Martos, and Josep Miquel Manzanaro, 3 vols. (Alicante: Institut Interuniversitari de Filologia Valenciana, 2005), 3:1218–32; Jonathan Wilson, "A Cistercian Point of View in the Portuguese Reconquista," *Journal of Medieval Monastic Studies* 8 (2019): 95–142. I am grateful to Jonathan Wilson for his suggestion of Nascimiento's work.

early phases of an "independent" Portuguese effort at expanding to the south in the twelfth century was overlaid with heavily sacralizing language which mimics, in many fashions, the style of liturgical sources.[8] Ritual practice for the coronation of kings in Iberia, both before and during the early crusade period suggests the development (albeit semi-independently) of sacral warfare; commemoration of royal and comital warfighting was overlaid with sacral imagery in art, charters, and chronicles of the period, too, reflecting the broader appeal of holy war as a lens for viewing the frontier and conflict with al-Andalus.[9] Taken together, these studies suggest that there are real viable grounds for the study of liturgical sources in the Iberian Peninsula and that, at least on the southwestern crusading frontier, the liturgical sources suggest realities congruent with other crusading theaters.

Northern crusading frontiers are often understood as being "the other side of the coin" from Iberian developments: they share an earlier heightened degree of royal involvement in campaigns followed by a wider phase of investment by middling nobles, widespread papal support for missionary activities and diocesan planting, and the programmatic settlement patterns to "Christianize" the frontier zones.[10] The Baltic Crusading theater, generally, has proven fruitful for

---

8   Luis Felípe Oliveira, "Guerra e Religiâo. As Narrativas de Conquista das Cidades do Sul," in *Hombres de religión y guerra. Cruzada y guerra santa en la Edad Media peninsular* (*siglos X–XV*), ed. Carlos de Ayala Martínez and J. Santiago Palacios Ontalva (Madrid: Silex, 2018), 513–40.

9   Carlos de Ayala Martinez, *Sacerdocio y Reino en la España Altomedieval. Iglesia y poder politico en el Occidente peninsular, siglos VII–XII* (Madrid: Silex, 2008), 131–270; Francisco García Fitz, *La Edad Media. Guerra e Ideología. Justificaciones religiosas y juridicas* (Madrid: Silex, 2003), 119–218; Alexander Pierre Bronisch, "La 'Chronica Adefonsi Imperatoris' entre guerra santa ibérica y cruzada," in *Hombres de religión y guerra*, 77–87; idem, "La (sacralización de la) guerra en las fuentes de los siglos X y XI y el concepto de guerra santa," in *Orígenes y desarrollo de la guerra santa en la Península Ibérica. Palabras e imágenes para una legitimación* (*siglos X–XIV*), ed. Carlos de Ayala Martínez, Patrick Henriet, and J. Santiago Palacios Ontalva (Madrid: Casa de Velázquez, 2016), 7–29; Helene Sirantoine, "La guerra contra los musulmanes en los diplomas castellanoleoneses (siglo XI-1126)," in ibid., 51–65; Carlos Laliena Corbera, "Rituales litúrgicos y poder real en el siglo XI," *Aragón en la Edad Media* 16 (2000): 467–76; Fermín Miranda García, "Sacralización de la guerra en el siglo X. La perspectiva pamplonesa," *Anales de la Universidad de Alicante. Historia Medieval* 17 (2011): 225–43.

10 Kurt Villads Jensen has made the comparison of these elements in an essay of considerable scope: Kurt Villads Jensen, "Crusading at the End of the World: The Spread of the Idea of Jerusalem after 1099 to the Baltic Sea Area and to the Iberian Peninsula," in *Crusading on the Edge: Ideas and Practice of Crusading in Iberia and the Baltic Region*, ed. Torben Kjersgaard Nielsen and Iben Fonnesberg-Schmidt, Outremer 4 (Turnhout: Brepols, 2016), 153–76. Livonian and Prussian campaigns seem to have favored the involvement of lower-ranking nobles and the creation of zones of territorial colonization by smaller groups:

the exploration of other parts of the wider fabric of clerical engagement with warfighting,[11] but investigations of liturgical traces of ecclesiastical bellicosity have offered preliminary results with cross-reading of chronicle evidence. Henry of Livonia, as Kaljundi and Undusk have both shown, deployed extensive liturgical vocabulary in his chronicle, so as to underline the sacrality of the Baltic campaigns and the ways in which their events shaped their liturgical commemorations. Thus, it appears that wider comparisons with other authors suggest that this was a common interest among chroniclers of the Baltic Crusades.[12] Anti Selart has read several of the miracle stories of the Livonian campaigns toward the Rus and even counter-actions against the Mongols as a kind of echo of the intercession sought through frequent liturgical actions devoted to Mary.[13] Marian devotion was also noticeable in the Płock miracles,

---

Astaf von Transehe-Roseneck, *Die ritterlichen Livlandfahrer des 13. Jahrhunderts. Eine genealogische Untersuchung*, Marburger Ostforschungen 12 (Marburg: Würzburg-Holzner Verlag, 1960); Aleks Pluskowski, *The Archaeology of the Prussian Crusade: Holy War and Colonisation* (Abingdon and New York: Routledge, 2013), 196–246; *The Teutonic Order in Prussia and Livonia: Political and Ecclesiastical Structures, 13th–16th century*, ed. Roman Czaja and Andrzej Radzimiński (Toruń: Towarzystwo Naukowe w Toruniu, 2015). I am grateful to Gregory Leighton for these references.

11   See, e.g., essays by Kotecki, Maciejewski, and Jensen in recent edited collection *Between Sword and Prayer: Warfare and Medieval Clergy in Cultural Perspective*, ed. Radosław Kotecki, Jacek Maciejewski, and John S. Ott, EMC 3 (Leiden and Boston MA: Brill, 2018): Radosław Kotecki, "Lambs and Lions, Wolves and Pastors of the Flock: Portraying Military Activity of Bishops in Twelfth-Century Poland," 303–40; Jacek Maciejewski, "A Bishop Defends His City, or Master Vincentius's Troubles with the Military Activity of His Superior," 341–68; Carsten Selch Jensen, "Bishops and Abbots at War: Some Aspects of Clerical Involvement in Warfare in Twelfth- and Early Thirteenth-Century Livonia and Estonia," 404–34.

12   Linda Kaljundi, "The Baltic Crusades and the Culture of Memory: Studies on Historical Representation, Rituals, and Recollection of the Past" (PhD thesis, University of Helsinki, 2016), 41, 43, 88; Jann Undusk, "Sacred History, Profane History: Uses of the Bible in the Chronicle of Henry of Livonia," in *Crusading and Chronicle Writing on the Medieval Baltic Frontier: A Companion to the Chronicle of Henry of Livonia*, ed. Marek Tamm, Linda Kaljundi, and Carsten Selch Jensen (Farnham and Burlington VT: Ashgate, 2011), 45–75.

13   Anti Selart, *Livonia, Rus' and the Baltic Crusades in the Thirteenth Century*, trans. Fionna Robb, ECEE 29 (Leiden and Boston MA: Brill, 2015), 104; Marian Dygo, "The Political Role of the Cult of the Virgin Mary in Teutonic Prussia in the Fourteenth and Fifteenth Centuries," *JMH* 15.1 (1989): 63–80; Jüri Kivimäe, "'Servi Beatae Marie Virginis': Christians and Pagans in Henry's Chronicle of Livonia," in *Church and Belief in the Middle Ages: Popes, Saints, and Crusaders*, ed. Kirsi Salonen and Sari Katajala-Peltomaa, CB 3 (Amsterdam: Amsterdam University Press, 2016), 201–26; Linda Kaljundi, "Livonia as a Mariological Periphery: A Comparative Look at Henry of Livonia's Representations of the Mother of God," in *Livland—eine Region am Ende der Welt? Forschungen zum Verhältnis zwischen Zentrum und Peripherie im späten Mittelalter*, ed. Anti Selart and Matthias Thumser, QSBG 27 (Cologne, Weimar, and Vienna: Böhlau, 2017), 431–60; Gregory Leighton, "'Reysa

studied by Skwierczyński, where processions seemed to have provoked the miraculous and shaped the response of Mary to contemporary urgent needs.[14] The Teutonic Order, by estimates from a later period, seem to have incorporated a strong Marian bent to their spirituality from the beginning.[15] Although the liturgical studies of how these interventions (studied more below) were invoked are less widely available, their increasing inclusion within bibliographies of crusading liturgies and liturgies in holy wars points toward a bright future.

Beyond the Iberian and Baltic contexts, there is considerable evidence in the continental environment for liturgical intercession in the traditional "core" of medieval European histories. In M. Cecilia Gaposchkin's recent book, she has forcefully argued that both the Advent and Epiphany liturgies formed the foundation of the feasts that celebrated the Capture of Jerusalem.[16] Gaposchkin has shown that the Northern Franks invested considerable intellectual and human resources in crafting a complete liturgical support effort for the process of crusading to Outremer, going so far as to invest enormous energy in the rituals for departure with the hope of spurring the pilgrim on toward success.[17] William Jordan, too, noted that there was substantial evidence for liturgical ceremony accompanying royal departures for war among the Capetian dynasty's many monarchs; even the *chansons des gestes* present strong evidence for the ways that liturgy suffused the tasks that accompanied crusading.[18] English liturgical commemorations showed that the practice for taking the Cross for a crusading mission was evident from the mid-twelfth century onward and made specific

---

in laudem Dei et virginis Marie contra paganos': The Experience of Crusading in Prussia during the Thirteenth and Fourteenth Centuries," *ZfO* 69.1 (2020): 1–25.

14   Krzysztof Skwierczyński, "The Beginnings of the Cult of the Blessed Virgin Mary in Poland in the Light of the Płock Accounts of Miracles from 1148," *Studi Medievali*, Ser. 3 53.1 (2012): 117–61 at 119.

15   Anette Löffler "Die Liturgie des Deutschen Ordens in Preußen," in *"Cura animarum." Seelsorge im Deutschordensland Preußen*, ed. Stefan Samerski, FQKK 45 (Cologne: Bohlau, 2013), 161–84; eadem, "Die Rolle der Liturgie im Ordenskonvent. Norm und Wirklichkeit," in *Das Leben im Ordenshaus. Vorträge der Tagung der Internationalen Historischen Kommission zur Erforschung des Deutschen Ordens in Tallinn 2014*, ed. Juhan Kreem, QSGD 81 (Weimar: VDG, 2019), 1–20.

16   M. Cecilia Gaposchkin, *Invisible Weapons: Liturgy and the Making of Crusade Ideology* (Ithaca NY: Cornell University Press, 2017), 137–48.

17   M. Cecilia Gaposchkin, "From Pilgrimage to Crusade: The Liturgy of Departure, 1095–1300," *Speculum* 88.1 (2013): 44–91.

18   William C. Jordan, "The Rituals of War: Departure for Crusade in Thirteenth-Century France," in *The Book of Kings: Art, War, and the Morgan Library's Medieval Picture Bible*, ed. William Noel and Daniel H. Weiss (London: Walters Art Museum 2002), 99–105; idem, "'Etiam Reges', Even Kings," *Speculum* 90.5 (2015): 613–34 at 616.

textual notation of the protective power that liturgical ceremony conveyed for the crusader.[19] In the Holy Roman Empire, there is substantive evidence to suggest that the Holy Land Masses were incorporated into missals in the period, even if Linder noted that these texts appeared less frequently in Imperial codices than in contemporary French examples.[20] The wide array of liturgical support structures suggests that they were taken very seriously by pilgrims and that they provided real and necessary backing for those about to depart.

Even in the Latin East, where the evidence is scarcer, scholarship has shown that innovative traditions blended Latin and Greek liturgical traditions to ensure the survival of the Christian populations in the region. Joint processions, as MacEvitt demonstrated, "whose structure both created unity and displayed difference, that was peculiarly adapted to the exigencies of the blurred yet tense boundaries among Christian communities," suggest that there was a common need for sacralizing protection rituals in the Latin East.[21] The coronation liturgy's connection to the Pentecostal miracle and the appearance of the Sacred Fire, by Rubenstein's analysis, was powerful when present but shocking when it failed to appear and provoked considerable controversy; to which Simon John added the important note that "the monarchs of Jerusalem cultivated a spiritualized image of kingship by harnessing the liturgical practices of the Latins who inhabited the Holy City."[22] Cara Aspesi's discovery of a liturgical text recomposed at the Siege of Acre helps to situate how liturgies were *re*contextualized in the aftermath of the loss of Jerusalem in 1187.[23] Especially in the Latin East, connections between the *loca sancta* and the clergy—often monastic, but frequently also regulars of a different stripe—created long-standing liturgical connections that underscored the prestige of those clergy serving in the Kingdom of Jerusalem and doing much of the work to support the wider efforts within the Latin East proper.[24] The collection of even these

---

19 James A. Brundage, "'Cruce Signari': The Rite for Taking the Cross in England," *Traditio* 22 (1966): 289–310.
20 Amnon Linder, *Raising Arms: Liturgy in the Struggle to Liberate Jerusalem in the Late Middle Ages*, Cultural encounters in late Antiquity and the Middle Ages 2 (Turnhout: Brepols, 2003), 126, 182–86, and (Table 3.A) 193–95.
21 Christopher MacEvitt, "Processing Together, Celebrating Apart: Shared Processions in the Latin East," *JMH* 43.4 (2017): 455–69, quote at 469.
22 Jay Rubenstein, "Holy Fire and Sacral Kingship in Post-Conquest Jerusalem," *JMH* 43.4 (2017): 470–84; Simon John, "Royal Inauguration and Liturgical Culture in the Latin Kingdom of Jerusalem, 1099–1187," *JMH* 43.4 (2017): 470–84, quote at 501.
23 Cara Aspesi, "The 'libelli' of Lucca, Biblioteca Arcivescovile, MS 5: Liturgy from the Siege of Acre," *JMH* 43.4 (2017): 384–402.
24 Wolf Zöller, "The Regular Canons and the Liturgy of the Latin East," *JMH* 43.4 (2017): 367–83.

results makes a powerful case for the urgent need for more of the manuscript culture of the Latin East to be unraveled, and some of that work is already being done, but it does suggest that liturgical innovations on the frontiers of the Latin East may have been congruent with changes on the other borderlands of Christendom.

1.2   *Hagiographical Intervention*

Hagiographical accounts record copious cultural and social information encoded in their reports of holy people and their deeds. In this subsection of the chapter, I wish to broadly survey studies of the intervention of saints in battles and military engagements in a manner that will help provide a kind of complimentary counterbalance to the history of liturgical intercession from the previous subsection. Interventions in military affairs by saints provide a kind of response to the calls for assistance in liturgical prayer. Even in cases where wars were fought among Christians, however, saints were known to intervene, and the frequency with which they did so underscores the ways that religious sentiments formed the bedrock of identities that were worth fighting and dying for in medieval Christian communities.[25] For this chapter, a more narrow focus to the usual battlefront zones brings this point into greater contrast. Here, we examine the holy intervention of saints in the Iberian Peninsula, the Latin East, and the Northeastern European frontier.

Hagiographical accounts from the Iberian Peninsula place a small cadre of saints among an elite group of spiritual warriors intervening on behalf of the Christian kingdoms of the north. James (*qua* Santiago), Mary, Emilianus of Berceo (*qua* San Millan), and George all appear with enough frequency that they appear to have been favored for such a purpose by hagiographers. In the case of James, the invented Battle of Clavijo (allegedly fought in either 834 or 844) served as a crucial marker for long twelfth-century authors that James had been invested in the early wars against al-Andalus for several centuries, as did the intervention of Santiago at the siege of Coimbra led by Fernando I of León.[26] Purkis has noted that Santiago's miracles were also witnessed by

---

25   Augustine Thompson, *Cities of God: The Religion of the Italian Communes, 1125–1325* (University Park: Pennsylvania State University Press, 2005), 108–12, makes this point openly in the many instances of patron saints of Italian communes adopting saints in the aftermath of victories and defeats.

26   Thomas Deswarte, "St. James in Galicia (c.500–1300): Rivalries in Heaven and on Earth," in *Culture and Society in Medieval Galicia: A Cultural Crossroads at the Edge of Europe*, ed. James D'Emilio, MEMI 59 (Leiden and Boston MA: Brill, 2015), 477–511.

FIGURE 2.1 The Abbey of Santa María la Real de Las Huelgas in Burgos, Spain. A mural depicting the Battle of Las Navas de Tolosa (1212) by Pedro Ruiz de Camargo, ca. 1600. Christian army is led by the Canon Domingo Pascual with an archiepiscopal cross, Archbishop Rodrigo Jiménez de Rada of Toledo advises the King Alfonso VIII of Castile from the second line of the battle. Two Christian banners are prominently displayed, a banner with the image of the Blessed Virgin Mary, patroness of Toledo and all of Spain, and one depicting Christ on the Cross.
PHOTO REPRODUCED WITH THE KIND PERMISSION OF THE AUTHOR MARTÍN ALVIRA CABRER AND PATRIMONIO NACIONAL

or performed for warriors with peculiar frequency.[27] *Contra* Santiago, Toledan chronicling of Marian intervention in the campaigns against al-Andalus had a double-purpose: first, it shut out Santiago from claiming saintly credit for new campaigns; and, second, Toledo's standards and cathedral were both deeply linked to the cult of Mary.[28] The palpable presence of the saints on the battlefield at Las Navas, for example, is visible even in commemorative art produced for Las Huelgas (fig. 2.1) and for Santa Maria de Huerta (figs. 2.2a–b); in neither

27 William J. Purkis, *Crusading Spirituality in the Holy Land and Iberia, c.1095–c.1187* (Woodbridge: Boydell Press, 2008), 145–49.
28 Amy G. Remensnyder, *"La Conquistadora": The Virgin Mary at War and Peace in the Old and the New Worlds* (Oxford and New York: Oxford University Press, 2014), 35–36.

FIGURES 2.2A–B   The Abbey of Santa María de Huerta, Spain. Murals above the tomb of Archbishop Rodrigo Jiménez de Rada of Toledo by Bartolomé Matarana (ca. 1580) depicting scenes from the Battle of Las Navas de Tolosa (1212). a) field mass celebrated by Archbishop Rodrigo for the Christian army before the battle; b) the battle scene: Domingo Pascual with an archiepiscopal cross in the first line is followed by Archbishop Rodrigo and King Alfonso VIII of Castile. Toledan banner with the image of the Blessed Virgin Mary is visible in the background.
PHOTOS REPRODUCED WITH THE KIND PERMISSION OF THE AUTHOR MARTÍN ALVIRA CABRER

case should we write off the representation of saints on the field as being token or an artistic convention.[29]

To that same end, it is difficult to read the *Cantigas de Santa Maria* as anything other than a popularization of the preferred cult of the Andalusian campaigns of Alfonso X and his father, Fernando III, given the role that Mary plays as a *conquistadora*, albeit a few centuries before such a role would be catapulted to prominence in Spanish transatlantic colonial projects.[30] Henriet has noted that the early *vita* of Raymond of Roda, bishop of Roda-Bobastro, underscored his role as a protector of vulnerable Christians along the frontier.[31] The liberation of captives was a frequent trope within hagiographical accounts, such as those performed by Mary in the Iberian context, and demonstrates the urgency of captivity in military contexts.[32] Other saints, as Brodman has noted, followed Mary's lead. These include "St. Dominic [of Osma], St. Isidore of Seville, St. Anthony of Padua, Santo Domingo de la Calzada but particularly Santo Domingo de Silos."[33] Although a later monastic interpolation into earlier Compostelan forgeries, the involvement of Emelianus of Berceo was an important advancement for the fortunes of the Rioja monastery of San Millán de la Cogolla, whose role as a pilgrimage stop and a locus of Benedictine influence in the region underscores the breadth of intellectual and cultural networks in the wider peninsula.[34] In the Crown of Aragon, the intervention of St. George

---

29 The author is grateful to Martin Alvira Cabrer for his fine photography and equally sterling knowledge of the art historical context of these representations.

30 Edward L. Holt, "'Cantigas de Santa María', 'Cantigas de Cruzada': Reflections of Crusading Spirituality in Alfonso X's 'Cantigas de Santa María,'" *Al-Masaq* 27.3 (2015): 207–24.

31 Patrick Henriet, "L'Évêque Raymond de Roda (1126), défenseur des 'christicoles'. Á propos de la 'Vita Beati Raimundi Basbastrensis Antistitis' (BHL 7074)," in *Hombres de religión y guerra*, 17–28.

32 For the actions of the Virgin Mary as a liberator of captives, see: Amy G. Remensnyder, "Christian Captives, Muslim Maidens, and Mary," *Speculum* 82.3 (2007): 642–77 at 648–49, 650–54.

33 James W. Brodman, "Captives or Prisoners: Society and Obligation in Medieval Iberia," *Anuario de Historia de la Iglesia* 20 (2011): 201–19 at 212.

34 On the hagiography of San Millan de la Cogolla and his interventions in armed conflict, see David Peterson, "Genesis y significado de 'Los Votos de San Millan,'" in *De ayer y hoy. Contribuciones multidisciplinares sobre pseudoepígrafos literarios y documentales*, ed. Mikel Labiano, De falsa et vera historia 2 (Madrid: Ediciones Clásicas, 2019), 223–38 at 224–28; Erik Alder, "Subaltern Saints: Medieval Iberian Hagiography in Dialogue with Latin American Testimonio," (PhD Thesis, University of Kansas, 2017), 116–17. On the importance of the pilgrimage road for the double-monasteries' successes: José Ángel García de Cortázar, "El dominio del monasterio de San Millán de la Cogolla en los siglos X a XII," in *Estudios de historia medieval de La Rioja*, ed. José Ángel García de Cortázar and Ruiz de Aguirre (Logroño: Universidad de La Rioja Servicio de Publicaciones, 2009), 443–54. The relationships between San Millan de la Cogolla and Calahorra was particularly important

was less frequent, but the activities of several clergy on the front lines earned those same men the status of *beatus* and *sanctus* by local reckoning, which for later chroniclers muddled the boundaries between holy intervention of saints as spiritual actors and as physical agents.[35] Angelic patronage, too, was common enough on the Iberian frontier that it seems to have served as an important parallel to similar trends across Christendom.[36] Because of the diversity imposed by the variety of societies along the Iberian frontier, it seems no accident that there should be a blend of saints taking part in the spiritual warfighting along the same frontiers along which their cult devotees invested sieges and fought pitched battles.

Similar trends, albeit with more challenging evidence, can be traced in the Latin East. In some of the earliest miracles of Thomas Becket's hagiography—within days of his martyrdom (in 1170)—a prisoner was freed by the miraculous intervention of the martyred archbishop; a similar event was noted in the Danish theater, where a warship was freed from a wave that would have prevented the conclusion of its military mission.[37] While comparable trends might

---

for the success of both but major political shifts fractured their alliance and led to considerable and dynamic struggles for supremacy: Iván García Izquierdo and David Peterson, "The Abbot-Bishops of San Millán and Calahorra (1025–1065): A Marriage of Convenience and a Messy Divorce," in *Obispos y monasterios en la Edad Media. Trayectorias personales, organización eclesiástica y dinámicas materiales*, ed. Andrea Vanina Neyra and Mariel Pérez (Buenos Aires: Sociedad Argentina de Estudios Medievales, 2020), 221–40 at 232–36. I am grateful to Prof. David Peterson for his suggestions regarding the history of San Millán de la Cogolla.

35   On the cult of St. George in Aragon and its neighboring and influential territories: Stefano Maria Cingolani, *Sant Jordi. Una Llegenda Mil·lenària* (Barcelona: Editorial Base, 2014); Margarita Vallejo Girvés, "Inuentio y desarrollo del culto de San Jorge pre-militar y caballero en Galatia," *Polis* 13 (2001): 141–53; Enric Olivares Torres, *L'ideal d'evangelització guerrera. Iconografia dels cavallers sants* (PhD thesis, Universitat de València, 2016); Esther Dehoux, "'Saint George, noble chevalier, tres humblement, je vous requier'. Enseignes et badges, (in)signes de la dévotion à saint Georges (XIIIe–début XVIe siècle)," in *Autour d'Azincourt. Une société face à la guerre (v. 1370–v. 1420)*, ed. Alain Marchandisse and Bertrand Schnerb (Villeneuve d'Ascq: Revue du Nord, 2017), 49–68. I am grateful for these recommendations to Martín Alvira Carber.

36   Patrick Henriet, "'Protector et defensor omnium'. Le culte de Saint Michel en péninsule ibérique (haut Moyen Âge)," in *Culto e santuari di san Michele nell'Europa medievale*, ed. Pierre Bouet, Giorgio Otranto, and André Vauchez, Bibliotheca michaelica 1 (Bari: Edipuglia, 2007), 113–32; Fermín Miranda García, "Ascenso, auge y caída de San Miguel como protector de la monarquía pamplonesa, siglos X–XII," in *Mundos medievales. Espacios, sociedades y poder. Homenaje al profesor José Ángel García de Cortázar y Ruiz de Aguirre*, ed. Beatriz Arizaga Bolumburu, Dolores Mariño Veiras, and Carmen Diéz Herrera, 2 vols. (Santander: Publican, 2012), 1:759–68.

37   The hagiography of Thomas Becket provides a window into the way hagiographical traditions exploded along the trade routes of the region, but the liberations of captives echo

not have spurred Archbishop Berenguer de Vilademuls of Tarragona toward sanctity, other interventions in the holy land—like the freeing of Bohemond from captivity in 1103—were an important buttress for crusader claims in the Latin East.[38] Elisabeth Lapina has shown that St. Demetrius of Thessaloniki, for example, emerged as an intervening presence at the Siege of Antioch in 1098. She has connected this pattern of intervention to an episode in Robert of Clari's chronicle, where Robert makes St. Demetrius responsible for the death of the Bulgarian Tsar Kalojan.[39] Mary appeared to defend crusaders in battle.[40] Defense of cities through reliquaries represented another extension of the kind of work that saints could do for their adherents: the Latin Emperors of Constantinople deployed the Madonna of Hodegetria in defense of the Queen of Cities; the Latin Kingdom of Jerusalem used the True Cross in battle for its apotropaic power in a similar fashion; similar use by Georgian military leaders saw relics of the True Cross staged as force protection in the theaters in which they fought.[41] Even a forged relic like the Rood of Bromholm was remem-

---

the importance of military miracles, even in an overwhelming corpus: *Miracula Sancti Thomae Cantuariensis, Auctore Benedicto, Abbate Petriburgensi*, in *Materials for the History of Thomas Becket, Archbishop of Canterbury*, vol. 2, ed. James Craigie Robertson, Rolls Series 67 (London: Longman & Co., 1876), 21–298 at 270–82. For the ship incident, see Ane L. Bysted, Carsten Selch Jensen, Kurt Villads Jensen, and John H. Lind, *Jerusalem in the North: Denmark and the Baltic Crusades, 1100–1522*, Outremer 1 (Turnhout: Brepols, 2012), 102.

38 On the murder of Berenguer de Vildamuls by Guillem Ramon de Moncada in 1194, see Damian J. Smith, "The Reconciliation of Guillem Ramon de Montcada, the Albigensian Crusade and Fourth Lateran," in *The Fourth Lateran Council and the Crusade Movement: The Impact of the Council of 1215 on Latin Christendom and the East*, ed. Jessalyn L. Bird and Damian J. Smith, Outremer 7 (Turnhout: Brepols, 2018), 131–50. For the release, for example, of Bohemond in 1103 from captivity: Nicholas Paul, "A Warlord's Wisdom: Literacy and Propaganda at the Time of the First Crusade," *Speculum* 85.3 (2010): 534–66 at 557–58; Yvonne Friedman, "Miracle, Meaning, and Narrative in the Latin East," *SCH* 41 (2005): 123–34.

39 Elizabeth Lapina, "Demetrius of Thessaloniki: Patron Saint of Crusaders," *Viator* 40.2 (2009): 93–112 at 93–94, 109–10.

40 Alison More, "'Milites Christi in hortis liliorum domini?': Hagiographic Constructions of Masculinity and Holiness in Thirteenth-Century Liege" (PhD thesis, University of Bristol, 2004), 112.

41 Alan V. Murray, "'Mighty against the enemies of Christ': The Relic of the True Cross in the Armies of the Kingdom of Jerusalem," in *The Crusades and their Sources: Essays Presented to Bernard Hamilton*, ed. John France and William G. Zajac (Aldershot and Burlington VT: Ashgate, 1998), 217–38; Robert Lee Wolff, "Footnote to an Incident of the Latin Occupation of Constantinople: The Church and the Icon of the Hodegetria," *Traditio* 6 (1948): 319–27; Mamuka Tsurtsumia, "The True Cross in the Armies of Georgia and the Frankish East," *Crusades* 12 (2013): 91–102; Elizabeth Eliott Lockhard, "Remembering Things: Transformative Objects in Texts about Conflict, 1160–1390" (PhD thesis, Columbia

bered as having had a real impact on warfighting in the eastern Mediterranean, long after it had been translated to England.[42] In Sicily, relics of St. Matthew turned back an effort by William I to destroy Salerno, although the use of reliquaries in wars against the non-Christians in the pre-Norman period needs further study.[43] Hagiographical interventions at Ramla, as James MacGregor showed, underscored the importance of warrior-saints, especially George, among the early crusaders.[44] Along the Eastern Mediterranean frontiers, then, there is some evidence that relics and saintly interventions played a role in injecting additional sacralizing energies into the wider theater of conflict.

Along the northern crusading frontiers, we find a similar pattern of hagiographical interpolation into the campaigns against non-Christians. As Anu Mänd has shown, the cult of Mary was of enormous consequence in Livonia, thanks in part to her frequently attested and widely celebrated interventions in the Livonian campaigns, as well as her strong ties to the military orders in the region.[45] Skwierczyński has shown that the role played in Livonia by the Virgin was in parallel to the work done in Poland, and miraculous interventions there were part of the sacralizing work of conversion-by-conquest and supported the wider missionary warfighting in the region.[46] The evidence from Livonia and Estonia's early Christian history suggests that miracles occurred in the same theaters as warfighting, but mirabilographical evidence underscores the intensity of Marian devotion and Mary's role in the wider success of

---

University, 2014), 87–89; Fanny Caroff, "L'affrontement entre chrétiens et musulmans. Le rôle de la vraie Croix dans les images de croisade (xiiie–xve siècle)," in *Chemins d'outremer. Études d'histoire sur la Méditerranée médiévale offertes à Michel Balard*, ed. Damien Coulon and Michel Balard, Byzantina Sorbonensia 20 (Paris: Publications de la Sorbonne, 2004), 99–114. I am grateful to John Giebfried, Andrew Buck, Greg Leighton, Radek Kotecki, and C. Matthew Philips for several of these references.

42   John Giebfried has argued in a conference paper that the Bromholm Rood is a forgery, but David Perry is the most recent treatment that has been published. See John Giebfried, "The Holy Forgery of Bromholm," Paper Presented at Fourth International Symposium on Crusade Studies, Saint Louis University, Saint Louis MO, 20 June 2018; David Perry, *Sacred Plunder: Venice and the Aftermath of the Fourth Crusade* (University Park: Pennsylvania State University Press, 2015), 39.

43   Graham A. Loud, *The Latin Church in Norman Italy* (Cambridge and New York: Cambridge University Press, 2007), 373–74.

44   James B. MacGregor, "Negotiating Knightly Piety: The Cult of the Warrior-Saints in the West, ca.1070–ca.1200," *ChH* 73.2 (2004): 317–45 at 333.

45   Anu Mänd, "Saints' Cults in Medieval Livonia," in *The Clash of Cultures on the Medieval Baltic Frontier*, ed. Alan V. Murray (Aldershot and Burlington VT: Ashgate, 2009), 191–226 at 194–99.

46   Skwierczyński, "The Beginnings," 117–62. See also, n. 12–14 above.

both the missionizing and warfighting in the Baltic theater.[47] Mary encouraged the conversion of a Danish king, and the story was a part of Cistercian mirabilographies from the Livonian campaigns from there onward.[48] The notion that the wider region was protected by, because the inherited and special property of, the Virgin Mary made the Marian hagiographical corpus a bridge for communicating both the sacred qualities of mercy (a typical Marian attribute) and vengeance (paradigmatic for crusades in the later twelfth century). Hungarian sources suggest a strongly similar tradition under the Árpad dynasty, too, as Zupka has recently demonstrated.[49] The Teutonic Order followed a similarly Marian track, with both visions and protective acts attested in the records of the thirteenth centuries and after.[50] In addition to the influence of Mary, there is also strong evidence, as Kotecki has argued, for the role of angelic intercession along the northern and northeastern frontiers.[51] Even the toponymical record attests to the importance of Mary in this early period.[52] St. Barbara, too, played a role, both as intercessor and in the protective power of her relics, as Leighton has argued.[53] The role, then, of intercessors was clearly both broad and deep in the Medieval Christian world.

---

47   For a survey of the Marian miracles in the process of conversion of Estonia and Livonia in precisely this same period as the "hearts and minds" front in holy wars in the region, see Marek Tamm, "Les miracles en Livonie et en Estonie à l'époque de la christianisation (fin XIIème–début XIIIème siècles)," in *"Quotidianum Estonicum": Aspects of Daily Life in Medieval Estonia*, ed. Jüri Kivimäe and Juhan Kreem, Medium aevum quotidianum. Sonderband 5 (Krems: Medium Aevum Quotidianum, 1996), 29–78.
48   Marek Tamm, "The Livonian Crusade in Cistercian Stories of the Early Thirteenth Century," *Crusading on the Edge*, 365–89 at 382–83; Barbara Bombi, "The Authority of Miracles: Cesarius of Heisterbach and the Livonian Crusade," in *Aspects of Power and Authority in the Middle Ages*, ed. Brenda Bolton and Christine Meek, International medieval research 14 (Turnhout: Brepols, 2007), 481–98.
49   Dušan Zupka, "Religious Rituals of War in Medieval Hungary Under the Árpád Dynasty," in *Christianity and War in Medieval East Central Europe and Scandinavia*, ed. Radosław Kotecki, Carsten Selch Jensen, and Stephen Bennett (Leeds: ARC Humanities Press, 2021), 141–57 at 145–49.
50   Gregory Leighton, "Did the Teutonic Order Create a Sacred Landscape in Thirteenth-Century Prussia?" *JMH* 44.4 (2018): 457–83.
51   Radosław Kotecki, "Pious Rulers, Princely Clerics, and Angels of Light: 'Imperial Holy War' Imagery in Twelfth-Century Poland and Rus'," in *Christianity and War*, 159–88.
52   See, e.g., the work of Mentzel-Reuters on Marienburg as a proof of the extent of hagio-toponymical trends: Arno Mentzel-Reuters, "Zur Sakraltopologie der Marienburg," in *"Castrum sanctae Mariae." Die Marienburg als Burg, Residenz und Museum*, ed. Arno Mentzel-Reuters and Stefan Samerski (Göttingen: Vandenhoeck & Ruprecht, 2019), 99–178.
53   See Gregory Leighton, "The Relics of St Barbara at Althaus Kulm: History, Patronages, and Insight into the Teutonic Order and the Christian Population in Prussia (Thirteenth–Fifteenth Centuries)," *ZH* 85.1 (2020): 5–50, esp. 10–17, 22–27, 40–43.

In the preceding section, I have attempted to sketch many of the elements of the wider "sacralization" of warfighting that occurred in the long twelfth century. It is clear that a number of important influences played out in local and regional contexts. Liturgical practices folded in the conduct of warfighting into the wider area of religious expression, and the intervention in military affairs by saints demonstrated that there was, at least from some sacral corners, approval for this development. Saints would not intervene to promote unholiness, nor would liturgical intercessions land as strongly on ears unused to hearing about the intentions of the divine; we must assume that, given all this evidence and the analysis of expert scholars, the real manifest urgency of religious feeling on the crusading path was not posturing but actual devotion.

2 Sacralized Warfighting and Religious History: Engaging the Lay with the Clerical

In this second section, two paired trends are also presented. First, preaching the crusade represented the recruitment of temporary soldiers for the crusade movement demonstrates keenly that sacralized warfare was an iterative movement, remade with each instance but also shaped by the causes that provoked it. Second, the more permanent institution that the military orders comprised were a way of providing for a standing contingent of holy wars, effectively intersecting the monasticization of twelfth-century society with sacralized military fraternities.[54] The work of recruiting and retaining active forces for the *negotium Christi* was a constant struggle, and the development of more sophisticated and professionalized strategies—eventually resulting in the distinctions between the *passagium generale* and *passagium particulare*—was in part a response to the effective deployment but underwhelming results of these multifarious efforts.[55]

---

[54] While I am quite aware of the perils around applying Constable's *Reformation of the Twelfth Century* beyond its original scope, I think that, especially in Conedera's recent work, this is a fair connection between Conedera's framework of sacralized knighthood and an understanding of the ways in which the religious thought of the period was transposed to a wider audience: Giles Constable, *The Reformation of the Twelfth Century* (New Haven CN: Yale University Press, 1998), 74–75; Sam Zeno Conedera, SJ, *Ecclesiastical Knighthood: The Military Orders in Castile, 1150–1350* (New York: Fordham University Press, 2015), 1–19, 141–44.

[55] Norman J. Housley, *The Avignon Papacy and the Crusades, 1305–1378* (Oxford: Clarendon Press, 1986), 3, 15; idem, "The Franco-Papal Crusade Negotiations of 1322–3," *Papers of the British School at Rome* 48 (1980): 166–85. I have elsewhere argued that this is partly the reason that clerics retreated from active leadership of armies on a routine basis

2.1 Crusade Preaching and Recruitment

The work of recent historians has highlighted the ways in which crusade preaching was shaped both by local conditions and by the variety of theological themes that were directly resonant with the audience for that preaching. While the collections of sermons that have been edited are still few in number, the quality of the scholarship produced is far too excellent to ignore in this opening chapter. In this sub-section, my intent is to examine some of the thematic elements deployed by crusade preachers, as studied by the most important scholars working on the subject. Crusade preaching developed over the long twelfth century in a fashion that suggests that it was an ongoing phenomenon, changing to meet contemporary and localized circumstances, and that the content of the preaching preserves echoes of the audience the sermons were oriented toward. The development of these themes recommends the sermons and preaching records as a window for understanding how the laity was enrolled in the work of the clerical thinkers about these campaigns.

Reports of preaching for the First Crusade suggest that, while the antecedents for the campaign were rich, the preachers engaged in recruitment were breaking new ground. The various reports of the Clermont sermons show the dynamic enrollment of the lesser nobility in a sacralizing and clericalizing project retrenched the notion of pilgrimage as key to the campaign and the status of the warriors as pilgrims under clerical protection.[56] Even in his ill-fated efforts, accounts of Peter the Hermit's recruitment efforts were part of a wider framework that enrolled the laity in the *negotium Christi*, but that he "mobilized all kinds of person, from senior clergy to the worst of criminals" made his crusading appeals more successful because they cultivated such a broad constituency.[57] Jay Rubenstein has argued that the apocalypticism of the First Crusade underlines how non-clerical participants were engaged in the salvific enterprise that theoretically suffused the projects of clergy in the Medieval Latin West.[58] Marcus Bull, of course, made this question—how the piety of

---

in the thirteenth century campaigns in Iberia and that warfighting's increasing professionalization can be traced in part along similar trajectories using that body of evidence. See Kyle C. Lincoln, "'In exercitu locus pontificalia exercet': Warrior Clerics in the Era of Fernando III," in *The Sword and the Cross*, 85–104, esp. 95–99.

56 Jonathan Riley-Smith, *The First Crusade and the Idea of Crusading* (Philadelphia PA: University of Pennsylvania Press, 1986), 24–25.

57 Conor Kostick, *The Social Sructure of the First Crusade*, MMED 76 (Leiden and Boston MA: Brill, 2008), 106.

58 Although provocative with respective to the sources and illustrative for a popular audience, it is telling that in his copy of the volume, Jonathan Riley-Smith expressed some doubt as to how deeply penetrative these ideas were for scholarly analysis. See Jay Rubenstein, *Armies of Heaven: The First Crusade and the Quest for Apocalypse* (New

the middle nobility drove the projects of crusading forward—central to his seminal *Knightly Piety and the First Crusade*, and it is worth noting that crusade preaching was contributing to an already developed framework for the warriors of the Limousin.[59] Beyond the First Crusade itself, the first half-century of crusading spurred increasingly specific developments of both the practice of preaching the crusade and the messages conveyed to listeners. Penny Cole noted that the call for preaching for the Second Crusade was in many ways conservative but was met with the kind of contemporary enthusiasm that could be as useful (in the case of Bernard of Clairvaux) or toxifying (in the case of Ralph, a Cistercian who preached in the Upper Rhineland to anti-Judaic and anti-authoritarian effect) as had been the case in the pursuit of the first crusade.[60]

Academic work regarding preaching, especially at Paris, suggests that the close of the first century of crusading history had already spurred enormous development along these earlier lines of innovation. Preachers in the buildup to the Second Crusade emphasized, along with papal letter-writing to the same effect, the normalcy of the work of crusading and that the liturgical formulae were effectively standardized by the Second Crusade. Those standards were widespread by the Third Crusade.[61] By this mid-century period, Smith has noted that "the language of spiritual battle might be applied to *bellatores*

York: Basic Books, 2011) (Personal copy of Jonathan Riley-Smith held in the Jonathan Riley-Smith Crusades Collection at Oakland University, Rochester, MI. Shelf mark 224 KL, inside cover).

[59] "It would be a mistake to underestimate the vitality of laymen's religious sentiments around the time of the First Crusade. One of the most important features of the piety of eleventh century arms-bearers ... was that it was associative, passive to the extent that It was inspired and sustained by the spiritual resources of a monastic or clerical elite. ... No popular religious culture is embraced by all people at all times with equal enthusiasm. But, on the other hand the existence of a sliding scale of piety in eleventh Aquitaine and Gascony is itself significant, for it was defined and perpetuated by the ideas and enthusiasms of those at its upper limits: men (and women) who were the most vigorous (and so conspicuous) supporters of a system of religious value which extended beyond them to touch the lives of most of their peers. It is difficult to imagine that [they] were so exceptional in their devotion that they departed from the norms which governed the society in which they lived. Ion the basis of what is known about their support for local ecclesiastical centers, they may be regarded as representative of the associative but potentially deep arms-bearing piety of their age ... it is not surprising that all these men, and many others like them, also went on the First Crusade": Marcus Bull, *Knightly Piety and the Lay Response to the First Crusade: The Limousin and Gascony* (Oxford: Clarendon Press, 1993), 285, 288.

[60] Penny Cole, *The Preaching of the Crusades to the Holy Land, 1095–1270* (New York: Medieval Academy of America, 1991), 41–48.

[61] M. Cecilia Gaposchkin, "The Place of Jerusalem in Western Crusading Rites of Departure (1095–1300)," *CHR* 99.1 (2013): 1–28 at 4.

as well as *oratores*" and this suggests that the language of sermons was creating real synergies between appeals for supporting the campaigns both with arms and with prayer.[62] The evidence from the Iberian Peninsula in the period shows that the holy wars there from the period between the First and Second Crusade involved full legations of cardinals to locally preach sermons (now lost) to recruit volunteers, as well as an invitation to the archbishop-elect of Tarragona to preach at the First Lateran Council (1123) to help generate external support for these parallel campaigns.[63] The poetic evidence from the Almeria campaigns in 1147, which likely colored the 1148 campaigns against Jaen about which less is known, suggests that there were some considerable successes in the cultivation of a similar ethos for crusading in the peninsula and that episcopal preaching was widespread in the buildup to the fighting.[64] Wilson has shown that the chronicles for the Portuguese campaigns against Lisbon, Alcacer do Sal, and Santarem were especially focused on portraying holy violence as justified, and their ultramontane Cistercian author's zeal for warfighting likely point to a fashion of crusade-fighting that was divergent from local traditions but that was nevertheless commensurate with contemporary norms elsewhere.[65] Similarly, the northeastern frontiers of Christendom saw the use of military force as a conversionary exercise, similarly underscoring the impact of the sermons that enrolled the lay warrior as agents of spiritual change.[66] The continued stimulation of these developments by the long duration of the campaigns suggests that preachers who framed the campaigns in question as holy wars succeeded in attracting warriors but the evidence shows that local traditions colored much of the proceedings of these campaigns, regardless of the point of the sermons preached to them.

At the turn of the thirteenth century, sermons and preaching reports for the Fourth Crusade, Albigensian Crusade and the Crusade of Las Navas provide exceptional data about how the idea of crusade was evolving to meet the peculiar circumstances of campaigns outside Outremer. Research on the

62 Katherine A. Smith, "Saints in Shining Armor: Martial Asceticism and Masculine Models of Sanctity, ca.1050–1250," *Speculum* 83.3 (2008): 572–602 at 581.
63 Joseph F. O'Callaghan, *Reconquest and Crusade in Medieval Spain* (Philadelphia: University of Pennsylvania Press, 2004), 38–39; Carlos de Ayala Martínez, "The Episcopate and Reconquest in the Times of Alfonso VII of Castile and León," in *Between Sword and Prayer*, 207–32 at 208–12.
64 Purkis, *Crusading Spirituality*, 172–76; Simon Barton, "A Forgotten Crusade: Alfonso VII of León-Castile and the Campaign for Jaén (1148)," *Historical Research* 73.182 (2000): 312–20.
65 Jonathan Wilson, "A Cistercian Point of View"; idem, "Enigma of the 'De Expugnatione Lyxbonensi,'" *JMIS* 9.1 (2017): 99–129.
66 Iben Fonnesberg-Schmidt, *The Popes and the Baltic Crusades, 1147–1254*, TNW 26 (Leiden and Boston MA: Brill, 2007), 28–52.

Fourth Crusade's sources makes clear that sermons shaped much of the humbler crusader's understanding of the ways in which their work as warriors was engaging with the developing narrative around the campaign, retaining and redirecting much of the initial energy that underscored the campaign well into the project of a new Latin Empire of Constantinople.[67] Some crusade preaching must have been effective in Bologna to inspire several thousand to leave in 1188, but Augustine Thompson has argued the northern city-states of Italy were more frequently engaged in defensive wars in their region that were sacralized against the Empire or against heresy than they did in Europe.[68] Venetian crusading enthusiasm, too, must have been stirred by preaching, and Madden has argued that Venice's early connections to the movement were pivotal in the formation of their own civic identity.[69] Preaching on the Albigensian front engaged the laity to consider how their frameworks of knightly loyalty were in play as the supporters of the heresies in the region were framed as traitors to God.[70] While the early Dominicans were active in the Albigensian theater, they also seem to have spread quickly to the northeastern reaches of Christendom, promoting the crusades in the Baltic along with campaigning at the other boundary places of Christendom.[71] The preaching for Las Navas, on both sides of the Pyrenees, suggests that the campaign was framed as a way to subdue the internecine conflicts between the Christian monarchs of Iberia. Having done so, they might converting martial combat between neighbors into the wider framework of spiritual warfighting on the peninsular frontier between Christians and Muslims.[72] Campaigns in Livonia, which received considerable attention at Fourth Lateran Council, were shaped by contemporary administrative reforms and the reinvigoration of combined missionary/military activities that were eventually supported by the Danish monarchy.[73] After 1213, Danish

---

67 Nikolas Chrissis, "The City and the Cross: The Image of Constantinople and the Latin Empire in Thirteenth-Century Papal Crusading Rhetoric," *Byzantine and Modern Greek Studies* 36.1 (2012): 20–37. I am grateful to John J. Giebfried for this reference.
68 Thompson, *Cities of God*, 108.
69 Thomas Madden, *Enrico Dandolo and the Rise of Venice* (Baltimore MD: Johns Hopkins University Press, 2003), 13–16, 117–32.
70 Beverly Mayne Kienzle, *Cistercians, Heresy, and Crusade in Occitania, 1145–1229* (Woodbridge: York Medieval Press in association with Boydell Press, 2001), 78–173.
71 Johnny G.G. Jakobsen, "Preachers of War: Dominican Friars as Promoters of the Crusades in the Baltic Region in the Thirteenth Century," in *Christianity and War*, 97–115.
72 Miguel Gómez, "Alfonso VIII and the Battle of Las Navas de Tolosa," in *King Alfonso VIII of Castile: Government, Family, and War*, ed. Miguel Gómez, Kyle C. Lincoln, and Damian J. Smith (New York: Fordham University Press, 2020), 143–71 at 152–57.
73 Alan V. Murray, "Adding to the Multitude of Fish: Pope Innocent III, Bishop Albert of Riga and the Conversion of the Indigenous Peoples of Livonia," in *The Fourth Lateran Council,*

preachers in the region should conclude, by papal mandate, their sermons with notations of pagan offenses and a general exhortation for parishioners to take up the Cross.[74] Legates, both from the wider Scandinavian region itself and dispatched from Rome, preached the crusade regularly in the early decades of the thirteenth century, and their work seems to have had a noticeable impact on those campaign's successes.[75] Similar work was being done in the 1230s by papal agents who were concerned about the regions around Hungary, and there were serious incursions made into the region by crusading forces.[76] By the time the drive for the Fifth Crusade was beginning to generate real momentum, many of these same thematic elements—converting non-Christians, recruitment through patterned sermons, and the pan-Christian appeal for combined campaigns—were already standard for crusade recruitment sermons and the ideological frameworks for crusade fighting in the period.[77]

The first century and a half of the crusading movements' military iterations suggests that the campaigns that pushed the boundaries of Christendom were driven as much by their recruitment efforts as by their fundraising: recruitment was necessary to bring soldiers to the battlefield. In the preceding section, a preliminary exploration of some of the scholarship about crusade preaching and recruitment suggests that the religious sources about crusading generate considerable data about the social and cultural draw of the crusading movement. Where individual crusaders were recruited by sermons and served for specific durations—either campaigns or predetermined measures

---

153–70 at 158–62, 167–70; Fonnesburg-Schmidt, *Popes*, 100–3, 113–19; Torben Kjersgaard Nielsen, "The Virgin at the Lateran—The Baltic Crusades, Rome and the Mother of God," in ibid., 171–192 at 172–73, 186–88.

74 Bysted et al., *Jerusalem in the North*, 91.

75 Anthony Perron, "Metropolitan Might and Papal Power on the Latin-Christian Frontier: Transforming the Danish Church Around the Time of the Fourth Lateran Council," *CHR* 89.2 (2003): 182–212; Carsten Selch Jensen, Kurt Villads Jensen, and John H. Lind, "Communicating Crusades and Crusading Communications in the Baltic Region," *Scandinavian Economic History Review* 49.2 (2001): 5–25 at 15.

76 John A. Fine, Jr., *The Bosnian Church: A New Interpretation. A Study of the Bosnian Church and Its Place in State and Society from the 13th to the 15th Centuries* (New York: Columbia University Press, 1975), 137–48; Ivan Majnarić, "Tending the Flock: Clergy and a Discourse of War in the Wider Hinterland of the Eastern Adriatic during the Late Twelfth and Thirteenth Century," in *Between Sword and Prayer*, 435–70.

77 Pierre-Vincent Claverie, "'Totius populi Christiani negotium': The Crusading Conception of Pope Honorius III, 1216–1221," in *The Fifth Crusade in Context: The Crusading Movement in the Early Thirteenth Century*, ed. E.J. Mylod et al. (Abingdon and New York: Routledge, 2017), 27–39; Barbara Bombi, "The Fifth Crusade and the Conversion of the Muslims," in ibid., 68–91; Jessalynn Bird, "Crusade and Reform: The Sermons of Bibliotheque Nationale, MS nouv. Acq. Lat. 999," in ibid., 92–114.

of time—there were, of course, more permanent forces (represented by the military orders) that supported temporary crusaders.

2.2 *Military Orders*

The historiography around the military orders is, to be charitable, superabundant. In this sub-section, it is most important that we highlight how the military orders, whether international or regional, provide evidence of the monasticization of warfighting. While a comprehensive survey of the literature about the military orders would run too many pages, here I wish to highlight the development of the international Orders of the Temple and the Hospital; early Iberian Orders of Santiago, Aviz/Évora, and Calatrava; and the early history of the Teutonic Order. The military orders, across their various regional and pan-Christian endeavors, proved to be one of the more effective methods of channeling individual enthusiasm and collective military resources in the crusading movement. In most cases, enrolling lay warfighters into "ecclesiastical knighthoods" involved both the "pull" factor of the prestige of monastic rules as a factor and the "push" factors of familial recruitment into the social networks of the orders themselves.

The Temple and the Hospital were, of course, the most pertinent examples of the ways that these new military confraternities were able to reshape the religious and political engagements of their contemporaries.[78] The establishment of the two Orders in the Holy Land in the late eleventh and early twelfth century was, in many ways, one of the stronger validators for Giles Constable's "monasticization" thesis, as Conedera has later demonstrated that the clericalization of knighthood brought with it much of the disciplinary rigor expected of regular religious. The recruitment of their members into the Order took a variety of means but there were a few predictable patterns. Forey's study of the recruitment and novitiate periods suggests that volunteers for the Hospital took their vows immediately and that the Temple had a short period for recruits to serve briefly in a testing period but that disappeared by the mid-twelfth century; in both cases, it seems that the orders recruited from family circles and social networks.[79] While the customs of both the Hospital and the Temple, as

---

[78] For a balanced history of the two Orders in their earliest period: Malcolm C. Barber, *The New Knighthood: A History of the Order of the Temple* (Cambridge and New York: Cambridge University Press, 1994); Jonathan Riley-Smith, *The Knights Hospitaler in the Levant, c.1070–1309* (New York: Palgrave MacMillan, 2012).

[79] Alan J. Forey, "Novitiate and Instruction in the Military Orders during the Twelfth and Thirteenth Centuries," *Speculum* 61.1 (1986): 1–17 at 1–3, 5, 8; Scott Jessee, "Crusaders and Templars: Robert the Burgundian Lord of Craon and Sablé and His Descendents, 1095–1192," *Medieval Prosopography* 30 (2015): 31–58 at 34–36, 53–54.

Brodman has argued, had their origins in the caritative functions—maintaining *hospitia* and protecting the holy places and roads—both had adopted more explicitly-militarized regulations and practices by the third quarter of the twelfth century.[80] Given the breadth of military obligations that were already incumbent on both the Temple and the Hospital, the absence of direct provisions before the thirteenth century suggests that the Orders were still struggling to embody and inculcate a monastic-knight dichotomy and privileging their monasticism rather than their bellicosity.[81] Even in the Iberian Peninsula, where the competition for lands, patronage, and recruits between the Temple and Hospital (on the one hand) and the Iberian Orders (on the other hand), the essential function of hospitality and protecting sacralized conquests and their Christian residents was preserved in the Iberian theater.[82]

Indeed, the Iberian Peninsula was the site of considerable innovation and exploration of the wider frame-space created by the Temple and Hospital's foundations in the Latin East. The early rules for the Orders of Santiago, Calatrava, Montjoy/Monfrague, Alcantara, and Avis/Évora suggest a diversity of approaches to the *modus vivendi* of Military Orders in the Iberian Peninsula. The life enjoined by the Rule of the Order of Santiago has been suggested as one of the sources of prestige that underscored their recruitment efforts, and the innovative provision that brothers could remain married and celibate has often been pointed to as a reason that Santiago grew so rapidly.[83] The Order of Mountjoy/Monfrague, founded by Count Rodrigo Álvarez in 1174, as a more rigorous version of the Order of Santiago, which had witnessed considerable success in the decades beforehand, that forbade its members to remain married.[84] As an Order that was connected more formally to the Castilian monarchy, Calatrava's rule should have been more militarized, but its foundations by monks and laity affiliated with and admiring of the Cistercians suggests that their historical trajectory aligned with the Temple given their emergence from

---

80   James W. Brodman, "Rule and Identity: The Case of the Military Orders," *CHR* 87.3 (2001): 383–400 at 385–86.
81   On this point, Malcolm C. Barber, "The Social Context of the Templars," *Transactions of the Royal Historical Society* 34 (1984), 27–46 at 35–36.
82   Enrique Rodríguez-Picavea, "The Military Orders and Hospitaller Activity on the Iberian Peninsula during the Middle Ages," *Mediterranean Studies* 18 (2009): 24–43 at 24–26; José Valente, "The New Frontier: The Role of the Knights Templar in the Establishment of Portugal as an Independent Kingdom," *Mediterranean Studies* 7 (1998): 49–65 at 58–60.
83   Sastre Santos Eutimio, "La Orden de Santiago y su Regla" (PhD thesis, Universidad Complutense, 1981), 172, 224–27.
84   Alan J. Forey, "The Order of Mountjoy," *Speculum* 46.2 (1971): 250–66 at 251–52.

similar circumstances.[85] The Order of Évora/Aviz is often conflated in historical analysis with Calatrava, since it was subsumed by a bull of filiation in 1201 with Calatrava, and much historical work contrasts the two orders in their trajectories.[86] Alcantara, although less frequently studied, preserved much of the same Cistercian emphasis that was typical as well of Calatrava, although it generally followed the same contours of the other contemporary orders in recruiting from common familial and social networks.[87] Recruitment for the Orders, as with the Temple and the Hospital, appears to have been regional, social, and familial—effectively following the same pattern in Iberia as in the Latin East.[88] While they emerged from their own unique circumstances, it seems quite clear that the overwhelming importance of crusading theologies folded many laymen into the work of these ecclesiastical knighthoods, much as they had in the Latin East.

The work of military orders in the Baltic theater was enormously impactful later in the thirteenth century than this paper confines itself, but even in the early work of the crusade movement in the region, the orders played a key role in clericalizing the campaign's warfighters. The missionary activities of the northern churches laid much of the groundwork for the colonial efforts of the military orders in the Baltic theater generally, and many of the clergy themselves appeared to have engaged in warfighting.[89] The Livonian Sword Brothers, following their double foundations in 1202 and 1204 (first episcopally and second papally), appear to have drawn from local populations, and played an active role in the hodgepodge of early colonial governance in the Baltic crusading theater.[90] The Teutonic Order, too, demonstrated the depth of

85   Conedera, *Ecclesiastical Knights*, 62–77.
86   Maria Cristina Almeida e Cunha, *Estudos sobre a Ordem de Avis, (séc. XII–XV)* (Porto: Universidad da Porto. Faculdade de Letras, 2009), 17–30, 37–59.
87   Luis Corral Val, "La orden de Alcántara. Organización institucional y vida religiosa en la Edad Media" (PhD thesis, Universidad Complutense, 2003), 544–50, 582–88.
88   Forey, "Novitiate," 1–17; Brodman, "Rule and Identity," 383–400; Clara Estow, "The Economic Development of the Order of Calatrava, 1158–1366," *Speculum* 57.2 (1982): 267–91 at 273–74.
89   Examples of the complex missionary-warfighting portraits of prelates in the region include the work by Torben Nielsen and Carsten Jensen: Torben Kjersgaard Nielsen, "The Missionary Man: Archbishop Anders Sunesen and the Baltic Crusade, 1206–21," in *Crusade and Conversion on the Baltic Frontier, 1150–1500*, ed. Alan V. Murray (Aldershot and Burlington VT: Ashgate, 2001), 95–117; Jensen, "Bishops," 404–30.
90   Selart, *Livonia*, 54 and 54n.138; Ēvalds Mugurēvičs, "The Military Activity of the Order of the Sword Brethren (1202–1236)," in *The North-Eastern Frontiers of Medieval Europe: The Expansion of Latin Christendom in the Baltic Lands*, ed. Alan Murray, The expansion of Latin Europe, 1000–1500 4 (Farnham: Variorum, 2014), 117–23.

their enmeshment in the wider region, although much of that earlier period is colored by their later territory-building and cultural leadership enterprises in the region.[91] Still, the conceptualization of the territory as being especially the property of the Virgin Mary as a key ideological underpinning for their conquest was part of the wider clericalization of the military orders generally.[92] In Prussia and Livonia, the efforts of the Teutonic knights appear almost colonial, and scholarly estimates make their efforts—however numerically small they might have been—to have made an outsized impact given their resources.[93] Although unique to their specific geographical and demographic concerns, the Sword Brothers and the Teutonic Order, much like their Iberian counterparts, underline the importance of these larger sacralizing efforts that constrained and shaped bellicosity into producing large territorial estates, nuanced law codes, and complex socio-cultural efforts at entrenching the Christian norms of the contemporary Church were part of the wider efforts sustained by these enterprises.

For both the term-limited crusader, recruited by a local or itinerant preacher for a specific campaign, and those permanently adjacent to *crucesignati*, because enrolled in a military order, the influence of crusading ideology is beyond question. What is clear, too, is that scholarship has started closing a number of gaps to explain where and how and when recruitments recurred. In the later essays of this collection, then, we would do well to remember this backdrop: crusades and holy wars did not just happen, but were caused to happen by papal mandate, royal initiative, and regional geopolitics. Nevertheless, the humans that took part in these enterprises did so for innately human reasons, often because they felt pressures from family members, were concerned for their salvation, or perceived real and actionable threats in their world that these campaigns might alleviate in some measure.

---

91   The recruitment of local warriors by the Teutonic Order has been well-studied by Militzer: Klaus Militzer, "The Recruitment of Brethren for the Teutonic Order in Livonia, 1237–1562," in *The Military Orders: Fighting for the Faith and Caring for the Sick*, ed. Malcolm Barber (Farnham: Variorum, 1994), 270–77. The historiography about this period and its many policized pitfalls is surveyed by Ekdahl: Sven Ekdahl, "Crusades and Colonisation in the Baltic: A Historiographic Analysis," trans. Helen Nicholson, in *The North-Eastern Frontiers*, 1–42, esp. 3–7, 25–29. I am grateful to Gregory Leighton for his suggestion of this paper, which led to also the excellent work in the volume that contains it.

92   On the hagiotoponymical evidence, see above, n. 50.

93   Bysted et al., *Jerusalem in the North*, 254–60.

3 Conclusions and Looking Ahead

In many treatments of medieval Latin Christendom, the nobility are described as belonging to a warrior aristocracy, and fairly enough. For scholars working on much of the legacy of this medieval world, there is a large body of evidence to suggest the deep enmeshment of the militarism of the aristocracy with the complex legacies—intellectual, religious, and social—of the Christian tradition. Having left the abbacy of Citeaux, Archbishop Arnau Amalric's letter to the General Chapter describing the Las Navas campaign noted that Christendom was beset on three sides by enemies: heretics to the south, pagans to the north, and Muslims to the east.[94] The ways in which the clergy in Latin Christendom approached their world were full of martial imagery, and the crusades only further increased the frequency with which they deployed this language and the ways in which the two spheres of Duby's *oratores* and *bellatores* overlapped.

There are also many places where these intersections have been explored in a less direct fashion. Although much of the material above was viewed by medieval readers and thinkers as being factual, or at the very least verisimilar enough to be easily construed as such, the body of medieval thought often extended beyond this envelope. We know, for example, that many medieval thinkers used imaginative literature to present events that, while not accurate in a factual sense because they were inventive at their core, felt authentic to the lived experience of contemporaries. While based on a real historical figure from an earlier century, for example, the vernacular language *Cantar de Mio Cid*, its predecessor in Latin called the *Historia Roderici Campidocti*, and the charters produced for the historical Rodrigo Diaz de Vivar are sources of different types: the charters describe what *was happening*, the *Historia Roderici* recounted what *did happen*, and the *Cantar* presented how later Castilians *thought it might have happened*.[95] Extending this notion across a wider array of sources—for example Guilhelm de Tudela and his continuator's *Chansons de le Croisade Albigeois*, the charters produced for the early movement that produced the Order of Preachers, and the *Cronica* of Guillaume de Puylarens—would perhaps bear out how much of an interpretive impact

---

[94] The letter has been translated by many scholars, but was edited in the *Selecta e variis chronicis ad Philippi-Augusti regnum pertinentibus*, ed. Michel-Jean-Joseph Brial, Recueil des Historiens des Gaul et de la France 19 (Paris: Palmé, 1880), 239–66 at 250–54.

[95] On the relationship between these texts, see Richard A. Fletcher, *The Quest for El Cid* (New York: Oxford University Press, 1991); David Porrinas González, *Historia y mito de un hombre de guerra* (Madrid: Desperta Ferro Ediciones, 2019); Simon Barton, "El Cid, Cluny, and the Spanish Reconquest," *English Historical Review* 126.520 (2011): 517–43.

imaginative literature might have had on the way that contemporaries interpreted events around them. The body of scholarship about chivalric epics, *chansons des gestes*, and fictional works from the period generally would occupy many additional chapters' space here, but it is worth noting that such a body of literature does contribute useful nuance to the more declarative body of sources under formal consideration above.[96] The ways in which these texts influenced their contemporaries portrayals of events are too many to be considered in this short precis of scholarship, but it is worth noting that comparisons in this collection to broader cultural "norms" as presented in the literary works from the period should be welcomed as yet another angle by which scholarship can consider the influence of warfighting on religious culture and vice versa. Although it was the primary lens for scholarly interpretation here, it was not the only viewpoint for medieval thinkers.

One of the challenges set before this chapter was to sketch some of the trends of scholarship, so that subsequent chapters can investigate new avenues of research and add new layers of meaningful discourse to scientific investigations. With the attention paid to warrior clerics in recent years, it is not surprising that this work has found a welcoming publisher that recognizes the value of new scholarship building on a recent trend. Still, so much of the work done in this collection is a special advancement along similar lines with the special attention paid to the war-related rituals and religious practices and it is expected that the non-specialist might find fruitful parallels. By way of a scholarly confession, I have found much of this work terribly useful but only after "discovering" it in the process of being asked to do so for this collection. As a bibliographical essay, there is surely quite a lot that is missing—no bibliographic essay of any scope can really be comprehensive, after all—and there are a number of language barriers that prevent me from considering some regions altogether were it not for the occasional translated essay that makes available a scholarly conversation in, say, Hungarian or Polish, which would otherwise be incomprehensible to someone whose research investigates the Castilian church.

It has been my wider goal for this essay that it could provide a survey of some of the scholarship that might stand in the background of the chapters

---

96   Broad survey guides for scholars are available on these subjects, generally, but *exempli gratia*: Anthony Bale, ed., *The Cambridge Companion to the Literature of the Crusades* (Cambridge and New York: Cambridge University Press, 2019); Corinne Saunders, ed., *A Companion to Medieval Poetry* (Malden MA: Wiley Blackwell, 2010). More specifically, see Christine Grieb, *Schlachtenschilderungen in Historiographie und Literatur (1150–1230)*, Krieg in der Geschichte 87 (Paderborn: Schöningh, 2015), where chap. 7 is on religion and war.

that follow. Given how infrequently medieval studies scholars are driven to make use of *comparanda* that fits only in some fashions and not in others, there are a great number of chapters left to be written. Because the chapters that follow present original scholarship rather than a summary bibliographic essay like this one, I have hoped that by providing better background and useful discursive framing, the essays that follow will receive a share of the credit that this chapter would have received, had it been of a more original sort. If this short essay can offer a more fertile foreground for non-specialist readers to frame the work that follows, it will have achieved its core objective.

Bibliography

Primary Sources

Miracula Sancti Thomae Cantuariensis, Auctore Benedicto, Abbate Petriburgensi. In *Materials for the History of Thomas Becket, Archbishop of Canterbury.* Vol. 2. Edited by James Craigie Robertson, 21–298. Rolls series 67. London: Longman & Co., 1876.

Otto of Friesing. *The Deeds of Frederick Barbarossa.* Translated, annotated, and introduction by Charles Christopher Mierow. Records of civilization 49. New York: Columbia University Press, 1953.

Selecta e variis chronicis ad Philippi-Augusti regnum pertinentibus. Edited by Michel-Jean-Joseph Brial, 239–66. Recueil des Historiens des Gaul et de la France 19. Paris: Palmé, 1880.

Secondary Sources

Alder, Erik. "Subaltern Saints: Medieval Iberian Hagiography in Dialogue with Latin American Testimonio." PhD thesis, University of Kansas, 2017.

Almeida e Cunha, Maria Cristina. *Estudos sobre a Ordem de Avis, (séc. XII–XV).* Porto: Universidad da Porto. Faculdade de Letras, 2009.

Alvira Cabrer, Martín. "Conmemorando la victoria. La 'Fiesta del Triunfo de la Santa Cruz.'" In *Memoria y fuentes de la guerra santa peninsular (siglos X–XV).* Edited by Carlos de Ayala Martínez, Francisco García Fitz, and J. Santiago Palacios Ontalva, 435–62. Madrid: Trea, 2021.

Alvira Cabrer. "El 'Triunfo de la Santa Cruz' en los 'flores sanctorum'. Pervivencia en castellano de un texto latino medieval." *e-Spania* 26 (2017): doi.org/10.4000/e-spania.26450.

Alvira Cabrer. *Las Navas de Tolosa 1212. Idea, liturgía y memoria de la batalla.* Madrid: Sílex, 2013.

Aspesi, Cara. "The 'libelli' of Lucca, Biblioteca Arcivescovile, MS 5: Liturgy from the Siege of Acre." *JMH* 43.4 (2017): 384–402.

Ayala Martínez, Carlos de. "The Episcopate and Reconquest in the Times of Alfonso VII of Castile and León." In *Between Sword and Prayer: Warfare and Medieval Clergy in Cultural Perspective*. Edited by Radosław Kotecki, Jacek Maciejewski, and John S. Ott, 207–32. EMC 3. Leiden and Boston MA: Brill, 2018.

Ayala Martínez, Carlos de. *Sacerdocio y Reino en la España Altomedieval. Iglesia y poder Político en el Occidente peninsular, siglos VII–XII*. Madrid: Sílex, 2008.

Bale, Anthony, ed. *The Cambridge Companion to the Literature of the Crusades*. Cambridge and New York: Cambridge University Press, 2019.

Barber, Malcolm C. *The New Knighthood: A History of the Order of the Temple*. Cambridge and New York: Cambridge University Press, 1994.

Barber, Malcolm C. "The Social Context of the Templars." *Transactions of the Royal Historical Society* 34 (1984), 27–46.

Barton, Simon. "A Forgotten Crusade: Alfonso VII of León-Castile and the Campaign for Jaén (1148)." *Historical Research* 73.182 (2000): 312–20.

Barton, Simon. "El Cid, Cluny, and the Spanish Reconquest." *English Historical Review* 126.520 (2011): 517–43.

Bird, Jessalynn. "Crusade and Reform: The Sermons of Bibliotheque Nationale, MS nouv. Acq. Lat. 999." In *The Fifth Crusade in Context: The Crusading Movement in the Early Thirteenth Century*. Edited by E.J. Mylod et al., 92–114. Abingdon and New York: Routledge, 2017.

Bombi, Barbara. "The Authority of Miracles: Cesarius of Heisterbach and the Livonian Crusade." In *Aspects of Power and Authority in the Middle Ages*. Edited by Brenda Bolton and Christine Meek, 481–98. International medieval research 14. Turnhout: Brepols, 2007.

Bombi, Barbara. "The Fifth Crusade and the Conversion of the Muslims." In *The Fifth Crusade in Context: The Crusading Movement in the Early Thirteenth Century*. Edited by E.J. Mylod et al., 68–91. Abingdon and New York: Routledge, 2017.

Brodman, James W. "Captives or Prisoners: Society and Obligation in Medieval Iberia." *Anuario de Historia de la Iglesia* 20 (2011): 201–19.

Brodman, James W. "Rule and Identity: The Case of the Military Orders." *CHR* 87.3 (2001): 383–400.

Bronisch, Alexander Pierre. "La 'Chronica Adefonsi Imperatoris' entre guerra santa ibérica y cruzada." In *Hombres de religión y guerra. Cruzada y guerra santa en la Edad Media peninsular (siglos X–XV)*. Edited by Carlos de Ayala Martínez and J. Santiago Palacios Ontalva, 77–87. Madrid: Sílex, 2018.

Bronisch, Alexander Pierre. "La (sacralización de la) guerra en las fuentes de los siglos X y XI y el concepto de guerra santa." In *Orígenes y desarrollo de la guerra santa en la Península Ibérica. Palabras e imágenes para una legitimación (siglos X–XIV)*. Edited by Carlos de Ayala Martínez, Patrick Henriet, and J. Santiago Palacios Ontalva, 7–29. Madrid: Casa de Velázquez, 2016.

Brundage, James A. "'Cruce Signari': The Rite for Taking the Cross in England." *Traditio* 22 (1966): 289–310.

Bull, Marcus. *Knightly Piety and the Lay Response to the First Crusade: The Limousin and Gascony*. Oxford: Clarendon Press, 1993.

Burger, Michael, *The Shaping of Western Civilization* (Toronto: University of Toronto Press, 2003).

Bysted, Ane L., Carsten Selch Jensen, Kurt Villads Jensen, and John H. Lind. *Jerusalem in the North: Denmark and the Baltic Crusades, 1100–1522*. Outremer 1. Turnhout: Brepols, 2012.

Caroff, Fanny. "L'affrontement entre chrétiens et musulmans. Le rôle de la vraie Croix dans les images de croisade (XIIIe–XVe siècle)." In *Chemins d'outre-mer. Études d'histoire sur la Méditerranée médiévale offertes à Michel Balard*. Edited by Damien Coulon and Michel Balard, 99–114. Byzantina Sorbonensia 20. Paris: Publications de la Sorbonne, 2004.

Chrissis, Nikolas. "The City and the Cross: The Image of Constantinople and the Latin Empire in Thirteenth-Century Papal Crusading Rhetoric." *Byzantine and Modern Greek Studies* 36.1 (2012): 20–37.

Cingolani, Stefano Maria. *Sant Jordi. Una Llegenda Millenària*. Barcelona: Editorial Base, 2014.

Claverie, Pierre-Vincent. "'Totius populi Christiani negotium': The Crusading Conception of Pope Honorius III, 1216–1221." In *The Fifth Crusade in Context: The Crusading Movement in the Early Thirteenth Century*. Edited by E.J. Mylod et al., 27–39. Abingdon and New York: Routledge, 2017.

Cole, Penny. *The Preaching of the Crusades to the Holy Land, 1095–1270*. New York: Medieval Academy of America, 1991.

Conedera, SJ, Sam Zeno. *Ecclesiastical Knighthood: The Military Orders in Castile, 1150–1350*. New York: Fordham University Press, 2015.

Constable, Giles. *The Reformation of the Twelfth Century*. New Haven CN: Yale University Press, 1998.

Corral Val, Luis. "La orden de Alcántara. Organización institucional y vida religiosa en la Edad Media." PhD thesis, Universidad Complutense, 2003.

Dehoux, Esther "'Saint George, noble chevalier, tres humblement, je vous requier'. Enseignes et badges, (in)signes de la dévotion à saint Georges (XIIIe–début XVIe siècle)." In *Autour d'Azincourt. Une société face à la guerre (v.1370–v.1420)*. Edited by Alain Marchandisse and Bertrand Schnerb, 49–68. Villeneuve d'Ascq: Revue du Nord, 2017.

Deswarte, Thomas. "St. James in Galicia (c.500–1300): Rivalries in Heaven and on Earth." In *Culture and Society in Medieval Galicia: A Cultural Crossroads at the Edge of Europe*. Edited by James D'Emilio, 477–511. MEMI 59. Leiden and Boston MA: Brill, 2015.

Duby, Georges. *The Three Orders: Feudal Society Imagined.* Translated by Arthur Goldhammer. Chicago: University of Chicago Press, 1980.

Dygo, Marian. "The Political Role of the Cult of the Virgin Mary in Teutonic Prussia in the Fourteenth and Fifteenth Centuries." *JMH* 15.1 (1989): 63–80.

Ekdahl, Sven. "Crusades and Colonisation in the Baltic: A Historiographic Analysis." Translated by Helen Nicholson. In *The North-Eastern Frontiers of Medieval Europe: The Expansion of Latin Christendom in the Baltic Lands.* Edited by Alan Murray, 1–42. The expansion of Latin Europe, 1000–1500 4. Farnham: Variorum, 2014.

Eliott Lockhard, Elizabeth. "Remembering Things: Transformative Objects in Texts about Conflict, 1160–1390." PhD thesis, Columbia University, 2014.

Estow, Clara. "The Economic Development of the Order of Calatrava, 1158–1366." *Speculum* 57.2 (1982): 267–91.

Fine, Jr., John A. *The Bosnian Church: A New Interpretation. A Study of the Bosnian Church and Its Place in State and Society from the 13th to the 15th Centuries.* New York: Columbia University Press, 1975.

Fitz, Francisco Garcia. *La Edad Media. Guerra e ideologia. Justificaciones religiosas y juridicas.* Madrid: Sílex, 2003.

Fletcher, Richard A. *The Quest for El Cid.* New York: Oxford University Press, 1991.

Fonnesberg-Schmidt, Iben. *The Popes and the Baltic Crusades, 1147–1254.* TNW 26. Leiden and Boston MA: Brill, 2007.

Forey, Alan J. "Novitiate and Instruction in the Military Orders during the Twelfth and Thirteenth Centuries." *Speculum* 61.1 (1986): 1–17.

Forey, Alan J. "The Order of Mountjoy." *Speculum* 46.2 (1971): 250–66.

Friedman, Yvonne. "Miracle, Meaning, and Narrative in the Latin East." *SCH* 41 (2005): 123–34.

Gaposchkin, M. Cecilia. "From Pilgrimage to Crusade: The Liturgy of Departure, 1095–1300." *Speculum* 88.1 (2013): 44–91.

Gaposchkin, M. Cecilia. *Invisible Weapons: Liturgy and the Making of Crusade Ideology.* Ithaca NY: Cornell University Press, 2017.

Gaposchkin, M. Cecilia. "The Place of Jerusalem in Western Crusading Rites of Departure (1095–1300)." *CHR* 99.1 (2013): 1–28.

García de Cortázar, José Ángel. "El dominio del monasterio de San Millán de la Cogolla en los siglos X a XII." In *Estudios de historia medieval de La Rioja.* Edited by José Ángel García de Cortázar and Ruiz de Aguirre, 443–54. Logroño: Universidad de La Rioja Servicio de Publicaciones, 2009.

García Izquierdo, Iván, and David Peterson, "The Abbot-Bishops of San Millán and Calahorra (1025–1065): A Marriage of Convenience and a Messy Divorce." In *Obispos y monasterios en la Edad Media. Trayectorias personales, organización eclesiástica y dinámicas materiales.* Edited by Andrea Vanina Neyra and Mariel Pérez, 221–40. Buenos Aires: Sociedad Argentina de Estudios Medievales, 2020.

Giebfried, John. "The Holy Forgery of Bromholm." Paper Presented at Fourth International Symposium on Crusade Studies, Saint Louis University, Saint Louis MO, 20 June 2018.

Gómez, Miguel. "Alfonso VIII and the Battle of Las Navas de Tolosa." In *King Alfonso VIII of Castile: Government, Family, and War.* Edited by Miguel Gómez, Kyle C. Lincoln, and Damian J. Smith, 143–71. New York: Fordham University Press, 2020.

Henriet, Patrick. "L'évêque Raymond de Roda (1126), défenseur des 'christicoles'. Á propos de la 'Vita Beati Raimundi Basbastrensis Antistitis' (BHL 7074)." In *Hombres de religión y guerra. Cruzada y guerra santa en la Edad Media peninsular (siglos X–XV).* Edited by Carlos de Ayala Martínez and J. Santiago Palacios Ontalva, 17–28. Madrid: Sílex, 2018.

Henriet, Patrick. "'Protector et defensor omnium'. Le culte de Saint Michel en péninsule ibérique (haut Moyen Âge)." In *Culto e santuari di san Michele nell'Europa medievale.* Edited by Pierre Bouet, Giorgio Otranto, and André Vauchez, 113–32. Bibliotheca michaelica 1. Bari: Edipuglia, 2007.

Holt, Edward L. "'Cantigas de Santa María', 'Cantigas de Cruzada': Reflections of Crusading Spirituality in Alfonso X's 'Cantigas de Santa María.'" *Al-Masaq* 27.3 (2015): 207–24.

Holt, Edward L. "'Laudes regiae': Liturgy and Royal Power in Thirteenth-Century Castile-León." In *The Sword and the Cross: Castile-León in the Era of Fernando III.* Edited by Edward L. Holt and Teresa Witcombe, 140–64. MEMI 77. Leiden and Boston MA: Brill, 2020.

Holt, Edward L. "Crusading Memory in the Templar Liturgy of Barcelona." *Crusades* 18 (2019): 217–30.

Housley, Norman J. *The Avignon Papacy and the Crusades, 1305–1378.* Oxford: Clarendon Press, 1986.

Housley, Norman J. "The Franco-Papal Crusade Negotiations of 1322–3." *Papers of the British School at Rome* 48 (1980): 166–85.

Jakobsen, Johnny G.G. "Preachers of War: Dominican Friars as Promoters of the Crusades in the Baltic Region in the Thirteenth Century." In *Christianity and War in Medieval East Central Europe and Scandinavia.* Edited by Radosław Kotecki, Carsten Selch Jensen, and Stephen Bennett, 97–115. Leeds: ARC Humanities Press, 2021.

Jensen, Carsten Selch. "Bishops and Abbots at War: Some Aspects of Clerical Involvement in Warfare in Twelfth- and Early Thirteenth-Century Livonia and Estonia." In *Between Sword and Prayer: Warfare and Medieval Clergy in Cultural Perspective.* Edited by Radosław Kotecki, Jacek Maciejewski, and John S. Ott, 404–34. EMC 3. Leiden and Boston MA: Brill, 2018.

Jensen, Carsten Selch, Kurt Villads Jensen, and John H. Lind. "Communicating Crusades and Crusading Communications in the Baltic Region." *Scandinavian Economic History Review* 49.2 (2001): 5–25.

Jensen, Kurt Villads. "Crusading at the End of the World: The Spread of the Idea of Jerusalem after 1099 to the Baltic Sea Area and to the Iberian Peninsula." In *Crusading on the Edge: Ideas and Practice of Crusading in Iberia and the Baltic Region*. Edited by Torben Kjersgaard Nielsen and Iben Fonnesberg-Schmidt, 153–76. Outremer 4. Turnhout: Brepols, 2016.

Jessee, Scott. "Crusaders and Templars: Robert the Burgundian Lord of Craon and Sablé and His Descendents, 1095–1192." *Medieval Prosopography* 30 (2015): 31–58.

John, Simon. "Royal Inauguration and Liturgical Culture in the Latin Kingdom of Jerusalem, 1099–1187." *JMH* 43.4 (2017): 470–84.

Jordan, William C. "'Etiam Reges', Even Kings." *Speculum* 90.5 (2015): 613–34.

Jordan, William C. "The Rituals of War: Departure for Crusade in Thirteenth-Century France." In *The Book of Kings: Art, War, and the Morgan Library's Medieval Picture Bible*. Edited by William Noel and Daniel H. Weiss, 99–105. London: Walters Art Museum, 2002.

Kaljundi, Linda. "The Baltic Crusades and the Culture of Memory: Studies on Historical Representation, Rituals, and Recollection of the Past." PhD thesis, University of Helsinki, 2016.

Kaljundi, Linda. "Livonia as a Mariological Periphery: A Comparative Look at Henry of Livonia's Representations of the Mother of God." In *Livland—eine Region am Ende der Welt? Forschungen zum Verhältnis zwischen Zentrum und Peripherie im späten Mittelalter*. Edited by Anti Selart and Matthias Thumser, 431–60. QSBG 27. Cologne, Weimar, and Vienna: Böhlau, 2017.

Kienzle, Beverly Mayne. *Cistercians, Heresy, and Crusade in Occitania, 1145–1229*. Woodbridge: York Medieval Press in association with Boydell Press, 2001.

Kivimäe, Jüri. "'Servi Beatae Marie Virginis': Christians and Pagans in Henry's Chronicle of Livonia." In *Church and Belief in the Middle Ages: Popes, Saints, and Crusaders*. Edited by Kirsi Salonen and Sari Katajala-Peltomaa, 201–26. CB 3. Amsterdam: Amsterdam University Press, 2016.

Kostick, Conor. *The Social Structure of the First Crusade*. MMED 76. Leiden and Boston MA: Brill, 2008.

Kotecki, Radosław. "Lambs and Lions, Wolves and Pastors of the Flock: Portraying Military Activity of Bishops in Twelfth-Century Poland." In *Between Sword and Prayer: Warfare and Medieval Clergy in Cultural Perspective*. Edited by Radosław Kotecki, Jacek Maciejewski, and John S. Ott, 303–40. EMC 3. Leiden and Boston MA: Brill, 2018.

Kotecki, Radosław. "Pious Rulers, Princely Clerics, and Angels of Light: 'Imperial Holy War' Imagery in Twelfth-Century Poland and Rus'." In *Christianity and War in Medieval East Central Europe and Scandinavia*. Edited by Radosław Kotecki, Carsten Selch Jensen, and Stephen Bennett, 159–88. Leeds: ARC Humanities Press, 2021.

Laliena Corbera, Carlos. "Rituales litúrgicos y poder real en el siglo XI." *Aragón en la Edad Media* 16 (2000): 467–76.

Lapina, Elizabeth. "Demetrius of Thessaloniki: Patron Saint of Crusaders." *Viator* 40.2 (2009): 93–112.

Le Goff, Jacque, ed. *The Medieval World*. Translated by Lydia G. Cochrane. New York: Collins and Brown, 1990.

Leighton, Gregory. "Did the Teutonic Order Create a Sacred Landscape in Thirteenth-Century Prussia?" *JMH* 44.4 (2018): 457–83.

Leighton, Gregory. "The Relics of St Barbara at Althaus Kulm: History, Patronages, and Insight into the Teutonic Order and the Christian Population in Prussia (Thirteenth-Fifteenth Centuries)." *ZH* 85.1 (2020): 5–50.

Leighton, Gregory. "'Reysa in laudem Dei et virginis Marie contra paganos': The Experience of Crusading in Prussia during the Thirteenth and Fourteenth Centuries." *ZfO* 69.1 (2020): 1–25.

Lincoln, Kyle C. "'In exercitu locus pontificalia exercet': Warrior Clerics in the Era of Fernando III." In *The Sword and the Cross: Castile-León in the Era of Fernando III*. Edited by Edward L. Holt and Teresa Witcombe, 85–104. MEMI 77. Leiden and Boston MA: Brill, 2020.

Linder, Amnon. *Raising Arms: Liturgy in the Struggle to Liberate Jerusalem in the Late Middle Ages*. Cultural encounters in late Antiquity and the Middle Ages 2. Turnhout: Brepols, 2003.

Löffler, Anette. "Die Liturgie des Deutschen Ordens in Preußen." In *"Cura animarum." Seelsorge im Deutschordensland Preußen*. Edited by Stefan Samerski, 161–84. FQKK 45. Cologne: Böhlau, 2013.

Löffler, Anette. "Die Rolle der Liturgie im Ordenskonvent. Norm und Wirklichkeit." In *Das Leben im Ordenshaus. Vorträge der Tagung der Internationalen Historischen Kommission zur Erforschung des Deutschen Ordens in Tallinn 2014*. Edited by Juhan Kreem, 1–20. QSGD 81. Weimar: VDG, 2019.

Loud, Graham A. *The Latin Church in Norman Italy*. Cambridge and New York: Cambridge University Press, 2007.

MacEvitt, Christopher. "Processing Together, Celebrating Apart: Shared Processions in the Latin East." *JMH* 43.4 (2017): 455–69.

MacGregor, James B. "Negotiating Knightly Piety: The Cult of the Warrior-Saints in the West, ca.1070–ca.1200." *ChH* 73.2 (2004): 317–45 at 333.

Maciejewski, Jacek. "A Bishop Defends His City, or Master Vincentius's Troubles with the Military Activity of His Superior." In *Between Sword and Prayer: Warfare and Medieval Clergy in Cultural Perspective*. Edited by Radosław Kotecki, Jacek Maciejewski, and John S. Ott, 341–68. EMC 3. Leiden and Boston MA: Brill, 2018.

Madden, Thomas. *Enrico Dandolo and the Rise of Venice*. Baltimore MD: Johns Hopkins University Press, 2003.

Majnarić, Ivan. "Tending the Flock: Clergy and a Discourse of War in the Wider Hinterland of the Eastern Adriatic during the Late Twelfth and Thirteenth Century." In *In Between Sword and Prayer: Warfare and Medieval Clergy in Cultural Perspective.* Edited by Radosław Kotecki, Jacek Maciejewski, and John S. Ott, 435–70. EMC 3. Leiden and Boston MA: Brill, 2018.

Mänd, Anu. "Saints' Cults in Medieval Livonia." In *The Clash of Cultures on the Medieval Baltic Frontier.* Edited by Alan V. Murray, 191–226. Aldershot and Burlington VT: Ashgate, 2009.

Mentzel-Reuters, Arno. "Zur Sakraltopologie der Marienburg." In *"Castrum sanctae Mariae." Die Marienburg als Burg, Residenz und Museum.* Edited by Arno Mentzel-Reuters and Stefan Samerski, 99–178. Göttigen: Vandenhoeck & Ruprecht, 2019.

Militzer, Klaus. "The Recruitment of Brethren for the Teutonic Order in Livonia, 1237–1562." In *The Military Orders: Fighting for the Faith and Caring for the Sick.* Edited by Malcolm Barber, 270–77. Farnham: Variorum, 1994.

Miranda García, Fermín. "Ascenso, auge y caída de San Miguel como protector de la monarquía pamplonesa, siglos X–XII." In *Mundos medievales. Espacios, sociedades y poder. Homenaje al profesor José Ángel García de Cortázar y Ruiz de Aguirre.* Vol. 1. Edited by Beatriz Arizaga Bolumburu, Dolores Mariño Veiras, and Carmen Diéz Herrera, 759–68. Santander: Publican, 2012.

Miranda García, Fermín. "Sacralización de la guerra en el siglo X. La perspectiva pamplonesa." *Anales de la Universidad de Alicante. Historia Medieval* 17 (2011): 225–43.

Moore, Robert Ian. "George Duby's Eleventh Century." *History* 69.225 (1984): 36–49.

More, Alison. "'Milites Christi in hortis liliorum domini?': Hagiographic Constructions of Masculinity and Holiness in Thirteenth-Century Liege." PhD thesis, University of Bristol, 2004.

Mugurēvičs, Ēvalds. "The Military Activity of the Order of the Sword Brethren (1202–1236)." In *The North-Eastern Frontiers of Medieval Europe: The Expansion of Latin Christendom in the Baltic Lands.* Edited by Alan Murray, 117–23. The expansion of Latin Europe, 1000–1500 4. Farnham: Variorum, 2014.

Murray, Alan V. "Adding to the Multitude of Fish: Pope Innocent III, Bishop Albert of Riga and the Conversion of the Indigenous Peoples of Livonia." In *The Fourth Lateran Council and the Crusade Movement: The Impact of the Council of 1215 on Latin Christendom and the East.* Edited by Jessalyn L. Bird and Damian J. Smith, 153–70. Outremer 7. Turnhout: Brepols, 2018.

Murray, Alan V. "'Mighty against the enemies of Christ': The Relic of the True Cross in the Armies of the Kingdom of Jerusalem." In *The Crusades and their Sources: Essays Presented to Bernard Hamilton.* Edited by John France and William G. Zajac, 217–38. Aldershot and Burlington VT: Ashgate, 1998.

Nascimiento, Aires A. "O Júbilo da Vitória. Celebração da Tomado de Santarém aos Mouros (A.D. 1147)." In *Actes del X Congrés Internacional de L'Associació Hispànica de Literatura Medieval*. Edited by Rafael Alemany, Josep Lluís Martos, and Josep Miquel Manzanaro, 3 vols., 3:1218–32. Alicante: Institut Interuniversitari de Filologia Valenciana, 2005.

Nielsen, Torben Kjersgaard. "The Missionary Man: Archbishop Anders Sunesen and the Baltic Crusade, 1206–21." In *Crusade and Conversion on the Baltic Frontier, 1150–1500*. Edited by Alan V. Murray, 95–117. Aldershot and Burlington VT: Ashgate, 2001.

Nielsen, Torben Kjersgaard. "The Virgin at the Lateran—The Baltic Crusades, Rome and the Mother of God." In *The Fourth Lateran Council and the Crusade Movement: The Impact of the Council of 1215 on Latin Christendom and the East*. Edited by Jessalyn L. Bird and Damian J. Smith, 171–192. Outremer 7. Turnhout: Brepols, 2018.

O'Callaghan, Joseph F. *Reconquest and Crusade in Medieval Spain*. Philadelphia: University of Pennsylvania Press, 2004.

Olivares Torres, Enric. *L'ideal d'evangelització guerrera. Iconografia dels cavallers sants*. PhD thesis, Universitat de València, 2016.

Oliveira, Luis Felípe. "Guerra e Religiâo. As Narrativas de Conquista das Cidades do Sul." In *Hombres de religión y guerra. Cruzada y guerra santa en la Edad Media peninsular (siglos X–XV)*. Edited by Carlos de Ayala Martínez and J. Santiago Palacios Ontalva, 513–40. Madrid: Sílex, 2018.

Paul, Nicholas. "A Warlord's Wisdom: Literacy and Propaganda at the Time of the First Crusade." *Speculum* 85.3 (2010): 534–66.

Perron, Anthony. "Metropolitan Might and Papal Power on the Latin-Christian Frontier: Transforming the Danish Church Around the Time of the Fourth Lateran Council." *CHR* 89.2 (2003): 182–212.

Perry, David. *Sacred Plunder: Venice and the Aftermath of the Fourth Crusade*. University Park: Pennsylvania State University Press, 2015.

Peterson, David. "Genesis y significado de 'Los Votos de San Millan.'" In *De ayer y hoy. Contribuciones multidisciplinares sobre pseudoepígrafos literarios y documentales*. Edited by Mikel Labiano, 223–38. De falsa et vera historia 2. Madrid: Ediciones Clásicas, 2019.

Porrinas González, David. *Historia y mito de un hombre de guerra*. Madrid: Desperta Ferro Ediciones, 2019.

Pluskowski, Aleks. *The Archaeology of the Prussian Crusade: Holy War and Colonisation*. Abingdon and New York: Routledge, 2013.

Purkis, William J. *Crusading Spirituality in the Holy Land and Iberia, c.1095–c.1187*. Woodbridge: Boydell Press, 2008.

Remensnyder, Amy G. "Christian Captives, Muslim Maidens, and Mary." *Speculum* 82.3 (2007): 642–77.

Remensnyder, Amy G. *"La Conquistadora": The Virgin Mary at War and Peace in the Old and the New Worlds*. Oxford and New York: Oxford University Press, 2014.

Riley-Smith, Jonathan. *The First Crusade and the Idea of Crusading*. Philadelphia: University of Pennsylvania Press, 1986.

Riley-Smith, Jonathan. *The Knights Hospitaler in the Levant, c. 1070–1309*. New York: Palgrave MacMillan, 2012.

Rodríguez-Picavea, Enrique. "The Military Orders and Hospitaller Activity on the Iberian Peninsula during the Middle Ages." *Mediterranean Studies* 18 (2009): 24–43.

Rosenwein, Barbara. *A Short History of the Middle Ages*. 5th ed. Toronto: University of Toronto Press, 2018.

Rubenstein, Jay. *Armies of Heaven: The First Crusade and the Quest for Apocalypse*. New York: Basic Books, 2011.

Rubenstein, Jay. "Holy Fire and Sacral Kingship in Post-Conquest Jerusalem." *JMH* 43.4 (2017): 470–84.

Sastre Santos, Eutimio. "La Orden de Santiago y su Regla." PhD thesis, Universidad Complutense, 1981.

Saunders, Corinne, ed., *A Companion to Medieval Poetry*. Malden MA: Wiley Blackwell, 2010.

Schmitz-Esser, Romedio. "The Bishop and the Emperor: Tracing Narrative Intent in Otto of Frtiesing's 'Gesta Frederici.'" *Medieval Chronicle* 9 (2014): 297–324.

Selart, Anti. *Livonia, Rus' and the Baltic Crusades in the Thirteenth Century*. Translated by Fionna Robb. ECEE 29. Leiden and Boston MA: Brill, 2015.

Sirantoine, Helene. "La guerra contra los musulmanes en los diplomas castellano-leoneses (siglo XI-1126)." In *Orígenes y desarrollo de la guerra santa en la Península Ibérica. Palabras e imágenes para una legitimación (siglos X–XIV)*. Edited by Carlos de Ayala Martínez, Patrick Henriet, and J. Santiago Palacios Ontalva, 51–65. Madrid: Casa de Velázquez, 2016.

Skwierczyński, Krzysztof. "The Beginnings of the Cult of the Bless Virgin Mary in Poland in the Light of the Płock Accounts of Miracles from 1148." *Studi Medievali*. Ser. 3. 53.1 (2012): 117–61.

Smith, Damian J. "The Reconciliation of Guillem Ramon de Montcada, the Albigensian Crusade and Fourth Lateran." In *The Fourth Lateran Council and the Crusade Movement: The Impact of the Council of 1215 on Latin Christendom and the East*. Edited by Jessalyn L. Bird and Damian J. Smith, 131–50. Outremer 7. Turnhout: Brepols, 2018.

Smith, Katherine A. "Saints in Shining Armor: Martial Asceticism and Masculine Models of Sanctity, ca.1050–1250." *Speculum* 83.3 (2008): 572–602.

Tamm, Marek. "The Livonian Crusade in Cistercian Stories of the Early Thirteenth Century." *Crusading on the Edge: Ideas and Practice of Crusading in Iberia and the Baltic Region*. Edited by Torben Kjersgaard Nielsen and Iben Fonnesberg-Schmidt, 365–89. Outremer 4. Turnhout: Brepols, 2016.

Tamm, Marek. "Les miracles en Livonie et en Estonie à l'époque de la christianisation (fin XIIème–début XIIIème siècles)." In *"Quotidianum Estonicum": Aspects of Daily*

Life in Medieval Estonia. Edited by Jüri Kivimäe and Juhan Kreem, 29–78. Medium aevum quotidianum. Sonderband 5. Krems: Medium Aevum Quotidianum, 1996.

The Teutonic Order in Prussia and Livonia: Political and Ecclesiastical Structures, 13th–16th Century. Edited by Roman Czaja and Andrzej Radzimiński. Toruń: Towarzystwo Naukowe, 2015.

Thompson, Augustine. *Cities of God: The Religion of the Italian Communes, 1125–1325*. University Park: Pennsylvania State University Press, 2005.

Transehe-Roseneck, Astaf von. *Die ritterlichen Livlandfahrer des 13. Jahrhunderts. Eine genealogische Untersuchung*. Marburger Ostforschungen 12. Marburg: Würzburg-Holzner Verlag, 1960.

Tsurtsumia, Mamuka. "The True Cross in the Armies of Georgia and the Frankish East." *Crusades* 12 (2013): 91–102.

Undusk, Jann. "Sacred History, Profane History: Uses of the Bible in the Chronicle of Henry of Livonia." In *Crusading and Chronicle Writing on the Medieval Baltic Frontier: A Companion to the Chronicle of Henry of Livonia*. Edited by Marek Tamm, Linda Kaljundi, and Carsten Selch Jensen, 45–75. Farnham and Burlington VT: Ashgate, 2011.

Valente, José. "The New Frontier: The Role of the Knights Templar in the Establishment of Portugal as an Independent Kingdom." *Mediterranean Studies* 7 (1998): 49–65.

Vallejo Girvés, Margarita. "Inuentio y desarrollo del culto de San Jorge pre-militar y caballero en Galatia." *Polis* 13 (2001): 141–53.

Wilson, Jonathan. "A Cistercian Point of View in the Portuguese Reconquista." *Journal of Medieval Monastic Studies* 8 (2019): 95–142.

Wilson, Jonathan. "Enigma of the 'De Expugnatione Lyxbonensi.'" *JMIS* 9.1 (2017): 99–129.

Wolff, Robert Lee. "Footnote to an Incident of the Latin Occupation of Constantinople: The Church and the Icon of the Hodegetria." *Traditio* 6 (1948): 319–27.

Zöller, Wolf. "The Regular Canons and the Liturgy of the Latin East." *JMH* 43.4 (2017): 367–83.

Zupka, Dušan. "Religious Rituals of War in Medieval Hungary Under the Árpád Dynasty." In *Christianity and War in Medieval East Central Europe and Scandinavia*. Edited by Radosław Kotecki, Carsten Selch Jensen, and Stephen Bennett, 141–57. Leeds: ARC Humanities Press, 2021.

Northern Europe and the Baltic

CHAPTER 3

Battle Psalms and War Liturgy in the Medieval Gaelic World and Its Neighbors before 1200

Jesse Patrick Harrington

Christianity influenced the theory and practice of warfare in medieval Britain and Ireland from an early date.[1] When religious writing from the post-Roman Insular world re-emerges over the course of the seventh century, Christianity had already been planted in the Gaelic world for two centuries since the arrival of St. Patrick. It was confidently expanding into its nearest neighbors, Pictish Scotland and "Anglo-Saxon" Northumbria. With the spread of the new religion came both new rules and new rituals appropriate to war and its conduct.

By far the most celebrated intervention of the Gaelic church in the conduct of warfare was the seventh-century *Lex Innocentium* (*The Law of Innocents*) of the Irish abbot and lawmaker, St. Adomnán of Iona, which later bore his name as *Cáin Adomnáin* (*The Law of Adomnán*). Promulgated at the Synod of Birr in 697, the law has been described as a medieval forerunner of the modern Geneva Conventions. It sought to protect both church property and *innocentes*—women, children, and clerics—whom it stipulated were to be treated as non-combatants. The substantial guarantor list suggests that secular and clerical leaders throughout the expanding Gaelic world, which then encompassed Ireland and the Western Isles of Scotland—as well as leaders beyond that world, insofar as the list includes Pictish rulers—wished to be associated with the principle.[2] The canons attributed to Adomnán additionally prohibited

[1] I would like to thank the editors and anonymous reviewer for their erudite suggestions, as well as Prof. Máire Ní Mhaonaigh, Prof. John Carey, and Dr. Brigid Ehrmantraut, for generously sharing further valuable observations, some of which go beyond the scope of the present piece. Any remaining omissions or errors are my own.

[2] *Adomnán's "Law of the Innocents," Cáin Adomnáin: A Seventh Century Law for the Protection of Non-Combatants*, trans. Gilbert Márkus (Kilmartin: Kilmartin House Trust, 2008); Thomas O'Loughlin, ed., *Adomnán at Birr, AD 697: Essays in Commemoration of the "Law of the Innocents"* (Dublin: Four Courts Press, 2011); James E. Fraser, "Adomnán and the Morality of War," in *Adomnán of Iona: Theologian, Lawmaker, Peacemaker*, ed. Jonathan M. Wooding et al. (Dublin: Four Courts Press, 2010), 95–111; Gilbert Márkus, *Conceiving a Nation: Scotland to AD 900* (Edinburgh: Edinburgh University Press, 2017), chap. 4. For the impact and endurance of the law into the twelfth century, see James W. Houlihan, *Adomnán's "Lex Innocentium" and the Laws of War* (Dublin: Four Courts Press, 2020), 141–64.

© KONINKLIJKE BRILL NV, LEIDEN, 2023 | DOI:10.1163/9789004686366_004

the receipt of cattle taken by plunder and may be interpreted as an attempt to limit plundering. Adomnán's *Vita S. Columbae* depicts the excommunication of raiders and offers "a nuanced moral reaction to violence and warfare and those who orchestrated them."[3] Adomnán was involved in the liberation of Irish hostages taken by Northumbrian raiders in the 680s, and the liberation of captives was an activity for which other clerics had showed concern as early as the time of the fifth-century missionary, St. Patrick.[4] Other clerics acted as peacemakers or peacebrokers between warring parties, as elsewhere in Christendom.[5] The Gaelic church provided sanctuary protection from an early date, though these protections came under increasing pressure from the eleventh century onward.[6]

Nonetheless, as Gilbert Márkus and James E. Fraser have reminded, neither Adomnán nor other Christian clerics of the same period sought to stop the fact of war, so much as to limit and regulate its effects. This was in keeping with contemporary clerical attitudes elsewhere toward war and violence.[7] Warfare in this period ranged from low-level violence among private parties to larger expeditions mounted by kings, with the rich Irish historical tradition of annals, hagiography, and saga literature abundantly detailing both sets of activity.[8] Violence was not held to be intrinsically immoral, and individual acts existed on a moral spectrum of human activity; given the right circumstances, killing on the battlefield could even be held to be sinless. Adomnán could write

---

[3] Fraser, "Adomnán," 97–98, 101, quoted at 101.

[4] *The Annals of Ulster (to A.D. 1131)*, ed. Sean Mac Airt and Gearoid Mac Niocaill (Dublin: Dublin Institute for Advanced Studies, 1983), 150–51 (s.a. 687.5); Fraser, "Adomnán," 96; David N. Dumville, "Coroticus," in *Saint Patrick, AD 493–1993*, ed. David N. Dumville and Lesley Abrams, SCelH 13 (Woodbridge: Boydell Press, 1993), 107–15 at 107–9.

[5] Thomas M. Charles-Edwards, "Irish Warfare before 1100," in *A Military History of Ireland*, ed. Thomas Bartlett and Keith Jeffery (Cambridge: Cambridge University Press, 1996), 26–51 at 32–33.

[6] Kathleen Hughes, *The Church in Early Irish Society* (Ithaca NY: Cornell University Press, 1966), 238; Joan N. Radner, "The Significance of the Threefold Death in Celtic Tradition," in *Celtic Folklore and Christianity: Studies in Memory of William W. Heist*, ed. Patrick K. Ford (Santa Barbara CA: McNally and Loftin, 1983), 180–99 at 193 and 198; Thomas M. Charles-Edwards, *Early Christian Ireland* (Cambridge: Cambridge University Press, 2000), 120; Wendy Davies, "'Protected Space' in Britain and Ireland in the Middle Ages," in *Scotland in Dark Age Britain*, ed. Barbara E. Crawford, St. John's house papers 6 (Aberdeen: Scottish Cultural Press, 1996), 1–19.

[7] *Adomnán's "Law of the Innocents,"* 8; Fraser, "Adomnán," 96, 100, 102, quoted at 100: "whether in Ireland or in Latin Christendom generally, it would be surprising in this period for a cleric to object to war in principle, and there is a great deal of evidence to suggest that Adomnán did not."

[8] Charles-Edwards, "Irish Warfare," 26–28.

of the outcomes of battles or decapitations "without feeling compelled to moralize." Crucially, the degree of sin ascribed to an act of violence "depended to a greater extent on the spiritual condition of the perpetrator," and to some extent, that of the victim "than upon the specific details of the act itself."[9]

Clerics were directly involved in the initiating and justifying processes of early medieval violence and warfare. While kings were earmarked with the divine duty of necessary warfare, clerics provided prayers in support. In the constellation of rulers in the early medieval Insular world, each king "had his own clerical phalanx that upheld the justice of his own causes, and condemned his enemies … as perpetrators of injustice themselves, against whom they had a duty to make war."[10] For example, Adomnán's *Vita Columbae* depicted his abbatial predecessor Columba promising his protection and victory to the Dalriadan king Áedán mac Gabráin, to Oswald of Northumbria, as well as to other kings.[11] One of Adomnán's English contemporaries, Stephen of Ripon, depicted the Northumbrian war effort as underpinned by the prayers and intercessions of its bishop, Wilfrid of York, a view notably extended by Wilfrid's hagiographers in the late eleventh and early twelfth centuries.[12] Such prayers and intercessions might take place not only at a distance, but on the battlefield itself, where the presence of the clergy provided visible support. Bede's *Historia Ecclesiastica* refers to the early seventh-century massacre of British monks who had been present on the field of Battle of Chester to pray for victory.[13] Fraser has suggested that *Cáin Adomnáin* may have been written in part to prevent the "calculated massacre" of clerics who, in providing support to fighting men, had been seen by some military leaders as legitimate targets for violence.[14] If this was its aim, it did not ultimately detach clerics from the direct experience of war and violence. Indeed, rivalry between religious houses was one notable cause of armed conflict. Particularly between the late eighth and early ninth centuries, battles took place between powerful ecclesiastical settlements, and between churches and Irish kings, including the conflict between the

---

9   Fraser, "Adomnán," 100–3, quoted at 101–2. For later, continental consideration of the problem, see also David S. Bachrach, *Religion and the Conduct of War, c. 300–1215* (Woodbridge: Boydell Press, 2003), 98–106.
10   Fraser, "Adomnán," 101–4, quoted at 109.
11   Miho Tanaka, "Iona and the Kingship of Dál Riata in Adomnán's 'Vita Columbae,'" *Peritia* 17–18 (2003), 199–214; Fraser, "Adomnán," 99, 103–4.
12   Jesse Patrick Harrington, "Vengeance and Saintly Cursing in the Saints' Lives of England and Ireland, c.1060–1215" (PhD thesis, University of Cambridge, 2018), 54–55.
13   Bede, *Ecclesiastical History of the English People*, ed. Bertram Colgrave and R.A.B. Mynors, 2 vols. (Oxford: Clarendon Press, 1967), 1:140–41.
14   Fraser, "Adomnán," 98–99.

supporters of the prominent churches of Clonmacnoise and Birr in 760. Raiding of churches became "a recurrent feature" of early medieval Irish warfare.[15]

In this cultural and political environment, ritual specialists in the Gaelic world and its neighbors had a wide variety of ritual tools, instruments, and practices for providing support to armies and their leaders. Among these were three broad categories which will be discussed in what follows: rituals of fasting, prayer, and psalm litanies; the ritual procession of relics and other holy objects as "battle talismans;" and the delivery of suitable harangues to direct the armies spiritually and militarily and to boost morale. These practices had key biblical precedents. Prominent were the narratives of Moses raising his arms and staff in prayer during the battle against the Amalekites at Rephidim (Exodus 17:8–14), the deployment of the Ark of the Covenant to manifest God's presence on the battlefield (Joshua 6:4–6:15), and the campaign harangues delivered by the Hasmonean Maccabees (e.g., 1 Maccabees 2–3). These biblical influences provided a shared framework with practices elsewhere in Christendom and will be given due consideration later in what follows.

The Gaelic world was far from static in its military, political, or religious culture. The period of study notably overlaps two key periods of transition in Irish military history. The first is the Viking Age, from the 830s on until around 1100. This period saw sporadic outbreaks of violence on a limited scale by both royal and non-royal authority. It also witnessed the introduction of pagan Scandinavian raiders and settlers. These became Christianized over time and increasingly integrated into the Gaelic world, but they could initially be seen as destructive barbarians and heathens intruding upon the Gaelic Christian social order, and thus as legitimate targets for Christian violence. As political and technological conditions advanced, it included the introduction of the battle-axe, the increasing importance of archery, improvement in the quality and availability of swords and armor, and the emergence of naval power in Irish warfare.[16]

The second period of transition is that of the increasing militarization of Irish and Scottish society after 1100. This period saw the organization of larger armies under increasingly consolidated "over-kingships" and included the wars among the provincial over-kings in twelfth-century Ireland, the "Davidian revolution" in the Kingdom of Scotland (1124–1153) and the Scottish invasions of England during the "Anarchy" (1136–1153), and the Anglo-Norman invasion of Ireland in 1169. It is in this same period of increasing militarization that

---

15 Clare Downham, *Medieval Ireland* (Cambridge: Cambridge University Press, 2018), 91, 138–40, quoted at 91.
16 Downham, *Medieval Ireland*, 89.

increased concern is shown by clerical authors for the importance of church sanctuary protections and their violation. The present essay offers a thematic survey, which does not attempt to give a general account of military practice in Ireland or to chart diachronic change. Nonetheless, it must be noted that both Gaelic society and the societies of its neighbors did change over time.

1 Psalms and Prayers

As elsewhere in the Latin West, the psalter was of fundamental importance in Irish Christianity. It was central to the Irish monastic system and represented the most read and studied book of the Bible.[17] Psalters were among the most important physical productions of the early Irish church, and historical and literary narratives in medieval Ireland were suffused with the language and motifs drawn from the psalms.[18] For medieval Irish clerics, the 150 poems that comprise the psalter were committed to memory in the first two or three years of their training and recited weekly as part of the divine office. For the non-religious, selections from the psalter were heard at every mass, "either as complete poems or as the excerpted verses that formed part of the introit, gradual, alleluia, offertory, and communion *formulae*."[19] Elsewhere in Latin Christendom, the psalter might additionally be known to the vernacular laity, as in England, where an Old English translation of the first fifty psalms can be attributed to the royal translation program of Alfred the Great.[20] Though no vernacular translation of the psalter survives from medieval Ireland, the psalms were probably also known to the laity in vernacular form. This conclusion can be reasonably inferred from the oral teaching of the psalms in the Irish church, the vernacular glossing of sacred verse in the *Liber Hymnorum*, and the extensive vernacular quotation from individual psalms in the twelfth-century

---

17 Martin McNamara, *The Psalms in the Early Irish Church*, Journal for the Study of the New Testament supplement series 165 (Sheffield: Sheffield Academic Press, 2000), 20.
18 Harrington, "Vengeance," 152–54; idem, "Sinners, Saints, Psalms, and Curses in 'Aided Diarmata meic Cerbaill' ('The Death-Tale of Diarmait mac Cerbaill')," in *Proceedings of Defining the Boundaries of Celtic Hagiography: Textual Sources Outside Lives and Martyrologies Conference, Dublin Institute for Advanced Studies, 25–26 May 2018*, ed. Sarah Waidler (Dublin: Dublin Institute for Advanced Studies, forthc. 2023).
19 Daniel M. Wiley, "The Maledictory Psalms," *Peritia* 15 (2001): 261–79 at 261.
20 For the situation elsewhere in Latin Christendom, see Theresa Gross-Diaz, "The Latin Psalter," in *The Bible from 600 to 1450*, ed. Richard Marsden and E. Ann Matter, The new Cambridge history of the Bible 2 (Cambridge: Cambridge University Press, 2012), 427–45 at 439–43.

saga *Aided Diarmata meic Cerbaill* (*The Death-tale of Diarmait mac Cerbaill*), which addressed a mixed clerical and lay audience.[21]

Because of their breadth as a compendium of Christian life and experience, the psalms were invoked frequently, and especially in times of tribulation. This "could take any number of forms from the impromptu recitation of a few appropriate verses to the performance of a more formal, stylized ritual."[22] A well-known example of such a ritual performance would be the Irish *sailm escaine*, or psalms of malediction, a cursus of some twenty or so psalms drawn from the psalter and the Book of Deuteronomy, compiled by at least the late seventh century to allow the Irish clergy to curse their enemies. These so-called "cursing psalms," which had their continental analogue in the Benedictine *clamor*, were used to enforce ecclesiastical sanction against lawbreakers, until such time as they made restitution, and to uphold the peace against illegitimate violence.[23] One of the most notable instances of their threatened use is in the cursus of psalms which form the later (possibly ninth-century) sanction clause of *Cáin Adomnáin*, for those who might break the tract's legal prescriptions.[24] The Irish annals record other instances of the clergy invoking the curses of God and the saints against those who had committed unlawful acts of violence, and such rituals would have included both fasting and psalm-singing by the clergy.[25]

---

21 McNamara, *Psalms*, 24–25; Máire Herbert, "Crossing Historical and Literary Boundaries: Irish Written Culture Around the Year 1000," *Cambrian Medieval Celtic Studies* 53–54 (2007): 87–101 at 88–90; Marie-Luise Ehrenschwendtner, "Literacy and the Bible," in *The Bible from 600 to 1450*, 704–21 at 704–5 and 710–11; Harrington, "Sinners."
22 Wiley, "Maledictory Psalms," 262.
23 Pádraig Ó Néill, "A Middle Irish Poem on the Maledictory Psalms," *Journal of Celtic Studies* 3 (1981): 40–58; Wiley, "Maledictory Psalms." For the *clamor*, see esp. Lester K. Little, *Benedictine Maledictions: Liturgical Cursing in Romanesque France* (Ithaca NY and London: Cornell University Press, 1993), 20–26.
24 Little, *Maledictions*, 170–71; Wiley, "Maledictory Psalms," 263–66.
25 See, e.g., *The Annals of Tigernach*, trans. Whitley Stokes, 2 vols. (Felinfach: Llanerch Publishers, 1993), 1:383 and 2:28 (s.a. 1043.8 and 1108.10); *The Annals of Inisfallen MS. Rawlinson B. 503*, ed. Seán Mac Airt (Dublin: Dublin Institute for Advanced Studies, 1951), 266–67 (s.a. 1108.4); *"Annala Uladh": Annals of Ulster Otherwise "Annala Senait," Annals of Senat: A Chronicle of Irish Affairs from A.D. 431 to A.D. 1540*, ed. William M. Hennessy and Batholomew Mac Carthy, 4 vols. (Dublin: Thom & Co., 1887–1901), 1:154–55 (s.a. 1166.10); *The Annals of Loch Cé*, RS 54, ed. William M. Hennessy, 2 vols. (London: Longman, 1871; rprt. Dublin: Stationery Office, 1939), 122–25 (s.a. 1128.4); *"Annála Ríoghachta Éireann": Annals of the Kingdom of Ireland, by the Four Masters*, ed. John O'Donovan, 7 vols. (Dublin: Hodges, Smith, 1854; rprt. New York: AMS Press, 1966), 2:844–45, 988–89, 1092–93 (s.a. 1043.12, 1109.6, 1109.7, 1150.15).

The attribution of the psalms' authorship to the biblical David, king of Israel, meant that their recitation was not confined to narrowly clerical interests or performers, but that they could also see wider use, extending both to the laity and to the battlefield.[26] In particular, David's status as a quintessential biblical warrior king made his psalms appropriate for recitation in martial contexts. Furthermore, the structure of many of the psalms, as prayerful petitions that complained of oppressive enemies and invoked a punitive God to vindicate the petitioner, only added to their perceived appropriateness for such settings. Michael McCormick offers the paradigmatic scholarly study of the continental use of the psalms as part of a Carolingian liturgy of war. For the Avar campaign of 791, the Frankish army prepared for war on the bank of the Enns River with three days of litanies and abstinence, accompanied by clerical recitations of the psalms in blocks of fifty.[27] The practice was an innovation on the use of a propitiatory liturgy in times of military crisis that appears to have been deeply rooted in Roman liturgical custom going back at least to the sixth century, and to have become established in Francia with papal support from the mid-eighth century onwards.[28] Although the burden of this liturgy seems to have fallen most heavily on the clergy and other non-combatants, from the 790s onwards prayers were also to be performed by the army itself, with instructions that the importance of the liturgies was to be communicated to their lay participants through vernacular preaching.[29]

There has also been investigation of the introduction of war liturgy in England. In a study of Alfred's *Prose Psalms*, Lucrezia Pezzarossa has suggested that "the absence of virtually any reference to these practices in Anglo-Saxon [historical] sources suggests that, unlike in Charlemagne's territories, liturgies of war were nearly unknown in Alfredian England."[30] An important exception

---

26 Harrington, "Sinners."
27 Michael McCormick, "The Liturgy of War in the Early Middle Ages: Crisis, Litanies, and the Carolingian Monarchy," *Viator* 15 (1984): 1–24 at 8–10; idem, *Eternal Victory: Triumphal Rulership in Late Antiquity, Byzantium, and the Early Medieval West* (Cambridge: Cambridge University Press, 1986), 347–55; Bachrach, *Religion*, 34, 39.
28 McCormick, "Liturgy of War," 17–21; idem, *Eternal Victory*, 342–47; Bachrach, *Religion*, 32–36.
29 McCormick, "Liturgy of War," 11–12; idem, *Eternal Victory*, 252–54; Bachrach, *Religion*, 32–43.
30 Lucrezia Pezzarossa, "The Ideology of War in Early Medieval England: Three Case Studies in Anglo-Saxon Literature" (PhD thesis, University of York, 2013), 111; eadem, "Bibbia, guerra e liturgia. Una nuova prospettiva sulla traduzione alfrediana del 'Libro dei Salmi,'" in *La Bibbia nelle letterature germaniche medievali*, ed. Marina Buzzoni, Massimiliano Bampi, and Omar Khalaf, Filologie medievali e moderne Rie occidentale 6 (Venice: Ca' Foscari, 2015), 37–50 at 40.

is the account in Asser's *Life of Alfred* that that the young Alfred had to stand alone against a Viking army at the Battle of Ashdown in 871, because Aethelred, his elder brother and king of Wessex, "was indeed still ... in the tent at prayer, hearing Mass and declaring firmly that he would not leave that place alive before the priest had finished Mass."[31] Pezzarossa concluded that while "this passage might very well be a masterly cover-up of a diplomatic incident, Asser's words still portray the king's devotion as being contrary to both common sense and usual practice—therefore reinforcing the impression that, at least in the second half of the ninth century, liturgies of war were not usually performed in England."[32] Nonetheless, attention to Alfred's *Prose Psalms* suggests the attempt to import Carolingian ideology and rituals of war into the Insular world.[33] English use of liturgy to secure military victory is most prominent in the desperate years of Aethelred II. At some point in ca. 995–1008, the bishops of England collectively instituted a nationwide program of prayer and fasting, with a mass *contra paganos*, in response to Viking raids.[34] Another nationwide program was instituted, partly under the influence of Archbishop Wulfstan II of York, in response to the raids of 1009. This required of all adult Christians in England daily fasting, almsgiving, and barefoot procession to the local church to receive confession, for the three days leading up to Michaelmas. The secular clergy were each instructed to sing thirty masses, and every monk was to recite the psalter thirty times. In addition, each religious community was to lie prostrate before the altar and sing Psalm 3 at each of the hours, with the collect *contra paganos*.[35] Simon Keynes has observed that the combination of these practices in response to a specific emergency "reeks of Carolingian antecedent and analogy," and that "when, in 1009, Wulfstan advocated a three-day programme of processions and prayer, he probably did so in full awareness that he was doing as the Franks had done in the past."[36] Wulfstan's provisions were later generalized for potential use in future emergencies.[37]

There is little reason to suppose that the Irish would have been any less willing to invoke the psalms similarly. Indeed, the well-attested Irish use of the

---

31   *Asser's Life of King Alfred, Together with the Annals of Saint Neots Erroneously Ascribed to Asser*, ed. William Henry Stevenson and Dorothy Whitelock (Oxford: Clarendon Press, 1959), 29.
32   Pezzarossa, "Ideology of War," 111; Pezzarossa, "Bibbia," 40.
33   Pezzarossa, "Bibbia."
34   Simon Keynes, "An Abbot, an Archbishop, and the Viking Raids of 1006–7 and 1009–12," *Anglo-Saxon England* 36 (2007): 151–220 at 171.
35   Keynes, "Viking Raids," 177–90.
36   Ibid., 184, 186.
37   Ibid., 189.

psalms in more general rituals of blessing and cursing mean one should almost expect to find similar ritual psalmody on and near the battlefield. After all, the binary relationship of blessing and cursing as perfect opposites made both particularly suitable for martial use, since the psalms' blessing of victory for one's allies had its inescapable corollary in the curse of defeat for one's enemy.[38] Some of the clearest examples of clerics reinforcing armies on the battlefield can be found in hagiographical and heroic literature. The importance of such appearances is not for the historical image of the saints and heroes that these texts purport to describe often at several centuries' remove. Hagiography is an imaginative and inventive rhetorical genre, designed to demonstrate the sanctity of its subject according to accepted, conventional standards contemporary with its authors and audiences. Rather, the importance of such texts is for the wider cultural and social realities that they reveal as intelligible to those audiences, and thus as plausible for the later period in which they were composed. As John France has argued, saints' lives can be "very valuable in themselves for what they tell us of clerical attitudes … to war," though what they tell us about the conduct of war itself is "much more fragmented and only becomes comprehensible taken in conjunction with other source material."[39]

The twelfth-century vernacular saga *Buile Suibhne* (*The Madness of Sweeney*) ostensibly concerns the wandering tribulations of the seventh-century Suibne mac Colmáin, king of Dál nAraidi in the north, who was driven insane by the curse of the monastic founder-saint Rónán Finn. Early in the narrative, the saga depicts Rónán, with his church bell and eight psalmists of his community, sprinkling holy water on the host of Suibne in preparation for the Battle of Mag Rath, fought in 637.[40] Gille (Gilbert) of Limerick, a twelfth-century Irish bishop, noted that "psalmist" was not a distinct clerical grade, since anyone could be authorized to intone a psalm.[41] Thus, the description here most probably refers to the immediate activity of ritual psalm recitation, to accompany the sacramentals of bell and holy water before battle, rather than to the status of the clerical performers.[42]

---

38   For the binary opposition, see Lester K. Little, "Blessings and Curses," *Memoirs of the American Academy in Rome* 51–52 (2006): 1–4.
39   John France, "War and Sanctity: Saints' Lives as Sources for Early Medieval Warfare," *JMMH* 3 (2005): 14–22 at 22.
40   "Buile Suibhne": "The Frenzy of Suibhne," Being the Adventures of Suibhne Geilt, a Middle Irish Romance, ed. J.G. O'Keeffe, Irish Texts Society 12 (London: Nutt, 1913), 10–11.
41   Marie Therese Flanagan, "Reform in the Twelfth-Century Irish Church: A Revolution of Outlook?" Kathleen Hughes Memorial lectures 9 (Cambridge: Hughes Hall and the Department of Anglo-Saxon, Norse, and Celtic, University of Cambridge, 2012), 32.
42   Bells were used not only for exorcism, malediction, and excommunication, but also for gathering community, enforcing compacts, oaths, and tribute, and as battle-talismans

Other idealized literary depictions of clerical involvement on the battlefield suggest such support—or opposition—was perceived as important in the high medieval period. The twelfth-century vernacular *Betha Finnchua Brí Gobunn* (*The Life of Finnchú of Brí Gobann*), ostensibly concerning the seventh-century warrior saint Finnchú, depicts clerics accompanying lay warriors into battle.[43] The twelfth-century saga *Aided Diarmata*, in line with earlier annalistic claims, depicts the battlefield prayers of St. Columba as instrumental and decisive in routing the army of his opponent, Diarmait, king of Tara, at the Battle of Cúil Dreimne.[44] *Betha Colaim Chille*, the sixteenth-century vernacular life of the saint attributed to Maghnus Ua Domnaill, makes Columba similarly decisive in the rout. In this later narrative, the saint fasts the night before the battle and, on the day itself, remains in the rear of the army with his arms raised in *croisfigill* ("cross-vigil") in their support, while the rival St. Finnian briefly does the same on behalf of Diarmait on the opposite side.[45] It is a complex narrative that is at least partly modelled on the performance of Moses against the Amalekites at Rephidim in Exodus.[46] Nor was the martial decisiveness of prayer confined to literature. The vernacular *Fragmentary Annals of Ireland*, copied in the seventeenth century but compiled perhaps as early as the eleventh, credit the routing of the Norse armies in Ireland in the early tenth century to "the fasting and prayers of the holy man, Céle Dabaill," abbot of Bangor.[47] The perceived power of such clerical and saintly prayers was doubtless an extension of belief in the power of clerical and saintly curses, developed into rituals suitable for deployment on or near the battlefield.

---

in war. See e.g., Lucas, "Social Role," 14–15, 18–28, 32–34; John H. Arnold and Caroline Goodson, "Resounding Community: The History and Meaning of Medieval Church Bells," *Viator* 43.1 (2012), 99–130; Cormac Bourke, *The Early Medieval Hand-bells of Ireland and Britain* (Dublin: National Museum of Ireland, 2020), chap. 10.

43 *Lives of Saints from the Book of Lismore*, ed. Whitley Stokes, Anecdota Oxoniensia 5 (Oxford: Clarendon Press, 1890), 89, 91–97, 236, 238, 240–44.

44 "An Edition of 'Aided Diarmata meic Cerbaill' from the Book of Uí Maine," ed. Dan M. Wiley (PhD Thesis, Harvard University, 2000), 130–31, 156–57.

45 *"Betha Colaim Chille": "Life of Columcille." Compiled by Manus O'Donnell in 1532*, ed. Andrew O'Kelleher and Gertrude Schoepperle, University of Illinois Bulletin 15.48 (Urbana IL: University of Illinois, 1918), 180–83.

46 Compare Radosław Kotecki, "With the Sword of Prayer, or How the Medieval Bishop Should Fight," *QMAN* 21 (2016): 341–69; idem, "Lions and Lambs, Wolfs and Pastors of the Flock: Portraying Military Activities of Bishops in Twelfth Century Poland," in *Between Sword and Prayer: Warfare and Medieval Clergy in Cultural Perspective*, ed. Radosław Kotecki, Jacek Maciejewski, and John S. Ott, EMC 3 (Leiden and Boston MA: Brill, 2018), 303–40.

47 *Fragmentary Annals of Ireland*, ed. Joan N. Radner (Dublin: Dublin Institute for Advanced Studies, 1978), 166–69.

While clerics were undoubtedly ritual specialists, the use of prayer and psalmody in search of military victory was not limited to the clergy. The nationwide participation of all adult Christians in almsgiving, fasting, and the sacraments in England in 1009 has already been noted. The *Fragmentary Annals* credit a similar, joint clerical and lay ritual response in Gaelic Scotland with earlier victories over Norse armies in 904 and 918, during the reign of Constantine II of Scotland.

> The men of Alba, lay and clergy alike, fasted and prayed to God and Columba until morning, and beseeched the Lord, and gave profuse alms of food and clothing to the churches and to the poor, and received the Body of the Lord from the hands of their priests, and promised to do every good thing as their clergy would best urge them, and that their battle-standard in the van of every battle would be the Crozier of Columba (*Bachall Cholaim Cille*).[48]

Another extended account of martial psalmody by laymen can be found in the retrospective royal saga *Cogad Gáedel re Gallaib* (*The War of the Irish with the Foreigners*).[49] Written in the early twelfth century on behalf of the ruling Uí Briain dynasty of Munster, the saga depicts the wars of their dynastic founder Brian Bóruma, king of Munster and high king of Ireland, against the Norse and the Kingdom of Leinster in Ireland. It culminates in the Battle of Clontarf in 1014, presented as a holy war between the Christian Irish and the pagan Norse. In this engagement, Brian was killed, but his army was victorious. In its account of Clontarf, the saga claims that Brian did not join the heat of the battle, but that he instead stayed on the side-lines, in prayer and fasting; praying the entire psalter, in three blocks of fifty, with a collect and *paternoster* to accompany each psalm. This description is analogous with the psalm performances mandated by Charlemagne and Aethelred II. In this ritual performance, Brian is said to have been alone, except for a single attendant to keep watch over the battle and to give him a report in between each block of

---

48 *Fragmentary Annals*, 168–71. See also the comments by Thomas Owen Clancy, "Columba, Adomnán and the Cult of Saints in Scotland," in *"Spes Scotorum," "Hope of Scots": Saint Columba, Iona and Scotland*, ed. Dauvit Broun and Thomas Owen Clancy (Edinburgh: T&T Clark, 1999), 3–33 at 26–27. For this narrative, see also comments by Robert Bubczyk and Radosław Kotecki in their respective chapters included to this collection (vol. 1, chap. 5 and vol. 2, chap. 3).

49 *"Cogadh Gaedhel re Gallaibh": "The War of the Gaedhil with the Gaill," or, the Invasions of Ireland by the Danes and Other Norsemen*, ed. James Henthorn Todd, Rolls series 48 (London: Longmans, Green, Reader, and Dyer, 1867).

fifty psalms.[50] Given the propagandistic nature of the text, this should not be taken as a reliable historical record of the period it describes. A key subtext is its claim that Brian was something resembling a royal saint and martyr for his ultimate propitiatory sacrifice at Clontarf, approaching the sacrifice of Christ for his people.[51] On the other hand, as a reflection of wider cultural attitudes and religious frames of reference, the episode shows again that recitation of psalms by the laity—or at least, anointed royalty—could be understood as providing effective, even decisive, support on the battlefield.

Cogad Gáedel evokes the entire psalter, but some psalms were undoubtedly better suited to military settings than others. Some indications of which psalms might have been regarded as suitable can be inferred from incidental references in hagiography. The earliest appearances of psalms in a martial setting can be found in the seventh-century hagiography of St. Patrick. Once again, this is revelatory not of the historical "reality" of the fifth-century missionary that these texts purport to describe, but rather of the cultural attitudes of the later authors who wrote them. In Muirchú moccu Machthéni's seventh-century *Vita S. Patricii*, the saint is depicted invoking Psalm 67, *Exsurgat Deus*, when facing the army of the pagan king Lóegaire mac Néill set against him. It reads:

> Then seeing impious gentile men about to rush against him, the holy Patrick rose and with a clear voice said: "Exsurgat Deus et dissipentur inimici eius et fugiant qui oderunt eum a facie eius" [Psalm 67:2: "Let God arise, and let his enemies be dissipated, and let those who have hated him flee from his face"]. And immediately, shadows and a certain horrible commotion rushed on; and the impious men fought amongst themselves, one rising up against another; and a great earthquake was made and made the axles of their chariots collide in the same place; and it drove them with force; and the chariots and horses hurled themselves headlong through the flatness of the plain, until at the end, few of them escaped half alive to the Mount of Mondorn. And there were laid flat by this plague before the king (because of his own words at Patrick's cursing) seven-times-seven men, until [Patrick] himself had remained with

---

50   Ibid., clxxxvi–clxxxvii, 196–200.
51   Jesse Patrick Harrington, "A Land Without Martyrs? St. Odrán, Gerald of Wales, and Christian Martyrdom in Medieval Ireland," *History Ireland* 28.3 (May/June 2020): 14–17 at 15.

only four men—[the king] himself and his wife, and two others among the *Scoti* [Irish]—and they feared greatly.[52]

Psalm 67 was considered a powerful psalm in the Insular world. Psalm 67:2 is close to that spoken by Moses in Numbers 10:35, before the elevation of the Ark of the Covenant; the psalmist imagines himself as Moses celebrating God's presence among the Israelites. Both are close to a probable cross inscription found in the Staffordshire Hoard, a hoard of martial items buried in England in the seventh century, and Psalm 67:2 is also invoked prophetically by the St. Guthlac in the *Vita S. Guthlaci*, written in England in ca. 730–740.[53] In the Patrician *vita*, the earthquake and heavens darkening give narrative expression to the motifs and images of Psalm 67:9, suggesting that the audience was meant to understand the entirety of the psalm as having been invoked, and not just the head of the psalm. Setting aside the miraculous outcome of the narrative, the text's author and audience seem to have found it natural that the cleric should recite the psalms to invoke God's aid in the impending battle.

Such imaginative literary accounts of psalms invoked in self-defense are expanded in *Bethu Phátraic* (the so-called *Vita Tripartita Sancti Patricii* or *Tripartite Life of St. Patrick*), the vernacular apogee of Patrician hagiography. This text appears to have achieved a stable narrative core by the tenth century, with subsequent homiletic revision into the twelfth century.[54] In it, Patrick separately invokes three psalms directly to enact, in each case, a miraculous self-defense and vindication: Psalms 19, 67, and 73. Psalm 19:8 is described as *fers fáithech*, "a prophetic verse," invoked to contrast Lóegaire's trust in chariots and horses with Patrick's trust in God: "hii in curribus et hii in equis, nos autem in nomine Domini Dei nostri magni" ("Some [trust] in chariots, and some in

---

52   Muirchú Moccu Machténi, *"Vita Sancti Patricii": Life of Saint Patrick*, ed. and trans. David Howlett (Dublin and Portland OR: Four Courts Press, 2006), 78–79.
53   Chris Fern, Tania Dickinson, and Leslie Webster, ed., *The Staffordshire Hoard: An Anglo-Saxon Treasure* (London: Society of Antiquaries of London, 2019), 102–8, 293–99. See also Sarah Foot, "Bede's Kings," in *Writing, Kingship and Power in Anglo-Saxon England*, ed. Rory Naismith and David A. Woodman (Cambridge: Cambridge University Press, 2017), 25–51 at 30.
54   *The Tripartite Life of Patrick: With Other Documents Relating to that Saint*, ed. Whitley Stokes, 2 vols., Rolls series 89 (London: Eyre and Spottiswoode, 1887); *"Bethu Phátraic": The Tripartite Life of Patrick*, ed. Kathleen Mulchrone (Dublin: Hodges Figgis & Co.; London: Williams and Norgate, 1939). For the date of the text, see Kenneth Hurlstone Jackson, "The Date of the Tripartite Life of St. Patrick," *Zeitschrift für celtische Philologie* 41 (1986): 5–45 at 5–12, 15–16; Francis J. Byrne and Pádraig Francis, "Two Lives of Saint Patrick: 'Vita Secunda' and 'Vita Quarta,'" *JRSAI* 124 (1994): 5–117 at 6–7, 14–5; Charles-Edwards, *Early Christian Ireland*, 11–13.

horses, but we in the name of the Lord our mighty God"). This is followed later in the narrative by the invocation of Psalm 67, which as before, enacts a violent earthquake that scatters the chariots and horses of the saint's opponents. Psalm 19:19 is similarly described as a prophetic verse—"ne tradas, Domine, bestiis animas confitentes tibi" ("Deliver not up to beasts, o Lord, the souls that confess thee")—protecting the saint from dogs set on him by his opponents.[55]

In these accounts, the saint stands apart from any explicit armed support, and his miraculous defense or vindication is worked without any intermediate agent. This is not surprising when one considers that the subject of hagiography was the figure of the saint as an autonomous power, set in direct relationship with the clerical and secular rulers whom the saint encountered. It was in the hagiographer's interest to emphasize the saint's miracles, which might come at the expense of references to the mutual support of clerics and their armies. Nonetheless, one can attempt to read between the lines to suggest that just such a mutual relationship might otherwise be presupposed. For example, the invocation of Psalm 67 might be seen elsewhere as implicit in the miraculous confusion and scattering of those that stand against the saint: as in the defeat and madness of Diarmait mac Cerbaill in *Aided Diarmata*, or in the scattering of the armies of Áed mac Ainmuirech and of Conall Derg in the twelfth-century *vitae* of the early monastic saints Máedóc of Ferns and Laisrén of Daiminis.[56] In other words, a specific martial ritual practice might perhaps be inferred as an assumed part of the background culture of the hagiographer and his audience, which makes sense of the miraculous outcomes of these narratives. It should also be noted that this exchange could be bidirectional. Hagiography described a cultural world intelligible to its author and audience, but it also could be written to provide precedent for contemporary religious practice.

For indirect evidence of the martial use of the psalms by lay warriors in the Christian Gaelic world, one can also refer to the vernacular heroic literature of medieval Ireland that is not ostensibly set in the Christian era. *Táin Bó Cuailnge (The Cattle-raid of Cooley)* is the central saga of the Ulster Cycle of Irish vernacular heroic literature and perhaps the best-known literary text of medieval Ireland, which developed in multiple recensions over several centuries. Its setting is the pre-Christian Irish "heroic age" of the first century,

---

55 *Tripartite Life*, 1.36, pp. 44–46; "*Bethu Phátraic*," 24, 28–30.
56 *Vitae sanctorum Hiberniae partim hactenvs: ineditae ad fidem codicvm manvscriptorvm recognovit prolegomenis notis indicibvs instrvxit*, ed. Charles Plummer, 2 vols. (Oxford: Clarendon Press, 1910), 2:134–5, 149, 301; "An Edition of 'Aided Diarmata meic Cerbaill,'" 129–38, 156–64.

concerning a legendary invasion of the Kingdom of Ulaid by the neighboring Connachta, supported by exiled warriors of the Ulaid. Nonetheless, the saga contains anachronisms, particularly in warfare, which are among the features which date its composition to the Christian period.[57] Its earliest manuscripts are of the twelfth century. The first recension is typically dated to the ninth century, the second to the twelfth.[58] In the final battle of the saga narrative, the pagan warriors of the legendary king of Ulaid, Conchobar mac Nessa, make a striking pre-battle boast in reply to his instruction to stand their ground. "'We shall hold the spot where we now stand,' said the warriors, 'but unless the ground quakes beneath us or the heavens fall down on us, we shall not flee from here.'"[59]

The boast is the third variation of a phrase that appears three times in *Táin Bó Cuailnge*. It appears first in the rhetorical question of Súaltaim, father of the warrior Cú Chulainn, in response to the invasion of the Connachta ("Is it the sky that cracks, or the sea that overflows its boundaries, or the earth that splits, or is it the loud cry of my son fighting against odds?"),[60] and second, in the oath Conchobar made when mustering the warriors of Ulaid, in response to Súaltaim's warning of the invasion ("By the sea before them, the sky above them, the earth beneath them, I shall restore every cow to its byre and every woman and boy to their own homes after victory in battle").[61] Kenneth Jackson took the boast as a sign of the warriors' courage, conceived in terms of a proverbial expression which he held to be common across Celtic culture.[62] His conjecture drew on classical ethnographic sources which would have been

---

57 James P. Mallory, "The World of Cú Chulainn: The Archaeology of 'Táin Bó Cúailnge,'" in *Aspects of the Táin*, ed. James P. Mallory (Belfast: December Publications, 1992), 103–59 at 111–13, 131–41, 151–53.

58 For the first and second recensions, see *"Táin Bó Cúalnge" from the Book of Leinster*, ed. Cecile O'Rahilly, Irish Texts Society 49 (Dublin: Dublin Institute for Advanced Studies, 1967); *"Táin Bó Cúailnge": Recension 1*, ed. Cecile O'Rahilly (Dublin: Dublin Institute for Advanced Studies, 1976). For its development, see Ruairí Ó hUiginn, "The Background and Development of 'Táin Bó Cúailnge,'" in *Aspects of the Táin*, 29–67.

59 *"Táin Bó Cúailnge": Recension 1*, 121, 234 (ll. 4043–44): "'Gébma-ne íarom i mbale i tám', ar na hóca, 'acht mani maidi in talam found nó an nem anúas foraind, nícon memsam-ne de sund.'"

60 Ibid., 103, 216 (ll. 3415–16): "In nem maides fa muir thar chrícha fa thalam conscara fa gáir mo maic se ... re n-éccomlonn?"

61 Ibid., 104, 217 (ll. 3448–50): "Muir ara cendaib, in nem húasa mbennaib, talum foa cosaib, dobér-sa cech mboin ina hindis díb 7 cach mben 7 cech mac dia tig iar mbúaid chatha."

62 Kenneth Hurlstone Jackson, *The Oldest Irish Tradition: A Window on the Iron Age* (Cambridge: Cambridge University Press, 1964), 13, 31–32.

unknown in medieval Ireland.[63] More recent scholarship has challenged the notion that the saga represents "a window on the Iron Age," as Jackson saw it.[64] Thus, the boast need not stem from a pre-Christian root. One can imagine it as a recognizably heroic claim in any cultural setting: the kind of expansive martial cry that could be given in any battle oration or its response.

Subsequent scholars, notably William Sayers, Liam Mac Mathúna, and John Shaw, focused on the literary aspects of the motif. They elaborated the theory that the boast reflected an inherited "threefold division of the cosmos" and represented the dissolution of the cosmic order.[65] There may be, however, an alternative, Christian narrative interpretation of the warriors' boast, specifically suited to its martial setting. An author, reader, or copyist reared on the memorization and daily recitation of the biblical psalms could scarcely have missed the immediate resonance of Psalm 45: "Deus noster refugium et virtus adiutor in tribulationibus quae invenerunt nos nimis, propterea non timebimus dum turbabitur terra et transferentur montes in cor maris" ("Our God is our refuge and strength: a helper in troubles, which have found us exceedingly. Therefore, we will not fear, when the earth shall be troubled; and the mountains shall be removed into the heart of the sea"[66]). The phrase fits well with the narrative economy of the saga. In the Milan Commentary on the psalter, which may be taken as evidence for Irish exegesis as expounded at Bangor or at related schools from about the eighth century onwards, the psalm was situated in the historical context of the reign of King Ahaz of Judah, in the aftermath of the siege of Jerusalem by the Aramites in alliance with the Ten

---

63 James J. Tierney, "The Celtic Ethnography of Posidonius," *Proceedings of the Royal Irish Academy. Section C: Archaeology, Celtic Studies, History, Linguistics, Literature* 60 (1959–1960): 189–275, at 194–95; David Rankin, *Celts and the Classical World* (London and New York: Routledge, 1987, rprt. 1996), 59.

64 Mallory, "The World," 108, 151–53.

65 William Sayers, "'Mani Maidi an Nem …': Ringing Changes on a Cosmic Motif," *Ériu* 37 (1986): 99–117; Liam Mac Mathúna, "The Christianization of the Early Irish Cosmos? 'Muir mas, nem nglas, talam cé' (Blathm. 258)," *Zeitschrift für celtische Philologie* 49–50 (1997): 532–47; idem, "Irish Perceptions of the Cosmos," *Celtica* 23 (1999): 174–87; idem, "The Irish Cosmos Revisited: Further Lexical Perspectives," in *Celtic Cosmology: Perspectives from Ireland and Scotland*, ed. Jacqueline Borsje et al., Papers in medieval studies 26 (Toronto: Pontifical Institute of Mediaeval Studies, 2014), 10–33 at 12–15; John Shaw, "A Gaelic Eschatological Folktale, Celtic Cosmology and Dumézil's 'Three Realms,'" in ibid., 34–52 at 42–45. These scholars have maintained that the motif was pre-Christian in origin but had been given a suitably Christianized literary repackaging, surviving ultimately as an eschatological folktale.

66 The quotation is from the *Gallicanum* psalter. The *Gallicanum* was the psalter text that was prevalent in Ireland, according to McNamara, *Psalms*, 33.

Tribes of Israel.[67] The psalm was accordingly interpreted in both the Latin commentary and the vernacular glosses as a psalm of thanksgiving for deliverance from hostile alienated kindred.[68] An evocation of the psalm would thus have been fitting in *Táin Bó Cuailnge*, in which the beleaguered Ulaid face invasion from their own exiled kinsmen in alliance with a foreign kingdom. It is perhaps notable that in the warning that elicits Conchobar's speech before the mustering of the Ulaid (in the first recension of *Táin Bó Cuailnge*), Súaltaim refers explicitly to the Connachta being led with the guidance of the Ulaid exile Fergus mac Róig.[69]

Beyond the meta-narrative, there is the additional possibility that the warrior's boast was a vernacular stock phrase that a warrior might plausibly have invoked before facing combat. Psalm 45 had a long history as a martial hymn: it is little coincidence that in sixteenth-century Germany, the vernacular form of Psalm 45 became a popular battle hymn, as Martin Luther's "Ein feste Burg ist unser Gott."[70] The respectively historical and literary interpretations of the boast in *Táin Bó Cuailnge* need not be mutually exclusive. A warrior might evoke a psalm before going into battle, but the choice of psalm by the author could speak directly to narrative context. This is a question of verisimilitude, and it speaks more to the Christian context in which *Táin Bó Cuailnge* was composed than it does the distant past or the context it purports to represent. The foregoing consideration of the importance of the psalms in a martial context suggests that the warriors' attributed evocation of Psalm 45 in the first recension of *Táin Bó Cuailnge* may have not only existed in the literary allusions of a clerical scribe; instead, it may have drawn on a common stock of imagery available to warrior and churchman alike at the time when the epic was set down in writing.

2   Saints, Relics, and Standards

In addition to the use of psalms, victory was also sought through the departed saints, their relics, and their banners, as was common elsewhere in

---

67   *"Thesaurus Palaeohibernicus": A Collection of Old-Irish Glosses, Scholia, Prose, and Verse*, ed. Whitley Stokes and John Strachan, 3 vols. (Cambridge: Cambridge University Press, 1901–1903), 1:224–27. See also McNamara, *Psalms*, 43–49.
68   *"Thesaurus Palaeohibernicus,"* 1:224.
69   *"Táin Bó Cúailnge": Recension 1*, 104, 217 (ll. 3431–36).
70   John Julian, *A Dictionary of Hymnology: Setting Forth the Origin and History of Christian Hymns of All Ages and Nations*, 2nd rev. ed., 2 vols. (New York: Dover, 1907; rprt. 1957), 1:322–25.

Christendom.[71] The deployment of holy objects in war had its universal Christian theological paradigm in the biblical Ark of the Covenant: which contained golden jars holding manna, the tablets of the covenant, and the Staff of Aaron, and was carried by the priestly Levites into battle.[72] The Gaelic world had a particularly rich cast of saints upon whom to call. In Ireland alone, the feast of a native saint was celebrated on all but twenty-one days of the year.[73] The extant hagiographical record from before the sixteenth century includes a hundred or so Latin *vitae* of about sixty Irish saints, and about fifty vernacular *bethada* (lives) of forty Irish saints.[74] Most of these Irish saints were reputed to have lived before about 700, and all before 1200. The role of saints in war has been better served by scholarship than other religious rituals of war in the Gaelic world. Their relics, which might include their portably enshrined remains, personal effects, or authority symbols (such as crosses, croziers, handbells, or psalters), were sometimes referred to as *meirge* or *vexilla* ("standards").[75] In addition to the provision of miraculous assistance that was expected of them, they gave a clear focus of morale on the battlefield. As Anthony T. Lucas has observed in his survey of the use of relics as "battle talismans" in the Irish historical record, the custom of carrying relics into battle appears to have been standard practice. He argued that the preliminary ritual, attested in some sources but probably observed in all cases, "involved carrying the relic three times round the combatants in the auspicious sunwise [i.e., clockwise] direction." The relics themselves were entrusted to representatives of the family which acted as their hereditary custodians. The sources usually refer to these custodians as "clerics," which Lucas suggested was a deliberate choice to enhance the relics' safety on the battlefield by entrusting them to those designated as non-combatants.[76]

By far the best known of these relic-standards is *An Cathach*, "The Battler" of Columba (fig. 3.1). After Patrick and Brigit, Columba was ranked the third of the great saints of Ireland. He was especially regarded as a patron of the Northern Uí Néill and of the influential Columban federation of monastic

---

71 See, e.g., Carl Erdmann, *The Origin of the Idea of Crusade*, trans. Marshall W. Baldwin and Walter Goffart (Princeton NJ: Princeton University Press, 1977), 35–56; Robert Bartlett, *Why Can the Dead Do Such Great Things? Saints and Worshippers from the Martyrs to the Reformation* (Princeton NJ: Princeton University Press, 2013), 321–24, 378–83.
72 Joshua 6:4–6:15; Hebrews 9:4. See also the discussion in the final chapter to this collection by Radosław Kotecki (vol. 2, chap. 8).
73 Pádraig Ó Riain, *A Dictionary of Irish Saints* (Dublin: Four Courts Press, 2011), 652–60.
74 Richard Sharpe, *Medieval Irish Saints' Lives: An Introduction to "Vitae Sanctorum Hiberniae"* (Oxford: Clarendon Press, 1991), 5–7.
75 Anthony T. Lucas, "The Social Role of Relics and Reliquaries in Ancient Ireland," *JRSAI* 116 (1986): 5–37 at 17.
76 Ibid., 20. The full survey covers pp. 17–20.

houses throughout Ireland and Scotland, and as the "apostle" and patron saint of the Scots and their kings. Columba's special association with war in both the historical and literary traditions of the Gaelic world has already been alluded to. Thomas Owen Clancy has suggested that the saint's persistent association in historical tradition with the Battle of Cúil Dreimne, combined with Adomnán's claims of him gaining victories for the kings Áedán and Oswald, may stand at the roots of his "reputation as an effective saint of war."[77] His "battler," which is still extant, was a celebrated psalter attributed to his own hand. It may date to the sixth or seventh century, and it was enshrined by the eleventh.[78] The sixteenth-century *Betha Colaim Chille* recorded the use of the psalter as a relic carried three-times sunwise around an army to ensure victory. By this time, the psalter was held by the Uí Domnaill (O'Donnells), kings of the Northern Uí Néill lineage of Cenél Conaill.[79] The annals mention *An Cathach* under 1497, when its hereditary keeper brought it on an expedition by Conn Ua Domnaill against Mac Diarmata of Magh Luirg. Conn was defeated, the relic captured, and its keeper slain. When the two sides made peace in 1499, the relic was restored to the Uí Domnaill.[80]

The dates at which *An Cathach* acquired its name or saw its first use in battle are unknown. Martin McNamara has suggested that the belief in the miraculous power of books written in the saint's hand, mentioned several times in Adomnán's *Vita S. Columbae*, may explain the psalter's use in battle, which might suggest its use at a comparatively early date.[81] In addition, the psalms' existing martial association and battlefield use may have made the physical psalter appropriate as a "textual shield."[82] The idea of the physical object of a sacred text serving such use had its biblical precedent, of course, in the tablets of the law contained in the Ark of the Covenant. The psalter represented another such biblical promise. Such "textual shields" did not have to be limited to the psalter, however. Another book with a Columban connection, the *Soiscéla Martain* (*The Gospel of Martin*), seems to have been paraded as a relic in war in the second half of the twelfth century.[83] This book had a double

77 Clancy, "Cult of Saints," 26.
78 Lucas, "Social Role," 9, 17.
79 "*Betha Colaim Chille*," 182–85; McNamara, *Psalms*, 29–30.
80 "Annala Uladh," 3:420–21, 444–45 (s.a. 1497.20, 1499.19); "Annála Ríoghachta Éireann," 4:1232–33, 1252–53 (s.a. 1497.7, 1499.15).
81 McNamara, *Psalms*, 29–30.
82 Faith Pennick Morgan, *Dress and Personal Appearance in Late Antiquity: The Clothing of the Middle and Lower Classes*, Late Antique archaeology supplementary series 1 (Leiden and Boston MA: Brill, 2018), 63.
83 Lucas, "Social Role," 18–19; John Bannerman, "'Comarba Coluim Chille' and the Relics of Columba," *IR* 44.1 (1993): 14–47 at 41, 44–45.

FIGURE 3.1 The portable reliquary shrine of *An Cathach* ("The Battler"), an early medieval psalter and one of many relics traditionally associated with the sixth-century abbot and "warrior saint" Columba. This psalter is by far the most celebrated of the relic-standards known to have been used in war in the Gaelic world. National Museum of Ireland
LICENSE: CC BY-SA 2.0. REPRODUCED FROM: BIT.LY/3PADJIP

association. As a sacred text, it was most probably a copy of one of the Gospels, as its name suggests, containing the promise of Christ, to whom all other biblical promises pointed as their final end As a holy object, it was maintained that the book had been brought by Columba from the tomb of St. Martin at Tours to the Columban monastery of Derry, where it served as the chief relic and insignia for Columba's abbatial successors.[84] As well as being a model monk,

---

84 Máire Herbert, *Iona, Kells, and Derry: The History and Hagiography of the Monastic "familia" of Columba* (Oxford: Clarendon Press, 1988), 188–93, 231, 256; Bannerman, "'Comarba,'" 40–41, 44–45. Bannerman, "'Comarba,'" 44, has conjectured that *Soiscéla Martain* may have been a copy of Sulpicius Severus' *Life, Epistles, and Dialogues* on St. Martin, which would interestingly extend the use of sacred texts as martial covenants in Ireland beyond the biblical canon. Nonetheless, the relic's name and the story of its recovery from Martin's tomb make it natural to regard it as "Martin's Gospel." Other Gospel books were known to have been placed in the tombs of churchmen and later recovered, the most famous example being the seventh-century St. Cuthbert Gospel, recovered at Durham in

Martin was a paradigmatic soldier saint, whose patronage was sought for providing miraculous aid in war, and whose cape the Frankish kings carried into battle to assure victory.[85] The *Soiscéla Martain* was thus arguably symbolic of two implied battlefield covenants mediated through the saints: God's covenant with the people of Martin and his covenant with the people of Columba. That *An Cathach* and the *Soiscéla Martain* should be used to represent and re-enact on the battlefield the covenants of the psalms and the saints should thus come as no surprise.

Columba's relics were neither limited to books nor to Ireland. In Scotland, his crozier acquired the name *Cathbuaid* ("Battle Victory"), because the Scots often attained victory after parading it as a standard before their armies, as against the Norse in 904 and 918. The staff is now lost, but it may have been superseded as a battle standard by a reliquary of Columba, the *Brecbennach* (fig. 3.2).[86] This reliquary first appears in 1211, when it passed to the Abbey of Arbroath along with land to support it, and those monks had a duty of bringing it with the Scottish royal army on campaign.[87] The vernacular literary tradition reports further martial relics of Columba and elaborates on the expectations of their potential users. An episode in the twelfth-century *Book of Leinster* attributes to him the promise that a Northern Uí Néill king, Áed mac Ainmuirech, would not die in battle for as long as he wore the saint's cowl.[88] On one level, the episode may attest the special protections afforded to those of visibly clerical status on the battlefield, or stand as an anagogical motif for the salvific importance of adopting and maintaining clerical life. However, it also invokes the miraculous power of the saint for those clothed—literally—with his protective graces. In this respect, it is perhaps similar with the use of St. Martin's

---

1104. Another seems to have been exhumed from the tomb of the sixth-century St. Lubin at Chartres by the tenth century, see Yves Delaporte, *Le Voile de Notre Dame* (Chartres: Maison des Clercs, 1927), 16n1, 28, 32. I am grateful to Dr. Vedran Sulovsky for bringing the last example to my attention.

85   See McCormick, *Eternal Victory*, 357; Klaus Schreiner, *Märtyrer, Schlachtenhelfer, Friedenstifter. Krieg und Frieden im Spiegel mittelalterlicher und frühneuzeitlicher Heiligenverehrung*, OFVK 18 (Opladen: Springer, 2000), 63–70; Bachrach, *Religion*, 39; Daniel Rupp, "Der heilige Martin als Schlachtenhelfer im Mittelalter," in *Martin von Tours. Krieger—Bischof—Heiliger* (Saarbrücken: Universitätsverlag des Saarlandes, 2013), 27–42; Bartlett, *Why Can the Dead*, 321. Compare also James Lloyd, "The Priests of the King's Reliquary in Anglo-Saxon England," *JEH* 67.2 (2016): 265–87 at 272.

86   *Fragmentary Annals*, 168–71; Bannerman, "'Comarba,'" 29; Clancy, "Cult of Saints," 26–27.

87   David H. Caldwell, "The Monymusk Reliquary: The 'Breccbennach' of St Columba?" *Proceedings of the Society of Antiquaries of Scotland* 131 (2001): 267–82 at 270–6; Bartlett, *Why Can the Dead*, 231–32.

88   *Lives of Saints from the Book of Lismore*, 306.

FIGURE 3.2 The Monymusk Reliquary, an eighth-century reliquary made of wood covered in bronze and silver plates with enameled bronze mounts, possibly similar to other reliquaries carried on campaigns in the medieval Gaelic world. This reliquary was formerly identified with the *Brecbennach*, though there is little to substantiate the conjecture. National Museum of Scotland
LICENSE: CC BY-SA 4.0. REPRODUCED FROM: W.WIKI/5AWY

cape in battle.[89] In the twelfth-century vernacular *Betha Choluim Chille* (*The Life of Columba*), the Irish saint's blessed cowl is given with the same promise to Áed Sláne, son of Diarmait mac Cerbaill, with a conditional prophecy that

---

89   Compare n. 85, above.

he should die of old age unless he should commit parricide. The *betha* observes that Áed Sláne eventually killed his father, before proceeding on a raid without the cowl. The two errors seal his death that day.[90] In this way, the saint's word and deed reach their common, fated conclusion, with the cowl acting as a kind of sacramental, mediating and fulfilling the saint's prophecy.

Other aspects of Columba's relics have ritual parallels elsewhere in Ireland. There were other medieval Irish relics called *cathaig* ("battlers"), such as the *Cathach* of St. Iarlaithe, which appears in the annals in the 1130s.[91] They need not all have been books as in the case of Columba's *Cathach*. The *Cathach* of St. Caillín is described as "a hazel cross to be cut, and its top through its middle."[92] The sunwise turn of Columba's *Cathach* may be analogous with the traditional Irish practice of cursing stones, the sites and practice of which survived down to the nineteenth century in many parts of Ireland. These always had "an early ecclesiastical association, typically invoking the power of an early Christian saint," and "always involved ritual turning," often preceded by ritual fasting and accompanied by prayer.[93] They were often associated with hereditary keepers in much the same manner as other relics.[94] In the twelfth-century *Vita S. Declani*, Declán of Ardmore blesses a stone on behalf of Dercán, a wealthy pagan of Déisi Muman, with the prophetic instruction that if the armies of his people solemnly march around it, victory will be guaranteed to them.[95] *Aided Diarmata* has Columba observe Diarmait's army march around a cairn before Cúil Dreimne, perhaps another reference to the practice.[96] There is arguably also a literary reflex of the turning practice in the first recension of *Táin Bó Cuailnge*, in the right turn of a chariot before an army to produce a good omen.[97] In the binary engagement of the battlefield, it should come as no surprise that the practices for cursing and for securing good martial omen are so close. These medieval accounts may well reflect martial practices current at the time of their writing, onto which the authors of those texts were

---

90   *Lives of Saints from the Book of Lismore*, 28, 176; Herbert, *Iona*, 233, 258.
91   "Chronicum Scotorum": *A Chronicle of Irish Affairs, From the Earliest Times to A.D. 1135*, ed. William M. Hennessy, Rolls series 46 (London: Longmans, Green, Reader, and Dyer, 1866), 284–87 (s.a. 1134, 1135); *Annals of Tigernach*, 2:151–52 (s.a. 1134.8); Lucas, "Social Role," 18.
92   Lucas, "Social Role," 19.
93   Christiaan Corlett, "Cursing Stones in Ireland," *Journal of the Galway Archaeological and Historical Society*, 64 (2012): 1–20.
94   Ibid., 17–18.
95   *Vitae sanctorum Hiberniae*, 2:51; Liam de Paor, *Saint Patrick's World: The Christian Culture of Ireland's Apostolic Age* (Dublin: Four Courts Press, 1993), 262–63. See also Lucas, "Social Role," 20; Corlett, "Cursing Stones," 15–16.
96   "An Edition of 'Aided Diarmata meic Cerbaill,'" 130, 157.
97   "*Táin Bó Cúailnge": Recension 1*, 1:126, ll. 25–28.

concerned to project a venerable antiquity. Nonetheless, such ritual practices should not be understood as pagan holdovers or superstitions. They were an integral part of the fabric of medieval Christianity, and should be considered in the same way as other relics.[98] As Clancy has reminded in his discussion of the performance of 918: "[w]e should picture ... not simply a superstitious reliance on a [relic] to win a battle, but a contract much like that involved in the relic circuits ... where during plagues and famine, the relics of saints toured, not just enforcing law but also reinforcing a sense of order and security."[99] A special ceremony embodying the idea of an ordered community was a procession that followed splendid reliquary cross, like twelfth-century Cross of Cong (figs. 3.3–4). Processional crosses were among the most versatile and obvious holy objects to have been used as battle standards in the medieval world.[100]

The annals record other relics being used as battle standards. One was the *Bacall Ísu* ("The Staff of Jesus"), the most prestigious relic in Ireland, referred to in the annals repeatedly until its destruction at the Reformation in 1538.[101] This staff was traditionally believed to have belonged to Jesus during his earthly ministry, to have been left with a pair of beatifically unageing custodians until the time of St. Patrick, and to have been received by the saint from God himself atop Mount Hermon, alongside other divine promises to Patrick concerning his mission to the Gaels.[102] As Lucas has noted, the importance of "the saint's staff or *bachall* was ... because it was thought of as the principal vehicle of his power, a kind of spiritual electrode through which he conveyed the holy energy by which he wrought the innumerable miracles attributed to him."[103] The use of holy staffs in battle, moreover, had clear biblical associations. Moses had raised his staff to assure the Israelite victory at Rephidim in Exodus 17:9, while the Ark of the Covenant had contained the Staff of Aaron. The corresponding value of a saint's staff in martial affairs was seized upon early in medieval Ireland. In *Bethu Phátraic*, Patrick is said to have extended his military protection to the royal Uí Néill dynasty while giving Conall, legendary

---

98   Corlett, "Cursing Stones," 17–18.
99   Clancy, "Cult of Saints in Scotland," 27.
100 See, e.g., John A. Cotsonis, *Byzantine Figural Processional Crosses*, Dumbarton Oaks Byzantine Collection publications 10 (Washington DC: Dumbarton Oaks, 1994), 11–12; Mamuka Tsurtsumia, "The True Cross in the Armies of Georgia and the Frankish East," *Crusades* 12.1 (2013): 91–102; Holger A. Klein, "Objektkultur und Kultobjekte im kaiserlich-byzantinischen Prozessionswesen," in *"Palatium sacrum"—Sakralität am Hof des Mittelalters. Orte, Dinge, Rituale*, ed. Manfred Luchterhandt and Hedwig Röckelein (Regensburg: Schnell & Steiner, 2021), 77–100.
101 Lucas, "Social Role," 9.
102 *Tripartite Life*, 1:28–30; "*Bethu Phátraic*," 18–9.
103 Lucas, "Social Role," 8–9.

FIGURE 3.3 The Cross of Cong, an Irish ornamented processional cross crafted ca. 1123 for Tairdelbach Ua Conchobair, king of Connacht (r. 1106–1156), to contain a relic of the True Cross. Front view. National Museum of Ireland
LICENSE: CC BY-SA 2.0. REPRODUCED FROM: BIT.LY/3DGNFYT

FIGURE 3.4
The Cross of Cong close up. Back view. A piece of the wood inside is believed to be a relic of the True Cross. National Museum of Ireland
LICENSE: CC BY-SA 2.0.
REPRODUCED FROM: BIT.LY
/3C4UZDJ

ancestor of the eponymous Cenél Conaill branch of Uí Néill, the protection of his crozier on his shield.[104] The *Fragmentary Annals* record a raid of 868 by Niall, "king of Ireland," on Flann mac Conaing, king of Brega. Flann, gathering help, pursued Niall, whom he found waiting with "six standards (*meirge*), the cross of the Lord, and the Staff of Jesus." Lucas observes that "there is no doubt about the status of the Staff of Jesus as a relic and 'the cross of the Lord' may well have been a relic of the True Cross. A relic carried to battle is sometimes referred to as a 'standard' ... and since the six 'standards' are here associated with one, and, possibly, two relics, they may well have been relics too."[105] The *Cronicon Scotorum* records another *bachall*, the *Mada Ciaráin* (Staff of Ciarán), deployed by the Connachta in an engagement of 1087. It was borne by its keeper: "Cormac Ua Cillín, chief vice-abbot of Síl Muiredaigh, with the staff of Ciarán in his hand before the battle when it was being fought between the Connachta and the Conmaicne."[106] *Bachaill* were also used not just for war, but for swearing compacts and making peace. Thus, in 1113, the southern armies of Muirchertach Ua Briain faced the northern armies of Domnall Ua Lochlainn

---

104   *Tripartite Life*, 1:138; "*Bethu Phátraic*," 85.
105   Lucas, "Social Role," 17.
106   "*Chronicum Scotorum*," 252–53 (s.a. 1087); Lucas, "Social Role," 14.

for a month until Cellach, "successor of Patrick, and the Staff of Jesus also made peace of a year between them."[107]

Naturally, the role of saints in war is given even greater prominence in the hagiography than in the annalistic record. The lives of Patrick had the saint promise blessing and victory in future military endeavors. In *Bethu Phátraic*, the saint offered both protection to the Uí Néill lineages and opposition to their hereditary enemies, the Connachta, in war. He cursed the Grecraige, a branch of the Connachta, always to be routed after they opposed him.[108] He cursed the Callraigi of Cúle-Cernadán to always be routed, though not to lose more than five men in each rout, after they struck spears against their shields to intimidate Patrick but repented.[109] With Brigit, he blessed the descendants of Eógan mac Néill's line, Cenél nEógain of Northern Uí Néill, till Doomsday: "So long as field shall be under crops, victory in battle (*búaid catha*) on their men. The head of the men of Ireland's hosts to their place, they shall attack every hill."[110] Patrick's depicted association and friendship with Eógan was natural, as the king represented the dynasty associated most with the saint's traditional shrine at Armagh.[111]

Betha Finnchua claimed that the Munstermen refused to go into battle without the saints: "The Munstermen entrusted themselves to their saints, to win victory from the Uí Néill, since they had no champion of battle against them."[112] Scannal of the Eóganachta "would not go until the valiant warrior [Finnchú] who dwelt in Munster should come with him." The *betha* depicts the formula: one royal champion of the Eóganachta and seven of their saints. "Then the Munstermen with their saints rise up against them; and though the Uí Néill were more numerous, they were routed in the battle by the strengths of the saints and the champions."[113] Finally, the *betha* reports that Finnchú established a blessed covenant with Cashel's kings: that in return for alms and tribute to the saint and his successors, any battles fought by the Éoganachta would be delivered victory in the name of God and Finnchú, and that "if one of his relics go with them into the contest that they will have the victory."[114]

---

107 *Annals of Ulster*, 1:554–55 (s.a. 1113.7); *Annals of Loch Cé*, 102–3 (s.a. 1113.6); "*Annála Ríoghachta Éireann*," 2:994–97 (s.a. 1113.10); Lucas, "Social Role," 18.
108 *Tripartite Life*, 1:138; "*Bethu Phátraic*," 85.
109 *Tripartite Life*, 1:142; "*Bethu Phátraic*," 87.
110 *Tripartite Life*, 1:154; "*Bethu Phátraic*," 93.
111 Charles-Edwards, *Early Christian Ireland*, 51.
112 *Lives of Saints from the Book of Lismore*, 96, 243.
113 Ibid., 96–97, 244.
114 Ibid., 97, 245.

Holy objects also saw martial deployment in England, as throughout medieval Europe. It has been suggested that the inscription of Psalm 67 found in the Staffordshire Hoard might have been part of a cross or portable reliquary intended to be borne into battle in the seventh century.[115] The English deployed crosses and relics as part of the ritual response to the Norse raids of 1009, and the swearing of oaths on relics was used to enforce compliance with the ritual mandates.[116] At the Battle of Hastings in 1066, Duke William of Normandy wore around his neck the relics on which his adversary King Harold of England had sworn his oath to him, thus summoning the saints to vindicate him against the man whom he regarded as a perjurer.[117] Perhaps most famously, Archbishop Thurstan of York deployed the northern saints at the Battle of the Standard at Northallerton in 1138, in response to an invasion of the north of England by David I of Scotland.[118] Central to Thurstan's effort was the deployment of the standard from which the battle took its name. Analogous with the contemporary Italian *carroccio*, this was a war cart, mounted with a mast bearing the English royal standard and a pyx containing the eucharistic host, surrounded by the consecrated banners of the saints John of Beverley, Wilfrid of Ripon, and Peter of York. In many respects, the English rally was given the character of a defensive holy war.[119] Contemporary chroniclers commented that the deployment made Christ the northern English defenders' *dux belli*, with the additional promise that the angels, saints, and martyrs would fight with them. One, Aelred of Rievaulx, envisioned the Standard as a latter day Ark of the Covenant, with the eucharistic host as the new manna, manifesting God's presence and victory on behalf of his Christian people with whom he had made his Covenant.[120] Thurstan had intended for these holy objects to compensate

---

115   Alan Thacker, "The Church and Warfare: The Religious and Cultural Background to the Hoard," in *The Staffordshire Hoard: An Anglo-Saxon Treasure*, ed. Chris Fern, Tania Dickinson, and Leslie Webster (London: Society of Antiquaries of London, 2019), 293–99. See also Foot, "Bede's Kings," 30.

116   Keynes, "Viking Raids," 181, 186–88.

117   Bartlett, *Why Can the Dead*, 322.

118   For modern accounts of this campaign, see Paul Dalton, *Conquest, Anarchy, and Lordship: Yorkshire, 1066–1154*, CSML, 4th ser. 27 (Cambridge: Cambridge University Press, 1994), 148–52, 205–6; Jim Bradbury, *Stephen and Matilda: The Civil War of 1139–53* (Stroud: Sutton, 1996), 33–36; David Crouch, *The Reign of King Stephen, 1135–1154* (Harlow: Longman, 2000), 81–82; and Bachrach, *Religion*, 153–60.

119   Donald Nicholl, *Thurstan: Archbishop of York (1114–1140)* (York: Stonegate Press, 1964), 221–28; Bachrach, *Religion*, 94–95, 154–61; Xavier Storelli, "Les harangues de la bataille de l'Étendard (1138)," *Médiévales* 57 (2009): 15–32 at 21–22, 24, 30–31.

120   Jesse Patrick Harrington, "Harangue or Homily? Walter Espec and the Deuteronomic Covenant in Aelred of Rievaulx's 'Relatio de Standardo,'" *HSJ* 32 (2020): 163–83 at 180–83. For the importance of the Eucharist to soldiers, see also Bachrach, *Religion*, 113–18, 159–60.

for the absence of the English king, Stephen of Blois, then distracted by rebellion in the distant south, and to shore up the flagging morale of the fractious northern baronage.[121] In these respects, Thurstan's logic was the same as that stated in *Betha Finnchua*. In the absence of a battle champion, an army should entrust itself to God and the saints, whom the clergy—with their holy banners, relics, and sacramentals—could readily manifest on the battlefield.[122]

Later chroniclers and hagiographers projected the role of English saints in war into the early medieval past. The eleventh and twelfth centuries saw the development of the legend of St. Cuthbert's appearance to Alfred of Wessex in a dream before the Battle of Edington in 878, promising him victory over the Norse.[123] The saint's appearance in the dream, carrying a Gospel adorned with gold and gems, may suggest that such books were presented as potential battle talismans, similar to the *Soiscéla Martain*.[124] More concretely, the legend contributed to the Banner of St. Cuthbert, a holy banner which first appears at Durham from the 1160s. Over the course of the thirteenth to sixteenth centuries, this banner saw recurring deployment against the Scots and gained a reputation as "the most popular—and on the whole the most effective—battle ensign in England."[125] The twelfth century also saw the first instance of the legend of John of Beverley's appearance in a dream to Alfred's grandson, Æthelstan, with a promise of victory over the Northumbrians and Scots in 934, in return for which the king granted the saint's shrine at Beverley many gifts

---

121   Nicholl, *Thurstan*, 221–27; Bachrach, *Religion*, 154–55; Storelli, "Les harangues," 24, 26–30.
122   Compare with Daniel M.G. Gerrard, "Fighting Clergy, Church Councils and the Context of Law: The Cutting Edge of Orthodoxy or the Ambiguous Limits of Legitimacy?" in *Heresy and the Making of European Culture: Medieval and Modern Perspectives*, ed. Andrew P. Roach and James R. Simpson (Farnham and Burlington VT: Ashgate, 2013), 275–88 at 284–85; idem, *The Church at War: The Military Activities of Bishops, Abbots, and Other Clergy in England, c.900–1200* (Abingdon and New York: Routledge, 2016), 118–22; Kotecki, "Lions and Lambs," 320.
123   John R.E. Bliese, "Saint Cuthbert and War," *JMH* 24.3 (1998): 215–41 at 215–26.
124   *Symeonis monachi opera omnia*, ed. Thomas Arnold, 2 vols., Rolls series 75 (London: Longman, 1882–1885), 1:204–5, 231–32; Aelred of Rievaulx, *Relatio de Standardo*, in *Aelredi Rievallensis Opera omnia VI. Opera Historica et Hagiographica*, ed. Domenico Pezzini, CCCM 3 (Turnhout: Brepols, 2017), 3–56 at 28–29; with translation in Aelred of Rievaulx, *The Historical Works*, ed. Marsha L. Dutton, trans. Jane Patricia Freeland, Cistercian Fathers series 56 (Kalamazoo MI: Cistercian Publications, 2005), 80–81. The book in question would presumably not have been understood as the so-called "St. Cuthbert Gospel," whose recovery from the saint's coffin in 1104 appears to postdate the earliest version of the legend, and whose original leather binding does not match the treasure binding described. For the earliest of these texts and their dates, see Bliese, "Saint Cuthbert," 217–21.
125   R.B. Dobson, *Durham Priory 1400–1450*, CSML, 3rd ser. 6 (Cambridge: Cambridge University Press, 1973), 27; Bliese, "Saint Cuthbert," 235–40.

and liberties.[126] Aelred contributed significantly to both legends: the legend of John of Beverley, indeed, first appears in Aelred. He may have been influenced by the events of 1138 in claiming that the special reliance of the northern frontier on the protection of the saints long predated the Normans' arrival in England.[127] Nonetheless, these developments indicate the degree to which the English were increasingly conscious of the importance of holy banners, relics, and saints in war, as the age marched on.

This shared cultural world explains the prominence with which Ireland's traditional saints, relics, and "standards" were deployed in resistance to the Anglo-Norman invaders in the 1170s and thereafter, as well as the urgency with which the invaders sought to secure and appropriate those same saints and relics on their arrival. At some point before 1177, the Anglo-Normans captured and removed the *Bacall Ísa* from Armagh to Dublin.[128] In 1178, during John de Courcy's conquest of Ulster, the Anglo-Normans captured the *Bachall Fínghin* and *Bachall Rónáin Fhinn* from the Ulaid who fled the field. Later, in another battle, they captured the *Canóin Pátraic* and *Ceolán Tighearnaigh*. In 1182, the invaders defeated Domnall Ua Lochlainn in Dál Riata and captured the *Soiscéla Martain* from his army.[129] In ca. 1185, John de Courcy commissioned the English Cistercian hagiographer Jocelin of Furness to write a new *Vita S. Patricii*, to promote his conquest of Armagh and Down and the subsequent providential discovery and translation of the bodies of their patron saints, Patrick, Brigit, and Columba.[130] In this comprehensive *vita*, the traditional stories of Patrick's miraculous curses, protections in war, and even the special blessing of the shields which bore his crozier remained intact, implicitly reworked in the new conqueror's favor.[131] The power of Patrick—which, it was implied, could easily

---

126 Susan E. Wilson, "King Athelstan and John of Beverley," *Northern History* 40.1 (2003): 5–23; Tomasz Tarczyński, "The King and the Saint against the Scots: The Shaping of English National Identity in the 12th Century Narrative of King Athelstan's Victory over His Northern Neighbours," in *Imagined Communities: Constructing Collective Identities in Medieval Europe*, ed. Andrzej Pleszczyński et al., EMC 8 (Leiden and Boston MA: Brill, 2018), 85–102.

127 Wilson, "King Athelstan," 10, 20.

128 Helen Birkett, *The Saints' Lives of Jocelin of Furness: Hagiography, Patronage and Ecclesiastical Politics* (Woodbridge: York Medieval Press in association with The Boydell Press, 2010), 144–45.

129 Lucas, "Social Role," 18–9; Bannerman, "'Comarba,'" 44–45.

130 For discussion, see Birkett, *Saints' Lives*, 141–70.

131 For the shields, see *Vita auctore Iocelino monacho de Furnesio. Patricius episcopus, apostolus & primas Hiberniæ*, in *Acta Sanctorum* Martii 2, ed. Godfrey Henskens and Daniel Papebroch (Antwerp: Meursius, 1668), 0540B–0580D at 0565C. For translation, see *The Most Ancient Lives of Saint Patrick: Including the Life by Jocelin*, ed. James O'Leary (New York: Kennedy, 1883), 286–87.

have resisted de Courcy on the field of battle—instead legitimized the adventurer's conquest and blessed his future martial endeavors. The rupture of the conquest of 1169 and its aftermath represented less of a fundamental shift in religious culture than it did in the personnel of those who held political proprietorship. Moreover, as the cases of *An Cathach* and the *Brecbennach* show, the ritual use of relics in war persisted in the Gaelic world long after the conquest period.

3 Harangue and Homily

In addition to reciting psalms, clerics mobilizing or supporting an army might preach in the lead-up to the campaign or give pre-battle orations, as part of the liturgy and to encourage those going into battle. With the record of such orations, one is always in uncertain territory. As Derek Baker and John Bliese have argued, the pre-battle orations recorded in medieval chronicles are often the imagined rhetorical set-pieces of their individual chroniclers, whose historicity as events outside the imaginations of their chroniclers cannot be easily established. While they may convey genuine insights into the psychology of the protagonists of the battle, they reflect foremost the concerns of the chroniclers who report them and of the audiences to whom those chronicles are directed.[132]

Nonetheless, some recorded instances do seem to align with demonstrable historical practice. The most celebrated and well-attested instance is recorded on the edge of the Gaelic world, at the Battle of the Standard at Northallerton in August 1138. In Henry of Huntingdon's account, a pre-battle oration and absolution was delivered to the English army by Ralph Nowell, bishop of Orkney, deputizing for Archbishop Thurstan.[133] In Aelred of Rievaulx's account, Ralph also delivered an oration and absolution, but the main oration is attributed to Walter Espec, high sheriff of Yorkshire and founder of Rievaulx.[134] Both Henry

---

[132] Derek Baker, "Aelred of Rievaulx and Walter Espec," *HSJ* 1 (1989): 91–98 at 95–98; John R.E. Bliese, "Aelred of Rievaulx's Rhetoric and Morale at the Battle of the Standard, 1138," *Albion* 20.4 (1988): 543–56 at 545–46, 552, 554–56; idem, "The Battle Rhetoric of Aelred of Rievaulx," *HSJ* 1 (1989): 99–107 at 99, 102; idem, "Rhetoric and Morale: A Study of Battle Orations from the Central Middle Ages," *JMH* 15 (1989): 201–26 at 203–4, 217–19, 220n3; idem, "The Courage of the Normans: A Comparative Study of Battle Rhetoric," *Nottingham Medieval Studies* 35 (1991): 1–26 at 2.

[133] Henry of Huntingdon, *"Historia Anglorum": The History of the English People*, 10.7–9, ed. Diane Greenway (Oxford: Oxford University Press, 1996), 712–17.

[134] Aelred of Rievaulx, *Relatio de Standardo*, in *Aelredi Rievallensis Opera omnia* VI, 59–73 at 62–65; with translation in Aelred of Rievaulx, *The Historical Works*, 251–57.

and Aelred had reasons to be well-informed of the battle and of the campaign leading up to it. Henry was based in the diocese of Lincoln and kept himself abreast of events in the neighboring archdiocese, while Aelred had personally known most of the noble participants on both sides of the battle, which took place beside abbey lands within twenty miles of Rievaulx.[135] On the other hand, neither account can be taken as a disinterested, fully reliable historical record. Both chroniclers had their own polemical reasons to attribute orations to Ralph and Walter respectively, and each showed literary invention and partisan interest on behalf of his chosen orator.[136] Both speeches are notable, however, in taking the implicit form of a biblical homily. Ralph's oration represents a homily on 1 Maccabees 2–3, while Walter's oration offers a meditation on the Mosaic covenant of Deuteronomy 11.[137] These orations can be profitably read against what is known of the battle.

Read against the month-long leadup to the battle, Ralph's speech is especially interesting. In response to the invasion of the north of England by David of Scotland, Archbishop Thurstan ordered the preaching of a defensive holy war throughout the York diocese on 27 July. Speeches which the chroniclers place at the Standard may reflect speeches delivered over many days or weeks leading up to the battle.[138] Significantly, Thurstan's order was issued in time to take advantage of the liturgical feast of the Maccabean martyrs on 1 August.[139] Sermons preached as part of the mobilization efforts for the campaign probably took as their theme this biblical example of a beleaguered few's miraculous defense against invasion by a "sacrilegious" multitude. The structure of the sermon attributed to Bishop Ralph seems to fit this pattern. Although the form of the sermon as transmitted may be the imagined rhetorical set-piece of its chronicler, it might nonetheless afford a genuine glimpse into the general mobilization efforts and the theme of clerical sermons delivered in the campaign leading up to the battle.

As orator, Ralph exhorts his army to remember the heroic deeds and martial reputation of their Norman ancestors in diverse times and places, from

---

135 Mariann Garrity, "'Hidden Honey': The Many Meanings of Aelred of Rievaulx's 'De Bello Standardii,'" *Cistercian Studies Quarterly* 44 (2009): 57–64 at 59; Jean A. Truax, *Aelred the Peacemaker: The Public Life of a Cistercian Abbot* (Collegeville MN: Cistercian Publications, 2017), 131–34.

136 Harrington, "Harangue or Homily?" 171–72; idem, "Northern Maccabees: The Battle Oration of Ralph Nowell, Bishop of Orkney, at the Battle of the Standard," *Northern Studies* 53 (2022): 27–42 at 29–38.

137 Harrington, "Harangue or Homily?" 168–70, 172–77; idem, "Northern Maccabees," 33–38.

138 Storelli, "Les harangues," 24–26. For the preparations, see also Bachrach, *Religion*, 153–56.

139 Harrington, "Northern Maccabees," 35.

Scotland to Jerusalem; contrasts them with the rashness of their ill-disciplined and lawless enemy; and assures that there is no cause to fear the people of Scotland, who should, by customary order, be subject to them. He states that he has been deputized by Thurstan and declares that this most recent invasion is providential, so that the invaders may be punished in England for their violation of the temples of God, bloodshed upon the altars, and indiscriminate murder of priests, children, and pregnant women. He proclaims that God himself will act through the English army and that the rashness of their ill-equipped and naked enemy is no match for their own heavy armor, courage, or the presence of God. He asserts that the enemy's numerical superiority is less important than the merit of the few and that the size of the enemy host is a hindrance to them. He concludes with a summary appeal to the army's ancestral glory, regular training, and military discipline in overcoming the enemy, observes that the enemy are already rushing forward in disorder, and grants absolution to all who fall while avenging God's house, priests, and people. While each aspect of the speech aligns with the canon of rhetoric identified in Bliese's study of battle speeches, they also notably align with order of the biblical themes in 1 Maccabees 2–3. They show the way in which biblical homily and battle harangue could be blended into a stirring oration as part of the religious ritual on the eve of battle.

Although attributed to a lay rather than clerical orator, Walter's homily on the Deuteronomic covenant is similarly befitting of its time and place. It aligns closely with the perception of the Standard as the new Ark of the Covenant, symbolic of the promises set forth in Deuteronomy 11.[140] Deuteronomy was also suitable for a martial harangue. In rituals of malediction, chapters of Deuteronomy were often invoked as cursing psalms.[141] Deuteronomy 11 invoked meditation on the deeds of the past, which allows Walter to introduce the deeds of his Norman ancestors as a promise of future victory. It set before the people of God a blessing and a curse: a blessing for those who obey the commandments and a curse for those who break them, along with the future promise of passing over the Jordan to possess the land beyond. It establishes the biblical terms by which victory is given to the orator's people *quasi in feudum* ("as if in fee"), provided they act on that divine promise according to the terms of the covenant.[142] The harangue was also a suitable setting for the invocation of relevant martial psalms. Walter's claim that "earth has not devoured [David of Scotland's army], heaven has not blasted them, the seas

---

140   Harrington, "Harangue or Homily?" 180–83.
141   Little, *Maledictions*, 61; Wiley, "Maledictory Psalms," 265; Harrington, "Vengeance," 201–2.
142   Harrington, "Harangue or Homily?" 172–77.

have not overwhelmed them, for no other reason than to save them for your victories, so that they may die at your hands," not only evokes the relevant terms of Deuteronomy 11:13–7 but echoes the apocalyptic imagery of Psalm 45 already discussed.[143] Walter's harangue also invokes, near its conclusion, the promise of Psalm 34 in its Christian interpretation: "that Christ himself will take up arms and shield and will rise to our aid."[144] Once again, regardless of whether it was ever delivered in the form which Aelred presents, it is at least a plausible representation of the kind of homily on the necessity of battle and the promise of victory that might have been delivered during the mobilization efforts or on the campaign.

On the Northumbrian side, then, religion was clearly an important unifier of a historically culturally mixed and fluid frontier zone: with a Norman-born archbishop mobilizing an army of Northumbrian English, putatively addressed by an Anglo-Norman high sheriff and an Anglo-Scandinavian bishop.[145] The English chroniclers of the Standard unfortunately omit any comparable religious homilies or rituals of war on the part of David of Scotland's equally mixed army, being concerned instead to present the barbarism and irreligion of the invader.[146] Given the invaders' reported violations of church sanctuary during the invasion and those of preceding generations, it must have been unimaginable for the English chroniclers to do otherwise. In Aelred's account, Walter dismisses David's army as an unholy mob: "Before them go actors (*histriones*), dancers, and dancing girls; before us go the cross of Christ and the relics of the saints."[147] The *histriones* who purportedly accompanied David's army may represent professional Gaelic poets, reciters, and storytellers, who proclaimed the past deeds of the army, its leaders, and their ancestors to strengthen morale. Ironically, they might thus be little different from the role Walter assumes for himself in telling the deeds of his own Norman ancestors.[148]

---

143   Aelred, *Relatio de Standardo*, 64; English translation: idem, *Historical Works*, 255–56.
144   Aelred, *Relatio de Standardo*, 65: "ipse Christus apprehendet arma et scutum, et exsurget in adiutorium nobis"; English translation: idem, *Historical Works*, 257.
145   For Ralph's Norse connexions and probable Anglo-Scandinavian (York Orcadian) background, see Christopher Norton, *St. William of York* (Woodbridge: York Medieval Press in association with Boydell Press, 2006), 229–31; and Haki Antonsson, *St. Magnús of Orkney: A Scandinavian Martyr-Cult in Context*, TNW 29 (Leiden and Boston MA: Brill, 2007), 93–96.
146   Among David's army were the Scots (the Gaelic-speakers from north of the Forth), and the men of Lothian, Galloway, Cumbria, Teviotdale, and the Isles.
147   Aelred, *Relatio de Standardo*, 65: "Illos histriones, saltatores et saltatrices, nos crux Christi et reliquie sanctorum antecedunt"; English translation: idem, *Historical Works*, 257.
148   For the comparable interpretation of the Anglo-Latin *histriones* as referring to performers of heroic, historical narratives, see Jesse Patrick Harrington, "Vain Spells or Vain Songs?

Aelred is the only chronicler to attribute the commanders in David's army with orations of their own. These, however, are delivered not to the army but privately in the royal tent, and they appear to be much more secular in tone.[149] Moreover, among David's ethnically composite army, the Gaelic fighters attract the least sympathy from Aelred.[150] Nonetheless, the Scots had asserted the righteousness of their own cause, defending the oaths which they had sworn to uphold the royal claim of David's niece Matilda and to punish the perjurers who enabled the usurpation of her throne by her cousin Stephen.[151] One should also recall what Aelred records elsewhere in his eulogic *vita* for David: that the Scottish king was an assiduous founder and patron of religious houses, who had devoted himself from his youth to masses, prayers, and psalmody.[152] Given this political and religious background, it seems highly probable that the mobilization of the Scottish army was accompanied by its own, analogous religious rituals, harangues, and homilies that the English chroniclers chose not to record.

There has been less study of similar speeches in the Gaelic world than among their English or Norman neighbors, though the shared influence of Psalm 45 on the speeches at the Standard and in *Táin Bó Cuailnge* may be noted.[153] In addition, *Betha Finnchua* can be studied for its clerical battle orations. While these imagined harangues lack the contemporary historical basis of the

---

The Meaning of the 'vanissima carmina et friuoleas incantationes' in the Hagiography of Saint Dunstan of Canterbury, 997–1130," *Quaestio Insularis* 17 (2016): 101–26 at 105–14. For the role of professional poets and storytellers in Gaelic society specifically, see Katharine Simms, *From Kings to Warlords: The Changing Structure of Gaelic Ireland in the Later Middle Ages*, SCelH 7 (Woodbridge: Boydell Press, 1987), 5; idem, "Images of Warfare in Bardic Poetry," *Celtica* 21 (1990): 608–19; Kenneth W. Nicholls, *Gaelic and Gaelicised Ireland in the Middle Ages*, 2nd rev. ed. (Dublin: Lilliput Press, 2003), 93–95; Ruairí Ó hUiginn, "In Song and in Story: Aspects of the Performance of Medieval Irish Saga Literature," *Quaestio Insularis* 19 (2018): 1–29.

149 Aelred, *Relatio de Standado*, 65–71; English translation: idem, *Historical Works*, 257–65.

150 William M. Aird, "'Sweet Civility and Barbarous Rudeness': A View from the Frontier. Abbot Ailred of Rievaulx and the Scots," in *Imagining Frontiers, Contesting Identities*, ed. Steven G. Ellis and Lud'a Klusáková (Pisa: Edizioni Plus and Pisa University Press, 2007), 59–75 at 64–67.

151 Aelred, *De sancto rege Scotorum David epitome*, in *Aelredi Rievallensis Opera Omnia* VI, 5–21 at 11; English translation: idem, *Historical Works*, 54. Aelred acknowledges this in his *vita* of David but does not allow such a possibility in his main account of the Standard, describing the invasion as unlawful aggression and making no mention of Matilda; see Harrington, "Harangue or Homily?" 178–80.

152 Aelred, *De sancto rege*, 7–8, 11; English translation: idem, *Historical Works*, 48–49, 55.

153 For a notable study of literary Irish accounts of battle incitement, albeit focusing on incitement by insult, see Proinsias Mac Cana, "Laíded, Gressacht: 'Formalized Incitement,'" *Ériu* 43 (1992): 69–92.

orations at the Standard, they are nonetheless composed according to canons of rhetoric which allow comparison with the English examples. Moreover, a Cistercian authorship has been proposed as a possibility for the text, which invites comparison with possible common themes in the oration imaginatively attributed to Walter by the Cistercian Aelred.[154] The Irish text gives two notable orations.

In the first instance, the saint is summoned to assist the army of Leinster during an invasion by the legendary Énnae Cennselach, the eponymous, putative royal ancestor of the south Leinster dynasty of Uí Chennselaig. The initial overtures of peace recommended by Finnchú fail, and the saint marches with the Leinster army in its van. A final effort by Finnchú to secure pledges from Cennselach fails. At this point, the Leinster army arose with Finnchú, who is then said to have given a harangue to the men. The harangue as reported in the Book of Lismore is very brief: "Follow me, o men of Leinster, *et reliqua*."[155] The copy probably abbreviates from its exemplar, so it is unfortunately not possible to elaborate on the rhetoric originally provided in the twelfth century.

The second and more extensive oration is set in the Kingdom of Munster during an invasion by the Uí Néill. In this instance, the saint is with the Munster army, supporting the southerners against the northerners. The narrative tells of the fear of the Munstermen against their northern adversary and of the pair of harangues given by the cleric Finnchú and the Eóganacht prince Coirpre Crom ("The Stooping") mac Crimthainn, to hearten them:

> The Munstermen, save Finnchú only, flinch from the fight in horror of the Uí Néill, and because of the abundance of their heroes and their accoutrements. And Finnchú gave counsel to the men of Munster and said that not a homestead of their territory would be left to them if there was any flinching. The Munstermen said: "The Uí Néill are thrice our number." Finnchú told them to slay the surplus till the numbers were equal, and when they were equal, that each of the Munstermen should then slay his opponent. Howbeit, Finnchú and Coirpre Crom heartened and strengthened the Munstermen to the battle, for Coirpre was not shunning it.

---

154   Ó Riain, *Dictionary*, 336–37; Karen E. Overbey, *Sacral Geographies: Saints, Shrines, and Territory in Medieval Ireland*, Studies in the visual cultures of the Middle Ages 2 (Turnhout: Brepols, 2012), 169. Note however the contrary assessment of Sarah Waidler, "Sanctity and Intertextuality in Medieval Munster: The Unusual Life of Findchú of Brí Gobann," *Peritia* 30 (2019): 215–34 at 225–26.
155   *Lives of Saints from the Book of Lismore*, 91, 238.

The Munstermen accepted the battle through shame and through the encouragement of Finnchú and Coirpre.[156]

Compared with the harangues at the Standard, these examples are short and show little that is overtly and specifically religious—or at least, no unifying homiletic theme that has yet been identified. Nonetheless, this compressed narrative contains at least three key elements of a medieval pre-battle oration. The men are told the necessity of defending their homeland from the invader and warned that victory belongs only to the courageous. They are told that the superior numbers of those facing them are no object. Finally, the army are set the positive example of their leaders and are driven to fight by both shame and encouragement. Individually, there are biblical analogues for each of these key themes, whether in the courage of Joshua or the victories of the outnumbered Maccabees. Moreover, each of these key themes is also prominent in the contemporary English accounts of the Standard. Together, they show one more way in which Christian clerics in both cultural zones could easily be imagined as providing the decisive elements of battlefield morale to armies in dire straits.

4 Conclusions

The Gaelic world possessed a rich and diverse tradition of religious ritual performance adaptable for military situations—including prayer and psalmody, relics and holy banners, and biblically inspired harangues and homilies—to invoke God and the saints to their aid. These rituals provided an important element of morale, both on the battlefields of Ireland and Britain and in the campaigns leading up to them. As a sign of their depth and power, one need only look to the geographical spread and longevity of these practices, which had roots deep within the Judaeo-Christian tradition, transcended cultural and period boundaries within the Insular world, and lasted from their first emergence down to the end of the medieval period. They could be taken both seriously and sympathetically by those on the outside of Gaelic culture. As such, such practices invite systematic attention in future, not least for

---

156   Ibid., 96–97, 244: "Locuid fir Mhuman in cath re gráin Clainni Néill 7 ar imut a laech 7 a trealaim, acht Finnchua a aenar. Et comairliged Finnchua fir Mhuman, 7 adubairt nach leicfithe baile dia bferunn doibh damad locad leo. Doraidhset fir Muman: 'Atait Clanna Néill ar tri coimlín-ne.' Aspert Finnchua a n-imarcraidh do shlaidhi comtis coimlina, et o robheitis comhlín cach do mharbhadh a fhair chomhlin iarsin. Cidh tra, rogress 7 ronert Finnchua 7 Cairbri Crom fir Mhuman 'cum an chatha, áir ni raibhe Cairpre ara imghabáil.' Roaemsat fir Mumhan in cath tria naire 7 tria nertadh Finnchua 7 Cairbri."

comparison of analogous practices in cultural zones which are sometimes treated in isolation from each other. Anyone seeking to understand the medieval Gaelic world and its neighbors—in all their hopes, fears, divisions, and interconnexions—"would do well, in their historical imaginations, to join the procession."[157]

Bibliography

Primary Sources

Adomnán's "Law of the Innocents," Cáin Adomnáin: A Seventh Century Law for the Protection of Non-Combatants. Translated by Gilbert Márkus. Kilmartin: Kilmartin House Trust, 2008.

Aelred of Rievaulx. *De sancto rege Scotorum David epitome*. In *Aelredi Rievallensis Opera omnia VI. Opera historica et hagiographica*. Edited by Domenico Pezzini, 5–21. CCCM 3. Turnhout: Brepols, 2017.

Aelred of Rievaulx. *Genealogia regum Anglorum*. In *Aelredi Rievallensis Opera omnia VI: Opera historica et hagiographica*. Edited by Domenico Pezzini, 3–56. CCCM 3. Turnhout: Brepols, 2017.

Aelred of Rievaulx. *The Historical Works*. Edited by Marsha L. Dutton. Translated by Jane Patricia Freeland. Cistercian Fathers series 56. Kalamazoo MI: Cistercian Publications, 2005.

Aelred of Rievaulx. *Relatio de Standardo*. In *Aelredi Rievallensis Opera omnia VI: Opera historica et hagiographica*. Edited by Domenico Pezzini, 59–73. CCCM 3. Turnhout: Brepols, 2017.

"An Edition of 'Aided Diarmata meic Cerbaill' from the 'Book of Uí Maine.'" Edited by Dan M. Wiley. PhD thesis, Harvard University, 2000.

"Annála Ríoghachta Éireann": Annals of the Kingdom of Ireland, by the Four Masters. Edited by John O'Donovan. 7 vols. Dublin: Hodges, Smith, 1854. Rprt. New York: AMS Press, 1966.

"Annala Uladh": Annals of Ulster Otherwise "Annala Senait," Annals of Senat: A Chronicle of Irish Affairs from A.D. 431 to A.D. 1540. Edited by William M. Hennessy and Batholomew Mac Carthy. 4 vols. Dublin: Thom. & Co., 1887–1901.

The Annals of Inisfallen MS. Rawlinson B. 503. Edited by Seán Mac Airt. Dublin: Dublin Institute for Advanced Studies, 1951.

The Annals of Loch Cé, RS 54. Edited by Wiliam M. Hennessy. 2 vols. London: Longman, 1871. Rprt. Dublin: Stationery Office, 1939.

---

157   Keynes, "Viking Raids," 188.

The Annals of Tigernach. Translated by Whitley Stokes. 2 vols. Felinfach: Llanerch Publishers, 1993.
The Annals of Ulster (to A.D. 1131). Edited by Sean Mac Airt and Gearoid Mac Niocaill. Dublin: Dublin Institute for Advanced Studies, 1983.
Asser's Life of King Alfred, Together with the Annals of Saint Neots Erroneously Ascribed to Asser. Edited by William Henry Stevenson and Dorothy Whitelock. Oxford: Clarendon Press, 1959.
Bede. *Ecclesiastical History of the English People*. Edited by Bertram Colgrave and R.A.B. Mynors. 2 vols. Oxford: Clarendon Press, 1967.
"Betha Colaim Chille": "Life of Columcille." Compiled by Manus O'Donnell in 1532. Edited by Andrew O'Kelleher and Gertrude Schoepperle. University of Illinois bulletin 15.48. Urbana IL: University of Illinois, 1918.
"Bethu Phátraic": *The Tripartite Life of Patrick*. Edited by Kathleen Mulchrone. Dublin: Hodges Figgis & Co.; London: Williams and Norgate, 1939.
"Buile Suibhne": "The Frenzy of Suibhne," Being the Adventures of Suibhne Geilt, a Middle Irish Romance. Edited by J.G. O'Keeffe. Irish Texts Society 12. London: Nutt, 1913.
"Chronicum Scotorum": *A Chronicle of Irish Affairs, From the Earliest Times to A.D. 1135*. Edited by William M. Hennessy. Rolls series 46. London: Longmans, Green, Reader, and Dyer, 1866.
"Cogadh Gaedhel re Gallaibh": "The War of the Gaedhil with the Gaill," or, the Invasions of Ireland by the Danes and Other Norsemen. Edited by James Henthorn Todd. Rolls series 48. London: Longmans, Green, Reader, and Dyer, 1867.
Fragmentary Annals of Ireland. Edited by Joan N. Radner. Dublin: Dublin Institute for Advanced Studies, 1978.
Henry of Huntingdon. "Historia Anglorum": *The History of the English People*. Edited by Diane Greenway. Oxford: Oxford University Press, 1996.
Life of St. Declan of Ardmore and, Life of St. Mochuda of Lismore. Edited by Patrick Power. Irish Texts Society 16. London: Nutt, 1914.
Lives of Saints from the Book of Lismore. Edited by Whitley Stokes. Anecdota Oxoniensia 5. Oxford: Clarendon Press, 1890.
Jocelin of Furness. *Vita auctore Iocelino monacho de Furnesio: Patricius episcopus, apostolus & primas Hiberniæ*. In *Acta Sanctorum* Martii 2. Edited Godefry Henskens and Daniel Papebroch, cols. 0540B–0580D. Antwerp: Meursius, 1668.
The Most Ancient Lives of Saint Patrick: Including the Life by Jocelin, Hitherto Unpublished in America, and his Extant Writings. Edited by James O'Leary. New York: Kennedy, 1883.
Muirchú Moccu Macthéni. *Vita Sancti Patricii: Life of Saint Patrick*. Edited by David Howlett. Dublin: Four Courts Press, 2006.
Symeonis monachi opera omnia. Edited by Thomas Arnold. 2 vols. Rolls series 75. London: Longman, 1882–1885.

"Táin Bó Cúailnge": Recension 1. Edited by Cecile O'Rahilly. Dublin: Dublin Institute for Advanced Studies, 1976.

"Táin Bó Cúalnge" from the Book of Leinster. Edited by Cecile O'Rahilly. Irish Texts Society 49. Dublin: Dublin Institute for Advanced Studies, 1967.

"Thesaurus Palaeohibernicus": A Collection of Old-Irish Glosses, Scholia, Prose, and Verse. Edited by Whitley Stokes and John Strachan. 3 vols. Cambridge: Cambridge University Press, 1901–1903.

The Tripartite Life of Patrick: With Other Documents Relating to that Saint. Edited by Whitley Stokes, 2 vols. Rolls series 89. London: Eyre and Spottiswoode, 1887.

Vitae sanctorvm Hiberniae partim hactenvs: ineditae ad fidem codicvm manvscriptorvm recognovit prolegomenis notis indicibvs instrvxit. Edited by Charles Plummer. 2 vols. Oxford: Clarendon Press, 1910.

Secondary Sources

Aird, William M. "'Sweet Civility and Barbarous Rudeness': A View from the Frontier. Abbot Ailred of Rievaulx and the Scots." In *Imagining Frontiers, Contesting Identities*. Edited by Steven G. Ellis and Lud'a Klusáková, 59–75. Pisa: Edizioni Plus and Pisa University Press, 2007.

Antonsson, Haki. *St. Magnús of Orkney: A Scandinavian Martyr-Cult in Context.* TNW 29. Leiden and Boston MA: Brill, 2007.

Arnold, John H., and Caroline Goodson. "Resounding Community: The History and Meaning of Medieval Church Bells." *Viator* 43.1 (2012): 99–130.

Bachrach, David S. *Religion and the Conduct of War, c. 300–1215.* Woodbridge: Boydell Press, 2003.

Baker, Derek. "Aelred of Rievaulx and Walter Espec." *HSJ* 1 (1989): 91–98.

Bannerman, John. "'Comarba Coluim Chille' and the Relics of Columba." *IR* 44.1 (1993): 14–47.

Bartlett, Robert. *Why Can the Dead Do Such Great Things? Saints and Worshippers from the Martyrs to the Reformation.* Princeton NJ: Princeton University Press, 2013.

Birkett, Helen. *The Saints' Lives of Jocelin of Furness: Hagiography, Patronage and Ecclesiastical Politics.* Woodbridge: York Medieval Press in association with The Boydell Press, 2010.

Bliese, John R.E. "Aelred of Rievaulx's Rhetoric and Morale at the Battle of the Standard, 1138." *Albion* 20.4 (1988): 543–56.

Bliese, John R.E. "The Battle Rhetoric of Aelred of Rievaulx." *HSJ* 1 (1989): 99–107.

Bliese, John R.E. "The Courage of the Normans: A Comparative Study of Battle Rhetoric." *Nottingham Medieval Studies* 35 (1991): 1–26.

Bliese, John R.E. "Rhetoric and Morale: A Study of Battle Orations from the Central Middle Ages." *JMH* 15 (1989): 201–26.

Bliese, John R.E. "Saint Cuthbert and War." *JMH* 24.3 (1998): 215–41.

Bourke, Cormac. *The Early Medieval Hand-bells of Ireland and Britain*. Dublin: National Museum of Ireland, 2020.

Bradbury, Jim. *Stephen and Matilda: The Civil War of 1139–53*. Stroud: Sutton, 1996.

Byrne, Francis J., and Francis, Pádraig. "Two Lives of Saint Patrick: 'Vita Secunda' and 'Vita Quarta.'" *JRSAI* 124 (1994): 5–117.

Caldwell, David H. "The Monymusk Reliquary: The 'Breccbennach' of St Columba?" *Proceedings of the Society of Antiquaries of Scotland* 131 (2001): 267–82.

Charles-Edwards, Thomas M. *Early Christian Ireland*. Cambridge: Cambridge University Press, 2000.

Charles-Edwards, Thomas M. "Irish Warfare before 1100." In *A Military History of Ireland*. Edited by Thomas Bartlett and Keith Jeffery, 26–51. Cambridge: Cambridge University Press, 1996.

Clancy, Thomas Owen. "Columba, Adomnán and the Cult of Saints in Scotland." In *"Spes Scotorum," "Hope of Scots": Saint Columba, Iona and Scotland*. Edited by Dauvit Broun and Thomas Owen Clancy, 3–33. Edinburgh: T&T Clark, 1999.

Corlett, Christiaan. "Cursing Stones in Ireland." *Journal of the Galway Archaeological and Historical Society* 64 (2012): 1–20.

Cotsonis, John A. *Byzantine Figural Processional Crosses*. Dumbarton Oaks Byzantine Collection publications 10. Washington DC: Dumbarton Oaks, 1994.

Crouch, David. *The Reign of King Stephen, 1135–1154*. Harlow: Longman, 2000.

Dalton, Paul. *Conquest, Anarchy, and Lordship: Yorkshire, 1066–1154*. CSML 4th ser. 27. Cambridge: Cambridge University Press, 1994.

Gerrard, Daniel M.G. *The Church at War: The Military Activities of Bishops, Abbots, and Other Clergy in England, c.900–1200*. Abingdon and New York: Routledge, 2016.

Gerrard, Daniel M.G. "Fighting Clergy, Church Councils and the Context of Law: The Cutting Edge of Orthodoxy or the Ambiguous Limits of Legitimacy?" In *Heresy and the Making of European Culture: Medieval and Modern Perspectives*. Edited by Andrew P. Roach and James R. Simpson, 275–88. Farnham and Burlington VT: Ashgate, 2013.

Davies, Wendy. "'Protected Space' in Britain and Ireland in the Middle Ages." In *Scotland in Dark Age Britain*, St. John's house papers 6. Edited by Barbara E. Crawford, 1–19. Aberdeen: Scottish Cultural Press, 1996.

Delaporte, Yves. *Le Voile de Notre Dame*. Chartres: Maison des Clercs, 1927.

De Paor, Liam. *Saint Patrick's World: The Christian Culture of Ireland's Apostolic Age*. Dublin: Four Courts Press, 1993.

Dobson, R.B. *Durham Priory 1400–1450*, CSML, 3rd ser. 6. Cambridge: Cambridge University Press, 1973.

Downham, Clare. *Medieval Ireland*. Cambridge: Cambridge University Press, 2018.

Dumville, David N. "Coroticus." In *Saint Patrick, AD 493–1993*. Edited by David N. Dumville and Lesley Abrams, 107–115. SCelH 13. Woodbridge: Boydell Press, 1993.

Ehrenschwendtner, Marie-Luise. "Literacy and the Bible." In *The Bible from 600 to 1450*. Edited by Richard Marsden and E. Ann Matter, 704–21. The new Cambridge history of the Bible 2. Cambridge: Cambridge University Press, 2012.

Erdmann, Carl. *The Origin of the Idea of Crusade*. Translated by Marshall W. Baldwin and Walter Goffart. Princeton NJ: Princeton University Press, 1977.

Fern, Chris; Dickinson, Tania; Webster, Leslie, ed. *The Staffordshire Hoard: An Anglo-Saxon Treasure*. London: Society of Antiquaries of London, 2019.

Flanagan, Marie Therese. "Reform in the Twelfth-Century Irish Church: A Revolution of Outlook?" Kathleen Hughes Memorial lectures 9. Cambridge: Hughes Hall and the Department of Anglo-Saxon, Norse, and Celtic, University of Cambridge, 2012.

Foot, Sarah. "Bede's Kings." In *Writing, Kingship and Power in Anglo-Saxon England*. Edited by Rory Naismith and David A. Woodman, 25–51. Cambridge: Cambridge University Press, 2017.

France, John. "War and Sanctity: Saints' Lives as Sources for Early Medieval Warfare." *The JMMH* 3 (2005): 14–22.

Fraser, James E. "Adomnán and the Morality of War." In *Adomnán of Iona: Theologian, Lawmaker, Peacemaker*. Edited by Jonathan M. Wooding et al., 95–111. Dublin: Four Courts Press, 2010.

Garrity, Mariann. "'Hidden Honey': The Many Meanings of Aelred of Rievaulx's 'De Bello Standardii.'" *Cistercian Studies Quarterly* 44 (2009): 57–64.

Márkus, Gilbert. *Conceiving a Nation: Scotland to AD 900*. Edinburgh: Edinburgh University Press, 2017.

Gross-Diaz, Theresa. "The Latin Psalter." In *The Bible from 600 to 1450*. Edited by Richard Marsden and E. Ann Matter, 427–45. The new Cambridge history of the Bible 2. Cambridge: Cambridge University Press, 2012.

Harrington, Jesse Patrick. "Harangue or Homily? Walter Espec and the Deuteronomic Covenant in Aelred of Rievaulx's 'Relatio de Standardo.'" *HSJ* 32 (2020): 163–83.

Harrington, Jesse Patrick. "A Land Without Martyrs? St. Odrán, Gerald of Wales, and Christian Martyrdom in Medieval Ireland." *History Ireland* 28.3 (May/June 2020): 14–17.

Harrington, Jesse Patrick. "Northern Maccabees: The Battle Oration of Ralph Nowell, Bishop of Orkney, at the Battle of the Standard." *Northern Studies* 53 (2022): 27–41.

Harrington, Jesse Patrick. "Sinners, Saints, Psalms, and Curses in 'Aided Diarmata meic Cerbaill' ('The Death-Tale of Diarmait mac Cerbaill')." In *Proceedings of Defining the Boundaries of Celtic Hagiography: Textual Sources Outside Lives and Martyrologies Conference, Dublin Institute for Advanced Studies, 25–26 May 2018*. Edited by Sarah Waidler. Dublin: Dublin Institute for Advanced Studies. Forthc. 2023.

Harrington, Jesse Patrick. "Vain Spells or Vain Songs? The Meaning of the 'vanissima carmina et friuoleas incantationes' in the Hagiography of Saint Dunstan of Canterbury, 997–1130." *Quaestio Insularis* 17 (2016): 101–26.

Harrington, Jesse Patrick. "Vengeance and Saintly Cursing in the Saints' Lives of England and Ireland, c.1060–1215." PhD thesis, University of Cambridge, 2018.

Herbert, Máire. "Crossing Historical and Literary Boundaries: Irish Written Culture Around the Year 1000." *Cambrian Medieval Celtic Studies* 53–54 (2007): 87–101.

Herbert, Máire. *Iona, Kells, and Derry: The History and Hagiography of the Monastic "familia" of Columba*. Oxford: Clarendon, 1988.

Houlihan, James W. *Adomnán's "Lex Innocentium" and the Laws of War*. Dublin: Four Courts Press, 2020.

Hughes, Kathleen. *The Church in Early Irish Society*. Ithaca NY: Cornell University Press, 1966.

Jackson, Kenneth Hurlstone. "The Date of the Tripartite Life." *Zeitschrift für celtische Philologie* 41 (1986): 5–45.

Jackson, Kenneth Hurlstone. *The Oldest Irish Tradition: A Window on the Iron Age*. Cambridge: Cambridge University Press, 1964.

Julian, John. *A Dictionary of Hymnology: Setting Forth the Origin and History of Christian Hymns of all Ages and Nations*. 2nd rev. ed. 2 vols. New York: Dover, 1907. Rprt. 1957.

Keynes, Simon. "An Abbot, an Archbishop, and the Viking Raids of 1006–7 and 1009–12." *Anglo-Saxon England* 36 (2007): 151–220.

Klein, Holger A. "Objektkultur und Kultobjekte im kaiserlich-byzantinischen Prozessionswesen." In *"Palatium sacrum"—Sakralität am Hof des Mittelalters. Orte, Dinge, Rituale*. Edited by Manfred Luchterhandt and Hedwig Röckelein, 77–100. Regensburg: Schnell & Steiner, 2021.

Kotecki, Radosław. "Lions and Lambs, Wolfs and Pastors of the Flock: Portraying Military Activities of Bishops in Twelfth Century Poland." In *Between Sword and Prayer: Warfare and Medieval Clergy in Cultural Perspective*. Edited by Radosław Kotecki, Jacek Maciejewski, and John S. Ott, 303–40. EMC 3. Leiden and Boston MA: Brill, 2018.

Kotecki, Radosław. "With the Sword of Prayer, or How the Medieval Bishop Should Fight." *QMAN* 21 (2016): 341–69.

Little, Lester K. *Benedictine Maledictions: Liturgical Cursing in Romanesque France*. Ithaca NY and London: Cornell University Press, 1993.

Little, Lester K. "Blessings and Curses." *Memoirs of the American Academy in Rome* 51–52 (2006): 1–4.

Lloyd, James. "The Priests of the King's Reliquary in Anglo-Saxon England." *JEH* 67.2 (2016): 265–87.

Lucas, Anthony T. "The Social Role of Relics and Reliquaries in Ancient Ireland." *JRSAI* 116 (1986): 5–37.

Mac Cana, Proinsias. "Laíded, Gressacht: 'Formalized Incitement.'" *Ériu* 43 (1992): 69–92.

Mac Mathúna, Liam. "The Christianization of the Early Irish Cosmos? 'Muir mas, nem nglas, talam cé' (Blathm. 258)." *Zeitschrift für celtische Philologie* 49–50 (1997): 532–47.

Mac Mathúna, Liam. "Irish Perceptions of the Cosmos." *Celtica* 23 (1999): 174–87.

Mac Mathúna, Liam. "The Irish Cosmos Revisited: Further Lexical Perspectives." In *Celtic Cosmology: Perspectives from Ireland and Scotland*. Edited by Jacqueline Borsje et al., 10–33. Papers in medieval studies 26. Toronto: Pontifical Institute of Mediaeval Studies, 2014.

Mallory, J.P. "The World of Cú Chulainn: The Archaeology of Táin Bó Cúailnge." In *Aspects of the Táin*. Edited by J.P. Mallory, 103–59. Belfast: December Publications, 1992.

McCormick, Michael. *Eternal Victory: Triumphal Rulership in Late Antiquity, Byzantium, and the Early Medieval West*. Cambridge: Cambridge University Press, 1986.

McCormick, Michael. "The Liturgy of War in the Early Middle Ages: Crisis, Litanies, and the Carolingian Monarchy." *Viator* 15 (1984): 1–24.

McNamara, Martin. *The Psalms in the Early Irish Church*, Journal for the Study of the New Testament supplement series 165. Sheffield: Sheffield Academic Press, 2000.

Morgan, Faith Pennick. *Dress and Personal Appearance in Late Antiquity: The Clothing of the Middle and Lower Classes*. Late Antique Archaeology supplementary series 1. Leiden and Boston MA: Brill, 2018.

Nicholl, Donald. *Thurstan: Archbishop of York (1114–1140)*. York: Stonegate Press, 1964.

Nicholls, Kenneth W. *Gaelic and Gaelicised Ireland in the Middle Ages*. 2nd rev ed. Dublin: Lilliput Press, 2003.

Norton, Christopher. *St. William of York*. Woodbridge: York Medieval Press in association with The Boydell Press, 2006.

O'Loughlin, Thomas, ed. *Adomnán at Birr, AD 697: Essays in Commemoration of the Law of the Innocents*. Dublin: Four Courts Press, 2001.

Ó hUiginn, Ruairí. "The Background and Development of Táin Bó Cúailnge." In *Aspects of the Táin*. Edited by J.P. Mallory, 29–67. Belfast: December Publications, 1992.

Ó hUiginn, Ruairí. "In Song and in Story: Aspects of the Performance of Medieval Irish Saga Literature." *Quaestio Insularis* 19 (2018): 1–29.

Ó Néill, Pádraig. "A Middle Irish Poem on the Maledictory Psalms." *Journal of Celtic Studies* 3 (1981): 40–58.

Ó Riain, Pádraig. *A Dictionary of Irish Saints*. Dublin: Four Courts Press, 2011.

Overbey, Karen E. *Sacral Geographies: Saints, Shrines, and Territory in Medieval Ireland*. Studies in the visual cultures of the Middle Ages 2. Turnhout: Brepols, 2012.

Paor, Liam de. *Saint Patrick's World: The Christian Culture of Ireland's Apostolic Age*. Dublin: Four Courts Press, 1993.

Pezzarossa, Lucrezia. "Bibbia, guerra e liturgia. Una nuova prospettiva sulla traduzione alfrediana del 'Libro dei Salmi.'" In *La Bibbia nelle letterature germaniche medievali*.

Edited by Marina Buzzoni, Massimiliano Bampi, and Omar Khalaf, 37–50. Filologie medievali e moderne Rie occidentale 6. Venice: Ca' Foscari, 2015.
Pezzarossa, Lucrezia. "The Ideology of War in Early Medieval England: Three Case Studies in Anglo-Saxon Literature." PhD thesis, University of York, 2013.
Radner, Joan N. "The Significance of the Threefold Death in Celtic Tradition." In *Celtic Folklore and Christianity: Studies in Memory of William W. Heist*. Edited by Patrick K. Ford, 180–99. Santa Barbara CA: McNally and Loftin, 1983.
Rankin, David. *Celts and the Classical World*. London and New York: Routledge, 1987. Rprt. 1996.
Rupp, Daniel. "Der heilige Martin als Schlachtenhelfer im Mittelalter." In *Martin von Tours. Krieger—Bischof—Heiliger*, 27–42. Saarbrücken: Universitätsverlag des Saarlandes, 2013.
Sayers, William. "'Mani Maidi an Nem …': Ringing Changes on a Cosmic Motif." *Ériu* 37 (1986): 99–117.
Schreiner, Klaus. *Märtyrer, Schlachtenhelfer, Friedenstifter. Krieg und Frieden im Spiegel mittelalterlicher und frühneuzeitlicher Heiligenverehrung*. OFVK 18. Opladen: Springer, 2000.
Sharpe, Richard. *Medieval Irish Saints' Lives: An Introduction to "Vitae Sanctorum Hiberniae."* Oxford: Clarendon Press, 1991.
Shaw, John. "A Gaelic Eschatological Folktale, Celtic Cosmology and Dumézil's 'Three Realms.'" In *Celtic Cosmology: Perspectives from Ireland and Scotland*. Edited by Jacqueline Borsje et al., 34–52. Papers in medieval studies 26. Toronto: Pontifical Institute of Mediaeval Studies, 2014.
Simms, Katharine. *From Kings to Warlords: The Changing Structure of Gaelic Ireland in the Later Middle Ages*. SCelH 7. Woodbridge: Boydell Press, 1987.
Simms, Katharine. "Images of Warfare in Bardic Poetry." *Celtica* 21 (1990): 608–19.
Storelli, Xavier. "Les harangues de la bataille de l'Étendard (1138)." *Médiévales* 57 (2009): 15–32.
Tanaka, Miho. "Iona and the Kingship of Dál Riata in Adomnán's 'Vita Columbae.'" *Peritia* 17–18 (2003): 199–214.
Tarczyński, Tomasz. "The King and the Saint against the Scots: The Shaping of English National Identity in the 12th Century Narrative of King Athelstan's Victory over His Northern Neighbours." In *Imagined Communities: Constructing Collective Identities in Medieval Europe*. Edited by Andrzej Pleszczyński et al., 85–102. EMC 8. Leiden and Boston MA: Brill, 2018.
Thacker, Alan. "The Church and Warfare: The Religious and Cultural Background to the Hoard." In *The Staffordshire Hoard: An Anglo-Saxon Treasure*. Edited by Chris Fern, Tania Dickinson, and Leslie Webster, 293–99. London: Society of Antiquaries of London, 2019.

Tierney, James J. "The Celtic Ethnography of Posidonius." *Proceedings of the Royal Irish Academy. Section C: Archaeology, Celtic Studies, History, Linguistics, Literature* 60 (1959–1960): 189–275.

Truax, Jean A. *Aelred the Peacemaker: The Public Life of a Cistercian Abbot.* Collegeville MN: Cistercian Publications, 2017.

Tsurtsumia, Mamuka. "The True Cross in the Armies of Georgia and the Frankish East." *Crusades* 12.1 (2013): 91–102.

Waidler, Sarah. "Sanctity and Intertextuality in Medieval Munster: The Unusual Life of Findchú of Brí Gobann." *Peritia* 30 (2019): 215–34.

Wiley, Daniel M. "The Maledictory Psalms." *Peritia* 15 (2001): 261–79.

Wilson, Susan E. "King Athelstan and John of Beverley." *Northern History* 40.1 (2003): 5–23.

CHAPTER 4

Religious Rites and Integrated Warfare in Civil War Era Norway (1130–1240)

Max Naderer

Prior to engaging in battle with his rival and sitting king in Norway Magnus Erlingsson, King Sverre Sigurdsson exclaimed: "Our strength lies entirely in God and His saints and not in our numbers."[1] Sverre's faction, the Birkibeinar, emerged victorious from this battle, while Magnus had to flee wounded and was shortly believed to have fallen. This was but one battle among these two, and several other competing kings and claimants to the Norwegian throne. Between 1130 and 1240 a series of conflicts, internal struggles, and wars were waged in Norway, which became known as civil wars constituting a distinct period in Norwegian history. The reliance on God and his saints nor their invocation or the employment of spiritual means have been the center of attention of research investigating the period. The article presents, therefore, a first attempt at considering religious rituals, spiritual weapons, and their utilization as an integrated part of warfare during the civil war period in Norway.

1 Integrated Warfare

According to Philippe Contamine, "it is clear that Christianity and war, the church and the military, far from being antithetical, on the whole got on well together [and] existed in a state of constant symbiosis."[2] Religious rites were frequently employed before a pitched battle—such as confession, Holy Communion, mass, and the sign of the cross—as well as during the battle itself when clerics prayed for the success of their party. The clergy accompanying an army was not merely expected to care for the warriors' souls but to

---

1 *Sverris saga*, ed. Þorleifur Hauksson, Íslenzk fornrit 30 (Reykjavík: Hið íslenska fornritafélag, 2007), 84: "várt traust, sem allra annarra, er allt undir Guð ok hans helgum mǫnnum en eigi undir liðsfjǫlða."
2 Philippe Contamine, *War in the Middle Ages*, trans. Michael Jones (Oxford and Cambridge MA: Blackwell, 1984), 296.

partake in battle and "fight with the sword of prayer."[3] The combatants themselves may have invoked heavenly assistance through their war cry. The secular and spiritual spheres influenced and permeated one another. In the long term, beginning with Emperor Constantine the Great, this led to a sacralization of war, a Christianization of the warrior's function, and a reinforcement as well as transformation of the prestige of warriors and their profession.[4] Concomitantly, it made it possible to translate and transfer the struggle from one battlefield onto another, from the temporal to the spiritual and vice versa. Thus, a knight entering a monastery was presented as entering a battlefield on a higher level, yet still be at war.[5] Spiritual life, in particular in a monastery, was compared to a constant and merciless struggle between heavenly and demonic forces—and those in their service—, between virtues and vices. Monks frequently understood themselves in martial rhetoric and belligerent imagery as soldiers of Christ. With the First Crusade as major turning point the boundaries between temporal and spiritual warfare became increasingly blurred. The crusaders as *milites Christi* embraced the double nature of their fight. The foundation of the first military orders reflects the merging of temporal and spiritual warfare as well as knightly and monastic life within a single ideal. While the crusaders' warfare was implicit of a double nature, that of the Templars was explicitly so.[6] One of the clearest examples presents the Knights Templar who, according to Bernard of Clairvaux in his famous *Praise of the New Knighthood*, were fighting not men but evil and, thus, combining temporal and spiritual warfare: "Truly, he who kills a malefactor is not a homicide but, if I may say so, a malicide and is clearly held to be the avenger of Christ in regard to those who do evil, and the defender of Christians."[7] Not only were boundaries blurred

---

3 See here esp. the wide-ranging article by Radosław Kotecki, "With the Sword of Prayer, or How the Medieval Bishop Should Fight," *QMAN* 21 (2016): 341–69.
4 Barbara Rosenwein, "Feudal War and Monastic Peace: Cluniac Liturgy as Ritual Aggression," *Viator* 2 (1971): 145–57; Contamine, *War in the Middle Ages*, 296–302.
5 Katherine Allen Smith, *War and the Making of Medieval Monastic Culture* (Woodbridge: Boydell Press, 2011), 39–111; Daniel M.G. Gerrard, *The Church at War: The Military Activities of Bishops, Abbots, and Other Clergy in England, c.900–1200* (Abingdon and New York: Routledge, 2016), 5–7.
6 Smith, *War*, 102–11. See on the spiritual fights of monks also Rosenwein, "Feudal War." She mentions the change after the First Crusade at p. 157.
7 Bernard of Clairvaux, *Ad milites Templi. De laude novae militiae*, in *Bernard von Clairvaux. Sämtliche Werke lateinisch/deutsch 1*, ed. Gerhard B. Winkler (Innsbruck: Tyrolia-Verlag, 1990), 217: "Sane cum occidit malefactorem, non homicidia, sed, ut ita dixerim, malicida, et plane Christi vindex in his qui male agunt, et defensor christianorum reputatur." See for further context Tomaž Mastnak, *Crusading Peace: Christendom, the Muslim World, and Western Political Order* (Berkeley CA and Los Angeles: University of California Press, 2002), 154–68. Quotation at 161.

and the spheres of battlefields conflated, but the Christian population at large also became increasingly involved in war, as liturgy became a part and weapon of warfare. M. Cecilia Gaposchkin has traced how they, through liturgical and paraliturgical rituals, wielded the invisible weapons of prayer and supplication. In that way, the men and women of the church took part in the fighting. Liturgy became a part of the organization of warfare and was perceived to have an impact on its outcome. Success and failure of the Crusades as holy wars against visible and invisible enemies became the responsibility of all of *christianitas*.[8]

In particular, Daniel Gerrard has argued to consider Contamine's concept and its implications in the study of medieval military campaigns, which incorporates the application of spiritual power to temporal warfare.[9] That means that "all discussion of strategy and tactics should engage with contemporary, rather than modern concepts of military utility, and so we must recall the important part played by the supernatural in contemporary military planning and practice."[10] Thus, for instance, rites and prayers undertaken both by the troops and accompanying clerics before battle, religious war cries, blessings of weapons as well as benefactions made in gratitude for victory, constitute an additional component of warfare and its strategy that was meant to have an effect and secure success. Fighting clerics may be the ultimate expression of that concept, "integrated war," as they could engage enemies on both spiritual and temporal levels, and take part in warfare in more ways than usually recognized. At the same time, conceptualizing warfare as integrated and taking place in different spheres simultaneously, thus effectively merging psychological, devotional, strategic, and economic aspects, blurs the line of what is meant potentially by "fighting clergy." The use of spiritual weapons, thus, becomes an integral part of military history.

Medieval armies had clerics among them, who were responsible to take care of the spiritual health of the warriors. The two primary duties of clerics accompanying any army were likely rather basic priestly functions, that is hearing confession and the proper treatment of the dead. There may be, however, occasions when the clergy intervened in the course of war by spiritual means

---

8   M. Cecilia Gaposchkin, *Invisible Weapons: Liturgy and the Making of Crusade Ideology* (Ithaca NY: Cornell University Press, 2017).
9   For the following, see Gerrard, *The Church at War*, 1–26, 113–35, 250–56; Daniel Gerrard, "Why Study Fighting Clergy? Knight Service, Integrated War, and the Bounds of English Military History, c.1000–1200," in *Between Sword and Prayer: Warfare and Medieval Clergy in Cultural Perspective*, ed. Radosław Kotecki, Jacek Maciejewski, and John S. Ott, EMC 3 (Leiden and Boston MA: Brill, 2018), 117–158.
10 Gerrard, "Why Study Fighting Clergy?" 150.

in order to achieve victory over the enemy. They were the foremost servants of God after all. The language and concept of *militia Christi* blurred the line between prayer and combat. The most explicit prohibition on the participation in war for clerics regards the shedding of blood. The designation of prayers and tears as the clergy's weapons may not have been understood merely metaphorically. No matter how unbelievable or inefficient those powers and measures may appear from a modern and secular perspective, the clergy and religious rites were expected to influence the outcome of military encounters. One problem, however, is that though the presence of clerics occasionally noted, the reason for their presence is only rarely explicitly stated. Yet, considering the ideological background and framing of some conflicts, it appears more likely that the participation of clerics was to secure divine support, pray for saintly intercession, and ultimately to aid in gaining victory over the enemy in battle and war.

As Bjørn Bandlien has argued, the civil war period in Norway was more profoundly influenced by ideas of holy war and crusading than earlier assumed. This affected and changed the perception of warfare as well as the legitimation of one's cause in it, but did not transform it absolutely but existed rather in a polyphonic discourse.[11] The civil wars have long been most interpreted as rivalry between aristocratic networks of families and friends, classes, regions or competing claimants to the throne fighting over the control of resources and the royal power.[12] In a similar vein, Hans Jacob Orning emphasized the impact of the introduction of the so-called Gregorian reform following the establishment of the Norwegian archbishopric in Nidaros (nowadays Trondheim) in 1153/1154. With the crowning of King Magnus Erlingsson in 1163/1164, his alliance with the church, and the promotion of the *rex iustus* ideal, it gave elite actors an ideological foundation to pursue and treat their rivals and enemies

---

11   Bjørn Bandlien, *Man or Monster? Negotiations of Masculinity in Old Norse Society* (Oslo, 2005), 290–348; idem, "Civil War as Holy War? Polyphonic Discourses of Warfare during the Internal Struggles in Norway in the Twelfth Century," in *Christianity and War in Medieval East Central Europe and Scandinavia*, ed. Radosław Kotecki, Carsten Selch Jensen, and Stephen Bennett (Leeds: ARC Humanities Press, 2021), 227–43.

12   See for an historiographical overview Sverre Bagge, "The Structure of the Political Factions in the Internal Struggles of the Scandinavian Countries during the High Middle Ages," *Scandinavian Journal of history* 24 (1999), 299–320. See further on the underlying causes on the outbreak of the civil wars, and whether internal or external elements explain it, Sverre Bagge, "Borgerkrig og statsutvikling i Norge i middelalderen," *HT* 65.2 (1986): 145–97; Hans Jacob Orning, "Borgerkrig og statsutvikling i Norge i middelalderen—en revurdering," *HT* 93.2 (2014), 193–216; Sverre Bagge, "Borgerkrig og statsutvikling—svar til Hans Jacob Orning," *HT* 93.1 (2015): 91–110; Hans Jacob Orning, "Hvorfor vant kongene?" *HT* 94.2 (2015): 285–92.

harsher eliminating them rather than seeking reconciliation. In short, the church provided the king with a black-and-white image of the enemy, which equated submission to God with submission to the king, effectively setting aside the traditional system of shared and inherited kingship based on being a former king's son only.[13] The implications and consequences are twofold. On one hand, it paved the way to construct the period as times of crisis and its conflicts as civil wars and, at least in part, holy wars.[14] On the other hand, this had an impact on the practice of warfare and the means actors sought to employ. Religious rites became more frequent, political factions claimed increasingly divine favor and authority for their cause, and the clerics became involved by wielding spiritual but also temporal weapons.[15] In short, warfare in Norway became more integrated.

2 Religious Rites and Spiritual Weapons in Warfare in Norway

The sagas narrate several rites employed before a battle that may have served to invoke spiritual powers. Not always is a purpose explicitly stated in the saga narratives nor is a direct connection drawn to their function and relation to military encounters. In what follows, the use of relics, prayers, kissing of churches, and finally, excommunication and their context will be discussed as the most prominent and significant religious rites and spiritual weapons that were performed and employed in warfare in Norway during the civil war period.

---

13   Hans Jacob Orning, *Unpredictability and Presence: Norwegian Kingship in the High Middle Ages*, TNW 38 (Leiden and Boston MA: Brill, 2008), 66–68; idem, "Borgerkrig," 208–12.
14   The arguments for the construction of the period as a time of crisis, in particular in retrospect, cannot be fully presented here, see esp. Hans Jacob Orning and Frederik Rosén, "'Sverris saga': A Manifesto for a New Political Order," in *Medieval and Modern Civil Wars*, ed. Jón Viðar Sigurðsson and Hans Jacob Orning, History of warfare 135 (Leiden and Boston MA: Brill, 2021), 69; Hans Jacob Orning, *Dei norske borgarkrigene 1130–1240* (Oslo: Samlaget, 2021), 23–43, 82–91.
15   On clerical behavior and its acceptance during the conflicts, see Louisa Taylor, "Bishops, War, and Canon Law: The Military Activities of Prelates in High Medieval Norway," *Scandinavian Journal of History* 45.3 (2020): 263–85. See also on the connection of (perceived) crises as well as means of spiritual support and intercession with God, in particular in the form of the liturgy and in the context of the crusades Christoph T. Maier, "Crisis, Liturgy and the Crusade in the Twelfth and Thirteenth Centuries," *JEH* 48.4 (1997): 628–57. See also Gaposchkin, *Invisible Weapons*, 29–64, 192–225.

2.1 The Use of Relics

One of the earliest instances of rites that aimed at securing divine aid and approval during the civil war period is the use of the True Cross in battle. After Sigurd Jórsalafari had died in 1130, both his son Magnus and his alleged half-brother Harald were elected and pronounced king at different things. Magnus rushed to Oslo in order to secure himself his father's treasure, among which possibly was the relic of the True Cross. After a short period of unease and tense coregency, the two kings met in battle at Fyrileif (nowadays Färlev, Sweden) in 1134, where "King Magnus had the Holy Cross carried before him in battle."[16] The purpose of Magnus having the Cross borne before him in battle is not explicitly stated in the saga, but it is plausible that it was a way to secure victory also by spiritual means. Alan V. Murray argued in the context of the relic's use in the Levant that its main purpose in battle was a morale-raising one. In this respect, it stood in a long tradition of other relics and sacred objects that were being used in warfare in Christian Europe. The psychological effect derived from the belief that it brought divine favor and protection.[17] In that way, it was likely used by Magnus in Norway as well. At the same time, it may have been used to visually signify Magnus's greater legitimacy to the throne in competition with Harald, as Lukas Raupp has argued.[18] Magnus had the superior forces, won this battle, and forced Harald to flee. Whether the relic was thought to have had any influence on the outcome of the battle is not stated, but the fact that its usage was noted is significant in itself. In the end, Harald came back, supported by Danish forces provided by the Danish King

---

16 *Heimskringla III*, ed. Bjarni Aðalbjarnarson, Íslenzk fornrit 28 (Reykjavík: Hið íslenzka fornritafélag, 1951), 281: "Magnús konungr lét bera fyrir sér krossinn helga í orrostu." *Heimskringla III*, ed. Bjarni Aðalbjarnarson, Íslenzk fornrit 28 (Reykjavík: Hið íslenzka fornritafélag, 1951), 281.

17 Alan V. Murray, "'Mighty against the enemies of Christ': The Relic of the True Cross in the Armies of the Kingdom of Jerusalem," in *The Crusades and Their Sources: Essays Presented to Bernard Hamilton*, ed. John France and William G. Zajac (Abingdon and New York: Routledge, 1998), 217–38. See also Klaus Schreiner, "'Signa Victricia': Heilige Zeichen in kriegerischen Konflikten des Mittelalters," in *Zeichen—Rituale—Werte. Internationales Kolloquium des Sonderforschungsbereichs 496 an der Westfälischen Wilhelms-Universität Münster*, ed. Gerd Althoff, Symbolische Kommunikation und gesellschaftliche Wertesysteme 3 (Münster: Rhema, 2004), 261–72; Gaposchkin, *Invisible Weapons*, 53–62. For a comparative analysis of several sacred objects, in particular the spear and the cross, used during expeditions, see further Radosław Kotecki, "Pious Rulers, Princely Clerics, and Angels of Light: Imperial Holy War Imagery in Twelfth-Century Poland and Rus'," in *Christianity and War*, 159–88.

18 Lukas Raupp, "Importing Jerusalem: Relics of the True Cross as Political Legitimation in Early Twelfth-Century Denmark and Norway," in *Tracing the Jerusalem Code. Volume 1: The Holy City Christian Cultures in Medieval Scandinavia (ca.1100–1536)*, ed. Kristin B. Aavitsland and Line M. Bonde (Berlin and Boston MA: De Gruyter, 2021), 140–165 at 162.

Erik Emune, and managed to win against and seize Magnús in Bergen in 1135. After his victory, Harald tried unsuccessfully to get his hands on the Cross relic, which had remained in the possession of Magnús, possibly as insignia, personal talisman or for protection:[19] "Magnús had had the Holy Cross with him since the Battle of Fyrileif had taken place, and he would not tell where it had got to now."[20] Its importance to Harald is further emphasized by the fact Bishop Reinald, one of Magnús's closest associates, got hanged, when he did not reveal the whereabouts of the relic. As Raupp argues taking the relic from Magnús would have meant "both a form of denunciation of the legitimacy of his rule as well as a legitimation of Harald's claim in this context."[21] Beyond that, Harald may have been interested in gaining the relic as phylactery and a token of divine assistance and protection.

The power of the Cross relic is demonstrated by another saga episode telling of an attack by Wendish heathens. After Sigurd Jórsalafari reportedly had received the piece of the True Cross from King Baldwin I of Jerusalem, he had the relic placed in Konungahella (nowadays Kungälv, Sweden)—contrary to his promise of bringing the relic to St. Olav's grave in Nidaros. The placement was strategic at the borderlands to the heathen population and suggests that Sigurd may have laid claim to the disputed area and may have thought of it as a crusading area. The town and church of Konungahella were to serve as a relying point for future expeditions into heathen territory; the relic itself may have been used to sacralize the place and secure it against non-Christian enemies, thus mirroring its function in the Kingdom of Jerusalem.[22] Indeed, the town was attacked and plundered by Wendish forces in 1135.

When the Wendish warriors under King Racibor I ransacked the town and burnt many of its buildings, not least the fortification, the Cross displayed its power. The church itself seems to have been protected from the fire so that it had to be destroyed by hand by the Wendish: "But the fire that they had kindled in the church went out twice. Then they knocked down the church."[23] Subsequently, as *Heimskringla* tells, the Cross turned its power against the

---

19　Ibid., 162.
20　*Heimskringla III*, 287: "Krossinn helga hafði Magnús haft með sér, síðan er Fyrileifarorrosta hafði verit, ok vildi hann ekki til segja, hvar þá var kominn"; English translation after Snorri Sturluson, *Heimskringla. Volume 3: Magnús Óláfsson to Magnús Erlingsson*, trans. Alison Finlay and Anthony Faulkes (London: Viking Society for Northern Research, University College London, 2015), 176.
21　Raupp, "Importing Jerusalem," 162.
22　Ibid., 162; Janus Møller Jensen, "Korstog mod de hedenske svenskere. Nye perspektiver på Kalmarledingen 1123/24," *Collegium Medievale* 31 (2018): 151–76.
23　*Heimskringla III*, 295: "En sá eldr, er þeir hǫfðu tendrat í kirkjunni, slokknaði tysvar. Þá hjoggu þeir ofan kirkjuna."

heathens themselves, seemingly in the form of the fire they wanted to burn down the church with:

> Then the priest Andreas and his companions went to the king's ship and took with them the Holy Cross. Then the heathens were struck with fear because of the portent whereby such a great heat came over the king's ship that they all felt they were almost burning. The king told the interpreter to ask a priest why this was. He said that almighty God, in whom Christians believed, was sending them a sign of his anger, in that they, who refused to believe in their creator, dared to take in their hands the sign of his Passion.[24]

In that way, the power of the Cross relic is shown to have an effect and God working through it. The episode in Konungahella does demonstrate the power and effect of spiritual means in warfare in another aspect as well. Before the destruction of the church, the saga mentions a warrior who was protected by magic, so that no weapon could hurt him. The blessing of a weapon by a priest turned out to be an effective solution, however. As *Heimskringla* reads:

> So the priest Andreas took consecrated fire and made the sign of the cross over it and cut tinder and set it on fire and fastened it on an arrow point and gave it to Ásmundr, and he shot this arrow at the man skilled in magic, and this shot pierced him so that he was completely done for, and he fell dead to the ground.[25]

The blessing and preparation of a weapon to hurt and kill a magically protected enemy do demonstrate the use of spiritual means in warfare, though this episode seems to be singular in that instance. What this scene further shows are the significance and effect of spiritual means against heathen forces and magic. This becomes relevant against the background that several factions

---

24 Ibid., 295: "Þá fóru þeir Andréás prestr á konungsskipit ok með krossinn helga. Þá kom ótti yfir heiðingja af þeiri bending, er yfir konungsskipit kom hiti svá mikill, at allir þeir þóttusk nær brenna. Konungr bað túlkinn spyrja prest, hví svá varð. Hann sagði, at almáttigr guð, sá er kristnir menn trúðu á, sendi þeim mark reiði sinnar, er þeir dirfðusk þess at hafa með hǫndum hans píslamark, þeir er eigi vilja trúa á skapara sinn"; English translation after Snorri Sturluson, *Heimskringla*, 3:181.

25 *Heimskringla III*, 293: "Þá tók Andréás prestr vígðan eld ok signaði ok skar tundr ok lagði í eld ok setti á ǫrvarodd ok fekk Ásmundi, en hann skaut þessi ǫru at inum fjǫlkunnga manni, ok beit þetta skot svá, at honum vann at fullu, ok fell hann dauðr á jǫrð"; English translation after Snorri Sturluson, *Heimskringla*, 3:180.

accused each other of non-Christian practices and being in alliance with the devil, which would both justify the use of spiritual powers as well as mark the opponent as a legitimate target of these forces.

Heimskringla is somewhat inconsistent in regards to the relic of the True Cross. Assuming it is the same relic, which was brought to Norway by King Sigurd, placed in Konungahella, used during the Battle of Fyrileif, and then warded off the Wendish attackers, it does not indicate how the Cross was recovered after King Magnus and Bishop Reinald refused to reveal its location. After the Wendish attack on Konungahella, *Heimskringla*, tells that the priest Andreas brought the Cross "to a place of good safety,"[26] while *Ágrip* has an unnamed priest taking the Cross north to the shrine of St. Olav, where it has remained ever since.[27] *Ágrip*, thus, seems to suggest that the relic has come to where it belonged and not even a king was entitled to St. Olav's possession. That applies in particular against the backdrop of the danger that the relic could have come into the wrong hands. When *Ágrip* was written around 1190 by an anonymous author with a probable connection to the see of Nidaros, King Sverre Sigurdsson was in conflict with the archbishops, and the loss of the True Cross in the Battle of Hattin was fresh and shocking news that reached the Christian realms.[28] The Cross relic may, therefore, as Raupp hints at,[29] have become a point of conflict between the exiled Archbishop Erik and his see on one hand, and the soon-to-be excommunicated King Sverre, in which the former wanted to be sure that Sverre could not make use of the relic.

Sverris saga gives evidence that King Sverre Sigurdsson made use of other relics in the course of the civil war period. Before rising to power and defeating his main rival King Magnus Erlingsson, he had a large ship built, which he had outfitted with relics and hoped would be receiving divine aid and favor. When the ship was launched, the saga has Sverre giving a speech:

---

26   *Heimskringla III*, 295: "Andréás flutti krossinn til góðrar varðveizlu."
27   *Ágrip af Nóregskonunga sǫgum*, in *Ágrip af Nóregskonunga sǫgum. Fagrskinna, Nóregs konunga tal*, ed. Bjarni Einarsson, Íslenzk fornrit (Rekjavík: Hið Íslenzka fornritafélag, 1985), 1–54 at 48: "Ok með því at prestinum þótti eigi heilt at setja hann annat sinni undir sama váða, þá flutti hann krossinn á launungu norðr til staðarins til ins helga Óláfs, sem hann var svarinn ok nú er hann síðan." One may also note that both sagas give an inverted order of the events. *Heimskringla* ends with the Wendish attack on Konungahella, while in *Ágrip* this attack seems to happen before the Battle of Fyrileif.
28   On the loss of the Cross and its effects, see Megan Cassidy-Welch, "Before Trauma: The Crusades, Medieval Memory and Violence," *Journal of Media & Cultural Studies* 31.5 (2017): 619–27.
29   Raupp, "Importing Jerusalem," 163.

"I commit this ship to the care and keeping of the Holy Mary, and name it Maríusúð; and I pray that the Holy Virgin Mary will keep watch and guard over it. And in token hereof, I devote to Mary precious gifts better suited to God's service; mass-robes, in which the archbishop will be gloriously arrayed on festivals, if he will wear them. And I hope, in return, that she will look on these gifts with favour, and grant her help and good fortune to the ship and the crew, and to all who sail upon it." In the carved beaks of the ship, both fore and aft, the King caused holy relics to be placed.[30]

The saga notes that the Maríusúð could be launched without demolishing buildings despite some doubts due to the ship's unusually large size. This stands somewhat in contrast to the Kuflungar's failed attempt to launch the ship in Sogn, where Sverre had beached the ship for the winter. Though the saga does not give explicitly religious reasoning, the Maríusúð did not move, so the Kuflungar set fire to her and burned her, thus committing a sacrilege. Immediately afterwards, the saga gives an episode of the Kuflungar attacking Áskell týza, the leading man of the Birkibeinar in Bergen, while he was celebrating mass in church. Subsequently, one of the Kuflungar was slain by a falling stone and the Holy Rood in that church sweated miraculously blood with drops falling on the altar.[31] In that way, the saga narrative depicts the Kuflungar not only transgressing Christian norms, breaking church peace and polluting the sacred space of the church—an accusation directed at the Birkibeinar at a later point by the same faction's leader—, but hints simultaneously at the spiritual aid Sverre and his Birkibeinar received. The Maríusúð obeyed the Birkibeinar and was valuable to them; it refused itself to the Kuflungar, the opponents of Sverre.

The Maríusúð was the only ship explicitly mentioned as embellished with relics. *Sverris saga* mentions, however, another ship that Sverre managed to capture from King Magnus Erlingsson, the Óláfssúð.[32] The name may be significant itself, as these two ships were named and most likely dedicated to the two most important saints who were addressed in prayers and received thanks. Even though Óláfssúð may not have been equipped with relics like the Maríusúð—at least there is no mention of it—it might have been dedicated to

---

30 *Sverris saga*, 123–24. "Vil ek ok þetta skip gefa á traust ok trúnað innar helgu Marie ok kalla þetta skip Máríusúðina. Vil ek ok þess biðja at in Helga mær María sé vǫrn ok gæzla fyrir þessu skipi. Ok hér til jartegna vil ek gefa Máríu þá gripi er meirr falla til Guðs þjónustu, en þat eru messufǫt þau er erkibyskup er sœmiliga búinn um hátíðir þótt hann beri, ok vænta þar í mót at hon mun á líta þessar gjafar ok veita sinn styrk ok gæfu bæði skipinu ok þeim ǫllum er með því fara'. Konungr lét grafa í ennispáninn, bæði fram ok aftr, helga dóma."
31 Ibid., 156–57.
32 Ibid., 61.

its eponymous saint and possibly bestowed with gifts in order to win St. Olav's help and support.[33]

Before being burnt by the Kuflungs, the last thing the saga tells about the Maríusúð is its use in the Battle of Fimreite in 1184, in which Sverre managed to overcome his rival King Magnus Erlingsson and become sole king of Norway, as the saga points out.[34] Thus, it may have served its primary purpose of bringing fortune to those who were fighting on it and for the rightful king, though the saga does not draw a direct connection between the ship's sanctified nature and its success in battle. However, this is indicated by the fact that the Maríusúð is only mentioned in the saga, when Sverre orders the ship to be built, embellished it with relics and dedicated it to the Virgin Mary, the Battle of Fimreite, and finally her burning by the Kuflungar.[35] Thus, the ship stands in connection to spiritual powers and symbolism—either due to Sverre's sacralization of the ship and his by God sanctioned path to kingship or the miracles mark the religious transgression of his enemies.

Bjørn Bandlien has made the case that the ship could be likened to the legendary sword Durendal, which Roland used in the service of Charlemagne. It also contained relics—a tooth of St. Peter, the blood of St. Basil, hairs of St. Denis, and a piece of St. Mary's clothing. Thus, the ship and the sword became reliquaries designed for battle.[36] However, the ship was not a weapon in the same way. The Maríusúð was an unusually large ship that not only served as fighting platform but with its higher rails almost like a floating castle during sea battles. This may speak to a tendency of Sverre to sacralize spaces that were expected to have a connection to fighting, battles, and sieges. He let built a castle in Nidaros, which he dubbed Sion. This further manifested the analogous parallel between him and David, which in itself was set up by the saga narrative in several ways.[37] That did not only present him as God's chosen ruler over Norway, but may have provided some spiritually beneficial battleground in the same vein as the Maríusúð. The saga mentions the building of both castle and ship in one breath.[38]

---

33   The standard of St. Olav does apparently not play a larger role, despite the saga telling that the saint provided Sverre his standard in a prophetic dream. In this dream, St. Olav called him also Magnus like his son, fought and protected him against King Magnus and Jarl Erling foreboding his way to royal power. Later, the Birkibeinar are said to conquer the actual standard of St. Olav, which was carried into battle by the townsmen of Nidaros. Thereafter, it is not mentioned. Ibid., 8–9, 25.
34   Ibid., 141–42, 54–55.
35   Ibid., 113, 23–25, 38, 41–42, 56.
36   Bandlien, *Man or Monster?* 329; idem, "Civil War," 229.
37   *Sverris saga*, 166. See also Bandlien, *Man or Monster?* 329.
38   *Sverris saga*, 113, the castle is named Sion at 66.

2.2 Prayers

Other than relics, prayers were a way of (*pre-*)battle rites that were employed to secure spiritual aid and to secure victory. These constituted probably the most common ritual. Yet, it needs to be noted there occur some differences as well. Prayers take place rather unspecific, in connection with concrete promises for granted victories, and/or as expression of thanks after success in battle. *Heimskringla*, for instance, tells that when Erling Skakki and his troops met Jarl Sigurd af Reyri for battle at Re in 1163 both sides sang each their prayer before engaging in battle:

> Erlingr said that his men should sing the *Paternoster* and pray that the side should be victorious that was most proper. Then they [i.e. Sigurd's men] all sang the *Kyrie* in a loud voice and all beat their weapons on their shields. And at that noise three hundred men of Erlingr's troop shot off and fled. Erlingr and his troop went across the river, and the jarl's men shouted a war cry.[39]

Ultimately, Jarl Sigurd fell in this battle, while Erling and his troops won and only "lost few men," as the saga notes. The saga, again, does not note any direct spiritual influence that brought victory to Erling and his men. However, Jarl Sigurd and his men were accused of having gained their prior victories relying on magic and fighting shamefully under the cover of the darkness of night.[40] It was Erling, who uttered this accusation against his enemies to his men the day before the battle. One cannot treat this as an intended factual statement, but needs to treat it, therefore, with caution and suspicion. In another instance, the saga author is more explicit in his own uncertainty and that he merely reports some rumors rather than facts. King Håkon II (herðibreiðr) was said to rely on a bearded woman, a certain Þórdís skeggja, who was to secure his victory over King Ingi, whom Erling supported. As long as the battle was performed at night, Håkon's troops would be successful, the promise was.[41] However, the

---

39   *Heimskringla III*, 389: "Þá mælti Erlingr, at hans men skyldi syngva 'Pater noster' ok biðja, at þeir hefði gagn, er betr gegndi. Þá sungu þeir kirjál allir hátt ok bǫrðu vápnum allir á skjǫldu sína. En við þann gný skutusk á brot ok flýðu þrjú hundruð manna af Erlings liði. Gekk Erlingr ok hans lið yfir ána, en jarls men œpðu heróp"; English translation after Snorri Sturluson, *Heimskringla*, 3:243–44.
40   *Heimskringla III*, 387.
41   Ibid., 366. William of Newburgh writes that King Sverre relied on the support of a witch he calls "daughter of the devil" (*filia diaboli, potentem in maleficiis*), and in *Sverris saga* he is accused of getting help from a "gautish woman" (*kyflan gauzka*) by Bishop Nicholas Arnesson, which mirrors likely similar accusations. (William of Newburgh, *Historia rerum Anglicarum*, in *Chronicles of the Reigns of Stephen, Henry II and Richard I*, ed. R. Howlett, Rerum Britannicarum medii aevi scriptores 82 (London: Longman & Co., n.p., 1884), 231;

saga states explicitly that this is something "people say ..., but I don't know the truth of it."[42] With some ambiguity, the saga implies in these ways that Erling's foes might have made use of unchristian practices and magic and Erling's side, therefore, may have enjoyed God's favor.

The *Kyrie* is otherwise mentioned sung by King Sverre Sigurdrsson with his men only once celebrating the imminent victory towards the end of the Battle of Fimreite, when the defeated King Magnus's men fled, connecting his triumph further to spiritual aid.[43] Here, the opposition between alleged support by God or the devil becomes even more apparent. William of Newburgh writes that Sverre had in his retinue a powerful "daughter of the devil" (*filia diaboli*) skilled in magic, who paved the way to victory in the Battle of Fimreite against King Magnus Erlingsson by manipulating the elements: "the calm sea opened her mouth, and, in the sight of the enemy, swallowed up the greater portion of the royal fleet."[44] In contrast, *Sverris saga* has its protagonist thanking God rather than demonic magic. Thus, he also points to a supernatural and spiritual element that supposedly aided him and his men in battle. It does not give any specifics, however, but just states that the own men had been strengthened to win against the superior forces of King Magnus: "He granted us strength and might. We cannot claim this victory as ours in any other way than as it comes through God's will and disposal."[45] Though there existed categorical distinctions between miracles and marvels as well as miracles and magic, as Robert Bartlett has pointed out, such distinctions are seldom clear-cut, widely acknowledged beyond the circles of theologians, or easy to uphold.[46] Accusations of making use of demonic magic and witchcraft and the attempt to win divine favor and beneficial intervention were ultimately two sides of the same coin, trying to make use of spiritual powers in battle while mistrusting and

---

Sverris saga, 197). As another parallel, according to *Hákon Hákonssons saga*, in 1263 the Scots were said to use magic against King Hakon's army. *Hákonar saga Hákonarsonar II*, in *Hákonar saga Hákonarsonar II. Magnúss saga lagabœtis*, ed. Sverrir Jakobsson, Þorleifur Hauksson, and Tor Ulset, Íslenzk fornrit 32 (Reykjavík: Hið íslenzka fornritafélag, 2013), 3–267 at 249–50.

42 *Heimskringla III*, 366: "Svá segja men ... en eigi veit ek sann á því."
43 *Sverris saga*, 144.
44 William of Newburgh, *Historia rerum Anglicarum*, 231: "tranquillum mare os suum aperiens, in conspectus hostium, majorem regiæ classis partem absorbuit."
45 *Sverris saga*, 145: "hann hefir nú miklu berara en fyrr veitt oss sinn styrk ok kraft í þessi orrustu. Ok eigi megum vér kenna oss þenna fagra sigr annan veg en þetta hafi farit eftir Guðs vilja ok hans tilskipun."
46 Robert Bartlett, *The Natural and the Supernatural in the Middle Ages: The Wiles Lectures given at the Queen's University of Belfast, 2006* (Cambridge: Cambridge University Press, 2008), 17–27.

denying this one's enemy, which can get transmitted in a propagandistic and biased fashion. Such rumors and allegations, then, may stem from actual attempts of winning and securing divine favor on one side and attempts to deny this to the other side as the flip side of sacralized and integrated warfare, but that remains unprovable. Ultimately, this attests to the belief in spiritual powers affecting the events on the battlefield and the integrated nature of warfare. Further, it indicates an element of planning, or a concern thereof, as allegations of the use of magic were expressed in pre-battle contexts, and more importantly, true or not, sorcerers and clerics alike had to accompany troops in order to affect the outcome of a battle.

Other prayers addressed God and His saints more directly, probably asking for aid, intercession, or support in a less formulaic, yet still ritualized fashion than the *Paternoster* or *Kyrie*. Harald Gilli, before attacking his rival Magnus Sigurdrsson in Bergen in the winter of 1134/1135, made a promise to St. Olav if he would aid him in the upcoming battle: "King Haraldr vowed to the blessed King Óláfr in return for victory for himself to have Óláfskirkja [Church of St. Olav] built there in the town at his own expense."[47] Prior to this, Harald refused to fight during the time of Christmas and thus honored the sanctity of that time, in contrast to Magnus, who let make preparations, so that "no more than three days over Yule were kept sacred."[48] Harald appears, thus, more pious than his rival and therefore probably also more worthy of spiritual support.

Two features are important in this respect. Firstly, spiritual aid needed to be earned and reciprocated. Most often, the thanks for granted help, be it by God or the saints, are unspecified and may have been performed primarily as prayers, but included the proper treatment and sparing of one's enemies as well.[49] However, at other times, asking for help already came along with a promise made, such as in the case of Harald Gilli who pledged to build a church for St. Olav in Bergen in exchange for his assistance. That leads to the second feature. This scene sets Harald in a tradition of miracles in which St. Olav intervenes in battles and helps rulers to gain victory after they had made promises to him. Significantly, one of the first miracles that are narrated in the *Passio Olavi* tells of a chieftain in Ireland, who was Norwegian by birth, overcoming

---

47 *Heimskringla III*, 286: "Haraldr konungr hét á inn Helga Óláf konung til sigrs sér at láta gera Óláfskirkju þar í býnum með sínum eins kostnaði"; English translation after Snorri Sturluson, *Heimskringla*, 3:175.
48 *Heimskringla III*, 286: "ok eigi meirr en þrjá daga var heilagt haldit um jólin."
49 See here explicitly Sverre's victory speech to his men in *Sverris saga*, 145–46. See also at 26, where Sverre showed his thankfulness to God, the Virgin Mary and St. Olav by granting mercy to everyone who asked for it.

an unjust Irish king in battle thanks to the aid of Christ and the intervention of the saint. This chieftain had promised to have a silver cross made for the church of the martyr before the battle. Further, in the next miracle, the Byzantine Emperor is told to have vowed to build a church in Constantinople in the name of St. Olav and honor of Virgin Mary if he would aid him and his men in battle. The Byzantine Christian army subsequently won against the heathen enemy with St. Olav appearing as standard-bearer and leading the Christians into battle.[50] Bishop Nicholas Arnesson may have set himself in the same tradition, when he set up a tent, sang mass, and promised to erect a great stone church just after and before entering into battle again with his Baglar against Sverre and his Birkibeinar.[51]

Besides St. Olav, it is seldom explicitly stated who was addressed, but the repeated thanks to certain saints after battles for granting victory indicate that the prayers may have been directed at them. In a speech to his men, the saga has King Sverre declaring: "I make my prayers to God, St. Olav, and St. Sunnifa."[52] At several other instances Sverre prayed to and/or gave thanks to God, the Virgin Mary and St. Olav.[53] These may be the most important authorities of spiritual aid. The Virgin Mary who is further attested through Sverre's ship, the Maríusúð. St. Olav was further frequently invoked through the Birkibeinar's war-cry: "Forward all, Christ's men, men of the cross, and men of King Olav the Saint."[54] Even though for the most part the descriptions of battles in the narrative do not tell of a direct intervention of saints or God, the fact that Sverre thanked and attributed victory to them multiple times, according to the saga, is significant in itself.[55]

What was asked for is equally seldom stated. As was the case in the context of the crusades, the psalms and prayers were likely of both a penitential and an intercessory nature, asking God for his mercy and forgiveness of sins as well as for his assistance against enemies.[56] Yet, one can almost safely assume that there existed differences as well, at least temporarily during the struggle between King Sverre Sigurdsson, on one hand, and King Magnus Erlingsson

50   *Passio et miracula beati Olaui*, ed. Frederick Metcalfe (Oxford: Clarendon Press, 1881), 75–78.
51   *Sverris saga*, 224.
52   Ibid., 84: "Skýt ek nú mínu máli til almáttigs Guðs ok ins helga Óláfs konungs ok innar helgu Sunnefu."
53   Ibid., 25–26, 35, 123.
54   Ibid., 254; *Hákonar saga Hákonarsonar II*, 92.
55   *Sverris saga*, 35, 39, 52, 54, 58, 74, 83, 84, 135, 38, 39, 45, 46, 49, 279. It is striking that most of the references occur in the first hundred chapters, before Sverre rose to sole royal power and had overcome King Magnus Erlingsson, likely belonging to the first part of the saga denominated *Grýla*, which possibly came about under Sverre's supervision.
56   Compare with Maier, "Crisis," 632.

and his father Jarl Erling Skakki on the other. Only the latter side claimed to offer salvation for the men dying in battle, as will be shown shortly. As a general point, one can tacitly assume that, as a further analogue to the crusader context,[57] there was for the most part no sense of what form possible aid would take in a specific context. Examples range from direct interventions of St. Olav in battle to more abstract allusions that one's own side got strengthened and won thanks to spiritual support. As an aside, excommunication may have been expected to weaken the banned and opponent side, or at least render their weapons less effective, as will be shown below.

Prayers did have an effect. This was not only communicated through miracles in *vitae* and saints' lives but is also suggested by the saga literature, in which in particular St. Olav was invoked and intervened.[58] Further, a few instances in *Sverris saga* present miraculous situations to its readers. The initial stages of his struggle for kingship were defined by some marches through wilderness and some distress. Once, when the exhausted Birkibeinar crossed a large lake in a forest with self-built rafts, the saga notes the miraculous nature of the raft sinking like a stone just after Sverre had left the raft as the last men safely arrived at the shore.[59] When Sverre and his men face a severe winter storm on a mountain, and some considered killing themselves, Sverre's prayers and God's mercy turned the storm into mild summer weather.[60] Perhaps most importantly in the context of battle and warfare, Sverre and his men were saved during a battle with his rival Magnus, who had superior forces, due to a fog that suddenly appeared prompted by Sverre's prayers. As Magnus's were faster and coming close, Sverre betook himself therefore to prayer, and called upon King Olav the Saint pleading for his men with much eloquence. And at that instant, a mist came down on the sea, so thick that they could not see from one ship to another.[61]

2.3 *The Kissing of Churches*

The polarization and the attempt to make use of prayers and other spiritual weapons seem to have been most prevalent during the conflict between the

---

57 James B. MacGregor, "Negotiating Knightly Piety: The Cult of the Warrior-Saints in the West, ca.1070–ca.1200," *ChH* 73.3 (2004): 317–45 at 341.
58 See, apart from earlier examples, *Morkinskinna I*, ed. Þórður Ingi Guðjónsson and Ármann Jakobsson (Reykjavík: Hið íslenzka fornritafélag, 2011), 58–59 (Duke Ótti gets healed through St. Olav's belt), 60–63 (St. Olav appears in a dream relating to a subsequent battle and in battle itself).
59 *Sverris saga*, 21–22.
60 Ibid., 34–35.
61 Ibid., 52.

RELIGIOUS RITES AND INTEGRATED WARFARE IN CIVIL WAR ERA   133

kings Sverre Sigurdsson and Magnus Erlingsson, and after the latter's death the Baglar led by Bishop Nicholas. One ritual related to prayers and thanksgiving and these conflicts occur in *Sverris saga* and appears as somewhat unique. The kissing of churches is mentioned three times in *Sverris saga*; other sagas don't mention it. How unique and idiosyncratic the ritual was, however, is hard to determine. It may be that only the author of *Sverris saga* found it noteworthy enough, yet it may have appeared in other contexts as well.

In one instance, it is most clearly intended to grant divine support before a battle. Prior to the Battle of Kalvskinnet in 1179, after a night of excessive drinking, Jarl Erling Skakki summoned his troops to meet the approaching Birkibeinar ready for battle. The saga tells that

> the jarl ... marched through the town along the street to Christ Church, which he kissed. He was here joined by King Magnus with his standard, by Sigurd Nikolásson, Jon of Randaberg, and Ivar Horti, with their companies. Many of the men fell on their knees and said their prayers. The jarl then turned away to leave the church, saying to his men: "Stand up and take your weapons. Some of us maybe will have the opportunity of resting here after a while."[62]

As in other cases, it is not stated who, if anyone, was directly addressed and what was asked for. It is thinkable that Erling and his men asked for divine aid in battle, yet is even more plausible that the prayers aimed also at forgiveness for sin and personal salvation. The prayers of Erling's men may also be understood in the context of the promised salvation that King Sverre mentions after his victory and at the burial of the Erling directly after this battle. Interestingly and in contrast to their opponents, the prayers on the side of the Birkibeinar seem to have been performed only by Sverre himself. As the saga reads, "And when he came across the hill at Feginsbrekka [Hill of Grace], he [i.e. Sverre] alighted from his horse, fell upon his knees, and said his prayers."[63]

This may highlight some differences regarding the authorities and performances of prayers between the two opposing factions. Erling Skakki fell in battle and during the following burial in Nidaros Sverre hold a speech. Here,

---

62   Ibid., 59: "Ok er jarl kom á land ok skipsǫgn hans ok merki gekk hann upp um bœinn at stræti ok minntisk til Kristkirkju. Ok þar kom þá til hans Magnús konungr með sínu merki ok sveit, Sigurðr Nikolásson ok Jón af Randabergi, Ívarr horti. Lǫgðusk þá margir menn á kné ok báðusk fyrir. Því næst snerisk jarl frá kirkjunni ok mælti til sinna mann: 'Standið upp ok takið vápn yður. Vera kann at nǫkkurum sé kostr at liggja hér um hríð.'"
63   Ibid., 57: "Ok er hann kom yfir ásinn á Feginsbrekku þá steig hann af baki ok fell á kné ok baðsk fyrir."

the saga has him mentioning the promise made to the men fighting on behalf of King Magnus Erlingsson:

> For, indeed, it is known to many that Archbishop Øystein and many other learned men have constantly said concerning all who die fighting for King Magnus and defending his land, that their souls will enter Paradise before their blood is could upon the ground. We may here rejoice at the sanctity of many men who have become saints, if what the Archbishop said is true, and all these have become saints who died fighting under Jarl Erling.[64]

The sarcastic tone has been noted,[65] implying that the followers of Erling and Magnus had been deceived into believing they would enter paradise and attain salvation if they died in the struggle against him. Given that the saga was composed relatively close in time and at least in part under guidance of Sverre himself, one can assume that the speech in the saga reflects what he actually said in Nidaros or what he wanted the audience to believe he had said. This refers to the promise of salvation credible. It also echoes the promise of the *Canones Nidrosienses*, article 2, that those who were killed fighting for the *patria* were granted eternal salvation.[66] Although an exact date cannot be safely established, it is generally assumed that Archbishop Øystein was involved in the creation of *Canones Nidrosienses*.[67] As Haki Antonsson has argued, this suggests that, firstly, the clause from the *Canones Nidrosienses* 2 was used in the propaganda war between the rival factions during the Norwegian civil war. This, he points out, constitutes a remarkably early example of the church offering spiritual rewards to those fighting Christian enemies. However, one might

---

64 Ibid., 61–62: "En þat er sem mǫrgum man kunnigt vera at Eysteinn erkibyskup ok margir aðrir lendir menn hafa jafnan sagt, at allir þeir menn er berðisk með Magnúsi konungi ok verði land hans ok létisk með því, at sálur þeira manna allra væri fyrr í Paradísu en blóðit væri kalt á jǫrðunni. Nú megum vér allir fagna hér svá margra manna heilagleik sem hér munu helgir hafa orðit ef þetta er svá sem erkibyskup hefir sagt, at allir sé þeir orðnir helgir menn er fallit hafa með Erlingi jarli."

65 Peter Foote, "Secular Attitudes in Early Iceland," in *"Aurvandilstá": Norse Studies*, ed. Michael Barnes, Hans Bekker-Nielsen, and Gerd Wolfgang Weber (Odense: Odense University Press, 1984), 31–46 at 40–42; Haki Antonsson, "Some Observations on Martyrdom in Post-Conversion Scandinavia," *Saga-Book* 28 (2004): 70–94 at 88–89.

66 *Latinske dokument til norks historie fram til år 1204*, ed. Eirik Vandvik (Oslo: Det norske samlaget, 1959), 42–44 (no. 7); Vegard Skånland, *Det eldste norske provinsialstatutt* (Oslo: Universitetsforlaget, 1969), 188–89.

67 The creation of the document has been connected to the establishment of the archbishopric of Nidaros in 1152/1153, Magnus Erlingsson's coronation, the latter part of Magnus's reign, or the early years of King Sverre Sigurdsson. See with references Antonsson, "Some Observations," 80.

note that this is the context which it may have made it important to associate one's enemies with unchristian behavior, the use of magic, and being in alliance with the devil. Secondly, rhetorical and emotive language was likely used to convey this message to King Magnus's followers; this language may well be close to the formulations Sverre shall have used in his speech. Lastly, it seems that the distinction between eternal salvation and martyrdom would have become blurred at the height of the civil war period, which constitutes a parallel to the crusades.[68]

The noted differences in the mode of prayer as well as the archbishop's highlighted role may be significant and suggest two things. Firstly, the collective nature of the prayer of Erling's men may not be that significant, as there are other instances of men praying collectively and that appears to have been fairly common. However, considering the promise of salvation in connection to the idea of martyrdom, this indicates that the men may have prayed rather for forgiveness for sins and personal salvation in case they may die in battle. The Birkibeinar fighting on Sverre's behalf may have prayed for similar things, at least in terms of the forgiveness for sins, but it is hardly likely that they would have fought in the same hope of their own salvation. Secondly, the collective nature of Erling's followers stands in contrast to Sverre praying individually, without his men mentioned or—seemingly—partaking. Thus, Sverre is singled out as pious, yet the scene may also indicate something further. Sverre acted in the position of the Birkibeinar's spiritual leader in the same vein as Archbishop Øystein was the spiritual leader of his opponents. As Sverre's speech at Erling's burial suggests, it was Archbishop Øystein who should procure spiritual help in battle. In a mocking tone, according to the saga, he noted that "his intercessions with the almighty God would be a big help to men, if so be that the archbishop was not somewhat biased in his pleading when he uttered the words."[69] It seems, thus, that intercessions and pleas for success in battle may have primarily been performed by clerics for the collective body of the army, while they could be supplemented by the warriors' prayers. Sverre, in this instance, embraced his double role as both secular and spiritual leader of his men, as he also explicitly stated,[70] proving himself as the more effective intercessor before God.[71]

---

68   Antonsson, "Some Observations," 89.
69   *Sverris saga*, 62: "Megum vér þat ætla at hans árnaðarorð mun verða mikil hjálp við allsvaldanda Guð, ef eigi er þat at erkibyskup hafi nǫkkut vinhallr verit í málinu þá er hann sagði þetta."
70   This will be discussed in more detail further down below.
71   His closer connection is otherwise attested, according to the saga, through his foresight in his dreams. For his dreams, see esp. Lars Lönnroth, "Sverrir's Dreams," *Scripta Islandica* 57 (2006): 97–110. As Orning and Rosén point out, *Sverris saga*, for the most part, "creates

At other times the kissing of churches was more intended to signify gratitude for the achieved victory. After repelling peasants, initially taken for King Magnus and his men, Sverre, "gave quarter to all who asked; and as he marched through the town he kissed all the chief churches."[72] Sverre kissing the churches in Bergen may then give expression to his thanks for the divine help he thought was granted him and secured victory without any loss against a foe much bigger, as the saga emphasizes: "no expedition so imposing in magnitude as theirs [i.e. the peasants] had ever fared worse."[73] This episode may be meaningful in showing Sverre's thankfulness, mercy, and divine favor. However, it gains in significance because it stands in contrast to a somewhat similar episode, in which some Birkibeinar who wanted to show their gratitude when having gained victory against peasants; "and many kissed the church. And the king said: 'You Birkibeinar are much more devout now than before. You behave as if you must lick every church you come near. It is not your habit to pay much regard to churches.'"[74] There are two points to Sverre's criticism. The gratitude was dishonest and undeserved, as it came without commitment in battle since these men had sought shelter in a church. Their flight marked them as cowards and showed their lack of trust in spiritual aid. Trust and belief always come with a degree of and despite uncertainty.[75] The apparent lack of trust and, subsequently, also lack of honest piety is echoed in Sverre's criticism. Concomitantly, it was premature. The battle was not yet over, and still the men who had not properly fought thanked God and the saints, and behaved as if the fighting was over.

2.4   Excommunication

The Norwegian civil war period was determined by different lines of conflicts. It did not only constitute a war of succession between different rivalling kings but was also fought over different claims and notions of authority over the church. Soon after the foundation of the archbishopric in Nidaros in 1152 or 1153, Archbishop Øystein managed to obtain the privileges and royal

---

an ambiguity around the question of whether Sverrir's success derives from his personal power or from God." Orning and Rosén, "*Sverris saga*," 77.

72   *Sverris saga*, 79: " ok gaf hann ǫllum grið er á hans vald kómu. Gekk konungr út um bœinn ok minntisk þá til allra hǫfuðkirkna."

73   Ibid., 79: "at aldri varð verri ferð farin en sú við jafnmiklu liði."

74   Ibid., 258: "en margir menn minntusk til kirkna. Þá mælti konungr: 'Miklu eru þér nú, Birkibeinar, trúmeiri en fyrr. Þér látið nú sem þér skulið sleikja hverja kirkju er þér komið til. Er at þér rœkið lítt kirkjur.'"

75   Ian Forrest, *Trustworthy Men: How Inequality & Faith Made the Medieval Church* (Princeton NJ and Oxford: Princeton University Press, 2018), 15–32, esp. 18–21, 30.

approval in regards to the self-administration the church demanded due to an arrangement with the then sitting King Magnus and his father Erling Skakki in exchange for the crowing of the young king in 1163/1164. The newly gained privileges were, however, soon threatened by the royal pretender Sverre Sigurdsson, who propagated rather an older system of proprietary churches, built and controlled by secular powers. Thus, he came into conflict with the ecclesiastical actors, especially the Archbishops Øystein and Erik Ívarsson, with whom Sverre disputed also the archbishops' need for and legitimacy of an armed military following. The dispute was eventually settled by Sverre's son Håkon who reconciled with the Norwegian bishops and confirmed the privileges they had obtained.[76] Denying the granted privileges and freedoms, King Sverre threatened the power and position of the church in Norway, thus providing the reason for ecclesiastical actors to side with his opponents and partake in the military affairs during that time. This is the issue that became increasingly prevalent and that led to his excommunication in the conflicts after he had defeated King Magnus.[77]

Erik Ívarsson became archbishop in 1188. Already two years he fled Norway and went into exile, where he stayed with Archbishop Absalon in Lund. Neither Absalon nor King Knut of Denmark were willing to support the fight against Sverre with troops, therefore the conflict was fought with "spiritual weapons," as Alexander Bugge noted already in 1916. Despite his observation and formulation, Bugge reduces the effects of excommunication as spiritual weapon to a significant reduction in support Sverre received, in particular from ecclesiastical actors.[78] This is significant but ignores other implications. As will be shown, this was meant to have an effect on the physical aspects of warfare as well. Archbishop Erik stayed outside of Norway and his diocese for the rest of Sverre's reign. In 1194 he placed Sverre under ban with backing of Pope Celestine III. The latest in 1199 all the other Norwegian bishops seem to

---

76 Bǫglunga saga, in Hákonar saga Hákonarsonar I: Bǫglunga saga, ed. Þorleifur Hauksson, Sverrir Jakobsson, and Tor Ulset, Íslenzk Fornrit 31 (Reykjavík: Hið íslenzka fornritafélag, 2013), 3–146, here 4; Kong Haakon Sverresöns Retterbod om Kirkens Friheder, in Norges gamle love indtil 1387, ed. R. Keyser et al. (Christiania: Chr. Gröhndahl, 1846), 444–45.

77 See on the disputes and the issue of libertas ecclesiae in Norway, among others, Sverre Bagge, "Den heroiske tid—kirkereform og kirkekamp 1153–1214," in "Ecclesia Nidrosiensis." Søkelys på Nidaroskirkens og Nidarosprovinsens historie, ed. Steinar Imsen (Trondheim: Tapir Akademisk Forlag, 2003); Jón Viðar Sigurðsson, Det norrøne samfunnet. Vikingen, kongen, erkebiskopen og bonden (Oslo: Pax Forlag, 2008), 161–76.

78 Alexander Bugge, Norges historie andet binds anden del tidsrummet 1103–1319 (Kristiania: Aschehoug & Co., 1916), 192–213. He notes that Erik employed spiritual weapons ("aandelige vaaben"), ultimately meaning excommunication, at 192.

have left the country and joined the archbishop in Denmark in order to avoid banishment for themselves.[79]

Significantly, after Archbishop Erik had sailed to Denmark, he lost his sight and became blind. Blindness is a punishment that has fallen on enemies of God in scripture, but maybe even more importantly in the Norse context, it has fallen on an enemy of St. Olav in at least one instance as well.[80] When the saga tells of Sverre's excommunication, which was proclaimed every Sunday in the chancel, it has Sverre responding that the ban was the reason for Erik's blindness turning his curse on himself: "The ban and curse, ... which he has uttered against me have fallen upon his own eyes, and he is now blind through them. Those who do the work of banning will fall under the ban."[81] In his propagandistic defense *A Speech against the bishops*, probably written 1198, Sverre rhetorically employed a body metaphor to describe different functions to members of society. The eyes represent the bishops "who should point us to the right way and the safe road ... and should moreover have a careful oversight of all members." Yet, "our bishops and other rulers, who should watch over Christianity, are blinded by covetousness, excess, ambition, arrogance, and injustice."[82] All of the Norwegian bishops were struck by metaphorical blindness that had them neglect their duty. This blindness made them unable to wield the spiritual sword, especially against the rightful king of Norway, who they should accept as the highest authority: "The King is set above all other dignitaries; for the King has to direct the bishop or the archbishop to do justice."[83] The archbishop, in addition, was struck by an actual blindness, as he was not only a sinner and unjust, but tried to wield spiritual means against the king, which turned against himself.

The excommunication of Sverre and the Birkibeinar was expected to have an effect in physical battle. Prior to a battle in Oslo in 1197 between the Birkibeinar and the Baglar factions, Bishop Nicholas, leader of the Baglar, assured his men that, due to the excommunication, the weapons of the Birkibeinar will be

---

79　See also Kåre Lunden, *Norge under Sverreætten 1177–1319*, ed. Knut Mykland, Norges Historie 3 (Oslo: J.W. Cappelens Forlag, 1976), 83.

80　Gen 19:11; Deut 28:28, 2 Kings 6:18. See pain to the eyes as punishment for speaking threateningly to St. Olav in his shrine. *Heimskringla III*, 232.

81　*Sverris saga*, 187: "ok þat sama bann ok blótan, segir hann, er hann nefnir mik til, þat hefir nú drifit í augu hans, ok er hann nú fyrir því blindr. Munu þeir í banni vera er bannsverk gera."

82　*En tale mot biskopene: En sproglig-historisk undersøkelse*, ed. Anne Holtsmark (Oslo: Dybwad, 1931), 2: "Ok blíndar nu biskupa vara ok aðra hofdíngia þa er kristní skilldi gæta, fesínkí ok vhof agírnd, dramb ok ranglæte."

83　Ibid., 12: "Kononngr er skipaðr ífuir allar aðrar tignir þuí at kononngr skall her stíorna till retlætes biskupi æðr erchibiskupi."

ineffective and may also have a discouraging effect: "The Birkibeinar are under ban so that their swords will not bite, and they will not dare to begin the attack. Be of good courage, therefore; if Sverre attacks us, the hand of death is upon him."[84] Nicholas's statement may have been meant to motivate and embolden his men and one may want to be careful not to take it at face value, not least as it is ascribed to the bishop by an unsympathetic author. However, one should not dismiss the statement out of hand either. Pre-battle speeches in historiography are usually invented, that is the case for saga literature as well.[85] Yet, they still mirror the values deemed most motivating and appreciated by contemporary warriors as well as their relative hierarchy in which related to each other. Even though Nicholas's statement is likely not to be understood literally, the saga seems to reflect an expectation that excommunication should have weakened the Birkibeinar. Excommunication wouldn't have turned the Birkibeinar's weapons useless—merely one hurt man could be seen as sufficient evidence against that—, but there seems to have been an expectation to render the weapons less effective. However, this turned not out to be the case in the course of battle, which the Birkibeinar won. The saga reads:

> A man spoke to the bishop: "Ride forward, Sire, and hard," he said, "our men need you to strengthen them; the Birkibeins' swords seem to us to be biting now." But the bishop replied: "Let us ride off as fast as we can, the devil got loose."[86]

It is not entirely clear what was expected of Nicholas, how he should "strengthen" his men. The saga does note that he was accompanied by several clerics when the battle began and both sides raised their war cry. It is possible that he was not only to act as commander of his troops but spiritual support and intercessor before God and the saints, supporting his men with his prayers. What can be said based on this account with some certainty, however,

---

84   *Sverris saga*, 202: "Eru Birkibeinar svá bannsettir at sverðin þeira munu ekki bíta, ok eigi munu þeir þora at at leggja. Verði þér nú vel við. Feigr mun hann nú, Sverrir, ef hann leggr at."
85   Hallvard Lie, *Studier i Heimskringlas stil. Dialogene og talene*, Skrifter utgitt av Det Norske Videnskaps-Akademi i Oslo II. Hist.-Filos. Klasse. 1936 5 (Oslo, 1937), 105–5, 22–25 and passim; James E. Knirk, *Oratory in the King's Sagas* (Oslo: Universitetsforlaget, 1981), 114–18, 229–30 and passim.
86   *Sverris saga*, 202: "Einn maðr mælti til byskups: 'Herra, ríðið nú fram hart, því at várir menn þurfu nú at þeir treystið þá. Lízk oss svá sem Birkibeinum bíti nú sverðin'. Þá mælti byskup: 'Ríðum undan nú. Lauss er djǫfullinn nú orðinn.'"

excommunication did play a role in military strategizing and was expected to have some effect on the physical encounter during battle, as the saga indicates.

Another episode, in contrast, does not indicate a direct influence of excommunication on military events. When Bishop Nicholas and his men laid siege to the castle held by Birkibeinar in Nidaros sometime after the battle in Oslo that same year, he threatened Thorstein kúgaðr: "It is unwise to hold the castle and to be under the ban. You will suffer more in another place."[87] The statement functions here as a threat in a twofold way. On one hand, Thorstein is possibly and rather subtly told that he will suffer in hell. On the other hand, quite explicitly, Nicholas threatens that he will burn and plunder Thorstein's properties and homestead. In any case, the excommunication was not meant to have a physical effect during the fighting, but rather have an effect as deterrent and ideological justification. As an outlaw who stood outside the Christian community and society, one could not blame those who would potentially kill Thorstein. Dying while under ban, he would eventually end up in hell. Thus, it seems Nicholas threatened Thorstein with spiritual and temporal consequences if he would not comply with the bishop's demands, but there's no sign of an expectation of an advantage in the case of combat or siege. The threat may have worked, as the saga tells that Thorstein betrayed his men and abandoned the castle to Nicholas and his men.[88]

Sverre was clearly bothered by the excommunication, despite that no losses or defeats could be attributed to it, according to the saga. However, as the saga also tells, Sverre presents letters exonerating him, which he claims to have been intercepted. The letters, he claimed, were sent by the pope writing that the king spoke more truthfully than the archbishop.[89] At the end of his life, he instructed his son Håkon to seek reconciliation with the church. According to the saga, he wanted that his body to be displayed with his face uncovered so that people could see the marks that the excommunication would have left on it—or the lack of it. The saga reports that all who saw his body could give the testimony of never having seen a more beautiful corpse.[90] The saga, then, does not explicitly call Sverre a saint but depicts him as having all the qualities to be one.[91] In that way, it also denies that the excommunication was effective or justified, hinting at some suspicion or concern in this regard.

---

87   Ibid., 206: "Óráðligt er þér at halda borgina ok vera í banni."
88   Ibid., 206–7.
89   Ibid., 193.
90   Ibid., 280.
91   It has also been noted that the *Grýla*, the first part of *Sverris saga*, contains significant hagiographic influences, which inscribed a religious and godly pattern into Sverre's biography. See with references ibid., lv–lviii.

3 Different Claims to Leadership in Integrated War and Ritual

In the course of the civil war period, several royal pretenders and rivalling kings claimed that their cause was hallowed by divine will. Frequently, this stands in contrast with allegations against the same pretenders and kings having provoked God's wrath, making use of unchristian practices, and of being in alliance with demonic force or even the devil. Harald Gilli's success, for instance, is described in Halldórr skvaldri's skaldic poem *Haraldsdrápa* as part of God's plan: "Now, wealth-sender, the whole of Norway has fallen under your sway. Your fortune lies on the green land. That is God's plan."[92] After his death, he was said to be a saint, which supposedly was to grant his sons legitimacy and secure support for them.[93] *Morkinskinna*, however, paints a rather different picture of Harald's way of gaining sole power in Norway. Here, the saga emphasizes that Harald's treatment of his rival Magnus and, in particular, Bishop Reinald put the whole of Norway under God's wrath, and is therefore responsible for the lengthy period of conflict, unrest and violence: "With this deed, the king grieved the hearts and minds of all good men, and it is probable that this crime doomed Norway and all who were implicated and were subject to excommunication and God's wrath."[94]

Significantly, these references to divine support and hallowed causes occur in opposition to one another and seldom entirely on their own, thus suggesting

---

[92] *Morkinskinna II*, ed. Þórður Ingi Guðjónsson and Ármann Jakobsson (Reykjavík: Hið íslenzka fornritafélag, 2011), 163: "Nús, auðsendir, undir / allr Nóregr þik fallinn; / þín liggr gipt á grœnu /—Goðs ráð er þat—láði"; English translation after Foote, "Secular Attitudes," 36.

[93] *Heimskringla III*, 303. Reportedly, Harald was killed lying in bed with his mistress. Ibid., 300–1. Harald was hardly unique in gaining a reputation as a saint. Throughout Scandinavia, martyr-cults were promoted by dynastic branches and factions in order to consolidate their power and grant the often young heirs of a late king legitimacy and rallying point for followers. As many rival kings suffered a violent death during the civil war period, and this seems to have been the only real prerequisite to be considered a martyr, several deceased kings were apparently considered holy by parts of the population. See Antonsson, "Some Observations," 71–77.

[94] *Morkinskinna II*, 162: "Hryggði hann í þessu allra góðra mann hugi ok hjǫrtu, ok er glíkligt at þetta óverkan hafi dregit Nóreg til mikillar ógiptu ok þeim er gerðu ok fellu með í bann ok Guðs reiði." Here, it is in agreement with other sources such as Theodoricus Monachus's chronicle who blames Harald Gilli for the disorder, injustice, and atrocities of the civil war period and refuses to write about the time after his arrival. Theodoricus, *"De antiquitate regum Norwagiensium." On the Old Norwegian Kings*, ed. Egil Kraggerud (Oslo: Novus, 2018), 126–27. On the depiction of Harald Gilli in different sources and historiography, see Knut Arstad, "'… han var svag af Chrakteer og uden ringeste Herskergaver, hvilket også fremgaar af hele hans Historie'. En undersøkelse av Harald Gilles ettermæle," *HT* 78.4 (1999): 435–60.

a polarization based on mutual religious claims and allegations, at least at times. Harald's victory over Magnus Sigurdsson and his claim that this was rooted in God's plan stand in contrast with Magnus's use of the True Cross in the Battle of Fyrisleif as well as his condemnation in *Morkinskinna*. Sverre's claims of enjoying divine support and his thanks to God and the saints for it stand in contrast to claims of his enemies of having just and sacred cause; accusations of him being apostate and in alliance with the devil are mirrored by the alliance of church and crown in person of Archbishop Øystein and King Magnus. This may speak for an increased tendency to seek spiritual aid in warfare during the twelfth-century civil war period and its character as, at least in part, holy war on one hand; and on the other hand, it suggests that claims of having a divinely justified cause and divine support stood in competition to one another. These claims were claimed for one's own faction, denied the opponent's side, and stood in the context of different claims to legitimacy and authority.

Such competing claims at the height of an ideological conflict may have led to enhanced modes of distinction in contrast to opposing factions. This seems to be true, in particular, of the conflicts of King Sverre on one side, and at first King Magnus, later Bishop Nicholas on the other side. It is important to note that this stands in connection to the involvement of the church and Sverre's opposition to the freedoms and privileges that were granted to it but does not seem typical for the whole civil war period in Norway. It is especially Sverre's reign and the resistance he faces in which the use of spiritual weapons and arguments appear as most frequent and prevalent.

The conflict between King Magnus, on one hand, and his contender Sverre, on the other, is depicted in an almost shismogenic fashion, that is as a mutual self-definition against the values of each other.[95] According to *Sverris saga*, Magnus had a reputation as a heavy drinker (*drykkjumaðr mikill*) as well as a notorious womanizer (*kvennamaðr mikill*).[96] Several claimants to the throne claimed to be his son, despite he appears to have never married and the

---

95 The term schismogenesis was coined by Gregory Bateson to describe people's tendency to define themselves against each other in a process where individual and groups exaggerate the differences between them and distance themselves from the other group by adapting different habits, ideologies, or moralities. Gregory Bateson, "Culture Contact and Schismogenesis," *Man* 35 (1935): 178–83. See also David Graeber, "Culture as Creative Refusal," *The Cambridge Journal of Anthropology* 31.2 (2013): 1–19.

96 *Sverris saga*, 151. In his polemic *A Speech against the Bishops*, Sverre accused clerics, among other crimes, of seducing other men's wives (*konor*), daughters (*dóttr*), and other kinswomen (*frendkonor*). By that logic Sverre was even more in line with Christian law and virtue than the clerics of the Norwegian church. *En tale mot biskopene*, 3.

importance of legitimate sons born in wedlock in the law of succession that was issued in the context of his crowing in 1163/1164. These features do not necessarily need to be understood as negative traits,[97] but they stand in striking contrast to the counter-image that is drawn of Sverre, who appears as more modest and pious. In an almost monkish fashion, Sverre supposedly had no other relationship to women other than his wife.[98] He never drank too much and supposedly only ate one meal a day.[99] From his men, he demanded very much the same, moderation regarding the consumption of alcohol as well as proper behavior in times of peace. "All things should be accompanied by moderation. Warriors in times of peace should be gentle as lambs, but in war fierce as lions," as *Sverris saga* has him summarizing in a speech.[100] The lion-and-sheep-allegory reminds of Bernard Clairvaux's description of the Knights Templar as marvelous hybrids of monks and knights: "Indeed, in a wondrous and unique manner they appear gentler than lambs, yet fiercer than lions."[101] This seemed to underlie the notion of warrior ideal that Sverre had, according to the saga, though a direct influence cannot be proven.[102]

In addition, the two rivals represent two sides in regard to the issue of *libertas ecclesiae*. While Magnus was allied with the archbishop of Norway, who would take the lead of the spiritual side in the warfare, Sverre claimed that same position for himself. At the burial of Magnus's father Jarl Erling, supposedly the real leader and decision-maker up until this point, Sverrre is reported stating: "Times are greatly changed, as you may see, and have taken a marvelous turn, when one man stands in the place of three; of king, of jarl, of archbishop, and I am that one."[103]

---

97 Bagge understands them as "essential part of the culture of traditional kingship;" and for Bandlien they have "a flavour of a traditional warrior ethos." Sverre Bagge, *From Gang Leader to the Lord's Anointed: Kingship in "Sverris saga" and "Hákonar saga Hákonarsonar,"* The Viking collection 8 (Odense: Odense University Press, 1996), 73; Bandlien, *Man or Monster?* 324.
98 For accusations of having had a woman before her, see *Sverris saga*, 188. See further Bjørn Bandlien, *Strategies of Passion: Love and Marriage in Medieval Iceland and Norway*, MTCN 6 (Turnhout: Brepols, 2005), 53–61.
99 *Sverris saga*, 280.
100 Ibid., 160: "Því at ǫllum hlutum skyldi stilling fylgja. Hermenn skyldu vera hógværir í friði sem lamb, en í ófriði ágjarnir sem león."
101 Bernard of Clairvaux, *Ad milites Templi. De laude novae militiae*, 221: "Ita denique miro quodam ac singulari modo cernuntur et agnis mitiores, et leonibus ferociores."
102 See also Bandlien, *Man or Monster?* 328.
103 *Sverris saga*, 61: "Aldaskipti er mikit orðit, sem þér meguð sjá, ok er undarliga orðit er einn maðr er nú fyrir þrjá: einn fyrir konung ok einn fyrir jarl, einn fyrir erkibyskup, ok em ek sá."

Sverre's claim to represent the three highest authorities of Norway is unique. This may represent a reaction to his rival's close alliance with the church as well as build on Sverre's education and the critique he faced because of it. King Magnus was crowned lacking the traditional grounds of legitimacy of being a former king's son and in exchange for privileges to the church. In addition, Archbishop Øystein was said to be Magnus's dearest and most intimate friend (*inn mesti ástvin*) indicating the close partnership between the two.[104] Sverre, in contrast, was clerically educated and possibly ordained as priest.[105] Therefore, he faced constant criticism; his opponents referred to him as "priest" or "priest of the devil" (*djǫfulsprestr*), effectively denouncing every legitimacy of his claims to the throne.[106] Rather than conceding his claims to the throne, it seems Sverre embraced the possibility to claim and combine the highest secular and spiritual authorities in the Norwegian realm in his person, at least for some time. After Sverre had won over Magnus in 1184 and gained sole kingship for some time, other rivals rose up against him who seem to have face the same criticism by Sverre's Birkibeinar due to their past as monks.[107] In particular before 1184, then, Sverre seems to have laid claim to rightfully wield both temporal and spiritual swords as well as having privileged access to God and his saints, which is reflected in the miracles and his role when giving praying mostly alone in favor of his faction.

The conflict between Sverre and Bishop Nicholas Arnesson, by contrast, demonstrated not Sverre's spiritual leadership but rather the ineffectiveness of spiritual weapons that were unjustly employed against him and his men. Nicholas and Sverre had a somewhat tense relationship beforehand, yet for a brief period they reconciled and Nicholas took part in the crowning ceremony of Sverre. After Nicholas had reconciled with Archbishop Erik in Denmark, he returned to Norway and in 1196 took on the leadership of the Baglar faction in open conflict against Sverre, while the latter was excommunicated. As previously shown, the excommunication was expected to have some effect in physical combat. Yet as *Sverris saga* emphasizes, it did not turn out to an efficient or powerful means against the Birkibeinar in battle.

The fight for the *libertas ecclesiae*, Sverre's excommunication, and in extension the framing of the conflicts, at least in part, as holy war provided the context in which Bishop Nicholas saw himself allowed to act beyond what

---

104   Ibid., 7.
105   For a discussion on that, see Magnús Stefánsson, "Kong Sverre—prest og sønn av Sigurd Munn?" in *Festskrift til Ludvig Holm-Olsen på hans 70-årsdag den 9. juni 1984* (Øvre Ervik: Alvheim & Eide Akademisk Forlag, 1984), 287–307.
106   *Sverris saga*, 55, 58, 129, 53, 232, 36.
107   Ibid., 156–57, 75–76.

was usually permitted clerics in warfare. Accordingly, *Sverris saga* reports him bearing physical weapons—a sword and a shield—challenging Sverre to a duel allegedly with the pope's approval. No explicit papal authorization is known. Correspondence between the Norwegian archbishops and the papacy reflects, however, ongoing debates on proper clerical conduct in Norway in the late twelfth century, in which various popes forbid the interaction and support for excommunicates, bearing of weapons, or commanding of ships. The clerics' weapons were prayers and tears, and "no warrior of God should involve himself in secular affairs," as Clement III made clear.[108] However, an 'impending grave necessity', mentioned in a letter of Celestine III from 1194, may have permitted Bishop Nicholas to fight for the church's freedom and privileges.[109] Despite bearing weapons and being willing to use them, he is not depicted actively taking part in physical combat. Evidence for his commanding troops is clearer. As such, he was responsible for the burning of churches and the city of Bergen in 1198, which he justified with the pollution of those places due to the presence of the excommunicated Birkibeinar.[110] The same year Pope Innocent III called Sverre an excommunicated, apostate, enemy of God and the saints in a letter to the Icelandic bishops.[111]

Sverris saga suggests that accusations of being unchristian, in alliance with the devil, and the employment of spiritual weapons were of mutual character. In this vein, Nicholas, the leader of the Baglar, was accused of being a "false bishop" (*villubyskup*), while the Baglar were said to be "devil's men" (*djǫfulsmenn*) and under ban.[112] The saga gives this information in a speech by Thorstein kúgaðr, the man who had surrendered the castle in Nidaros to the Baglar in secret, and who in this scene fell to the king's feet and begged for his pardon. Thus, ascribed to a man in distress, the saga still leaves some ambiguity and it implies that Thorstein simply told what Sverre wanted to hear. That the Baglar were under ban is further testified by a skaldic verse in response to a verse in which the Baglar mock the Birkibeinar.[113] It is not clear

---

108 *Latinske dokument*, 84 (no. 24): "Cum arma clericorum iuxta sacre scripture testimonium orationes et lacrime iudicentur. ... Nemo militans deo implicat se negotiis secularibus."
109 *Latinske dokument*, 98 (no. 29): "... prohibemus ne aliquis episcopus abbas seu clericus ... arma sumere vel in expedicionem ire vel ad hoc quicquam de suo impendere compellantur nisi forte necessitas tam grauis immineat ... permittatur."
110 *Sverris saga*, 228, reports: "The bishop said that the Birkibeinar had polluted all the churches and they were frequented by men under ban, thus, they were not more sacred than brothels" ("Byskup sagði svá at Birkibeinar hefði saurgat kirkjur allar ok bannsettir men væri inni, svá at eigi væri þær helgari en porthús ǫnnur").
111 *Latinske dokument*, 114 (no. 35).
112 *Sverris saga*, 233–34.
113 Ibid., 231.

who, if anyone, would have issued the ban, though it is neither entirely implausible nor implausible that it might have been Sverre in his self-ascribed role as asserted sovereign of the Norwegian church and "man in the place of three." Significantly, in both *Sverris saga* as well as the polemic *A Speech Against the Bishops* it is made clear that those who directed a ban unjustly will themselves fall under the ban.[114]

In addition, Bishop Nicholas's status as "false bishop" may be subtly and symbolically confirmed in the saga narration. In 1198/1199 he and the Baglar attacked the town of Nidaros unsuccessfully, and Nicholas could only narrowly escape. The saga tells that Bishop Nicholas threatened to burn down a monastery, and forced the prior and canons to give aid in the fight. The nature of the support they were expected to give is not specified in the narration. However, they were to be close to the battle itself and not allowed to be guarded by the monastery's walls, as "they then went away with them, and were on board his ship."[115] It may be that they were supposed to support the Baglar by prayers, though that must remain speculation. Towards the end of the battle, the Bishop managed to flee, while his lost miter was kept as a token of the Birkibeinar's victory. The saga author may, thus, have wanted to symbolically confirm that Nicholas was indeed a "false bishop," as stated earlier, or may have lost all his suitability and dignity as bishop, the latest when he forced the canons of Helgasetr to take part in the battle. Thereafter, he had to flee Norway. In that way, the saga symbolically turned the arguments against Sverre on its head and directed it against his enemies. The ban cursed them rather than him, and rather than Sverre being a false king, Nicholas was a false bishop. His lost miter became a symbol of this and the Birkibeinar's victory.

In effect, integrated warfare in Norway and the framing of the conflicts as holy war have led to a merging of leadership roles and expansion of authority claims. For some time, a secular ruler, King Sverre appears to have laid claim to act as spiritual leader, probably in reaction to his rivals backing by the church and his own clerical education. As such, he seems to have been in charge of the ritual employment of spiritual weapons through prayers. Similarly, a cleric in extraordinary circumstances, Bishop Nicholas Arnesson, took on the role of secular leadership bearing weapons and commanding troops in a fight against excommunicates for the *libertas ecclesiae*. However, they remain exceptional,

---

114   Compare with *Konungs skuggsjá* stating: "the bishop's sword only bites when it is rightfully used; when it is wrongfully used, it injures him who smites with it, not him who is stricken" ("Enn byskupins suerd bitr ei nema Rettliga se hogguit med. Enn ef hann hoggr Rangliga med / þui þa uerdr þeim mein at er hoggr. enn eigi uerdr þeim mein at er firi uerdr."). *Konungs Skuggsiá*, ed. Ludvig Holm-Olsen, Norrøne tekster 1 (Oslo: Norsk Historisk Kjeldeskrift-Institutt, 1983), 126.
115   *Sverris saga*, 238: "Síðan fóru þeir brot með honum ok váru á hans skipi."

one more than the other.[116] Written in the middle of the thirteenth century, the *Konungs skuggsjá* (*King's Mirror*) suggests a stricter division. The king shall wield the temporal word and the bishop the spiritual one; "and he shall smite with words but not with hands like the king."[117]

4   Conclusions

The civil war period was marked by increased use of spiritual means to influence battles and secure divine favor. The use of relics, prayers, at times in combination with the kissing of churches, and the excommunication of the enemy were the spiritual weapons that should aid one's own and weaken the opponents' side. Along with the use of spiritual means came the denunciation of the enemy as making use of unchristian magic and relying on demonic forces. Such accusations probably turned the opposite side's attempt to rely on divine aid on its head, but would also justify the own cause and use of spiritual means. Despite its evident utilization from the very beginning of the civil war period, warfare as thoroughly integrated culminated after King Magnus Erlingsson's elevation to king of God's grace in alliance with the Norwegian church and, in particular, with King Sverre Sigurdsson's ascent to kingship and the resistance he faced, that is between 1160 and 1200. Notably, at its height the merging of battlefields and enemies, visible and invisible, led to a temporary conflation of leadership roles. In general, references to spiritual aid remain sparse. A more wide-ranging and comparative analysis would cast light on how exceptional the presented evidence may be.

---

116   For parallel examples of warring bishops in the twelfth and early thirteenth centuries, see Timothy Reuter, "'Episcopi cum sua militia': The Prelate as Warrior in the Early Staufer Era," in *Warriors and Churchmen in the High Middle Ages: Essays Presented to Karl Leyser*, ed. Timothy Reuter (London and Rio Grande OH: Hambledon Press, 1992), 111–26; Kyle C. Lincoln, "Beating Swords Into Croziers: Warrior Bishops in the Kingdom of Castile, c.1158–1214," *JMH* 44.1 (2018): 83–103; Craig M. Nakashian, *Warrior Churchmen of Medieval England, 1000–1250: Theory and Reality* (Woodbridge: Boydell Press, 2016); Radosław Kotecki, "Lions and Lambs, Wolfs and Pastors of the Flock: Portraying Military Activities of Bishops in Twelfth Century Poland," in *Between Sword and Prayer*, 303–40; Taylor, "Bishops." See also several chapters in Radosław Kotecki, Carsten Selch Jensen, and Stephen Bennett, ed., *Christianity and War in Medieval East Central Europe and Scandinavia* (Leeds: ARC Humanities Press, 2021).
117   *Konungs Skuggsiá*, 126: "Enn (sa) Refsingar (vondr) er byskup hefir. þa skal j munni hafa / ok med ordum hoggua."

Bibliography

Primary Sources

Ágrip af Nóregskonunga sǫgum. In *Ágrip af Nóregskonunga sǫgum. Fagrskinna, Nóregs konunga tal.* Edited by Bjarni Einarsson, 1–54. Íslenzk fornrit 35. Rekjavík: Hið Íslenzka fornritafélag, 1985.

Bernard of Clairvaux. *Ad milites Templi. De laude novae militiae.* In *Bernard von Clairvaux. Sämtliche Werke lateinisch/deutsch I.* Edited by Gerhard B. Winkler, 267–326. Innsbruck: Tyrolia-Verlag, 1990.

Bǫglunga saga. In *Hákonar saga Hákonarsonar I. Bǫglunga saga.* Edited by Þorleifur Hauksson, Sverrir Jakobsson, and Tor Ulset, 3–146. Íslenzk Fornrit 31. Reykjavík: Hið íslenzka fornritafélag, 2013.

Hákonar saga Hákonarsonar II. In *Hákonar saga Hákonarsonar II. Magnúss saga lagabœtis.* Edited by Sverrir Jakobsson, Þorleifur Hauksson, and Tor Ulset, 3–267. Íslenzk fornrit 32. Reykjavík: Hið íslenzka fornritafélag, 2013.

Heimskringla III. Edited by Bjarni Aðalbjarnarson. Íslenzk fornrit 28. Reykjavík: Hið íslenzka fornritafélag, 1951.

En tale mot biskopene. En sproglig-historisk undersøkelse. Edited by Anne Holtsmark. Oslo: Dybwad, 1931.

Kong Haakon Sverresöns Retterbod om Kirkens Friheder. In *Norges gamle love indtil 1387.* Vol. 1. Edited by R. Keyser et al., 444–445. Christiania: Gröhndahl, 1846.

Konungs Skuggsiá. Edited by Ludvig Holm-Olsen, Norrøne tekster 1. Oslo: Norsk Historisk Kjeldeskrift-Institutt, 1983.

Latinske dokument til norks historie fram til år 1204. Edited by Eirik Vandvik. Oslo: Det norske samlaget, 1959.

Morkinskinna I. Edited by Þórður Ingi Guðjónsson and Ármann Jakobsson. Reykjavík: Hið íslenzka fornritafélag, 2011.

Morkinskinna II. Edited by Þórður Ingi Guðjónsson and Ármann Jakobsson. Reykjavík: Hið íslenzka fornritafélag, 2011.

Passio et miracula beati Olaui. Edited by Frederick Metcalfe. Oxford: Clarendon Press, 1881.

Snorri Sturluson. *Heimskringla. Vol. 3: Magnús Óláfsson to Magnús Erlingsson.* Translated by Alison Finlay and Anthony Faulkes. London: Viking Society for Northern Research, University College London, 2015.

Sverris saga. Edited by Þorleifur Hauksson. Íslenzk fornrit 30. Reykjavík: Hið íslenska fornritafélag, 2007.

Theodoricus. "De antiquitate regum Norwagiensium." *On the Old Norwegian Kings.* Edited and translated by Egil Kraggerud. Oslo: Novus, 2018.

William of Newburgh. *Historia rerum Anglicarum.* In *Chronicles of the Reigns of Stephen, Henry II and Richard I.* Edited by R. Howlett. Rerum Britannicarum medii aevi scriptores 82. London: n.p. Longman & Co. 1884.

Secondary Sources

Antonsson, Haki. "Some Observations on Martyrdom in Post-Conversion Scandinavia." *Saga-Book* 28 (2004): 70–94.

Arstad, Knut. "'... han var svag af Chrakteer og uden ringeste Herskergaver, hvilket også fremgaar af hele hans Historie'. En undersøkelse av Harald Gilles ettermæle." *HT* 78.4 (1999): 435–60.

Bagge, Sverre. "Borgerkrig og statsutvikling i Norge i middelalderen." *HT* 65.2 (1986): 145–97.

Bagge, Sverre. "Borgerkrig og statsutvikling—svar til Hans Jacob Orning." *HT* 93.1 (2015): 91–110.

Bagge, Sverre. *From Gang Leader to the Lord's Anointed. Kingship in "Sverris saga" and "Hákonar saga Hákonarsonar."* The Viking collection 8. Odense: Odense University Press, 1996.

Bagge, Sverre. "Den heroiske tid—kirkereform og kirkekamp 1153–1214." In *"Ecclesia Nidrosiensis." Søkelys på Nidaroskirkens og Nidarosprovinsens historie*. Edited by Steinar Imsen, 51–80. Senter for Middelalderstudier, NTNU. Skrifter 15. Trondheim: Tapir Akademisk Forlag, 2003.

Bagge, Sverre. "The Structure of the Political Factions in the Internal Struggles of the Scandinavian Countries during the High Middle Ages." *Scandinavian Journal of History* 24 (1999): 299–320.

Bateson, Gregory. "Culture Contact and Schismogenesis." *Man* 35 (1935): 178–83.

Bugge, Alexander. *Norges historie andet binds anden del tidsrummet 1103–1319*, Norges historie fremstillet for det norske folk. Kristiania: Aschehoug & Co., 1916.

Bandlien, Bjørn. "Civil War as Holy War? Polyphonic Discourses of Warfare during the Internal Struggles in Norway in the Twelfth Century." In *Christianity and War in Medieval East Central Europe and Scandinavia*. Edited by Radosław Kotecki, Carsten Selch Jensen, and Stephen Bennett, 227–43. Leeds: ARC Humanities Press, 2021.

Bandlien, Bjørn. *Man or Monster? Negotiations of Masculinity in Old Norse Society*. Acta Humaniora. Oslo: University of Oslo, Faculty of Humanities Unipub, 2005.

Bandlien, Bjørn. *Strategies of Passion: Love and Marriage in Medieval Iceland and Norway*, MTCN 6. Turnhout: Brepols, 2005.

Bartlett, Robert. *The Natural and the Supernatural in the Middle Ages. The Wiles Lectures Given at the Queen's University of Belfast, 2006*. Cambridge: Cambridge University Press, 2008.

Cassidy-Welch, Megan. "Before Trauma: The Crusades, Medieval Memory and Violence." *Journal of Media & Cultural Studies* 31.5 (2017): 619–27.

Contamine, Philippe. *War in the Middle Ages*. Translated by Michael Jones. Oxford and Cambridge MA: Blackwell, 1984.

Foote, Peter. "Secular Attitudes in Early Iceland." In *"Aurvandilstá": Norse Studies*. Edited by Michael Barnes, Hans Bekker-Nielsen, and Gerd Wolfgang Weber, 31–46. Odense: Odense University Press, 1984.

Forrest, Ian. *Trustworthy Men: How Inequality & Faith Made the Medieval Church.* Princeton, Oxford: Princeton University Press, 2018.

Gaposchkin, M. Cecilia. *Invisible Weapons: Liturgy and the Making of Crusade Ideology.* Ithaca NY: Cornell University Press, 2017.

Gerrard, Daniel M.G. *The Church at War. The Military Activities of Bishops, Abbots, and Other Clergy in England, c.900–1200.* Abingdon and New York: Routledge, 2016.

Gerrard, Daniel M.G. "Why Study Fighting Clergy? Knight Service, Integrated War, and the Bounds of English Military History, c.1000–1200." In *Between Sword and Prayer: Warfare and Medieval Clergy in Cultural Perspective.* Edited by Radosław Kotecki, Jacek Maciejewski, and John S. Ott, 117–58. EMC 3. Leiden and Boston MA: Brill, 2018.

Graeber, David. "Culture as Creative Refusal." *The Cambridge Journal of Anthropology* 31.2 (2013): 1–19.

Jensen, Janus Møller. "Korstog mod de hedenske svenskere. Nye perspektiver på Kalmarledingen 1123/24." *Collegium Medievale* 31 (2018): 151–76.

Knirk, James E. *Oratory in the King's Sagas.* Oslo: Universitetsforlaget, 1981.

Kotecki, Radosław. "Lions and Lambs, Wolfs and Pastors of the Flock: Portraying Military Activities of Bishops in Twelfth Century Poland." In *Between Sword and Prayer: Warfare and Medieval Clergy in Cultural Perspective.* Edited by Radosław Kotecki, Jacek Maciejewski, and John S. Ott, 303–40. EMC 3. Leiden and Boston MA: Brill, 2018.

Kotecki, Radosław. "Pious Rulers, Princely Clerics, and Angels of Light: Imperial Holy War Imagery in Twelfth-Century Poland and Rus'." In *Christianity and War in Medieval East Central Europe and Scandinavia.* Edited by Radosław Kotecki, Carsten Selch Jensen and Stephen Bennett, 159–88. Leeds: ARC Humanities Press, 2021.

Kotecki, Radosław. "With the Sword of Prayer, or How the Medieval Bishop Should Fight." *QMAN* 21 (2016): 341–69.

Kotecki, Radosław, Carsten Selch Jensen, and Stephen Bennett, ed. *Christianity and War in Medieval East Central Europe and Scandinavia.* Leeds: ARC Humanities Press, 2021.

Lie, Hallvard. *Studier i Heimskringlas stil. Dialogene og talene.* Skrifter utgitt av Det Norske Videnskaps-Akademi i Oslo II. Hist.-Filos. Klasse. 1936 5. Oslo, 1937.

Lincoln, Kyle C. "Beating Swords into Croziers: Warrior Bishops in the Kingdom of Castile, c.1158–1214." *JMH* 44.1 (2018): 83–103.

Lönnroth, Lars. "Sverrir's Dreams." *Scripta Islandica* 57 (2006): 97–110.

Lunden, Kåre. *Norge under Sverreætten 1177–1319.* Edited by Knut Mykland. Norges Historie 3. Oslo: J.W. Cappelens Forlag, 1976.

MacGregor, James B. "Negotiating Knightly Piety: The Cult of the Warrior-Saints in the West, ca.1070–ca.1200." *ChH* 73.3 (2004): 317–45.

Maier, Christoph T. "Crisis, Liturgy and the Crusade in the Twelfth and Thirteenth Centuries." *JEH* 48.4 (1997): 628–57.

Mastnak, Tomaž. *Crusading Peace: Christendom, the Muslim World, and Western Political Order*. Berkeley CA and Los Angeles: University of California Press, 2002.

Murray, Alan V. "'Mighty against the enemies of Christ': The Relic of the True Cross in the Armies of the Kingdom of Jerusalem." In *The Crusades and Their Sources: Essays Presented to Bernard Hamilton*. Edited by John France and William G. Zajac, 217–38. Abingdon and New York: Routledge, 1998.

Nakashian, Craig M. *Warrior Churchmen of Medieval England, 1000–1250: Theory and Reality*. Woodbridge: Boydell Press, 2016.

Orning, Hans Jacob. "Borgerkrig og statsutvikling i Norge i middelalderen—en revurdering." *HT* 93.2 (2014): 193–216.

Orning, Hans Jacob. "Hvorfor vant kongene?" *HT* 94.2 (2015): 285–92.

Orning, Hans Jacob. *Dei norske borgarkrigene 1130–1240*. Oslo: Samlaget, 2021.

Orning, Hans Jacob. *Unpredictability and Presence: Norwegian Kingship in the High Middle Ages*. TNW 38. Leiden and Boston MA: Brill, 2008.

Orning, Hans Jacob, and Frederik Rosén. "'Sverris saga': A Manifesto for a New Political Order." In *Medieval and Modern Civil Wars*. Edited by Jón Viðar Sigurðsson and Hans Jacob Orning, 62–93. History of warfare 135. Leiden and Boston MA: Brill, 2021.

Raupp, Lukas. "Importing Jerusalem: Relics of the True Cross as Political Legitimation in Early Twelfth-Century Denmark and Norway." In *Tracing the Jerusalem Code. Volume 1: The Holy City Christian Cultures in Medieval Scandinavia (ca.1100–1536)*. Edited by Kristin B. Aavitsland and Line M. Bonde, 141–65. Berlin and Boston MA: De Gruyter, 2021.

Reuter, Timothy. "'Episcopi cum sua militia': The Prelate as Warrior in the Early Staufer Era." In *Warriors and Churchmen in the High Middle Ages: Essays Presented to Karl Leyser*. Edited by Timothy Reuter, 111–26. London and Rio Grande OH: The Hambledon Press, 1992.

Rosenwein, Barbara. "Feudal War and Monastic Peace: Cluniac Liturgy as Ritual Aggression." *Viator* 2 (1971): 129–57.

Schreiner, Klaus. "'Signa Victricia'. Heilige Zeichen in kriegerischen Konflikten des Mittelalters." In *Zeichen—Rituale—Werte. Internationales Kolloquium des Sonderforschungsbereichs 496 an der Westfälischen Wilhelms-Universität Münster*. Edited by Gerd Althoff, 259–300. Symbolische Kommunikation und gesellschaftliche Wertesysteme 3. Münster: Rhema, 2004.

Sigurðsson, Jón Viðar. *Det norrøne samfunnet. Vikingen, kongen, erkebiskopen og bonden*. Oslo: Pax Forlag, 2008.

Skånland, Vegard. *Det eldste norske provinsialstatutt*. Oslo: Universitetsforlaget, 1969.

Smith, Katherine Allen. *War and the Making of Medieval Monastic Culture*. Woodbridge: Boydell Press, 2011.

Stefánsson, Magnús. "Kong Sverre—prest og sønn av Sigurd Munn?" In *Festskrift til Ludvig Holm-Olsen på hans 70-årsdag den 9. juni 1984*, 287–307. Øvre Ervik: Alvheim & Eide Akademisk Forlag, 1984.

Taylor, Louisa. "Bishops, War, and Canon Law: The Military Activities of Prelates in High Medieval Norway." *Scandinavian Journal of History* 45.3 (2020): 263–85.

CHAPTER 5

Religiosity and Religious Rituals in the Battle of Bannockburn, 1314

Robert Bubczyk

Due to its great significance as a turning point in Anglo-Scottish relations, the Battle of Bannockburn in 1314 has long been subject to intensive research scrutiny, particularly by military historians. Analyzes have been conducted in terms of the armed operations launched by the respective sides, their strategies, military formations, tactics, weaponry, and strength of respective units; in-depth reconstructions aim to recreate the respective stages of the battle and situate the same relative to the local topography. Medievalists also consider the impact of this military engagement on the subsequent political changes in Anglo-Scottish relations and underline its ideological importance as a formative event for the Scottish national identity.[1] What in many works devoted to the military confrontation between England and Scotland in 1314 still remains in short supply, however, is an analysis of the religious aspects of the battle, including the directly associated ritual behavior of the soldiers. Meanwhile, as confirmed by some historians, the mutual ties between Christian religion and military action were very strong in the Middle Ages and constituted a near indispensable element of any armed confrontation.[2] Indeed, it was believed

---

1   The most important studies devoted to the Battle of Bannockburn in 1314 include: William Mackay Mackenzie, *The Battle of Bannockburn: The Study of Medieval Warfare* (Glasgow: MacLehose and Sons, 1913); John E. Morris, Bannockburn (Cambridge: Cambridge University Press, 1914); Barrie Goedhals, "John's Barbour's 'The Bruce' and Bannockburn," *Unisa English Studies* 2 (1968): 40–58; William Scott, *Bannockburn Revealed: A Reappraisal* (Rothesay: Elenkus, 2000); Peter Amstrong, *Bannockburn: Robert Bruce's Great Victory* (Oxford: Osprey, 2002); Aryeh Nusbacher, *The Battle of Bannockburn, 1314* (Stroud: Tempus, 2005); Michael Brown, *Bannockburn: The Scottish War and the British Isles, 1307–1323* (Edinburgh: Edinburgh University Press, 2008); David Cornell, *Bannockburn: The Triumph of Robert the Bruce* (New Haven CN and London: Yale University Press, 2009); Peter Reese, *Bannockburn: Scotland's Greatest Victory* (Edinburgh: Canongate Books, 2014); Michael Penman, ed., *Bannockburn, 1314–2014: Battle and Legacy* (Donington: Tyas, 2016).

2   For religion, the medieval clergy and war, see David S. Bachrach, *Religion and the Conduct of War, c.300–1215* (Woodbridge: Boydell Press, 2003); idem, "The Medieval Military Chaplain and His Duties," in *The Sword of the Lord: Military Chaplains from the First to the Twenty-First Century*, ed. Doris L. Bergen (Notre Dame IN: University of Notre Dame Press, 2004), 69–88; idem, "Military Chaplains and the Religion of War in Ottonian Germany, 919–1024," *RSS* 39.1

that religiously-tinted gestures and rituals were crucial for any military expedition to succeed.[3] Their purpose was to ensure divine favor and support for the respective undertakings. Pious knights would take pains to thoroughly prepare for war even before they set out into the field, and those efforts were in equal measure martial and spiritual. To this end, they made endowments to churches, settled disputes and resolved conflicts as well as distributed alms, thus hoping to eliminate any obstacles to receiving a blessing from members of the clergy. The typical religious rituals observed at various stages of preparation for a military engagement included: confession, Holy Communion, and participation in a mass, sometimes also fasting. During a battle, priests would pray for victory

---

(2011): 13–21; Laurence G. Duggan, *Armsbearing and the Clergy in the History and Canon Law of Western Christianity* (Woodbridge: Boydell Press, 2013); Philippe Buc, *Holy War, Martyrdom, and Terror: Christianity, Violence, and the West* (Philadelphia: University of Pennsylvania Press, 2015); Craig M. Nakashian, *Warrior Churchmen of Medieval England, 1000–1250: Theory and Reality* (Woodbridge: Boydell Press, 2016); Daniel M.G. Gerrard, *The Church at War: The Military Activity of Bishops, Abbots and Other Clergy in England, c. 900–1200* (Abingdon and New York: Routledge, 2017), and in particular most recent studies on this subject: Radosław Kotecki, Jacek Maciejewski, John S. Ott, ed., *Between Sword and Prayer: Warfare and Medieval Clergy in Cultural Perspective*, EMC 3 (Leiden and Boston MA: Brill, 2018); Radosław Kotecki and Jacek Maciejewski, "Ideals of Episcopal Power, Legal Norms and Military Activity of the Polish Episcopate between the Twelfth and Fourteenth Centuries," KH 127.Eng.-Language Edition 4 (2020): 5–46; Radosław Kotecki, Carsten Selch Jensen, and Stephen Bennet, ed., *Christianity and War in Medieval East Central Europe and Scandinavia* (Leeds: ARC Humanities Press, 2021).

3   For rituals in history, their definitions and examples, see Michael McCormick, *Eternal Victory: Triumphal Rulership in Late Antiquity, Byzantium, and the Early Medieval West* (Cambridge: Cambridge University Press, 1986); idem, "Liturgie et guerre des Carolingiens à la première croisade," in *"Militia Christi" e crociata nei secoli XI–XIII*, Miscellanea del Centro di studi medioevali 13 (Milan: Vita e pensiero, 1992), 209–40; Roy A. Rappaport, *Ritual and Religion in the Making of Humanity* (Cambridge: Cambridge University Press, 2012); Barbara Stollberg-Rilinger, *Rituale. Historische Einführungen*, Historische Einführungen 16 (Frankfurt and New York: Campus Verlag, 2013). On the role of religious rituals in executing the royal power, see David Cannadine, Simon Price, ed., *Rituals of Royalty: Power and Ceremonial in Traditional Societies* (Cambridge: Cambridge University Press, 1993); Gerd Althoff, *Die Macht der Rituale* (Darmstadt: Wissenschaftliche Buchgesellschaft, 2013); Mark W. Ormrod, "The English Monarchy and the Promotion of Religion in the Fourteenth Century," in *Religion and Politics in the Middle Ages: Germany and England by Comparison*, ed. Ludger Körtner and Dominik Waßenhoven, Prince Albert studies 29 (Berlin and Boston MA: De Gruyter, 2013), 205–17 at 206–9; for rituals, liturgy and medieval warfare, see, among others, Jacek Banaszkiewicz, "Włócznia i chorągiew. O rycie otwierania bitwy w związku z cudem kampanii nakielskiej Bolesława Krzywoustego (Kadłubek, III,14)," KH 94.4 (1987): 3–24, repr. in idem, *W stronę rytuałów i Galla Anonima* (Cracow: Avalon, 2018), 79–110; M. Cecilia Gaposchkin, *Invisible Weapons: Liturgy and the Making of Crusade Ideology* (Ithaca NY and London: Cornell University Press, 2017); and recently Kotecki, Jensen, and Bennet, ed., *Christianity and War*, chaps. 7–11.

in the field, continuously maintaining the warriors' conviction of fighting the good fight. Soldiers themselves also commonly implored God and saints to aid them. Religious inscriptions were carved onto swords and charging armies would call upon their patron saints when it was time to attack. It was genuinely believed that assistance from holy patrons could be secured by carrying their relics onto the field, both in the form of actual body parts and consecrated banners bearing their names, likenesses, or attributes. Participants in a battle saw it as a form of trial by combat, a judicial duel—divine judgement (*iudicium Dei*) wherein God himself determined whose cause was just. Once the fighting was over, funerary rites were performed for the dead and war trophies were offered to God: banners, weaponry and elements of equipment were later stored in churches as votive offerings.[4] To better understand the medieval notions of piety as well as the narratives and vivid descriptions of battlefields provided by the authors of respective accounts, one should approach many of such military engagements in terms of the accompanying, religiously motivated efforts, gestures and rituals. The following essay will discuss the religious aspects of the Battle of Bannockburn fought on 23 and 24 June 1314.

The surviving narrative accounts from the period provide the basic sources of information on the battle itself—they will also be the focal point of the analysis conducted herein. Chronologically speaking, the works closest to the events in question include chronicles, mainly English ones, such as the

---

4   Sven Ekdahl, *Die "Banderia Prutenorum" des Jan Długosz, eine Quelle zur Schlacht bei Tannenberg 1410. Untersuchungen zu Aufbau, Entstehung und Quellenwert der Handschrift* (Göttingen: Vandenhoek & Ruprecht, 1976), 8–30; Jan Frans Verbruggen, *The Art of Warfare in Western Europe during the Middle Ages: From the Eighth Century to 1340*, 2nd ed. (Woodbridge: Boydell Press, 1998); Philippe Contamine, *War in the Middle Ages* (Oxford: Blackwell, 1999), 98–302; Matthew Strickland, *War and Chivalry: The Conduct and Perception of War in England and Normandy, 1066–1217* (Cambridge: Cambridge University Press, 1996), 58–67; Malte Prietzel, *Kriegführung im Mittelalter. Handlungen, Erinnerungen und Bedentungen*, KG 32 (Paderborn: Schöningh, 2006). For the war perceived as the *iudicium dei*, see Kelly DeVries, "God and Defeat in Medieval Warfare: Some Preliminary Thoughts," in *The Circle of War in the Middle Ages: Essays on Medieval Military and Naval History*, ed. Donald J. Kagay and L.J.A. Villalon (Woodbridge: Boydell Press, 1999), 87–97; Rudolf Schieffer, "'Iudicium Dei'. Kriege als Gottesurteile," in *Heilige Kriege. Religiöse Begründungen militärischer Gewaltanwendung. Judentum, Christentum und Islam im Vergleich*, ed. Klaus Schreiner and Elisabeth Müller-Luckner, SHKK 78 (Munich: Oldenbourg, 2008), 219–28; Martin Clauss, "Der Krieg als Mittel und Thema der Kommunikation. Die narrative Funktion des Gottesurteils," in *Gottes Werk und Adams Beitrag. Formen der Interaktion zwischen Mensch und Gott im Mittelalter*, ed. Thomas Honegger, Gerlinde Huber-Rebenich, and Volker Leppin, Das Mittelalter. Perspektiven mediävistischer Forschung. Beihefte 1 (Berlin: De Gruyter, 2014), 128–41.

anonymous *Vita Edwardi Secundi* (covering the period from 1307 to 1325)[5] and the *Chronicle of Lanercost* (1272–1346),[6] as well as *Scalacronica* (1066–1363) by Thomas Gray (or Grey) of Heton,[7] who was particularly invested from an emotional perspective in the battle (his father was captured by the Scots on the first day of the hostilities). Unfortunately, the fragment of his chronicle relevant to this point focuses only on a description of the military engagement, rendering it somewhat less valuable in the specific context of the religious aspects of the battle. Another English source about the Battle of Bannockburn is the relatively less known *Chronicon Angliae temporibus Edwardi II et Edwardi III* written by Geoffrey le Baker of Swinbrook.[8] A fairly sizeable mention of the discussed event was also included in *Chronica monasterii S. Albani*, a chronicle written by the English Benedictines associated with the monastery in Tynemouth and St. Albans Abbey.[9] It remains unclear whether the authorship of the fragment referring to the Battle of Bannockburn can be attributed to John of Trokelowe, or whether he was only a scribe working for another Benedictine, William Rishanger.[10] Either way, this particular account is of lesser value to our present deliberations as its author, similarly to Thomas Gray, described only events related to the actual fighting, and thus mostly neglected the religious context found in other texts. The key facts related to the battle, albeit written from a somewhat more distant chronological perspective, were

---

5   *Vita Edwardi Secundi*, ed. and trans. Wendy R. Childs (Oxford: Clarendon Press, 2005); on the chronicle and its possible authorship, see Antonia Gransden, *Historical Writing in England II: C.1307 to the Early Sixteenth Century* (London and Henley: Routledge and Kegan Paul, 1982), 3, 31–37.

6   *The Chronicle of Lanercost*, ed. and trans. Herbert Maxwell (Glasgow: Maclehose and Sons, 1913); on the authorship of the chronicle, see Andrew G. Little, "The Authorship of the 'Lanercost Chronicle,'" *English Historical Review* 31.122 (1916): 269–79 and 32.125 (1917): 48–49; also see Gransden, *Historical Writing*, 12–17.

7   Thomas Gray, *Scalacronica*, ed. and trans. Andy King, Publications of the Surtees Society 209 (Woodbridge: Boydell Press, 2005); Gransden, *Historical Writing*, 92–96.

8   Geoffrey le Baker, *Chronicon Galfridi le Baker de Swynebroke*, ed. Edward Maunde Thompson (Oxford: Clarendon Press, 1889); for the English translation, see *The Chronicle of Geoffrey le Baker*, trans. Richard Barber, intro. and notes David Preest (Woodbridge: Boydell Press, 2012); on the author, his work, and its sources, see Richard Barber in the introduction to the English translation, ibid., xiii–xxvii; see also Gransden, *Historical Writing*, 4, 37–42.

9   *Chronica monasterii S. Albani. Johannis de Trokelowe, et Henrici de Blaneforde, monachorum S. Albani, necnon quorundam anonymorum, chronica et annals, regnantibus Henrico Tertio, Edwardo Primo, Edwardo Secundo, Ricardo Secundo, et Henrico Quarto*, ed. Henry Thomas Riley (London: Longmans, Green, Reader, and Dyer, 1866). The passages on the Battle of Bannockburn are included in the part of this volume entitled *Johannis de Trokelowe Annales*, 84–87.

10   Gransden, *Historical Writing*, 4–6.

also discussed in two Scottish sources. The first is the epic work presenting the heroic acts of the Scottish king, Robert I, written by the archdeacon of Aberdeen, John Barbour. In around 1375, the author created a rhymed poem entitled *The Bruce* which contained, among other things, a suggestive account of the victory won by the Scots commanded by Robert the Bruce over the English.[11] Another source, written around the mid-fifteenth century, is a narrative piece known as the *Scotichronicon* (1447)[12] written by the abbot of the Canon Regular monastery in Inchcolm Walter Bower as a continuation of John of Fordun's *Chronica gentis Scotorum*.[13]

Information pertinent to these deliberations, i.e. contributing to the reconstruction of the religious context of the events of June 1314 that culminated with the English defeat in the Battle of Bannockburn, at times emerges in some of the works cited above also outside the narrative accounts related specifically to the battle itself (be it in the form of a chronicler's portrayal of Edward II's army's preparations for the impending engagement, or the authors' comments on the result thereof). The anonymous lay clerk believed to be the author of *Vita Edwardi Secundi* observed in his retelling of the events of June 1314 that approximately one week prior to the Nativity of St. John the Baptist (24 June), King Edward II departed from Berwick, heading towards Stirling with a over two thousand knights and an unspecified number of infantry, as well as the accompanying convoy. The military might of the English expedition emboldened the king, at the same time undermining his vigilance and boosting confidence in his imminent victory to the point that he chose not to lead his army onwards in line with accepted military strategy, proceeding as if on a religious pilgrimage to Santiago and not towards a clash with a mortal enemy. This alleged nonchalance of the ruler was not without negative consequences. Stops for sleep and food were brief, causing considerable exhaustion among the troops even before they faced their Scottish adversaries.[14] Further details as to the circumstances of the English army's departure to meet the enemy were provided by the author of the *Chronicle of Lanercost*, who suggestively

---

11   John Barbour, *The Bruce*, ed. and trans. Archibald A. McBeth Duncan, Canongate classics 78 (Edinburgh: Canongate Books, 1997); Gransden, *Historical Writing*, 80–83.
12   Walter Bower, *Scotichronicon*, 9 vols., ed. John MacQueen et al. (Aberdeen: Aberdeen University Press, 1993–1999).
13   Gransden, *Historical Writing*, 82.
14   "Rex igitur, de tanta et tam clara multitudine confisus et animosus effectus, de die in diem festinanter ad locum prefixum est profectus, non tamquam exercitum ducturus ad bellum set magis profecturus ad Sanctum Iacobum. Breuis erat mora capiendi sompnum, set breuior erat mora sumendi cibum; unde equi, equites et pedites, labore et fame fatigati, si minus bene rem gererent non errant culpandi": *Vita Edwardi Secundi*, 88.

contrasted the behavior of Edward II with the pre-battle practices of his father, Edward I.[15] Whenever the latter marched against Scotland, he would prepare by seeking God's blessing through the intercession of all saints whose sanctuaries he passed and piously visited along the way. There, praying at the graves of St. Thomas of Canterbury, Edmund, Hugon, William, and Cuthbert, he would make generous offerings not just to the patrons themselves, but also to the monasteries tending to their graves; he would also give alms to the poor. Meanwhile, unlike the father, who always remembered to carry out adequate religious rites when faced with a campaign in Scotland, the son and heir to the English throne made no effort to secure the favor of God and his saints for the military objective of in his attempts at crushing the Scottish rebellion, nor to elevate the morale of his own troops.[16] Quite the contrary in fact: when Edward II led his massive army to the north in June 1314, his behavior stood in stark contrast to the Christian custom and practice which was highly esteemed by clerical authors:

---

15   Edward I was very well-known by the monks of the Cumbrian Lanercost monastery, especially that he tended that priory and made a few visits to that place in the latter part of his reign, see Michael Prestwich, *Edward I* (London: Methuen, 1988), 507, 509, 556.

16   Edward II's light-heartedness in this respect was emphasized by David Cornell, who aptly noted that the king had failed to ceremoniously take the banners of renowned northern saints St. Cuthbert and St. John of Beverley, which "would have had an enormous spiritual effect on troops about to go to war" as well as boosted the morale of his army, see Cornell, *Bannockburn*, 147. Indeed, from 1296 onwards it was customary that the banners of St. Cuthbert and St. John of Beverley were taken by King Edward I on his Scottish military expeditions. Edward II made a promise to the monks of Durham that he would always take the banner of St. Cuthbert to his wars. In 1307 the king paid the banner-bearer. In 1310 the king demanded that the archbishop's vicar from Beverley, John Rolleston, carry the banner of John of Beverley in the Scottish campaign. There is no evidence, however, that any of the two banners was taken to the Battle of Bannockburn, see Richard Sharpe, "Banners of the Northern Saints," in *Saints of North-East England, 600–1500*, ed. Margaret Coombe, Anne Mouron, and Christiana Whitehead, MCS 39 (Turnhout: Brepols, 2017), 245–301 at 281–84. The importance of the cults of different saints for propaganda reasons during military efforts of Edward I as well as Robert Bruce was stressed by Michael Penman, "'Sacred Food for the Soul': In Search of the Devotions to Saints of Robert Bruce, King of Scotland, 1306–1329," *Speculum* 88.4 (2013): 1035–62; For the cult of St. John of Beverley in England, see Susan E. Wilson, *The Life and After-Life of St. John of Beverley: The Evolution of the Cult of an Anglo-Saxon Saint* (Aldershot and Burlington VT: Ashgate, 2006); Tomasz Tarczyński, "The King and the Saint against the Scots: The Shaping of English National Identity in the 12th Century Narrative of King Althestan's Victory over His Northern Neighbours," in *Imagined Communities: Constructing Collective Identities in Medieval Europe*, ed. Andrzej Pleszczyński et al., EMC 8 (Leiden and Boston MA: Brill, 2018), 85–102.

Marching with great pomp and elaborate state, he took goods from the monasteries on his journey, and, as was reported, did and said things to the prejudice and injury to the saints. In consequence of this and other things it is not surprising that confusion and everlasting shame overtook him and his army, which was foretold at the time by certain religious men of England.[17]

It seems likely that the chronicler's emphasis and downright homiletic portrayal of the religious errors and negligence of Edward II on the eve of the decisive battle with the Scots was intended by the author as a way to aid the reader in better understanding the reasons of the English defeat as, from the strictly military standpoint, the evident martial advantage of the English ought to have led to an entirely different outcome.[18] But—as the author suggests—it did not because the southern invaders had failed to adequately propitiate Divine Providence. An even more forthright interpretation of his countrymen's defeat was presented by the author of the already cited *Vita Edwardi Secundi*, whose parallel of the history of ancient military conflicts served to uncompromisingly accuse Edward II's army of giving in to sin, specifically that of pride (*superbia*) and greed.[19] The author used the reference to the defeat at Bannockburn as a telling example in a more general theological reflection on the disastrous consequences of transgressing God's commandments, including through condescension or lust for another's property.[20]

---

17 *The Chronicle of Lanercost*, 206.
18 On the estimated number of the troops participating in the battle on both sides, see Geoffrey W.S. Barrow, *Robert Bruce: And the Community of the Realm of Scotland*, 4th ed. (Edinburgh: Edinburgh University Press, 2005), 268–73; compare with Cornell, *Bannockburn*, 138–47.
19 Referring to this account, Antonia Gransden remarked that the sins of pride and avarice were among favorite themes of medieval preachers. See Gransden, *Historical Writing*, 33.
20 "Sic homines nostri, qui in superbia et abusione uenerunt, in ignominia et confusione redierunt. Certe superba nostrorum presumpcio Scotos fecit gaudere triumpho. De superbia modernorum, et quis fructus inde proueniat, modicum si placet lector aduertat. Hodie pauper et tenuis, qui nec obolum habet in bonis, maiorem se contempnit, et maledictum pro maledicto referre non metuit. Set ex rusticitate forsan hoc accidit. Veniamus igitur ad eos qui se putant eruditos. Quis putas maiori rixa in alium excandescit quam curialis? Dum forte rancore tumescit inferiorem non respicit, parem fascidit, maiori par fieri semper intendit. Nam armiger militem, miles baronem, baro comitem, comes regem, in omni fere cultu antecedere nititur et laborat. Porro dum sumptus deficit, quia patrimonium non sufficit, ad predam se conuertunt, uicinos spoliant, subditos expilant, et in ipsos Dei ministros infamem questum exercent. Hinc est quod magnates terre uel cadunt in bello, uel moriuntur sine filio, aut sexus femineus hereditatem diuidit, et nomen patris imperpetuum euanascit": *Vita Edwardi Secundi*, 98.

Similar sentiments regarding the English expedition of 1314 were expressed by Geoffrey le Baker of Swinbrook in Oxfordshire. In his description of Edward II's royal army and their behavior on the eve of the battle, the author observed the indifferent, downright arrogant and ostentatious transfer onto the battlefield of not just the warriors but also the vast convoy accompanying it, carrying lavish accessories as if they were heading for a banquet and not a clash with a mortal enemy. This was likely due to the misplaced, as would soon become evident, conviction that victory was within easy reach. The chronicler suggested that the English had been guilty of pride and overconfidence, clearly evidenced—he argues—by their behavior even during the night immediately preceding the decisive confrontation between the two opposing armies. Unlike the Scots, who fasted and awaited, in devout reverence, the opportunity to fight for the freedom of their homeland, Edward II's warriors devoted their spare time to drinking, shouting and swearing.[21]

The general opinions of English chroniclers regarding the character of the Battle of Bannockburn and the reasons for Edward II's defeat were not particularly far removed from those voiced, somewhat later, by Scottish authors. *The Bruce*, a chivalric poem written by the archdeacon of Aberdeen, John Barbour, in around 1375, contains a passage wherein the titular hero speaks to the gathered lords at the close of the first day of battle (23 June 1314). The Scottish king encourages his commanders to intensify their efforts, listing all the reasons for which they are bound to be victorious. Above all, he claims, that they are in the right and God always stands on the side of the righteous.

---

21 "Illuc Anglicorum pompa, usque tunc solita in equis belligerare, copias adduxit cursantium dextrariorum, armorum radiancium, milicianque copiosam, cuius temeritas nimium presumptuosa, sibi ipsi blandiendo promittens victoriam quam de suis viribus desperantibus solet Imperator universi conferre, de sua Securitate adeo fuerat confisa ut, preter necessariam reii militari equorum et armorum atque victualium habundanciam, vasa quoque aurea et argentea, quibus qualibus pacis tempore solent mundi principum convivia luxuriare, secum facerent deferri. Nunquam tunc presents antea vel post tantam nobilitatem tam nobilem apparatum tanta superbia intumentem viderunt solo guerre Martis favori commendare, ut pauper ille Carmelita, frater R. Bastone, in suis heroicis de eodem bello, quo presens a Scotis captus, deplanxit luctuose. Vidisses illa nocte gentem Anglorum, non angelorum more vivencium set vino madencium, crapulam eructancium, 'Wassayl' et 'Drinkhail' plus solito intonancium; econtra Scotos silentem sanctam vigiliam ieiunio celebrantes, et amore patrie libertatis licet iniusto, tamen acri et in mortem parato, estuantes": Geoffrey le Baker, *Chronicon Galfridi*, 7; *The Chronicle of Geoffrey*, 7. On the pompous advancements of the English army towards the Scots, accompanied by numerous wagons with rich provisions and precious furnishings, see also Bower, *Scotichronicon*, 362. Compare with similar contrasting description of preparation for Battle of Northallerton in 1138 by Aelred of Rievaulx discussed by Jesse Partick Harrington in volume.

Meanwhile—the literary Bruce continues—the English stand as the very contradiction of integrity: they are driven solely by pride and desire for dominance. At the end of his speech, the Scottish leader invokes God, pleading for his support.[22] In another section of the poem, Barbour mentions the deteriorating morale of the English soldiers who, having been bested during the first day of the battle, start to sense the possibility of ultimate defeat as they realize that they are fighting against the righteous, thus gravely offending God.[23] In writing those words, John Barbour evoked the archetypical doctrine of just war, one that had existed since Antiquity and continued to be widely debated in the Middle Ages.[24] At the same time, he suggested that the military action taken by the English was unjust, both in terms of human and divine laws. In the opinion of some researchers, the overriding intention of the poem's author was to present the conflict in an analogy to the hostilities between Christians and pagans along the Muslims during the crusades. The archdeacon of Aberdeen perceived the Scots' struggle for independence as fully justified and consistent with God's design, which, in a way, made them equal to knights fighting as crusaders elsewhere, whereas the English transgressed the principles of just war, and were thus more akin to infidels. As a consequence of such an interpretation

---

22   "For we haff thre gret avantagis / The first is that we haf the rycht / And for the rycht ay God will fycht. ... For thoucht our fayis haf mekill mycht / Thai have the wrang, and succudry / And covatys of senyoury / Amovys thaim foroutyn mor. ... God help us that is maist of mycht": John Barbour, *The Bruce*, 460–65.

23   "The Inglishmen sic abasing / Tuk and sic drede of that tithing / That in five hunder placis and ma / Men mych se samyn routand ga / Sayand, 'Our lordis for thar mycht / Will allgate fecht aganc the rycht / Bot quha-sa werrayis wrangwysly / Thai fend God all to gretumly / And thaim may happyn to mysfall, / And swa may tid that her we sall'": ibid., 467.

24   On the issue of the legitimization of violence, and so called just and unjust war, which provoked a heated debate among medieval intellectuals, especially in the context of the crusading movement, see among others Frederick H. Russell, *The Just War in the Middle Ages* (Cambridge, New York, and Melbourne: Cambridge University Press, 1975), 4–8, 18–19; Jonathan Riley-Smith, "Crusading as an Act of Love," *History* 65.214 (1980): 177–92; Richard W. Kaeuper, *Chivalry and Violence in Medieval Europe* (Oxford: Oxford University Press, 1999), 63–88; Contamine, *War*, 282–84; Thomas Scharff, *Die Kämpfe der Herrscher und der Heiligen. Krieg und historische Erinnerung in der Karolingerzeit* (Darmstadt: Wissenschaftliche Buchgesellschaft, 2002); Christopher Tyerman, *God's War: A New History of the Crusades* (Cambridge MA: Belknap Press of Harvard University Press, 2006); Jean Flori, *La guerre sainte. La formation de l'idée de croisade dans l'Occident chrétien* (Paris: Aubier, 2009); Carsten Selch Jensen, "Gods War: War and Christianisation on the Baltic Frontier in the Early 13th Century," *QMAN* 16 (2011): 123–47; Kurt Villads Jensen, "Holy War—Holy Wrath! Baltic Wars Between Regulated Warfare and Total Annihilation Around 1200," in *Church and Belief in the Middle Ages: Popes, Saints, and Crusaders*, ed. Kirsi Salonen and Sari Katajala-Peltomaa, CB 3 (Amsterdam: Amsterdam University Press, 2016), 227–50.

of the Scottish war of independence, Barbour was inclined to defend various acts of cruelty committed by Robert the Bruce and his companions against the English (not only on the Bannockburn battlefield), similarly to the way that medieval Europe was glad to absolve Christian knights of the violence inherent in the military operations in the Holy Land.[25]

Another account discussing the circumstances surrounding the battle and offering a deeper insight into the religious aspects of the Battle of Bannockburn is the opinion voiced by Walter Bower in his *Scotichronicon*. The chronicler begins the description of this key point in his nation's history by discussing the reasons behind the English defeat and Scottish victory, framing the same primarily in religious terms. This section of the chronicle informs the reader that the Scottish king, Robert the Bruce, surrendered the fate of the military conflict to God and defeated the English through God's grace. On the contrary, Edward II perceived the outcome only in earthly terms, placing his unwavering confidence in the numbers and might of his human military force. This had been evident ever since he set out with great pomp to finally conquer the whole of Scotland. Of this—as the author observes—God did not approve.[26] Among the reasons responsible for the southern invaders' defeat, Bower also goes on to include the unjust character of the English expedition to Scotland, and in

---

[25] Joachim Schwend, "Religion and Religiosity in 'The Bruce,'" in *Scottish Language and Literature, Medieval and Renaissance*, ed. Dietrich Strauss and Horst W. Drescher (Frankfurt am Main, Bern, and New York: Peter Lang, 1984), 207–15; Sonja Cameron, "Chivalry and Warfare in Barbour's 'Bruce,'" in *Armies, Chivalry and Warfare in Medieval Britain and France*, ed. Matthew Strickland, Harlaxton medieval studies 7 (Stamford: Watkins, 1998), 13–29; Sarah Tolmie, "Making Memories: Barbour and Bannockburn," in *Bannockburn, 1314–2014*, 139–51. For a range of interpretations of *The Bruce*, in particular as a key to understanding the wider nationalistic, social and cultural concerns of late medieval Scots, presented in an interdisciplinary manner, see Steve Boardman and Susan Foran, ed., *Barbour's Bruce and its Cultural Contexts: Politics, Chivalry, and Literature in Late Medieval Scotland* (Rochester NY: Brewer, 2015). For the detailed analyzes of the literary creations of the main character, i.e. Robert the Bruce and his companions as showed by John Barbour in the historical and cultural context (especially in the so-called collective memory), see Wojciech Michalski, *Robert Bruce i jego kompania w eposie pióra Johna Barboura. "The Bruce" około 1376* (Lublin: Wydawnictwo Uniwersytetu Marii Curie-Skłodowskiej, 2020).

[26] "Beneplacitum est Domino super timentes eum. Speravit autem rex Robertus in Deo, et non est fraudatus a desiderio suo. Speravit et Eadwardus in tumultuoso exercitu suo. Cuius caterva circumvallatus et Gloria humane potencie confisus, Scociam hostiliter intravit, et ipsam circumquaque devastans usque Bannokburne pervenit. Regi etenim Anglie Rex Scocie cum paucis intrepide occurrens, non in multitudine populi sed in Domino, ut premissimus, spem ponens, cum antedicto rege duplici bello tam in vigilia quam festo Nativitatis Sancti Johannis Baptiste viriliter conflixit, et ipsum cum suis ipsom auxiliante cuius est victoriam dare in fugam convertit": Walter Bower, *Scotichronicon*, 352, see also 360.

doing so evokes, similarly to John Barbour, the doctrine of just war. Furthermore, the author of the *Scotichronicon* accuses the English king of committing a godless act driven by his contempt for his equal (the Sottish monarch) and invading a country without just cause. Thus, Bower continues, Edward II was met with God's punishment for spilling innocent blood.[27]

Given the above analysis from both English and Scottish sources, contemporaries highlighted the religious elements of the Battle of Bannockburn in addition to the martial one. The efforts made by the opposing sides to win God's favor before the battle, and the attitudes adopted (in the case of Robert the Bruce) or neglected (Edward II), were believed to have influenced the eventual outcome of the engagement. Even before presenting the details of the battle itself, authors of English accounts as well as their Scottish counterparts emphasized the religiosity of Robert the Bruce and his soldiers. They also contrasted these with the lack thereof on the part of the English expedition, particularly King Edward II himself.

This non-religious, non-Christian attitude of the southern invaders was, in the opinion of clergymen writing the relevant narrations, revealed in the fact that they had succumbed to cardinal sins, especially pride and greed. In all probability the authors employed established *cliches* of presenting combating sides in terms of good and bad Christians. Scottish sources were even more adamant in emphasizing the negative perception of the English, accusing the army of transgressing upon the principles of just war. As a consequence, the audiences reading about the particulars of the battle were introduced to this subject, even before considering details related to the battle's respective stages, in a way that likely hinted at the ultimate result of the engagement as well as better understanding why the significantly stronger contingent of the well trained and armed southern troops had been defeated by the Scottish army weaker, poorly armed, and seemingly bound to fail. Alongside the authors' general comments on the Battle of Bannockburn, telling information related to its various religious aspects is also provided in more or less detailed descriptions of the armed engagement of 23 and 24 June 1314 itself. Narrative sources suggest that the religious contexts of the military conflict entailed some characteristic religious rituals performed by the warriors themselves, as

---

27 "Huiusmodi Victoria Scotis cessit, ut creditor, in hoc bello diversis ex causis: tum primo quia rex Anglie injustum contra Scotos movit bellum, quia injusta de causa et iniquo animo; tum quia Deum non timuit nec in ipso congressu eum pre oculis habuit; tum eciam quia parem suum regem Scotorum contempsit; tum [quia] in potencia virtutis sue et in multitudine bellatorum presumpsit; tum quia injuste terram alienam et in alieno solo innocuous invasit; tum eciam propter innocentis sanguinis effusionem vindictam Dei expertus est sicut in sequenti veridico relatu patet manifeste": ibid., 354.

well as the active presence (albeit likely not in a martial capacity) of a sizeable group of priests at the site of the battle. The significance of the latter and their functions in the context of military campaigns throughout the Middle Ages cannot be overstated. The presence of clergymen in a military contingent was crucial to the preservation of the fighting men's morale. By evoking religion, the priests helped the soldiers to better understand the reasons for combat, ensuring them of the divine favor for the particular cause about to be settled through the force of arms, as well as the promise of reward in the form of eternal life. The activity of military chaplains served many crucial psychological purposes—in particular, it helped to alleviate the natural and potentially overpowering fear of death, harm, or capture.[28] It is hardly surprising, therefore, that generals acknowledged the significance of the ecclesiastical contributions and went to great lengths to ensure the participation of men of the cloth in their expeditions. The likely significant involvement of clergymen in the Battle of Bannockburn, particularly on the Scottish side, was hinted at by the authors of the cited narrative sources and is partially also supported by several indirect arguments.[29] A short reference to the presence of some,

---

28 Alastair J. Macdonald, "Courage, Fear and the Experience of the Later Medieval Scottish Soldier," *Scottish Historical Review* 92.235 (2013): 179–206. On the wounds sustained in medieval combat and the causes of death on the battlefield in the context of late medieval sources, see Ian A. MacInnes, "Heads, Shoulders, Knees and Toes: Injury and Death in Anglo-Scottish Combat, c.1296–c.1403," in *Wounds and Wound Repair in Medieval Culture*, ed. Larissa Tracy and Kelly DeVries, EMC 1 (Leiden and Boston MA: Brill, 2015), 102–27; idem, "'On Man Slashes, One Slays, One Warns, One Wounds': Injury and Death in Anglo-Scottish Combat, c.1296–c.1403," in *Killing and Being Killed: Bodies in Battle. Perspectives on Fighters in the Middle Ages*, ed. Jörg Rogge, Mainz historical cultural sciences 38 (Mainz: Transcript, 2017): 61–78.

29 For example, offering confession to thousands of soldiers before the Battle of Bannockburn, both on the first and second day (confirmed by contemporary sources), required the presence of a significant number of priests on the battlefield, whose ratio to soldiers, according to Michael A. Penman's estimates, may have been 1:40. In addition, priests were responsible for celebrating masses and providing warriors with the protection of some saints through their relics, banners and blessings. All this involved a personal engagement in a war of not only "ordinary" military chaplains but also of some prominent clergymen, such as prelates and members of their chapters. The confirmation of a certain involvement of priests, both secular and monastic, in military endeavors is not only confirmed by narratives. In some documentary sources, such as financial accounts, payments were made to priests for their service and the dates of such entries coincided with military campaigns, see Michael A. Penman, "Faith in War: The Religious Experience of Scottish Soldiery, c.1100–c.1500," *JMH* 37.3 (2011): 295–303. On the role and functions of the clergy in the pastoral care of soldiers as well as theological and legal justification of the engagement of clerics in medieval warfare, see esp. David. S. Bachrach, "The Organisation of Military Religion in the Armies of King Edward I of England (1272–1307)," *JMH* 29.4

unnamed, bishops and "other men of religion" in the English army is found in the account by Geoffrey le Baker.[30] Walter Bower's chronicle mentions—as discussed below—the names of two Scottish priests who played important roles during the battle. The key religious rituals performed by the Scottish soldiers immediately before the engagement, both on the first and second day of the battle, included: confession, Holy Communion, and participation in a mass. Other ritual religious gestures common among the Scots included fasting on the first day and kneeling on the ground before the decisive engagement on the second day. References to those gestures and rituals are found in both Scottish and English sources, although the former are understandably more detailed. In his poem, John Barbour mentions that on Sunday morning (23 June), immediately after sunrise, a mass was consecrated in the camp of Robert the Bruce's army, during which many of the soldiers went to confession. The participants prayed and fasted on only bread and water to celebrate St. John's Eve which happened to fall on that date.[31] On the very same day, which concluded with a victorious engagement between a part of the Scottish army and the enemy's vanguard forces, including the famed armed confrontation between Robert the Bruce himself and Henry de Bohun during which the latter was killed,[32] the Scottish king addressed the surrounding lords giving the already mentioned speech rife with religious connotations. It is noteworthy that the monarch not only emphasized his unwavering faith in God's favor for their cause as, he argued, God always favors the just—which promised a decisive victory for the Scots; but he also called upon the gathered men to properly prepare for the engagement by partaking in the mass to be consecrated the following morning.[33] And they did; Barbour writes that at dawn on 24 June, Scottish soldiers prayed during the mass even before having some food and

[ ] (2003): 265–86; idem, "The Friars Go to War: Mendicant Military Chaplains, 1216–c.1300," *CHR* 90.4 (2004): 617–33; Bernard S. Bachrach and David S. Bachrach, *Warfare in Medieval Europe, c.400–1453* (Abingdon and New York: Routledge, 2017), 323–28; see also works cited in n. 2 above.
[30] *The Chronicle of Geoffrey*, 8.
[31] "On Sonday than in the morning / Weile sone after the sone rising / Thai hard thar mes commounaly / And mony thaim schraiff full devotly / That thocht to dey in that melle / Or than to mak thar contré fre. / To God for thar rycht prayit thai, / Thar dynit nane of thaim that that day / Bot for the vigil off Sanct Jhane / Thai fastyt water and breid ilkan": John Barbour, *The Bruce*, 425.
[32] *Vita Edwardi Secundi*, 88; John Barbour, *The Bruce*, 450.
[33] "Sua that we be the sone-rysing / Haff herd mes and buskyt weill / Ilk man intill his awn eschell": John Barbour, *The Bruce*, 459. On the practice of orations before medieval pitched battles, their importance and functions, see Prietzel, *Kriegführung*, 64–65; Bachrach and Bachrach, *Warfare*, 326–28.

making ready for the fight itself. Immediately before advancing against the enemy, the defenders of independence kneeled and prayed to God, imploring the Creator to aid them. Commenting on this gesture, Edward II suggested that the kneeling Scots were asking the English for mercy, to which one of the accompanying magnates, Sir Ingram, replied that they were indeed pleading for mercy but from God rather than the English king. The knight further stated that their enemies would either win or die in combat, but would certainly not kneel before death.[34] Thus, he acknowledged the evident valor and bravery of the opponents.

A wealth of details related to the religious aspects of Scottish preparations are provided in the *Scotichronicon*. Some coincide with the information included in the *Chronicle of Lanercost*[35] as well as Barbour's account summarized above, while others shed new light on some of the particulars. According to Walter Bower's description, on the first day of the battle, King Robert called upon his soldiers to go to confession, devoutly participate in the Holy Mass, accept Communion, and entrust their fate to God. Next, the Scottish chronicler relates the account by Abbot Bernard of Arbroath, who was present at the camp during the battle, of the events which took place the following morning, shortly before the decisive engagement. As told by the monk—and recounted by Bower—at dawn, masses were celebrated throughout the camp as per the king's order. Afterwards, the monarch himself addressed his men, emphasizing the importance of the military struggle for Scottish independence, preserving honor, avenging fallen compatriots killed by the invaders, and liberating others, both laymen and men of religion, who still suffered the indignity of captivity. Robert the Bruce also forcefully declared that the soldiers gathered on the field of battle would not lose hope as they had placed their trust in God.[36] Next, the

---

34   According to *Vita Edwardi Secundi*, 90, Robert Bruce ordered bread and wine to be distributed among his soldiers in that morning; John Barbour described that morning with these words: "The Scottismen quhen it wes day / Thar mes devoutly gert thai say / Syne tuk a sop and maid thaim yar. … The Scottismen commounaly / Knelyt all doune to God to pray / And a schort prayer thar maid thai / To God to help thaim in that fycht, / And quhen the Inglis king had sycht / Off thaim kneland he said in hy, / 'Yone folk knelis to ask mercy'. / Schyr Ingrahame said, 'Ye say suth now, / Thai ask mercy bot nane at you, / For thar trespass to God thai cry. / I tell you a thing sekyrly, / That yone men will all wyn or de, / For doute of dede thai sall nocht fle'": John Barbour, *The Bruce*, 469, 473.

35   *The Chronicle of Lanercost*, 207 includes the following passage: "Now when the two armies had approached very near each other, all the Scots fell on their knees to repeat 'Pater noster', commending themselves to God and seeking help from Heaven; after which they advanced boldly against the English." This scene was repeated and further elaborated by Walter Bower in his *Scotichronicon*, see n. below.

36   Walter Bower, *Scotichronicon*, 362–64.

king emphasized that the day of the decisive battle—24 June—was also the feast day of St. John, suggesting that the opportune coincidence would prove fortunate for the Scottish army gathered on the fields of Bannockburn, thanks to the intercession of the martyr himself as well as other saints of the church and Christ, their leader:

> Happy is this day! John the Baptist was born on it;[37]
> and St Andrew and Thomas who shed his blood
> along with the saints of the Scottish fatherland will fight today
> for the honor of the people, with Christ the Lord in the van.
> Under this leader you will conquer and make an end to war.

As observed by Bower, the king's speech roused the Scots, who expressed their enthusiasm by blowing horns and lifting their banners. The author of *Scotichronicon* also mentioned the subsequent events in the Scottish camp. The next to address the warriors was Abbot Maurice of Inchaffray, who had been busy since early morning hearing the king's confession and celebrating a mass. The priest's words echoed those of Robert the Bruce. The clergyman emphasized the need to defend freedom and preserve the laws broken by the English. It is therefore not surprising that the concise oration was met with equal enthusiasm by Scottish soldiers. Next, Abbot Maurice, clad in liturgical vestments and with a crucifix in his hand, stood barefoot before the army preparing for battle, telling them to kneel and pray for God's favor, which they did. Upon seeing this telling gesture, some of the English started to loudly quip that the Scots were kneeling before them in fear, ready to surrender without a fight.

---

37   According to the author of *Vita Edwardi Secundi*, some English knights perceived St. John's Day as the time not proper for the fight, because it was a feast and also because the soldiers were tired after the night of vigilance, and the earl of Gloucester personally advised their king to postpone the pitch battle till the next day, allowing his army to rest and fully recuperate. This suggestion was rejected both by the monarch and some younger knights as a sign of cowardice and even treachery, see: "Mane autem facto certo cercius compertum est Scotos paratos ad prelium cum magna multitudine armatorum. Unde homines nostri, milites scilicet ueterani, et hii qui magis errant experti, consilium dederunt ipso die non esse pungnaturum, set diem crastinum magis expectandum, tum propter solempne festum, tum propter laborem preteritum. Utile quidem et honestum erat consilium apud iuuenes reprobatum, inhers et ignauum reputatum. Comes autem Gloucestrie consuluit regi ne ipso die in bellum prodiret, set propter festum pocius uacaret, et exercitum suum ualde recrearet. Set rex consilium comitis spreuit, et prodicionem et preuaricacionem sibi imponens in ipsum uehementer excanduit": *Vita Edwardi Secundi*, 90. On the relations between religious holidays and battles, see Hans M. Schaller, "Der heilige Tag als Termin mittelalterlicher Staatsakte," *Deutsches Archiv für Erforschung des Mittelalters* 30 (1974): 1–24; Prietzel, *Kriegführung*, 66–67.

Meanwhile, as Bower tells it, "An older English knight, Ingram de Umfraville, offered a more sound interpretation of this, and replied to them saying: 'You are right that they are surrendering, but to God, not to you.'" Immediately after those words, the author of *Scotichronicon* continues the battle that would end in Scottish victory commenced. Information about its course is provided not only in Bower's work but also in other medieval accounts cited herein.[38]

The details discussed in the above paragraphs, originating from source texts whose authors focused, to varying degrees, on the religious aspects of the Battle of Bannockburn, encourage one to ask some questions regarding the motivations, character, and historical and cultural context of the actions taken by the combatants. Any potentially accessible answer to this will be significant in providing a deeper insight into the role and functions served by religion, not only in the context of the battle discussed here, but also more broadly—in the history of medieval armed conflicts.

The participation of soldiers preparing for battle in religious rituals such as mass, confession, and Communion, was a widespread practice in the Christian societies of medieval Europe. Chronicle accounts mentioning the same date back to the Frankish monarchy in at least the eight century. During the great reformatory synod convoked by Majordomo Carloman, famous *Concilium Germanicum* of 742, it was decided that every military unit should have a chaplain assigned in order to facilitate confession and absolution. The possibility of actively engaging in religious rituals allowed those facing the necessity of combat to gain the conviction, actively supported by their confessors, that the events about to unfold were indeed the will of God. This helped to reduce the tension and fear before the battle. Confession and Communion served a cleansing and motivational function by encouraging the penitents' hope for the greatest of all prizes upon the death of the body—the eternal salvation

---

38   Walter Bower, *Scotichronicon*, 6:363–65. The Battle of Bannockburn was reconstructed by its eye-witness, a Carmelite friar and poet, Robert Baston, whose poem, written in Latin, was included by Bower in his work. Baston was originally supposed to commemorate the expected victory of the English army to the shame of the Scots. After the defeat of the army of Edward II, he became a prisoner of the winners and was commissioned by Robert the Bruce to describe the battle in a way free from ambiguity and bias in exchange for his release, and he did so, see Walter Bower, *Scotichronicon*, 6:366–74. On the identity of the author, pp. 458–59; see also a detailed description of the battle by John Barbour, *The Bruce*, 473–99. On the retreat of Edward II and his army after the lost battle, see *Vita Edwardi Secundi*, 94–95. Geoffrey le Baker wrote in his chronicle that Edward II, fleeing for his life from the battlefield, vowed to God and the Holy Virgin that he would fund a monastery where twenty-four Carmelite friars would stay and study theology as a votive offering for his safe return to England, which was later fulfilled by the king and approved of by Pope John XXII, see *The Chronicle of Geoffrey*, 8–9.

of the soul. The practice of confession before a battle most certainly became more widespread after the Fourth Lateran Council, where canon 21 imposed the obligation to go to confession and receive the Eucharist at least once a year on all Christians. This significantly increased the demand for priestly services. An important argument in favor of attaching chaplains to military expeditions was voiced by Thomas Aquinas, who supported the practice in his *Summa Theologiae*.[39] Apart from confessions, churchmen also conducted field masses. It was assumed that prayer under a priest's leadership immediately before a battle could serve to persuade God to endorse the given side's reasons to engage in the same. This was achieved through, e.g., dedicated formulas that enriched the liturgy celebrated at such times. Portable altars used when celebrating masses in the field were engineered in a way that facilitated their easy transport. However, the use of portable altars could also prove troublesome as a special dispensation from the pope was required to transport the same. In the later medieval period, it was also difficult to enlist parish clergy to participate in military expeditions as this required removing them from their service to local communities they were directly assigned to, and as such could be met with protests from diocesan bishops. As a result, when organizing a campaign late medieval rulers often called on the assistance of monks, particularly from mendicant orders, since they usually had no such parish obligations. This was also true in the case of the Battle of Bannockburn, where, as sources confirm, a number of monks were present.[40] At the same time, there is no written information to suggest any jurisdictional or procedural problems, or legal disputes between rulers and members of the clergy that would be related to the participation of men of the cloth in the battle, either on the English or Scottish side.

As already mentioned, one of the most significant ritual gestures, mentioned in three separate accounts pertaining to the events of 24 June 1314, was the Scottish soldiers' act of kneeling directly before the decisive clash of arms. The author of the *Chronicle of Lanercost*, John Barbour, and later also Walter Bower, all insisted that the telling gesture of the Scots had allowed them to say a short prayer (the first of said accounts identified it as "Our Father") intending to surrender themselves to God's grace and ask for God's protection. In Bower's account, the relevant fragment introduces the character of Abbot Maurice of Inchaffray, who is credited with initiating the gesture. Kneeling or prostrating oneself (Greek *proskynesis*) was a long-established practice dating back to

---

39   Bachrach, "The Friars," 621.
40   David S. Bachrach, "Confession in the 'Regnum Francorum' (742–900): The Sources Revisited," *JEH* 54.1 (2003): 3–22; idem, "The Organization," 268–85; idem, "The Friars," 618–30; Prietzel, *Kriegführung*, 65–67.

Antiquity and signifying deep veneration. In the Early Christian period, the followers of Christ adopted the old Roman and Greek gesture, incorporating it into their worship. In the Middle Ages, falling to one's knees directly onto the ground was also perceived as a symbolic act of humility. It was to represent the lowly condition of humans—beings raised from the ground and bound to return to it. In his deliberations on the etymology of the word *humilitas*, Isidore of Seville noted its symbolic association, also observed by the Romans, with the word *humus* meaning ground or soil. The high and late Middle Ages were rife with iconographic representations of *proskynesis* depicted as the act of absolute humility in surrendering oneself to God.

The scene of soldiers dropping to their knees included in the narrative accounts on the Battle of Bannockburn fits right into these Christian pragmatics. The alleged misunderstanding of the gesture by the English, as presented in Barbour's telling of the story and later repeated almost word for word by the author of *Scotichronicon*, may have been a literary device employed to further contrast the deep faith of the Scots and the irreligious, of the enemy—Edward II and some of his soldiers. Also, the fact that Abbot Maurice (this time in Bower's account) stood barefoot before the Scottish troops should be considered in the context of Christian symbolism rooted in the cultural heritage of pagan Antiquity. Both in ancient times and medieval Christianity it was believed that only a man not wearing shoes, standing barefoot, could truly be unblemished and pure (in the spiritual sense). Animal skin from which shoes were made stood in contradiction to this, signifying impurity. Early Christian texts portray barefoot angels, as well as apostles being instructed by Christ himself to take off their shoes while preaching. Images of Christ and his mother, Mary, standing barefoot are common in medieval iconography.[41] The symbolic significance of bare feet evoked by Walter Bower in his description of the Scottish religious

---

41 The meaning and functions of the ritual gesture of falling on one's knees and on appearing barefooted in medieval religious symbolism are discussed by Przemysław Mrozowski, "Klęczenie w kulturze Zachodu średniowiecznego. Gest ekspiacji—postawa modlitewna," *KH* 95.1 (1988): 37–60; Jacek Maciejewski, "'Nudo pede intrat urbem': Research on the Adventus of a Medieval Bishop Thorach the First Half of the Twelfth Century," *Viator* 41.1 (2010): 89–100; Klaus Schreiner, "'Nudis pedibus'. Barfüßigkeit als religiöses und politisches Ritual," in *Rituale, Zeichen, Bilder: Formen und Funktionen symbolischer Kommunikation im Mittelalter*, ed. Ulrich Meier, Gerd Schwerhoff, and Gabriela Signori, Norm und Struktur 40 (Cologne: Böhlau, 2011), 125–205; Donat de Chapeaurouge, *Einführung in die Geschichte der christlichen Symbole*, 6th ed. (Darmstadt: Wissenschaftliche Buchgesellschaft, 2012). In military context, on the symbolism of bare feet in pagan traditions, see Jacek Banaszkiewicz, "'Nadzy wojownicy'—o średniowiecznych pogłosach dawnego rytu wojskowego," in *Człowiek, sacrum, środowisko. Miejsca kultu we wczesnym średniowieczu*, ed. Sławomir Moździoch, Spotkania Bytomskie 4 (Wrocław:

rituals before the battle was consistent with the presented narration, suggesting to the reader that the conduct of the Scots was exemplary, Christian—that no transgressions could be attributed to them. Thus, the God-fearing soldiers placed themselves in God's hands before combat, not neglecting to perform all the appropriate rituals and gestures, including prostration and prayer, accompanied and instructed as they were by a more than competent priest whose irreproachable behavior was evidenced, among other things, by the fact that he wore no shoes. Under those circumstances, given the satisfaction of all religious conditions of good preparation for battle, victory was all but guaranteed.

In the context of the campaign under discussion that culminated with the decisive Battle of Bannockburn and its religious aspects, there is also one other issue worth consideration. One cannot fail to notice Robert the Bruce's attempt to enlist the support of some saints for the military endeavors of his soldiers. As mentioned above, Walter Bower describes the monarch's prediction in his pre-battle address that alluded to the opportune coincidence with the birthday of St. John as a sign that apart from Christ himself as their leader, St. Andrew and St. Thomas, as well as some other unnamed Scottish saints, would fight on their side. This fact reveals one of the aspects of Robert and his army's religiosity, while at the same time hinting at the need to consider the wider context of patron saints and their involvement in military conflicts.

We are inclined to agree with those biographers of the Bannockburn victor who suggest that his relationship with the church, while undoubtedly driven by pragmatism, was also rooted in the man's authentic faith. He expressed this in a way characteristic of his epoch by dutifully embodying certain specific religious practices. The former was, at least to an extent, the result of a tragic episode which happened in the Scottish ruler's life in 1306. It was then that he had been forced to seek aid from local church hierarchs having blasphemously murdered his political rival, John Comyn, which aroused the wrath of the English monarchy and ultimately led Edward I to attempt the conquest of Scotland. Bruce, who crowned himself as the king of the Scots in March of the same year, brought the bishops of Glasgow, St. Andrews, and Moray to his side. In exchange for absolution of the sin of murder committed on sacred ground (granted personally by the bishop of Glasgow), subsequent aid in terms of diplomacy and propaganda, as well as open support for his political ambitions, Robert the Bruce repaid the Scottish church in various ways. These included commitment to protect its independence, inclusion of some churchmen into

---

Werk, 2000), 11–25, rprt. in idem, *Takie sobie średniowieczne bajeczki* (Cracow: Avalon, 2012), 361–89 at 366–67.

his closest circles of power, endowments to the existing ecclesiastical institutions and foundation of new places of worship.

The efforts made by the ruler in the years preceding the battle discussed in this paper, preceding and succeeding it, clearly show that Robert was acutely aware of the significance of the cult of the saints and religious rituals as powerful tools for achieving political and military goals. One of the most telling examples illustrating the king's understanding of such dependencies was his particular favor extended to Arbroath Abbey dedicated to the archbishop of Canterbury, St. Thomas Becket—a famous victim of English "tyranny." His martyrdom at the hands of Henry II's thugs in 1170 made the saint a symbolic ally to Scottish aspirations towards independence. This was likely one of the reasons why St. Thomas's name was included by Robert in his speech before the battle of 24 June 1314, as well as why Bernard, the abbot of Arbroath was present at the camp. In fact, the latter was there not only as the propagator of St. Thomas's worship and custodian of the saint's memory but also in the official capacity of royal chancellor and a member of the king's closest circle of power. He also carried some form of a material remnant of St. Columba in the form of an object he had brought with him to Bannockburn. It is possible, of which more below, that Arbroath Abbey held some relic of the saint which, in Bernard's hands, made its way, carried in a dedicated reliquary, to Stirling castle on the eve of the battle; a banner dedicated to Columba may have also been flown at the camp.

Another good example of King Robert's devotional practices was the renovation (or foundation) of a priory at Kirkton of Strath Fillan dedicated to St. Fillan in Strathearn, maintained by the Canon Regulars of Inchaffray Abbey. This allowed for the previously scattered relics of the saint to be gathered in a single location. Tradition has it that the endowment in question was an expression of Robert the Bruce's gratitude for St. Fillan's protection during, among other engagements, the Battle of Bannockburn. Notably, the superior of the monastery in Inchaffray, Maurice, was one of the two abbots mentioned in source texts by name as participants in the battle. Bower made him, likely for a good reason, one of the main characters in his retelling of the story, identifying him as the king's confessor before the clash with Edward II's army. Maurice was also an orator contributing to rousing the soldiers' morale, as well as a chaplain performing important religious rites at the Scottish camp during the key stage of preparations for the final battle. Numerous arguments supporting Robert the Bruce's dedication to devotional practices, which may have been due to the king's authentic religiosity, are also provided by his conduct in the years that followed the Battle of Bannockburn until his death in 1329, including his pilgrimage to St. Ninian at Whithorn undertaken in the same year, as well as his wish (sadly unheeded) to have his heart transported by James Douglas to the Holy Land.[42]

Given both the piety of Robert the Bruce, whose extent and character were outlined above, and the overall popularity of the cults of some saints in medieval Scotland, historical studies have been conducted to determine the potential role of such aspects in the Battle of Bannockburn. The Scots' appeal for St. Andrew and St. Thomas's aid seems evident, not only because their names were specifically mentioned by Bower, who—fully aware of the significance of such worship—placed the suitable words in king Robert's mouth. St. Andrew was one of the New Testament apostles that enjoyed the greatest reverence in Scotland where his relics had been most likely present since as early as the fourth century. It was at that time, according to some medieval Scottish accounts, that St. Regulus (also known as St. Rule) had brought them to the country from Greece and erected a church at the location of the later city of St. Andrews. It was exactly due to the presence of St. Andrew's relics that the city became an important pilgrimage destination in the Middle Ages. To accommodate the growing numbers of arriving pilgrims, the decision was made to replace the old church with a large cathedral, whose construction began in 1158 and ended in 1318. Robert the Bruce took part in the consecration of this largest church in Scotland and, according to the *Scotichronicon*, donated

---

42 Tomasz Kapitaniak, *Bannockburn 1314* (Łódź, Ibidem, 2002), 79–104; Michael Penman, "Christian Days and Knights: The Religious Devotions and Court of David II of Scotland, 1329–71," *Historical Research* 75.189 (2002): 249–72 at 251–52; idem, "'Sacred Food,'" 1039–48; Michalski, *Robert Bruce*, 164–77. The most important biographies of Robert the Bruce are the following: Ronald McNair Scott, *Robert the Bruce: King of Scots* (New York: Barnes and Noble, 1982); Chris Brown, *Robert the Bruce: A Life Chronicled* (Stroud: Tempus, 2004); Barrow, *Robert Bruce*, as in n. 18; Michael Penman, *Robert the Bruce: King of the Scots* (New Haven CN: Yale University Press, 2014); Colm McNamee, *Robert Bruce: Our Most Valiant Prince, King and Lord* (Edinburgh: Birlinn, 2018). On the cult of St. Fillan in Scotland, see Simon Taylor, "The Cult of St. Fillan in Scotland," in *The North Sea World in the Middle Ages: Studies in the Cultural-History in North-Western Europe*, ed. Thomas R. Liszka and Lorna E.M. Walker (Dublin: Four Courts Press, 2001), 175–210. For a general overview of functions of saints and their relics in medieval religiosity, including their role in military conflicts, where they were regarded as aids, see František Graus, "Der Heilige als Schlachtenhelfer—Zur Nationalisierung einer Wundererzählung in der mittelalterlichen Chronistik," in *Festschrift für Helmut Beumann zum 65. Geburtstag*, ed. Kurt-Ulrich Jäschke and Reinhard Wenskus (Sigmaringen: Thorbecke, 1977), 330–48; Robert Bartlett, *Why Can the Dead Do Such Great Things? Saints and Worshippers from the Martyrs to the Reformation* (Princeton NJ and Oxford: Princeton University Press, 2013), 282–332, 379–83. For military interventions of angels through their revelations before some medieval battles, see Radosław Kotecki, "Pious Rulers, Princely Clerics, and Angels of Light: 'Imperial Holy War' Imagery in Twelfth-Century Poland and Rus'," in *Christianity and War*, 159–88.

the generous annual amount of 100 marks to the cathedral priory as thanks to St. Andrew's assistance in the Battle of Bannockburn. St. Andrew became a symbol of independent Scotland and sovereign royal power, particularly in the turbulent times of the late thirteenth and early fourteenth centuries. His aid is known to have been successfully evoked already during the Battle of Stirling Bridge in 1297. The saint's subsequent effective intercession came in 1314 at Bannockburn.[43]

As already mentioned, the fact that on 24 June 1314, Robert the Bruce also elected to call upon another saint, St. Thomas, may have been, at least partially, due to the symbolic and political significance attributed to this English martyr—a victim of Henry II's terror—in the context of Scottish independence aspirations. In the opinion of Michael Penman, Robert the Bruce may have exploited the worship of Becket as a tool facilitating the efforts to gain papal support for his war against England. It is not without significance that the mention of the saint's name was attributed to Robert in Bower's citation of Bernard of Arbroath, whose abbey, consecrated in 1197, was dedicated to none other than St. Thomas. Given his affiliation with the patron saint, the abbot, as an eyewitness to the events, may have wanted to underscore Becket's significance by mentioning him by name, alongside St. Andrew, in his account of the battle. Thomas Becket had been among the most venerated saints among the Scottish population long before 1314, and Arbroath Abbey was hardly the only place dedicated to the English archbishop and his worship. His cult had been widely popularized in twelfth- and thirteenth-century Scotland, as evidenced by the prevalence of altars and chapels devoted to the saint scattered throughout the country, as well as the documented efforts of the powers to promote his worship, undertaken by several Scottish monarchs—including Robert the Bruce and his predecessors William I, Alexander II, and Alexander III, as well as by local magnates and supporters of the Bannockburn victor, e.g., Thomas Randolph, earl of Moray and Sir David Lindsay of Crawford.[44]

---

43 Marinell Ash and Dauvit Broun, "The Adoption of St Andrew of Patron Saint of Scotland," in *Medieval Art and Architecture in the Diocese of St Andrews*, ed. John Higgit, British Archaeological Association conference transactions 23 (Leeds: British Archaeological Association, 1994), 16–24 at 18–21; Penman, "Sacred Food," 1050; Mairi Cowan, "'The Saints of the Scottish Country Will Fight Today': Robert the Bruce's Alliance with the Saints at Bannockburn," *International Review of Scottish Studies* 40 (2015): 1–32 at 5–8. On the participation of Robert Bruce in the consecration of the Cathedral of St. Andrews, see Walter Bower, *Scotichronicon*, 413; Tom Turpie, *Kind Neighbours: Scottish Saints and Society in the Later Middle Ages*, TNW 70 (Leiden and Boston MA: Brill, 2015), 29–30.

44 Michael Penman, "The Bruce Dynasty, Becket and Scottish Pilgrimage to Canterbury, c.1178–c.1404," *JMH* 32.4 (2006): 346–70; idem, "Sacred Food," 1046–49; Cowan, "'The Saints,'" 8–10. On the cult of saints among Scottish royalty and aristocracy, particularly

Apart from the two saints directly named by Bower as patrons evoked at the Battle of Bannockburn, one would be relatively safe in assuming that many other Christian saints would have been prayed to for assistance before the engagement. The most likely, albeit not directly confirmed in the sources, the addressee of prayers for mediation with God would have been St. Columba, whose spiritual presence and intercession during the battle of 1314 was to be assured by the abbot of Arbroath, Bernard. In a document dating back to 1211, signed in Aberdeen by William I, the Scottish king confirmed the previously established right of Arbroath Abbey to keep and protect a mysterious object described as *Breccbennach*, directly associated in the charter with St. Columba. The document states that concerning the confirmation of the already held privilege, King William I endowed the monks with the land of Forglen in Banffshire, but under the condition that should the leaseholders of the land ever be called upon by the king to stand at arms, they would be obliged to carry *Breccbennach* with them. Clearly, it was intended as a way of ensuring some form of St. Columba's presence in hope of securing the saint's assistance directly on the field of battle in the event of a military conflict. The actual nature of *Breccbennach* continues to be a subject of contention among historians. Until recently, the most prevalent opinion, dating back to nineteenth-century deliberations, identified the object as the currently empty eight-century reliquary, also known as the Monymusk Reliquary, currently displayed at the National Museum of Scotland in Edinburgh. Were one to follow this train of thought, it would be natural to assume that *Breccbennach* originally contained some sort of St. Columba's relic and that the monks of Arbroath were charged with protecting them.

However, this conclusion has been challenged of late as it is argued, there is no evidence to suggest any association between *Breccbennach* and the Monymusk Reliquary. A recent hypothesis states that the mysterious name may have not referred to a reliquary at all, but rather to a banner bearing the saint's image. Unfortunately, given the present state of knowledge, it is impossible to positively verify any of the proposed answers as to what *Breccbennach* actually was. It is plausible, however, that the object directly related to the cult of St. Columba—whatever its exact nature—was used during the Battle of Bannockburn. This is supported by the generally uncontested fact that Abbot Bernard, was present at the site. And due to the obligation imposed on his

---

in the later Middle Ages, see Matthew H. Hammond, "Royal and Aristocratic Attitudes to Saint and the Virgin Mary in Twelfth- and Thirteenth-Century Scotland," in *The Cult of Saints and the Virgin Mary in Medieval Scotland*, ed. Steve Boardman and Eila Williamson, SCelH 28 (Woodbridge: Boydell Press, 2010), 61–85; Turpie, *Kind Neighbours*.

abbey years before, he would have been expected, as its superior, to ensure St. Columba's spiritual contribution to the war effort. The opportunity to do just that came in June 1314, and what better way to do so than to evoke the saint, his presence manifested in one form or another, in the very field of imminent battle.[45]

The likelihood that Abbot Bernard of Arbroath implored St. Columba to aid Robert the Bruce's troops in the Battle of Bannockburn seems high not only considering indirect source references to this fact and historical determinations made to date but also given the significant popularity of the saint's worship and his perceived affinity for matters related to protecting Scotland against its enemies. As observed by Robert Bartlett in his book on medieval veneration of saints and religion, relics of St. Andrew and St. Columba served, in the discussed period as well as previously, as symbols of Scottish national unity.[46] The life and activity of St. Columba, an Irish monk and missionary spreading the word of Christ in Scotland (the founder and first abbot of Iona Abbey) were popularized soon after his death through the efforts of his hagiographer, Adomnán, the ninth abbot of Iona, in his *Vita Columbae*. The hagiography described the first miracles performed by Columba, both in life and after death. His relics could be effectively used to call down rain during a time of drought, protect a community against plague, and secure victory in a military engagement. The saint's miraculous intercessions continued to be mentioned in later accounts. An Irish text dating back to the early tenth-century mentions, for example, a Viking raid led against Scotland by King Ivarr (Imar). Faced with the threat, the defenders performed some religious rituals, calling for divine intervention. To this end, they prayed to God and St. Columba, fasted, distributed alms to churches and the poor, received Communion, and pledged to always carry St. Columba's crosier before a battle as a sign of victory.

45   Francis Eeles, "The Monymusk Reliquary or Brecbennoch of St Columba," *Proceedings of the Society of the Antiquaries of Scotland* 68 (1934): 433–38; David H. Caldwell, "The Monymusk Reliquary: The 'Breccbennach' of St Columba?" *Proceedings of the Society of the Antiquaries of Scotland* 131 (2001): 267–82; Penman, "Christian Days," 251; idem, "Faith in War," 298; Cowan, "'The Saints,'" 11; Richard Sharpe, "King William and the Brecc Bennach in 1211: Reliquary or Holy Banner?" *IR* 62.2 (2015): 163–90; idem, "Banners." The author points at a meaningful lack of any evidence for the presence of banners of any English saints during the Battle of Bannockburn, despite the promise, confirmed by sources, made by Edward II to carry on his military expedition to Scotland the banners of St. Cuthbert and St. John of Beverley respectively, see Sharpe, "Banners," 249, 283. Compare n. 16 above. On the cult of St. Columba in Scotland, the *Breccbennach* and its uncertain connection with the Battle of Bannockburn, see also Turpie, *Kind Neighbours*, 33–34.

46   Hammond, "Royal and Aristocratic Attitudes," 75; Bartlett, *Why Can the Dead*, 231–32.

After that, the anonymous author reports, they were able to not only prevail over the Viking invaders in battle but also win several subsequent military confrontations. It was likely due to this and other similar stories that the cult of St. Columba gradually spread and solidified throughout Scotland, continuing well into the following centuries. An antiphoner dating back to the first half of the fourteenth century, used by the monks of the Inchcolm monastery and known as the *Inchcolm Antiphoner*, contains hymns of praise for the saint, referred to as the patron saint of the whole of Scotland. It also contains prayers imploring him to protect the land against English aggression. In his *Scotichronicon*, Bower lists some miracles performed through St. Columba's intercession in the fourteenth century, and although his possible contribution to the Battle of Bannockburn is not directly mentioned, there is much to suggest that such assistance was nonetheless sought by the Scots.[47]

Apart from the confirmed or at least highly likely inclusion of the saints mentioned above in the prayers for assistance performed by the participants in the Battle of Bannockburn, it could be hypothesized that other beatified individuals were also invoked. As already mentioned above, one of the saints believed to be partial to the Scottish cause may have been St. Fillan, whose involvement in the battle should be considered, among other indications, based on the *ex post facto* argument that in 1318, Robert the Bruce renovated and expanded the Augustine chapel of Inchaffray dedicated to St. Fillan in Strathearn. The donation was, according to tradition, an expression of the king's gratitude for the support granted by the saint during the 1314 Bannockburn military conflict with the English.[48] Another plausible hypothesis could also suggest the

---

47 Walter Bower, *Scotichronicon*, 7:108–11, 118–21, 398–403; Jean-Michel Picard, "The Purpose of Adomnán's 'Vita Columbae,'" *Peritia* 1 (1982): 160–77; Thomas O. Clancy, "Columba, Adomnán and the Cult of Saints in Scotland," in *"Spes Scotorum." "Hope of Scots": Saint Columba, Iona and Scotland*, ed. Dauvit Broun and Thomas O. Clancy (Edinburgh: T&T Clark, 1999), 3–33; Bartlett, *Why Can the Dead*, 30; Cowan, "'The Saints,'" 12. For St. Columba as patron saint and military aide in Gaelic world, see also discussion by Jesse Patrick Harrington in this collection (vol. 1, chap. 3).

48 Taylor, "The Cult of St. Fillan," 184, 187; Penman, "Sacred Food," 1040; Cowan, "'The Saints,'" 19–20. Tom Turpie refers in his work on Scottish medieval saints to the story about St. Fillan's miraculous manifestation shortly before the Battle of Bannockburn as told by Hector Boece (1465–1536) in his *Historia Gentis Scotorum* (Hector Boethius, *Scotorum Historia (1575 Version): A Hypertext Critical Edition*, 14.36, ed. Dana F. Sutton (2010), philological.bham.ac.uk/boece/14lat.html) written in 1527. According to the Scottish chronicler, the silver case including the relic of St. Fillan opened (and then closed of its own volition) in front of the astonished King Robert the Bruce and his men-at-arms, which they interpreted as a good omen. This story, which may be used to augment the assumption about St. Fillan's participation in the Battle, cannot be verified by other accounts, see Turpie, *Kind Neighbours*, 128–29.

spiritual presence at the Bannockburn battlefield of St. Ninian, a (most likely) fifth-century missionary among the Picts, as confirmed by at least one anthology. According to an account in *Orygynale Cronikil of Scotland* (early 1400s/ fifteenth century) by Andrew of Wyntoun, prayers for the saint's aid were made by Scottish soldiers before the victorious Battle of Roslin fought against the English in 1303. It is not unlikely that a similar practice took place eleven years later at Bannockburn. Robert the Bruce's reverence for St. Ninian is beyond doubt. In his later years, already weakened by illness, he undertook a pilgrimage to the saint's grave in Whithorn in the region of Galloway. Notably, that journey likely precipitated the king's death only several months later (in 1329). In the late Middle Ages, St. Ninian enjoyed widespread veneration throughout Scotland and beyond.[49]

A warranted hypothesis in the context of imploring saints to aid troops during the discussed battle relates to the alleged intercession of St. Margaret, a Scottish queen and wife to King of Scotland Malcolm III, whom pope Innocent IV beatified in 1250 in recognition of her sainthood. Robert the Bruce was among the advocates of her cult, having extended his support to the Dunfermline Abbey in Fife, where the queen was buried by her own choice (even though her heart was laid to rest at Melrose Abbey). Originally, the cult of St. Margaret had only regional outreach but gradually spread to the whole of Scotland. Innocent V, who encouraged the faithful to go on pilgrimages to her grave, aided in further popularizing her cult. The *Scotichronicon* provides two descriptions of miracles performed through her intercession. According to Bower's text, the first took place during the attempted translation of the queen's earthly remains in 1250, but the second sheds more insight on her potential involvement in the Battle of Bannockburn. In 1263, Scotland was invaded by a Norwegian force led by King Håkon IV, who put forward claims to a part of the territory. At the time, writes Walter Bower, a mighty but unwell Scottish knight named John Wemyss experienced a vision in his dream, wherein long dead Margaret in the company of her husband, King Malcolm, and their three sons, stood in her full majesty in the doorway of the church in Dunfermline. The woman introduced herself to the knight and when asked about her intentions, informed him that she was about to accompany her husband and sons to Largs where, in a great battle against the Norwegians, they would stand in defense of the country against the usurper seeking to unlawfully subjugate the land. St. Margaret further explained to the awestruck man that only her own

---

49   Penman, "Sacred Food," 1036, 1052–53; Cowan, "'The Saints,'" 12–14; Daphne Brooke, *Wild Men and Holy Places: St. Ninian, Whithorn and the Medieval Realm of Galloway* (Edinburgh: Birlinn, 2001); Thomas O. Clancy, "The Real St Ninian," *IR* 42.1 (2001): 1–28 at 21–25.

dynasty, and not the usurper's, has a legitimate claim to the rule of Scotland, as it was granted to herself and her heirs by God himself. As soon as he woke up and despite his illness, the knight traveled to the abbey where the queen's grave was located and described his vision to the prior, after which he paid homage to the saint's relics and was miraculously healed. At the same time, a messenger arrived in Dunfermline to inform the monks of the victorious battle fought by Scottish troops against the Norwegian army at Largs. Bower's narration suggests that in the Scottish national tradition, as well as the collective awareness of the late Middle Ages, St. Margaret was perceived as significantly invested in the protection of the legitimacy and sovereignty of Scottish rule. In this context, as well as given the well documented, personal commitment of Robert the Bruce to popularizing the saint's cult, one would be justified in assuming the likelihood of St. Margaret's name also having been evoked in the prayers for spiritual assistance said during the Battle of Bannockburn in 1314.[50]

Researchers studying the question of Robert the Bruce's religiosity also mention, in the context of the Battle of Bannockburn, the possibility of at least one more saint's name having been evoked. This was St. Kentigern, also known as Mungo, the first bishop of Glasgow. There are several arguments to potentially support this claim. Kentigern was known, as reflected in medieval writing, as another saint whose intercession allegedly aided the Scots in defending their territories against foreign invaders. In a twelfth-century poem

50   *The Miracles of Saint Aebbe of Coldingham and St Margaret of Scotland*, ed. Robert Bartlett (Oxford: Clarendon Press, 2003); 87–89; Walter Bower, *Scotichronicon*, 5:336–39; Penman, "Sacred Food," 1056–58; Cowan, "The Saints,'" 14–17; for the biography of St. Margaret, see Catherine Keene, *Saint Margaret, Queen of the Scots: A Life in Perspective* (New York: Palgrave Macmillan, 2013). The importance of the cult of St. Margaret for preserving and spreading the idea of national identity and sovereignty of the Scots can be also related to the fact that the queen was associated with a very sought-after holy relic, which remained in her personal possession and later, after the queen's death, in the custody of her successors. The object in question was a reliquary holding a fragment of the True Cross, brought by St. Margaret on her arrival in Scotland. The reliquary is known as the Black Rood. Believed to be an authentic fragment of the True Cross—as described and confirmed by Aelred of Rievaulx, this holy relic was regarded by medieval Scottish people to be a particularly significant symbol of the collective memory of the sacred monarchy and sovereignty. This was based on the belief, which prevailed in medieval Christianity, that the possession of relics holding splinters of the True Cross by a monarch testified to the support given by God to their sovereign rule. The English king, Edward I, who was perfectly aware of the meaning of the Black Rood for the Scots, ordered the relic to be taken away from them and placed this symbolic object in the custody of the English (in the castle of Berwick in 1291). Earlier, i.e. after conquering Wales in 1284, Edward had done the same with the holy cross of the Welsh, known as the Croes Naid. The Black Rood did not return to Scotland until 1328, see Julianna Grigg, "The Black Rood of Scotland: A Social and Political Life," *Viator* 48.3 (2017): 1–26.

attributed to a man named Willelmus, entitled *Carmen de Morte Sumerledi*, one may find a reference to exactly such intervention during the second invasion of Scotland led by Somerled of Argyll (Battle of Renfrew in 1164).[51] In the late Middle Ages, the great piety and sainthood of Kentigern, as well as miracles performed through his intercession were described by Walter Bower in his *Scotichronicon*.[52] According to the 1432 inventory of the saint's burial place at the Glasgow Cathedral, which had been erected in his honor, it contained a collection of relics, including St. Kentigern's bones, combs and fragments of clothing. One cannot exclude the possibility that some of the items could have been brought to the Bannockburn battlefield in 1314. King Robert the Bruce may have done so not only to further bolster the numbers of saints leading his army to victory over the English. Robert Wishart, the bishop of Glasgow between 1271 and 1316, personally charged with preserving the relics of St. Kentigern kept at the site, was among the king's key supporters in the struggle for Scottish independence. Wishart demonstrated such a stance already in 1306 when, as already mentioned, he absolved his namesake of the crime of John Comyn's murder. The bishop's involvement in the battle, as well as the presumed presence of St. Kentigern's relics at the site, may have served as not only confirmation of the prelate's prominent position in the then system of political power. It could also serve as an expression of the king's gratitude for loyal services rendered. Robert the Bruce is known to have personally supported the cult of St. Kentigern, as evidenced by his actions in the years following the victorious battle.[53]

The above deliberations, based on the available sources pertaining to the Battle of Bannockburn, point to the conclusion that the religiosity of its participants significantly affected their actions at the respective stages of military engagement. Considering the surviving accounts, various elements of religious

---

51 There were at least two attacks on Scotland carried out by Somerled and his allies, one in 1153 and the other one—in 1164. In the first recorded military onslaught, as it was written in the poem in question, St. Kentigern failed to protect the Cathedral of Glasgow and its congregation, despite the prayers for his intervention. This finally happened, however, which was suggested in the second part of the poem, in 1164, when the Scottish forces led by the bishop of Glasgow, Herbert, and the sheriff of Lanark, Baldwin of Biggar, defeated the invaders in the Battle of Renfrew, see Alex Woolf, "The Song of the Death of Somerled and the Destruction of Glasgow in 1153," *Sydney Society for Scottish History Journal* 14 (2013): 1–11. On the life and cult of St. Kentigern in Scotland, see John R. Davies, "Bishop Kentigern among the Britons," in *Saints' Cults in the Celtic World*, ed. Steve Boardman, John Reuben Davies, and Eila Williamson, SCelH 25 (Woodbridge: Boydell Press, 2009), 66–90.

52 Walter Bower, *Scotichronicon*, 2:78–87.

53 Penman, "Sacred Food," 1050–51; Cowan, "'The Saints,'" 17–19.

behavior took forms typical of medieval battlefields in general, and involved rituals such as participation in the mass, confession, Communion, fasting, pre-battle blessing, and other ritual gestures, such as kneeling immediately before the battle's commencement. One must note the presence of numerous members of the clergy, mainly monks, at the military camp. Their task was to ensure the soldiers' adequate spiritual preparation for combat. Indeed, priests played several roles at Bannockburn: from their direct involvement in the performance of specific rites and caring for holy relics and other symbols of divine presence, to strengthening the combatants' belief in standing on the side of good and justice, as well as their expectation of due spiritual reward.

Given the knowledge we currently possess, our analysis of narrative sources related to the Battle of Bannockburn still proves insufficient to decisively determine the extent to which the authors, writing from sometimes rather distant chronological perspectives, based their accounts of the battle on actual facts, such that were known to them. It is not possible to tell precisely to what degree the narrations related to the events in question were products of specific ideological and political agendas that were bound to have affected all descriptions of the Battle of Bannockburn. The selection and emphasis on particular aspects of the battle were certainly conditioned by specific political allegiances, but also patriotism, the intellectual formation and institutional affiliation of authors such as John Barbour or Walter Bower, whose accounts of the event must also be perceived through the prism of collective memory and development of the national mythos.[54] Further research is needed in terms of religiosity and the extent to which clergy were involved on the English side of the 1314 conflict.[55] Our current knowledge on the topic, as presented in the above analysis of the relevant source texts, shows a clear disproportion in this respect in favor of emphasizing the religious behavior of the Scots, while almost entirely neglecting to present the same from the perspective of the English. This is partially because most of the battle's descriptions are found in Scottish sources whose authors, due to the victorious character of the encounter, were more inclined to focus on praising the accomplishments

---

54   On collective memory, see Maurice Halbwachs, *On Collective Memory*, trans. Lewis A. Coser (Chicago: University of Chicago Press, 1992, 1st ed. 1925); Jan Assmann, *Das kulturelle Gedächtnis. Schrift, Erinnerung und politische Identität in frühen Hochkulturen* (Munich: Beck, 2007, 1st ed. 1992).

55   Gerrard, *The Church at War*, chap. 4, recently conducted in his study an in-depth analysis of spiritual aspects of English clerical participation in warfare (the use of sacred banners, crosses, relics, as well as excommunication), but he did not cover the period after 1200.

of their countrymen[56] and setting them against a broader, also religious, context. In turn, Edward II's ignominious defeat may have effectively discouraged English chroniclers from going into too much detail regarding this episode in the country's history, however significant for future Anglo-Scottish relations. It appears that they would much rather forget it had even happened.

Bibliography

Primary Sources

Chronica monasterii S. Albani. Johannis de Trokelowe, et Henrici de Blaneforde, monachorum S. Albani, necnon quorundam anonymorum, chronica et annals, regnantibus Henrico Tertio, Edwardo Primo, Edwardo Secundo, Ricardo Secundo, et Henrico Quarto. Edited by Henry Thomas Riley. London: Longmans, Green, Reader, and Dyer, 1866.

The Chronicle of Geoffrey le Baker. Translated by Richard Barber. Introduction and notes by David Preest. Woodbridge: Boydell Press, 2012.

Chronicon Galfridi le Baker de Swynebroke. Edited by Edward Maunde Thompson. Oxford: Clarendon Press, 1889.

Hector Boethius [Boece]. *Scotorum Historia (1575 Version): A Hypertext Critical Edition.* Edited by Dana F. Sutton (2010). philological.bham.ac.uk/boece.

John Barbour. *The Bruce.* Edited and translated by Archibald A. McBeth Duncan. Canongate classics 78. Edinburgh: Canongate Books, 1997.

The Chronicle of Lanercost. Edited and translated by Herbert Maxwell. Glasgow: Maclehose and Sons, 1913.

The Miracles of Saint Aebbe of Coldingham and St Margaret of Scotland. Edited by Robert Bartlett. Oxford: Clarendon Press, 2003.

Thomas Gray. *Scalacronica.* Edited and translated by Andy King. Publications of the Surtees Society 209. Woodbridge: Boydell Press, 2005.

Vita Edwardi Secundi. Edited and translated by Wendy R. Childs. Oxford: Clarendon Press, 2005.

Walter Bower. *Scotichronicon.* 9 vols. Edited by John MacQueen et al. Aberdeen: Aberdeen University Press, 1987–1998.

---

56   It was common practice that the victorious side in a medieval battle hyped its outcome, see Philippe Contamine, "Die Schlacht im Abendland am Ende des Mittelalters, Vorstellung, Kampfhandlung, Bericht, Bild, Erinnerung," in *Tannenberg—Grunwald - Žalgiris 1410. Krieg und Frieden im späten Mittelalter,* ed. Werner Paravacini, Rimvydas Petrauskas, and Grischa Vercamer, DHIW 26 (Wiesbaden: Harrassowitz, 2012), 69–88.

Secondary Sources

Althoff, Gerd. *Die Macht der Rituale*. Darmstadt: Wissenschaftliche Buchgesellschaft, 2013.

Amstrong, Peter. *Bannockburn. Robert Bruce's Great Victory*. Oxford: Osprey Publishing, 2002.

Ash, Marinell, and Broun, Dauvit. "The Adoption of St Andrew of Patron Saint of Scotland." In *Medieval Art and Architecture in the Diocese of St Andrews*. Edited by John Higgit, 18–21. British Archaeological Association conference transactions 23. Leeds: The British Archaeological Association, 1994.

Bachrach, Bernard S., and David S. Bachrach. *Warfare in Medieval Europe, c.400–1453*. Abingdon and New York: Routledge, 2017.

Bachrach, David S. "Confession in the 'Regnum Francorum' (742–900): The Sources Revisited." *JEH* 54.1 (2003): 3–22.

Bachrach, David S. "The Friars Go to War: Mendicant Military Chaplains, 1216–c.1300." *CHR* 90.4 (2004): 617–33.

Bachrach, David S. "The Medieval Military Chaplain and His Duties." In *The Sword of the Lord: Military Chaplains from the First to the Twenty-First Century*. Edited by Doris L. Bergen, 69–88. Notre Dame IN: University of Notre Dame Press, 2004.

Bachrach, David S. "Military Chaplains and the Religion of War in Ottonian Germany, 919–1024." *RSS* 39.1 (2011): 13–21.

Bachrach, David S. "The Organization of Military Religion in the Armies of King Edward I of England (1272–1307)." *JMH* 29 (2003): 265–86.

Bachrach, David S. *Religion and the Conduct of War, c.300–125*. Woodbridge: Boydell Press, 2003.

Banaszkiewicz, Jacek. "'Nadzy wojownicy'—o średniowiecznych pogłosach dawnego rytu wojskowego." In *Człowiek, sacrum, środowisko. Miejsca kultu we wczesnym średniowieczu*. Edited by Sławomir Moździoch, 11–25. Spotkania Bytomskie 4. Wrocław: Werk, 2000. Rprt. in Jacek Banaszkiewicz. *Takie sobie średniowieczne bajeczki*. 361–89. Cracow: Avalon, 2012.

Banaszkiewicz, Jacek. "Włócznia i chorągiew. O rycie otwierania bitwy w związku z cudem kampanii nakielskiej Bolesława Krzywoustego (Kadłubek, III, 14)." *KH* 94.4 (1987): 3–24. Reprinted in Jacek Banaszkiewicz. *W stronę rytuałów i Galla Anonima*. 79–110. Cracow: Avalon, 2018.

Barrow, Geoffrey W.S. *Robert Bruce: And the Community of the Realm of Scotland*. 4th ed. Edinburgh: Edinburgh University Press, 2005.

Bartlett, Robert. *Why Can the Dead Do Such Great Things? Saints and Worshippers from the Martyrs to the Reformation*. Princeton NJ and Oxford: Princeton University Press, 2013.

Boardman, Steve and Susan Foran, ed. *Barbour's Bruce and its Cultural Contexts: Politics, Chivalry, and Literature in Late Medieval Scotland*. Rochester: Brewer, 2015.

Brooke, Daphne. *Wild Men and Holy Places: St. Ninian, Whithorn and the Medieval Realm of Galloway.* Edinburgh: Birlinn, 2001.

Brown, Chris. *Robert the Bruce: A Life Chronicled.* Stroud: Tempus, 2004.

Brown, Michael. *Bannockburn: The Scottish War and the British Isles, 1307–1323.* Edinburgh: Edinburgh University Press, 2008.

Buc, Philippe. *Holy War, Martyrdom, and Terror: Christianity, Violence, and the West.* Philadelphia: University of Pennsylvania Press, 2015.

Caldwell, David H. "The Monymusk Reliquary: The 'Breccbennach' of St Columba?" *Proceedings of the Society of the Antiquaries of Scotland* 131 (2001): 267–82.

Cameron, Sonja. "Chivalry and Warfare in Barbour's 'Bruce.'" In *Armies, Chivalry and Warfare in Medieval Britain and France.* Edited by Matthew Strickland, 13–29. Harlaxton medieval studies 7. Stamford: Watkins, 1998.

Cannadine, David and Simon Price, ed. *Rituals of Royalty: Power and Ceremonial in Traditional Societies.* Cambridge: Cambridge University Press, 1993.

Chapeaurouge, Donat de. *Einführung in die Geschichte der christlichen Symbole.* 6th ed. Darmstadt: Wissenschaftliche Buchgesellschaft, 2012.

Clancy, Thomas O. "Columba, Adomnán and the Cult of Saints in Scotland." In *"Spes Scotorum." "Hope of Scots": Saint Columba, Iona and Scotland.* Edited by Dauvit Broun and Thomas O. Clancy, 3–33. Edinburgh: T&T Clark, 1999.

Clancy, Thomas O. "The Real St Ninian." *IR* 42.1 (2001): 1–28.

Clauss, Martin. "Der Krieg als Mittel und Thema der Kommunikation. Die narrative Funktion des Gottesurteils." In *Gottes Werk und Adams Beitrag. Formen der Interaktion zwischen Mensch und Gott im Mittelalter.* Edited by Thomas Honegger, Gerlinde Huber-Rebenich, and Volker Leppin, 128–41. Das Mittelalter. Perspektiven mediävistischer Forschung. Beihefte 1. Berlin: De Gruyter, 2014.

Contamine, Philippe. "Die Schlacht im Abendland am Ende des Mittelalters, Vorstellung, Kampfhandlung, Bericht, Bild, Erinnerung." In *Tannenberg—Grunwald—Žalgiris 1410. Krieg und Frieden im späten Mittelalter.* Edited by Werner Paravacini, Rimvydas Petrauskas, and Grischa Vercamer, 69–88. DHIW 26. Wiesbaden: Harrassowitz, 2012.

Contamine, Philippe. *War in the Middle Ages.* Translated by Michael Jones. Oxford: Blackwell, 1999.

Cornell, David. *Bannockburn: The Triumph of Robert the Bruce.* New Haven CN and London: Yale University Press, 2009.

Cowan, Mairi. "'The Saints of the Scottish Country Will Fight Today': Robert the Bruce's Alliance with the Saints at Bannockburn." *International Review of Scottish Studies* 40 (2015): 1–32.

Davies, John R. "Bishop Kentigern Among the Britons." In *Saints' Cults in the Celtic World.* Edited by Steve Boardman, John Reuben Davies, and Eila Williamson, 66–90. SCelH 25. Woodbridge: Boydell Press, 2009.

DeVries, Kelly. "God and Defeat in Medieval Warfare: Some Preliminary Thoughts." In *The Circle of War in the Middle Ages: Essays on Medieval Military and Naval History*. Edited by Donald J. Kagay and L.J.A. Villalon, 87–97. Woodbridge: Boydell Press, 1999.

Duggan, Laurence G. *Armsbearing and the Clergy in the History and Canon Law of Western Christianity*. Woodbridge: Boydell Press, 2013.

Eeles, Francis. "The Monymusk Reliquary or Brecbennoch of St Columba." *Proceedings of the Society of the Antiquaries of Scotland* 68 (1934): 433–38.

Ekdahl, Sven. *Die "Banderia Prutenorum" des Jan Dlugosz, eine Quelle zur Schlacht bei Tannenberg 1410. Untersuchungen zu Aufbau, Entstehung und Quellenwert der Handschrift*. Göttingen: Vandenhoek & Ruprecht, 1976.

Gaposchkin, M. Cecilia. *Invisible Weapons: Liturgy and the Making of Crusade Ideology*. Ithaca NY and London: Cornell University Press, 2017.

Gerrard, Daniel M.G. *The Church at War: The Military Activity of Bishops, Abbots and Other Clergy in England, c. 900–1200*. Abingdon and New York: Routledge, 2017.

Goedhals, Barrie. "John's Barbour's 'The Bruce' and Bannockburn." *Unisa English Studies* 2 (1968): 40–58.

Gransden, Antonia. *Historical Writing in England II: C.1307 to the Early Sixteenth Century*. London and Henley: Routledge and Kegan Paul, 1982.

Graus, František. "Der Heilige als Schlachtenhelfer—Zur Nationalisierung einer Wundererzählung in der mittelalterlichen Chronistik." In *Festschrift für Helmut Beumann zum 65. Geburtstag*. Edited by Kurt-Ulrich Jäschke and Reinhard Wenskus, 330–48. Sigmaringen: Thorbecke, 1977.

Grigg, Julianna. "The Black Rood of Scotland: A Social and Political Life." *Viator* 48.3 (2017): 1–26.

Hammond, Matthew H. "Royal and Aristocratic Attitudes to Saint and the Virgin Mary in Twelfth- and Thirteenth-Century Scotland." In *The Cult of Saints and the Virgin Mary in Medieval Scotland*. Edited by Steve Boardman and Eila Williamson, 61–85. SCelH 28. Woodbridge: Boydell Press, 2010.

Jensen, Carsten Selch. "Gods War: War and Christianisation on the Baltic Frontier in the Early 13th Century." *QMAN* 16 (2011): 123–47.

Jensen, Kurt Villads. "Holy War—Holy Wrath! Baltic Wars Between Regulated Warfare and Total Annihilation Around 1200." In *Church and Belief in the Middle Ages: Popes, Saints, and Crusaders*. Edited by Kirsi Salonen and Sari Katajala-Peltomaa, 227–50. CB 3. Amsterdam: Amsterdam University Press, 2016.

Kaeuper, Richard W. *Chivalry and Violence in Medieval Europe*. Oxford: Oxford University Press, 1999.

Kapitaniak, Tomasz. *Bannockburn 1314*. Łódź: Ibidem, 2002.

Keene, Catherine. *Saint Margaret, Queen of the Scots: A Life in Perspective*. New York: Palgrave Macmillan, 2013.

Kotecki, Radosław. "Pious Rulers, Princely Clerics, and Angels of Light: 'Imperial Holy War' Imagery in Twelfth-Century Poland and Rus'." In *Christianity and War in Medieval East Central Europe and Scandinavia*. Edited by Radosław Kotecki, Carsten Selch Jensen, and Stephen Bennet, 159–88. Leeds: ARC Humanities Press, 2021.

Kotecki, Radosław, and Jacek Maciejewski. "Ideals of Episcopal Power, Legal Norms and Military Activity of the Polish Episcopate Between the Twelfth and Fourteenth Centuries." *KH* 127. Eng.-Language Edition 4 (2020): 5–46.

Kotecki, Radosław, Jacek Maciejewski, and John S. Ott, ed. *Between Sword and Prayer: Warfare and Medieval Clergy in Cultural Perspective*. EMC 3. Leiden and Boston MA: Brill, 2018.

Little, Andrew G. "The Authorship of the 'Lanercost Chronicle.'" *English Historical Review* 31.122 (1916): 269–79 and 32.125 (1917): 48–49.

Macdonald, Alastair J. "Courage, Fear and the Experience of the Later Medieval Scottish Soldier." *Scottish Historical Review* 92.235 (2013): 179–206.

MacInnes, Iain A. "Heads, Shoulders, Knees and Toes: Injury and Death in Anglo-Scottish Combat, c.1296–c.1403." In *Wounds and Wound Repair in Medieval Culture*. Edited by Larissa Tracy and Kelly DeVries, 102–27. EMC 1. Leiden and Boston MA: Brill, 2015.

MacInnes, Iain A. "'One Man Slashes, One Slays, One Warns, One Wounds'. Injury and Death in Anglo-Scottish Combat, c.1296–c.1403." In *Killing and Being Killed: Bodies in Battle. Perspectives on Fighters in the Middle Ages*. Edited by Jörg Rogge, 61–78. Mainz historical cultural sciences 38. Mainz: Transcript, 2017.

Mackay Mackenzie, William. *The Battle of Bannockburn: The Study of Medieval Warfare*. Glasgow: MacLehose and Sons, 1913.

McCormick, Michael. *Eternal Victory: Triumphal Rulership in Late Antiquity, Byzantium, and the Early Medieval West*. Cambridge: Cambridge University Press, 1986.

McCormick, Michael. "Liturgie et guerre des Carolingiens à la première croisade." In *"Militia Christi" e crociata nei secoli XI–XIII*, 209–40. Miscellanea del Centro di studi medioevali 13. Milano: Vita e pensiero, 1992.

McNamee, Colm. *Robert Bruce: Our Most Valiant Prince, King and Lord*. Edinburgh: Birlinn, 2018.

Michalski, Wojciech. *Robert Bruce i jego kompania w eposie pióra Johna Barboura. "The Bruce" około 1376*. Lublin: Wydawnictwo Uniwersytetu Marii Curie-Skłodowskiej, 2020.

Morris, John E. *Bannockburn*. Cambridge: Cambridge University Press, 1914.

Nakashian, Craig M. *Warrior Churchmen of Medieval England, 1000–1250: Theory and Reality*. Woodbridge: Boydell Press, 2016.

Nusbacher, Aryeh. *The Battle of Bannockburn, 1314*. Stroud: Tempus, 2005.

Ormrod, Mark W. "The English Monarchy and the Promotion of Religion in the Fourteenth Century." In *Religion and Politics in the Middle Ages: Germany and*

England by Comparison. Edited by Ludger Körtnger and Dominik Waßenhoven, 205–17. Prince Albert studies 29. Berlin and Boston MA: De Gruyter, 2013.

Penman, Michael. "The Bruce Dynasty, Becket and Scottish Pilgrimage to Canterbury, c.1178–c.1404." *JMH* 32.4 (2006): 346–70.

Penman, Michael. "Christian Days and Knights: The Religious Devotions and Court of David II of Scotland, 1329–71." *Historical Research* 75.189 (2002): 249–72.

Penman, Michael. "Faith in War: The Religious Experience of Scottish Soldiery, c.1100–c.1500." *JMH* 37.3 (2011): 295–303.

Penman, Michael. *Robert the Bruce: King of the Scots*. New Haven CN: Yale University Press, 2014.

Penman, Michael. "'Sacred Food for the Soul': In Search of the Devotions to Saints of Robert Bruce, King of Scotland, 1306–1329." *Speculum* 88.4 (2013): 1035–62.

Penman, Michael, ed. *Bannockburn, 1314–2014: Battle and Legacy*. Donington: Shaun Tyas, 2016.

Picard, Jean-Michel. "The Purpose of Adomnán's 'Vita Columbae.'" *Peritia* 1 (1982): 160–77.

Prestwich, Michael. *Edward I*. London: Methuen, 1988.

Prietzel, Malte. *Kriegführung im Mittelalter. Handlungen, Erinnerungen und Bedentungen*. KG 32. Paderborn: Schöningh, 2006.

Rappaport, Roy A. *Ritual and Religion in the Making of Humanity*. Cambridge: Cambridge University Press, 2012.

Reese, Peter. *Bannockburn. Scotland's Greatest Victory*. Edinburgh: Canongate Books, 2014.

Riley-Smith, Jonathan. "Crusading as an Act of Love." *History* 65.214 (1980): 177–92.

Russell, Frederick H. *The Just War in the Middle Ages*. Cambridge, New York, and Melbourne: Cambridge University Press, 1975.

Schaller, Hans M. "Der heilige Tag als Termin mittelalterlicher Staatsakte." *Deutsches Archiv für Erforschung des Mittelalters* 30 (1974): 1–24.

Scharff, Thomas. *Die Kämpfe der Herrscher und der Heiligen. Krieg und historische Erinnerung in der Karolingerzeit*. Darmstadt: Wissenschaftliche Buchgesellschaft, 2002.

Schieffer, Rudolf. "'Iudicium Dei'. Kriege als Gottesurteile." In *Heilige Kriege. Religiöse Begründungen militärischer Gewaltanwendung. Judentum, Christentum und Islam im Vergleich*. Edited by Klaus Schreiner and Elisabeth Müller-Luckner, 219–28. SHKK 78. Munich: Oldenbourg, 2008.

Schwend, Joachim. "Religion and Religiosity in 'The Bruce.'" In *Scottish Language and Literature, Medieval and Renaissance*. Edited by Dietrich Strauss and Horst W. Drescher, 207–15. Frankfurt am Main, Bern, and New York: Peter Lang, 1984.

Scott, Ronald McNair. *Robert the Bruce: King of Scots*. New York: Barnes and Noble, 1982.

Scott, William. *Bannockburn Revealed: A Reappraisal*. Rothesay: Elenkus, 2000.

Sharpe, Richard. "Banners of the Northern Saints." In *Saints of North-East England, 600–1500*. Edited by Margaret Coombe, Anne Mouron, and Christiana Whitehead, 245–301. MCS 39. Turnhout: Brepols, 2017.

Sharpe, Richard. "King William and the Brecc Bennach in 1211: Reliquary or Holy Banner." *IR* 62.2 (2015): 163–90.

Stollberg-Rilinger, Barbara. *Rituale. Historische Einführungen*. Historische Einführungen 16. Frankfurt and New York: Campus Verlag, 2013.

Strickland, Matthew. *War and Chivalry: The Conduct and Perception of War in England and Normandy, 1066–1217*. Cambridge: Cambridge University Press, 1996.

Tarczyński, Tomasz. "The King and the Saint against the Scots: The Shaping of English National Identity in the 12th Century Narrative of King Althestan's Victory over His Northern Neighbours." In *Imagined Communities: Constructing Collective Identities in Medieval Europe*. Edited by Andrzej Pleszczyński et al., 85–102. EMC 8. Leiden and Boston MA: Brill, 2018.

Taylor, Simon. "The Cult of St. Fillan in Scotland." In *The North Sea World in the Middle Ages: Studies in the Cultural-History in North-Western Europe*. Edited by Thomas R. Liszka and Lorna E.M. Walker, 175–210. Dublin: Four Courts Press, 2001.

Tolmie, Sarah. "Making Memories: Barbour and Bannockburn." In *Bannockburn, 1314–2014: Battle and Legacy*. Edited by Michael Penman, 139–51. Donington: Shaun Tyas, 2016.

Turpie, Tom. *Kind Neighbours: Scottish Saints and Society in the Later Middle Ages*. TNW 70. Leiden and Boston MA: Brill, 2015.

Tyerman, Christopher. *God's War: A New History of the Crusades*. Cambridge MA: Belknap Press of Harvard University Press, 2006.

Verbruggen, Jan Frans. *The Art of Warfare in Western Europe during the Middle Ages: From the Eighth Century to 1340*. 2nd ed. Woodbridge: Boydell Press, 1998.

Wilson, Susan E. *The Life and After-Life of St. John of Beverley: The Evolution of the Cult of an Anglo-Saxon Saint*. Aldershot and Burlington VT: Ashgate, 2006.

Woolf, Alex. "The Song of the Death of Somerled and the Destruction of Glasgow in 1153." *Sydney Society for Scottish History Journal* 14 (2013): 1–11.

Zupka, Dušan. "Religious Rituals of War in Medieval Hungary Under the Árpád Dynasty." In *Christianity and War in Medieval East Central Europe and Scandinavia*. Edited by Radosław Kotecki, Carsten Selch Jensen, and Stephen Bennet, 141–57. Leeds: ARC Humanities Press, 2021.

Zupka, Dušan. *Ritual and Symbolic Communication in Medieval Hungary Under the Árpád Dynasty, 1000–1301*. ECEE 39. Leiden and Boston MA: Brill, 2016.

CHAPTER 6

Invocations by Knights for Supernatural Aid in the Sources of the Baltic Crusades, Medieval Poland and the *Chansons* of the Crusades

Sini Kangas

The historical sources of the crusades were written to propagate the unity of Catholic Christendom under the Roman pontificate. The beginning of the crusading era at the turn of the twelfth century was interlinked with the rising papal call for the plenitude of power, and despite the political setbacks gnawing at the foundations of papal power after the heyday of the reign of Innocent III, the clerical grasp over the production of the sources related to crusading remained strong throughout the thirteenth and fourteenth centuries.

The clerical quills shaping the history of crusades underlined the performance of religious rituals under the guidance of ecclesiastical leadership. The function of worship was to contribute to the victories by maintaining the purity of intention and dogma among the warriors. The depictions define devotions in terms of collective and public experience supervised by clerics, whereas the displays of individual religiosity and popular belief have to be read between the lines. However, scattered references show that both forms of devotion affected the notions and actions of crusaders beyond clerical instigation.

In their everyday life, medieval laymen did not draw a line between the official and doctrinally correct teaching of the church and the more local belief systems. They were inseparable. The great majority of the population being illiterate, religious norms and practices were mostly communicated orally and visually by preaching, recital, liturgy, and ecclesiastical art. Many knights and lower clergy were literate to a degree, but theological and philosophical discussion of religion would have been beyond both groups. The Bible was usually available only in individual books of excerpts. Psalters, missals, breviaries, and other types of partial editions were more common than complete volumes until the thirteenth century, while many knew the Bible through popular and often inaccurate retellings of biblical events.[1] Lay people, for example, would not have been able to tell, which saints were mentioned in the Scriptures and

---

1 Thomas J.H. McCarthy, "Scriptural Allusion in the Crusading Accounts of Frutolf of Michelsberg and His Continuators," in *The Uses of the Bible in Crusader Sources*, ed. Elizabeth

which not, nor would this information have been crucial to them. Local cults were popular.

The same conclusions concern the conceptual making of the crusades in the minds of medieval contemporaries. Although fervent in their crusading zeal, for the crusaders, religiosity was much more than the concept of Christian holy war. Moreover, the network of ideas related to this concept did not form an isolated entity but contributed flexibly within various systems of belief affected by the social and cultural environment of the believers.[2] A telling argument is that there was no fixed term for the crusade until relatively late when the expeditions had been occurring for over a century.[3]

This article discusses the expressions of lay piety with an emphasis on prayer and the invocations for supernatural help in the sources of the Baltic Crusades and the vernacular *chansons* of the crusades.[4] In addition to the modern literal sense of the term "prayer," the invocations in the medieval framework

---

Lapina and Nicholas Morton, Commentaria 7 (Leiden and Boston MA: Brill, 2017), 152–75 at 164.

2 Richard W. Kaeuper, *Holy Warriors: The Religious Ideology of Chivalry* (Philadelphia: University of Pennsylvania Press), 92–93, 171.

3 In the twelfth century there did not yet exist any particular term for the crusade. The Latin sources most often use words *iter* (pilgrimage or journey), *peregrinatio* (pilgrimage), and *expeditio* (military expedition), whereas the Old French *chansons* speak about the march to Jerusalem, the visit to the Holy Sepulcher, and the battle to avenge Christ. The term *crucesignatus* with an indication of a pilgrim on his way to Jerusalem appears in the sources from the 1180s onward. Michael Markowski, "'Crucesignatus': Its Origins and Early Usage," *JMH* 10.3 (1984): 157–64 at 160–64. The first extant mention in Old French, *croiserie/croisee/croisie*, emerge in the Old French translations of William of Tyre's chronicle describing the events of 1219–1239. Benjamin Weber, "Conceptualizing the Crusade in Outremer: Uses and Purposes of the Word 'Crusade' in the Old French Continuation of William of Tyre," *Crusades* 20 (2021): 151–64; Mireille Issa, *La version latine et l'adaptation française de "l'Historia rerum in partibus transmarinis gestarum" de Guillaume de Tyr*, The medieval translator 13 (Turnhout: Brepols, 2010), 211–12. By the thirteenth century, the term *crucesignatus* had evolved to mean a crusader, that is, someone who had taken the crusading vow and was wearing the cross badge, thus being "signed with a cross." The concept was used in the model sermons of Humbert of Romans, Jacques de Vitry, Gilbert of Tournai, and Eudes de Chatêauroux. Christoph T. Maier, *Crusade Propaganda and Ideology: Model Sermons for the Preaching of the Cross* (Cambridge: Cambridge University Press, 2000), 52–53, 210–12; Miikka Tamminen, *Crusade Preaching and the Ideal Crusader*, Sermo 14 (Turnhout: Brepols, 2018), Introduction.

4 The crusades generated a discernible group of vernacular epic poems disseminating the exploits of the champions of the holy war and their entourage. The *chansons* of the crusades waver between historiography and storytelling tradition, forming a connective between the more fictional *chansons de geste* and historical chronicles. Unlike the *chansons de geste* situated in the more remote past, they describe their contemporary history, even if they take considerable liberties with the historical facts.

relate to a variety of devotions soliciting divine intercession in the forms of visions, dreams, and the veneration of saints.

Whereas crusader chronicles written in Latin generally limit their descriptions of solitary prayers with any detailed content to the prayers said by bishops, adding occasional references to lay invocations for supernatural aid to spice up the narrative, the fictional *chansons* frequently include detailed depictions of knights absorbed in prayer. Although no exact genre equivalent to the *chansons* is extant from the Eastern or Central European traditions, among the chronicles *Kronike von Pruzinlant* and the so-called Gallus Anonymus contain interesting examples of lay communications with supernatural powers, which can be supplemented by the bits and pieces scattered in other sources.

The caveat remains that the observations are mostly limited to the warrior aristocracy. The contents relate only sporadically and briefly to the religious notions of the lower classes. In these cases, the accounts of lay belief show compatibility between the ideas of the nobility and commoners. On the other hand, the sources forming the major sample for this article were composed for the use of knights, whether rulers, their vassals, or members of the military orders, and in the case of crusader *chansons* they were also commissioned by them.

The *Cronicae et gesta ducum sive principum Polonorum* by the so-called Gallus Anonymus (ca. 1115) is the oldest surviving chronicle of Poland, treating the history of the Piast dynasty from the middle of the tenth century up to ca. 1113.[5] The work is likely to have been composed in the milieu of the court of Duke Bolesław III Wrymouth, either at the commission of the duke himself, or someone from his immediate entourage. Of the author, not much is known other than that he was not Polish. The text was written in honor of Duke Bolesław and to support the duke's claim for power in a difficult political situation after Bolesław had imprisoned and blinded his older half-brother Zbigniew, who had died because of the mutilation. The series of events remaining unclear, Bolesław was sharply criticized for the death of his brother, and was compelled to atone for his sins and perform major works of penance in public. The chronicle by Gallus was aimed at restoring the ducal authority and legitimizing Bolesław's claim for power as a ruler chosen by God, a member of an ancient ruling dynasty, and a guarantee of restoring Poland's greatness.

---

[5] For an edition and English translation, see Gallus Anonymus, *Gesta principum Polonorum*, ed., trans., and ann. Paul W. Knoll and Frank Schaer, CEMT 3 (Budapest and New York: Central European University Press, 2003) (hereafter Gallus, *Gesta*). For a research on Gallus, see Eduard Mühle, "Neue Vorschläge zur Herkunft des Gallus Anonymus und zur Deutung seiner 'Chronik,'" *ZfO* 60.2 (2011): 267–85.

In this framework, especially the ducal victory in the Battle of Nakło (1109) against the pagan Pomeranians as well as against German king Henry V in the same year was seen as an important token of divine favor.[6]

Nicolaus of Jeroschin was a cleric and herald in the service of the Teutonic Order. His *Kronike von Pruzinlant* (ca. 1341),[7] dedicated to the Virgin Mary and commissioned by the Grand Master of the Order, is a Middle High German verse translation of the *Chronicon terrae Prussiae* by Peter of Dusburg (fl. 1326), another priest brother in the service of the Teutonic Order.[8] Instead of translating Peter's chronicle word for word, Nicolaus extends Peter's treatise up to 1331 and makes several additions to the original text. The most interesting of these emerge at the end of *Di Kronike*, including anecdotes and stories of knights who encounter supernatural characters, whether benign or menacing. In some instances, the knights actively evoke divine assistance by prayers.

Lay religiosity and belief play an important role in *Di Kronike*, because Nicolaus intended his work for the use of the knights in the service of the Teutonic Order. The text was written to motivate both the brothers and seasonal crusaders (*Kriegsgäste*) in their fight against the Prussians and Lithuanians according to contemporary chivalric models. Based on the number of surviving

---

6   Roman Michałowski, "'Restauratio Poloniae' dans l'idéologie dynastique de Gallus Anonymus," *APH* 52 (1985): 5–43; Jacek Banaszkiewicz, "Gallus as a Credible Historian, or Why the Biography of Bolesław the Brave is as Authentic and Far from Grotesque as Bolesław the Wrymouth's," in *Gallus Anonymous and his Chronicle in the Context of Twelfth-Century Historiography from the Perspective of the Latest Research*, ed. Krzysztof Stopka (Cracow: Polish Academy of Arts and Sciences, 2010), 19–33 at 19–21; Grischa Vercamer, "'Boleslavus non solum aurem correctoribus non adhibuit [...]'—War Gallus Anonymus dem polnischen Fürsten Bolesław III. Schiefmund wirklich vorbehaltlos positiv Eingestellt?" *Studia Maritima* 32 (2019): 45–88. See also Zbigniew Dalewski, "A New Chosen People? Gallus Anonymus's Narrative about Poland and Its Rulers," in *Historical Narratives and Christian Identity on a European Periphery: Early History Writing in Northern, East-Central and Eastern Europe (c.1070–1200)*, ed. Ildar H. Garipzanov, MTCN 26 (Turnhout: Brepols, 2011), 145–66.

7   Nicolaus von Jeroschin, *Di Kronike von Pruzinlant des Nicolaus v. Jeroschin*, ed. Ernst Strehlke, SrP 1 (Leipzig: Hirzel, 1861), 303–624 (hereafter Jeroschin, *Di Kronike*); *The Chronicle of Prussia by Nicolaus von Jeroschin: A History of the Teutonic Knights in Prussia, 1190–1331*, trans. Mary Fischer, CTT 20 (Aldershot and Burlington VT: Ashgate, 2010), 4–6, 10–12.

8   The *Chronicon terrae Prussiae* was the first major narrative history of the Teutonic Order written in Prussia. The work was dedicated to the Grand Master Werner von Orseln. Peter von Dusburg, *Chronicon terrae Prussiae*, ed. Max Töppen, SrP 1 (Leipzig: Hirzel, 1861), 24–219 (hereafter Dusburg, *Chron. Pr.*); *The Chronicle of Prussia by Nicolaus von Jeroschin*, 10–12; Gregory Leighton, "Did the Teutonic Order Create a Sacred Landscape in Thirteenth-Century Prussia?" *JMH* 44.4 (2018): 457–83 at 459–60.

medieval copies, *Di Kronike von Pruzinlant* was distributed widely during the fourteenth century.[9]

In addition to historiography, the crusades to the Holy Land, beginning with the First Crusade, produced a rich layer of vernacular sources known as the first and second crusade cycles. The earliest surviving versions of these tales, including the trilogy of *La chanson d'Antioche, Les chétifs* and *La chanson d'Jérusalem*, remain in the retelling (or commission) by Graindor of Douai (late 1170s to early thirteenth century).[10] Whereas the *Chanson d'Antioche*, concentrating on the two sieges of Antioch and its capture by the crusaders in 1097–1098, includes a lot of historical characters and events, the second, *Les Chétifs* is a

---

[9] Peter of Dusburg was writing a sacred history of the Teutonic Order, perhaps to legitimize the Order for the papal curia, or with an intention to produce material for the preachers of the Baltic Crusades. Jeroschin, although also sacralizing the warfare by the Order on the Baltic front, includes much more references to physical warfare. As such, he might have been writing principally to knights. The hypothesis that either of the chronicles was aimed at members of the Order as part of the *Tischlesung*, texts read out during the meals for spiritual purposes has been refuted. See Leighton, "Did the Teutonic Order," 460. In his analysis of the *Livonian Rhymed Chronicle* (ca. 1290), the oldest extant *Ordensgeschichte* written for the Teutonic Order, Alan Murray pointed out that the rules of the Order stated that the knights should silently listen to the word of God during their meals, not lay chronicles. Alan V. Murray, "The Structure, Genre and Intended Audience of the 'Livonian Rhymed Chronicle,'" in *Crusade and Conversion on the Baltic Frontier, 1150–1500*, ed. Alan V. Murray (Aldershot and Burlington VT: Ashgate, 2001), 235–51. The rules of the Order clearly support this view: "Preterea observandum est, ut in omnibus domibus, ubi numerus fratrum et integritatem conventus est completus (ut scilicet XII fratres et tercius decimus preceptor eorum ibidem morentur secumdum numerum discipulorum Christi), leccio continue ad mensam habeatur, quam omnes in mensa edentes sub silencio audiant, ne sole eis fauces sumant cibum, sed et aures esuriant Dei verbum; poterunt tamen submisse et brevi oracione in mensa constituti de necessariis loqui": *Die Statuten des Deutschen Ordens nach den ältesten Handschriften*, chap. 13, ed. Max Perlbach (Halle: Niemeyer, 1890), 41 (hereafter *Statuten*). Obedience to the *Rule* explains the great number of translations of the stories of the Bible, especially the Maccabees and Judith, produced for the use of the Order. Mary Fischer, "Biblical Heroes and the Uses of Literature: The Teutonic Order in the Late Thirteenth and Early Fourteenth Centuries," in *Crusade and Conversion*, 261–76.

[10] Graindor remains an obscure character. In the extant manuscripts of *Chanson d'Antioche* he is referred to as Graindor de Brie, Jendeus de Brie, Gautier de Douai, or Graindor de Dijon. The places of origin of the manuscripts and the similarities with the chronicles of Robert the Monk and Albert of Aachen support the assumption that Graindor of Douai came from northern France and was writing in his native the dialect of Picardy. Duparc-Quioc dates Graindor's text to ca. 1177 and Edgington and Sweetenham to no later than the early thirteenth century. *La Chanson d'Antioche*, ed. Suzanne Duparc-Quioc (Paris: L'Académie des inscriptions et belles-lettres, 1976–1978), 133–37; *The "Chanson d'Antioche": An Old French Account of the First Crusade*, trans. Susan B. Edgington and Carol Sweetenham, CTT 22 (Farnham and Burlington VT: Ashgate, 2011), 34, 47.

fictional account of the crusaders kept captives by the Turkish leader Corbaran d'Oliferne.[11] After a series of heroic exploits including a judicious duel against two Turkish champions, slaying the dragon Sathanas and rescuing Corbaran's nephew from the wild beasts and bandits, the captives win back their freedom and are able to join the rest of the army besieging Jerusalem.[12]

La chanson d'Antioche may have been based on the stories told by the first crusaders on their return home. The point of view is northern French; Duparc-Quioc has connected Graindor's work with the family of St-Pol and the comitial house of Flanders under Philip of Alsace, who may have used the work against the rival house of Champagne-Blois; the cowardly and treacherous Stephen of Blois is the arch-villain of the story.[13] An early version of Les chétifs was possibly written under the auspices of Raymond of Poitiers, prince of Antioch, by 1149.[14] Situated in the framework of the First Crusade, the text draws together hostage stories from several expeditions between 1100–1102.

1 The Ecclesiastically Approved Framework of Prayer in the Sources of the Crusades

In his bull *Quia maior* for the preparations for the Fifth Crusade from 1213, Pope Innocent III encouraged the participation of the whole population to gain spiritual benefits and support the forthcoming enterprise. The pope ordered intercessory processions and prayers to be organized throughout the Latin Christendom. All men and women were instructed to prostrate themselves and pray for the crusades every day at mass after the kiss of peace. The prayers were to be accompanied by the recitation of Psalms 78(79) *Deus venerunt gentes*.[15]

---

11 The character is loosely based on the Turkish atabeg Kerbogha. The heroic crusader knights include Richard of Chaumont, Baldwin and Ernoul of Beauvais and Harpin of Bourges.
12 The third poem, *Chanson de Jérusalem* tells the tale of the capture of the city by the crusaders and their subsequent victory of the Battle of Ascalon. *La Chanson de Jérusalem*, ed. Nigel Thorp, OFCC 6 (Tuscaloosa AL: University of Alabama Press, 1992).
13 *La Chanson d'Antioche*, 86–87 (ll. 1438–45); 90–91 (ll. 1527–39); 92–93 (ll. 1576–80); 94–95 (ll. 1610–25); 284–86 (ll. 5604–49); 348–50 (ll. 7021–53).
14 *The "Chanson des Chétifs" and "Chanson de Jérusalem": Completing the Central Trilogy of the Old French Crusade Cycle*, trans. Carol Sweetenham, CTT 29 (Aldershot and Burlington VT: Ashgate, 2016), 10–11; *Les Chétifs*, ed. Geoffrey M. Myers, OFCC 5 (Tuscaloosa AL: University of Alabama Press, 1981).
15 *Innocentii III regesta sive epistolæ* (continuation), ed. Jacques-Paul Migne, PL 216 (Paris: Apud J.-P. Migne Editorem, 1855), 817–20; James Brundage, "A Transformed Angel (x 3.31.18): The Problem of the Crusading Monk," in *Studies in Medieval Cistercian History*

In addition, once in a month men and women, preferably in separate groups, were to process from church to church calling for help for the crusaders, and all Christians were to devote themselves to prayer, fasting, and almsgiving during these days.[16] Innocent himself arranged three processions in Rome. Laymen gathered at the church of Santa Anastasia, women at Santa Maria Maggiore, and clergy at Santi Apostoli. From these points the groups processed toward the Lateran church. After gathering there, laymen attended the mass in the Lateran church with the pope, whereas women continued to their mass in the basilica of Santa Croce in Gerusalemme.[17]

The requests outlined in *Quia maior* reveal two important aims. Firstly, everyone was to contribute to crusading. Innocent wished to engage the whole community. Secondly, the devotions were organized in public under the coordination and control of the church. To quote Allington, Innocent was "promoting a more extensive type of piety that aimed at a broader program of reform than devotion to the individual saints of a particular city."[18] In other words, individual adaptations or exclusivity were not sought in the rituals.

The tendency to exclude intimate or improvised forms of worship is clearly present in the clerical sources of the crusades. The rules of the Teutonic Order

---

Presented to Jeremiah F. O'Sullivan, ed. ed. John R. Sommerfeldt, Cistercian studies 13 (Spencer MA: Cistercian Publications, 1971), 55–62; Amnon Linder, *Raising Arms: Liturgy in the Struggle to Liberate Jerusalem in the Late Middle Ages*, Cultural encounters in Late Antiquity and the Middle Ages 2 (Turnhout: Brepols, 2003), 37–41; Richard Allington, "Crusading Piety and the Development of Crusading Devotions," in *The Fourth Lateran Council and the Crusade Movement*, ed. Jessalynn Bird and Damian Smith, Outremer 7 (Turnhout: Brepols, 2018), 13–40.

16 Innocent renewed the orders dictated by the bull *Audita tremendi*, launched by Pope Gregory VIII in 1187 after the defeat of Hattin and the consequent loss of Jerusalem to Saladin. According to the *Audita*, special prayers were to be said for the liberation of the Holy Land and for the release of Christian captives. The Fourth Lateran Council reaffirmed these regulations in 1215. *Gregorii VIII pontifici Romani Epistolæ et privilegia*, ed. Jacques-Paul Migne, PL 202 (Paris: Apud J.-P. Migne Editorem, 1855), 1539–42; Helmut Roscher, *Papst Innocenz III. und die Kreuzzüge*, Forschungen zur Kirchen- und Dogmengeschichte 21 (Göttingen: Vandenhoeck & Ruprectht, 1969), 140–46.

17 *Innocentii III Regesta sive Epistolæ*, 698–99; Allington, "Crusading Piety"; Christoph T. Maier, "Crisis, Liturgy and the Crusade in the Twelfth and Thirteenth Centuries," *JEH* 48.4 (1997): 628–57 at 633; Susan Twyman, "The 'Romana Fraternitas' and Urban Processions at Rome in the Twelfth and Thirteenth Centuries," in *Pope, Church, and City: Essays in Honour of Brenda Bolton*, ed. Frances Andrews, Christoph Egger, and Constance M. Rousseau, MMED 56 (Leiden and Boston MA: Brill, 2004), 205–21.

18 Allington, "Crusading Piety," 23.

from 1264[19] state that the brothers shall attend together the divine services and hours day and night. The services are sung or read aloud by the priests either from breviaries or from books written for the use of the Order. The quality and number of prayers said daily is precise: thirteen *Paternosters* for matins, nine for vespers, and seven for other canonical hours for the lay brothers, and the same number of *Paternosters* for the hours of the Virgin Mary,[20] the patron saint of the Order. The statutes particularly mention that if the lay brothers are literate enough, they may recite Psalms or other texts pertaining to clerical office with the priests on the canonical hours or the hours of Our Lady and be excused from saying the corresponding *Paternosters* required from them.[21] During the oratories they should stand and bow at every *Gloria Patri* bending their bodies properly. It was strictly forbidden to disturb the prayer of others by whispering, talking aloud, or by prostrating or genuflecting (praying) in a disorderly manner at variance with the regulations of the church.[22]

Furthermore, the brothers prayed for the souls of their deceased brethren. Whereas the responsibility of the priest brothers was to read the office of the dead from the breviary of the Order, each lay brother was obliged to recite one hundred *Paternosters* for the recently deceased brothers of their convent or house and fifteen *Paternosters* for all the brothers who had passed away among the Order. Finally, lay brothers' daily duties included the recitation of thirty *Paternosters* for the living benefactors, servants, and friends of the Order, and the same number (thirty) *Paternosters* for the deceased members of those groups. This obligation was removed during times of fasting.[23]

---

19 The oldest extant statutes of the Teutonic Order date from 1264. The Order had been authorized by the pope twenty years earlier to write their own rules. See *Statuten*, LI. The rule was based upon the rules of the Templars, with modifications and additions made for the Teutonic Order. See Indrikis Sterns, "The Teutonic Knights in the Crusader States," in *The Impact of the Crusades on the Near East*, ed. Norman P. Zacour and Harry W. Hazard, in *A History of the Crusades*, vol. 5, ed. Kenneth M. Setton (Madison WI: University of Wisconsin Press, 1985), 315–78 at 323–25.

20 The first prayers were said at Matins before dawn. Thereafter services were held once every three hours until the final office just before going to sleep. See *The Chronicle of Prussia by Nicolaus von Jeroschin*, 93n3.

21 "Aliis ad officium pertinentibus dicere voluerint": *Statuten*, chap. 8, p. 35.

22 "Veniarum inordinacione orantes perturbet": *Statuten*, chap. 8, pp. 33–35, the quotation on p. 34. In the light of the old French and German variants included in Perlbach's edition, this rule forbids such physical movements during praying that might easily disturb the concentration of others. The adverb *inordinate* is very interesting, referring to something that varies from the Testament, the divine law, or the rules of the church. Compare with *Mediae Latinitatis lexicon minus*, ed. Jan F. Niermeyer, 2nd rev. ed., 2 vols. (Leiden and Boston MA: Brill, 2002), 1:707.

23 *Statuten*, chap. 10, pp. 36–38.

Such an exacting daily prayer routine had been planned as suitable for the needs of the Order. The phrasing suggests a clear division between the practices followed by brothers of clerical and lay background. Especially for the latter group, prayer indicated monotonous repetition dozens of times every day in a definite position, in unison with the brethren. According to Stefan Kwiatkowski, the regulations of the Teutonic Order reflect the clericalization of ritual that had taken place by the thirteenth century. Whereas priests organized and led the rituals, brothers engaging in warfare passively prayed according to given formulas.[24] Kwiatkowski's findings can be further applied to the chronicles written for the Order. In the texts, the clerical narrator's calls for divine help for the knights are far more common than depictions of the knights taking the initiative and praying themselves.

In the *Livonian Rhymed Chronicle* (ca. 1290),[25] prayers, though numerous, remain brief and mostly unspecified in content. In a typical example, everyone praises God and/or the Virgin Mary after a military victory or a successful escape from danger. The identified cases of praying knights represent the leadership of the order. They pray aloud, the brethren together with their brothers in arms. Brother Bernard of Haren is depicted setting out for an expedition with the brothers: "They prayed to God in heaven that He watch over them and give them eternal life," "the Master gave great thanks to God and His dear Mother, the Queen of Heaven, who are worthy of all praise and honour."[26] Whereas prayers said privately by individuals are absent from the *Livonian Rhymed Chronicle*, heathens do not pray at all. Prayer is an exclusive group activity restricted to the crusaders and not used by their enemies.[27]

The given frames of prayer were not limited to the crusaders but applied to all Christians. The descriptions of devotional practices in crusader chronicles

---

24   Stefan Kwiatkowski, "Verlorene Schlachten und Gefallene in der geistigen Tradition des Deutschen Ordens," *OM* 16 (2011): 141–57.
25   The scope of the chronicle is 1143–ca. 1290. The author(s) does not reveal his personality. The text is written in Middle High German verse. *The Livonian Rhymed Chronicle*, trans. Jerry C. Smith and William L. Urban (Bloomington IN: Indiana University Press, 1977).
26   *The Livonian Rhymed Chronicle*, 61, 120. Translation is based upon *Livländische Reimchronik*, ed. Leo Meyer (Paderborn: Schöningh, 1876), rr. 4783–85, 9898. The chronicle discusses the conquest and colonization of Livonia in 1180–1290. Devotions to the Virgin Mary, the patron of the Order, are mentioned passim in the chronicle.
27   The chronicles do sometimes mention the pagan Gods by name. In the chronicle of Henry of Livonia pagans call for help from Tharapita (Taara), whereas the crusaders cry out for Christ: "Gaudet exercitus christianorum, exclamant, Deum exorant. Clamanet et illi, gaudentes in Tarapitha suo. Illi nemus, isti Iesum invocant." *Heinrici Chronicon Livoniae*, 3.4, ed. Leonid Arbusow and Albert Bauer, MGH SS rer. Germ. 31 (Hannover: Hahn, 1955), 218.

from Eastern, Central, and Western Europe similarly emphasize the collective and public nature of prayer, orchestrated by authorized clergymen, preferably by a bishop. Helmold of Bosau recounts in his *Chronicle of the Slavs*[28] Bishop Vicelin, who implored the intercession of all the saints, especially that of St. Nicholas to whose service he had in particular committed himself, when he was free to pray.[29] The text does not explain the wording, but the context seems to allude to moments when he was not taking care of his duties as a minister of a church. In Helmold's chronicle, such freedom of prayer is an episcopal prerogative, commoners are not mentioned to pray privately.

2   Knightly Observance of Religious Rituals in Public

The medieval institutions of knighthood and the clergy both drew their members from the aristocracy and relied on the support of the military magnates. Therefore, the coexistence of the two estates was labeled by the recognition of mutual benefits even during the times of competition over land and titles. In the words of Ramon Llull, the offices of the cleric and knight were the two most honorable and noble vocations, and thus a perpetual friendship ought to exist between the members of these groups.[30]

From the beginning of the crusading era, the idea of crusader knights as the protectors of the church and Christendom prevails in the sources.[31] In opposition to knightly violence against Christians, albeit within the limits of canon law, the reform papacy gained political weight by even closer collaboration with the nobility than in the early Middle Ages.[32] By strengthening ties, the

---

28   The chronicle treats the conquest and conversion of the Slavs living along the River Elbe. Helmold of Bosau was a deacon ca. 1150 in Segeberg, writing at the instigation of Bishop Gerold of Oldenburg. The chronicle was finished by 1172 in Bosau. Helmold von Bosau, *The Chronicle of the Slavs*, trans. Francis J. Tschan, Records of civilization 21 (New York: Columbia University Press, 1935), 19.

29   "Orationi etiam interdum vacans, omnium sanctorum suffragia efglagitabat, precipue vero beati Nicolai, cuius obsequio specialius sese manciparat": Helmold von Bosau, *Chronica Slavorum*, 1.42, ed. Johann M. Lappenberg. MGH SS 21 (Hannover: Hahn, 1869), 1–99 at 45. Bishop Vicelin was the predecessor of Gerold as the bishop of Oldenburg. He was renowned for his missionary work among the Slavs and even called their apostle.

30   Ramon Llull, *Llibre de l'Ordre de Cavalleria*, ed. Antonio Cortijo Ocaña (Amsterdam and Philadelphia PA: John Benjamins Publishing Company, 2015), 2.4, 68.

31   Paul Rousset, *Histoire d'une idéologie. La croisade* (Lausanne: L'Age d'Homme, 1983), 31.

32   Christopher Tyerman, *The Invention of the Crusades* (Hampshire: Macmillan, 1998), 10–11; Richard W. Kaeuper, *Medieval Chivalry* (Cambridge: Cambridge University Press, 2016), 275.

clergy successfully increased its spiritual foothold in the ceremonial traditions of the warrior aristocracy. In the chronicles and *chansons* alike, the bold bishop features as the collaborator and spiritual adviser of the princes.[33]

The observance of religious rituals in public had been an ordinary part of warfare in medieval Europe for at least two hundred years before the crusades. Priests accompanied the armies, celebrating masses, leading prayers, making battle orations, performing litanies and safeguarding the relics.[34] Before

---

33 For the military activities of the bishops in twelfth-century Poland, see Radosław Kotecki, "Lions and Lambs, Wolfs and Pastors of the Flock: Portraying Military Activities of Bishops in Twelfth Century Poland," in *Between Sword and Prayer: Warfare and Medieval Clergy in Cultural Perspective*, ed. Radosław Kotecki, Jacek Maciejewski and John S. Ott, EMC 3 (Leiden and Boston MA: Brill, 2018); 303–40. For a comparison of episcopal activities on the eastern and western fronts of crusades, see Sini Kangas, "The Image of 'Warrior-Bishops' in the Northern Tradition of the Crusades," in *Christianity and War in Medieval East Central Europe and Scandinavia*, ed. Radosław Kotecki, Carsten Selch Jensen, and Stephen Bennett (Leeds: ARC Humanities Press, 2021), 57–73.

34 On penitential and liturgical practices during the First Crusade see *Gesta Francorum et aliorum Hierosolymitanorum*, ed. and trans. Rosalind Hill (London: Nelson & Sons, 1962), chap. 8, 67–68; chap. 9, 81, 90, 91, 94; *Die Kreuzzugsbriefe aus den Jahren 1088–1100*, ed. Heinrich Hagenmeyer (Innsbruck: Verlag des Wagnerschen Universitäts-Buchhandlung, 1901), 167, 171 (nos. 17–18); Raymond of Aguilers, *Historia Francorum qui ceperunt Iherusalem*, ed. Jacques Bongars, RHC HO 3 (Paris: L'Académie des Inscriptions et Belles-Lettres, 1866), 231–309, at chap. 20, 296–97, 300; Fulcher of Chartres. *Historia Hierosolymitana (1095–1127)*, 1.18, ed. Heinrich Hagenmeyer (Heidelberg: Winters Universitätsbuchhandlung, 1913), 238; Albert of Aachen, *Historia Iherosolimitana*, 4.52 and 53, ed. and trans. Susan Edgington (Oxford: Clarendon Press, 2008), 330 and 332–34; Guibert of Nogent, *Dei gesta per Francos*, 6.18 and 7.6, ed. Robert B.C. Huygens, CCCM 127A (Turnhout: Brepols, 1996), 253 and 276; Robert of Rheims, *Historia Iherosolimitana*, ed. Philippe le Bas, RHC HO 3 (Paris: L'Académie des Inscriptions et Belles-Lettres, 1866), 721–882 at 827–28; *The "Historia Ierosolimitana" of Baldric of Bourgeuil*, ed. Steven Biddlecombe (Woodbridge: Boydell Press, 2014), 79, 115 107; William of Tyre, *Chronicon*, 4.22, 6.16, 8.11, 9.11, ed. Robert B.C. Huygens, CCCM 63–63A (Turnholt: Brepols, 1986), 264, 329, 400, 433; *La Chanson d'Antioche*, chap. 105, p. 381 (ll. 7665–68). See also M. Cecilia Gaposchkin, *Invisible Weapons: Liturgy and the Making of Crusade Ideology* (Ithaca NY: Cornell University Press, 2017), 96–99, 112, 115, 122–24. Raymond of Aguilers and Fulcher of Chartres were chaplains, who marched east with the Provençals lead by Count Raymond of St. Gilles (Raymond) and forces from Flanders and France under Robert of Flanders and Stephen of Blois (Fulcher). The anonymous author of the *Gesta Francorum* has commonly been interpreted as having been a lesser vassal, who took up the cross with the Southern-Italian Norman contingent under Duke Bohemond of Taranto. Albert of Aachen wrote his work by ca. 1120 based upon the accounts of returning German crusaders. Baudri of Dol, Robert of Rheims, and Guibert of Nogent were Benedictine historians writing in France by ca. 1108, whereas William, archbishop of Tyre, was writing the royal history of the Kingdom of Jerusalem by 1186.

entering the battles, warriors confessed their sins and received Communion.[35] Warriors serving under the Carolingian rulers had been encouraged to participate in these activities,[36] and not only crusaders, but many contemporary armies continued the tradition.

Devotional practices were understood to contribute positively to the outcome of battle, whether fought against pagans or fellow Christians. Hence, before launching the attack against the pagan Pomeranians in Kołobrzeg (1103), Bolesław III took Holy Communion and had mass celebrated. During this victorious campaign, he introduced a custom of holding the Little Office of the Virgin Mary before joining the battle.[37] Albeit the last practice was rather to serve his private devotion,[38] at the same time massive religious preparations for battle are reported from his campaign to Bohemia in 1110.[39]

In addition, religious practices served to maintain cohesion within the troops as well, on condition that the whole army participated in worship. According to Baudri of Dol (or Baudri of Bourgueil), a Benedictine chronicler of the First Crusade and the absentee bishop of Dol, devotions were meaningless unless everyone in the camp was in attendance.[40] The respect felt by the men in arms for authority, whether clerical or martial, helped to reach the

---

35 In the course of the twelfth and thirteenth centuries confession before entering the battle had become the norm. Martin Aurell, *Le chevalier lettré. Savoir et conduite de l'aristocratie aux XII*^{e} *et XIII*^{e} *siècles* (Paris: Fayard, 2007), 413; David S. Bachrach "Lay Confession to Priests in Light of Wartime Practice (1097–1180)," RHE 102.1 (2007): 76–99; see also Xavier Storelli, "Les chevaliers face à la mort soudaine et brutale. L'indispensable secours de l'Église?" in *Chevalerie et christianisme aux XII*^{e} *et XIII*^{e} *siècles*, ed. Martin Aurell and Catalina Girbea (Rennes: Presses Universitaires de Rennes, 2011), 149–77.

36 David S. Bachrach, *Religion and the Conduct of War c.300–c.1215* (Woodbridge: Boydell Press, 2003), 83, 62, 64; Janet L. Nelson, "The Church's Military Service in the Ninth Century: A Contemporary Comparative View?" SCH 20 (1983): 15–30.

37 Gallus, *Gesta*, 3.28, pp. 167–69.

38 In other place of the chronicle the duke is said to celebrate this office "cum episcopis et capellanis": ibid., 3.25, 158.

39 In the account on Bohemian expedition, the duke is also mentioned praying privately in his tent which may be another reference to the *officium parvum*. See Radosław Kotecki, "Bishops and the Legitimisation of War in Piast Poland until the Early Thirteenth Century," PH 111.3 (2020): 437–70 at 450–51. The Little Office, sometimes referred to as the *cursus matutinarium*, began to gradually expand as a supplement to the night canonical hours of the breviary. In Gallus's chronicle this characteristic element is still visible, as the chronicler links the office with the time of the canonical *Matutinum*. Compare with Rachel Fulton Brown, *Mary and the Art of Prayer: The Hours of the Virgin in Medieval Christian Life and Thought* (New York: Columbia University Press, 2018), 8, 10, 14, 17, where, however, no mention on evidence in Gallus's chronicle.

40 Baudri was the abbot of St. Pierre-de-Bourgueil and Bishop of Dol. *The "Historia Ierosolimitana" of Baldric of Bourgeuil*, 69.

military objectives set for the campaign. During the First Crusade, the deceased papal legate, Bishop Adhemar of Le Puy, was reported to have manifested in a vision and given precise orders for the conquest of Jerusalem in July 1099. The crusaders were to turn their backs on sin, take off their shoes and walk around the city in procession, pray aloud for divine aid, and fast. The city was taken after nine days.[41]

Vice versa, by neglecting confession, individual warriors exposed themselves to great danger. The *Miracula beati Egidii* by Peter Guillaume (composed between 1122–1166) includes a story of Bolesław's cupbearer (*pincerna*) named Sieciech who during the expedition to Pomerania forgot to confess his sins to the priest before the battle, even if he had promised to do so. After a couple of days of fighting, he mentioned of the matter to his comrades, but did not mend his ways. He did not come to his senses even when St. Giles warned him in a dream of the grave consequences of his negligence. Some days after, the cupbearer was gravely wounded by a wisent during a hunt and would have perished without the intercessory prayers by St. Giles. Only after the saint had informed the knight of his miraculous survival in another vision, the sinner repented. On his recovery, the cupbearer made a pilgrimage to the grave of the saint in Provence.[42]

Within Latin Christendom, ethnic and linguistic boundaries did not affect knightly piety. Above all, their religiosity was adaptive and flexible. Professional warriors selected religious ideas that best supported their military aims and complied with the practice of warfare.[43] At the same time, exemplary knighthood comprised genuine devoutness. Geoffroi de Charny and William the Marshal were respected for their religiosity both before and besides their involvement in crusading.[44] Vice versa, even the mightiest among the military aristocracy were not exempt from religious sanctions. In the case of Landgrave

---

41 "Sanctificamini ab immunditiis vestris et revertatur unusquisque ab operibus suis pravis. Et post haec, nudis pedibus circuite civitatem Iherusalem invocantes Deum, et jejunabitis. Si sic egeritis, et oppugnaveritis civitatem viriliter usque ad novem dies, capietur": Raymond of Aguilers, *Historia Francorum*, chap. 20, p. 296; *Gesta Francorum*, chap. 9, p. 90.

42 *Miracula beati Egidii auctore Petro Guillelmo*, ed. Georg Heinrich Pertz, MGH SS 12 (Hannover: Hahn, 1856), 316–23 at 320–21.

43 Kaeuper, *Medieval Chivalry*, 172–79, 388–91; Kaeuper, Richard W., "Piety and Independence in Chivalric Religion," in *Kings, Knights and Bankers: The Collected Articles of Richard W. Kaeuper*, ed. Christopher Guyol, Later medieval Europe 13 (Leiden and Boston MA: Brill, 2016), 327–41; Samuel A. Claussen, "Chivalric and Religious Valorization of Warfare in High Medieval France," in *Prowess, Piety, and Public Order in Medieval Society: Studies in Honor of Richard W. Kaeuper*, ed. Craig M. Nakashian and Daniel P. Franke, Later medieval Europe 14 (Leiden and Boston MA: Brill, 2017), 199–217.

44 Aurell, *Le chevalier lettré*, 288–89.

Conrad of Thuringia, the penitent prince was subjected to public penance after having plundered the town of Fritzlar and having much of its population killed in 1232. After the campaign he confessed and repented the sins he had committed when capturing Fritzlar. With a shaved head and barefoot, the penitent knight walked around the churchyard and asked people he met there to beat him with a rod he was carrying in his hand. As none of them was willing to do so, he continued through the town shedding tears and falling on his knees at every door, begging for a beating. Finally, an old woman agreed to hit him to take vengeance for his sins. She gave him a proper blow that drew his blood.[45] The penitent landgrave entered the Teutonic Order and served later as the Grand Master in 1239–1240.

Knightly piety did not essentially differ from the spirituality of the lower classes. The scale and scope of resources invested in religious institutions and charitable activities, as well as the publicity attained from these activities were more grandiose, but the forms of religiousness remained the same. Nobility and commoners alike heard the mass and partook in the Communion, listened to the Bible and religious texts being read aloud, gave alms to people poorer than themselves, prayed and sang hymns and psalms. They venerated saints, participated in pilgrimages and crusades according to their budget, hoped to end their days after confessing their sins, and expected to be buried in the consecrated ground or straight into the church, if possible. Charny owned the Shroud of Turin, and Marshal joined the Templars on his deathbed. These actions required networks, wealth, and good name, but both the veneration of saints and willingness to connect with a religious order were common qualities among medieval Christians. Patron saints were important for knightly families and could have a remarkable role in the family history.

In many cases both local and foreign cults were revered. Prince Bolesław was blessed by fortune and victory by St. Giles, whose cult originated in the lower Rhône area. According to the Gallus's chronicle, a "Polish bishop" Franco, perhaps of Poznań diocese, advised the parents of the future prince, who had long hoped for an offspring. Despite their ardent prayers, fasting, and generosity to the poor, their wish was not fulfilled. Franco counselled them to turn to St. Giles in the land of Provence, to whom they should without delay send an image of pure gold resembling a boy. The image and a cup were prepared immediately and sent forth along with a rich gift of silver, robes, holy garments, and a royal letter asking humbly for the holy prayers of the saint. The request

---

45   Dusburg, *Chron. Pr.*, 4.33, 198; Jeroschin, *Di Kronike*, 410 (ll. 9309–54).

was granted and a son was born to the great joy of the prince and his wife.[46] The moral of the story is that laymen, however pious, need specialized clergymen to guide them with the proper observance of spiritual mysteries.[47]

Jeroschin relates a story of a pilgrim from Meissen who had not atoned for a past sin properly during his crusading in Prussia. When he died on his way back home, no rest was granted for him, but his grave suddenly opened, and the dead man jumped out to the astonishment of the local bishop. The crusader had been condemned to hell for stealing the field of his neighbor and was now consigned to purgatory waiting his damnation. The punishment had not been executed immediately, because the sinner had taken the cross during his lifetime. The poor soul was rescued by his son, who traveled east to find out what had happened to his father and, on arriving to the open grave, swore to give the field back to its lawful owner. The pit closed and the pilgrim found his rest.[48]

The partial clericalization of the ritual of knighting, as well as the promotion of penitential practices such as pilgrimage among the nobility, were other small victories for the clergy.[49] The ceremony originated in the pagan German tribal custom of granting arms to young warriors and initiating them into manhood.[50] In the early Middle Ages, the West Frankish bishops placed

---

46 Gallus, *Gesta*, Epylogus and 1.30–31, pp. 10–11 and 104–8; Radosław Kotecki and Jacek Maciejewski, "Writing Episcopal Courage in Twelfth-Century Poland: Gallus Anonymous and Master Vincentius," in *Episcopal Power and Personality in Medieval Europe, 900–1480*, ed. Peter Coss et al., MCS 42 (Turnhout: Brepols, 2020), 35–61 at 43–44. For the importance of St. Giles to Bolesław, see Michałowski, "'Restauratio Poloniae,'" 25–31; Jacek Banaszkiewicz, "Książę polski Bolesław i szkocki rycerz Desiré. Dwie opowieści o potomkach zrodzonych za wstawiennictwem św. Idziego (Gall, 'Epylogus' i ks. I, rozdz. 30–31 oraz 'Le lai de Desiré' koniec XII w.)," in *W stronę rytuałów i Galla Anonima* (Cracow: Avalon, 2018), 344–76.

47 John of Salisbury elaborates the concept in his *Policraticus*. He concludes that whether literate or illiterate, a prince must depend on episcopal and clerical guidance in all matters of faith and especially what becomes to the receiving of the sacraments. John of Salisbury, *Policraticus*, 4.3 and 4.6, ed. Katherine S.B. Keats-Rohan, CCCM 118 (Turnhout: Brepols, 1993), 236 and 248, 251–52.

48 Jeroschin, *Di Kronike*, 396–98 (ll. 8155–8264).

49 Martin Aurell, "From Episcopal Dubbing to Sacrament of Confirmation (Twelfth–Fourteenth Centuries)," *Viator*, forthc.

50 Nithard provides an early example of the ritual, describing the dubbing of Charles the Bald in Quierzy in September 838. Nithard, *Vita Karoli*, 1.6, ed. and trans. Philippe Lauer and Sophie Glansdorf, in *Histoire des fils de Louis le Pieux*, Classiques de l'histoire au Moyen Âge 51 (Paris: Les Belles Lettres, 2012), 26; Janet L. Nelson, *The Frankish World 750–900* (London and Rio Grande OH: Hambledon Press, 1996), 84; Kaeuper, *Medieval Chivalry*, 81, 104.

the ritual within a Christian framework,[51] to which ritual blessings and vigil were added over time. Accolade during a mass, often integrated into a religious feast, became standard practice during the twelfth century.[52] Prince Władysław Herman, seeing that his son would be capable of ruling and fighting, had young Bolesław girded with the sword during the feast of the Assumption of the Virgin Mary in Płock, where the cathedral dedicated to Virgin Mary was located close to the princely court.[53] Frederick Barbarossa arranged the knighting of his two sons in 1184 during great Pentecost festivities in Mainz.[54]

3   Private Invocations by Knights

In most of the references discussing knightly piety an ordained cleric acts as an intercessor between the deity or a saint and a lay person. The cleric may either actively promote worship or be prompted to do so in collaboration with the knight. Without clerical advice, the ritual may easily be prolonged or go askew, as in the cases of Bolesław's parents or Conrad. In addition, the sources contain a few instances of straight communication between God, saints, and laymen. In comparison with the basic case administered by the clergy, these events often take place in private. Typically, the potential recipient of divine help either actively pleads for supernatural protection or remains a passive recipient of divine intercession through a vision or other sort of miracle. In the sources produced by the clergy, the depictions of such individual experiences of holiness are sparser and briefer than in the texts produced by or under a lay patron.

Prayers said individually by knights in great peril are thereby rarely mentioned in the sources of the Baltic Crusades, whereas in the vernacular *chansons* of the crusades they are relatively common. Based on the few available examples, the context of the ritual intercession is fairly similar in Eastern and Western European texts; the calls for aid are directed to God and/or the

---

51   Nelson, "Church's Military Service," 29; Georges Duby, *The Three Orders: Feudal Society Imagined* (Chicago: The University of Chicago Press, 1980), 358.
52   Aurell, *Le chevalier lettré*, 26, 296–97; Kaeuper, *Medieval Chivalry*, 81.
53   Gallus, *Gesta*, 2.18, pp. 152–53; For an analysis of the knighting of Bolesław, see Zbigniew Dalewski, "The Knighting of Polish Dukes in the Early Middle Ages: Ideological and Political Significance," *Acta Polonia Historica* 80 (1999): 15–43 at 25–27; see also Kotecki, "Bishops," 448.
54   Aurell, *Le chevalier lettré*, 158–59. For other similar examples, see Max Lieberman, "Knighting in the Twelfth and Thirteenth Centuries," *Anglo-Norman Studies* 43 (2020): 151–76 at 153, 154, 156.

saints at a critical moment during battles, raids, and sieges. Whereas God and Christ were the primary objects of veneration in both groups, the sample of saints included in the pleas is variable. The Virgin Mary was very popular in eastern, central, and western European texts alike, but on the whole, the invocations in the *chansons* involved far more saints than the sources of the Baltic Crusades.

The selection of the Mother of God as a principal source of aid was natural, especially in the eastern case: not only was Mary nominated the patroness of the Teutonic Order, but the protector of the Baltic Crusades in general. In addition, St. Barbara and St. Lawrence were called on for help several times. The Devil, too, had a role in the Baltic sources by carrying out acts that inadvertently assisted in the work of God. Other holy persons mentioned included St. George,[55] the Maccabees, St. Catherine of Alexandria, St. Mary Magdalene, St. Giles, St. Sebastian, and St. Stephen, as well as the regional saints Elizabeth of Thuringia and Elizabeth of Hungary.[56]

While raiding the lands of Sudargus's (Neman in the Kaliningrad region), Teutonic Knight Albrecht of Hagen fell from his horse and was concussed. When he recovered consciousness, he found himself horseless and alone. In his great distress he implored God and the Virgin Mary to rescue him from the imminent danger. In return he would thenceforth serve them as well as he could, even better than before. After making the sign of the cross to ward off all harm, Albrecht began to walk in the direction of the town Ragnit (Lith. Ragainė, Rus. Neman), where he hoped to find his knightly brothers. It was a long walk, and Albrecht had to stop to ask the way from a village he passed. When he had left, the peasants realized that they had left an enemy go freely and came after him with dogs. The knight was very scared and hid in the bushes. The pursuers and dogs passed him several times within touching distance but could not

---

55 Wigand of Marburg mentions lay crusaders riding under the banner of St. George, while the knights of the Teutonic Order gathered under the banners of Mary and the Order, marked with the cross and the eagle. Wigand von Marburg, *Nowa kronika Pruska*, chap. 139, 294, 296, ed. and trans. Sławomir Zonenberg and Krzysztof Kwiatkowski (Toruń: Towarzystwo Naukowe w Toruniu, 2017), 318, 504, 506. For the cult of St. George in Prussia and the popularity of the saint among the supporters of the Order, see Werner Paravicini, *Die Preußenreisen des europäischen Adels*, vol. 1, Beihefte der Francia 17.1 (Sigmaringen: Thorbecke, 1989).

56 Nicholas Jaspert, "Culte des saints," in *Prier et combattre. Dictionnaire européen des orders militaires au Moyen Âge*, ed. Nicole Bériou et al. (Paris: Fayard, 2009), 835; Hans Hettler, *Preussen als Kreuzzugsregion. Untersuchungen zu Peter von Dusburg's "Chronica terre Prussie" in Zeit und Umfeld* (Frankfurt: Peter Lang, 2014), 462–67.

see him because God blinded them. The knight safely reached Ragnit and gave thanks to God and His Mother.[57]

Before taking the habit of the Teutonic Order, brother Johannes of Ilberstedt had been a pernicious knight. Once he fell seriously ill and received holy sacraments, but instead of concentrating on prayer and contemplation, he raped a servant girl who was looking after him. Still, on the scene of crime, God made the devil lift the sinner up in the air and reprimand him for his grave error. The knight called to Mary for help in his great agony and swore to join the Order if only she saved him from the danger. When he enunciated the word "Order," the devil dropped him in a bog some half a mile away from his sickbed. As proof of the story's veracity, his bedclothes were later found in the bog.

In the case of noble fighting men, the protagonists usually survive the threat. Women and commoners do not fare so well. In a story resembling that of Johannes, a Lithuanian heathen warrior intended to rape a nun during a raid on Frankfurt. She prayed for help from Christ, her true husband, who helped her by tricking the assailant into cutting off her head before touching her body, thus saving her purity for eternal joy.[58] The incident was part of the lengthy conflict over the rule of Pomerelia and the Kingdom of Poland between Władysław the Elbow (Łokietek) and John of Luxembourg, king of Bohemia, in which the Teutonic Order supported the latter claimant. In response to the alliance between the Order and Count Palatine Louis of Wittelsbach (from 1328 Holy Roman Emperor Louis IV), the army of Władysław and his pagan Lithuanian allies launched an attack in 1326 on the lands of the Margraviate of Brandenburg reaching as far as Frankfurt and Berlin. The intended rape of a nun might have been added to the text to underline the depravity of the enemy of the Order.

Peter of Dusburg and Nicolaus of Jeroschin recount the miraculous finding of the head of St. Barbara in the stronghold at Sartowice (Germ. Sartowitz) held by the men of Świętopełk, duke of East Pomerania at the beginning of the first Prussian Uprising (1242–1249). The Teutonic Knights under the command of Marshal Dietrich of Bernheim[59] had managed to enter the castle by

---

57 Jeroschin, *Di Kronike*, 590–91 (ll. 24871–24937).
58 Ibid., 609–10 (ll. 26535–81).
59 Besides the master, the marshal was the official responsible for the preparations for the battle and for the leadership during the fighting. *Statuten*, chap. 19–30, pp. 105–107. The memory of Dietrich as the key factor in the discovery of St. Barbara's relics and leader of the procession to Althaus Kulm survived into the fifteenth century also beyond the area of the Teutonic Order. *Die aeltere Hochmeisterchronik*, ed. Max Töppen, SrP 3 (Frankfurt am Mein: Hirzel, 1866), 519–709 at 547–48; Gregory Leighton, "The Relics of St Barbara at Althaus Kulm: History, Patronages, and Insight into the Teutonic Order

surprise, scaling the wall by ladders and overcoming the garrison, killing them in the battle that ensued. In the cellars of the castle they found a silver casket containing a head of a maiden, attached with a written document claiming that the head belonged to St. Barbara,[60] hacked off by her pagan father in ancient times in Egypt.[61] Among the prisoners they found an old woman who told them that their victory was a gift from the saint. The old lady herself had fervently prayed for Barbara to save her folk from the invading crusaders and had in response had a vision in her sleep. The maiden showed that her skirts were hitched up, ready to leave the place. Her purpose was to go and hear mass in Althaus Kulm (Pol. Starogród) the same day. After appearing to the woman thrice, Barbara commended her to God, because she was leaving immediately and could not offer her protection any longer. The woman woke up so unhappy that she fell out of her bed. She tried to go after the saint, but Barbara had disappeared. While looking for her, she found out that the castle was under attack and shouted to the guards to wake up. While telling her story, she now understood with great sadness, that the prayers of the knights to St. Barbara had been heard instead of her own. The brothers took the head relic to Althaus Kulm in solemn procession, the clerics singing hymns, the bells ringing, and the commoners following barefoot with banners and burning candles in their hands. After the mass was said, the relic was taken up to the castle, where it was greatly honored up to the day when Nicolaus was writing his chronicle.[62]

---

and the Christian Population in Prussia (Thirteenth–Fifteenth Centuries)," *ZH* 85.1 (2020): 5–50.

[60] For the cult of St. Barbara in Poland, see Agnieszka Błażewicz, "Skarb relikwiarzowy z kościoła zamkowego w czasach krzyżackich. Dzieje relikwii św. Barbary," in *Spotkania malborskie im. Macieja Kilarskiego*, ed. Artur Dobry, 3 vols. (Malbork: Muzeum Zamkowe w Malborku, 2004–2008), 2(2006):93–111 at 99–101; Waldemar Rozynkowski, "Św. Barbara—święta 'od wody'. O patrociniach św. Barbary w średniowiecznej Polsce," in *Město a voda. Praha, město u vody*, ed. Olga Fejtová, Václav Ledvinka, and Jiří Pešek (Prague: Scriptorium, 2005), 231–42 at 239; Leighton, "The Relics." For the castle and cult site, see *Die Bau- und Kunstdenkmäler der Provinz Westpreussen*, vol. 2: *Kulmerland und Löbau*, ed. Johannes Heise (Danzig: 1887–1895), 16n41.

[61] The finding of the relic led to the establishment of St. Barbara's cults in many parts of Prussia, especially in Culm. Nicolaus mentions that the life and miracles of St. Barbara were translated into German by Luder von Braunschweig, who was the patron of Nicolaus and the grand master of the Order. No life of Barbara by him has survived. See *The Chronicle of Prussia by Nicolaus von Jeroschin*, 94 n. 1.

[62] Dusburg, *Chron. Pr.*, 3.36, pp. 69–70; Jeroschin, *Di Kronike*, 375–79 (ll. 6307–6670). For that story, see Maria Starnawska, "The Role of the Legend of Saint Barbara's Head in the Conflict of the Teutonic Order and Swietopolk, the Duke of Pomerania," in *The Military*

The account of the late thirteenth-century *Galician-Volhynian Chronicle* of the attack of the Mongols in 1259/1260 on the Polish town Sandomierz likewise ends in a tragedy. According to the text, the Tatars forded over the Wisła River and began to ravage the Polish lands. They came to Sandomierz and laid siege to the city surrounding it from all sides and bombarding its walls with their machines day and night. On the fourth day they managed to breach the city wall and pour into the city, where they started a fire and began to slaughter the inhabitants with their spears. Those who could seek protection in the keep, with the consequence that many were crushed to death in the gates and other fell from the drawbridge to the deep moat. A large crowd had also gathered in the church and perished there in the flames. The fire got out of hand, driving the attackers out of the city to wait for the flames to die off.

The next day the abbots, priests, and deacons assembled, sang mass with the clergy, and began to distribute Holy Communion first to the clergy, then to the nobles with their wives and children, and thereafter to everyone present. Many people confessed their sins. Holding crosses, candles and censers in their hands, the crowd left the city. The nobles' servants came first carrying the children, followed by the nobles and their wives marching dressed in their "wedding attire." Many of the people were crying; the husbands wept for their wives, mothers for their children, brothers for brothers. It was all in vain because God's wrath was upon them. The Tatars slaughtered all of them, men and women, while they were advancing towards the monastery of the Holy Trinity on Łysa Góra Mountain (Łysiec, Święty Krzyż), which was destroyed similarly.[63]

The Gallus chronicle contains a similar report of Prince Bolesław III's raid on the border of Poland and Pomerania. The prince was besieging the stronghold of Nakło with his army and war engines on the frontier of Poland and

[63] *Orders*, vol. 6.2: *Culture and Conflict in Western and Northern Europe*, ed. Jochen Schenk and Mike Carr (Abingdon and New York: Routledge, 2017), 203–13; Leighton, "The Relics."
Chronica Galiciano-Voliniana (Chronica Romanoviciana), ed. Dariusz Dąbrowski and Adrian Jusupović, MPH NS 16 (Cracow: Polska Akademia Umiejętności, 2017), 421–27; English translation in *The Hypatian Codex II: The Galician-Volynian Chronicle*, trans. George A. Perfecky, Harvard series in Ukrainian studies 16.2 (Munich: Fink, 1973), 79–80. My compliments to Radosław Kotecki for sharing the extract. For traces of similar religious practices in the *acta* of 1339, concerning the trial between Poland and the Teutonic Order accusing the Order of the desecration of churches during the raids in Poland ca. 1330, see Radosław Kotecki, "The Desecration of Holy Places According to Witnesses' Testimonies in the Polish-Teutonic Order Trials of the 14th Century," in *Arguments and Counter-Arguments: The Political Thought of the 14th- and 15th Centuries during the Polish-Teutonic Order Trials and Disputes*, ed. Wiesław Sieradzan (Toruń: Wydawnictwo Naukowe Uniwersytetu Mikołaja Kopernika, 2012), 69–110 at 101–2.

Pomerania on St. Lawrence's Day.[64] The people inside had negotiated a truce with the Poles on the condition that if no rescue force appeared by the nominated day, they would surrender the town. On hearing about the treaty, the Pomeranian leaders made a plot, and abandoning their horses and the network of roads, approached the Polish army from the depth of the forest. The attack began on the Day of St. Lawrence, at the hour of the celebrations of the mass for the holy martyr. Though outnumbered by the enemy, Bolesław divided his warriors into two commands, one under himself and the other under his Count Palatine Skarbimir, and appealed to the courage of his troops, God and St. Lawrence in these words: "My unconquerable young friends, let your mettle and the pressing danger and your love of your country, rather than any words from me, stir your hearts. Today, with God's favor and the intercession of St. Lawrence may the idolatry of the Pomeranians and their martial pride be crushed by your swords." And soon, after a fierce confrontation, the Pomeranians' line, mostly comprising of foot soldiers, was broken by Skarbimir and surrounded and demolished by Bolesław's men. The Polish victory was owed to the help of God stirred by the prayers of St. Lawrence. "Those present were amazed how such a great slaughter could so quickly have been made by less than a thousand warriors."[65]

Martin, Archbishop of Gniezno, was likewise miraculously rescued from the Pomeranians when they were looting in Poland. The old archbishop was confessing to a priest before setting out for a journey, his horse already waiting saddled outside. Suddenly one of the priests ran indoors crying out that the Pomeranians were attacking them. The archbishop and his men were not armed and had no time to flee. One of them, an archdeacon, left the sanctuary and thus lost his chance to escape. When he was trying to reach the horses, he was seized by the enemy. Since the enemy mistook him to be the archbishop, he was treated well and guarded reverently. In the meanwhile, the frightened archbishop prayed to God, blessed himself with the sign of the cross and climbed up the altar, having miraculously been given strength that a fragile old man would not otherwise have possessed. The priest hid behind the altar. The majesty of God blinded the pagans rushing into the church so that they did not search the altar properly but were content to leave with the relics and the

---

64 The description of the siege and capture of Nakło was important, and it was later developed by Master Vincentius at the turn of the thirteenth century. In both stories Bolesław is shown as the slayer of pagans and a Christian hero. See Kotecki and Maciejewski, "Writing Episcopal Courage," 44–45; Kotecki, "Bishops," 446; idem, "Pious Rulers, Princely Clerics, and Angels of Light: Imperial Holy War Imagery in Twelfth-Century Poland and Rus'," in *Christianity and War*, 159–88.
65 Gallus, *Gesta*, 3.1, pp. 224–25.

archbishop's travel altar, as well as the archdeacon they had captured outside. God Almighty later returned the treasures undefiled and complete to the archbishop. The archdeacon was released safe and healthy.[66]

God also heard the petitions of the blessed Czesław Odrowąż, a Dominican friar who, according to a later source from ca. 1470, prayed for the people of Wrocław during the Mongol invasion of Poland in 1241. Czesław comforted the terrified people who were hiding in the citadel, never ceasing to pray for divine protection. At the critical moment when the Mongols were preparing to scale the ramparts, Czesław appeared upon the wall just as a fireball fell from the heavens onto the heads of the enemy, who turned in flight, leaving the city intact (fig. 6.1).[67]

The cases of Czesław, Martin, and also that of Sandomierz are conventional. The prayer is initiated by a member of the higher clergy and in the first and last case attended by a faceless crowd, which plays only a supporting role as beneficiaries of the divine intervention requested by a clergyman. The distress and fear felt by the people in such a situation are filtered to heaven by clerical invocation and left thenceforth to the mercy of divine judgment.

In the *chansons* of the crusades also, devotions typically take place at official sites or events of worship, where the armies or other narratively important groups gather to worship under authorized preachers. Besides these standard practices, individual knights are frequently depicted absorbed in prayer, calling directly for supernatural aid before taking part in especially difficult or dangerous ventures, either when combat is about to begin or amidst battle, that is, at moments when it is clearly not possible to consult any member of the clergy. More often than not, these prayers save their lives. They represent the topos of

---

66 Ibid., 2.43, 196–99; Kotecki and Maciejewski, "Writing Episcopal Courage," 43.
67 "Beatus Ceslaus natione Polonus a Dominico una cum Jacintho Romae habitum Ordinis suscepit, et in Polonia et Silesia miris signis et prodigijs effulsit. Hic circa annum Domini 1241 cum Tartarorum Rabie Polonia et Silesia devastaretur, existens in castro inclitae Civitatis Wratislaviensis cum alijs Christi fidelibus orationibus suis civitatem ab eorum insania potenter defendit. Ipso namque orante globus igneus super caput ejus apparuit, quo perterritae tartarorum legiones fugae praesidia assumpserunt et abeuntes civitatem intactam dimiserunt. Ad ejus etiam venerabile sepulchrum usque hodie mortui resuscitantur, et varijs oppressi languoribus ad invocationem nominis ejus meritis ipsius gratiose liberantur." Biblioteka Uniwersytetu Wrocławskiego, IV Q 194, k. 6r; Archivio Segreto Vaticano, Archivum Congregationis Sacrorum Rituum, Processus 3620, *Sacrorum Rituum Congregatione Wratislaviensis Beatificationis et Canonisationis Servi Dei Ceslai Odrovansij Ordinis Praedicatorum*, 208–9, 224–25. Cited after Wojciech Kucharski, *"Beatus Ceslaus natione Polonus." Dzieje kultu błogosławionego Czesława*, Studia i źródła Dominikańskiego Instytutu Historycznego w Krakowie 10 (Cracow: Esprit, 2012), 90, where (pp. 85–113) is a detailed discussion of this source as compared with other accounts on the Blessed Czesław. My compliment to Radosław Kotecki for pointing out the fragment.

INVOCATIONS BY KNIGHTS FOR SUPERNATURAL AID

FIGURE 6.1 Blessed Czesław defending Wrocław from Mongols in 1241. Copperplate print from Dominicus Frydrychowicz's *S. Hyacinthvs Odrovasivs* ... (Cracow: Typis Universitatis, 1688), 194
LICENSE: PUBLIC DOMAIN. REPRODUCED FROM:
BIT.LY/3WG4NWK

the *prière du plus grand peril*, prayer in mortal peril, danger which the knights hope to overcome through the miraculous intervention by Christ, saints, or other biblical characters.[68]

These prayers belong to solitary, voluntary and informal acts of piety. They are sometimes related to rather unorthodox adaptations of the Christian rites, such as making the cross out of blades of grass or using the sword to make the sign of the cross, thereby improvising with a weapon to make the blessing to invoke magical protection.[69] Such references to the *ad hoc* fabricated crosses such references can be found nowhere else than in fictional *chansons*:

During the Battle of Antioch in June 1098, Rainald of Toul lost his horse and had to continue the fight on foot. After killing many enemies, he noticed that he had lost so much blood that he would soon die. The brave knight prayed to God to have mercy on his soul, made a cross out of three blades of grass, confessed his sins to God and died. The angels carried his soul to heavenly joy singing *Te deum laudamus*.[70]

In the *chansons*, the prayers said at moments of danger invariably contain memorized lists of biblical characters and saints as well as a paraphrase of the *credo*. The content and length of the lists of names vary according to the person saying the prayer, some of them being rather long. Besides the Virgin Mary, also Mary Magdalen, Lazarus, and Nicholas are popularly petitioned for aid. Although these saints were prominent among the contemporary laity, references to them remain of little significance in the Latin chronicles of the crusades produced in the west. Another group mentioned regularly were those military heroes of the Old Testament who miraculously survived from almost certain death with the help of God. This group contains David, Moses, the Maccabees, Joshua, Job and Judith, the slayer of Holofernes. Among the sources for the Baltic Crusades, the text by Nicolaus of Jeroschin has a similar selection of saints to those prominent in the western European tradition of the crusades. In addition to his namesake St. Nicholas, he relates to David (and his combat with Goliath, several times), Saul, Jonathan, the Maccabees (Judas Maccabeus several times), Joab, Gideon, Isaac, Esau, Joshua, Jacob, Job, Judith (and her killing of Holofernes, twice), Abraham, Solomon and St. Elizabeth of

---

68 The "Chanson des Chétifs" and "Chanson de Jérusalem," 81–82n30; see also Marie Pierre Koch, *An Analysis of the Long Prayers in Old French Literature with Special Reference to the "Biblical-Creed-Narrative" Prayers*, Studies in Romance languages and literatures 19 (New York: AMS Press, 1969).

69 For examples of an improvised confession and the topos of the cross made out of three blades of grass, see Storelli, "Les chevaliers."

70 *La Chanson d'Antioche*, cccxxxiv, 420–21 (ll. 8520–41).

Thuringia. Nicolaus also compares the Galindians to Pharaoh, the enemy of Moses.[71]

In *Les chétifs*, the knight Richard of Chaumont was chosen to represent his captor Corbaran of Oliferne in a judicial combat against the Turkish champions Sorgalé and Goliath in front of the Sultan of Persia. Richard agreed on condition that he and his fellow crusaders would gain back their freedom, should he win the fight. When he saw his adversaries, he prostrated himself in a cross on the ground and prayed to God, the Father, Alpha and Omega and Lord of all. Richard's invocation reminded God of the many miracles he had implemented through mortals. He had given mankind a way to free itself of the burden of the original sin through Mary, he had sent Christ to the world to preach to the people, though Pilate and Barabbas rejected his teaching. Furthermore, he had released many mortal men: Adam and Eve after they sinned, Noah from the flood, Abraham, Abel, Jacob, and Esau, Joseph, and finally Moses by sending the daughter of Pharaoh to rescue him when he was a baby. Because of these divine favors and miraculous rescues, Richard dared to ask God to let him kill in the forthcoming fight his two mighty enemies.[72]

Richard survived the fight as the victor and Corbaran kept his word. On their way back to Oliferne, Corbaran's fief, the crusaders nevertheless lost their way in a storm and ended up at Mount Tigris, where the horrible dragon Sathanas kept its lair. A Turkish nobleman of the region also had Christian captives. One of them was Ernoul of Beauvais who, sent for an errand by his captor, had similarly got lost with the regrettable result of encountering the dragon. Ernoul prayed to God and Lady Mary, from whom he sought protection in his attempt to slay a dragon. He appealed to the bleeding wounds of Christ and to His suffering on the cross to free the weak captives of hell. After praying, he picked a blade of grass and began to cross himself, eventually eating the blade in place of the Body of Our Lord to secure His aid at the Day of Judgement.[73]

The unfortunate Ernoul was swallowed by the beast, but only after his brother Baldwin of Beauvais in the retinue of Richard of Chaumont and Corbaran had heard his cries. Leaving his comrades behind, Baldwin hurried after Ernoul. On his way he halted to pray several times, beginning already while climbing the mountain in quest of the dragon's lair:

---

71 Jeroschin, *Di Kronike*, l 331–43, 347 (ll. 2406, 2415, 2418–19, 2427, 2487, 2514, 2519, 2563, 2566, 2584, 2604, 2614, 2654–55, 2698–99, 2772, 2796, 2838, 2844, 2890, 2895, 2940–41, 2978, 3008, 3020, 3088, 3135, 3166, 3178, 3282, 3320, 3322, 3332, 3337, 3534, 3555, 3864).
72 *Les Chétifs*, 21–22 (ll. 830–83).
73 Ibid., 44–45 (ll. 1892–1938).

"Ah God!" said Baldwin, "in Your holy pity and by Our Lady the Virgin Mary, offer me your aid. Ah, noble St Nicholas, take pity on me. Lord God, come to my help so that I do not get attacked and eaten and devoured by this serpent."[74]

A bit later he prayed again, this time for much longer than the first time. Again, he commenced by calling on God and St. Nicholas and proceeded to recite a makeshift *credo*, beginning with the creation and paradise entrusted to Adam and Eve, the Fall and the condemnation of mankind, the harrowing of hell, and the miraculous release of souls by Christ. Baldwin carried on with the life of Christ, mentioning his birth, the visit of the three kings, and the main events of Easter. After relating to the visit of the three Marys to the Savior's grave, he repeated the breaking of the gates of hell and the saving of the souls of Adam and Eve, Noah and Abraham, Moses and Jonah, Jacob and Esau, as well as Joseph. The prayer concluded with the encounter of Christ and Mary Magdalen after the resurrection, and a reminder for Christ that he had promised his blessing for all those who truly believed in him. Since he had also saved Susanna and Daniel, would he not protect Baldwin from the dragon? After having prayed, Baldwin crossed himself in the name of God, son of the Virgin Mary.[75]

Before entering the battle with the beast, Baldwin prayed for the third time to God. This time St. Michael manifested in the shape of a dove and told him not to lose faith, reminding him of Lazarus brought from death to life. Baldwin was overjoyed, crossed himself four times, and wandered on until he found the head of Ernoul and the body of his donkey strangled by the dragon. Baldwin made one last sign of the cross on his chest and after having called out to Father God and Jesus Christ, commanded the beast not to devour nor hurt him in the name of St. Denis, St. George, St. Maurice, St. Peter, St. Lawrence, St. Leonard, St. Nicholas, St. James, St. Giles, and all the Apostles, the Holy Cross and the Holy Sepulcher. Baldwin kept attacking the beast bravely all the time calling God for his help. The fight was fierce and long, and once an angel had to place himself in front of Baldwin to protect him, but finally the hero pierced the stony heart of the dragon with his sword and destroyed it.[76]

Harpin of Bourges, another crusader captive in the group of Richard and Baldwin, seeing lions coming towards him, was terrified by the prospect of imminent death. He implored Christ, who had allowed Longinus to strike him

---

74   Ibid., 53 (ll. 2279–83). English translation after *The "Chanson des Chétifs,"* 111.
75   *Les Chétifs*, 54–56 (ll. 2306–2406).
76   Ibid., 57–59 (ll. 2473–2555) and 65–66 (ll. 2806–52).

with the lance, died willingly on the cross, and redeemed from hell Baal, Elisha, Abel, Noah, and Abraham, not to let him die. With his sword he drew a ring around him large enough for his horse to step into and blessed the ring with the sign of the cross loudly calling on the name of Jesus. The lions were not able to cross the line he had drawn because God protected him and his horse.[77] When Harpin was later threatened twice by Saracens armed with knives and bows, he was again miraculously saved by invoking God, St. Mary and St. Nicholas.[78]

Fulcher the Orphan,[79] who was the first among the crusaders to climb over the city wall of Antioch, rested for a moment under the siege ladder to implore protection from God:

> My Lord and father, I invoke your holy name. You were born of the Blessed Virgin, you saved St. Jonah from the belly of the whale, you brought St. Lazarus back from the dead. You pardoned Mary Magdalen ... You pardoned him [the centurion] and forgave his sins. You were laid in the Sepulchre and kept under guard like a thief. Three days later you rose from the dead and went down to Hell, which could not stand against you; you released your own, Noah and Aron ... let me climb up the ladder for my salvation, and save the Franks from death and captivity by letting us conquer the town and the citadel. He raised his hand in a sign of blessing, then seized the ladder and climbed up.[80]

Godfrey of Bouillon, the famous leader of one of the armies of the First Crusade and the future advocate of the Holy Sepulcher and *de facto* first Frankish ruler of Jerusalem, with a deep wound piercing his liver and lungs, prayed to God

---

77 Ibid., 79–80 (ll. 3449–69).
78 Ibid., 82–84 (ll. 2543–50, 3581–3615, 3615–23).
79 Fulcher the Orphan is not mentioned in any other source. His nickname indicates humble, although probably still knightly origin. The description and context pair him with other crusader knights. *La Chanson de Jérusalem* refers to certain Joseran, Thomas, and Fulk of Melun as the three crusaders to enter Antioch. This is probably a confusion, since Fulk of Melun occurs several times in the *Chanson d'Antioche* with that name and without any indication to orphanhood. Fulk was a common name. *La Chanson de Jérusalem*, 109 (ll. 3516–17).
80 "Damedex, sire pere, par ton saintisme non, Ki de sainte Virgene presistes naquison, Et saint Jonas salvastes el ventre del poisson, De mort resuscitates le cors saint Lazeron. Marie Madeleine fesistes le pardon ... Tu li fesis pardon et grant remission; El sepucre fus mis et gaitiés a laron, Al tierc jor en aprés eüs surexion; A infer en alastes, n'i ot deffension, Vos amis en jetastes: Noé et Aron. ... Si me laisiés monter a me salvation et garisses François de mort et de prison, que nos puissons conquerre le vile et le donjon." "Lors a levé sa main, si fist beneïçon, puis se prist a l'esciele, si est alés amon": *Les Chanson d'Antioche*, chap. 253, pp. 305–6 (ll. 6097–6101, 6113–17). English text after *The "Chanson d'Antioche,"* 247–48.

to save him from what would otherwise be certain death, like he had saved Lazarus and Mary Magdalen. Renaut Porcet, another hero of crusader conquest of Antioch who was captured and decapitated by the Muslims, also mentioned the resurrection of Lazarus in an appeal, as well as the rescues of Daniel from the cave of the lions and Jonah from the stomach of the big fish, while remaining captive.[81]

The biblical characters mentioned in the fragments were all heroes of famous stories known by medieval audiences since childhood. Lazarus had lost his life, whereas Daniel and Jonah had certainly been faced with a serious risk of perishing. For warriors fearing for their lives in times of battle, their miraculous survival unharmed from seemingly certain death was an appealing source of consolation, as well as an object of identification.[82] Mary Magdalen might look like a peculiar choice among the list of saints mentioned by the crusaders. In the Middle Ages she was confused with Mary of Bethany, the sister of Lazarus, and this explains why her name often appears with Lazarus.[83] After the alleged recovery of the bones of Mary Magdalen by the monks of the Abbey of Sainte-Marie-Madeleine in Vézelay in ca. 1050, her cult had become very popular in the west.

The prayers in peril function in both western and eastern European tradition as the markers of a turning point of the narrative. The appeal to God and the subsequent recital of the litany of saints indicate the beginning of a great battle, allowing the audience a moment to focus on the forthcoming chivalric fighting with many dramatic turns and miraculous escapes.

Visions form another group of miraculous effects added to the texts to highlight the story. As in the case of direct prayers to God and his saints, the inclusion of the event, whether active prayer or passive reception of a divine message, had two objectives. The immediate aim was to keep up the curiosity of the audience with exciting details, but primarily both types of invocations are in the narratives to remind the audience of the Christian morals and the

---

81   *La Chanson d'Antioche*, 456 (ll. 9288–9301) and 229–30 (ll. 4364–70).

82   Sini Kangas, "Scripture, Hierarchy, and Social Control: The Uses of the Bible in the Twelfth- and Thirteenth-Century Chronicles and 'Chansons' of the Crusades," in *Transcultural Approaches to the Bible: Exegesis and Historical Writing in the Medieval Worlds*, ed. Matthias M. Tischler and Patrick S. Marschner, TMS 1 (Turnhout: Brepols, 2021), 109–44.

83   The error was originally made by Pope Gregory the Great. He incorporated Mary the disciple of Christ, Mary of Bethany and the unnamed sinful woman whom Christ pardoned at the well of Sychar into one person, the unhistorical Mary Magdalene, known as a former prostitute. *Sancti Gregorii Magni Romani pontificis XL homiliarum in Evangelia libri duo*, ed. Jacques-Paul Migne, PL 76 (Paris: Apud J.-P. Migne Editorem, 1857), 1238–46.

ever-present omnipotence of God. In crusading, they also had an important role in inciting new pilgrims to take up the cross.

During the First Crusade, the major turning points at the siege of Antioch, the ensuing Battle of Antioch, the second siege of Antioch and the conquest of Jerusalem, were marked by visions and miracles. In Antioch, Peter Bartholomew, a preacher of unclear background marching among the Provençal army under count Raymond of St. Gilles, saw in a vision Christ, St. Mary and St. Andrew, who told him in which place he could find the Holy Lance with which Longinus had pierced the side of Christ hanging on the cross. The genuineness of the discovery was doubted until Peter proved he was telling the truth in an ordeal by fire. He was injured and later died from the further harm done by hysterical crusaders, who wanted to take secondary relics from him after he had survived the ordeal.[84] The other very famous miracle took place during the Battle of Antioch in June 1098, when St. George, St. Mercurius and St. Demetrius were reported to have descended from the mountains mounted on white horses and leading the legions from heaven under white banners, helping the crusaders to rout the army of the Turkish Atabeg Kerbogha.[85]

Battlefield visions and miracles were also reported from the eastern crusader fronts. In 1242 Duke Świętopełk stirred up the Prussian chieftains to revolt against the Teutonic Order in the First Prussian Uprising. In 1244 they raided Culm (Pol. Chełmno) and killed the garrison, the German settlers and

---

84 The descriptions of the miracle of the Holy Lance reveal a difference of opinion between Provençals and Normans. Raymond of Aguilers depicts the miracle as a genuine one, while Ralph of Caen, a chaplain in the service of Bohemond of Taranto and Tancred de Hauteville, remains entirely skeptical. Raymond of Aguilers, *Historia Francorum*, chap. 13, p. 265; chap. 17–18, pp. 279–82, 284, 285–87; Ralph of Caen, *Gesta Tancredi*, chap. 49, pp. 676–69; Guibert of Nogent, *Dei Gesta per Francos*, 6.22, pp. 263–64.

85 "Exibant quoque de montaneis innumerabiles exercitus, habentes equos albos, quorum vexilla omnia erant alba ... cognoverunt esse adjutorium Christi, cujus ductores fuerunt sancti Georgius, Mercurius et Demetrius": *Gesta Francorum*, chap. 8, 69; *Les Chanson d'Antioche*, 262–63 (l. 9062) (Maurice, George, Mercurius, and Demetrius). Heavenly warriors on white horses are also mentioned by Robert of Rheims, *Historia Iherosolimitana*, 796 (George, Demetrius, Maurice), 832 (George, Maurice, Mercurius and Demetrius); Baudri of Dol, *Historia Jerosolimitana*, 81 (George, Mercurius and Demetrius); Guibert of Nogent, *Dei Gesta per Francos*, 6.9, p. 240 (George, Mercurius and Demetrius); alleged Patriarch of Jerusalem in a letter to westerners, *Epistulae et chartae*, 147 (George, Demetrius, Theodore and Blaise). For discussion of those miracles, see Elizabeth Lapina, "Crusades, Memory, and Visual Culture: Representations of the Miracle of Intervention of Saints in Battle," in *Remembering the Crusades and Crusading*, ed. Megan Cassidy-Welch (Abingdon and New York: Routledge, 2016), 49–72; Beth C. Spacey, *The Miraculous and the Writing of Crusade Narrative* (Woodbridge: Boydell Press, 2020).

the allies of the Order.[86] When a citizen of Culm was lying mortally wounded on the battlefield, he was comforted by the Virgin Mary, who was walking among the dying and blessing them with holy smoke. She revealed to the dying man that all his suffering would end on the third day, when he would receive the heavenly wages in great joy. On the third day after this the man died.[87]

Hermann Sarrazin, a brother of the Teutonic Order in Königsberg (Rus. Kaliningrad), was a pious man devoted to the Virgin Mary even before joining the Teutonic Order. Once he threatened to kill another knight he was keeping as his captive, if the man would not be able to gather a large enough ransom. When the captive pleaded to him in the name of the Virgin to set a lower ransom, he released the man without demanding any payment at all. When the same Hermann was later on his way to receive the habit and the blessing to join the Order, he halted to fight in a tournament, where he slew the boldest and most skillful of the knights in the name of Lady Mary, unseating his opponent with his lance at the first attempt and winning his arms and horse, which he gave to the poor.[88]

Before his last battle Hermann saw a vision in which St. Mary was inviting him to her son's table. Hermann went to his brothers before riding off to the battle and prayed aloud for them:

> My dear brothers, may God take care of you and bless you in all eternity. You will never see me alive again because I have been invited by the dear mother of God to leave here and share eternal joy. May God grant my dearest wish, that you and I meet again in the kingdom of heaven. Amen.

Later that year a farmer had a vision of St. Mary, angels and virgins leading the soul of Hermann Sarrazin and his comrade-in-arms to heaven.[89]

---

86   Peter of Dusburg, *Chronicon terrae Prussiae*, 3.40–41, pp. 73–74.
87   Jeroschin, *Di Kronike*, 386 (ll. 7219–92).
88   Ibid., 422 (ll. 10325–70). Hermann was an exemplary knight in his devotion to the Virgin. Appealing to a vision from the mother of God, he criticized the texts chosen for the *Tischlesung* for being too worldly. Dusburg, *Chron. Pr.*, 3.81, p. 95; Marcus Wüst, *Studien zum Selbstverständnis des Deutschen Ordens im Mittelalter* (Weimar: VDG, 2013), 101; Arno Mentzel-Reuters, *"Arma Spiritualia." Bibliotheken, Bücher und Bildung im Deutschen Orden* (Petersberg: Harrassowitz, 2003), 78.
89   Jeroschin, *Di Kronike*, 422–23, 427 (ll. 10371–10414, 10733–64). English translation after *The Chronicle of Prussia by Nicolaus von Jeroschin*, 133; Marcus Wüst, "Zu Entstehung und Rezeption der 'Chronik des Preussenlandes' Peters von Dusburg," in *Neue Studien zur Literatur im Deutschen Ordens*, ed. Bernhart Jähnig and Arnold Mentzel-Reuters (Stuttgart: Hirzel, 2014), 206.

Not surprisingly, churches were appropriate places for visions in both eastern and western traditions alike. Brother Heinrich Stange was in a state of great anguish for the well-being of his soul. He went to church and prayed fervently to God, asking for a sign that he would be worthy of grace. Immediately a statue of Christ on the cross released its hand from the nail and blessed him with a sign of the cross. The miracle was later made public by a priest brother at Christburg (Pol. Dzierzgoń).[90]

Near the end of his chronicle, Nicolaus of Jeroschin includes two interesting adaptations of the basic experience of heavenly vision. In these cases, the devil appeared to a crusader in a dream or a dreamlike atmosphere instead of a holy person. In the first instance, he bit the toe of a Bavarian bowman living in Ragnit when he was going to sleep. The reason for the attack was that the soldier had made the sign of the cross inadequately when going to bed; having made the mistake of not covering himself properly, a toe sticking out, he left a target for the devil. We are told that had he been entirely uncovered the devil would have eaten him altogether. Thereafter the Bavarian made big signs of the cross correctly every night.[91]

Another example is that of brother Heinrich of Kunzen, who as a young man had been a rapacious and sinful knight, guilty of killing, robbing, thieving, swindling, committing arson and much else. One day, at dusk, a warrior riding on a black horse came to him, promising to take him to the richest plunder ever. Heinrich followed. As they went through difficult terrain, his horse became more and more unwilling to proceed and finally stopped completely. Heinrich tried to kick the horse onwards and finally lost his temper shouting aloud "in God's name go forward!" The spell broke with these words: the rider on the black horse was the devil, who had tricked Heinrich into approaching the verge of an abyss, into which he would have plunged, had his horse and God not saved him. Heinrich praised God and went home frightened but unharmed. Sometime thereafter he had another vision at dusk. God appeared to him as a stern judge, around whom many people were crying for justice for the evil deeds Heinrich had done to them. The judge asked Heinrich to step forward and answer the accusations. Heinrich could not do anything except stand silent, because he was guilty of all the crimes of which he was accused. Only when God sentenced him to death, did Heinrich finally manage to speak. When he promised to change his ways and join the Teutonic Order, the judge and the crowd disappeared.

---

90 Jeroschin, *Di Kronike*, 415–16 (ll. 9799–9832).
91 Ibid., 582 (ll. 24110–55).

Heinrich happened to have a young and beautiful wife, who did not give him her consent to take the habit. When the devil, too, visited Heinrich once again, promising worldly riches, he began to waver in his decision. At that point a series of further miracles took place. Every night, when Heinrich and his wife tried to go to bed, they heard loud knocking and hammering on the walls and a voice calling: "Heinrich, stop sleeping, get up and go to prayer because your brothers are up!" The wife was so frightened that she not only changed her mind about Heinrich joining the Order but took the veil herself.[92]

Visions emerge in many genres of medieval sources and are also common in the sources of the crusades irrespective of the author's background or the place of origin. They constitute an interesting group of intercessory episodes by combining elements from both the major categories of clerically instigated and privately initiated invocations. During the experience, the divine protector addresses the unconscious recipient directly, offering assistance and information crucial to overcome grave difficulties. An active plea is not necessary, although the vision may also be preceded by conscious prayer, fasting, and confession.

In the chronicles written by clerics, the private prayers of laymen were far more sparse than visions sent to them. Although the crusaders' enemies showed no tendency to pray, even they could receive supernatural sights sent by God.[93] It is possible that clerical authors preferred to replace or interpret private prayers as visions in the case of laymen because visions did not challenge clerical authority and experience as intercessors. By contrast, direct initiatives to solve problems without spiritual intermediaries, even if such initiatives usually occurred only in contexts in which clerical assistance could not be relied on, might be taken to suggest that secular people did not need clerical assistance. A layman experiencing divine power through a vision remained a passive recipient of the mysteries of faith without any hint that he was usurping a clerical prerogative.

Under the pretext of a vision, people without formal status could, in exceptional cases, even legitimately intervene in the powers of the pontificate. According to Albert of Aachen, William of Tyre and the *Chanson d'Antioche*, the First Crusade was initiated by Peter the Hermit, a charismatic preacher from Amiens. Peter had traveled to Jerusalem as a pilgrim already several years before the crusade. When he prayed exhausted in the Church of the Holy

---

92 Dusburg, *Chron. Pr.*, 3.284, pp. 168–69; Jeroschin, *Di Kronike*, 562–64 (ll. 22384–22627); English translation after *The Chronicle of Prussia by Nicolaus von Jeroschin*, 246–47.

93 Jeroschin, *Di Kronike*, 351, 461 (ll. 4265–4312, 13734–48); *Les Chanson d'Antioche*, 290–91, 327–28 (ll. 5737–59, 6609–32).

Sepulcher, he fell asleep and had a vision of Christ, who advised him to ask for a letter of holy mission from the patriarch of Jerusalem with the seal of the holy cross, take the letter home and stir the hearts of the believers to march east to cleanse the holy sites in Jerusalem: the gates of Paradise would open to those who would be chosen to participate in the expedition. After receiving the letter from the patriarch, Peter made haste to travel to Rome, where he met Pope Urban II who listened to him carefully and set out across the Alps to preach the crusade, mobilizing the bishops of the Frankish kingdom as well as many princes, dukes and counts.[94] Although the Benedictine historians omit Peter's role in instigating the expedition, emphasizing the role of the pope as the initiator of the crusade, the story turned out to be lasting and popular, emerging also in the chronicles of Peter of Dusburg, Nicolaus of Jeroschin and Helmold of Bosau.[95]

4 Conclusions

The samples in this paper fall into two groups. The larger of these consisted of prayers, recitals, and hymns displayed in public under the supervision of ordained clerics. This group also included some cases, in which laymen adopted a more active role while still acting in collaboration with the clergy. Ritual action was, for instance, initiated by a lay person but could not achieve its aim without clerical expertise, as in case of Bolesław's parents praying for a child or the penitent Master Conrad, who made efforts to atone for his sins but had great difficulties for completing the task. Even if these people acted in good faith, they seemed to lack the necessary knowledge to perform the rites properly. In the case of brother Heinrich Stange, the miracle had taken place genuinely but was published by a priest brother. Such examples apparently strengthened the impression of the priority of clerical authority in the preparation and exercise of ritual practices and were strongly represented in the sources written by clerics.[96]

With a few exceptions, the invocations thus entailed at least some co-operation between knights and clerics, the two leading groups in medieval

---

[94]   Albert of Aachen, *Historia Iherosolimitana*, 1.2–6, pp. 2–8, William of Tyre, *Chronicon*, 8.23, p. 416; *Chanson d'Antioche*, 30–36 (ll. 266–377).
[95]   Dusburg, *Chron. Pr.*, 4.78, pp. 206–7; Jeroschin, *Di Kronike*, 52–54 (ll. 21517–21666); Helmold von Bosau, *Chronica Slavorum*, 1.31, pp. 33–34. Helmold omits any reference to the pope. According to him, Peter was a monk of Spanish background.
[96]   Compare with the information about pre-battle rituals during duke Bolesław's campaign against the Bohemians in 1110, Kotecki, "Bishops," 453.

communities. The finding was in line with the overall strengthening of ties between clergy and lay aristocracy from the late eleventh century onward. Clerical involvement in the ritual activities of the warrior aristocracy increased during the twelfth century, including not only the various practices related to crusading and pilgrimage but also for instance the ceremony of knighting and the growing trend to confess and receive Holy Communion before engaging in military conflict.[97]

The alliance is apparent in the sources for the crusades, which propagate the exploits of the knights through clerical quills. The texts were invariably intended for the use of the clergy and the warrior aristocracy, and the contents thus reflect themes of interest to both target groups: Christian morality and the glory of God intertwined with lengthier descriptions of warfare. The themes were by no means contradictory, the knights being genuinely religious and most of the clerics stemming from the same aristocratic background.

The other group, which consisted of far fewer cases, concerns spontaneous prayers said by knights in mortal peril. The longest and most detailed examples are found in the *chansons* of the crusades, *Chétifs* and *Chanson d'Antioche*. There is no extant epic poetry representing the central and eastern European tradition of the crusades, and hence no closely corresponding sources written or commissioned by lay warriors to compare. Among the sources produced for the Teutonic Order, especially Nicolaus of Jeroschin's *Kronike von Pruzinlant* includes prayers and visions that have some interesting similarities with the western *chansons*.[98] Also in Nicolaus's text, knights are compelled to invoke supernatural help when finding themselves alone in mortal peril. In all these cases, the lay crusaders' invocations were motivated either by acute danger or unconsciously. The current situation, rather than active planning, regulated the action taken. Clerical instigation was simply unavailable in the given contexts. In these cases, lay invocations were mostly successful. Direct appeals to God and the saints resulted in miraculous survival, or the advice received in a dream opened a new path to salvation.

Unlike the compilers of the chansons, the clerical authors of the chronicles preferred visions to prayers said in private while describing direct communications between laymen and their heavenly patrons. This might be explained by the fact that the recipients of visions had a passive role without challenging clerical intermediation and guidance.

---

97 Kaeuper, *Holy Warriors*, 53–55.
98 To some extent, this conclusion can be applied to Peter von Dusburg's *Chronicon terrae Prussiae*, which Nicolaus extended. However, the additions by Nicolaus were especially important for the content of this article.

In the solitary prayers of the knights, the selection of saints and other biblical characters was greater and differed somewhat from that of the clerical chronicles. They also included quasi-magical improvisation of Christian practices, such as fabricating the cross out of grass or drawing a protective sign of the cross on the ground, clearly deriving from popular beliefs and practice rather than the official teachings of the church. On the other hand, the structure of the knightly implorations for supernatural aid showed a conscientious effort to follow the Scriptures. The verbal contents of the appeals recalled parts of the *credo* and well-known stories of the Bible.

The core ritual for religious invocation consisted of a prayer and the sign of the cross in all kinds of sources. In the case of the vernacular *chansons*, the sign of the cross confirmed the blessing. Without the physical seal, the prayer was not complete. The making of the cross was therefore described carefully, and the knights invested remarkable effort in the making of the gesture even in a moment of emergency.

The materials studied here were almost exclusively limited to males, references to women's prayers remaining extremely rare in the chronicles and *chansons*. Only one prayer by a nun under attack and one vision by an old woman can be found in the sources selected for this paper. The former case ended in violent death, albeit followed by eternal life, the latter case in captivity. No generalizations can be made from such isolated cases. It is possible that Peter of Dusburg and Nicolaus of Jeroschin, who intended their texts for audiences largely consisting of males, did not consider expressions of female piety an interesting subject in this context.

Acknowledgments

I would like to thank Prof. Martin Aurell and the CESCM for the opportunity to finish this chapter as an invited researcher at the Université de Poitiers. Dr. Philip Line has corrected the English language of this chapter and given many helpful comments on the content.

Bibliography

Primary Sources

Die aeltere Hochmeisterchronik. Edited by Max Töppen. SrP 3. 519–709. Frankfurt am Mein: Hirzel, 1866.

Albert of Aachen. *Historia Iherosolimitana*. Edited and translated by Susan Edgington. Oxford: Clarendon Press, 2008.

Baudri of Dol. *The "Historia Ierosolimitana" of Baldric of Bourgeuil.* Edited by Steve Biddlecombe. Woodbridge: Boydell Press, 2014.

Chronica Galiciano-Voliniana (Chronica Romanoviciana). Edited by Dariusz Dąbrowski and Adrian Jusupović. MPH NS 16. Cracow: Polska Akademia Umiejętności, 2017.

La Chanson d'Antioche. Vol. 1. Edited by Suzanne Duparc-Quioc. Paris: L'Académie des inscriptions et belles-lettres, 1976–1978.

La Chanson de Jérusalem. Edited by Nigel Thorp. OFCC 6. Tuscaloosa AL: University of Alabama Press, 1992.

The "Chanson d'Antioche": An Old French Account of the First Crusade. Translated by Susan B. Edgington and Carol Sweetenham. CTT 22. Aldershot and Burlington VT: Ashgate, 2011.

The "Chanson des Chétifs" and "Chanson de Jérusalem": Completing the Central Trilogy of the Old French Crusade Cycle. Translated by Carol Sweetenham. CTT 29. Aldershot and Burlington VT: Ashgate, 2016.

Les Chétifs. Edited by Geoffrey M. Myers. OFCC 5. Tuscaloosa AL: The University of Alabama Press, 1981.

Fulcher of Chartres. *Historia Hierosolymitana (1095–1127).* Edited by Heinrich Hagenmeyer. Heidelberg: Carl Winters Universitätsbuchhandlung, 1913.

Gesta Francorum et aliorum Hierosolimitanorum. Edited and translated by Rosalind Hill. London: Nelson & Sons, 1962.

The Hypatian Codex II: The Galician-Volynian Chronicle. Translated by George A. Perfecky. Harvard series in Ukrainian studies 16.2. Munich: Fink, 1973.

Gallus Anonymus. *Gesta principum Polonorum.* Translated and annotated by Paul W. Knoll and Frank Schaer, with the preface by Thomas N. Bisson. CEMT 3. Budapest and New York: Central European University Press, 2003.

Gregorii VIII pontifici Romani Epistolæ et privilegia. Edited by Jacques-Paul Migne, 1539–42. PL 202. Paris: Apud J.-P. Migne Editorem, 1855.

Guibert of Nogent. *Dei gesta per Francos.* Edited by Robert B.C. Huygens. CCCM 127/A. Turnhout: Brepols, 1996.

Helmold von Bosau. *Chronica Slavorum.* Edited by Johann Martin Lappenberg, 1–99. MGH SS 21. Hannover: Hahn, 1869.

Helmold von Bosau. *The Chronicle of the Slavs.* Translated by Francis Joseph Tschan. Records of civilization 21. New York: Columbia University Press, 1935.

Innocentii III Regesta sive Epistolæ. Edited by Jacques-Paul Migne. PL 216. Paris: Apud J.-P. Migne Editorem, 1855.

John of Salisbury. *Policraticus.* Edited by Katherine S.B. Keats-Rohan. CCCM 118. Turnhout: Brepols, 1993.

Die Kreuzzugsbriefe aus den Jahren 1088–1100. Edited by Heinrich Hagenmeyer. Innsbruck: Verlag des Wagnerschen Universitäts-Buchhandlung, 1901.

Livländische Reimchronik. Edited by Leo Meyer. Paderborn: Schöningh, 1876.

The Livonian Rhymed Chronicle. Translated by Jerry C. Smith and William L. Urban. Bloomington IN: Indiana University Press, 1977.

Miracula beati Egidii auctore Petro Guillelmo. Edited by Georg Heinrich Pertz. MGH SS 12. 316–23. Hannover: Hahn, 1856.

Nicolaus von Jeroschin. *The Chronicle of Prussia by Nicolaus von Jeroschin: A History of the Teutonic Knights in Prussia, 1190–1331.* Translated by Mary Fischer. CTT 20. Aldershot and Burlington VT: Ashgate, 2010.

Nicolaus von Jeroschin. *Di Kronike von Pruzinlant des Nicolaus v. Jeroschin.* Edited by Ernst Strehlke. SrP 1. 303–624. Leipzig: Hirzel, 1861.

Nithard. *Vita Karoli.* Edited by Philippe Lauer and Sophie Glansdorf. In *Histoire des fils de Louis le Pieux.* Classiques de l'histoire au Moyen Âge 51. 2–144. Paris: Les Belles Lettres, 2012.

Peter von Dusburg. *Chronicon terrae Prussiae.* Edited by Max Töppen. SrP 1. 24–219. Leipzig: Hirzel, 1861.

Ralph of Caen. *Gesta Tancredi.* Edited by Ludovico Antonio Muratori. RHC HO 3. 603–716. Paris: Imprimerie Impériale, 1866.

Ramon Llull. *Llibre de l'Orde de Cavalleria.* Edited by Antonio Cortijo Ocaña. Amsterdam and Philadelphia PA: John Benjamins Publishing Company, 2015.

Raymond of Aguilers. *Historia Francorum qui ceperunt Iherusalem.* Edited by Jacques Bongars. RHC HO 3. 231–309. Paris: Imprimerie Impériale, 1866.

Robert of Rheims, *Historia Iherosolimitana.* Edited by Philippe le Bas. RHC HO 3. 721–882. Paris: L'Académie des Inscriptions et Belles-Lettres. Imprimerie Nationale, 1866.

Robert of Rheims's History of the First Crusade. Translated by Carol Sweetenham. CTT 11. Aldershot and Burlington VT: Ashgate, 2005.

Sancti Gregorii Magni Romani pontificis XL homiliarum in Evangelia libri duo. Edited by Jacques-Paul Migne. PL 76. 1075–1312. Paris: Apud J.-P. Migne Editorem, 1857.

Die Statuten des Deutschen Ordens nach den ältesten Handschriften. Edited by Max Perlbach. Halle: Niemeyer, 1890.

William of Tyre. *Chronicon.* Edited by Robert B.C. Huygens. CCCM 63–63A. Turnhout: Brepols, 1986.

Wigand von Marburg. *Nowa kronika Pruska.* Edited and translated by Sławomir Zonenberg and Krzysztof Kwiatkowski. Toruń: Towarzystwo Naukowe w Toruniu, 2017.

Secondary Sources

Allington, Richard. "Crusading Piety and the Development of Crusading Devotions." In *The Fourth Lateran Council and the Crusade Movement.* Edited by Jessalynn Bird and Damian Smith, 13–40. Outremer 7. Turnhout: Brepols, 2018.

Aurell, Martin. "From Episcopal Dubbing to Sacrament of Confirmation (Twelfth–Fourteenth Centuries)." *Viator*. Forthc.

Aurell, Martin. *Le chevalier lettré. Savoir et conduite de l'aristocratie aux XIIe et XIIIe siècles*. Paris: Fayard, 2007.

Bachrach, David S. "Lay Confession to Priests in Light of Wartime Practice (1097–1180)." *RHE* 102.1 (2007): 76–99.

Bachrach, David S. *Religion and the Conduct of War c.300–c.1215*. Woodbridge: Boydell Press, 2003.

Banaszkiewciz, Jacek. "Gallus as a Credible Historian, or Why the Biography of Bolesław the Brave is as Authentic and Far from Grotesque as Bolesław the Wrymouth's." In *Gallus Anonymous and his Chronicle in the Context of Twelfth-Century Historiography from the Perspective of the Latest Research*. Edited by Krzysztof Stopka, 19–33. Cracow: Polish Academy of Arts and Sciences, 2010.

Banaszkiewicz, Jacek. "Książę polski Bolesław i szkocki rycerz Desiré: Dwie opowieści o potomkach zrodzonych za wstawiennictwem św. Idziego (Gall, 'Epylogus' i ks. I, rozdz. 30–31 oraz 'Le lai de Desiré' koniec XII w.)." In Jacek Banaszkiewicz. *W stronę rytuałów i Galla Anonima*. 344–76. Cracow: Avalon, 2018.

Błażewicz, Agnieszka. "Skarb relikwiarzowy z kościoła zamkowego w czasach krzyżackich. Dzieje relikwii św. Barbary." In *Spotkania malborskie im. Macieja Kilarskiego*. 3 vols. Edited by Artur Dobry, 2:93–111. Malbork: Muzeum Zamkowe w Malborku, 2010.

Brundage, James. "A Transformed Angel (X 3.31.18): The Problem of the Crusading Monk." In *Studies in Medieval Cistercian History Presented to Jeremiah F. O'Sullivan*. Edited by John R. Sommerfeldt, 55–62. Cistercian studies 13. Spencer MA: Cistercian Publications, 1971.

Claussen, Samuel A. "Chivalric and Religious Valorization of Warfare in High Medieval France." In *Prowess, Piety, and Public Order in Medieval Society: Studies in Honor of Richard W. Kaeuper*. Edited by Craig M. Nakashian and Daniel P. Franke, 199–217. Later medieval Europe 14. Leiden and Boston MA: Brill, 2017.

Dalewski, Zbigniew. "The Knighting of Polish Dukes in the Early Middle Ages: Ideological and Political Significance." *Acta Polonia Historica* 80 (1999): 15–43.

Dalewski, Zbigniew. "A New Chosen People? Gallus Anonymus's Narrative about Poland and Its Rulers." In *Historical Narratives and Christian Identity on a European Periphery: Early History Writing in Northern, East-Central and Eastern Europe (c.1070–1200)*. Edited by Ildar H. Garipzanov, 14–66. MTCN 26. Turnhout: Brepols, 2011.

Duby, Georges. *The Three Orders: Feudal Society Imagined*. Chicago: The University of Chicago Press, 1980.

Fischer, Mary. "Biblical Heroes and the Uses of Literature: The Teutonic Order in the Late Thirteenth and Early Fourteenth Centuries." In *Crusade and Conversion on the Baltic Frontier, 1150–1500*. Edited by Alan V. Murray, 261–76. Aldershot and Burlington VT: Ashgate, 2001.

Fulton Brown, Rachel. *Mary and the Art of Prayer: The Hours of the Virgin in Medieval Christian Life and Thought*. New York: Columbia University Press, 2018.

Gaposchkin, M. Cecilia. *Invisible Weapons: Liturgy and the Making of Crusade Ideology*. Ithaca NY: Cornell University Press, 2017.

Heise, Johannes, ed. *Die Bau- und Kunstdenkmäler der Provinz Westpreussen*. Vol. 2. *Kulmerland und Löbau*. Danzig: 1887–1895.

Hettler, Hans. *Preussen als Kreuzzugsregion. Untersuchungen zu Peter von Dusburg's "Chronica terre Prussie" in Zeit und Umfeld*. Frankfurt: Peter Lang, 2014.

Issa, Mireille. *La version latine et l'adaptation française de "l'Historia rerum in partibus transmarinis gestarum" de Guillaume de Tyr*. The medieval translator 13. Turnhout: Brepols, 2010.

Jaspert, Nicholas. "Culte des Saints." In *Prier et combattre. Dictionnaire européen des ordres militaires au Moyen Âge*. Edited by Nicole Bériou et al., 835. Paris: Fayard, 2009.

Jensen, Carsten Selch. "Bishops and Abbots at War: Some Aspects of Clerical Involvement in Warfare in Twelfth- and Early Thirteenth-Century Livonia and Estonia." In *Between Sword and Prayer: Warfare and Medieval Clergy in Cultural Perspective*. Edited by Radosław Kotecki, Jacek Maciejewski, and John S. Ott, 404–34. EMC 3. Leiden and Boston MA: Brill, 2018.

Kaeuper, Richard W. *Medieval Chivalry*. Cambridge: Cambridge University Press, 2016.

Kaeuper, Richard W. *Holy Warriors: The Religious Ideology of Chivalry*. Philadelphia: University of Pennsylvania Press, 2009.

Kaeuper, Richard W. "Piety and Independence in Chivalric Religion." In *Kings, Knights and Bankers: The Collected Articles of Richard W. Kaeuper*. Edited by Christopher Guyol, 327–41. Later medieval Europe 13. Leiden and Boston MA: Brill, 2016.

Kangas, Sini. "The Image of Warrior Bishops in the Northern Tradition of the Crusades." In *Christianity and War in Medieval East Central Europe and Scandinavia*. Edited by Radosław Kotecki, Carsten Selch Jensen, and Stephen Bennett, 57–73. Leeds: ARC Humanities Press, 2021.

Kangas, Sini. "Scripture, Hierarchy, and Social Control: The Uses of the Bible in the Twelfth- and Thirteenth-Century Chronicles and Chansons of the Crusades." In *Transcultural Approaches to the Bible: Exegesis and Historical Writing in the Medieval Worlds*. Edited by Matthias M. Tischler and Patrick S. Marschner, 109–44. TMS 1. Turnhout: Brepols, 2021.

Koch, Marie Pierre. *An Analysis of the Long Prayers in Old French Literature with Special Reference to the "Biblical-Creed-Narrative" Prayers*. Studies in Romance languages and literatures 19. New York: AMS Press, 1969.

Kotecki, Radosław. "Bishops and the Legitimisation of War in Piast Poland until the Early Thirteenth Century." *PH* 111.3 (2020): 437–70.

Kotecki, Radosław. "The Desecration of Holy Places According to Witnesses' Testimonies in the Polish-Teutonic Order Trials of the 14th Century." In *Arguments and Counter-Arguments: The Political Thought of the 14th- and 15th Centuries during the*

Polish-Teutonic Order Trials and Disputes. Edited by Wiesław Sieradzan, 69–110. Toruń: Wydawnictwo Naukowe Uniwersytetu Mikołaja Kopernika, 2012.

Kotecki, Radosław. "Lions and Lambs, Wolves and Pastors of the Flock: Portraying Military Activity of Bishops in Twelfth-Century Poland." In *Between Sword and Prayer: Warfare and Medieval Clergy in Cultural Perspective*. Edited by Radosław Kotecki, Jacek Maciejewski, and John S. Ott, 303–40. EMC 3. Leiden and Boston MA: Brill, 2018.

Kotecki, Radosław. "Pious Rulers, Princely Clerics, and Angels of Light: Imperial Holy War Imagery in Twelfth-Century Poland and Rus'." In *Christianity and War in Medieval East Central Europe and Scandinavia*. Edited by Radosław Kotecki, Carsten Selch Jensen, and Stephen Bennett, 159–88. Leeds: ARC Humanities Press, 2021.

Kotecki, Radosław, and Jacek Maciejewski. "Writing Episcopal Courage in Twelfth-century Poland: Gallus Anonymous and Master Vincentius." In *Episcopal Power and Personality in Medieval Europe, 900–1480*. Edited by Peter Coss et al., 35–61. MCS 42. Turnhout: Brepols, 2020.

Kucharski, Wojciech. *"Beatus Ceslaus natione Polonus." Dzieje kultu błogosławionego Czesława*. Studia i źródła Dominikańskiego Instytutu Historycznego w Krakowie 10. Cracow: Esprit, 2012.

Kwiatkowski, Stefan. "Verlorene Schlachten und Gefallene in der geistigen Tradition des Deutschen Ordens." *OM* 16 (2011): 141–57.

Lapina, Elizabeth. "Crusades, Memory, and Visual Culture: Representations of the Miracle of Intervention of Saints in Battle." In *Remembering the Crusades and Crusading*. Edited by Megan Cassidy-Welch, 49–72. Abingdon and New York: Routledge, 2016.

Leighton, Gregory. "Did the Teutonic Order Create a Sacred Landscape in Thirteenth-Century Prussia?" *JMH* 44.4 (2018): 457–83.

Leighton, Gregory. "The Relics of St Barbara at Althaus Kulm: History, Patronages, and Insight into the Teutonic Order and the Christian Population in Prussia (Thirteenth–Fifteenth Centuries)." *ZH* 85.1 (2020): 5–50.

Lieberman, Max. "Knighting in the Twelfth and Thirteenth Centuries." *Anglo-Norman Studies* 43 (2020): 151–76.

Linder, Amnon. *Raising Arms: Liturgy in the Struggle to Liberate Jerusalem in the Late Middle Ages*. Cultural Encounter in Late Antiquity and the Middle Ages 2. Turnhout: Brepols, 2003.

McCarthy, Thomas J.H. "Scriptural Allusion in the Crusading Accounts of Frutolf of Michelsberg and His Continuators." In *The Uses of the Bible in Crusader Sources*. Edited by Elizabeth Lapina and Nicholas Morton, 152–75. Commentaria 7. Leiden and Boston MA: Brill, 2017.

Maier, Christoph T. "Crisis, Liturgy and the Crusade in the Twelfth and Thirteenth Centuries." *JEH* 48.4 (1997): 628–57.

Maier, Christoph T. *Crusade Propaganda and Ideology: Model Sermons for the Preaching of the Cross*. Cambridge: Cambridge University Press, 2000.

Markowski, Michael. "'Crucesignatus': Its Origins and Early Usage." *JMH* 10.3 (1984): 157–64.

Mentzel-Reuters, Arno. *"Arma Spiritualia." Bibliotheken, Bücher und Bildung im Deutschen Orden* (Petersberg: Harrassowitz, 2003).

Michałowski, Roman. "'Restauratio Poloniae' dans l'idéologie dynastique de Gallus Anonymus." *APH* 52 (1985): 5–43.

Mühle, Eduard. "Neue Vorschläge zur Herkunft des Gallus Anonymus und zur Deutung seiner 'Chronik.'" *ZfO* 60.2 (2011): 267–85.

Nelson, Janet L. "The Church's Military Service in the Ninth Century: A Contemporary Comparative View?" *SCH* 20 (1983): 15–30.

Nelson, Janet L. *The Frankish World 750–900*. London and Rio Grande OH: Hambledon Press, 1996.

Paravicini, Werner. *Die Preußenreisen des europäischen Adels*. Vol. 1. Beiheifte der Francia 17.1. Sigmaringen: Thorbecke, 1989.

Roscher, Helmut. *Papst Innocenz III. und die Kreuzzüge*. Forschungen zur Kirchen- und Dogmengeschichte 21. Göttingen: Vandenhoeck & Ruprectht, 1969.

Rousset, Paul. *Histoire d'une idéologie. La croisade*. Lausanne: L'Age d'Homme, 1983.

Rozynkowski, Waldemar. "Św. Barbara—święta 'od wody'. O patrociniach św. Barbary w średniowiecznej Polsce." In *Město a voda. Praha, město u vody*. Edited by Olga Fejtová, Václav Ledvinka, and Jiří Pešek, 231–42. Prague: Scriptorium, 2005.

Starnawska, Maria "The Role of the Legend of Saint Barbara's Head in the Conflict of the Teutonic Order and Swietopolk, the Duke of Pomerania." In *The Military Orders*. Vol. 6.2: *Culture and Conflict in Western and Northern Europe*. Edited by Jochen Schenk and Mike Carr, 203–13. Abingdon and New York: Routledge, 2017.

Sterns, Indrikis. "The Teutonic Knights in the Crusader States." In *The Impact of the Crusades on the Near East*. Edited by Norman P. Zacour and Harry W. Hazard. In *A History of the Crusades*. Vol. 5. Edited by Kenneth M. Setton, 315–78. Madison WI: University of Wisconsin Press, 1985.

Storelli, Xavier. "Les chevaliers face à la mort soudaine et brutale: L'indispensable secours de l'Église?" In *Chevalerie et christianisme aux XIIe et XIIIe siècles*. Edited by Martin Aurell and Catalina Girbea, 149–177. Rennes: Presses universitaires de Rennes, 2011.

Tamminen, Miikka. *Crusade Preaching and the Ideal Crusader*. Sermo 14. Turnhout: Brepols, 2018.

Twyman, Susan. "The 'Romana Fraternitas' and Urban Processions at Rome in the Twelfth and Thirteenth Centuries." In *Pope, Church, and City: Essays in Honour of Brenda Bolton*. Edited by Frances Andrews, Christoph Egger, and Constance M. Rousseau, 205–21. MMED 56. Leiden and Boston MA: Brill, 2004.

Tyerman, Christopher. *The Invention of the Crusades*. Hampshire: Macmillan, 1998.

Vercamer, Grischa. "'Boleslavus non solum aurem correctoribus non adhibuit [...]'—War Gallus Anonymus dem polnischen Fürsten Bolesław III. Schiefmund wirklich vorbehaltlos positiv Eingestellt?" *Studia Maritima* 32 (2019): 45–88.

Weber, Benjamin. "Conceptualizing the Crusade in Outremer: Uses and Purposes of the Word 'Crusade' in The Old French Continuation of William of Tyre." *Crusades* 20 (2021): 151–64.

Wüst, Marcus. *Studien zum Selbstverständnis des Deutschen Ordens im Mittelalter*. Weimar: VDG, 2013.

Wüst, Marcus. "Zu Entstehung und Rezeption der 'Chronik des Preussenlandes' Peters von Dusburg." In *Neue Studien zur Literatur im Deutschen Ordens*. Edited by Bernhart Jähnig and Arnold Mentzel-Reuters, 197–210. Stuttgart: Hirzel, 2014.

CHAPTER 7

Rituals of War as Religious Markers during the Early Crusades in Livonia and Estonia in the Light of Henry's *Chronicon Livoniae*

Carsten Selch Jensen

God's War—that was the kind of war that the crusaders were fighting in Livonia and Estonia around 1200. At least according to one contemporary chronicler, Henry of Livonia. He was a priest who wrote very knowledgeably and with great enthusiasm about military affairs related to the submission and conversion of the local non-Christian, pagan people from the late twelfth century until the early thirteenth century—completing his chronicle in 1227 or shortly thereafter.[1] Quite often Henry seems to have accompanied the crusaders on campaign, performing his clerical duties among the fighting men who were actively engaged in this divinely sanctioned war. In that respect, Henry offers an eyewitness account of the military activities of the crusaders and the local Christian forces fighting their pagan foes in a war considered to be divinely approved and supported. It was no small thing to fight God's War and Henry ascribes certain rituals to the military activities of the crusaders. These rituals seemingly covered the full spectrum of military activities—from the initial taking of the cross and the plea for divine support through prayers and masses before the actual fighting commenced, through the battles themselves, and finally as part of the celebrations of victory or the mourning of a defeat.

---

1 Ane Bysted, Carsten Selch Jensen, Kurt Villads Jensen, and John H. Lind, *Jerusalem in the North: Denmark and the Baltic Crusades, 1100–1522*, Outremer 1 (Turnhout: Brepols, 2012), 75, 85, 140–42; Carsten Selch Jensen, *Med ord og ikke med slag. Teologi og historieskrivning i Henrik af Letlands krønike* (Copenhagen: Gads Forlag, 2019), 76–80, an English version of this work is being prepared for publication titled *Through Words, not Weapons: Theology and History Writing in the Chronicle of Henry of Livonia (ca.1227)* (Turnhout: Brepols, forthc. 2024). Edition of the chronicle used in this article is *Heinrici Chronicon Livoniae*, ed. Leonid Arbusow and Albert Bauer, MGH SS rer. Germ. 31 (Hannover: Hahn, 1955) (hereafter Henry, *Chron. Liv.*). Other standard bilingual, Latin and German, edition is Heinrich von Lettland, *Livländische Chronik*, ed. and trans. Albert Bauer, Ausgewählte Quellen zur deutschen Geschichte des Mittelalters. Freiherr vom Stein-Gedächtnisausgabe 24 (Darmstadt: Wissenschaftliche Buchgesellschaft, 1959). All quotations in English are from *The Chronicle of Henry of Livonia*, trans. James A. Brundage, 2nd ed. (New York: Columbia University Press, 2003).

Throughout the early years of the crusades in Livonia and Estonia, the military campaigns went hand in hand with intensive campaigns of preaching and baptizing: coercing the local people to adopt the Christian belief and a proper Christian way of life.[2] In the mind of Henry of Livonia there seems not to have been any conflict between what the crusaders did—namely fighting God's War—and what the missionaries did—preaching the word of God and baptizing the pagans. It was essentially two different but equally important ways of doing God's work. Other contemporary chroniclers referred to this duality of war and preaching simply as the "business of the faith and peace" (*negotium fidei et pacis*). Henry repeatedly stressed the fact that proper peace could only be obtained through the pagans acceptance of Christianity, since Christ was in essence the only true peace ("veram pacem, que Christus est").[3] On several occasions, Henry even refers to the Christian faith as a yoke that must be shouldered by the converts—not as a "harsh, unbearable burden, but rather the sweet and light yoke of the Lord."[4] In this way, the ritual of baptism became the primary sacramental ritual of the crusades and the entire mission in Livonia and Estonia and the ultimate sign that God's War had been won and the false deities defeated and destroyed.

The various rituals of war described in Henry's chronicle—the *Chronicon Livoniae*—were, however, not exclusively associated with the crusaders. On the contrary, there are some important rituals associated with the proper way of fighting which Henry ascribes to the enemies of the crusaders. These "pagan" rituals are most often used by Henry as part of a grander narrative first and foremost underlining an obvious duality between the forces of good and the forces of evil so essential to the narrative structure of the chronicle.[5] In the mind of Henry of Livonia he is not only describing some obscure historical events that took place in a remote border region between Christianity and paganism around 1200. Rather, he narrates how a divine history unfolds in these lands through the hands of God and his servants—the crusaders and the missionaries—encased in sacred rituals and combatting the pagans and their false but powerful and dangerous deities.

---

2 Jensen, *Med ord*, 80–84.
3 Beverly M. Kienzle, *Cistercians, Heresy and Crusade in Occitania, 1145–1229* (Woodbridge: York Medieval Press in association with The Boydell Press, 2001), 143; Henry, *Chron. Liv.*, 19.8, pp. 132–33.
4 Henry, *Chron. Liv.*, 29.3, p. 209: "gravaminis alicuius iugum importabile …, sed iugum Domini leve ac suave"; trans. Brundage, 231. Regarding *iugum Domini*, see as example ibid., 9.13, p. 32. Henry also refers to the yoke of the faith (*iugum fidei*) in 10.1, p. 33.
5 Jensen, *Med ord*, 114–18.

Thus, it is the aim of this article to show how rituals of war (and the narrative surrounding them) are used in Henry's chronicle to describe the conversion of the local pagans.

1   Preparing for War: The Taking of the Cross

In the manuscript used by Leonid Arbusow and Albert Bauer containing a major part of Henry of Livonia's chronicle, the narrative commences with a short hymn in which the chronicler implores God to give to the Christians the necessary power to defeat the carnal armies of the pagans and ensure that their false deities eventually will be destroyed. Furthermore, the sacramental ritual of baptism is presented as a holy treasure that must prevail so that all the pagans may accept Christianity.[6] It is not quite clear if this hymn was part of the original chronicle or constitutes a later addition. In the opening lines of the first proper chapter of the chronicle, however, the chronicler strikes a similar chord by placing the history of the Livonian crusades and the history of the Livonian church firmly within an overall biblical narrative. The crusaders were not simply (and for the most part) German knights who had chosen to go to Livonia to fight a worldly enemy for earthly possessions and/or power. Rather the crusaders walked in the footsteps of the major biblical characters continuously occupied with the holy task of fulfilling God's will. Like the Israelites in biblical times, the crusaders once again took upon themselves to fight God's enemies—this time, however, not in the Holy Land, but rather in Livonia and Estonia enshrined in specific rituals.[7]

This idea of the submission and conversion of the local pagans being essentially a continuation of a divine history is further emphasized in the chronicle when Henry states that Livonia was in fact the land of the Virgin Mary in contrast to the Holy Land, which belonged to her son, Jesus Christ.[8] In the chronicle

---

[6] Henry, *Chron. Liv.*, opening hymn found in the German editions, pp. 2–3. See also the discussion in Linda Kaljundi, "(Re)Performing the Past: Crusading, History Writing, and Rituals in the Chronicle of Henry of Livonia," in *The Performance of Christian and Pagan Storyworlds*, ed. Lars B. Mortensen and Tuomas M.S. Lehtonen, Medieval identities 3 (Turnhout: Brepols, 2013), 295–338 at 301–2.

[7] For a more in-depth discussion on the biblical models for the crusades, see as examples Nicholas Morton, "The Defence of the Holy Land and the Memory of the Maccabees," *JMH* 36 (2010): 275–93, and the collective volume by Elizabeth Lapina and Nicholas Morton, ed., *The Uses of the Bible in Crusader Sources*, Commentaria 7 (Leiden and Boston MA: Brill, 2017).

[8] Henry, *Chron. Liv.*, 19.7, pp. 131–32. Henry of Livonia has here a relative detailed section about Bishop Albert arguing for papal support during the Fourth Lateran Council in Rome 1215 enhancing the argument about Livonia being especially devoted to the Virgin Mary and under her guardianship.

there is a relatively detailed section describing how Bishop Albert argued for papal support of the Livonian church during his visit to Rome in 1215 during the Fourth Lateran Council. Bishop Albert claimed that Livonia was especially devoted to the Virgin Mary and hence was under her specific guardianship.[9] On a practical level, the crusaders and the entire army of Livonia would follow this idea whenever they went on a military expedition, often commencing on a feast day associated with the Virgin and taking with them banners dedicated to the Virgin bearing her image as a concrete sign of their special devotion to her and acknowledging her as the true guardian of Livonia. When conquering an enemy stronghold, the Christians would also ritually place the banner of the Virgin Mary on top of the battlements of the defeated enemy fortress as a manifest demonstration that the Virgin Mary and her Son, Jesus Christ, had once more defeated the pagans and their false deities (through the skilled arms of the Christian armies). Thus, the rituals associated with the banner of the Virgin Mary in the armies of the crusaders in Livonia and later also in Estonia in a very Strong way marked the crusaders and their fellow men-in-arms as God's champions in a truly holy war.[10]

As indicated in the opening paragraph of this chapter, Henry liked to refer to the crusaders as those who were fighting "God's Wars" (*prelia Domini*).[11] This particular type of warfare was not fought on behalf of any worldly powers, but solely on behalf of God and his church, primarily and specifically its Livonian branch. The competing powers of the Danish and Swedish magnates and ecclesiastical powers who were also actively involved in these crusades and missionary activities were viewed by Henry with the greatest mistrust. Essentially he regarded them more or less as false workers in the Lord's Vineyard unjustly encroaching on the work done by the true workers, namely the missioners (and the armies) serving the Livonian church.[12] Consequently, it was the crusaders who fought on behalf of the Livonian church who most properly fought this divine war and most willingly sat "themselves up as a wall for the Lord's house," as it is said in the chronicle.[13] Repeatedly, Henry makes these parallels

---

9   Ibid.
10 See, e.g., ibid., 11.6, pp. 145–46. See also Werner Paravicini, *Die Preussenreisen des europäischen Adels*, 2 vols., BF 17.1–2 (Sigmaringen: Thorbecke, 1989–1995), 2:139–52; Jensen, *Med ord*, 305–6.
11 *Henry, Chron. Liv.*, 11.5, p. 144.
12 See, e.g., ibid., 25.1, pp. 177–78.
13 Ibid., 27.1, p. 194: "et ad ponendum se murum pro domo Domini." Apart from the biblical reference to the wall around the Lord's house, Henry once again refers to the *prelia Domini* in this particular chapter. See also Nicholas Morton, "Walls of Defence for the House of Israel: Ezekiel 13:5 and the Crusading Movement," in *The Uses of the Bible*, 403–20.

between well-known biblical stories and references and current events that were unfolding in Livonia and Estonia, thereby repeatedly underlining the fact that he believed these events to be part of an ongoing sacred history.[14]

Like the crusades in general, the crusading activities in the eastern parts of the Baltic took place within a practical and strong theological-spiritual framing based on regional calls to arms, preaching campaigns among relevant partakers, promises of indulgence, crusader vows and of course the very important and concrete ritual of the taking of the cross.[15] Essentially these rituals associated with the crusades had evolved from ancient rituals related to the tradition of pilgrimaging that had a very long and strong history within Western Christendom. So close were the two types of penitential acts—pilgrimaging and crusading—that some of the very first tentative crusades were simply considered to be armed pilgrimages. Similarly, the crusaders themselves were often referred to as "pilgrims" as is the case in the chronicle of Henry of Livonia.[16] The third bishop in Livonia—the previously-mentioned vigorous Bishop Albert, who is a central character in Henry's chronicle, is famously known for his many journeys to Gotland, Denmark, Germany, and even to Rome—tirelessly promoting the crusades in Livonia and Estonia and gathering more volunteers for the continuous wars. His favorite tool was unsurprisingly his sermons and his persuasive preaching through which he attracted new crusaders for the seasonal campaigns in Livonia and Estonia. As part of these tours of preaching and recruiting, new volunteers would be marked (or marked themselves) with the cross as Bishop Albert moved from region to region and from town to town ritually setting them out as proper crusaders ready to fight the Lord's War.

---

14   Jensen, *Med ord*, 28–40, 115–18.
15   Kaljundi, "(Re)Performing the Past," 306–8. See also the discussions in Iben Fonnesberg-Schmidt, "Pope Honorius III and Mission and Crusades in the Baltic Region," in *The Clash of Cultures on the Medieval Baltic Frontier*, ed. Alan V. Murray (Farnham and Burlington VT: Ashgate, 2009), 103–22; idem, *The Popes and the Baltic Crusades 1147–1254*, TNW 26 (Leiden and Boston MA: Brill, 2007). With regards to the taking of the cross, see also James A. Brundage, "'Cruce signari': The Rite for Taking the Cross in England," *Traditio* 22 (1966): 289–310; Kenneth Pennington, "The Rite for Taking the Cross in the Twelfth Century," *Traditio* 30 (1974): 429–35; Michael Markowski, "'Crucesignatus': Its Origins and Early Usage," *JMH* 10.3 (1984): 157–65; and M. Cecilia Gaposchkin, *Invisible Weapons: Liturgy and the Making of Crusade Ideology* (Ithaca NY: Cornell University Press, 2017), 72–92.
16   For a few examples, see Henry, *Chron. Liv.*, 3.2, p. 12; 4.1, p. 13; 5.1, p. 15; 7.1, p. 19. See also Lean Ni Chleirigh, "'Nova Peregrinatio': The First Crusade as a Pilgrimage in Contemporary Latin Narratives," in *Writing the Early Crusades: Text, Transmission and Memory*, ed. Marcus Bull and Damien Kempf (Woodbridge: Boydell Press, 2014), 63–74.

It has been intensely discussed by historians if the crusades in the Baltic were in fact considered to be on an equal footing with the crusades who went to some of the major crusading theaters like the Iberian Peninsula or The Holy Land. It is a rather complicated discussion with no straightforward answers, as it seems to depend very much on when and how one evaluates the sources. Local or regional plans and ideas of a "proper" model for crusading might at times clash with official papal plans for a grander overarching crusader strategy covering not just remote regions like the Baltic but also the aforementioned campaigns in Spain, Palestine, Syria, or Egypt. Local needs and plans were often "made to fit" more official plans and ideas of crusading. In this respect, Henry puts a lot of effort into describing the crusading activities (and the entire work done by the Livonian church) in Livonia and Estonia as being as important as that which took place in any of the other crusading theaters—and certainly as an essential part of the fulfillment of a divine holy history.[17]

The idea of crusading became almost from the beginning an integrated part of the processes of conquest, submission, and conversion in Livonia and Estonia. From early in the chronicle, Henry refers to Christian armies that could be summoned to support the young Livonian church. Shortly before his death, the first Livonian bishop, Bishop Meinhard experienced a serious revolt among the local Livs of which some had embraced Christendom and accepted baptism. In Henry's chronicle, the armies are not specifically referred to as crusader armies per se, but merely as fighting men brought together by German, Danish, and Norwegian merchants trading in the region.[18] Not long after this incident—seemingly the merchant's army never came into action—Henry narrates the coming together of the first formalized crusades in Livonia (and the preparation thereof). Right after the appointment of a new bishop in Livonia—Bishop Berthold—the first proper crusaders seem to have arrived in Livonia. Following a short visit to his new bishopric in 1197 that nearly got him killed by the (still) rebellious Livs, Bishop Berthold hastily withdrew to Germany to gather armed support for his future work in Livonia. According to Henry, Pope Celestine III "granted remission of sins to all those who should take the cross and arm themselves against the perfidious Livonians."[19] This papal promise of indulgence formally turned the military campaigns in

---

17 Fonnesberg-Schmidt, *The Popes*, 56–65; Jensen, *Med ord*, 136. Recently, on the implementation the concept of the crusade on the frontiers of Western Christendom, see Paul Srodecki and Norbert Kersken, ed., *The Expansion of the Faith: Crusading on the Frontiers of Latin Christendom in the High Middle Ages*, Outremer 14 (Turnhout: Brepols, 2021).

18 Henry, *Chron. Liv.*, 1.11, pp. 5–6.

19 Ibid., 2.3, p. 9: "Igitur domnus papa cunctis signum crucis accipientibus et contra perfidos Lyvones se armantibus remissionem indulget peccatorum"; trans. Brundage, 32.

Livonia into proper crusades granting special privileges to those who promised to fight God's War and ritually took the cross, thus turning a person into a "cross-marked man" (*crusesignatus*).[20] As indicated above Henry uses in his chronicle a slightly different terminology, typically referring to the crusaders as "pilgrims" or "pilgrims in Livonia" (*perigrini/peregrini in Lyvoniam*).[21] Yet the taking of the cross still was the essential ritual for these new crusaders placing them firmly within the grander narrative of the medieval crusading movement. In the chronicle we are told that Berthold did manage to gather men (crusaders) for his second trip to Livonia which in turn led to his premature death—quite ironically—in the very first recorded battle between crusaders and a local Livonian host in the summer of 1198.[22] Berthold was soon followed by a new bishop—Bishop Albert—who thus became the third bishop of the Livonian church. He too immediately began to gather military support for the ensuing battles against the rebellious Livs. Having learned from his predecessors' mistakes, Bishop Albert did not go to Livonia before he had collected what seems to have been a sizable force of crusaders. Accordingly, he first went to Visby on Gotland, signing five hundred men with the cross before traveling to Denmark and asking for the support of the Danish king and archbishop. Not ready to go to Livonia quite yet, the bishop then went to Germany, signing many more with the cross in Magdeburg while assuring the newly crowned King Philip that the crusaders who went to Livonia would enjoy the same papal protection as those who went to the Holy Land. In his chronicle, Henry even let Bishop Albert declare that the Livonian pilgrims would enjoy the same "plenary remission of sins" (*plenariam peccaminum*) as was offered to those who went to Jerusalem to visit the Holy Sepulcher.[23] As indicated above, it is much debated whether the early crusades in Livonia were indeed considered to be as important as the crusades targeting, for example, the Iberian Peninsula or the Holy Land. Henry seems not to have had any such doubts—he clearly did what he could to maximize the legitimacy (and importance) of the Livonian church by suggesting unwavering

---

20   Kaljundi, "(Re)Performing the Past," 308. See also Markowski, "'Crusesignatus,'"; Christoph T. Maier, *Preaching the Crusades: Mendicant Friars and the Cross in the Thirteenth Century*, CSML, 4th ser. 28 (Cambridge: Cambridge University Press, 1994); James M. Powell, *Anatomy of a Crusade 1213–1221* (Philadelphia PA: University of Pennsylvania Press, 1986), esp. 51–65.

21   See, e.g., Henry, *Chron. Liv.*, 4.1, p. 13.

22   Ibid., 2.6–7, pp. 10 and 11. In the chronicle, Henry makes the slightly laconic remark that Bishop Berthold restrained his horse badly and by accident ended up among the Liv warriors, who grabbed the bishop and killed him, before they were eventually defeated by the crusaders.

23   Ibid., 3.2, p. 12, trans. Brundage, 35–36.

papal support even if that might not have been entirely true. Henry is not too fussy either about the actual indulgence promised to the Livonian crusaders or if in fact they did enjoy the same privileges and the same amount of indulgence as other crusaders, if he could ascertain the legitimation of the Livonian church as opposed to the competing powers of Denmark, Sweden, and Norway. For that same reason, he simply seems to ignore the fact that the popes at this early stage in the late twelfth century were more reactive than actually strictly active towards the crusading activities in the Baltic, responding more to regional requests for support and promises of indulgency than out of an overall papal strategical plan.[24] That would slowly change in the early thirteenth century, and Henry seems to be forestalling some of these events (too) early in his chronicle in an effort to maximize the importance and legitimacy of the German mission in Livonia from the very beginning. Thereby he clearly tries to oust and reject any later claims for supremacy from the side of the Danes or the Swedes that becomes more and more predominant as the events unfolds in the region and in the chronicle.[25] Of course, Henry had to accept and acknowledge that the Danish archbishops and their subordinate bishops had similar rights to call for crusades and grant indulgency as had the Livonian bishops. Eventually, the Danish archbishop Andrew Sunesen even became papal legate of the entire region.[26] Henry also relates how Andrew Sunesen as preparation for a Danish attack on the Estonian island of Saaremaa (Dan. Øsel, Germ. Swed. Ösel) in 1206 "for the remission of sins, had bestowed the sign of the cross upon a great multitude who were to take vengeance on the pagans and subject the nations to the Christian faith."[27] Regardless however of the different patterns in the organizational aspects of the crusading activities, both the German and the Scandinavian crusaders shared the same fundamental rituals concerning the crusader vows and the taking of crosses together with promises of indulgence before embarking on a crusade around 1200.

The crusaders from Denmark, Norway, or Sweden would have had their favored local harbors when embarking on a seaborne expedition targeting for example the northern provinces of Estonia. Most German crusaders however seems to have gathered in Lübeck with a stop-over in Visby on Gotland

---

24 Fonnesberg-Schmidt, *The Popes*, 65–74; Jensen, *Med ord*, 76–83.
25 Jensen, *Med ord*, 215–16.
26 Torben Kjersgaard Nielsen, "The Missionary Man: Archbishop Anders Sunesen and the Baltic Crusade, 1206–21," in *Crusade and Conversion on the Baltic Frontier 1150–1500*, ed. Alan V. Murray (Farnham and Burlington VT: Ashgate, 2001), 95–117.
27 Henry, *Chron. Liv.*, 10.13, p. 43: "qui in remissionem peccatorum infinitam multitudinem signo crucis signaverat ad faciendam vindictam in nationibus et ad subiugandas gentes fidei Christiane"; trans. Brundage, 64.

before continuing towards the estuary of the River Daugava (Germ. Düna, Rus. Dvina) in the present-day Gulf of Riga. Not infrequently, the crusaders from Scandinavia and the Germans would meet on Gotland or cross paths on the sea towards their favored destinations when not falling upon enemy raiders going the other way. As with any other crusades, the Scandinavian and German crusaders would have vowed to go on crusade for a specific period. Usually, the time set would cover a specific campaign or more generally, a longer period spent in a particular region. German crusaders coming to Livonia would often stay there for one season—arriving in Livonia in the early spring when the waters in the Baltic Sea were once again free from winter storms and heavy ice that otherwise made it impossible to navigate the waters around Livonia by ship. Having completed their season of service they would then return home on the arrival of a new seasons of crusaders traveling on the merchants' ships together with trading goods and military equipment.[28] This annual rhythm became so typical of the crusades in Livonia that Henry simply refers to it as a pilgrim's year during which the pilgrims had served under God's cross.[29]

Occasionally, some of the crusaders would renew their wows and stay in Livonia for another season, either out of piety and the desire to continue to do God's work or because of an acute need for more fighting men to defend the Livonian church against pagan attacks.[30] One such incident happened in 1207 when Bishop Albert was on his way to Germany for another preaching tour together with those crusaders who had already been in Livonia for one season. By chance (or divine providence!), a strong headwind kept the bishop and all the crusaders from leaving the estuary of the Daugava River forcing the ships to anchor and wait for the storm to pass. Probably the bishop and the more prominent among the crusaders had taken shelter in the nearby Cistercian Abbey of Dünamünde (Latv. Daugavgrīva) when messengers arrived and informed the bishop of a threatening attack against the city of Riga by a huge force of enemies.[31] Bishop Albert immediately summoned the crusaders, and in tears "he made known to them the damages to the church and invited them to become its defenders and strong auxiliaries by resuming the sign of the cross."[32] Since the crusaders had already fulfilled last year's vow they were no longer bound to stay in Livonia. The bishop therefore—according to Henry—had to use the best of his verbal skills to persuade the men to turn around and go back

---

28 See, e.g., ibid., 8.2, p. 24; 24.4, pp. 173–74.
29 See, e.g, ibid., 7.3, p. 20: "qui per annum illum in Lyvonia sub cruce sua Deo militaverant."
30 Ibid., 8.2, p. 24.
31 Ibid., 11.9, pp. 56–57.
32 Ibid., 11.9, p. 57: "ecclesie dampna lacrimando indicat et, ut fiant ecclesie defensores et fortes auxiliarii ipsos invitat"; trans. Brundage, 77–78.

to Riga: "he comforted them by reminding them of the previous plenary remission of their neglected sins, and, because of the greater labors they would now be undertaking on their long pilgrimage, he promised a greater indulgence and eternal life."[33] The importance of the ritual taking of the cross and the accompanying crusader vows is very clear from this particular case. The crusaders, having fulfilled their previous vow, now had to be persuaded to renew this vow and to take the cross once more to again become proper crusaders or "pilgrims" in the mind of Henry. According to his chronicle the crusaders had already received a plenary remission of sins—the highest and most absolute type of indulgence that could be bestowed on any crusader technically clearing them of all their guilt and any current demands for penitential acts. Still, the bishop seems to have felt that he could outdo that by promising them an even greater indulgence and eternal life. Probably it is the chronicler who gets a little carried away here by suggesting that the bishop could in fact go beyond a plenary indulgence.[34] It is most likely another attempt by Henry to enhance the legitimacy of the Livonian church against the rival powers of especially Denmark and Sweden. In the chronicle we are told that 300 individuals among the homebound crusaders renewed their vows and took up the cross once more, to serve God and the Livonian church and thus prepared themselves to return to Riga. Not entirely satisfied with the result, Bishop Albert accordingly "hired many more and sent them to Riga."[35] So, we have here proper crusaders bound by crusader vows and hired men—mercenaries—fighting side by side in the same godly war and perhaps even earning a similar indulgence without any particular reflection from the side of the chronicler.

As indicated above the Scandinavian crusaders seems to have had a slightly different rhythm in their campaigns as they initially lacked ecclesiastical and military powerbases like the urban (and fortified) centers of Üxküll (Est. Üksküla, Latv. Ikšķile) and Riga in the German-dominated parts of Livonia. No similar and relative secure places were available to the Danes or the Swedes during their initial expeditions into the region. Only in 1219 did the Danes establish a proper stronghold at Lyndanisse (nowadays Tallinn, Estonia; Germ. Reval), when they established a more permanent base for their continued

---

33   Ibid.: "et crucis signum resumere in plenariam ante neglectorum delictorum remissionem ammonendo confortat et ob maioris laboris sui longam peregrinationem maiorem indulgenciam et vitam promittit eternam"; trans. Brundage, 78.

34   Jensen, *Med ord*, 215–16. For a more general discussion on the indulgency granted in the Baltic, see Axel Ehlers, *Die Ablasspraxis des Deutschen Ordens im Mittelalter*, QSGD 64 (Marburg: Elvert, 2007).

35   Henry, *Chron. Liv.*, 11.9, p. 57: "insuper et multos mercede conducens episcopus Rigam remittit"; trans. Brundage, 78.

conquest, submission and conversion of the Estonian people that eventually became targeted from both north and south by encroaching crusader armies and foreign invaders: from the north by Danes and Swedes and from the south by Germans from Riga. An especially important goal for the Danish crusades was to eliminate—or at least contain—the extremely powerful naval powers of the Estonian islands of Saaremaa and Muhu. Alongside the Curs, these people raided far and wide in the Baltic, not shying away from attacking even the Danish provinces in the southern parts of modern-day Sweden, burning down churches, robbing and enslaving the locals.[36] In 1206, the Danish king Valdemar II had targeted Saaremaa in an attempt to subdue the islanders. A wooden fortress was quickly erected by the Danes and the king asked for volunteers among his men to stay behind to garrison the fortress when the rest of the Danish fleet prepared to return home. None of the Danish crusaders and men-at-arms, however, were inclined to stay behind—at least not according to Henry of Livonia. He seems to indicate that they did not fancy a long winter in complete isolation on an island swarming with hostile warriors infamously known for their bloodlust and hatred of the Christians. Consequently, King Valdemar had to give up his plans for a permanent presence on Saaremaa, returning instead to the usual pattern of seasonal expeditions that would last until 1219 and the establishment of a permanent Danish stronghold at Lyndanisse.[37] That is the overall narrative in the chronicle of Henry of Livonia, but I have elsewhere suggested that it may not at all have been the intention of the Danes to stay on Saaremaa for a longer period. Rather the attack should be seen as a demonstration of power from the side of the Danish king, that he had in fact the military (and naval) capability to strike against his enemies wherever and whenever he chose. Similarly the construction of the fortress and the (almost) immediate demolition should also be seen as an act of power and not as a prequel to a humiliating retreat from the side of the Danes even if Henry wants it to look that way.[38]

---

36 Ibid., 7.1, pp. 18–19. See also Carsten Selch Jensen, Marika Mägi, Kersti Markus, and Janus Møller Jensen, *Da Danskerne fik Dannebrog. Historien om de dansk-estiske relationer omkring år 1200* (Tallinn: Argo, 2019), 69–81 (parallel edition in Estonian under title *Taanlaste Ristisõda Eestis*). For a concise introduction to the long history of piracy in the eastern Baltic, see Marika Mägi, *The Viking Eastern Baltic* (Leeds: ARC Humanities Press, 2019), esp. 45–58.
37 Henry, *Chron. Liv.*, 10.13, pp. 43–44.
38 Carsten Selch Jensen, "Fighting in the Wilderness: Military Campaigning in 13th-Century Livonia with a Special Focus on Coastal and Riverine Warfare Summer and Winter," in *Material Culture of Medieval Warfare*, ed. Alan Murray and James Titterton (Leiden and Boston MA: Brill, forthc. 2024).

In the chronicle of Henry of Livonia, there is a reference to another type of ritual associated with the sign of the cross. In 1210, following some fierce fighting between Estonian, Livonian, and German forces, about hundred Christians were captured by the Estonians. Some of them were killed immediately, says Henry, but other were submitted to gruesome torture: "[the Estonians] roasted some alive, and, after stripping the others of their clothes and making crosses on their backs with their swords, they cut their throats, and thus, we hope, sent them into the heavenly company of the martyrs."[39] One particular aspect of the torture—the cutting of crosses directly into the naked flesh of the captives—seemingly became a sort of mock ritual in the mind of Henry, committed by the pagans with the intention of ridiculing Christianity in general and the wearing of the cross among the crusaders in particular. Henry however firmly believes that such a mock ritual would eventually help the Christians in achieving the crowns of martyrdom, thus essentially nullifying the pagan ritual.[40]

2 Casting of Lots: A Ritual between Paganism and Christendom

A ritual celebration among the crusaders would continue during their entire service in Livonia even if not all of them were engaged in actual fighting and certainly not on a constant basis. In some cases, crusaders seem to have been tasked primarily with the apparently less glorified work of repairing or guarding roads and bridges, improving the walls around castles and the major settlements and towns like Riga, etc. That was, however, not a work to scorn according to Henry: "The pilgrims of this year [1209] were always ready to obey in the matter of heightening the walls and in other things of service to God."[41]

---

39 Ibid., 14.8, p. 80: "quorum alios vivos assaverunt, alios nudantes vestimentis suis et gladiis suis in dorsis eorum crucibus factis iugulaverunt et in martyrum consorcio ut speramus in celum transmiserunt"; trans. Brundage, 102.

40 Similar narratives of pagans mocking Christians—especially captured clerics—or even sacrificing them, can be found in other chronicles like, e.g., *Magistri Adam Bremensis Gesta Hammaburgensis ecclesiae pontificum*, 2.43, ed. Bernhardt Schmeidler, MGH SS rer. Germ. 2 (Hannover and Leipzig: Hahn, 1917), 103–4; *Petri de Dusburg Chronicon terre Prussie*, 3.67, ed. Max Töppen, SrP 1 (Leipzig: Hirzel, 1861), 3–219 at 88; Wigand von Marburg, *Nowa kronika Pruska*, ed. and trans. Sławomir Zonenberg and Krzysztof Kwiatkowski (Toruń: Towarzystwo Naukowe w Toruniu, 2017), 330, 434. See also Karol Modzelewski, *Barbarian Europe*, trans. Ewa Macura (Frankfurt am Main and New York: Peter Lang, 2015), 21, 374.

41 Henry, *Chron. Liv.*, 13.3, p. 68: "Peregrini vero eiusdem anni in muri exaltatione et in aliis, quibus Deo servire poterant, obedire parati errant"; trans. Brundage, 90. See also ibid., 22.2, p. 148.

This manual labor could be as important as actual fighting a carnal enemy and was thus considered a proper and genuine service to God.[42]

When preparing for specific military expeditions further rituals were employed among the crusaders and the Livonian army in general. For example, we are told how Bishop Albert would summon the crusaders, the Sword Brethren, the fighting men of Riga, the local vassals and the various units and bands from among the local converts. The bishop had them all come together at a preplanned location that was tactical as well strategically well located with regards to the specific planned campaign. In the chronicle such places are often referred to by their Latvian name of *maias* and designated as places of prayers and counseling (*locus colloquiorum exercitus et orationum*) for the army to converge at.[43] When everybody had come together, the bishop would admonish everybody to fulfill their Christian duty to fight for the Lord before blessing the entire army and celebrating a full mass.[44] Such masses are mentioned from time to time in the chronicle indicating that the bishop or some other accompanying prelates would often resort to this particular sacramental ritual as a mean to assert God's blessing of the planned military expedition.[45] Those who did not show up when the army was summoned would be fined and the bishop also reminded everybody that only those who took part in the actual fighting would receive a share of the booty.[46] The booty would be any valuables taken from enemy farmsteads and villages like harvested crops, livestock or slaves (mostly women and young children of both sexes, since male enemies were normally killed on the spot).[47] This booty was not exclusively for the army to share as parts of it usually would be offered as thanks to the local churches following a successful campaign thereby securing a continuously divine support.[48]

---

42 At one point Henry even refers to Riga as the city of God and thus raises the importance of the manual work done by the pilgrims/crusaders, see ibid., 9.4, p. 28.
43 Ibid., 23.9, p. 165; see also 22.2, p. 148; 23.7, p. 160.
44 Ibid., 11.5, p. 52; 18.5, pp. 117–18; 22.2, p. 148.
45 Ibid., 23.9, p. 164. For some other evidence of preparatory rites before fighting administered by clerics in Livonia and Estonia, see Carsten Selch Jensen, "Clerics and War in Denmark and the Baltic: Ideals and Realities Around 1200," in *Fighting for the Faith: The Many Crusades*, ed. Carsten Selch Jensen, Janus Møller Jensen, and Kurt Villads Jensen, Scripta minora 27 (Stockholm: Runica et mediævalia, 2018), 187–217 at 201–4.
46 See, e.g., Henry, *Chron. Liv.*, 11.5, p. 53; 15.3, p. 91; 21.3, p. 143; 22.9, p. 153; 23.9, p. 167. Sometimes booty was a distraction making some of the warriors skip the actual fighting out of greed, see ibid., 15.3, p. 91.
47 See, e.g., 23.9, p. 166. For in-depth discussion of the practice of enslaving and plunder according to Henry's chronicle, see John Gillingham, "A Strategy of Total War? Henry of Livonia and the Conquest of Estonia, 1208–1227," *JMMH* 15 (2017): 186–214.
48 Henry, *Chron. Liv.*, 7.2, pp. 19–20 and 15.3, p. 91.

It was of course not only the crusaders or the Western Christians who had their rituals of war as a mean to ready themselves to fight God's War. Similarly the non-Christian people would have had their own rituals before going into war proper. On several occasions, Henry mentions how pagan warriors sought protection and guidance from their own deities before commencing on a military campaign.[49] A very common ritual that appears throughout the chronicle having also some biblical connotations seems to have been the casting of lots mentioned both as a ritual solely for the pagans, but also as a ritual used by the local Livs and Letts supporting the crusaders. They were in most cases formally Christianized, having accepted baptism and were thus fighting alongside the foreign crusaders. They would, however, still use the casting of lots as part of their ritual preparation for combat, as we shall see in the following examples.

In one of the first examples, however, the casting of lots was not in the first place associated with preparations for an upcoming military expedition. It was rather part of a narrative set up by Henry, in which the actual conversion of some of the local Lettish people from paganism into Christianity was decided—a little randomly, one should think—by the casting of lots. According to the chronicler, the randomness was however less of a problem in this particular case, since the Christian missionaries had prepared the locals through excessive sermons. And the actual decision to be made was not whether the Letts should accept Christianity. Rather, they had to decide if they should accept the Orthodox or rather the Latin rite: "they cast lots and asked the opinion of their gods as to whether ... they should submit to baptism of the Rusians of Pskov or, on the other hand, to that of the Latins." Quite ironically, Henry makes the pagan deities decide through the casting of lots which branch of Christendom was the preferable, and of course "the lot fell to the Latins."[50]

Another example from the chronicle places the ritual of casting lots in a genuinely warlike situation with crusaders and Sword Brethren seeking the alliance of some of the local Semgallians. They had not accepted Christianity at this early stage (1208) but were still ready to fight alongside the crusaders against their longtime Lithuanian enemies. The combined forces marched towards the Lithuanian territories and during a rest, the Semgallians decided to ask their deities for guidance and their favor in the ensuing fights. Again, the casting of lots became the ritual form through which the pagans approached their gods. They seem also to have a very "down-to-earth" sentiment towards

---

49 See, e.g., ibid., 12.2, p. 59. Compare with Kaljundi, "(Re)Performing the Past," 313.
50 Henry, *Chron. Liv.*, 11.7, p. 55: "missis tamen prius sortibus et requisito consensu deorum suorum, an Ruthenorum de Plicecowe ..., an Latinorum debeant subire baptismum" and "et cecidit sors ad Latinos"; trans. Brundage, 75.

their gods since they also asked them, if the Lithuanians already knew they were coming and was planning a counterattack or if they could rely on the element of surprise![51] Similarly, Henry also recalls how enemy attacks was thwarted because the pagan deities let the lots speak against such plans.[52] As such, Henry seems not to have opposed this ritual casting of lots and may simply have compared the local traditions with the Old Testament examples on how the Israelites adhered to the casting of lots when they sought help from God.[53] In this way, a local tradition was seemingly acceptable to the crusaders and the missionaries as a divine tool to seek out the will of the deities—whether pagan or Christian. Apparently so also because the Christian God could influence the outcome of the lots even when it was pagans who performed the ritual.

That the casting of lots was in fact acceptable to the Christians can be seen from one last example in the chronicle in which Henry relatively detailed described how the crusaders, the Sword Brethren and the local militias had come together in the preparation for yet another expedition into the lands of the Estonians in 1220. In this case, the army gathered during wintertime in a prearranged place, conveniently close to the areas that would soon to be attacked. Mass was said once again as was custom and the army was then divided "into three squadrons" (*in tres turmas*) as was the norm with medieval armies on the march or when deploying for battle. In the concrete case, however, the actual deployment was decided through the casting of lots which came to include the crusader units and the knights of the Sword Brethren, "and the [Livs] got the left-hand road, the Estonians got the road to the right by lot. The Germans with the Letts took the middle road, as was their custom."[54] On one side, the ritual casting of lots was performed in accordance with

---

51   Ibid., 12.2, p. 59. With regards to the widespread use of casting of lots among the pagan people, see Leszek P. Słupecki, "'Per sortes ac per equum': Lot-Casting and Hippomancy in the North after Saga Narratives and Medieval Chronicles," in *"Á Aaustrvega": Saga and East Scandinavia*, ed. Agneta Ney et al. 2 vols. (Gavle: Gävle University, 2009), 2:876–83; idem, "Prognostication in Pagan Beliefs Among Slavs in the Middle Ages," in *Prognostication in the Medieval World: A Handbook*, ed. Matthias Heiduk, Klaus Herbers, and Hans-Christian Lehner, 2 vols. (Berlin and Boston MA: De Gruyter, 2020), 1:85–108 at 97–102.
52   Henry, *Chron. Liv.*, 20.2, p. 136.
53   The casting of lots is a reoccurring theme in the Old Testament as a mean to discover the will of God, see, e.g., 1 Samuel 14:41–42. In the New Testament, following the crucifixion of Christ the solders divided his belongings between themselves by casting lots, Matthew 27:35; Mark 15:24; Luke 23:34. Another example is the selection of new apostles as narrated in the Acts 1:26.
54   Henry, *Chron. Liv.*, 23.9, p. 164: "et missis sortibus optinuerunt Lyvones viam ad sinistram, Esto-nes vero viam ad dextram sorte perceperunt; Theuthonici vero cum Lettis solito more sibi viam mediam usurparunt"; trans. Brundage, 183.

tradition, on the other side everything seemingly still played out according to custom with regards to the actual deployment of the individual units and the army as a whole was deployed according to the tactical norms of the period.

3 Spears and Swords in the Rituals of War

In some of the cases brought forward by Henry of Livonia, the casting of lots is mentioned alongside a ritual use of spears and other weapons as another way of asserting divine support among the non-Christian people. One such example happened already during the lifetime of Bishop Meinhard, when his "co-worker in Christ," a Cistercian monk by the name Theodoric, had the misfortune of being selected as an intended human sacrifice to the pagan gods by some angry Livs in Treiden. A flooding rain had ruined their harvest, whereas Theodoric's crops were untouched. Because of this the Livs decided they would offer Theodoric as a sacrifice to the gods—but only if the deities would accept such a sacrifice. According to Henry a spear (*lancea*) was placed on the ground and a horse was brought forth according to the custom of hippomancy known from other areas of the Baltic. Depending on which hoof went first towards the spear (or perhaps crossed the spear on the ground), Theodoric would either be killed or released. Miraculously it was "the hoof of life" (*pedem vite*) that went first, and Theodoric was thus saved. Henry (and the local Livs) firmly believed that it was the God of the Christians who had intervened in the ritual thereby saving the monk and making sure that he could continue his work as a missioner.[55] In this case, the spear seemingly played a minor role, merely symbolizing a marker or line to be crossed.

Later in the chronicle, Henry more specifically mentions spears as a symbol signifying either war or peace. For example, during peace negotiations between Estonians and Letts in 1208 they would brandish spears against each other in a threateningly manner.[56] Of course, it is no surprise that warriors would carry their weapons even during negotiations like the one just mentioned and the brandishing of spears might simply suggest an overly heated debate among proud warriors and not actual ritualistic use of weapons—in this case their spears—as specific symbolical markers that could initiate or end wars.[57] This practice however become a little more obvious through one of

---

55 Ibid., 1.10, p. 4, trans. Brundage, 27.
56 Ibid., 12.6, p. 62, trans. Brundage, 84.
57 See, e.g., Piotr Boroń, *Słowiańskie wiece plemienne* (Katowice: Wydawnictwo Uniwersytetu Śląskiego, 1999), 84, thanks to Dr. Radosław Kotecki for bringing this publication to my attention.

the other examples in the chronicle. In 1198, during Bishop Berthold's second visit in Livonia—this time backed by his newly recruited crusaders—we are told about a meeting between the bishop and the local Livs that also involved a ritual exchange of weapons. It is said in the texts that "the [Livs] offered and received a short armistice, exchanging [spears], according to the custom, to confirm the peace." The peace, however, was short-lived and immediately broken, says Henry, when the Livs killed some of the Germans who were foraging for their horses: "[t]he lord bishop, when he saw this, sent back their spear and called off the peace."[58] Quite ironically, the same Livs had shortly before the peace negotiations argued against the use of force in the continuous missionary work with a reference to the traditional position of St. Augustin that it was not allowed—not even possible—to force non-Christians into accepting Christianity. This is of course also a literary construction by Henry, having the local pagans quote an ancient Christian theologian and his arguments against conversion by force, as is the case here in the text. For Henry this was simply another way of legitimizing the preaching campaigns and the ensuing crusades that were to follow the very first incidents of armed clashes between the German crusaders and the local people.[59]

The specific reference to the ritual use of spears as a symbol of either peace or war however seems plausible and is further supported by other examples in the chronicle with ritual uses of weapons accepted by both the locals and the newcomers. This is for example the case in 1213 when spears were used once again to signal the ending of a truce—this time when a Lithuanian host of warriors came to the castle of Kokenhusen (nowadays Koknese) occupied by a garrison of German men-at-arms. The Lithuanians called out to the garrison and then threw a spear into the River Daugava "to abrogate their peace and friendship with the Germans" as it is said in the chronicle.[60]

---

[58] Henry, *Chron. Liv.*, 2.5, p. 10: "Interea colligende partis eorum causa breves dant et recipiunt inducias, missis invicem lanceis secundum morem ad confirmationem pacis" and "Quo viso domnus episcopus ipsorum lancea remissa paci contradixi"; trans. Brundage, 33.

[59] Jensen, *Med ord*, 13–14, 72–75. For a discussion on St. Augustin's view on war and mission, see Frederick H. Russell, "Love and Hate in Medieval Warfare: The Contribution of Saint Augustine," *Nottingham Medieval Studies* 31 (1987): 108–24.

[60] Henry, *Chron. Liv.*, 17.2, p. 113: "Letones ... vocatis quibusdam de castro Kukenois lanceam in Dunam miserunt, paci ac familiaritati Theuthonicorum contradicentes"; trans. Brundage, 133. Along a somewhat similar note, Henry also mentions the use of swords in a ritualistic way. Following a very long and gruesome story in the chronicle about the treacherous and brutal killings of some Christians—among them several priests—by marauding Estonian warriors, the chroniclers mentions that the Estonians sent the still bloodied swords they had used to kill the Christians to other Estonians, urging them to join this attack on their enemies among the Christians. The bloodied sword is mentioned in ibid., 26.7, p. 190.

4   Ritually Ending the War

As suggested in the opening paragraph, a successful military campaign had its own rituals—the placing of the crusaders' Marian banner for example on the upper rampart of a conquered enemy fortress was a very powerful symbol of victory. In one case the specific raising of the banner was even carried out by the conquered people themselves symbolizing first their wavering response to the crusaders' call for surrender—some hoisted the banner, others tore it down again—before finally agreeing to surrender by leaving the banner in place and thereby submitting themselves to the demands for conversion and baptism.[61] Thus the ritual hoisting of the Marian banner essentially preceded the more important ritual of baptism designating the pagans' submission to Christianity as an absolute Christian victory.[62]

Following the baptism of the defeated (pagan) enemies the crusaders and their fellow-men-in-arms would ceremonially praise God through hymns and prayers for having granted them another great victory.[63] Especially towards the ending of the chronicle, Henry seems to extol in these appraisals describing how huge amounts of booty—weapons, clothes, horses, captives—were taken from the field and brought back to Livonia to be distributed among those who had taken part in the campaign as indicated previously, but also as offerings to the local churches.[64] In this way the vocal appraisal of God, Jesus Christ, and the Virgin Marry took on a ritualistic form summarizing the overall notion of the ongoing crusades as essentially God's War. It was only fitting that a victory in such a war was followed by material offerings to the local churches in the form of valuables taken from the enemy.[65]

A victory (or a defeat—depending on the perspective) would generate other rituals according to Henry. In one case, he claims that a number of Lithuanian women had killed themselves when they learned that their husbands had been slain in battle. His source was a fellow priest who had been held captive by the Lithuanians. This priest allegedly told Henry that the said women—fifty

---

61   Ibid., 16.4, pp. 108–9.
62   See also Jüri Kivimäe, "'Servi Beatae Marie Virginis': Christians and Pagans in Henry's 'Chronicle of Livonia,'" in *Church and Belief in the Middle Ages: Popes, Saints, and Crusaders*, ed. Kirsi Salonen and Sari Katajala-Peltomaa, CB 3 (Amsterdam: Amsterdam University Press, 2016), 201–26 at 213–14.
63   Henry, *Chron. Liv.*, 28.6, p. 205.
64   See above, n. 48.
65   See, e.g., Henry, *Chron. Liv.*, 28.6, p. 205; 29.9, p. 215; 30.6, p. 221. Singing and even music accompanied the crusaders also in other situations, about which, see Alan V. Murray, "Music and Cultural Conflict in the Christianization of Livonia, 1190–1290," in *The Clash of Cultures*, 293–305.

in number—had hanged themselves because they firmly believed that they would be reunited with their dead husbands in the afterlife.[66]

On a more general level, the handling of the dead following a battle also took on ritualistic forms, again depending on whether it was the bodies of slain enemies or your own dead that had to be taken care of. In one case Henry tells that "there were about five hundred dead on the field of battle and many others fell on the plains, the roads, and elsewhere." The many dead people however seem almost exclusively to have been the bodies of the pagan enemies as Henry goes on to tell the reader that only four Christians had died in the fighting—two from among the Germans and two Lettish warriors. One of the Germans was a "young count from the bishop's household and one of the duke's knights. May their memory be blessed and may their souls rest in Christ."[67] Henry praises the dead Christian soldiers whereas his concern for the dead enemies seems to have been absolutely absent. In this particular case, the battle took place during wintertime and burying so many dead bodies (or even burning them in the case of the dead enemies) may simply have been impossible. Such a general *modus operandi* seems to have been the norm all year round however—you took great care of your own fallen comrades and fellow fighters whereas the bodies of the enemy were left to rot on the ground.[68]

In some cases, prominent persons among the dead would be honored with special rituals as was, for example, the case with Bishop Berthold following his death in 1198. As mentioned above he had been killed in a battle which took place during summertime and all the dead bodies soon started decaying—except for the bishop's body which was seemingly unaffected by the heat and had not been touched by any wild animals that would normally feast on the bodies of the dead following a battle. That is at least what we are told in the chronicle of Arnold of Lübeck.[69] This is also indirectly acknowledged by Henry since he tells us that Bishop Berthold came to rest in the church of

---

66   Henry, *Chron. Liv.*, 9.5, p. 28. The ritual of a woman's suicide after the death of her husband is well attested among the Slavs. For in-depth analysis of the sources concerning this rite and connected beliefs, see Tadeusz Lewicki, "Obrzędy pogrzebowe pogańskich Słowian w opisach podróżników i pisarzy arabskich głównie z IX–X w.," *Archeologia* 5 (1952–1953): 122–54.

67   Henry, *Chron. Liv.*, 23.9, p. 166: "Erant autem interfectorum in loco certaminis circiter quingenti, et alii plures per campos et per vias et alibi ceciderunt" and "comes iuvenis de familia episcopi milesque ducis unus, quorum memoria sit in benedictione et anime eorum requiescant in Christo"; trans. Brundage, 185.

68   See, e.g., ibid., 11.9, p. 57. With regards to the burning of the dead, see, e.g., ibid., 12.6, p. 65.

69   *Arnoldi Chronica Slavorum*, 5.30, ed. Johann Martin Lappenberg, MGH SS rer. Germ. 14 (Hannover: Hahn, 1868), 215.

Üxküll besides Bishop Meinhard; Berthold as a martyr and Meinhard as a confessor and thus both venerable men.[70]

Henry also implies that some pagans preferred to kill their wounded comrades during battle rather than leaving them behind for the enemy to capture or more likely to torture and kill. We are even told that they would cut off the heads of their fallen comrades to take them home for a ritual mourning commemorating the dead and securing for them a proper afterlife.[71]

A sort of "counter-ritual" was the desecrating of the dead bodies of your enemy as suggested by one of the previous examples from the chronicle. In these cases, enemy dead bodies could be left unburied on the ground, or perhaps thrown into a moat to make the water undrinkable during sieges.[72] A targeted desecration is also mentioned in the chronicle when Estonians raiders burned down churches in Livonia and desecrated the graves of the dead Christians: "When all the people stayed in the forts, [the Estonians] burned the empty villages and churches and, with their pagan sacrifices, committed many abominations around the churches and tombs of Christians."[73]

In other cases, various burial traditions—both Christian and pagan—would be used side by side when taking care of a people who had been killed for example during battle. A prominent example is that of the Livonia elder and nobleman, Caupo. He had accepted Christianity early on and allied himself with the German newcomers continuously waging war on his enemies. In 1217 Caupo was fatally wounded in battle—accordingly, he was run clear through by a lance—and with his last breath he expressed his Christian faith, gave away his worldly possession to the churches established in Livonia and for one last time enjoyed "the sacrament of the Lord's body" (*Dominici corporis sacramentis*) before expiring. According to the chronicle, he was on his deathbed surrounded by some very prominent persons—among them Count

---

70　Henry, *Chron. Liv.*, 10.6, p. 36. For the cult of Berhold, see Kristjan Kaljusaar, "Martyrdom on the Field of Battle in Livonia during Thirteenth Century Holy Wars and Christianization: Popular Belief and the Image of a Catholic Frontier," in *Christianity and War in Medieval East Central Europe and Scandinavia*, ed. Radosław Kotecki, Carsten Selch Jensen, and Stephen Bennett (Leeds: ARC Humanities Press, 2021), 245–62 at 253–57. Whether or not there actually was a local veneration of Meinhard and Bertold is much debated, see Anti Selart, "Meinhard, Berthold, Bernhard—kein Heiliger für Livland," in *"Credo." Christianisierung Europas im Mittelalter*, ed. Christoph Stiegemann, Martin Kroker, and Wolfgang Walter, 2 vols. (Petersberg: Imhof, 2013), 1: 434–40.

71　Henry, *Chron. Liv.*,.5, p. 77 and 9.4, p. 28. See also Jensen, *Med ord*, 13–14.

72　See, e.g., ibid., 20.7, p. 139.

73　Ibid., 14.10, p. 83: "et omni populo in castris existente ipsi villas vacuas et ecclesias incenderunt et nequicias multas circa ecclesias et sepulchra mortuorum christiano-rum immolaticiis suis exercuerunt"; see also 27.1, p. 193.

Albert of Lauenburg and Abbot Bernhard of Lippe of Dünemünde. The latter had been a renowned knight and former crusader before he gave up his secular life to become a Cistercian monk and missionary in Livonia eventually becoming bishop of Semgallia in 1218.[74] Surrounded by these important defenders of Western Christendom Caupo was accordingly "burned and the bones were taken away to Livonia and buried at Cubbesele."[75] Thus, the traditional burning of the dead among the non-Christian people of Livonia and Estonia was in some cases accepted by the Christians who normally condemned all such "pagan" rites. A certain amount of pragmatism seems to have prevailed with regards to which rituals to accept (and in what situations) and which rituals to condemn in the quest to defeat the enemies of God.

5   Baptism as an Imagined Counter-Ritual

As previously mentioned, the sacrament of baptism was fundamental in the overall narrative of Henry of Livonia focusing on the Christianization of the pagan people. Accepting or rejecting baptism was to Henry essentially the same as accepting or rejecting Christianity, thereby accepting or rejecting God, Christ and the Virgin Mary. In that sense, baptism became in a way the most powerful ritual for the Christians governing all their actions—when to preach or fight, and when to make peace. From a pagan perspective acceptance of baptism became the ultimate submission to the newcomers accepting not just new political (and military) masters, but essentially also a completely new worldview. Therefore, it is hardly surprising—at least not from the perspective of the pagans—that uprisings and revolts against the foreigners became of paramount importance and a recurring event throughout the chronicle: in the mind of Henry, it was the pagan deities who rose against the Christian God challenging some of the fundamental Christian rituals. Consequently, parts of his narrative become a sort of imagined pagan ritual resistance fight against

---

74   With regards to the fascination history of Bernhard of Lippe, see, e.g., Paul Johansen, "Lippstadt, Freckenhorst und Fellin in Livland. Werk und Wirkung Bernhards II. zur Lippe im Ostseeraum," in *Westfalen, Hanse, Ostseeraum*, ed. Luise von Winterfeld, Veröffentlichungen des Provinzialinstituts für Westfälische Landes- und Volkkunde 1, Wirtschafts- und verkehrswissenschaftliche Arbeiten 7 (Münster: Aschendorff, 1955), 97–160; Ulrich Meier, "'Der Eckstein ist gekommen ...'. Die Konsolidierung der Herrschaft Lippe im 13. Jahrhundert," in *Lippe und Livland. Mittelalterliche Herrschaftsbildung im Zeichen der Rose*, ed. Jutta Prieur (Detmold: Verlag für Regionalgeschichte, 2008), 45–64.

75   Henry, *Chron. Liv.*, 21.4, p. 144: "Et combustum est corpus eius, et ossa delata in Lyvoniam et sepulta in Cubbesele."

Christendom. For example, the local tradition of using bath houses—or to be more precise, saunas—in the everyday life among the Livs and Letts. There are in the chronicle two specific references to such bath houses/saunas and their use by the locals, and in both cases, Henry uses them to address or at least exemplify an overall struggle between Christianity and paganism as an essential part of the foundational story of the Livonian church that is at the very center of his chronicle.[76] The peculiar thing however is that Henry seems to view this local tradition from two completely different angles in the chronicle. In the first case, the use of baths houses and saunas among the locals seems to be the very quintessence of pagan behavior, whereas in the second case, it is what local Christians do right before they become martyrs!

The use of saunas is first mentioned in the chronicle immediately after Bishop Berthold was killed in a battle. Following the death of the bishop, the now leaderless army of crusaders took their revenge on the local Livs "with both horses and ships, fire and sword [and] laid waste the crops of the [Livs]."[77] The ferocity of the crusaders must have terrified the locals, forcing them into submission—at least for the time being—making them promise to renew the peace and accept Christian priests into their strongholds. They also promised to pay for the sustenance of these priests as long as they stayed among them. Following this, about one hundred Livs are said to have accepted baptism as an act of submission and atonement for the recent killing of the bishop and the subsequent defeat in battle by the crusaders.[78] A process for the appointment of a new bishop was also initiated and most of the crusaders now left Livonia and returned home. They left behind the local Christians, the priests and one single ship of merchants. At the very beginning of the chronicle, Henry notes that some of the merchants who traveled to and from Livonia regularly over the years had formed bonds of friendship with local traders among the Livs, so it seemed just naturally that some of them now opted to stay and continue with their businesses.[79] Neither can it be ruled out that a small contingent of men-at-arms—perhaps not more than a handful—may have stayed behind guarding the local fortified episcopal castle as they had done during the reign of Bishop Meinhard.[80] The most recent converts among the Livs, however, did not stay loyal to their new faith for very long. As soon as the crusaders left,

---

76   Jensen, *Med ord*, 299–300.
77   Henry, *Chron. Liv.*, 2.6, p. 10: "et tam equis quam navibus, tam igne quam gladio Lyvonum perdunt segetes"; trans. Brundage, 33.
78   Ibid., 2.7, pp. 10–11.
79   Ibid., 1.2, p. 2.
80   Carsten Selch Jensen, "The Nature of the Early Missionary Activities and Crusades in Livonia, 1185–1201," in *Medieval Spirituality in Scandinavia and Europe: A Collection of*

Henry mentions how "the treacherous [Livs], emerging from their customary baths, poured the water of the Daugava River over themselves, saying: 'We now remove the water of baptism and Christianity itself with the water of the river. Scrubbing off the faith we have received, we send it after the withdrawing Germans.'"[81] This is the first time in the chronicle that Henry mentions these local "customary baths" (*balneis consuetis*), and immediately interpreted them as some sort of (pagan) ritual and a specific way for the locals to cleanse themselves of the recent ritual of baptism and the faith of the Christians who had encroached on their lands and enforced upon them a new religion. *Balneis consuetis* is the term used by Henry, but it is not clear from the narrative if Henry basically was ignorant of the ancient traditions of using bathhouses and saunas in these parts of the world, or he simply choses to describe something well-known to him in a specific setting that underlines his overall narrative of Christianity versus paganism in his chronicle. It would seem odd if Henry did not know this local custom of using a sauna after having spent around twenty years in Livonia when he completed his chronicle in the late twelfth-twenties. It may of course be that he simply related some older legendary narratives from among the very first missionaries, who did not know the various local customs as well as later generations of clerics who settled in the region and like Henry became integrated into the society as a parish priest and very active interpreter and missioner. It cannot be ruled out either that the locals actually had some kind of religious ideas associated with the bathhouses and saunas and the concrete processes of cleansing that came from that, but Henry only has a couple of references to this traditional use of bathhouses throughout the entire chronicle. In this case, he continues to relate how the Livs not only cleansed themselves of the Christian baptism through the use of the "customary baths." He also tells how they performed a specific action associated with a wooden head of a man who had been cut into a tree by the crusaders who had now left the country. Following the allegedly ritual cleansing in the bath house/sauna the locals prepared a special brew of mead, which they drank before they (very carefully, it seems) cut loose the carved image from the tree. They then placed it on two logs which they had tied together on the Daugava River and "sent it as the god of the Germans, together with their Christian faith, after those who were going back to Gotland by sea."[82]

Essays in Honour of Tore Nyberg, ed. Lars Bisgaard et al., Odense University studies in history and social sciences 234 (Odense: Odense University Press, 2001), 121–37, esp. 127.
81   Henry, *Chron. Liv.*, 2.8, p. 11: "Hic iam baptismatis aquam cum ipsa christianitate removemus aqua fluminis et fidem susceptam exfestucantes post Germanes recedentes transmittimus"; trans. Brundage, 34.
82   Ibid., 2.8, p. 11.

Another incident involving a sauna took place in 1215 when the already Christianized Letts in one of the northernmost provinces of Livonia was attacked by the still pagan Estonians. In this specific case, we are told that a large army of Estonians had attacked a local Livonian stronghold but eventually withdraw again when they learned about a planned counterattack by a local force of Sword Brethren. During their retreat the Estonians once again passed through some of the deserted villages of the locals—they had all taken to the forest during the Estonians' initial attack. Most likely the Letts had brought with them their valuables with the aim of denying the enemy as much booty as possible. It so happened that one of the locals—a man called Talibald—just then decided to leave the relative safety of the forest because he wanted a bath. So, the primary (or perhaps even the sole) reason for Talibald to leave his safe hideout seemingly was an urge to have a bath/use the sauna, even though he knew that enemy raiders were roaming the countryside. It seems to indicate that the use of bathhouses and saunas was quite important among the locals, perhaps even in a religious sense holding some sort of spiritual meaning even after they had become Christians. For Talibald, it all ended very badly; he was apprehended by the Estonians who forced him to reveal to them where his valuable had been hidden (apparently not in the forest—more likely buried close to his farm) before "they put him again into the fire ... and roasted him like a fish, until he gave up the spirit and died." He would soon however be avenged by his sons, who initiated a series of brutal attacks on the nearby Estonians, killing and burning their way through the lands and taking as many women and children as possible as slaves. At the same time Talibald is praised by Henry as a true martyr so there seems to be no question about his loyalty to the Livonian church in the mind of the chronicler.[83]

Consequently, in one case we have the traditional use of bathhouses/saunas described as a sort of pagan counter-ritual against the sacramental ritual of baptism and in another case, the use of such bathhouses seems to have been fully accepted even among the Christians. It seems to support the notion that Henry in the early parts of his chronicles relies on legendary stories from when the missionaries were new to the local traditions or at least not have had time to incorporate former non-Christian traditions and habits into an overall Christian narrative.

---

83   Ibid., 19.3, pp. 124–25, trans. Brundage, 144.

6   Concluding Remarks

According to Henry of Livonia the wars fought in Livonia and Estonia around 1200 were always carried out within a certain ritualistic framework, covering all aspects of the wars from the very early preparations right until the celebration of victory or the mourning of defeat. In the *Chronicon Livoniae* Henry reflects on the use of these rituals both among the Christians and among the pagans, constantly seeing the specific rituals as part of an overall struggle between good and evil, between God and the pagan deities. Accordingly, the crusaders were all marked by the cross before they even went on a campaign setting them off as the "cross marked men" specially dedicated to fight the Lord's War with the promise of indulgence whereas the pagans would seek the support of their pagan deities for example through the casting of lots or similar rituals as a preparation for war. As such, the rituals are seen by Henry as essential to the outcome of the specific military campaigns, as well as to the overall struggle (from his perspective) against the enemies of God. Similarly, victory or defeat in battle was not simply the pragmatic outcome of an earthly encounter, but rather the consequence of a war fought between the heavenly powers of God and the aforementioned pagan demons. As an eyewitness, Henry must have been familiar with most of these rituals associated with the crusaders and the Christian armies supporting the Livonian church. He would have witnessed masses performed on the outset of a military campaign, perhaps even performed them himself, as well as having heard the admonishing sermons delivered by the bishops to the army awaiting battle, and also seen the banner of the Virgin Mary being unfolded by the army when its marched against the enemy. Surely he would also have experienced how the dead and wounded were treated after battle—both among the crusaders and among their enemies and seen how even the corpses would be submitted to certain rituals (or lack thereof) as a consequence of these divine wars.

Some of the rituals were specific to a military setting like for example the blessing of the armies before battle, the privileges granted to the crusaders, the specific use of the banner of the Virgin Mary, etc. Other rituals, however, were generally part of the overall missionary activities of the church for example the saying of masses, the rite of baptism and the burying of the dead in a properly Christian way and would have been considered essential in any Christian society of the time. Thus extraordinary religious rituals became intertwined with more common religious rituals in the world of Henry of Livonia forming a special setting around these wars.

Henry also had a first-hand experience with quite a lot of the rituals ascribed to the local people—for example, the use of weapons as part of certain rituals associated with the peace negotiations and the declarations of war, the casting of lots, the uses of bathhouses and saunas, and even the rather syncretistic burning of some of the dead local lords who had converted into Christianity. As such the chronicle is an extremely important source for the study of the culture of war among the traditional societies of the (early) medieval Livonia and Estonia when comparing Henry's textual descriptions of local rituals with both older and younger chronicles found within the same overall region. Of course such studies require very careful use of the textual evidence—preferably supplied with archaeological evidence—since the texts are almost exclusively written down by Christian chroniclers who most often upheld a strong dichotomy between Christianity and paganism that is also fundamental to the overall narrative of Henry of Livonia. Still, Henry is an important source to the way rituals of war were used in the early decades of the twelfth century among crusaders and others in Livonia and Estonia—at least as seen from the perspective of a priest, missioner and army chaplain.

Bibliography

Primary Sources

Arnoldi Chronica Slavorum. Edited by Johann Martin Lappenberg. MGH SS rer. Germ. 14. Hannover: Hahn, 1868.

The Chronicle of Henry of Livonia. Translated by James A. Brundage. 2nd ed. New York: Columbia University Press, 2003.

Heinrich von Lettland. *Livländische Chronik*. Edited and translated by Albert Bauer. Ausgewählte Quellen zur deutschen Geschichte des Mittelalters. Freiherr vom Stein-Gedächtnisausgabe 24. Darmstadt: Wissenschaftliche Buchgesellschaft, 1959.

Heinrici Chronicon Livoniae. Edited by Leonid Arbusow and Albert Bauer, MGH SS rer. Germ. 31. Hannover: Hahn, 1955.

Magistri Adam Bremensis Gesta Hammaburgensis ecclesiae pontificum. Edited by Bernhardt Schmeidler. MGH SS rer. Germ. N.S. 2. Hannover and Leipzig: Hahn, 1917.

Petri de Dusburg Chronicon terre Prussie. Edited by Max Töppen. SrP 1. 3–219. Leipzig: Hirzel, 1861.

Wigand von Marburg. *Nowa kronika Pruska*. Edited and translated [into Polish] by Sławomir Zonenberg and Krzysztof Kwiatkowski. Toruń: Towarzystwo Naukowe w Toruniu, 2017.

Secondary Sources

Boroń, Piotr. *Słowiańskie wiece plemienne*. Katowice: Wydawnictwo Uniwersytetu Śląskiego, 1999.

Brundage, James A. "'Cruce signari': The Rite for Taking the Cross in England." *Traditio* 22 (1966): 289–310.

Bysted, Ane, Carsten Selch Jensen, Kurt Villads Jensen, and John H. Lind. *Jerusalem in the North: Denmark and the Baltic Crusades, 1100–1522*. Outremer 1. Turnhout: Brepols, 2012.

Chleirigh, Lean Ni. "'Nova Peregrinatio': The First Crusade as a Pilgrimage in Contemporary Latin Narratives." In *Writing the Early Crusades: Text, Transmission and Memory*. Edited by Marcus Bull and Damien Kempf, 63–74. Woodbridge: Boydell Press, 2014.

Ehlers, Axel. *Die Ablasspraxis des Deutschen Ordens im Mittelalter*. QSGD 64. Marburg: Elvert, 2007.

Fonnesberg-Schmidt, Iben. "Pope Honorius III and Mission and Crusades in the Baltic Region." In *The Clash of Cultures on the Medieval Baltic Frontier*. Edited by Alan V. Murray, 103–22. Farnham and Burlington VT: Ashgate, 2009.

Fonnesberg-Schmidt, Iben. *The Popes and the Baltic Crusades 1147–1254*. TNW 26. Leiden and Boston MA: Brill, 2007.

Gaposchkin, M. Cecilia. *Invisible Weapons: Liturgy and the Making of Crusade Ideology*. Ithaca NY: Cornell University Press, 2017.

Gillingham, John. "A Strategy of Total War? Henry of Livonia and the Conquest of Estonia, 1208–1227." *JMMH* 15 (2017): 186–214.

Jensen, Carsten Selch. "Clerics and War in Denmark and the Baltic: Ideals and Realities Around 1200." In *Fighting for the Faith: The Many Crusades*. Edited by Carsten Selch Jensen, Janus Møller Jensen, and Kurt Villads Jensen, 187–217. Scripta minora 27. Stockholm: Runica et mediævalia, 2018.

Jensen, Carsten Selch. "Fighting in the Wilderness: Military Campaigning in 13th-Century Livonia with a Special Focus on Coastal and Riverine Warfare Summer and Winter." In *Material Culture of Medieval Warfare*. Edited by Alan Murray and James Titterton. Leiden and Boston MA: Brill, forthc. 2024.

Jensen, Carsten Selch. *Med ord og ikke med slag. Teologi og historieskrivning i Henrik af Letlands krønike*. Copenhagen: Gads Forlag, 2019.

Jensen, Carsten Selch. "The Nature of the Early Missionary Activities and Crusades in Livonia, 1185–1201." In *Medieval Spirituality in Scandinavia and Europe: A Collection of Essays in Honour of Tore Nyberg*. Edited by Lars Bisgaard et al., 121–37. Odense University studies in history and social sciences 234. Odense: Odense University Press, 2001.

Jensen, Carsten Selch. *Through Words, not Weapons: Theology and History Writing in the Chronicle of Henry of Livonia (ca.1227)*. Turnhout: Brepols, forthc. 2024.

Jensen, Carsten Selch, Marika Mägi, Kersti Markus, and Janus Møller Jensen. *Da Danskerne fik Dannebrog. Historien om de dansk-estiske relationer omkring år 1200*. Tallinn: Argo, 2019. Parallel edition in Estonian under title *Taanlaste Ristisõda Eestis*.

Johansen, Paul. "Lippstadt, Freckenhorst und Fellin in Livland. Werk und Wirkung Bernhards II. zur Lippe im Ostseeraum." In *Westfalen, Hanse, Ostseeraum*. Edited by Luise von Winterfeld, 97–160. Veröffentlichungen des Provinzialinstituts für Westfälische Landes- und Volkkunde 1, Wirtschafts- und verkehrswissenschaftliche Arbeiten 7. Münster: Aschendorff, 1955.

Kaljundi, Linda. "(Re)Performing the Past: Crusading, History Writing, and Rituals in the Chronicle of Henry of Livonia." In *The Performance of Christian and Pagan Storyworlds*. Edited by Lars B. Mortensen and Tuomas M.S. Lehtonen, 295–338. Medieval identities 3. Turnhout: Brepols, 2013.

Kaljusaar, Kristjan. "Martyrdom on the Field of Battle in Livonia during Thirteenth Century Holy Wars and Christianization: Popular Belief and the Image of a Catholic Frontier." In *Christianity and War in Medieval East Central Europe and Scandinavia*. Edited by Radosław Kotecki, Carsten Selch Jensen, and Stephen Bennett, 245–62. Leeds: ARC Humanities Press, 2021.

Kienzle, Beverly M. *Cistercians, Heresy and Crusade in Occitania, 1145–1229*. Woodbridge: York Medieval Press in association with The Boydell Press, 2001.

Kivimäe, Jüri. "'Servi Beatae Marie Virginis': Christians and Pagans in Henry's 'Chronicle of Livonia.'" In *Church and Belief in the Middle Ages: Popes, Saints, and Crusaders*. Edited by Kirsi Salonen and Sari Katajala-Peltomaa. CB 3. Amsterdam: Amsterdam University Press, 2016.

Lapina, Elizabeth, and Nicholas Morton, ed. *The Uses of the Bible in Crusader Sources*. Commentaria 7. Leiden and Boston MA: Brill, 2017.

Lewicki, Tadeusz. "Obrzędy pogrzebowe pogańskich Słowian w opisach podróżników i pisarzy arabskich głównie z IX–X w." *Archeologia* 5 (1952–1953): 122–54.

Mägi, Marika. *The Viking Eastern Baltic*. Leeds: ARC Humanities Press, 2019.

Maier, Christoph T. *Preaching the Crusades: Mendicant Friars and the Cross in the Thirteenth Century*. CSML, 4th ser. 28. Cambridge: Cambridge University Press, 1994.

Markowski, Michael. "'Crucesignatus': Its Origins and Early Usage." *JMH* 10.3 (1984): 157–65.

Meier, Ulrich. "'Der Eckstein ist gekommen …'. Die Konsolidierung der Herrschaft Lippe im 13. Jahrhundert." In *Lippe und Livland. Mittelalterliche Herrschaftsbildung im Zeichen der Rose*. Edited by Jutta Prieur, 45–64. Detmold: Verlag für Regionalgeschichte, 2008.

Modzelewski, Karol. *Barbarian Europe*. Translated by Ewa Macura. Frankfurt am Main and New York: Peter Lang, 2015.

Morton, Nicholas. "The Defence of the Holy Land and the Memory of the Maccabees." *JMH* 36 (2010): 275–93.

Morton, Nicholas. "Walls of Defence for the House of Israel: Ezekiel 13:5 and the Crusading Movement." In *The Uses of the Bible in Crusader Sources*. Edited by Elizabeth Lapina and Nicholas Morton, 403–20. Commentaria 7. Leiden and Boston MA: Brill, 2017.

Murray, Alan V. "Music and Cultural Conflict in the Christianization of Livonia, 1190–1290." In *The Clash of Cultures on the Medieval Baltic Frontier*. Edited by Alan V. Murray, 293–305. Farnham and Burlington VT: Ashgate, 2009.

Nielsen, Torben Kjersgaard. "The Missionary Man: Archbishop Anders Sunesen and the Baltic Crusade, 1206–21." In *Crusade and Conversion on the Baltic Frontier 1150–1500*. Edited by Alan V. Murray, 95–117. Farnham and Burlington VT: Ashgate, 2001.

Paravcini, Werner. *Die Preußenreisen des europäischen Adels*. 2 vols. BF 17.1–2. Sigmaringen: Thorbecke, 1989–1995.

Pennington, Kenneth. "The Rite for Taking the Cross in the Twelfth Century." *Traditio* 30 (1974): 429–35.

Powell, James M. *Anatomy of a Crusade 1213–1221*. Philadelphia PA: University of Pennsylvania Press, 1986.

Russell, Frederick H. "Love and Hate in Medieval Warfare: The Contribution of Saint Augustine." *Nottingham Medieval Studies* 31 (1987): 108–24.

Selart, Anti. "Meinhard, Berthold, Bernhard—kein Heiliger für Livland." *"Credo." Christianisierung Europas im Mittelalter*. Edited by Christoph Stiegemann, Martin Kroker, and Wolfgang Walter. 2 vols., 1:434–40. Petersberg: Imhof, 2013.

Słupecki, Leszek P. "'Per sortes ac per equum': Lot-Casting and Hippomancy in the North after Saga Narratives and Medieval Chronicles." In *"Á Aaustrvega": Saga and East Scandinavia*. Edited by Agneta Ney et al. 2 vols., 2:876–83. Gavle: Gävle University, 2009.

Słupecki, Leszek P. "Prognostication in Pagan Beliefs Among Slavs in the Middle Ages." In *Prognostication in the Medieval World: A Handbook*. Edited by Matthias Heiduk, Klaus Herbers, and Hans-Christian Lehner, 2 vols., 1:85–108. Berlin and Boston MA: De Gruyter, 2020.

Srodecki, Paul, and Norbert Kersken, ed. *The Expansion of the Faith: Crusading on the Frontiers of Latin Christendom in the High Middle Ages*. Outremer 14. Turnhout: Brepols, 2021.

CHAPTER 8

"Devotis oracionibus plusquam gladiis": Rituals and Sacralization of Warfare in the Teutonic Order's Prussian Lands

Gregory Leighton

When the faithful Maccabees advanced to their wars against the multitudes of infidels, it is read that they conquered many of them with divine prayers, in addition to conquering many of them with their swords, for victory is not to be found in our strength, but in fact it is from God who does not desert those who trust in Him.[1]

⁂

The above quote comes from a formulary originally housed in the Staats- und Universitätsbibliothek Königsberg (Pol. Królewiec, Rus. Kaliningrad), 101.[2] Nestled within a collection of texts attributed to Arnold of Zwrócona

---

1 *Das Formelbuch des Domherrn Arnold von Protzan*, ed. Wilhelm Wattenbach, Codex diplomaticus Silesiae 5 (Breslau: Max, 1862), 307: "Cum fideles Machabei contra turbam infidelium ad bella procederent, plerumque legitur eos vicisse devotis oracionibus plusquam gladijs, cum in virtutibus nostris non sit victoria, sed a deo qui sperantes in se non deserit." A version of Arnold's formulary is also kept in Gdańsk Library of the Polish Academy of Sciences, Mar. F 244, fols. 91–184, see Otto Günther, *Katalog der Handschriften der Danziger Stadtbibliothek*, pt. 5: *Die Handschriften der Kirchenbibliothek von St. Marien in Danzig* (Danzig: Kafemann, 1921), 273–75, though this version does not contain the quoted introductory passage. For the history of the Staats- und Universitätsbibliothek Königsberg, see Kurt Forstreuter, *Das Preußisches Staatsarchiv in Königsberg. Ein geschichtlicher Rückblick mit einer Übersicht über seine Bestände*, Veröffentlichungen der Niedersächsischen Archivverwaltung 3 (Göttingen: Vandenhoek & Ruprecht, 1955), 11–24.
2 Emil Julius Hugo Steffenhagen, *Catalogus codicum manuscriptorum bibliothecae Regiae et Universitatis Regimontiae*, vol. 1 (Königsberg: Schubert & Seidel, 1861), 44–45. This formulary was previously kept in Tapiau (Rus. Gvardeysk), the precursor to the Order's archives in Königsberg. See Eckhard Grunewald, "Das Register der Ordensliberei Tapiau aus den Jahren 1541–1543. Eine Quelle zur Frühgeschichte der ehem. Staats- und Universitätsbibliothek Königsberg," in *Berichte und Forschungen. Jahrbuch des Bundesinstituts für Ostdeutsche*

(Ger. Protzan),[3] a churchman from Wrocław (Ger. Breslau), the formulary is a copy of the original and dated to the turn of the fifteenth century.[4] The passage's subject concerns an expedition of crusaders and Teutonic Knights against the Lithuanians and a request that prayers be said for them. These campaigns, the *Reisen*, were aimed at converting the Lithuanians from paganism to Christianity and lasted well into the fifteenth century.[5]

The prayer request above might be connected to the campaign led in the winter of 1381 by Wigand of Baldersheim, commander of Ragnit castle (Lith. Ragainė, Rus. Neman).[6] According to Wigand of Marburg (fl. 1394), a herald in the service of the Order and author of the *Cronica nova Prutenica*, the commander's army included crusaders (*peregrini*).[7] The army departed from Ragnit and entered the lands of Pastów, raiding and plundering a series of villages, returning with spoils and captives.[8] In any case, the brief quotation highlights the powerful relationship of religious rituals to martial success in the southern Baltic zone. This was more than allegorical, though. Wigand, memorializing Winrich of Kniprode, grand master of the Teutonic Order, pointed out how he decreed an increase in prayers, votive masses, and solemn masses for the safety of those on campaigns "in the praise of God and the Virgin Mary against the pagans."[9]

Kultur und Geschichte, vol. 1, ed. Eckhard Grunewald (Munich: Oldenbourg, 1993), 55–92, at 66 for the formulary.

3   Steffenhagen, "Zu dem Thorner Formelbuche und dem Formelbuche Arnold's von Protzan," *Altpreußische Monatsschrift* 8 (1871): 531–34 at 533–34.
4   *Das Formelbuch des Domherrn Arnold von Protzan*, ix–x.
5   For the *Reisen*, see below, n. 7.
6   Johannes Voigt, *Namen-Codex der Deutsch-Ordens Beamten, Hochmeister, Landmeister, Großgebietiger, Komthure, Vögte, Pfleger, Hochmeister-Kompane, Kreuzfahrer und Söldner-Hauptleute in Preussen* (Königsberg: Bornträger, 1843), 46. See Wigand von Marburg, *Nowa kronika Pruska*, ed. Sławomir Zonenberg and Krzysztof Kwiatkowski (Toruń: Towarzystwo Naukowe w Toruniu, 2017), 444, 446 (Wigand, *Cron. Prut.*).
7   Wigand, *Cron. Prut.*, 444. For crusaders in Prussia ca. 1380–1381, see Werner Paravicini, *Die Preußenreisen des europäischen Adels*, Beihefte der Francia 17.1–2, 2 vols. (Sigmaringen: Thorbecke, 1989–1995), 1:186, 201n109, 239, 304. 1380–81 appears to have been a winter in which only a few noblemen came to Prussia, although there were crusaders. See *Franciscani Thorunensis Annales Prussici (941–1410)*, ed. Ernst Strehlke, SrP 3 (Leipzig: Hirzel, 1866), 57–316 at 113: "Anno 1380 non fuit reisa propter defectum nivis et glaciei ... Fuerunt in terra valentes milites, sed pauci barones." For the meaning of *peregrini*, see also Carsten Selch Jensen's chapter in this collection (vol. 1, chap. 7).
8   Wigand, *Cron. Prut.*, 446. For the location, see n. 1998.
9   Ibid., 482: "Quotiens indicta fuerat aliqua reysa in laudem Dei et virginis Marie contra paganos, tociens multiplicate sunt oraciones, staciones, missarum solempnia, signanter de sancta Trinitate, de omnibus sanctis et de beata Virgine in salutem transeuncium ad agones et bella etc." The use of *staciones* likely refers to processions. However, the recent edition of the

In any case, the small passage magnifies the power of religious rites in times of war on the southern Baltic frontier by reinforcing the power of prayer and its relationship to martial success. It cites the Maccabees and other figures from the Old Testament, proceeding to then reference Exodus 17:11, a verse with a lengthy history of use to sacralize conflicts before and at the time of the crusades, emphasizing the role of prayer in times of war as a means for obtaining salvation and divine aid.[10] In Exodus 17:11, Moses oversaw the battle of the Israelites against the Amalekites at Rephidim.[11] By keeping his arms raised to the Lord and praying for victory, the Israelites gained a foothold in the battle. As soon as he lowered his arms, the tides reversed. Therefore, Hur and Aron helped him to keep his arms to the sky, and the Israelites managed to conquer Amalek.[12] Our text reminds the reader that, just as Moses prayed for victory, so should the Christian people of Prussia pray for the "faithful knights of Christ" (*Milites nostri Christi fideles*) to achieve victory and return safely.[13] Thus, the people in the local parish churches, cathedrals, and monasteries in Prussia were as much a part of the war effort as the knights on the battlefield. In praying, they took on the roles of Aaron and Hur, supporting the soldiers with prayers and specific rituals to ensure their victory in war. The performance of a religious ritual on earth was directly related to victory coming from heaven, placing the temporal conflict in which the crusaders and knights in the Order found themselves within a sacred history.[14]

Taking this example as a point of departure, this chapter will begin with a consideration of existing scholarship on religious rituals in times of war in the southern Baltic at the time of the crusades. From here, it will discuss the evidence of letters, papal permissions, liturgical texts, reports of campaigns

---

chronicle by Sławomir Zonenberg and Krzysztof Kwiatkowski suggests that this refers to the votive masses, not processions. See ibid., 483n2242.

10 Radosław Kotecki, "With the Sword of Prayer, or How the Medieval Bishop Should Fight," *QMAN* 21 (2016): 341–69 at 346–49. Also see M. Cecilia Gaposchkin, *Invisible Weapons: Liturgy and the Making of Crusade Ideology* (Ithaca NY and London: Cornell University Press, 2016), 41–43. The use can be traced to the eighth century. See Michael McCormick, *Eternal Victory: Triumphal Rulership in Late Antiquity, Byzantium and the Early Medieval West* (Cambridge: Cambridge University Press, 1986), 344–45.

11 Kotecki, "With the Sword," 346–47.

12 *Das Formelbuch des Domherrn Arnold von Protzan*, 307: "Scimus enim quod pugnantibus filijs Israel Moyses deum elevatis in altum manibus exoravit pro victoria populi consequenda."

13 Ibid.: "Similiter faciamus et nos, preces ad dominum fundentes humiles, ut Milites nostri Christi fideles pro laude dei nostraque salute cum victoria revertantur."

14 The relationship here is between history and "sacred history" (*Heilsgeschichte*). See John Strange, "Heilsgeschichte und Geschichte. Ein Aspekt der Biblischen Theologie," *Scandinavian Journal of the Old Testament* 3.2 (1989): 100–13.

from the region, and objects associated with them to demonstrate that, in fact, the source material for the region has quite a lot to say about the performance of religious rituals in times of war. The last section discusses some select symbolic manifestations of these rituals and their perceived effects, highlighting the roles religious rituals in times of war played in the Christianization process and the perception of the region by contemporaries.

1   Background

To say that awareness of the northeastern frontier of the medieval world, e.g. the regions of present-day Estonia, Latvia, Lithuania, Poland, and Russia in western academic circles has increased in the past decades would be an understatement.[15] Anti Selart, Kurt Villads Jensen, Torben Kjersgaard Nielsen, Marek Tamm, Linda Kaljundi, Iben Fonnesberg-Schmidt, Carsten Selch Jensen, and Alan V. Murray, to name some of the most prominent scholars, have all produced studies ranging from the "traditional" histories analyzing the politics and military strategy of the crusaders in the Baltic, to broader considerations of the spread of the idea of crusading, be it in written or material culture.[16]

---

15   The key works remain William Urban, *The Baltic Crusade* (Dekalb: Northern Illinois University Press, 1975); idem, *The Prussian Crusade* (Lanham MD: University Press of America, 1982); Eric Christiansen, *The Northern Crusades: The Baltic and the Catholic Frontier (1100–1525)* (London: MacMillan, 1980); William L. Urban, *The Livonian Crusade* (Washington DC: University Press of America, 1989); idem, *The Samogitian Crusade* (Chicago: Lithuanian Research and Studies Center, 1989). For newer studies, see *Crusade and Conversion on the Baltic Frontier, 1150–1500*, ed. Alan V. Murray (Aldershot and Burlington VT: Ashgate, 2001); *The Clash of Cultures on the Medieval Baltic Frontier*, ed. Alan V. Murray (Farnham and Burlington VT: Ashgate, 2009); *The North-Eastern Frontiers of Medieval Europe: The Expansion of Latin Christendom in the Baltic Lands, 1000–1550*, ed. Alan V. Murray, The expansion of Latin Europe, 1000–1500 4 (Farnham and Burlington VT: Ashgate, 2014).

16   *Medieval History Writing and Crusading Ideology*, ed. Janne Malkki, Tuomas M.S. Lehtonen, and Kurt Villads Jensen, Studia Fennica. Historica 9 (Helsinki: Finnish Literary Society, 2005); Kurt Villads Jensen, "Sacralization of the Landscape: Converting Trees and Measuring Land in the Danish Crusades against the Wends," in *The Clash of Cultures*, 141–50; Torben Kjersgaard Nielsen, "Henry of Livonia on Woods and Wilderness," in *Crusading and Chronicle Writing on the Medieval Baltic Frontier: A Companion to the Chronicle of Henry of Livonia*, ed. Marek Tamm, Linda Kaljundi, and Carsten Selch Jensen (Farnham and Burlington VT: Ashgate, 2011), 157–78; Marek Tamm, "A New World into Old Words: The Eastern Baltic Region in the Cultural Geography of Medieval Europe," in *Clash of Cultures*, 11–36; idem, "Inventing Livonia: The Name and Fame of a New Christian Colony on the Medieval Baltic Frontier," *ZfO* 60.2 (2011): 186–209; Linda Kaljundi, "(Re)Performing the Past: Crusading, History Writing, and Rituals in the Chronicle of Henry of Livonia," in *The Performance of Christian and Pagan Storyworlds: Non-Canonical Chapters of the*

However, it is the steady output of scholarship from German and Polish scholars that is most conspicuous feature of the current state of study on the Teutonic Order and the conversion of the northeastern frontiers of Europe to Latin Christianity. Foundational works by Roman Czaja, Jürgen Sarnowsky, Krzysztof Kwiatkowski, and others, deserve special mention here. Their works cover the inner life and spirituality of the brothers of the Teutonic Order and the appeal of the southern Baltic to secular crusaders as a place to carry out service to God and the Latin Church as well as a desire for personal glory and adventure, all constituent elements of what is known by the German term as the *Reisen*.[17] Those campaigns served as a defining element of the Teutonic Order's role in the conversion of the southern Baltic region, reaffirming the status of the Order as a defender of Christianity even after the conversion of Lithuania in 1386, and the baptism in 1387 of Jogaila of Lithuania as Władysław II Jagiełło, king of Poland. In 1397, for example, the Grand Master of the Teutonic Order, Konrad of Jungingen, depicted his order as a defender of the whole of Christendom against paganism in a letter to the Order's procurator in Rome, Johann vom Felde.[18] Johann's letter to the grand master in 1403 also demonstrates the international characteristic of the campaigns, for he reported on

---

History of Nordic Medieval Literature, ed. Lars Boje Mortensen and Tuomas M.S. Lehtonen, Medieval identities 3 (Turnhout: Brepols, 2013), 295–338; Iben Fonnesberg-Schmidt, *The Popes and the Baltic Crusades, 1147–1254*, TNW 26 (Leiden and Boston MA: Brill, 2007). Also see the recent collection of studies *Crusading on the Edge: Ideas and Practices of Crusading in Iberia and the Baltic Region, 1100–1500*, ed. Torben Kjersgaard Nielsen and Iben Fonnesberg-Schmidt, Outremer 4 (Turnhout: Brepols, 2016).

17   Roman Czaja, "Das Selbstverständnis der geistlichen Ritterorden im Mittelalter. Bilanz und Forschungsperspektive," in *Selbstbild and Selbstverständnis der geistlichen Ritterorden*, ed. Roman Czaja and Jürgen Sarnowsky, OM 13 (Toruń: Wydawnictwo Naukowe Uniwersytetu Mikołaja Kopernika, 2005), 7–24; Krzysztof Kwiatkowski, "Die Selbstdarstellung des Deutschen Ordens in der Chronik Wigands von Marburg," in ibid., 127–38; Jürgen Sarnowsky, "Identität und Selbstgefühl der geistlichen Ritterorden," in *Ständische und religiöse Identitäten in Mittelalter und frühen Neuzeit*, ed. Stefan Kwiatkowski and Janusz Małłek (Toruń: Wydawnictwo Naukowe Uniwersytetu Mikołaja Kopernika, 1998), 109–30.

18   The authoritative study on these campaigns remains that of Paravicini's three-volume, *Die Preußenreisen des europäischen Adels*. For the third volume, see *Adlig leben im 14. Jahrhundert. Weshalb sie fuhren. Die Preußenreisen des europäischen Adels*, Vestigia Prussica. Forschungen zur ost- und westpreußischen Landesgeschichte 2 (Göttingen: Vandenhoeck & Ruprecht, 2019). Also see *Codex diplomaticus Prussicus*, ed. Johannes Voigt, 6 vols. (Königsberg: Bornträger, 1838–1861), 5(1857):117 (no. 92). For Johann vom Felde, see *Die Berichte der Generalprokuratoren des Deutschen Ordens an der Kurie*, vol. 1: *Die Geschichte der Generalprokuratoren von den Anfängen bis 1403*, ed. Kurt Forstreuter, Veröffentlichungen der Neidersächsischen Archivverwaltung 12 (Göttingen: Vandenhoeck & Ruprecht, 1961), 146–64.

how he publicized the Order's campaigns to the Italian nobility, in this case, Raimondo del Balzo Orsini.[19]

Truly international phenomena of the fourteenth- and fifteenth-century nobility, attracting warriors from Bohemia, the British Isles, France, Germany, Italy, the Low Countries, and Spain, these campaigns had a transformative effect on the integration within and communication of this region to Latin Europe.[20] On a broad level, the *Reisen* were responsible for the introduction to the southern Baltic zone not only of Latin Christianity (including religious rituals associated with war) to the region, but also chivalric culture.[21] New studies have shed light onto this previously "overlooked" region of Latin Christian world, which in Western scholarship has been rather neglected, with the notable exception of the works of Alan V. Murray, Mary Fischer, Helen J. Nicholson, and Nicholas Morton.[22]

Few works, however, have ventured beyond the major narrative texts (i.e., the chronicles) in order to study the crusades to Prussia and Lithuania during the thirteenth to fifteenth century, specifically the function of religious

---

19 Orsini was made a lay member (*confrater*; *mitbruder*) of the Order following his *Reise* in 1378. See *Berichte*, 378–79 (no. 269), here 378. Also see Paravicini, *Preußenreisen* 1:108, 328; idem, *Preußenreisen* 2:134. For a brief overview of Raimondo, see Hubert Houben, "Raimondo del Balzo Orsini e l'Ordine Teutonico," in *L'Ordine Teutonico tra Mediterraneo a Baltico incontri e scontri tra religioni, poplie e cultura*, Acta Theutonica 5 (Salento: Galatina, 2008), 195–218; Kristjan Toomaspeog, "Orsini del Balzo, Raimondo," *Dizionario Biografico degli Italiani* 79 (2013): bit.ly/3K3x2ea. I am thankful to Dr. Kristjan Toomaspeog (Università del Salento, Lecce) for pointing me to sources for Italian knights on the *Reisen*.

20 Paravicini, *Preußenreisen*, 1:45–142, for origins of crusaders who went to Lithuania in the fourteenth and fifteenth century.

21 Rimvydas Petrauskas, "Knighthood in the Grand Duchy of Lithuania from the Late Fourteenth to the Early Sixteenth Centuries," *Lithuanian Historical Studies* 11 (2006): 36–66 at 39–51 for elements of knighthood and their incorporation within Lithuanian royal culture. Also see Werner Paravicini, "Litauer. Vom heidnischen Gegner zum adligen Standesgenossen," in *Tannenberg—Grunwald—Žalgiris 1410. Krieg und Frieden im späten Mittelalter*, ed. Werner Paravicini, Rimvydas Petrauskas, and Grischa Vercamer, DHIW 26 (Wiesbaden: Harrassowitz, 2012), 253–84 at 265–67.

22 Mary Fischer, "Biblical Heroes and the Uses of Literature: The Teutonic Order in the Late Thirteenth and Early Fourteenth Centuries," in *Crusade and Conversion*, 261–75; eadem "The Books of the Maccabees and the Teutonic Order," *Crusades* 4 (2005): 59–71; Helen J. Nicholson, "Saints Venerated in the Military Orders," in *Selbstbild und Selbstverständnis*, 91–113; Nicholas Morton, "The Defence of the Holy Land and the Memory of the Maccabees," *JMH* 36.3 (2010): 275–93 at 290–91; idem, *The Medieval Military Orders, 1120–1314*, Seminar studies 1 (Abingdon and New York: Routledge, 2013), 80–85. Also see Gregory Leighton, "Did the Teutonic Order Create a Sacred Landscape in Thirteenth-Century Prussia?" *JMH* 44.4 (2018): 457–83; idem, "'Reysa in laudem Dei et virginis gloriose contra paganos': The Experience of Crusading in Prussia during the Thirteenth and Fourteenth Centuries," *ZfO* 69.1 (2020): 1–25.

rituals within them. Perhaps the best example of the potential for such research is the 2012 monograph of Krzysztof Kwiatkowski, *Zakon niemiecki jako "corporatio militaris,"* which presents a thorough analysis of the inner mentality of the Teutonic Order and how its members identified themselves within the framework of religious warfare.[23] Most significant for this chapter is that Kwiatkowski's study considers how conduct in war and military activity shaped the corporate identity of the Order, a theme continued in his 2017 *Wojska zakonu niemieckiego w Prusach 1230–1525*.[24] Paweł Gancarczyk and Anette Löffler have also contributed greatly to the understanding of the roles of ritual and, specifically, religious rituals, in this region of medieval Europe.[25] It is against the backdrop of this body of scholarship that the present chapter considers religious rituals in times of war and the ways in which they were understood, expressed, and communicated by contemporaries.

2   Religious Rites of War and the Teutonic Order in Prussia: Source Overview

The main information concerning rituals of war in the southern Baltic zone comes from the written material produced within and outside of the Teutonic Order, a body of sources that is complex and multi-referential. Its development reflects a historiographic tradition that emerged over centuries, reinforcing the core concepts of the collective identity of the Order as a religious corporation of knights of Christ. These works expressed this to members, supporters, and

---

23   Krzysztof Kwiatkowski, *Zakon niemiecki jako "corporatio militaris,"* pt. 1: *Korporacja i krąg przynależących do niej. Kulturowe i społeczne podstawy działalności militarnej zakonu w Prusach (do początku XV wieku)* (Toruń: Uniwersytet Mikołaja Kopernika, 2012), 22–40.

24   Ibid., 96–104; idem, *Wojska zakonu niemieckiego w Prusach 1230–1525. Korporacja, jej pruskie władztwo, zbrojni, kultura wojny i aktywność militarna* (Toruń: Wydawnictwo Naukowe Uniwersytetu Mikołaja Kopernika, 2017), 49–50. Also see Erich Weise, "Der Heidenkampf des Deutschen Ordens, Erster Teil," *ZfO* 12.1 (1963): 63–80; idem, "Der Heidenkampf des Deutschen Ordens, Zweiter Teil," *ZfO* 13.4 (1964): 401–20; Sarnowsky, "Identität," 114–15; Czaja, "Selbstverständnis," 9–13; Wüst, *Studien zum Selbstverständnis des Deutschen Ordens im im Mittelalter*, QSGD 73 (Weimar: VDG, 2013), 33–35, for a description of the role of this in the induction rituals of the Order.

25   Paweł Gancarczyk, "The Musical Culture of the Teutonic Order in Prussia Reflected in the 'Marienburger Tresslerbuch' (1399–1409)," in *The Musical Heritage of the Jagiellonian Era*, ed. Paweł Gancarczyk and Agnieszka Leszczyńska (Warsaw: Institute of Art at the Polish Academy of Sciences, 2012), 191–200 at 198–99; Anette Löffler, "Die Rolle der Liturgie im Ordenskonvent. Norm und Wirklichkeit," in *Das Leben im Ordenshaus. Vorträge der Tagung der Internationalen Historischen Kommission zur Erforschung des Deutschen Ordens in Tallinn 2014*, ed. Juhan Kreem, QSGD 81 (Weimar: VDG, 2019), 1–21.

critics of the Order.[26] Most, if not all, were produced by priests in the Order or, as in the case of Wigand of Marburg, by close affiliates.[27] They document the history of the Teutonic Knights from its origins in the Holy Land in the twelfth century, through its rise in Prussia during the thirteenth century, its campaigns against the Lithuanians, and to its decline in the fifteenth century following the Battle of Grunwald/Tannenberg on 15 July 1410.[28]

Chronicles documenting the history of the Teutonic Order's Prussian territory include Peter of Dusburg's *Chronicon terre Prussie* (ca. 1326),[29] Nicolaus of Jeroschin's *Di Kronike von Pruzinlant* (ca. 1341),[30] and Wigand of Marburg's chronicle (mentioned above).[31] The chronicle of Johannes of Posilge, a Pomesanian church official, recorded the history of Prussia until 1416,[32] and a series

---

26 Krzysztof Kwiatkowski, "Die 'Eroberung Preußens' durch den Deutschen Orden—ihr Bild unf ihre Wahrnehmung in der Literatur des Deutschen Ordens im 14. Jahrhundert," in *Kryziaus karu epocha Baltijos regiono tautu istorineje samoeje*, ed. Rita Regina Trimoniene and Robertas Jurgaitis (Siauliai: Delta, 2007), 131–69; Marcus Wüst, *Studien*, 48–140. This was also true for the Order's houses outside Livonia and Prussia, thus demonstrating how history writing was a means of communicating memory, commemoration, and unity within the Order's houses, as demonstrated in the work of Gustavs Strenga, "Remembering the Common Past: Livonia as a 'lieu de mémoire' of the Teutonic Order in the Empire," in *Livland—Eine Region am Ende der Welt? Forschungen zum Verhältnis zwischen Zentrum und Peripherie im späten Mittelalter*, ed. Anti Selart and Matthias Thumser, QSBG 27 (Cologne, Weimar, and Vienna: Böhlau, 2017), 347–71, esp. 361–66.

27 *Contra* Christiansen, *Northern Crusades*, 166, which calls Wigand "the Order's own annalist." See Sławomir Zonenberg, "Wstęp źródłoznawczy i historyczny," in Wigand, *Cron. Prut.*, 23–28 at 27–28 for Wigand's affiliation to the Teutonic Order. Also see Marcus Wüst, *Studien*, 105–6, for a summary of Wigand's origins and status.

28 Werner Paravicini, "Vom Kreuzzug zum Soldzug. Die Schlacht bei Tannenberg und das Ende der Preußenfahrten des europäischen Adels," in *"Conflictus magnus apud Grunwald" 1410. Między historią a tradycją*, ed. Krzysztof Ożóg and Janusz Trupinda (Malbork: Muzeum Zamkowe, 2013), 119–26.

29 "Chronicon terre Prussie" von Peter von Dusburg, ed. Max Töppen, SrP 1 (Leipzig: Hirzel, 1861), 3–219 (hereafter Dusburg, *Chron. Pr.*).

30 Nicolaus of Jeroschin, *Di Kronike von Pruzinlant*, ed. Ernst Strehlke, SrP 1, 303–624 (hereafter Jeroschin, *Di Kronike*). For the English translation, see *The Chronicle of Prussia: A History of the Teutonic Knights in Prussia, 1190–1331*, ed. and trans. Mary Fischer, CTT 20 (Farnham and Burlington VT: Ashgate, 2010).

31 Wigand, *Cron. Prut.*, 39. Also see Jarosław Wenta, *Studien über die Ordensgeschichtsschreibung am Beispiel Preußens*, Studia hisotriographica 2 (Toruń: Wydawnictwo Naukowe Uniwersytetu Mikołaja Kopernika, 2003), 160; Ralf G. Päsler, *Deutschsprachige Sachliteratur im Preußenland bis 1500. Untersuchungen zu ihrer Überlieferung*, Aus Archiven, Bibliotheken und Museen Mittel- und Osteuropas 2 (Cologne: Böhlau, 2003), 274; Zonenberg, "Wstęp," 23–28.

32 *Johannes von Posilge, Officials von Pomesanien, Chronik des Landes Preussen (von 1360 an, fortgesetzt bis 1419)*, ed. Ernst Strehlke, SrP 3 (Leipzig: Hirzel, 1866), 79–338.

of other texts are associated with the area of Sambia are also noteworthy.[33] The *ältere Hochmeisterchronik*, a continuation of Peter of Dusburg and Nicolaus of Jeroschin's chronicles of Prussia, written around 1440 by an unknown member of the Teutonic Order, demonstrates the development of the Order's historiographical tradition.[34]

The Teutonic Order thus played a foundational role in the perception, representation, and reception of Prussia's history. However, that history itself was framed within a deeper construction, namely the origins of the Teutonic Order and the status of its members as "knights of God" (*godes rittere*) and their status as the heirs of the Abraham, David, Joshua, and the Maccabees. The roots for those developments go back to the *Prologue* to the Order's Rule (ca. 1264), which emphasizes the Order's place in what may be regarded as "divine history." The *Prologue* is thus the beginning of a historiography, emphasizing the Order's biblical roots and the role of God in determining the course of its history.[35] This was expressed in the historical texts of the other military orders as well.[36] As this paper demonstrates, religious rituals and their symbolic meanings play a significant role in this historical representation of the Order.

Unique among the three international military orders, the Teutonic Order produced a significant body of spiritual literature in addition to the historical texts just mentioned.[37] This includes translations of the Bible and specific books from the *Apocrypha* in the Middle High German vernacular—Judith, Esther, Maccabees, and Job—in addition to the Book of Revelation.[38] As

---

33 *Canonici Sambiensis epitome gestorum Prussie*, ed. Max Töppen, SrP 1, 272–90. For a recent examination of this text, see Sławomir Zonenberg, "Kto był autorem 'Epitome gestorum Prussie'?" *ZH* 74.4 (2013): 85–102.

34 *Die ältere Hochmeisterchronik*, ed. Max Töppen, SrP 3, 540–637. For context, see Jochen Hermann Vennebusch, "Zentral Facetten der Spiritualität des Deutschen Orden sim Spiegel der 'älteren Hochmeisterchronik,'" *OM* 18 (2013): 243–318 at 254–59 for the liturgical characteristics of the text. Also see Wüst, *Studien*, 118–21.

35 Udo Arnold, "Die Anfänge der Ordensgeschichtsschreibung," in *Neue Studien zur Literatur im Deutschen Orden*, ed. Bernhart Jähnig and Arno Mentzel-Reuters, Zeitschrift für deutsches Altertum und deutsche Literatur. Beiheifte 19 (Berlin: LIT, 2014), 178–95. Also see Wüst, *Studien*, 48–49.

36 Helen J. Nicholson, "Memory and the Military Orders," in *Entre Deus e o Rei. O Mundo das Ordens Militares I: Arquivos e Memória*, ed. Isabel Cristina Gerreira Fernandes, Coleção ordens militares 8 (Palmela: Município de Palmela-GesOS, 2018), 17–28 at 20–25.

37 Arno Mentzel-Reuters, "'Deutschordensliteratur' im literarischen Kontext," in *Mittelalterliche Kultur und Literatur im Deutschordensstaat in Preussen. Leben und Nachleben*, ed. Jarosław Wenta, Sieglinde Hoffmann, and Gisela Vollmann-Profe, SBS 1 (Toruń: Uniwersytet Mikołaja Kopernika, 2008), 356–68.

38 Ralf G. Päsler, *Sachliteratur*, 282–84; Kwiatkowski, "Selbstdarstellung," 128–32; Zonenberg, "Wstęp," 38.

Marcus Wüst has demonstrated, those works were designed not for external supporters of the Order, as with Peter of Dusburg's Latin chronicle, which appears to have been aimed at supporters in the papal court at Avignon or, as suggested by Wenta, as a preaching manual for clergy in Prussia.[39] Instead, the translations were meant as edifying materials for the brethren, reinforcing concepts of fighting on behalf of God, and dying in his service.[40] This spiritual literature was likely meant to be read communally at meal times, as a form of the *Tischlesung* prescribed by the Order's *Rule*.[41]

Such a body of sources, historical and literary, reinforced the biblical lineage outlined in the *Prologue* to the Order's monastic rule. It, therefore, provides an important context necessary to study religious rites of war in the Order's southern Baltic territories, the role of these religious rituals in sacralizing warfare, and the communication of this understanding to the Order's supporters and inhabitants of the region. The institution of the Teutonic Order, according to the *Prologue*, finds its roots in Genesis 14:18–20, when Abraham received the blessing of Melchizedek after he had rescued Lot from Sodom.[42] In the context of this paper, the ritual of the blessing is connected not only to the combat endured by Abraham, but also with the wars that the Order carried out in the defense of *Christianitas*.[43] This legacy survived in various contexts, not only in

---

39   Jarosław Wenta, "Bemerkungen über die Funktion eines mittelalterlichen historiographischen Textes. Die Chronik des Peter von Dusburg," in *"De litteris, manuscriptis, inscriptionibus ..." Festschrift zum 65. Geburtstag von Walter Koch*, ed. Theo Kölzer et al. (Cologne, Weimar, and Vienna: Böhlau, 2007), 675–86 at 675–6; Marcus Wüst, "Zu Entstehung und Rezeption der 'Chronik des Preussenlandes' Peters von Dusburg," in *Neue Studien*, 197–211 at 200–2.

40   Wüst, *Studien*, 141–42; Jarosław Wenta, "Kazanie i historyczne egzemplum w późnośredniowiecznym Chełmnie," in *"Ecclesia et civitas." Kościół i życie religijne w mieście średniowiecznym*, ed. Halina Manikowska and Hanna Zaremska (Warsaw: Instytut Historii Polskiej Akademii Nauk, 2002), 473–82 at 478–79, for the analysis of *exempla* in the chronicle.

41   *Die Statuten des Deutschen Ordens nach den ältesten Handschriften*, chap. 13, ed. Max Perlbach (Halle: Niemeyer, 1890), 41. For debates on communal reading, see Karl Helm and Walther Ziesemer, *Die Literatur des Deutschen Ritter-Ordens*, Gießener Beiträge zur deutschen Philologie 94 (Gießen: Schmitz, 1951), 28–29; Päsler, *Sachliteratur*, 276; Arno Mentzel-Reuters, *"Arma Spiritualia." Bibliotheken, Bücher und Bildung im Deutschen Orden*, Beiträge zum Buch- und Bibliothekswesen 47 (Wiesbaden: Harrassowitz, 2003), 80–82. For arguments against *Tischlesungen*, see Wenta, *Studien*, 155–60.

42   Genesis 14:18–20. For the connection to Abraham, see *Die Statuten*, 23 (Prologue, 2): "An der widerverte begente ime Melchisidech mit sînem prîsante unde *dô offente der heilige geist, daz der, der die hôhesten stat in der ecclesien hat, wie liep er sule haben rittere ... Dô hûb sich ritterschaft von den geloubegen wider die ungeloubegen*." My italics.

43   *The Oxford Bible Commentary*, ed. John Barton and John Muddiman (Oxford and New York: Oxford University Press, 2001), 50.

wars against the Prussians, but also against the Kingdom of Poland, Lithuania, Turks, Walachaians, Tatars, and Rusians in which the Teutonic Order was depicted as a bulwark of Christianity (*antemurale Christianitatis*), or a shield of Christianity (*schild der cristenheit*).[44]

The *Prologue* then lists other Old Testament warriors whose battles were divinely approved and who performed the appropriate rituals in times of combat before securing victory. Moses receiving the Ark of the Covenant (Exodus 25), Joshua (Joshua 3), David, and the Maccabees (1 & 2 Maccabees) all were tied to the profession of the Order: it was from those figures that the "knighthood" (*ritterschaft*) of the Teutonic Knights originated, and was characterized as a new form of war against the unbelievers.[45] For the present chapter, the symbolic nature of religious rituals in these examples also would have been understood as in relation to their martial success. Thus, the importance of religious rites before, during, and after combat come to the forefront of the group identity and mission of the Teutonic Order.

The sources also allow for the consideration of the spaces in which religious rituals of war took place. As demonstrated later in this chapter, this allows us to comment on their perceived effects. Already in papal permissions issued in 1344, 1360, and 1366, it was stipulated that masses on campaign be held in the appropriate places and with the appropriate priests.[46] This indicates specific demarcated spaces, namely the *capelle* and *reisehuwte*, portable tents that the armies would bring with them on campaign and within which mass would be held. Tents of course held a practical function, namely to protect army camps and serve as shelter, as evidenced in the chronicle of Nicolaus of Jeroschin and Wigand of Marburg's chronicle.[47] Their religious purposes in Prussia appear already in the fourteenth century, namely in the context of the Teutonic

---

44 Paul Srodecki, "'Schilt der Cristenheite' i 'Scutum christianitatis'—spory polsko-krzyżackie a retoryka przedmurza / tarczy na początku XV wieku," in *Unia w Horodle na tle stosunków polsko-litewskich. Od Krewa do Zaręczenia wzajmnego Oboga Narodów*, ed. Sławomir Górzyński (Warsaw: DiG, 2015), 147–63 at 149–52. Also see *Tabulae Ordinis Theutonici*, ed. Ernst Strehlke (Berlin: Weidmann, 1869), 204–8 (no. 213).

45 *Die Statuten*, 24–25 (Prologue, 3).

46 *Codex diplomaticus Prussicus*, 3 (Königsberg: Bornträger, 1848):71–72 (no. 48), 126–27 (no. 96); *Avignonische Quellen zur Geschichte des Ordensland (1342–1366)*, ed. Arthur Motzki, Beilage zum Jahresbericht des Königlichen Gymnasiums zu Braunsberg, 1914 3 (Braunsberg Ostpr.: Heynes, 1914), 43 (no. 84).

47 Jeroschin, *Di Kronike*, 381 (ll. 6831–37), 391 (ll. 7720–25), 396 (ll. 8104–7), 398 (ll. 8326–31), 406 (ll. 8957–63), 431 (ll. 11,076–81), 463 (ll. 13,845–49), 474 (ll. 14,817–23); Wigand, *Cron. Prut.*, 160, 266, 326, 482, 580.

Order's attack of Tczew (Germ. Dirschau) in 1308.[48] According to a witness at the papal trial held in Warsaw and Uniejów in 1339, the Piast duke, Kazimierz of Gniewkowo, then governor of Tczew on behalf of Władyslaw the Elbow (Łokietek), came to the besieger, grand master Siegfried of Feuchtwangen, whom he found attending mass. Indeed, the source does not inform the mass was held in a tent, but there are grounds for thinking so, and Polish chronicler, Jan Długosz, referring to these very events, says that when Casimir arrived at the Teutonic camp, the master invited him to his tent (*tabernaculum magistri*) where he had just finished hearing a mass.[49] Nicolaus of Jeroschin also pointed to the symbolic roles of tents in his lament for the Holy Land: "your tents have been invaded, and your tabernacle destroyed," symbolizing the destruction of the Holy Land.[50] Thus, the tent was a portable *sacrum* in which pre-battle rituals could be observed.

Tents also emerge in other evidence for the period. In 1395, Konrad of Jungingen, as a sign of his thanks to Phillip the Bold, duke of Burgundy, sent a war tent, which would also have been used to observe mass on campaign.[51] The material concerning tents and their link to worship on campaign emerges throughout the fifteenth century with more regularity. In 1418, for example, the provost of Frauenburg Cathedral (Pol. Frombork) requested a tent from the grand master of the Order, Michael Küchmeister of Sternberg, along with a warning of impending war with Poland and Lithuania.[52] The link between these objects and religious rituals of war can also be seen in a letter from 1427 in the context of the wars against the Hussites, in which Nickil, a knight from

---

48 Jürgen Sarnowsky, *Der Deutsche Orden*, Wissen 24 (Munich: Beck, 2011), 45–46, for context. Also see Radosław Kotecki, "The Desecration of Holy Places According to Witnesses' Testimonies in the Polish-Teutonic Order Trials of the 14th Century," in *Arguments and Counter-Arguments: The Political Thought of the 14th–15th Centuries during the Polish-Teutonic Order Trials and Disputes*, ed. Wiesław Sieradzan (Toruń: Wydawnictwo Naukowe Uniwersytetu Mikołaja Kopernika, 2012), 69–111, esp. 73–76.

49 The witness was Anthony, a knight from Cuiavia and *familiarius* to Duke Casimir, also present in Tczew during the Teutonic invasion of Pomerania. See *Lites ac res gestae inter Polonos ordinemque Cruciferorum*, vol. 1, ed. Ignacy Zakrzewski (Poznań: Biblioteka Kórnicka, 1890), 296; *Ioannis Dlugossii Annales seu cronicae incliti regni Poloniae*, bk. 9, ed. Jan Dąbrowski (Warsaw: Państwowe Wydawnictwo Naukowe, 1978), 58.

50 Jeroschin, *Di Kronike*, 557 (l. 21,983), quoting Dusburg, *Chron. Pr.*, p. 208: "Factus est dominus inimicus ... dissipavit quasi ortum tentorium tuum, demolitus est tabernaculum tuum."

51 *Codex diplomaticus Prussicus*, 6 (Königsberg: Bornträger, 1861):14 (no. 15). Giving of luxurious tented chapels as a diplomatic gift was a widely practiced custom in the later Middle Ages.

52 Berlin, GStA PK, XX. HA, Ordensbriefarchiv (OBA), no. 2692.

Reibnitz in Germany, requested a tent, in addition to hats and gloves, for the performance of religious services.[53]

One can also consider how tents were used to demarcate a sacred space within the landscape for observing rites before war. This space was made sacred through the performance of the mass (and the observance of the liturgy by the participants) and the presence of specific objects, like altars and reliquaries. A well-known example is the portable reliquary of Tilo of Lorich, komtur of Elbing (Pol. Elbląg), produced sometime around 1388 (figs. 8.1a–b).[54] The metallic case contains a depiction of the key elements of the Teutonic Order's group identity in Prussia, showing Tilo the patron kneeling in reverence before the patroness of the Teutonic Knights, the Virgin Mary, dressed as a knight and his robe depicting the Order's cross.[55] The inventory books of the Teutonic Order's convents in addition to the book of the Order's treasurer (*Treßlerbuch*) provide descriptions of so-called *reisegeret*: objects brought on campaign for observing mass. These objects reflect the consistent presence of objects to be used in celebrating mass on the move throughout the later fourteenth and fifteenth century and particularly in times of war.

In 1399, a portable altar for the Grand Master was commissioned in Marienburg (Pol. Malbork).[56] In 1406, the commander of Ragnit, Friedrich of Zoller, commissioned the painter, Peter, to decorate a portable altar for his use.[57] Ragnit was one of the main points of departure for campaigns against the Lithuanians and, in the fifteenth century, the Samogitians, which would situate the commission of such a work within the context of the Order's martial activities.[58] As shown by Christofer Herrmann, the castle's appearance

---

53 Ibid., no. 4839.
54 Now housed in Warsaw, Muzeum Wojska Polskiego.
55 For context, see Michał Woźniak, "Dyptyk relikwiarzowy elbląskiego komtura domowego Thiele von Loricha," in *"Praeterita posteritati." Studia z historii sztuki i kultury ofiarowane Maciejowi Kilarskiemu*, ed. Mariusz Mierzwiński (Malbork: Muzeum Zamkowe, 2001), 481–500 at 484–87. Also see Udo Arnold, "Maria als Patronin des Deutschen Ordens im Mittelalter," in *"Terra Sanctae Mariae." Mittelalterliche Bildwerke der Marienverehrung im Deutschordensland Preußen*, ed. Gerhard Eimer et al., Kunsthistorische Arbeiten der Kulturstiftung der deutschen Vertriebenen 7 (Bonn: Kulturstiftung der deutschen Vertriebenen, 2009), 29–57 at 46–48.
56 *Das Marienburger Treßlerbuch der Jahre 1399–1409*, ed. Erich Joachim (Königsberg: Thomas & Oppermann, 1896), 15: "item 4 m. 7 sc. und 1 schilling vor eyne veniebank mit den pulten in des meisters capellen *und vor eynen reysealtar*." My italics.
57 Ibid., 402: "item 4 ½ m. Peter moler vor des groskumpthurs gemach zu molen und *vor eynen reysalter zu molen*." My italics.
58 Paravicini, *Preußenreisen*, 2:88–93; Kwiatkowski, "Wstęp historycznomilitarny," in Wigand, *Cron. Prut.*, 45–102 at 70 [add to bibliography], identifies the frequency with which

FIGURES 8.1A–B   Reliquary of Tilo of Lorich, probably taken as booty by the Polish king Władysław Jagiełło after the Battle of Grunwald/Tannenberg (1410) and given to Gniezno Cathedral
REPRODUCED WITH KIND PERMISSION OF MUZEUM WOJSKA POLSKIEGO, WARSAW, POLAND

(significantly altered at the turn of the fifteenth century) was aimed at the guests and recruiting continued support in the fifteenth century. Guillibert de Lannoy, one of the last "guests" to participate on the *Reisen*, commented on the castle's appearance: "[it] is a large castle with a small village fortified with wood, belonging to the brothers of the Teutonic Order, called Ragnit, and is both a convent and a commandery."[59] Though already heavily damaged by the eighteenth century, the visual program depicting the coats of arms of various officials of the Order (e.g., the marshal and grand master) would have also reinforced the messages of holy war communicated in the Order's written canon.[60] This places the portable altar commissioned there within a broader context of visual communication of the Order to its supporters, similar to the shrines throughout the *Ordensland* associated with the *Reisen*.[61]

Recently, Gregory Leighton has commented on the links between visual culture of the period (specifically, the church at Juditten [Rus. Mendeleevo]) and campaigns into Samogitia on portable altars from the Teutonic Order's Prussian lands.[62] A typical model of these objects depicts the Virgin Mary with

---

commanders of Ragnit, in addition to those of Königsberg, Brandenburg (Ushakovo, Kalinigrad oblast), and Balga (Veseloe, Kaliningrad oblast) appear throughout Wigand of Marburg's chronicle.

59   "Aus den voyaiges Guillibert de Lannoy, 1412," ed. Ernst Strehlke, SrP 3: 449: "Sy arryva a *ung gros chastel et petite ville fermee de bois, appartenant aux seigneurs de l'orde de Prusse, nomme Ranghenyt, qui est ung convent et commanderie*." My italics. Also see Loïc Chollet, *Les Sarrasins du Nord. Une histoire de la croisade Balte par la littérature (XII*^{e}*–XV*^{e} *siècle)* (Neuchâtel: Éditions Alphil and Presses Universitaires Suisses, 2019), 197–99.

60   Hans-Georg Tautorat, "Zur Baugeschichte des Ordenshauses Ragnit (1397–1409)," *Jahrbuch der Albertus-Universität zu Königsberg* 22 (1972): 423–37 at 435; Christofer Herrmann, *Mittelalterliche Architektur im Preußenland. Untersuchungen zur Kunstlandschaft und -geographie*, Studien zur internationalen Architektur- und Kulturgeschichte 56 (Petersberg: Imhof, 2007), 668; idem, "Ragnit, Neidenburg, Bütow—die letzten drei Deutschordensburgen in Preußen," in *Die Burg im 15. Jahrhundert. Kolloquium des Wissenschaftlichen Beirats der Deutschen Burgenvereinigung, Kronberg 2009*, ed. Hartmut Hofrichter and Joachim Zeune, Veröffentlichungen der Deutschen Burgenvereinigung 12 (Braubach: Braubacher Dr. Burgenvereinigung, 2011), 155–64 at 156–58.

61   Paravicini, *Preußenreisen*, 1:305; idem, "Verlorene Denkmäler europäischer Ritterschaft. Die heraldischen Malereien des 14. Jahrhunderts im Dom zu Königsberg," in *Kunst und Geschichte im Ostseeraum. Tagungen 1988 und 1989*, ed. Erich Böckler, Homburger Gespräche 12 (Kiel: Martin-Carl-Adolf-Böckler-Stiftung, 1990), 75–76; Janusz Trupinda, "Zespól heraldyczny z herbem von Jungingen w systemie dekoracji malarskiej piętra reprezentacyjnego Pałacu Wielkich Mistrzów w Malborku," in *Krzyżacy—szpitalnicy—kondotierzy*, ed. Błażej Śliwiński, Studia z dziejów średniowiecza 12 (Malbork: Muzeum Zamkowe, 2006), 397–423 at 401–2.

62   Gregory Leighton, "Crusading and Holy War in the Teutonic Order's Struggle for Žemaitija: Written and Visual Perspectives," *Acta Historica Universitatis Klaipedensis* 41 (2020): 25–52 at 38–46.

the Christ child on the left knee, and when opened, the interior depicts a crucified Christ along with a series of painted figures, including knights of the Order. This is the so-called *Schutzmantelmadonna*, a type of image that flourished in Prussia at the end of the fourteenth century with a highly devotional character. As shown above, the Marian emphasis of votive Masses requested in times of war in Prussia was important in expressing collective identities of the Teutonic Order, in addition to securing the prayers of the local population.[63] Given the patronage and commission of these objects by members of the Teutonic Order, the significance of observing these masses (and carrying out the appropriate rituals) carries over into the realm of visual culture. The function of at least some of these objects as portable altars serves to link, therefore, religious rituals, warfare, and the communication of both through the medium of visual culture.[64]

While it is clear that the Teutonic Order maintained the objects necessary for performing rituals in times of war, it is also important to contextualize their functions and perceived effects. As in other regions of the medieval world, the celebration of masses and the performance of chants and processions were a fundamental component to the experience of war in Prussia. From the thirteenth to the fifteenth century, soldiers would have heard the *missa contra paganos* and participated in its observance in times of war. Echoes of it can be seen in Peter of Dusburg's *Chronicon terre Prussie*. In his recollection of the privileges bestowed upon the Order by Pope Gregory IX, Peter cites the 1 Maccabees 2:62, the last words of Matathias: "And so observe, from generation to generation, that none of those who put their trust in Him will lack strength."[65] However, these echoes seem coincidental and do not appear within the context of warfare.

---

63 Corine Schleif, "Die Schreinmadonna im Diözesanmuseum zu Limburg. Ein verfemtes Bildwerk des Mittelalters," *Jahrbuch des Vereins für Nassauische Altertumskunde und Geschichtsforschung* 95 (1985): 39–54 at 45–46; Gudrun Radler, "Der Beitrag des Deutschordenslandes zur Entwicklung der Schreinmadonna (1390–1420)," in *Sztuka w kręgu zakonu krzyżackiego w Prusach i Inflantach*, ed. Michał Woźniak, Studia Borussica-Baltica Torunensia Historiae Artium 2 (Toruń: Wydawnictwo Naukowe Uniwersytetu Mikołaja Kopernika, 1995), 241–74 at 259–74; idem, "Die Schreinmadonnen des Deutschordenslandes Preußen," in *"Terra Sanctae Mariae,"* 199–212.

64 Radler, "Die Schreinmadonnen," 202, points out that some of these objects were quite large, and intended for use in church ceremonies, though others (such as that in the Musée de Cluny, Paris, and in the Diocesan Museum in Pelplin) were smaller, at less than 50cm in height.

65 Dusburg, *Chron. Pr.*, 2.6, p. 38. This appears to cite 1 Maccabees 2:62, which has echoes of the *Graduale* of the *missa contra paganos*: "sciant gentes." Also see 3.310, p. 176, which parallels the *Tractus*: "Nequando dicant Gentes: Ubi est Deus eorum?"

A reference to the *contra paganos* mass appears in the *ältere Hochmeisterchronik*. In describing the Battle of Rudau (Lith. Rūdava, Pol. Rudawa) (17 February 1370) between the Teutonic Knights and the Lithuanians, in which the marshal of the Order, Hennig Schindekopf, was killed. The text states that the battle took place "on the Sunday when one chants *Exsurge*."[66] It appears that the army observed the *missa contra paganos*, whose *Introitus* is *Exsurge, quare obdormis*, in the context of this fifteenth-century chronicle. However, to show how elusive main narrative texts can be, we cannot rule out that the reference to "when one chants *Exsurge*" might also simply refer to the date of the battle itself (i.e., Sexagesima Sunday, the second Sunday before Lent). Both contexts indeed make sense, and the performance of mass on campaign was surely part of the experience of crusaders on the battlefield and in the churches, though it is not so clear in this context.

Indulgences and formularies, especially those written by Heinrich Kuwal, bishop of Sambia, further demonstrate that the performance of the *missa contra paganos* in the Prussian cathedrals and churches was a regular element of daily life in the region. Four preserved requests from the late fourteenth century? specify that the votive masses be performed "for the warriors of the Christians" (*pro christianorum propugnatoribus*), i.e., crusaders. Specifically, they stipulate that the votive masses be to All Saints, the Blessed Virgin Mary, and the Holy Spirit, with the *Collect* prayer be *Omnipotens sempiterne Deus, in cuius manu sunt omnes potestates*.[67] The requests were sent to major cathedrals, such as Königsberg, in addition to important monasteries and pilgrimage centers, such as the Cistercian nunnery at Löbenicht (part of the city of Königsberg), the shrine of the Virgin Mary at Juditten, and that of St. Katherine at Arnau (Rus. Rodniki).[68] Votive masses were requested for the safe return of armies,

---

66 *Die ältere Hochmeisterchronik*, 565: "Also geschach is, das dy Littawen mit al irer macht am sontage, so man singet: *Exurge, quare obdormis domine etc* gar vruy uff Zamelant insprengeten bey dem hawsze Rawdaw." My italics. For the death of Schindekopf, see Kurt Lohmeyer, "Die Litauerrschlacht bei Rudau im Samland (1370), ihre gleichzeitige und ihre spätere Darstellungen," *Zeitschrift für preußische Geschichte und Landeskunde* 7 (1870): 349–63, esp. 355–57. Schindekopf was commemorated in various churches in the region of Sambia, including the local church in Laptau (Rus. Muromskoe) where an inscription commemorated the battle, and at Quednau (Rus. Severnaya Gora), where his armor was placed as a sort of shrine to the memory of the battle. See Herrmann, *Mittelalterliche Architektur*, 549, for the inscription. For the shrine, Lucas David, *Preussische Chronik*, ed. Ernst Hennig, vol. 7 (Königsberg: Hartnung, 1815), 87–89.

67 *Formularz z Uppsali. Późnośredniowieczna księga formularzowa biskuptw pruskich*, ed. Radosław Biskup, Fontes TNT 109 (Toruń: Towarzystwo Naukowe w Toruniu, 2016), 252–58 (nos. 322–26). For the *in cuius manu* prayer, see Gaposchkin, *Invisible Weapons*, 48.

68 The monastery at Löbenicht was built to commemorate the victory of the Teutonic Order at the Battle of the Streba (2 February 1348). See Wigand, *Cron. Prut.*, 240–45. Also see Gregory Leighton, "The Relics of St Barbara at Althaus Kulm: History, Patronages, and

too, thus reflecting the ways in which religious rituals of war were a communal experience and performance, much like other regions of medieval Europe.[69]

The performance of the *Contra paganos* mass appears in the context of wars against the Rusians (specifically those of Novgorod) and Turks. On 24 June 1447, Konrad von Erlichshausen decreed to the commanders of Elbing, Balga (Rus. Veseloe), Brandenburg (Rus. Ushakovo), Königsberg, Ragnit, and Memel (Lith. Klaipėda) that the *missa contra paganos* be recited once per week in their convents until Michaelmas (29 September). This was to ensure victory for the Livonian Branch of the Teutonic Order, headed by Heinrich Vincke of Overberg.[70] The Grand Master's letter also highlights the meaning of the rituals, namely in that they strengthen the position of the Order on the edges of Christendom and ensure God's help in achieving victory, and a similar request was sent in April of the same year, this time to Rome.[71] As I have argued elsewhere, the phrase of "the edges" (*grenitczen*) of Christendom is particularly important, for it further cements the relationship and continuity of the performance of those masses on the frontiers of the Latin Christian world. Indeed, a direct reference is made to "those new converts living on the boundaries [of Christendom]" ("die neuwen cristgelowbigen an den grenitczen gesessen"). In the context of border zones, the masses and the observance of the rituals are linked to the Christianization of formerly pagan (or non-Christian) lands.

3   Religious Rituals, Warfare, and Sacralization of the Landscape

Although the performance of masses in times of war is rare in the chronicles, we can use the above to elaborate on the symbolic elements of rituals that would have taken place in times of war. In doing so, we can further discern their effects (perceived and real). Peter of Dusburg's treatise on physical and

---

Insight into the Teutonic Order and the Christian Population in Prussia (Thirteenth–Fifteenth Centuries)," *ZH* 85.1 (2020): 5–50 at 29–30. For the pilgrimage shrines surrounding Königsberg, see Paravicini, *Preußenreisen*, 1:305–9.

69   *Formularz z Uppsali*, 257–58 (no. 326).

70   *Liv-, Est-, und Curländisches Urkundenbuch nebst Regesten*, ed. Friedrich Georg von Bunge et al., 2 vols. in 13 pts. (Reval, Riga and other cities: Kimmel and other publishers, 1853–2018), here 1.10:246–47 (no. 357).

71   Ibid.: "und also eyne nach der ander umbeczech Gote dem almechtigen zcu lobe, Marien der werden juncfrauwen, allen lieben heiligen zcu eren *und der gantczen cristenheit zcu merunge*." Also see ibid., 213–14 (no. 307): "Eyn solchs zcu vorstoren, Gote zcu lobe, der werden juncfrauwen Marien zcu eren, dem heiligen cristen geloben und allen deutschen landen zcu beschutczunge, *besundern den neuwen cristgelowbigen an den grenitczen gesessen zcu trostung und enthaldung* und zcu breytung des heiligen cristen geloubens haben wir mit dem gebietiger zcu Lieffland bestalt." My italics.

spiritual weapons is a case in point with respect to the relationship between religious rituals, objects used in war, and their perceived effects. The sword of the knight was symbolized by the gift of the prophet, Jeremiah, in the dream of Judas Maccabee (2 Macc. 15:16), which formed part of the battle preparations (sometimes described as a sermon) before the Battle of Adasa. Peter quotes this directly: "Take this sword as a gift from God, with which you shall drive out the enemies of my people."[72] In this context, the sword symbolizes the protection of the land of Israel, the swords of righteous soldiers such as Saul, and Gideon, and also reflects the "good works" that brothers in the Order were obligated to carry out.

This complex array of meanings reveals not only how, in Peter's mind, objects of warfare had profound religious symbolisms and contexts, they were also linked to religious rituals (e.g. prayer in times of war, or the blessing of weapons). There existed in the liturgy of the Teutonic Order prayers for blessing soldiers and their weapons.[73] Some of the earliest of these can be seen in the Order's *Rule*, namely the blessing of the sword and the blessing of the knight. Such blessings are also present in the *Pontificale Romanum*, which the Teutonic Order would have used. The *Aufnahmeritual*, the rites with which a new brother was sworn into the Order, highlights the Order's collective image and contextualizes how brothers in the Order might have understood religious rituals with respect to combat. For example, the formula *Benediccio ad militem* called upon God to acknowledge the knight, "who fights everyday willingly with his sword against the barbarity of the pagans."[74] His sword was also blessed, and it was prayed for that he never succumbs to the turbulence of war, but emerges victorious.[75] These rituals linked the knight and his sword to the broader world of Christendom, not just the Order's territories in Prussia, which is demonstrated in the Order's liturgy. In addition to praying for the Order's

---

72   Dusburg, *Chron. Pr.*, 2.8, p. 41: "De gladio dicitur Jeremias extendisse dextram et dedisse Jude gladium dicens: *accpie gladium sanctum munus a deo, quo deicies adversarios populi mei Israel.*" My italics. For the commentary on this scene, see *The Oxford Bible Commentary*, 749–50.

73   Arno Mentzel-Reuters, "Der Deutsche Orden als geistlicher Orden," in *"Cura animarum,"* 15–43 at 27.

74   *Die Statuen*, 129: "Exaudi, quesumus, Domine, preces nostras, ut hunc famulum tuum, *qui hodierna die militari ense te annuente precingitur*, bendicere dignare, *quatinus contra paganorum omniumque malignancium seviciam defensor sit.*" My italics.

75   Ibid.: "Benedic, Domine sancta pater, per invocacionem tui nominis et per adventum filii tui Domini nostri Ihesu Christi atque per donum sancti spiritus hunc ensem, quo hic famulus tuus hodierna die precingi desiderat, quatinus eo munitus nullis bellorum turbetur incursibus, sed felici victoria per omnia potitus semper illesus tuo presidio conservetur."

land, this included a prayer "for the whole of Christendom."[76] The blessing and their associated rituals had a multi-level meaning. Calling not just to the earthly duties of the knight of the Order to fight against pagans (*contra paganorum omnium*) but to all bad things (*omnia malignancia*), the ritual reflects the earthly and spiritual struggles of the brothers as part of the monastic corporation.[77] As Andreas Heinz has suggested, these blessings emphasized the calls for God's protection of the knight, holding a deeply spiritual meaning, in addition to reaffirming that the weapons were used justly, in defense of the church. The liturgy of the Teutonic Order provides some glimpses into the links between religious rituals and warfare in the southern Baltic zone. In this context, the weapons used by brothers in their martial encounters took on a dual role. They were used for both physical protection in combat, in addition to the spiritual protection of the brother as he fought on the battlefield against the enemies of the church.[78] Dušan Zupka's recent work on holy war discusses this at length.[79] Other objects, such as tents mentioned above, can be seen from a symbolic viewpoint. They were related directly to the performance of religious rituals, in this case, as the space in which the Ark of the Covenant was kept during the wandering of the Israelites through the desert recounted in the Book of Exodus.[80]

A variety of correspondences demonstrate the functions of religious rites of war in the southern Baltic as an important element in sacralizing the landscape through performing religious rituals.[81] These examples should be consid-

---

76 Ibid., 130: "Brûder, bittet unsern hêrren Got vor die heiligen cristenheit, daz er sie trôsten mit sînen gnâden unde vride gerûche sie zu bewaren vor allem ubele." For the prayers for the Order's land, see 132: "Bittet ouch vor alle die lant, die vor der heidenschaft legen, daz Got mit sîme râte und crafte zu hulfe kome, daz Gotes geloube und minne dâ inne gebreitet werde alsô daz sie allen iren vîenden mugen widerstên."
77 Kwiatkowski, *Zakon niemiecki*, 88–89.
78 See Carl Erdmann, *Die Entstehung des Kreuzzugsgedankens*. FKG 6 (Stuttgart: Kohlhammer, 1935), 329–33; also see Heinz, *Lebendiges Erbe. Beiträge zur abendländischen Liturgie- und Frömmigkeitsgeschichte*, Pietas liturgica. Studia 21 (Tübingen and Basel: Francke, 2010), 221–23.
79 Derek A. Rivard, *Blessing the World: Ritual and Lay Piety in Medieval Religion* (Washington DC: Catholic University of America Press, 2009), 156–74; Dušan Zupka, *Meč a kríž. Vojna a náboženstvo v stredovekej strednej Európe (10.–12. storočie)* (Bratislava: VEDA, 2020), 210–15. For sword in the rituals of war, see also Carsten Selch Jensen's chapter in this collection (vol. 1, chap. 7).
80 See, e.g., Christoph Dohmen, "Zelt, heiliges Zelt," in *Lexikon für Theologie und Kirche*, vol. 10, ed. Walter Kaspar (Freiburg: Herder Institut, 2001), 1419; Katherine Allen Smith, "Glossing the Holy War: Exegetical Constructions of the First Crusade, c.1099–c.1146," *Studies in Medieval and Renaissance History*, ser. 3 10.3 (2013): 1–39 at 21–22; eadem, *The Bible and Crusade Narrative in the Twelfth Century* (Woodbridge: Boydell Press, 2020), 135.
81 Wenta, *Studien*, 167–68.

ered alongside the many instances of war for the purposes of expanding the boundaries of Christianity or subjugating the non-Christian lands to Christian rule. Given that this region did not possess any shrines sacred to Christendom, but rather places sacred to paganism, religious rites also served to sacralize the spaces in which war occurred.[82] While surely true on a local level in the Baltic, expanding the borders of *Christianitas* was a fundamental component in the liturgy of war and *missa contra paganos*, in which the faithful also prayed that in subjugating the pagans and expanding the borders of Christianity, peace might be obtained.[83] This was a concept expressed in the blessings said for the German Emperors in the Sens Pontifical, highlighting the universal element of prayer rituals in times of war and their perceived impact.[84]

Many parallels to this can be seen in the sources associated with the Teutonic Order and the Christianization of the Baltic region, situating the performance of religious rites in times of war within a broader context and demonstrating their role in increasing the borders of Christendom. Papal encyclicals encouraging the preaching of the Prussian crusades are a suitable example. Throughout the 1230s and into the 1260s, especially following the defeat of the Teutonic Order on 13 July 1260 at the Battle of Durben (Latv. Durbe), calls for increased preaching of the crusades in Prussia and Livonia was tied directly with the expansion of Christianity's borders. A common phrase of these letters highlighted "the zeal of God and [campaigning] for the expansion of the Christian faith and taking of the land from the hand of the pagans."[85] These preaching campaigns were undertaken primarily by the Dominicans, with whom the Teutonic Order shared its liturgy.[86] Later, in the fourteenth century, Peter of

82 Leighton, "Did the Teutonic Order," 468–81.
83 *Agobardi archiepiscopi Lugundensis libri duo pro filiis et contra Iudith uxorem Ludovici Pii*, ed. Georg Waitz, MGH SS 15.1 (Hannover: Hahn, 1887), 274–79 at 275: "Cum enim deberent exercitus mitti *adversus exteras gentes, et ipse impertor adversus barbaras nationes dimicare, ut eas fidei subiugaret ad diliatandum terminum regni fidelium*—sic namque orat universalis ecclesia in solemnibus illis oracionibus diebus passionis dominicae pro imeratoribus." My italics.
84 Carl Erdmann, "Der Heidenkrieg in der Liturgie die Kaiserkrönung Ottos I," *Mitteilungen des Instituts für Österreichische Geschichtsforschung* 46 (1932): 129–42 at 141, a list of blessings from the Sens Pontifical: "Pedibus quoque vestris substernat inimicos christiani nominis, ut efferos animos retundere valeatis victricibus armis. Amen." Erdmann connected this version of the Sens Pontifical to a manuscript in Brussels (Hs. 391).
85 *Preußisches Urkundenbuch*, ed. Rudolf Philippi et al., 6 vols. in 9 pts. (Königsberg: Hartnung and other publishers, 1882–2000), here 1.1:62 (no. 81), 67 (no. 88), 111 (no. 146); 1.2:26 (no. 30), 88 (no. 103), 118 (no. 141), 133 (no. 158), 172 (no. 234).
86 Axel Ehlers, *Die Ablaßpraxis des Deutschen Ordens im Mittelalter*, QSGD 64 (Marburg: Elwert, 2007), 24–49, 41–44. Alexander Baranov, "Die Frühzeit des Deutschen Ordens in Livland und die Eroberung Kurlands. Ein peripheres Tätigkeitsfeld?" in *Livland—eine*

Dusburg wrote that the Order's wars in Prussia were carried out "for glorifying and expanding the borders of Christendom."[87] Contemporaries, such as King John I of Bohemia, in a letter from March 1335 confirming his protection of the Order, described "the most noble master and brothers of the Teutonic House who fight to extend the boundaries of Christianity (*durch breytunge des Cristengeloubis*) against the enemies of the cross, at their own expense and with their own blood, as we have seen ourselves."[88]

A further reflection of this is the Marian character of the masses and the content of some letters. They contextualize the reason for which masses were performed by the local population, in addition to the ways in which the Teutonic Order communicated its Marian identity (its patron saint was the Virgin Mary). The performances of the masses in the churches resulted from direct correspondence and appeals from higher officials in the Teutonic Order to church leaders. One example is a request for prayers recorded in the register of Grand Master Konrad of Jungingen. Before asking for the prayers, the small formula reads how "for the honor of God and to serve his blessed Mother we, with the counsel of our officials, sent out an army to the unbelievers."[89] Similar examples can also be found in the international correspondence of the Teutonic Order to the rulers of Christendom, such as a letter from Konrad Zöllner of Rotenstein to Wenceslas IV, King of Germany, around 1390. The letter documents a campaign done "for the love and honor of God and to serve His mother, Mary." It also points to the successful performance of mass both on the battlefield and in the Prussian churches, for it was "through the help of Our Lord that we returned safely, unharmed."[90]

Another letter from around 1400, this time from Konrad of Jungingen and describing a *Reise* to Wenceslas IV, should also be considered here. The letter

---

Region, 315–46. For the Order's liturgy and its connections to the Dominican Rite, see Anette Löffler, "Die Liturgie des Deutschen Ordens in Preußen," in *"Cura animarum,"* 161–84 at 161–62.

87 Dusburg, *Chron. Pr.*, 3.30, p. 66: "Longa et supra ingenii mei parvitatem esset singulariter enarre, quam potenter et magnifice, quam eleganter et strenue magister et fratres predicti, tamquam alteri Machabei, *in ampliando fines Cristianorum et dilatando* ... ingesserint manus suas." My italics.

88 *Preußisches Urkundenbuch*, 3.1:70 (no. 95): "Wand di erbarn geistlichin luyte der homeistir und di brudere des ordens des spittalis unser vrowen von dem duyczen huyse von Ierusalem, *durch breytunge des Cristengeloubis und merunge gotisdynstis* nicht alleyne tůn groze unzeliche kost und erbeit *kegen dy vynde cruycis heyden genang* in pfleclichen herverten ... als wir selbir haben gesehen und ervarin." My italics.

89 Berlin, Geheimes Staatsarchiv Preußischer Kulturbesitz, XX. Haputabteilung, Ordensfoliant (GStA PK, XX. HA, OF) 3, fol. 18.

90 *Codex diplomaticus Prussicus* 4 (Königsberg: Bornträger, 1853):114–15 (no. 80).

opens with the same formula, pointing out the connection of the expedition to serving God and the Virgin Mary, but also includes that the Marshal, Werner of Tettingen, arrived in Lithuania "on the Wednesday following Candlemas." This was one of the most important liturgical feasts of the Order's monastic calendar and, mentioned above, itself a day of commemoration of the Order's victory at the Strebe River in 1348. After an account of the campaign, the letter states that "with the help of God" (*mit der hulfe gotis*) the campaign was a success, indicating that the group of higher officials (*etliche kompthure mynes Ordens*) and guests (*etliche herren und geste*) would have observed the office of Candlemas either before leaving Königsberg, or even on the march itself, thus ensuring that they had performed the appropriate rituals before battle and that the local population on the home front had done the same.[91] While the letter could surely be seen to attempt to garner more support from Wenceslas, and to frame the Order in a positive light to ensure that this support would continue, it is important to note that the performance of religious rituals in the context of the Order's central purpose (i.e., fighting against the pagans) was a key component to solidifying its group identity and central mission.

While direct references to the performance of religious rituals on campaign for the southern Baltic zone are scant at best, a consultation of the Order's foundational texts, such as its *Rule*, in addition to letters, formularies, and other materials, demonstrates that these rituals were indeed foundational to the Crusade phenomenon in the Baltic and were perceived to have many different effects. Much like the extensive body of literature produced in the Order, these rituals were fundamental to the edification of the brothers and their collective identity as a religious corporation, particularly to the knights themselves, in addition to sacralizing the space in which their wars against the pagans took place. This final section will analyze the performance of these rituals, the spaces in which such rituals took place, in addition to the objects associated with them.

Delivering sermons to motivate combatants appears to have been a fundamental duty of the priest-brothers in the Teutonic Order, though Werner Paravicini has rightly noted that next to nothing survives concerning the

---

91   *Codex diplomaticus Prussicus* 6 (Königsberg: Bornträger, 1863), 98–99 (no. 96): "das ich gote unserm herren und synir werden muter czu lobe und czu eren, und merunge des heiligen cristglouben, den Obirsten Marschalk und etliche kompthure mynes Ordens, do ouch etliche herren und geste mete woren, eyn heer us mynes Ordens lande off di ungloubigen gesant hatte, die in der vynde landen quamen an der Mittewochen noch unser frawwen tage lichtmesse nehst vorgangen … also das sie mit der hulfe gotis vil der ungloubigen slugen und vyngen unt ettwifil gegenote in den landen betwungen, das sie sich czu dem cristenglouben und mynem Orden undirtenig dirgeben haben."

precise content within them.[92] According to the *Rule*, priests were expected to muster the brethren to war, reminding them to think of how Christ died on the Cross for them.[93] This would surely have occurred during sermons. In Livonia we know of a thirteenth-century copy of a preaching manual of Alanus de Insulis, *De arte praedicandi*, kept in the Cistercian monastery of Dünamünde (Latv. Daugavgrīva, Rus. Dwinsk). It perhaps belonged originally to the monastery in Padis (Est. Padise).[94] Among the various topics in the treatise includes preaching for knights (*ad milites*), in addition to sermons on bravery (*de fortitudine*), and on prayer itself (*Exhortatio ad orationem*). All of these refer to warfare or mention it. For example, the exhortation to prayer notes: "Just as the knight does not go out to battle without his weapons, so does the Christian no go out without prayer."[95] The sermon designed for preaching to knights, in particular, discusses the symbolism of weapons and their spiritual and physical functions, such as the shield as a symbol of faith (*lorica fidei*), the sword of the word of God (*gladium verbi Dei*), and others.[96] We know of some later examples in which sermons took place in times of war, in this case, after battle. This appears in Wigand of Marburg's account of the Siege of Kaunas (Pol. Rus. Kowno) in April of 1362. Wigand refers directly to a sermon (*sermo ad populum*), delivered presumably on the battlefield.[97]

Though evidence for sermons and their contents is vague, other sources indicate that the performance of masses on campaign was quite important, even a fundamental experience to warfare for the Teutonic knights. One of the earliest direct references comes from a bull of Clement VI, dated to 1344. Responding

---

92 Paravicini, *Adlig leben*, 526–28. Sermon materials do survive in Toruń, Archiwum Państwowe w Toruniu, Akta miasta Torunia, 69/248/o, but primarily for the period later than that covered in this study.

93 *Die Statuten*, 26 (Prologue, 4): "Under disen geliden sint ouch pfaffen, die ine werde unde eine nuzze stat hânt ... *Sô man aber striten sal, sô sulen sie die brûdere sterken zu dem strite unde manen sie, daz sie gedenken, wie Got ouch den tôt durch sie leit an dem crûce*." My italics.

94 Richard Newhauser, Tiina Kala, and Meelis Friedenthal, "The Work of an English Scribe in a Manuscript in Estonia," *Scriptorium. International Review of Medieval Studies* 62.1 (2008): 139–48, discuss the manual.

95 Alanus de Insulis, *Summa Magistri Alani doctoris universalis de arte praedicatoria*, PL 210, ed. Jacques-Paul Migne (Paris: Apud Editorem J.-P. Migne, 1855),168: "Sicut militi sine armis ad bellum non convenit, ita Christiano cuilibet sine oratione procedere non expedit."

96 Ibid., 185: "ita sunt duo gladiis pertinentes ad propulsandos diversos insultus hominum; materialis ... et spiritualis. ... Accingatur ergo miles exterius *ad reformandam violentiam pacem tempore; interius quoque gladio verbi Dei, ad restaurandam pacem proprii pectoris*." My italics.

97 Wigand, *Cron. Prut.*, 304.

to an appeal from the grand master of the Order, Ludolf König of Weizzau, Clement VI decreed that the Order, particularly the marshal (*capitaneus*), and its guests on their campaigns "against pagans and schismatic enemies to the Christian faith, for the defense and propagation of said faith" were allowed to observe mass before the light of day, due to the shortness of the days in the winter.[98] This also symbolized the conquest of Christianity (light) over paganism (darkness), a sentiment also echoed in the *Prologue* of the Order's *Rule*, where the brothers, like the guardians of the Litter of Solomon, have no fear of darkness.[99] Two subsequent examples concerning the celebration of mass on campaign appeared later. In October of 1360, Innocent VI granted Winrich of Kniprode, grand master of the Order, to observe mass on campaign before the light of day and on portable altars. This letter is slightly different to that of Clement VI, for it refers to the "banners and flags" of the Order's officers, but ultimately the imagery concerning the length of days in wintertime (the most popular time for the Order's *Reisen*) and the danger of the campaigns remains the same.[100] In September of 1368, Pope Urban V granted the same permissions not just to the Order in Prussia, but to its Livonian branch.[101] All three reflect contemporary views of how these rituals in times of war served to sacralize conflicts.

Indeed, while this paper has sought not to rely too much on chronicles, one example deserves mention here that links the above material quite well.

---

98 *Codex diplomaticus Prussicus* 3 (Königsberg: Bornträger, 1848), 71–72 (no. 48) at 71: "Nos itaque huiusmodi supplicatoinibus inclincati, quod Magister et Capitaneus exercitus christianorum Hospitalis eiusdem … possint et in Altari portatili missas per proprios vel alios udoneos sacerdotes, *in locis tamen congruentibus et honestis eciam antequam illucescat dies circa tamen diurnam lucem*, cum qualitas negociorum pro tempore ingruentium id exegerit in eorum presentia facere celebrari." My italics.

99 *Die Statuten*, 25 (Prologue, 3). For the importance of the symbolism of light in a military context, see Radosław Kotecki, "Pious Rulers, Princely Clerics, and Angels of Light: 'Imperial Holy War' Imagery in Twelfth-Century Poland and Rus'," in *Christianity and War in Medieval East Central Europe and Scandinavia*, ed. Kotecki, Carsten Selch Jensen, and Stephen Bennett (Leeds: ARC Humanities Press, 2021), 159–88. Also see Kotecki's contribution to this collection (vol. 2, chap. 3).

100 *Avignonische Quellen*, 43 (no. 84): "cum ipse ac preceptores et fratres dicti hospitalis parcium prusie et livonie pro defensione et exaltacione ac incremento fidei catholice cum exercitibus suis … non possint presertim yemali tempore, quo dies fiunt in illis partibus nimis breves … ortum diei pro audienda missa propter itineris et more pericula expectare, viginti preceptoribus dicti hospitalis parcium predictarum, propriis utentibus banderiis seu vexillis, ut in expedicionibus huiusmodi possint in locis congruentibus et honestis missas per proprios vel alios ydoneos sacerdotes, eciam antequam illucescat dies, circa tamen diurnam lucem, cum qualitas negociorum pro tempore ingruentium id exegerit."

101 *Codex diplomaticus Prussicus* 3 (Königsberg: Bornträger, 1848):126–27 (no. 96). The letter was issued on either 2 or 8 September.

Wigand of Marburg's description of the Siege of Kaunas in April of 1362 is one of the most important sources for understanding not only religious rituals and warfare but also their symbolic functions and how contemporaries understood them. Krzysztof Kwiatkowski, in particular, has demonstrated in two publications that the description served to reflect Wigand's own relationship to the Order (his patron) and crusaders (his audience),[102] in addition to the liturgical elements of warfare on the *Reisen*.[103] The account of Wigand refers, specifically, to a wide variety of performances and rites that served to place the physical siege of the castle within a spiritual context. The bishop of Sambia, Bartholomeus of Radam accompanied the army and performed a solemn mass after the siege of the castle ended. This is a rare description of a mass performed on the battlefield, but we know from the permissions granted to the Order that mass on the move was a key component to the experience of war in the region and was practiced regularly. Subsequent expeditions recorded in Wigand's chronicle demonstrate that church officials often accompanied armies on campaign.[104]

4   Conclusions

This chapter began with a quote from a small formulary concerning a request for prayers and a procession, most likely aimed at the local Christian population in Prussia. While not explicitly concerning the religious rituals of war on the battlefield, the introductory quote demonstrates that even on the northeastern "frontier" of Christendom, common practices of liturgical celebration and their connection to warfare formed an important element of religious life, much like in other regions of Western Europe. Following a brief overview of previous approaches to this topic, religious rituals were contextualized within the available source material. This section concluded that the presence of ritualization of warfare as a means to achieve God's blessing goes back to the

---

[102] Krzysztof Kwiatkowski, "Selbstdarstellung," 127–38 at 129–32. The relationship between Wigand as a herald and the participant on the *Reisen* has only recently been analyzed by Kwiatkowski and Zonenberg. See Zonenberg "Wstęp," 38.

[103] Krzysztof Kwiatkowski, "Prolog et Epilog 'temporis sanctis'. Die Belagerung Kauens 1362 in der Beschreibung Wigands von Marburg," *ZfO* 57.2 (2008): 238–54, esp. 250–52; idem, "'Christ ist erstanden …' and Christians Win! Liturgy and the Sacralization of Armed Fight against Pagans as Determinants of the Identity of the Members of the Teutonic Order in Prussia," in *Sacred Space in the State of the Teutonic Order in Prussia*, ed. Jarosław Wenta and Magdalena Kopczyńska, SBS 2 (Toruń: Wydawnictwo Naukowe Uniwersytetu Mikołaja Kopernika, 2013), 101–30.

[104] Wigand, *Cron. Prut.*, 304, 306, 320–22.

earliest texts produced in the Teutonic Order's historiography, namely the *Prologue* to its monastic Rule. The nature of the Teutonic Order as a religious institution, too, and the performance of the communal reading at mealtimes (*Tischlesung*), demonstrates that the concept of achieving God's favor formed a key element of the Teutonic Order's group identity.

From here, it considered the spaces in which such rituals took place. Particularly important are the delivery of sermons in times of war, in addition to an analysis of the inventories of the Teutonic Order's monasteries. These objects included war tents and portable altars, fundamental in demarcating a specific point in the landscape for the performance of religious rituals in times of war. The consideration of war liturgies, the blessing of soldiers and their weapons, and their presence in the available source material demonstrates that, just as in other regions of Europe, liturgical performance in times of warfare was a multi-dimensional way in which groups expressed support for the Teutonic Order and for visiting crusaders. Through analyzing the symbolic nature of the rituals and placing them within a broader framework, this chapter argues that religious rites served to sacralize conflicts and, indeed, the landscapes in which they took place. To conclude, and quote the introductory formula for a final time, it appears that warfare in the southern Baltic was understood at this time to involve not only swords but also prayer and ritual.

Bibliography

Manuscript Sources

Berlin, Geheimes Staatsarchiv Preußischer Kulturbesitz (GStA PK), XX. Hauptabteilung, Ordensbriefarchiv (OBA), Nr. 2692.

Berlin, GStA PK, XX. HA, OBA, Nr. 4839.

Berlin, GStA PK, Ordensfoliant (OF) 3.

Primary Sources

Agobardi archiepiscopi Lugdunensis libri duo pro filiis et contra Iudith uxorem Ludovici Pii. Edited by Georg Waitz, 274–79. MGH SS 15.1. Hannover: Hahn, 1887.

Die ältere Hochmeisterchronik. Edited by Max Töppen, 540–637. SrP 3. Leipzig: Hirzel, 1866.

"Aus den voyaiges Guillibert de Lannoy, 1412." Edited by Ernst Strehlke, 443–53. SrP 3. Leipzig: Hirzel, 1866.

Die Berichte der Generalprokuratoren des Deutschen Ordens an der Kurie. Vol. 1: *Die Geschichte der Generalprokuratoren von den Anfängen bis 1403*. Edited by Kurt

Forstreuter. Veröffentlichungen der Neidersächsischen Archivverwaltung 12. Göttingen: Vandenhoek & Ruprecht, 1961.

Canonici Sambiensis epitome gestorum Prussie. Edited by Max Töppen, 27–90. SrP 1. Leipzig: Hirzel, 1861.

Codex diplomaticus Prussicus. Edited by Johannes Voigt. 6 vols. Königsberg: Bornträger, 1836–1861.

Das Formelbuch des Domherrn Arnold von Protzan. Edited by Wilhelm Wattenbach. Codex diplomaticus Silesiae 5. Breslau: Max, 1862.

Formularz z Uppsali. Późnośredniowieczna księga formularzowa biskuptw pruskich. Edited by Radosław Biskup. Fontes TNT 109. Toruń: Towarzystwo Naukowe w Toruniu, 2016.

Franciscani Thorunensis Annales Prussici (941–1410). Edited by Ernst Strehelke, 57–316. SrP 3. Leipzig: Hirzel, 1866.

Ioannis Dlugossii Annales seu cronicae incliti regni Poloniae. Bks. 1–12. Edited by Consilium (Cracow: Państwowe Wydawnictwo Naukowe, 1964–2005). Fully accessible via National Digital Library Polona, dlugosz.polona.pl/en.

Johannes von Posilge, Officials von Pomesanien, Chronik des Landes Preussen (von 1360 an, fortgesetzt bis 1419). Edited by Ernst Strehlke, 79–338. SrP 3. Leipzig: Hirzel, 1866.

Lucas David. *Preussische Chronik*. Edited by Ernst Hennig. Vol. 7. Königsberg: Hartnung, 1815.

Lites ac res gestae inter Polonos ordinemque Cruciferorum. Vol. 1. Edited by Ignacy Zakrzewski. Poznań: Biblioteka Kórnicka, 1890.

Liv-, Est-, und Curländisches Urkundenbuch nebst Regesten. Edited by Friedrich Georg von Bunge et al. 2 vols. in 13 pts. Reval, Riga and other cities: Kimmel and other publishers, 1853–2018.

Das Marienburger Treßlerbuch der Jahre 1399–1409. Edited by Erich Joachim. Königsberg: Thomas & Oppermann, 1896.

Nicolaus of Jeroschin. *Di Kronike von Pruzinlant*. Edited by Ernst Strehlke, 303–624. Sriptores rerum Prussicarum 1. Leipzig: Hirzel, 1861.

Nicolaus of Jeroschin. *The Chronicle of Prussia: A History of the Teutonic Knights in Prussia, 1190–1331*. Edited and translated by Mary Fischer. CTT 20. Farnham and Burlington VT: Ashgate, 2010.

Petri de Dusburg Chronicon terre Prussie. Edited by Max Töppen, 3–219. SrP 1. Leipzig: Hirzel, 1861.

Preußisches Urkundenbuch. Edited by Rudolf Philippi et al. 6 vols. in 9 pts. Königsberg: Hartnung and other publishers, 1882–2000.

Die Statuten des Deutschen Ordens nach den ältesten Handschrifiten. Edited by Max Perlbach. Halle: Niemeyer, 1890.

Wigand von Marburg. *Nowa kronika Pruska*. Edited by Sławomir Zonenberg and Krzysztof Kwiatkowski. Toruń: Towarzystwo Naukowe w Toruniu, 2017.

Secondary Sources

Arnold, Udo. "Die Anfänge der Ordensgeschichtsschreibung." In *Neue Studien zur Literatur im Deutschen Orden*. Edited by Bernhart Jähnig and Arno Mentzel-Reuters, 178–95. Zeitschrift für deutsches Altertum und deutsche Literatur. Beiheifte 19. Berlin: LIT, 2014.

Arnold, Udo. "Maria als Patronin des Deutschen Ordens im Mittelalter." In *"Terra Sanctae Mariae." Mittelalterliche Bildwerke der Marienverehrung im Deutschordensland Preußen*. Edited by Gerhard Eimer et al., 29–57. Kunsthistorische Arbeiten der Kulturstiftung der deutschen Vertriebenen 7. Bonn: Kulturstiftung der deutschen Vertriebenen, 2009.

Baranov, Alexander. "Die Frühzeit des Deutschen Ordens in Livland und die Eroberung Kurlands. Ein peripheres Tätigkeitsfeld?" in *Livland—Eine Region am Ende der Welt? Forschungen zum Verhältnis zwischen Zentrum und Peripherie im späten Mittelalter*. Edited by Anti Selart and Matthias Thumser, 315–46. QSBG 27. Cologne, Weimar, and Vienna: Böhlau, 2017.

Barton, John and John Muddiman, ed. *The Oxford Bible Commentary*. Oxford and New York: Oxford University Press, 2001.

Chollet, Loïc. *Les Sarrasins du Nord. Une histoire de la croisade Balte par la littérature (XIIe–XVe siècle)*. Neuchâtel: Éditions Alphil and Presses Universitaires Suisses, 2019.

Czaja, Roman. "Das Selbstverständnis der geistlichen Ritterorden im Mittelalter. Bilanz und Forschungsperspektive." In *Selbstbild and Selbstverständnis der geistlichen Ritterorden*. Edited by Roman Czaja and Jürgen Sarnowsky, 7–24. OM 13. Toruń: Uniwerstet Mikołaja Kopernika, 2005.

Dohmen, Christoph. "Zelt, heiliges Zelt." In *Lexikon für Theologie und Kirche*. Vol. 10. Edited by Walter Kaspar, 1419. Freiburg: Herder Institut, 2001.

Ehlers, Axel. *Die Ablaßpraxis des Deutschen Ordens im Mittelalter*. QSGD 64. Marburg: Elwert, 2007.

Erdmann, Carl. *Die Entstehung des Kreuzzugsgedankens*. FKG 6. Stuttgart: Kohlhammer, 1935.

Erdmann, Carl. "Der Heidenkrieg in der Liturgie die Kaiserkrönung Ottos I." *Mitteilungen des Instituts für Österreichische Geschichtsforschung* 46 (1932): 129–42.

Fischer, Mary. "Biblical Heroes and the Uses of Literature: The Teutonic Order in the Late Thirteenth and Early Fourteenth Centuries." In *Crusade and Conversion on the Baltic Frontier, 1150–1500*. Edited by Alan V. Murray, 261–75. Farnham and Burlington VT: Ashgate, 2001.

Fischer, Mary. "The Books of the Maccabees and the Teutonic Order." *Crusades* 4 (2005): 59–71.

Fonnesberg-Schmidt, Iben. *The Popes and the Baltic Crusades, 1147–1254*. TNW 26. Leiden and Boston MA: Brill, 2007.

Forstreuter, Kurt. *Das Preußisches Staatsarchiv in Königsberg. Ein geschichtlicher Rückblick mit einer Übersicht über seine Bestände*. Veröffentlichungen der Niedersächsischen Archivverwaltung 3. Göttingen: Vandenhoek & Ruprecht, 1955.

Gancarczyk, Paweł. "The Musical Culture of the Teutonic Order in Prussia Reflected in the 'Marienburger Tresslerbuch' (1399–1409)." In *The Musical Heritage of the Jagiellonian Era*. Edited by Gancarczyk and Agnieszka Leszczyńska, 191–200. Warsaw: Institute of Art at the Polish Academy of Sciences, 2012.

Gaposchkin, M. Cecilia. *Invisible Weapons: Liturgy and the Making of Crusade Ideology*. Ithaca NY and London: Cornell University Press, 2017.

Grunewald, Eckhard. "Das Register der Ordensliberei Tapiau aus den Jahren 1541–1543. Eine Quelle zur Frühgeschichte der ehem. Staats- und Universitätsbibliothek Königsberg." In *Berichte und Forschungen. Jahrbuch des Bundesinstituts für Ostdeutsche Kultur und Geschichte*. Vol. 1. Edited by Eckhard Grunewald, 55–92. Munich: Oldenbourg, 1993.

Günther, Otto. *Katalog der Handschriften der Danziger Stadtbibliothek*. Pt. 5: *Die Handschriften der Kirchenbibliothek von St. Marien in Danzig*. Danzig: Kafemann, 1921.

Heinz, Andreas. *Lebendiges Erbe. Beiträge zur abendländischen Liturgie- und Frömmigkeitsgeschichte*. Pietas liturgica. Studia 21. Tübingen and Basel: Francke, 2010.

Helm, Karl, and Walther Ziesemer. *Die Literatur des Deutschen Ritter-Ordens*. Gießener Beiträge zur deutschen Philologie 94. Gießen: Wilhelm Schmitz, 1951.

Herrmann, Christofer. *Mittelalterliche Architektur im Preußenland. Untersuchungen zur Kunstlandschaft und -geographie*. Studien zur internationalen Architektur- und Kulturgeschichte 56. Petersberg: Imhof, 2007.

Herrmann, Christofer. "Ragnit, Neidenburg, Bütow—die letzten drei Deutschordensburgen in Preußen." In *Die Burg im 15. Jahrhundert. Kolloquium des Wissenschaftlichen Beirats der Deutschen Burgvereinigung, Kronberg 2009*. Translated by Hartmut Hofrichter and Joachim Zeune, 155–64. Veröffentlichungen der Deutschen Burgenvereinigung 12. Braubach: Braubach Dt. Burgenvereinigung, 2011.

Houben, Hubert. "Raimondo Del Balzo Orsini e l'Ordine Teutonico." In *L'Ordine Teutonico tra Mediterraneo a Baltico incontri e scontri tra religioni, poplie e cultura*. Edited by Houben, 195–218. Acta Theutonica 5. Salento: Galatina, 2008.

Jensen, Kurt Villads. "Sacralization of the Landscape: Converting Trees and Measuring Land in the Danish Crusades against the Wends." In *The Clash of Cultures on the Medieval Baltic Frontier*. Edited by Alan V. Murray, 141–50. Farnham and Burlington VT: Ashgate, 2009.

Kaljundi, Linda. "(Re)Performing the Past: Crusading, History Writing, and Rituals in the Chronicle of Henry of Livonia." In *The Performance of Christian and Pagan Storyworlds*. Edited by Lars Boje Mortensen and Tuomas M.S. Lehtonen, 295–338. Medieval identities 3. Turnhout: Brepols, 2013.

Kotecki, Radosław. "The Desecration of Holy Places According to Witnesses' Testimonies in the Polish-Teutonic Order Trials of the 14th Century." In *Arguments and Counter-Arguments: The Political Thought of the 14th–15th Centuries during the Polish-Teutonic Order Trials and Disputes*. Edited by Wiesław Sieradzan, 69–111. Toruń: Wydawnictwo Naukowe Uniwersytetu Mikołaja Kopernika, 2012.

Kotecki, Radosław. "Pious Rulers, Princely Clerics, and Angels of Light: 'Imperial Holy War' Imagery in Twelfth-Century Poland and Rus'." In *Christianity and War in Medieval East Central Europe and Scandinavia*. Edited by Kotecki, Carsten Selch Jensen, and Stephen Bennett, 159–88. Leeds: ARC Humanities Press, 2021.

Kotecki, Radosław. "With the Sword of Prayer, or How the Medieval Bishop Should Fight." *QMAN* 21 (2016): 341–69.

Kwiatkowski, Krzysztof. "'Christ ist erstanden …' and Christians Win! Liturgy and the Sacralization of Armed Fight against Pagans as Determinants of the Identity of the Members of the Teutonic Order in Prussia." In *Sacred Space in the State of the Teutonic Order in Prussia*. Edited by Jarosław Wenta and Magdalena Kopczyńska, 101–30. SBS 2. Toruń: Wydawnictwo Naukowe Uniwersytetu Mikołaja Kopernika, 2013.

Kwiatkowski, Krzysztof. "Die 'Eroberung Preußens' durch den Deutschen Orden—ihr Bild unf ihre Wahrnehmung in der Literatur des Deutschen Ordens im 14. Jahrhundert." In *Kryziaus karu epocha Baltijos regiono tautu istorineje samoeje*. Edited by Rita Regina Trimoniene and Robertas Jurgaitis, 131–69. Siauliai: Delta, 2007.

Kwiatkowski, Krzysztof. "Prolog et Epilog 'temporis sanctis'. Die Belagerung Kauens 1362 in der Beschreibung Wigands von Marburg." *ZfO* 57.2 (2008): 238–54.

Kwiatkowski, Krzysztof. "Die Selbstdarstellung des Deutschen Ordens in der Chronik Wigands von Marburg." In *Selbstbild und Selbstverständnis der geistlichen Ritterorden*. Edited by Roman Czaja and Jürgen Sarnowsky, 127–38. OM 13. Toruń: Wydawnictwo Naukowe Uniwersytetu Mikołaja Kopernika, 2005.

Kwiatkowski, Krzysztof. "Wstęp historycznomilitarny." In *Nowa kronika Pruska*. Edited by Sławomir Zonenberg and Krzysztof Kwiatkowski, 45–102. Toruń: Towarzystwo Naukowe w Toruniu, 2017.

Kwiatkowski, Krzysztof. *Zakon niemiecki jako "corporatio militaris."* Pt. 1: *Korporacja i krąg przynależących do niej. Kulturowe i społeczne podstawy działalności militarnej zakonu w Prusach (do początku XV wieku)*. Toruń: Uniwersytet Mikołaja Kopernika, 2012.

Leighton, Gregory. "Crusading and Holy War in the Teutonic Order's Struggle for Žemaitija. Written and Visual Perspectives." *Acta Historica Universitatis Klaipedensis* 41 (2020): 25–52.

Leighton, Gregory. "Did the Teutonic Order Create a Sacred Landscape in Thirteenth-Century Prussia?" *JMH* 44.4 (2018): 457–83.

Leighton, Gregory. "The Relics of St Barbara at Althaus Kulm: History, Patronages, and Insight into the Teutonic Order and the Christian Population in Prussia (Thirteenth–Fifteenth Centuries)." *ZH* 85.1 (2020): 5–50.

Leighton, Gregory. "'Reysa in laudem Dei et virginis gloriose contra paganos': The Experience of Crusading in Prussia during the Thirteenth and Fourteenth Centuries." *ZfO* 69.1 (2020): 1–25.

Lohmeyer, Kurt. "Die Litauerrschlacht bei Rudau im Samland (1370), ihre gleichzeitige und ihre spätere Darstellungen." *Zeitschrift für preußische Geschicte und Landeskunde* 7 (1870): 349–63.

Löffler, Anette. "Die Liturgie des Deutschen Ordens in Preußen." In *"Cura animarum." Seelsorge im Deutschordensland Preußen*. Edited by Stefan Samerski, 161–84. FQKK 45. Cologne: Böhlau, 2013.

Löffler, Anette. "Die Rolle der Liturgie im Ordenskonvent. Norm und Wirklichkeit." In *Das Leben im Ordenshaus. Vorträge der Tagung der Internationalen Historischen Kommission zur Erforschung des Deutschen Ordens in Tallinn 2014*. Edited by Juhan Kreem, 1–21. QSGD 81. Weimar: VDG, 2019.

McCormick, Michael. *Eternal Victory: Triumphal Rulership in Late Antiquity, Byzantium and the Early Medieval West*. Cambridge: Cambridge University Press, 1986.

Mentzel-Reuters, Arno. *"Arma Spiritualia." Bibliotheken, Bücher und Bildung im Deutschen Orden*. Beiträge zum Buch- und Bibliothekswesen 47. Wiesbaden: Harrassowitz, 2003.

Mentzel-Reuters, Arno. "Der Deutsche Orden als geistlicher Orden." In *"Cura animarum." Seelsorge im Deutschordensland Preußen*. Edited by Stefan Samerski, 15–43. FQKK 45. Cologne: Böhlau, 2013.

Mentzel-Reuters, Arno. "'Deutschordensliteratur' im literarischen Kontext." In *Mittelalterliche Kultur und Literatur im Deutschordensstaat in Preussen. Leben und Nachleben*. Edited by Jarosław Wenta, Sieglinde Hoffmann, and Gisela Vollmann-Profe, 356–68. SBS 1. Toruń: Wydawnictwo Naukowe Uniwersytetu Mikołaja Kopernika, 2008.

Motzki, Arthur. *Avignonische Quellen zur Geschichte des Ordensland (1342–1366)*. Beilage zum Jahresbericht des Königlichen Gymnasiums zu Braunsberg 1914 3. Braunsberg Ostpr.: Heynes, 1914.

Murray, Alan V., ed. *Crusade and Conversion on the Baltic Frontier, 1150–1500*. Farnham and Burlington VT: Ashgate, 2001.

Murray, Alan V., ed. *The North-Eastern Frontiers of Medieval Europe: The Expansion of Latin Christendom in the Baltic Lands, 1000–1550*. The expansion of Latin Europe, 1000–1500 4. Farnham and Burlington VT: Ashgate, 2014.

Malkkim, Jane, Tuomas M.S. Lehtonen, and Kurt Villads Jensen, ed. *Medieval History Writing and Crusading Ideology*. Studia Fennica. Historica 9. Helsinki: Finnish Literary Society, 2005.

Morton, Nicholas. "The Defence of the Holy Land and the Memory of the Maccabees." *JMH* 36.3 (2010): 275–93.

Morton, Nicholas. *The Medieval Military Orders, 1120–1314*. Seminar Studies 1. Abingdon and New York: Routledge, 2013.

Newhauser, Richard, Tiina Kala, and Meelis Friedenthal. "The Work of an English Scribe in a Manuscript in Estonia." *Scriptorium. International Review of Medieval Studies* 62.1 (2008): 139–48.

Nicholson, Helen J. "Memory and the Military Orders." In *Entre Deus e o Rei. O Mundo das Ordens Militares I. Arquivos e Memória*. Edited by Isabel Cristina Gerreira Fernandes, 17–28. Coleção ordens militares 8. Palmela: Município de Palmela-GEsOS, 2018.

Nicholson, Helen J. "Saints Venerated in the Military Orders." In *Selbstbild und Selbstverständnis der geistlichen Ritterorden*. Edited by Roman Czaja and Jürgen Sarnowsky, 91–113. OM 13. Toruń: Wydawnictwo Naukowe Uniwersytetu Mikołaja Kopernika, 2005.

Nielsen, Torben Kjersgaard. "Henry of Livonia on Woods and Wilderness." In *Crusading and Chronicle Writing on the Medieval Baltic Frontier: A Companion to the Chronicle of Henry of Livonia*. Edited by Marek Tamm, Linda Kaljundi, and Carsten Selch Jensen, 157–78. Farnham and Burlington VT: Ashgate, 2011.

Nielsen, Torben Kjersgaard, and Iben Fonnesberg-Schmidt, ed. *Crusading on the Edge: Ideas and Practices of Crusading in Iberia and the Baltic Region, 1100–1500*. Outremer 4. Turnhout: Brepols, 2016.

Paravicini, Werner. *Adlig Leben im 14. Jahrhundert. Weshalb sie fuhren? Die Preußenreisen des europäischen Adels, Teil 3*. Vestigia Prussica. Forschungen zur ost- und westpreußischen Landesgeschichte 2. Göttingen: Vandenhoek & Ruprecht, 2020.

Paravicini, Werner. "Litauer. Vom heidnischen Gegner zum adligen Standesgenossen." In *Tannenberg—Grunwald—Žalgiris 1410. Krieg und Frieden im späten Mittelalter*. Edited by Werner Paravicini, Rimvydas Petrauskas, and Grischa Vercamer, 253–84. DHIW 26. Wiesbaden: Harrassowitz, 2012.

Paravicini, Werner. *Die Preußenreisen des europäischen Adels*. 2 vols. BF 17.1–2. Sigmaringen: Thorbecke, 1989–1995.

Paravicini, Werner. "Verlorene Denkmäler europäischer Ritterschaft. Die heraldischen Malereien des 14. Jahrhunderts im Dom zu Königsberg." In *Kunst und Geschichte im Ostseeraum. Tagungen 1988 und 1989*. Edited by Erich Böckler, 67–123. Homburger Gespräche 12. Kiel: Martin-Carl-Adolf-Böckler-Stiftung, 1990.

Paravicini, Werner. "Vom Kreuzzug zum Soldzug. Die Schlacht bei Tannenberg und das Ende der Preußenfahrten des europäischen Adels." In *"Conflictus magnus apud Grunwald" 1410. Między historią a tradycją*. Edited by Krzysztof Ożóg and Janusz Trupinda, 119–26. Malbork: Muzeum Zamkowe, 2013.

Päsler, Ralf G. *Deutschsprachige Sachliteratur im Preußenland bis 1500. Untersuchungen zu ihrer Überlieferung*. Aus Archiven, Bibliotheken und Museen Mittel- und Osteuropas 2. Cologne: Böhlau, 2003.

Petrauskas, Rimvydas. "Knighthood in the Grand Duchy of Lithuania from the Late Fourteenth to the Early Sixteenth Centuries." *Lithuanian Historical Studies* 11 (2006): 36–66.

Radler, Gudrun. "Der Beitrag des Deutschordenslandes zur Entwicklung der Schreinmadonna (1390–1420)." In *Sztuka w kręgu zakonu krzyżackiego w Prusach i Inflantach*. Edited by Michał Woźniak, 241–74. Studia Borussica-Baltica Torunensia Historiae Artium 2. Toruń: Uniwersytet Mikołaja Kopernika, 1995.

Radler, Gudrun. "Die Schreinmadonnen des Deutschordenslandes Preußen." In *"Terra Sanctae Mariae." Mittelalterliche Bildwerke der Marienverehrung im Deutschordensland Preußen*. Edited by Gerhard Eimer et al., 199–212. Kunsthistorische Arbeiten der Kulturstiftung der deutschen Vertriebenen 7. Bonn: Kulturstiftung der deutschen Vertriebenen, 2009.

Rivard, Derek A. *Blessing the World: Ritual and Lay Piety in Medieval Religion*. Washington DC: Catholic University of America Press, 2009.

Sarnowsky, Jürgen. *Der Deutsche Orden*. Wissen 24. Munich: Beck, 2011.

Sarnowsky, Jürgen. "Identität und Selbstgefühl der geistlichen Ritterorden." In *Ständische und religiöse Identitäten in Mittelalter und frühen Neuzeit*. Edited by Stefan Kwiatkowski and Janusz Małłek, 109–30. Toruń: Uniwersytet Mikołaja Kopernika, 1998.

Schleif, Corine. "Die Schreinmadonna im Diözesanmuseum zu Limburg. Ein verfemtes Bildwerk des Mittelalters" *Jahrbuch des Vereins für Nassauische Altertumskunde und Geschichtsforschung* 95 (1985): 39–54.

Smith, Katherine Allen. *The Bible and Crusade Narrative in the Twelfth Century*. Woodbridge: Boydell Press, 2020.

Smith, Katherine Allen. "Glossing the Holy War: Exegetical Constructions of the First Crusade, c.1099–c.1146." *Studies in Medieval and Renaissance History*, ser. 3 10.3 (2013): 1–39.

Steffenhagen, Emil Julius Hugo. *Catalogus codicum manuscriptorum bibliothecae Regiae et Universitatis Regimontiae*. Vol. 1. Königsberg: Schubert & Seidel, 1861.

Steffenhagen, Emil Julius Hugo. "Zu dem Thorner Formelbuche und dem Formelbuche Arnold's von Protzan." *Altpreußische Monatsschrift* 8 (1871): 531–34.

Strange, John. "Heilsgeschichte und Geschichte. Ein Aspekt der Biblischen Theologie." *Scandinavian Journal of the Old Testament* 3.2 (1989): 100–13.

Strenga, Gustavs. "Remembering the Common Past: Livonia as a 'lieu de mémoire' of the Teutonic Order in the Empire." In *Livland—Eine Region am Ende der Welt? Forschungen zum Verhältnis zwischen Zentrum und Peripherie im späten Mittelalter*. Edited by Anti Selart and Matthias Thumser, 347–71. QSBG 27. Cologne, Weimar, and Vienna: Böhlau, 2017.

Tamm, Marek. "Inventing Livonia: The Name and Fame of a New Christian Colony on the Medieval Baltic Frontier." *ZfO* 60.2 (2011): 186–209.

Tamm, Marek. "A New World into Old Words: The Eastern Baltic Region in the Cultural Geography of Medieval Europe." In *The Clash of Cultures on the Medieval Baltic Frontier*. Edited by Alan V. Murray, 11–36. Farnham and Burlington VT: Ashgate, 2009.

Tautorat, Hans-Georg. "Zur Baugeschichte des Ordenshauses Ragnit (1397–1409)." *Jahrbuch der Albertus-Universität zu Königsberg* 22 (1972): 423–37.

Toomaspoeg, Kristjan. "Orsini del Balzo, Raimondo." In *Dizionario Biografico degli Italiani* 79 (2013), bit.ly/3K3x2ea.

Trupinda, Janusz. "Zespól heraldyczny z herbem von Jungingen w systemie dekoracji malarskiej piętra reprezentacyjnego Pałacu Wielkich Mistrzów w Malborku." In *Krzyżacy—szpitalnicy—kondotierzy*. Edited by Błazej Śliwiński, 397–423. Studia z dziejów średniowieczna 12. Malbork: Muzeum Zamkowe, 2006.

Urban, William. *The Baltic Crusade*. Dekalb IL: Northern Illinois University Press, 1975.

Urban, William. *The Livonian Crusade*. Washington DC: University Press of America, 1989.

Urban, William. *The Prussian Crusade*. Washington DC: University Press of America, 1982.

Urban, William. *The Samogitian Crusade*. Chicago: Lithuanian Research and Studies Center, 1989.

Vennebusch, Jochen Hermann. "Zentral Facetten der Spiritualität des Deutschen Ordens im Spiegel der 'älteren Hochmeisterchronik.'" *OM* 18 (2013): 243–318.

Voigt, Johannes. *Namen-Codex der Deutsch-Ordens Beamten, Hochmeister, Landmeister, Großgebietiger, Komthure, Vögte, Pfleger, Hochmeister-Kompane, Kreuzfahrer und Söldner-Hauptleute in Preussen*. Königsberg: Bornträger, 1843.

Wenta, Jarosław. "Bemerkungen über die Funktion eines mittelalterlichen historiographischen Textes. Die Chronik des Peter von Dusburg." In *"De litteris, manuscriptis, inscriptionibus ..." Festschrift zum 65. Geburtstag von Walter Koch*. Edited by Theo Kölzer et al., 675–86. Cologne, Weimar, and Vienna: Böhlau, 2007.

Wenta, Jarosław. "Kazanie i historyczne egzemplum w późnośredniowiecznym Chełmnie." In *"Ecclesia et civitas." Kościół i życie religijne w mieście średniowiecznym*. Edited by Halina Manikowska and Hanna Zaremska, 473–483. Colloquia medievalia Varsoviensia 3. Warsaw: Instytut Historii Polskiej Akademii Nauk, 2002.

Wenta, Jarosław. *Studien über die Ordensgeschichtsschreibung am Beispiel Preußens*. Studia hisotriographica 2. Toruń: Wydawnictwo Naukowe Uniwersytetu Mikołaja Kopernika, 2003.

Weise, Erich. "Der Heidenkampf des Deutschen Ordens, Erster Teil." *ZfO* 12.1 (1963): 63–80.

Weise, Erich. "Der Heidenkampf des Deutschen Ordens, Zweiter Teil." *ZfO* 13.4 (1964): 401–20.

Woźniak, Michał. "Dyptyk relikwiarzowy elbląskiego komtura domowego Thiele von Loricha." In *"Praeterita posteritati." Studia z historii sztuki i kultury ofiarowane Maciejowi Kilarskiemu*. Edited by Mariusz Mierzwiński, 481–500. Malbork: Muzeum Zamkowe, 2001.

Wüst, Marcus. *Studien zum Selbstverständnis des Deutschen Ordens im Mittelalter*. QSGD 73. Weimar: VDG, 2013.

Wüst, Marcus. "Zu Entstehung und Rezeption der 'Chronik des Preussenlandes' Peters von Dusburg." In *Neue Studien zur Literatur im Deutschen Orden*. Edited by Bernhart Jähnig and Arno Mentzel-Reuters, 197–211. Zeitschrift für deutsches Altertum und deutsche Literatur. Beiheifte 19. Berlin: LIT, 2014.

Zonenberg, Sławomir. "Kto był autorem 'Epitome gestorum Prussie'?" ZH 74.4 (2013): 85–102.

Zonenberg, Sławomir. "Wstęp źródłoznawczy i historyczny." In *Nowa kronika Pruska*. Edited by Sławomir Zonenberg and Krzysztof Kwiatkowski, 13–44. Toruń: Towarzystwo Naukowe w Toruniu, 2017.

Zupka, Dušan. *Meč a kríž. Vojna a náboženstvo v stredovekej strednej Európe (10.–12. storočie)*. Bratislava: VEDA, 2020.

Index

Aaron, Patriarch of Israel (biblical)   94, 215, 262
Abel (biblical)   213, 215
Aberdeen   157, 160–61, 175
Abraham (biblical), Hebrew patriarch   213–15, 268–69
Absalon, archbishop of Lund (1178–1192)   137
Acre, siege of (1189–1192)   36
Adam and Eve (biblical)   213–14
Adasa, battle of (161 BC)   278
Adhemar of Monteil, bishop of Le Puy (1082–1098), papal legate and crusader   201
Adomnán of Iona (saint), abbot, lawmaker and hagiographer   71–73, 89, 176
Áed Findliath mac Niall, high king of Ireland   96
Áed mac Ainmuirech, high king of the Northern (d. 598)   84, 91
Áed Sláne, son of Diarmait mac Cerbaill   92–93
Áedán mac Gabráin, king of Dál Riata (ca. 574–ca. 609)   73, 89
Aemilian of Cogolla (Berceo) (saint)   40
Aethelred I, king of Wessex (865–871)   78
Aethelred II / the Unready, king of the English (978–1013)   78, 81, 101
Aethelstan, king of England (924–939)   99
Aelred of Rievaulx, chronicler   98, 100–2, 104–6, 179n50
Ágrip af Nóregskonungasögum   123
Ahaz (biblical), king of Judah   86
Aided Diarmata meic Cerbaill, saga   76, 80, 84, 93
al-Andalus, Andalusia   33, 37–38, 40
Albert of Aix(-la-Chapelle) or of Aachen, chronicler   199n34, 220
Albert of Buxhövden, bishop of Livonia (1199–1229)   233n8, 234–35, 237, 239–40, 243
Albert von Lauenburg   251
Albrecht of Hagen, Teutonic knight   205
Alcacer do Sal, campaigns against (1147)   48
Alexander II, king of Scotland (1214–1249)   174

Alexander III, king of Scotland (1249–1286)   174
Alfonso I of Portugal / the Conqueror / Afonso Henriques, count of Portugal (1112–1139), king of Portugal (1139–1185)   32
Alfonso VIII of Castile / the Noble (El Noble), king of Castile and Toledo (1158–1214)   38–39
Alfonso X / the Wise of Castile, king of Castile and León (1252–1284)   40
Alfred the Great, king of Wessex (871–886), king of Anglo-Saxons (886–899)   75, 77–78, 99
Alfred's *Prose Psalms*   77
Allington, Richard   195
Almeria, campaigns in 1147   48
Alps   221
Althaus Kulm / Starogród   206n59, 207
Alvira Cabrer, Martín   32, 38–39, 40n29
Amalekites (biblical)   74, 80, 262
Amiens   220
Andrew Sunesen, archbishop of Lund (1201–1228)   238
Andreas, priest   123
Andrew (saint), apostle and patron of Scotland   167, 171, 173–74, 176, 217
angel, angels, angelic   170, 212, 218
   See also standard-bearers (miraculous); warrior-saints
   role in war, imagination of   41, 98, 173n42
   St. Michael, Archangel   214
Andrew of Wyntoun, chronicler   178
Anglo-Norman realm. *See* England, English
Anthony of Padua (saint)   40
Antioch, siege or battle of (1097/1098)   42, 212, 215, 215n79, 217
Antonsson, Haki   134
Apocrypha   268
Aquitaine   47n59
Aragon   40–41
Aramites (biblical)   86
Armagh   97, 100
Arnau Amalric, archbishop of Narbonne (ca. 1212–1225)   55

Arnold of Lübeck, chronicler 249
Arnold of Procan / Protzan / Zwrócona, canon of Wrocław, bishop's notary 260–61
Árpád (Hungarian dynasty) 44
Ashdown, battle of (871) 78
Áskell týza, the leading man of the Birkibeinar in Bergen 126
Aspesi, Cara 36
Asser, hagiographer 78
Audita tremendi, papal bull (1187) 195*n*16
Augustine (saint) 247, 247*n*59
Aurell, Martin 223
Avars 6, 77
Avignon 269

Baal 215
Bachall Fínghin 100
Bachall Ísu ("The Staff of Jesus") 94, 96–98, 100, 170
Bachall Rónáin Fhinn 100
Bachrach, David S. 5, 7
Baglar, faction or party during the Norwegian Civil Wars 131, 133, 144–46
Baker, Derek 101
Baldwin I, king of Jerusalem (1100–1118) 123
Baldwin and Ernoul of Beauvais, crusaders 194, 213, 214
Baldwin of Biggar, sheriff of Lanark 180*n*51
Balga / Veseloe 274*n*58, 277
Baltic, region 3, 10, 19–20, 33–35, 37, 44, 49, 53, 241, 246, 261–64, 266, 269, 279–80, 282, 286
Banaszkiewicz, Jacek 17
Bandlien, Bjørn 120, 127
Bangor 80, 86
Bannockburn, battle of (1314) 19, 153, 155–57, 158*n*16, 159–60, 162–64, 164*n*29, 166–68, 168*n*38, 169–76, 176*n*45, 177, 177*n*48, 178–81
Barabbas (biblical) 213
Barbara (saint) 44, 205–6, 206*n*59, 207, 207*n*60–61
Barcelona, county of 32
Bartholomeus of Radam, bishop of Sambia (1358–1378) 285
Bartlett, Robert 129, 176
Basil of Caesarea (saint) 127
Baudri of Dol, chronicler 199*n*34, 200, 200*n*40

Bavaria, Bavarian 219
Belarus 10
Benedictines (Order of St. Benedict) 156, 221
Berenguer de Vilademuls, archbishop of Tarragona (1174–1194) 42
Bergen 122, 130, 136, 145
Berlin 206
Bernard, abbot of Arbroath, bishop of the Isles (d. 1331) 166, 172, 174–76
Bernard of Clairvaux (saint), theologian and crusade preacher 47, 118, 143
Bernard of Haren, Teutonic brother 197
Bernhard of Lippe, abbot of Dünemünde 251, 251*n*74
Berthold, bishop of Livonia (1196–1198) 236–37, 237*n*22, 247, 249–50, 252
Berwick, castle of 157, 179*n*50
Betha Choluim Chille (*The Life of Columba*, twelfth-century) 92–93
Betha Colaim Chille (*The Life of Columba*, sixteenth-century) 80, 89
Betha Finnchua Brí Gobunn (*The Life of Finnchú of Brí Gobann*) 80, 97, 99, 105
Bethu Phátraic (the so-called *Vita Tripartita Sancti Patricii* or *Tripartite Life of St. Patrick*) 83, 94, 97
Bible, biblical 74–75, 77, 107, 189, 193*n*9, 202, 212, 223, 233, 233*n*7, 235, 245, 245*n*53, 262, 268
  Book of Deuteronomy 76, 102–4
  Book of Esther 268
  Book of Exodus 74, 80, 94, 262, 270, 279
  Book of Genesis 269
  Book of Job 268
  Book of Joshua 74, 88, 107, 270
  Book of Judith 193*n*9, 268
  Books of Maccabees, First and Second 74, 102–3, 107, 193*n*9, 268, 270, 275, 275*n*65, 278
  Book of Psalms 19, 74–76, 78–79, 81–84, 86–87, 98, 103–4, 194, 196
  Gospels 90, 99
Birkibeinar, faction or party during the Norwegian Civil Wars 117, 126, 127*n*33, 131–33, 135–36, 138–40, 145, 145*n*110
Birr, synod of (697) 71
Bliese, John 101

INDEX

Bohemia, Bohemians / *Bohemi*, Bohemian   3, 12–13, 200, 200*n*39, 221*n*96, 265
Boemond I of Antioch, prince of Taranto (1088–1111) and Antioch (1098–1111)   42, 199*n*34, 217*n*84
Bolesław III / the Wrymouth, prince of Poland (1102–1138)   191, 201–2, 203*n*46, 204, 204*n*53, 208, 209*n*64, 221, 221*n*96
Bologna   49
Book of Leinster   91
Brandenburg / Ushakovo   272*n*58, 277
Brian Bóruma, king of Munster (978–1014), high king of Ireland (1002–1014)   81–82
Brigit of Kildare (saint)   88, 97, 100
British Isles, Britain   5, 71, 73, 78, 83, 107, 265
Brodman, James W.   40, 52
Bruce, poem. See John Barbour
Bubczyk, Robert   19, 81*n*48
Bugge, Alexander   137
Buile Suibhne (*The Madness of Sweeney*), saga   79
Bull, Marcus   46
Byzantium, Byzantines, Byzantine.   See Roman Empire (Eastern, Byzantine)

Caillín (saint)   93
Cáin Adomnáin. See *Lex Innocentium*
Calahorra   40–41*n*34
Callraigi of Cúle-Cernadán   97
Canóin Pádraig (*Book of Armagh*)   100
Canones Nidrosienses   134
Cantar de Mio Cid   55
Cantigas de Santa Maria   40
Capetian (French dynasty)   35
Carloman, Frankish majordomo   168
Carmelites (The Order of the Brothers of the Blessed Virgin Mary of Mount Carmel)   168*n*38
Carmen de Morte Sumerledi by Willelmus   180
Carolingians (Frankish dynasty), Carolingian empire   4–5, 77–78, 200
Castile, Castilian   32, 52, 56
Catherina of Alexandria (saint)   205
Caupo, Livonian nobleman   250–51
Céle Dabaill, abbot of Bangor (ca. 868–927)   80
Celestine III, pope (1191–1198)   137, 145, 236
Cellach (saint), abbot and archbishop of Armagh (d. 1129)   97

Ceólán Tighernaigh (*Bell of Tigernach*)   100
Champagne-Blois family   194
Chanson d'Antioche. See Graindor of Douai
Chansons de le Croisade Albigeois   55
Chanson d'Jérusalem. See Graindor of Douai
Charlemagne, king of the Franks (768–814), of the Lombards (774–814), emperor (800–814)   77, 81, 127
Charles the Bald, Frankish king, emperor (875–877)   203*n*50
Chester, battle at (ca. 605–613)   73
Christburg / Dzierzgoń   219
Chronica gentis Scotorum   157
Chronica monasterii S. Albani   156
Chronica Slavorum. See Helmold of Bosau
Chronicle of Lanercost   156–57, 165, 169
Chronicon Angliae temporibus Edwardi II et Edwardi III   156
Chronicon Livoniae. See Henry of Livonia
Chronicon terrae Prussiae. See Peter of Dusburg
churches / monasteries
  at Arnau / Rodniki   276
  at Juditten / Mendeleevo   274, 276
  at Kirkton of Strath Fillan, priory   172
  at Whithorn, St. Ninian's priory   172, 178
  in Bergen, St. Olaf's church   130
  in Burgos, Santa María Real de las Huelgas, monastery   32, 38–39
  in Derry, monastery   90
  in Dunfermline, abbey   178–79
  in Frauenburg / Frombork, Cathedral of the Blessed Virgin Mary   271
  in Glasgow, Cathedral of St. Kentigern   180, 180*n*51
  in Gniezno, Cathedral of Sts. Mary and Adalbert   273
  in Inchaffray, abbey   172, 177
  in Inchcolm, monastery   157, 177
  in Jerusalem, Holy Sepulcher Church   220–21
  in Kalvskinnet   133
  in Königsberg, Cathedral of Virgin Mary and St. Adalbert   276
  in Königsberg, nunnery at Löbenicht   276
  in Lanercost, monastery   158*n*15
  in Melrose, abbey   178
  in Padis / Padise, monastery   283
  in Płock, Virgin Mary Cathedral   204

churches / monasteries (*cont.*)
  in Rome, Basilica of Santa Croce in Gerusalemme 195
  in Rome, Lateran archbasilica 195
  in Rome, Santa Anastasia 195
  in Rome, Santa Maria Maggiore 195
  in Rome, Santi Apostoli 195
  in San Millán de la Cogolla, San Millán de la Cogolla monastery 40, 40–41n34
  in Santa Maria de Huerta, Santa Maria de Huerta monastery 38
  in St Andrews, Cathedral of *St Andrew* 173
  in Strathearn, chapel 177
  in Tynemouth, monastery 156
  in Vézelay, Abbey of Sainte-Marie-Madeleine 216
  of Arbroath, abbey 91, 172, 174–76
  of Birr 74
  of Clonmacnoise 74
  of Dünamünde / Daugavgrīva, cistercian abbey 239, 283
  of Iona Abbey 176
  of Łysa Góra (Bald Mountain) / Łysiec / Święty Krzyż, monastery 208
  of St. Albans Abbey 156
  of St. Pierre-de-Bourgueil 200n40
Cistercians (Order of Cistercians) 52, 106
Citeaux (abbey) 55
Clancy, Thomas O. 7, 89, 94
Clavijo, battle of (fictional?) (834 or 844) 37
Clement III, pope (1187–1191) 145
Clement VI, pope (1342–1352) 283–84
clergy, clerical order
  authority of 221
  armsbearing by (or lack thereof) 119–20, 145
  chaplaincy and spiritual ministry to the army/rulers by 5, 31–32, 99, 102–3, 117, 119–20, 164, 164n29, 165–69, 171–72, 181, 199, 231, 243, 283, 285
    See also tented chapels and/portable altars, use in war
  participation / involvement in warfare (or lack thereof) 5, 10, 14, 19, 41, 73, 103, 117, 119–21, 134–35, 139, 145–46, 164–67, 169, 180–81, 181n55, 199, 222, 237, 285
  role in peace-making / restraining from war of by 72, 96–97
Clermont 46
Clontarf, battle at (1014) 81–82
Cogad Gáedel re Gallaib (*The War of the Irish with the Foreigners*), saga 81–82
Coimbra, siege of (1064) 37
Coirpre Cromm mac Crimthainn, the Eóganacht prince and king (d. 577) 106–7
Cole, Penny 47
Columba / Colum Cille (saint), abbot and missionary, patron of Scotland 73, 80, 88–90, 100, 172, 175–76, 176n45, 177
Conall Derg 84
Conall Gulban 94, 96
Concilium Germanicum (742) 168
Conchobar mac Nessa, legendary king of Ulaid 85, 87
Conedera, SJ, Sam Zeno 51
Conmaicne people 96
Conn Ua Domnaill, king of Ireland (956–980) 89
Connachata, Kingdom of 85, 87, 96–97
Conrad, landgrave of Thuringia (1231–1234), grand master of the Teutonic Order (1239–1240) 201–2, 204, 221
Constable, Giles 51
Constantine I / the Great, Roman emperor (306–337) 118
Constantine II of Scotland, king of Scotland (900–943) 81
Constantinople 131
  Latin Empire of 42, 49
Contamine, Philippe 17, 119
Corbaran d'Oliferne, emir 194, 213
Cormac Ua Cillín, chief vice-abbot of Síl Muiredaigh 96
Cornell, David 158n16
Cronica of Guillaume de Puylarens 55
Cronicae et gesta ducum sive principum Polonorum / *Chronicles and Deeds of the Dukes or Princes of the Poles* by Gallus Anonymus. *See* Gallus Anonymus

INDEX 301

Cronica nova Prutenica. See Wigand of Marburg
Cronicon Scotorum 96
crusades   161, 189–90, 199*n*33, 200, 222, 235–36, 239
　See also war, fighting (*also* ideology of): crusading ideology/notion of/propaganda, rhetoric and/or idea of; Holy Land, Outremer
　against Albigensians   48–49
　against Hussites (1420–1421)   271
　against Ottomans (1396, 1443/1444, 1456, 1526)   6*n*12
　in the Baltic region (1198–1503)   3, 13, 20, 32–34, 43, 189–90, 192, 193*n*9, 203–5, 212, 217, 231–33, 235–36, 239, 263, 265, 280, 282
　　First (1096–1099)   46–47, 47*n*59, 48, 118, 193–94, 199*n*34, 200–1, 215, 217, 220
　　Second (1145–1149)   47–48
　　Third (1189–1192)   47
　　Fourth (1202–1204)   48–49
　　Fifth (1217–1221)   50, 194
crusading ideology/notion of/propaganda   19, 46–50, 54, 120, 190, 190*n*3, 194–95, 235–36, 236*n*17, 239–40, 263, 280, 283, 286
Cubbesele / Kizbele   251
Cú Chulainn, warrior   85
Cúil Dreimne, battle of (ca. 555–561)   80, 89
Culm / Kulm / Chełmno   207*n*61, 217–218
cursing stones   93
Cuthbert of Lindisfarne (saint)   99, 158, 158*n*16, 176*n*45
Czaja, Roman   264
Czesław Odrowąż, Dominican friar   210–11

Dál Riata, Kingdom of   100
Daniel (biblical)   214, 216
Daugava / Düna / Dvina, river   239, 247, 253
David (biblical), Hebrew king   77, 127, 212, 268, 270
David I / the Saint, king of Scotland (1124–1153)   98, 102–5, 105*n*151
David Lindsay of Crawford, Scottish nobleman   174
Davidian revolution   74
De arte praedicandi by Alanus de Insulis   283

Declán of Ardmore (saint)   93
Demetrius of Thessaloniki (saint)   42, 217, 217*n*85
Denis (saint)   127, 214
Denmark, Danes, Danish   41, 44, 49–50, 122, 234–38, 240–41
Dercán, a wealthy pagan of Déisi Muman   93
devil. *See* Sathanas, dragon, devil
Diarmait mac Cerbaill, king of Tara (ca. 658/660–665)   80, 84, 92
Die ältere Hochmeisterchronik   268, 276
Dietrich of Bernheim, marshal of the Teutonic Orden   206, 206*n*59
Domingo Pascual, canon and archbishop elect of the Toledo   38–39
Dominic de la Calzada (saint)   40
Dominic of Osma (saint)   40
Dominic of Silos (saint)   40
Dominicans (Order of Preachers)   49, 55
Domnall Ua Lochlainn, king of Cenél Eogain, over-king of Ailech, and alleged high king of Ireland (d. 1121)   96, 100
Down   100
Dublin   100
Duby, Georges   55
Dunstan of Canterbury (saint)   105*n*148
Duparc-Quioc, Suzanne   194
Durben / Durbe, battle of (1260)   280
Durendal, legendary sword of Roland   127
Durham   90*n*84, 99, 158*n*16

East Central Europe / Central Europe   10, 13, 15, 198, 222
Eastern Europe   3–4, 6, 9, 11, 16, 198, 204, 216, 222
Edinburgh   175
Edington, battle of (878)   99
Edmund the Martyr (saint)   158
Edward I, king of England (1272–1307)   158, 158*n*15–16, 171, 179*n*50
Edward II, king of England (1307–1327)   157–58, 158*n*16, 159–60, 162–63, 166, 167*n*37, 168*n*38, 170, 172, 176*n*45, 182
Egypt   207, 236
Eirik Ivarsson, archbishop of Nidaros (1188–1205)   125
Elbe, river   198*n*28
Elbing / Elbląg   277

Elisha, Hebrew prophet (biblical)   215
Elizabeth of Hungary (saint)   205
Elizabeth of Thuringia (saint)   205, 213
Emilianus of Berceo (saint)   37
England, English   6–7, 43, 74, 77–78, 81, 83, 98–100, 102–4, 106, 153, 155–61, 163, 165–66, 166*n*35, 167, 167*n*37, 168*n*38, 169–70, 172, 176*n*45, 178, 180–82
Énnae Cennselach, legendary ancestor of Leinster dynasty   106
Enns, river   77
Eógan mac Néill, king of Connacht (d. ca. 465)   97
Eóganachta (Irish dynasty)   97, 106
Erdmann, Carl   6
Erik Ívarsson, archbishop of Nidaros (1188–1202)   137–38, 144
Erik II / the Emune, king of Denmark (1134–1137)   122
Erling Skakki, Norwegian jarl   127*n*33, 128–29, 132–34, 137, 143
Esau, son of Isaac   212–14
Estonia, Estonian, Estonians   43, 44*n*47, 231–36, 238, 241–42, 245–46, 247*n*60, 250–51, 254–56, 263
Eudes de Chatêauroux, theologian and cardinal (d. 1273)   190*n*3
excommunication   19, 132, 136–40, 144–47, 181*n*55
   See also rites of war: cursing the enemy
Eysteinn Erlendsson, archbishop of Nidaros (1161–1188)   134–37, 142–44

Feginsbrekka / Hill of Grace   133
Fergus mac Róig, legendary king of Ulaid   87
Fernando I of León / the Great (el Magno), count of León (1029–1037), king of León (1037–1065)   37
Fernando III of Castile / the Saint (el Santo), king of Castile and Toledo (1217–1252), king of León and Galicia (1230–1252)   40
Figurski, Paweł   16
Fillan of Munster (saint)   172, 177, 177*n*48
Fimreite, battle of (1184)   126, 129
Finnchú (saint)   80, 97, 106–7
Finnian (saint)   80
First Prussian Uprising (1242–1249)   217

Fischer, Mary   265
Flanders   194, 199*n*34
Flann mac Conaing, king of Brega (786–812)   96
Fonnesberg-Schmidt, Iben   263
Forey, Alan J.   51
Forglen in Banffshire (estate)   175
Fragmentary Annals of Ireland   81, 96
France, John   79, 199*n*34, 265
Franco, "Polish" bishop   202
Frankfurt (Oder)   206
Franks, Frankish   35, 77–78, 91, 168, 203, 215, 221
Fraser, James E.   72–73
Frederick I Barbarossa, king of Germany (1152–1190), of Burgundy (1152–1190), of Italy (1155–1190), Holy Roman Emperor (1155–1190)   30, 204
Friedrich of Zoller, commander of Ragnit   272
Fritzlar   202
Fulcher of Chartres, chaplain, crusader, and chronicler   199*n*34
Fulcher the Orphan, crusader   215, 215*n*79
Fyrisleif / Färlev, battle of (1134)   122–123, 142

Gaels, Gaelic   7–8, 19, 71, 74–75, 81, 84–85, 88–90, 94, 101, 104–5, 107–8
Galician-Volhynian Chronicle   208
Galindians   213
Gallus Anonymus, the so-called, chronicler   191, 202, 208
Gancarczyk, Paweł   266
Gaposchkin, M. Cecilia   6, 35, 119
Gascony   47*n*59
Gelasius, pope (492–496)   31
Geoffrey le Baker of Swinbrook, chronicler   156, 160, 165, 168*n*38
Geoffroi de Charny, French knight   201–2
George (saint)   37, 40–41, 43, 205, 205*n*55, 214, 217, 217*n*85
Georgia, Georgian   42
Germany, Germans, German   87, 203, 217, 233, 235–42, 245, 247, 249, 253, 264–65, 268
Gerold, bishop of Starigard / Oldenburg (1155–1163)   198*n*28
Gerrard, Daniel   119

INDEX

Gesta Francorum (*Deeds of the Franks* by anonymous)   199*n*34
Gideon (biblical)   212, 278
Gilbert of Tournai, French Franciscan friar (1284)   190*n*3
Giles the Hermit (saint)   201–2, 203*n*46, 205, 214
Gille (Gilbert) of Limerick, bishop of Limerick (1106–1140)   79
Glasgow   171
Gloucester   167*n*37
Gniezno   16, 273
Godfrey of Bouillon, leader of the First Crusade   215
Goliath (biblical)   212
Gotland, isle   235, 237–39, 253
Graindor of Douai, French troubadour, author of *chansons de geste*: *Chanson d'Antioche*, *Les Chétifs*, *Chanson d'Jérusalem*   193, 193*n*10, 194, 194*n*12, 213, 215*n*79, 216, 220, 222
Gregory I the Great, pope (590–604)   216*n*83
Gregory VIII, pope (1187)   195*n*16
Gregory IX, pope (1227–1241)   275
Grunwald / Tannenberg / Žalgiris, battle of (1410)   267, 273
Guibert of Nogent, chronicler   199*n*34
Guillibert de Lannoy, Prussian crusader   274
Guilhelm de Tudela (William of Tudela), writer   55
Gulf of Riga   239
Guthlac (saint)   83

Håkon II / Herdebrei, king of Norway (1147–1162)   128
Håkon III Sverisson, king of Norway (1202–1204)   140
Håkon IV Håkonsson, king of Norway (1217–1263)   178
Harald IV / Gille, king of Norway (1130–1136)   122–23, 130, 141, 141*n*93–94, 142
Haraldsdrápa, skaldic poem by *Halldórr skvaldri*   141
Harold Godwinson, king of England (1066)   98
Harpin of Bourges, crusader   194, 214–15
Harrington, Jesse Patrick   19

Hastings, battle of (1066)   98
Hattin, battle of (1187)   125, 195*n*16
Hector Boece, chronicler   177*n*48
Heimskringla, saga by Snorri Sturluson   123–25, 128–29
Heinrich Kuwal, bishop of Sambia (1387–1395)   276
Heinrich of Kunzen, brother of the Teutonic Order   219–20
Heinrich Stange, brother of the Teutonic Order   219, 221
Heinrich Vincke of Overberg, landmeister of Livonia (1438/1439–1450)   277
Heinz, Andreas   278
Helgasetr   146
Helmold of Bosau, chronicler   198, 198*n*28, 221, 221*n*95
Hennig Schindekopf, marshal of the Teutonic Order   276
Henriet, Patrick   40
Henry II Plantagenet, king of England (1154–1189)   172, 174
Henry V, king of Germany (1099–1125) and emperor (1111–1125)   192
Henry de Bohun, English knight   165
Henry of Huntingdon, chronicler   101–2
Henry of Livonia, chronicler   8, 20, 34, 231–33, 235–42, 243*n*42, 244–47, 247*n*60, 248–53, 255–56
Herbert of Selkirk, bishop of Glasgow (1147–1164)   180*n*51
Hermann Sarrazin, brother of the Teutonic Order   218, 218*n*88
Herrmann, Christofer   274
Hermon, mount   94
Historia Ecclesiastica by Bede   73
Historia Gentis Scotorum   177*n*48
Historia Roderici Campidocti   55
Hohenstaufen (Staufer) dynasty or empire   5
Holt, Edward L.   32
Holy Cross, Jerusalem relics of   214
Holy Land, Outremer, Latin East, Levant   19, 35–37, 41–43, 48, 51, 53, 122, 162, 173, 193, 195*n*16, 233, 236–37, 267, 271
Holy Sepulcher   214–15, 237
Holy Trinity   208
Hugo (saint)   158

Humbert of Romans, Dominican scholar (d. 1277) 190*n*3
Hungary, Hungarians (Magyars), Hungarian 3, 6, 13, 17, 44, 50, 56
Hur / Chur (biblical), companion of Moses and Aaron 262

Iarlaithe (saint) 93
Iberian Peninsula, Iberia, Iberian 32–33, 35, 37, 40–41, 48–49, 52–53, 236–37
Iceland, Icelandic 145
Inchcolm Antiphoner 177
Ingi, king of Norway (1136–1161) 128
Ingram de Umfraville, Scottish nobleman in English service 166, 168
Innocent III, pope (1198–1216) 145, 189, 194–95, 195*n*16
Innocent IV, pope (1243–1254) 178
Innocent V, pope (1276) 178
Innocent VI, pope (1352–1362) 284
Intervention/assistance of God/saints during war/battle 37, 40–42, 44, 91, 97–100, 106, 124, 130–132, 167, 171, 173*n*42, 174–77, 179, 209–12, 217
Ireland, Irish 7, 10, 71–76, 78, 80–81, 83–86, 88–90, 93, 95–96, 105*n*153, 107, 130, 131, 176
Isaac (biblical), son of Abraham 212
Isidore of Seville (saint), archbishop of Seville, theologian, and scholar 40, 170
Israel, Israelites, Israelite, Chosen People (ancient, biblical) 83, 87, 233, 262, 278
Italy 49, 265
Ivar Horti 133
Ivarr / Imar, king of Norsemen (857–873) 176

Jackson, Kenneth Hurlstone 85–86
Jacob (biblical), patriarch of the Israelites 212–14
Jacques de Vitry, theologian and cardinal (d. 1240) 190*n*3
Jaen, campaigns against (1148) 48
James Douglas, Scottish knight 173
James the Greater / Santiago (saint), apostle and patron of Spain 37–38, 214
Jan Długosz, historian 271
Jensen, Carsten Selch 8, 20, 263
Jensen, Kurt Villads 8, 263
Jeremiah (biblical), Hebrew prophet 278

Jerusalem, city and kingdom 6, 35–36, 42, 86, 103, 123, 190*n*3, 195*n*16, 199n34, 201, 215, 217, 220–21, 237
Jesus Christ 38, 82, 90, 104, 118, 131, 167, 170–71, 176, 190*n*3, 205–6, 212–15, 217–219, 221, 232, 234, 246, 248–49, 251, 266, 275, 283
Joab (biblical) 212
Job (biblical) 212
Jocelin of Furness, hagiographer 100
Jogaila. *See* Władysław II Jagiełło
Johann vom Felde, the Teutonic Order's procurator in Rome 264
Johannes, Lithuanian heathen warrior 206
Johannes of Posilge, church official and chronicler 267
John (saint), apostle, his feast 167, 167*n*37, 171
John Barbour, chronicler 157, 160–62, 162*n*25, 163, 165–66, 166*n*34, 169–70, 181
John Comyn III of Badenoch, Scottish magnate (d. 1306) 171, 180
John de Courcy, Anglo-Norman knight 100–1
John of Beverley (saint) 98–100, 158*n*16, 176*n*45
John of Fordun, chronicler 157
John of Luxembourg / the Blind, king of Bohemia (1310–1335) 206, 281
John of Salisbury, writer and scholar 203*n*47
John of Trokelowe, chronicler 156
John Rolleston, archbishop's vicar 158*n*16
John Wemyss, Scottish knight 178
Jon of Randaberg 133
Jonah / Jonas (biblical), Hebrew prophet 214–16
Jonathan (biblical) 212
Jordan, river 103
Jordan, William 35
Joseph (biblical) 213–14
Joshua (biblical), successor of Moses 212, 268, 270
Judith (biblical), slayer of Holofernes 212

Kaljundi, Linda 34, 263
Kalojan of Bulgaria, tsar of Bulgaria (1196–1207) 42
Kalvskinnet, battle of (1179) 133
Kangas, Sini 19

INDEX

Kaunas / Kowno, siege of (1362)   283, 285
Kazimierz son of Ziemomysł, duke of Gniewkowo (d. 1347/1353)   271
Kentigern / Mungo (saint), first bishop of Glasgow   179–80, 180n51
Kerbogha, Turkish atabeg   194, 217
Kirill, patriarch of Moscow   3
Knut VI, king of Denmark (1182–1202)   137
Kokenhusen / Koknese   247
Konrad von Erlichshausen, grand master of the Teutonic Order (1441–1449)   277
Konrad von Jungingen, grand master of the Teutonic Order (1393–1407)   264, 271, 281
Konrad Zöllner of Rotenstein, grand master of the Teutonic Order (1382–1390)   281
Konungahella / Kungälv   123–25
Konungs skuggsjá (*King's Mirror*)   147
Kotecki, Radosław   15, 44, 81n48
Königer, Albert M.   4
Königsberg / Kaliningrad   218, 272n58, 276–77, 282
Kronike von Pruzinlant. *See* Nicolaus of Jeroschin
Kuflungar people   126–27
Kwiatkowski, Krzysztof   9, 262n9, 264, 266, 285
Kwiatkowski, Stefan   197
Kyrie eleison (*Lord, have mercy*), chant   128–30

Laisrén of Daiminis (saint)   84
Lapina, Elisabeth   42
Largs, battle of (1263)   178–79
Las Navas de Tolosa, battle of (1212)   32, 38–39, 48, 55
Lateran Council, First (1123)   48
Lateran Council, Fourth (1215)   49, 169, 233n8, 234
Latvia, Latvian (Lettish), Latvians (Letts)   243–46, 249, 252, 254, 263
Lawrence (saint)   205, 209, 214
Lazarus of Bethany (saint)   212, 214–16
Leighton, Gregory   9, 20, 44, 274
Leinster, Kingdom of   81, 106
Leonard (saint)   214
Les Chétifs. *See* Graindor of Douai
Lex Innocentium (*Cáin Adomnáin*)   71, 73, 76
Liber Hymnorum   75
Life of King Alfred by Asser. *See* Asser
Limousin   47

Lincoln   102
Lincoln, Kyle   18–19
Linder, Amnon   36
Line, Philip   223
Lisbon, campaigns against (1147)   48
Lithuania, Lithuanians, Lithuanian, *also* Grand Duchy of Lithuania   6, 10, 192, 206, 244–45, 247–48, 261, 263–25, 270–72, 276, 282
Livonia, Livonian, Livs   8, 19–20, 34, 43–44, 44n47, 49, 54, 231–33, 233n8, 234–37, 240, 242, 244–47, 250–56, 280, 283
Livonian Rhymed Chronicle   193n9, 197
Lóegaire mac Néill, king of Tara and high king of Ireland (428–458)   82
Löffler, Annette   9, 266
Longinus, Roman soldier   214, 217, 217n84
Lot (biblical)   269
Louis of Wittelsbach, count Palatine of the Rhine, Holy Roman Emperor (1328–1347)   206
Low Countries   265
Lucas, Anthony T.   7, 88, 94
Luder von Braunschweig, grand master of the Teutonic Order (1331–1335)   207n61
Ludolf König of Weizzau, grand master of the Teutonic Order (1342–1345)   284
Lyndanisse / Tallinn / Reval   240–241
Łysa Góra (Bald Mountain) / Łysiec / Święty Krzyż   208

Mac Diarmata (dynasty of Magh Luirg)   89
Mac Mathúna Liam   86
Maccabees (Hasmonean dynasty)   74, 205, 212, 260, 262, 268, 270, 278
MacEvitt, Christopher   36
MacGregor, James   43
Maciejewski, Jacek   15
Madden, Thomas   49
Máedóc of Ferns (saint)   84
Mag Rath, battle of (637)   79
Magdeburg   237
Maghnus Ua Domnaill, hagiographer   80
Magnus Erlingsson, king of Norway (1161–1184)   117, 120, 125–127, 127n33, 129, 131, 131n55, 132–34, 136–37, 142–44, 147
Magnus IV Sigurdson/ the Blind, king of Norway (1130–1135)   122–25, 130, 141–42
Mainz   204

Malcolm III, king of Scotland (1058–1093) 178
Manthey, Jan 14
Margaret of Wessex (saint), Scottish queen (1070–1093) 178–79, 179n50
Margraviate of Brandenburg 206
Marienburg / Malbork, seat of the Teutonic Order 272
Maríusúð, ship 126–27, 131
Márkus, Gilbert 72
Martin, archbishop of Gniezno (d. 1115/1116) 209–10
Martin (saint), bishop of Tours 90, 90n84, 91, 92
Martin Luther 87
Mary Magdalene (saint, biblical) 205, 212, 214–16, 216n83
Mary of Bethany (biblical), sister of Lazarus 216, 216n83
mass against pagans (*missa contra paganos*) 5–6, 9, 78, 200, 275, 275n65, 276–77, 279–80
Matarana, Bartolomé, painter 39
Matathias, Jewish priest (biblical) 275
Matilda, Holy Roman Empress (1114–1125), claimant to the English throne (d. 1167) 105
Matthew the Evangelist 43
Maurice (saint) 214, 217n85
Maurice, abbot of Inchaffray, bishop of Dunblane (d. 1340s) 167, 169–70, 172
Mänd, Anu 43
McCormick, Michael 4–5, 12, 16, 77
McNamara, Martin 89
Meinhard, bishop of Livonia (1186–1196) 236, 246, 250, 252
Meissen 203
Melchizedek (biblical), king of Salem and priest of *El Elyon* 269
Memel / Klaipėda 277
Mercurius (saint) 217, 217n85
Michael, Archangel. *See* angel, angels, angelic: St. Michael, Archangel
Michael Küchmeister of Sternberg, grand master of Teutonic Order (1414–1422) 271
Milan 86
Military orders
　　Livonian Brother of the Sword / Livonian branch of Teutonic Order 53–54, 243–45, 254, 277
　　of Alcantara 52–53
　　of Aviz/Évora 51–53
　　of Calatrava 51–53
　　of the Hospital 51–53
　　of Montjoy/Monfrague 52
　　of Santiago 51–52
　　of the Temple 51–53, 118, 143
　　Teutonic Order (Order of Brothers of the German House of Saint Mary in Jerusalem) 8–9, 19–20, 35, 44, 51, 53–54, 192, 193n9, 195–196, 196n19, 197, 205, 205n55, 206, 206n59, 208n63, 217–18, 222, 260–62, 264, 267–72, 274–78, 280–82, 284–86
Miracula beati Egidii by Peter Guillaume 201
Mondorn, mount 82
Mongols, Mongol 34, 208, 210–11, 270
Moray, province of 171
Morkinskinna 141–42
Moroz, Irina 10
Morton, Nicholas 265
Moses (biblical), prophet and patriarch of Israel 74, 80, 83, 94, 102, 212–14, 262, 270
Muhu (island) 241
Muirchertach Ua Briain, king of Munster and high king of Ireland (1086–1119) 96
Muirchú moccu Machthéni (*Vita S. Patricii*) 82–83
Munster, Kingdom of, Munstermen 97, 106–7
Murray, Alan V. 122, 193n9, 263, 265
Muslims, Muslim 49, 55, 161, 216

Naderer, Max 19
Nakło, battle of (1109) 192, 208, 209n64
Nascimiento, Aires A. 32
Nedkvitne, Arnved 10
Nicholas (saint), bishop of Myra 198, 212, 215
Nicholas Arnesson, bishop of Oslo (1190–1225) 128n41, 131, 133, 138–40, 142, 144–46
Nicholson, Helen J. 264
Nickil, German knight 271–72
Nicolaus of Jeroschin, herald and chronicler 191–93, 193n9, 206–7, 207n61, 212, 219, 221–22, 222n98, 223, 267–68, 270–71

INDEX 307

Nidaros / Trondheim   120, 123, 125, 127,
    127*n*33, 133–34, 134*n*67, 136–37, 146
Nielsen, Torben Kjersgaard   8, 263
Ninian (saint), missionary   172, 178
Nithard, Frankish historian   203*n*50
Noah (biblical)   213–15
Normans, Norman   5, 7, 100, 102–4, 199*n*34,
    217*n*84
Norse. *See* Vikings
Northern Europe   3–4, 6, 9–11, 18–19, 37, 41,
    48, 264
Northumbria, Northumbrian   71–72, 99, 104
Norway, Norwegian, Norwegians   19, 117,
    120–21, 125, 127, 130, 134, 136–37, 141–42,
    142*n*96, 143–47, 178–79, 236, 238
Novgorod   277

Oder, river   206
Olaf (saint), king of Norway (d. 1030)
    123, 125–27, 127*n*33, 130, 130*n*49,
    131–32, 138
Óláfssúð, ship   126
omens, dreams, visions, prophetic signs
    (in connection with warfare)   191, 201,
    204, 207, 216–18, 218*n*88, 219–220,
    222–23, 278
Orning, Hans Jacob   120
Orygynale Cronikil of Scotland   178
Oslo, battle of (1197)   138, 140
Oswald of Northumbria, king of
    Northumbria (633–642)   73, 89
Otto of Friesing, bishop of Fiesing and
    chronicler   30
Ottonians (Saxon dynasty), Ottonian
    empire   5

pagan counter-ritual against baptism (using
    saunas and bathhouses)   251–54
pagans, pagan, paganism (*also* infidels,
    barbarians)   16, 93, 123–24, 128, 170, 197,
    206, 209*n*64, 217, 231–33, 242, 245*n*51,
    246–47, 249*n*66, 250–55, 261, 264, 277,
    280–82, 284
Palestine   236
Paravicini, Werner   282
Paris   47, 275*n*64
Passio Olavi   130
Pastów lands   261
Pater noster (*Our Father*)   130, 166*n*35, 169,
    196

Patrick (saint), missionary and bishop,
    patron of Ireland   71–72, 82–83, 88, 94,
    100
Penman, Michael   7
Persia   213
Peter, painter   272
Peter (saint), apostle   127, 214
Peter Bartholomew, preacher   217
Peter of Dusburg, chronicler   192, 193*n*9,
    206, 221, 222*n*98, 223, 267–269, 275,
    277–278, 280–281
Peter of York (saint)   98
Peter the Hermit (of Amiens), priest preacher
    and crusader   46, 220, 221*n*95
Peterson, David   41*n*34
Pezzarossa, Lucrezia   77
Philip I (of Alsace), count of Flanders
    (d. 1191)   194
Philip of Swabia, king of Germany
    (1198–1208)   237
Phillip the Bold, duke of Burgundy
    (1363–1404)   271
Piasts (Polish dynasty)   191
Picts, Pictish   71
Płock   34–35, 204
Poitiers   223
Poland, Poles, Polish   14–15, 56, 189, 199*n*33,
    206, 207*n*60, 208, 208*n*63, 209–10,
    263–64, 270–71
Policraticus. *See* John of Salisbury
Pomerania, Pomeranians, Pomeranian   192,
    201, 208–9
Pomerelia   206
Pomesania   267
Pontifical of Sens   280
Pontificale Romanum   278
Pontius Pilate, prefect of Judaea   213
portable altars. *See* tented chapels and/
    portable altars, use in war
Portugal, Portuguese   32–33, 48
Poznań   202
Praise of the New Knighthood. *See* Bernard of
    Clairvaux
prayers (in connection with war)   147, 194,
    199, 201, 222, 262, 278
    See also rites of war
    as thanksgiving / praise for victory   87,
        126, 128, 130–31, 133, 136, 197, 231
    before battle, combat and/or in war
        4–5, 10, 73, 78–81, 107, 117, 119, 128,

prayers (in connection with war) (*cont.*)
    132–33, 158, 167, 169, 171, 175, 178, 197,
    199–200, 210, 213, 231, 282
    See also rites of war: invocations of
    God/saints
  by the clergy (or lack thereof)   82–83,
    119–20, 139
    See also clergy, clerical order:
    chaplaincy and spiritual ministry
    to the army/rulers by
  for crusaders   194–95
  for forgiveness for sins and personal
    salvation   134–35, 200, 262
  for mercy, deliverance from the threat of
    death, protection, or safe return   132,
    166, 169, 176–177, 200, 210, 276
  for peace   5, 76
  for success in war by rulers' progenitors/
    relatives   73, 81, 128, 158
  for victory   5, 73, 80–81, 117, 120, 128, 135,
    154–55, 167, 178, 200, 262, 277
  in the Bible   74–76, 80
  in tent   78, 131
Provence, Provençal   199*n*34, 201–2, 217,
    217*n*84
Prussia, Prussians   8–9, 19–20, 54, 192, 203,
    207*n*61, 217, 260, 262, 265–70, 272,
    275–76, 278, 280–81, 284–85
Psalter   19, 75–76, 78, 81, 86, 88–90, 189
Pskov   244
Ptak, Jan   14
Purkis, William J.   37
Pyrenees   49

Quia maior, papal bull (1213)   194–95
Quierzy   203*n*50

Ragnit / Neman   205–6, 219, 261, 272,
    272*n*58, 277
Raimondo del Balzo Orsini, lay member of
    Teutonic Order   265, 265*n*19
Rainald of Toul, knight crusader   212
Ralph, Cistercian monk and preacher   47
Ralph Nowell (Radulf Novel), bishop of
    Orkney (d. ca. 1151)   101–2
Ralph of Caen, chaplain and writer
    (d. ca. 1120)   217*n*84
Ramla, battle of (1099)   43

Ramon Llull, theologian and scholar
    (d. 1315/1316)   198
Ratibor I (Racibor), duke of Pomerania
    (1135–1156)   123
Raupp, Lukas   122–23, 125
Raymond of Aguilers, chaplain and
    crusader   199*n*34, 217*n*84
Raymond of Poitiers, prince of Antioch
    (1136–1149)   194
Raymond of Roda, bishop of Roda-Bobastro
    (1076–1095)   40
Raymond IV of St. Gilles, count of
    Toulouse   199*n*34, 217
Re, battle at (1163)   128
Regulus / Rule (saint)   173
Reibnitz   272
Reinald, bishop of Stavanger (d. 1135)   123,
    125, 141
Renaut Porcet, crusader   216
Renfrew, battle of (1164)   180, 180*n*51
Rephidim (biblical), battle at   74, 80, 94, 262
Rhineland   47
Rhône, river   202
Richard of Chaumont, crusader   194*n*11,
    213–14
Rievaulx   101–2
Riga   240–41, 243, 243*n*42
Riley-Smith, Jonathan   46*n*58
rites of war (generally)   163–64, 168, 171, 181,
    233, 244, 263, 266, 270
  See also prayers (in connection with
    war); *signa victricia* (victory-bringing
    objects, war talismans)
  almsgiving   78, 81, 97, 158, 176, 195
  battle cries   118–19, 128, 131
  (pre-)battle speeches, sermons and
    exhortations   74, 77, 86–87, 101–7,
    125–26, 133–35, 139, 160–61, 165, 165*n*33,
    167, 171–72, 199, 209, 243, 255, 282–83,
    286
  (pre-)battle / before fighting religious
    rites   6, 107, 128, 131, 168, 181, 199–200,
    221*n*96, 143*n*42, 243*n*45
  blessing the arms/banners   6, 16, 100, 119,
    123, 181, 278–79
  blessing, clerical, before/during war to
    rulers/soldiers   3, 79, 103, 164*n*29, 181,
    243, 255, 278–79

INDEX

rites of war (generally) (*cont.*)
  carrying or using: relics, crosses, holy banners/standards   7, 9, 15, 19, 38–39, 42–44, 74, 87–89, 91–94, 96–101, 104, 107, 122–23, 125–27, 147, 155, 158*n*16, 164*n*29, 167, 172, 173*n*42, 175–76, 176*n*45, 180–81, 181*n*55, 199, 234, 248, 255, 272
    See also signa victricia (victory-bringing objects, war talismans); clergy, clerical order: chaplaincy and spiritual ministry to the army/ruler
  celebrating victory, return, *adventus/triumphus*   129
  chivalric   204–10, 212–21, 223
  confession and absolution/indulgence   5, 78, 81, 101, 103, 117, 119, 134, 154, 164*n*29, 165–69, 181, 200, 200*n*35, 201, 222, 237–38, 240
    See also clergy, clerical order: chaplaincy and spiritual ministry to the army/ruler
  crusading (characteristic of the crusades)   123, 131–32, 235
  crusading as armed pilgrimages   235, 237, 240
  cursing the enemy   76, 79–80, 82, 97, 100, 103
    See also excommunication
  depositing booty and/or captured banners in churches   155
  devotion / worship before and/or in war (or lack thereof)   10, 78, 81, 158, 199–200
  fasting   19, 74, 76, 78, 80–81, 154, 160, 165, 176, 181, 195, 201
  funerary / mourning   119, 155, 231, 249–50
  gestures (walking barefoot, rising hands, handshake, shaking spears)   78, 80, 167, 170, 170*n*41, 171, 201
  girding with a sword, knighting, becoming knight   203, 203*n*50, 204, 204*n*53, 222
  hoisting a (holy) banner as a sign of a conquest/subjugation to Christianity   248
  Holy Communion/Eucharist/*viaticum*, taking of   10, 81, 117, 154, 165–66, 168–69, 176, 181, 200, 222
    See also clergy, clerical order: chaplaincy and spiritual ministry to the army/ruler
  Holy Mass on the battlefield or on the way to it   39, 78, 117, 131, 154, 164*n*29, 165–69, 181, 199–200, 209, 231, 243, 245, 255, 270, 272, 275, 283–85
    See also clergy, clerical order: chaplaincy and spiritual ministry to the army/ruler
  invocations of God/saints   7, 76, 83, 86–87, 93, 97, 107, 120–21, 126, 131–32, 139, 155, 158, 161, 166, 169, 173, 176–78, 197, 201, 209, 213–16, 222–23, 279
  kissing churches   19, 132–36, 147
  liturgy of war (liturgical prayers)   6, 16, 19, 31–32, 35–36, 71, 77, 169, 200, 278–79, 286
  oaths on relics   98
  penitential   10, 131, 200, 235
  pilgrimages to, and/or visits in churches before/after war   158
  pouring tears, weeping, expression of grief   12, 208
  pre-Christian / pagan / magic   17, 85–86, 128, 128*n*41, 129–30, 141, 147, 197*n*27, 203, 232, 242, 244–47
  processions   19, 32, 74, 78, 94, 195, 201, 275
  profectio bellica (departure and march for war)   10–11, 15, 35
  propagandistic role of   74
  prostration / *proskynesis* / bowing down / kneeling in front of holy icon/person/relic or just on the ground, before going to war   165–71, 181, 213
  psalm litanies, psalmsinging or recitation   74, 76–79, 81–84, 101, 107, 131, 194, 199
  ringing of bells (or sound of bells)   79
  singing religious chants   128, 248*n*65, 275
    See also Kyrie eleison (*Lord, have mercy*), *Te deum Laudamus* (*We praise thee, O God*)

rites of war (*cont.*)
    sprinkling holy water on the host before battle   79
    submission to victors   208
    taking the cross by crusaders   35–36, 190*n*3, 203, 217, 231, 233, 235, 237, 240, 255
    taking vows to God/saints, if granted victory/success   128, 130–31, 168*n*38
    thanksgiving for victory   155, 248
    votive donations and/or foundations   119, 127, 158, 172, 177, 180, 248
    votive masses in times of war / home front   261, 262*n*9, 275–77, 282
Robert I / the Bruce, king of Scotland (1306–1329)   157, 160–62, 162*n*25, 163, 165–66, 166*n*34, 167, 168*n*38, 171–73, 177*n*48, 178–80
Robert Baston, Carmelite friar and poet   168*n*38
Robert of Clari, knight and chronicler   42
Robert II, Count of Flanders, crusader   199*n*34
Robert of Rheims, chronicler   199n34
Robert Wishart, bishop of Glasgow (1271–1316)   180
Rodrigo Álvarez, Galician nobleman and crusader   52
Rodrigo Diaz de Vivar (El Cid), Castilian knight, prince of Valencia (1094–1099)   55
Rodrigo Jiménez de Rada, archbishop of Toledo (1208–1247)   38–39
Roman Empire (Eastern, Byzantine)   5, 11, 11*n*32, 12, 15, 131
Roman Empire (Western, medieval), Holy Roman Empire   36
Romans   170
Rome   50, 195, 221, 234–35, 277
Rónán Finn (saint)   79
Roslin, battle of (1303)   178
Rubenstein, Jay   46
Rudau / Melnikovo, battle of (1370)   276
Ruiz de Camargo Pedro, painter   38
Rurikids (Rusian dynasty)   11
Rus, Rusians, Rusian   3, 10, 10*n*29, 10, 11, 15, 34, 244
Russia, Russians   3, 10, 263

Saaremaa / Øsel / Ösel, island   238, 241
sacrilege   126
Saladin, sultan of Egypt and Syria (1174–1193)   195*n*16
Salian dynasty or empire   5
Salomon (biblical), king of Israel   213, 284
Samogitia   274
Sandomierz   208, 210
Santarem, the conquest of (1147)   32, 48
Santiago de Compostela   157
Saracens   215
Sarnowsky, Jürgen   264
Sartowice   206
Sathanas, dragon, devil   205–6, 213–14, 219–20
Saul (biblical), king of Israel   212, 278
Sayers, William   86
Scalacronica   156
Scandinavia, Scandinavian   10, 19, 50, 74, 104, 238–40
Scannal of the Eóganachta   97
Scotichronicon   157, 162–63, 166–68, 170, 173, 177–78, 180
Scotland (*also* Alba), Scots, Scottish   3, 7, 10, 19, 71, 74, 81, 89, 91–92, 99, 103, 105, 105*n*151, 153, 156–58, 158*n*16, 159–65, 166*n*34, 167, 168*n*38, 169–76, 176*n*45, 177–79, 179*n*50, 180–82
Sebastian (saint)   205
Segeberg (village)   198*n*28
Selart, Anti   34, 263
Semgallia, Semgallians   244, 251
Shaw, John   86
Sicily   43
Sieciech, Bolesław III's cupbearer   201, 221
Siegfried of Feuchtwangen, grand master of the Teutonic Order (1303–1311)   271
signa victricia (victory-bringing objects, war talismans)   74, 88, 91, 94, 96–99, 123, 175–76, 278
    Ark of the Covenant (biblical)   74, 83, 88–89, 94, 98, 103, 270, 279
    Black Rood of Scotland   179*n*50
    Cross of Cong   94–96
    Cross of Neith / Croes Naid, holy cross of the Welsh   179
    Mada Ciaráin (Staff of Ciarán)   96
    Monymusk Reliquary   92, 175

signa victricia (*cont.*)
    Rood of Bromholm, forged relic   42–43, 43*n*4
    sign of the cross   212, 214, 219, 223, 238–39, 242
    St. Columba's *Brecbennach*   92, 101, 175, 176*n*45
    St. Columba's *Cathach* ("The Battler") 88–91, 93, 101
    St. Columba's crozier   81, 91, 176
    St. Martin's cape   91–92
    St. Olaf's banner   127*n*33
    St. Patrick's staff or crozier   94, 96–97, 100
    True Cross, relics of   42, 95–96, 104, 122–25, 142, 179*n*50
Sigurd af Reyri, Norwegian jarl   128
Sigurd Magnusson / Jórsalafari, king of Norway (1103–1130)   122–23, 125
Sigurd Nikolásson   133
Sion, castle in Nidaros   127, 140, 145
Skarbimir, count palatine of Polish prince   209
Skwierczyński, Krzysztof   43
Slavs, Slavic   6, 17, 198*n*28, 249*n*66
Smith, Katherine A.   47–48
Sodom (biblical)   269
Sogn (territory in Vestland)   126
Soiscéla Martain (*The Gospel of Martin*)   89, 90*n*84, 91, 99, 100
Sójka, Jerzy   14
Somerled of Argyll, king of the Isles (1158–1164)   180, 180*n*51
Sorgalé and Goliath, Turkish champions   213
Spain, Spanish   38, 221*n*95, 236, 265
Speech against the bishops   138, 144*n*96, 146
St Andrews   171, 173
St. Cuthbert Gospel   90*n*84, 99*n*124
Staffordshire Hoard   83, 98
Standard (at Northallerton), battle of the (1138)   7, 98, 101–7
standard-bearers (miraculous)   131, 217
standard-bearers (real, lay/clerical)   15, 96, 158*n*16
Stephen (deacon, saint)   205
Stephen of Blois, king of England (1135–1154)   99, 105, 194

St-Pol family   194
Stephen Henry, count of Blois and Chartres (d. 1102)   199*n*34
Stephen of Ripon, writer   73
Stirling, castle   157, 172
    battle of   174
Strebe / Streva, river, battle at (1348)   282
Súaltaim, father of Cú Chulainn   85, 87
Suibne mac Colmáin, king of Dál nAraidi   79
Summa Theologiae. *See* Thomas Aquinas, theologian   169
Sunnifa (saint)   131
Susanna (biblical)   214
Sverre Sigurdsson, king of Norway (1184–1202)   117, 125–26, 127*n*33, 128*n*41, 129, 130*n*49, 131, 131*n*55, 132–35, 136*n*71, 136–40, 142, 142*n*96, 143–44, 146–47
Sverris saga   129, 130*n*49, 132–34, 138, 140, 142–46
    Grýla, the first part of   131*n*55, 140*n*91
Sweden, Swedish   234, 238, 240–41
Świętopełk II the Great, duke of East Pomerania (1215–1266)   206, 217
Syria   236

Táin Bó Cuailnge (*The Cattle-raid of Cooley*), saga   84–85, 87, 93
Tairdelbach Ua Conchobair, king of Connacht (1106–1156)   95
Talibald, Liv   254
Tamm, Marek   263
Tancred de Hauteville, prince of Galilee (1099–1101, 1109–1112)   217*n*84
Tatars. *See* Mongols, Mongol
Tczew   271
Te Deum laudamus (*We praise thee, O God*), chant   212
tented chapels and portable altars, use in war   169, 270–72, 274, 284, 286
Teutonic Order. *See* Military orders: Teutonic Order
Teutonic Order's Rule   268–70, 278, 283–84, 286
Tigris, mount   213
Thacker, Alan   7
Theodoric, Cistercian monk   246
Theodoricus Monachus, chronicler   141*n*94

Thomas Aquinas, theologian   169
Thomas Becket (saint), archbishop of Canterbury (1162–1170)   41, 41*n*37, 158, 167, 171–74
Thomas Gray (or Grey) of Heton, chronicler   156
Thomas Randolph, earl of Moray   174
Thompson, Augustine   49
Thurstan of Bayeux, archbishop of York (1114–1140)   98–99, 101–3
Tilo of Lorich, komtur of Elbing / Elbląg   272–73
Toledo   38
Treiden   246
Turks, Turkish   213, 217, 270, 277
Turpie, Tom   177*n*48

Uí Briain (dynasty of Munster)   81
Uí Chennselaig (south Leinster dynasty)   106
Uí Domnaill (dynasty of the Northern Uí Néill lineage of Cenél Conaill)   89
Uí Néill (Irish dynasty)   88, 91, 94, 96–97, 106
Ukraine   3, 10
Ulaid, Kingdom of   85, 87, 100
Ulster (territory in Ireland)   100
Ulster Cycle   84
Undusk, Jann   34
Uniejów   268
Urban II, pope (1088–1099)   221
Urban V, pope (1362–1370)   284
Üxküll / Üksküla / Ikšķile   240, 250

Valdemar II, king of Denmark (1202–1241)   241
Venice   49
Veszprémy, László   12
Vicelin, bishop of Starigard / Oldenburg (1149–1154)   198
Vikings, Norse   74, 78, 80–81, 91, 98–99, 138, 176–77
Vincentius of Cracow / Master Vincentius / Kadłubek, bishop of Cracow and chronicler   209*n*64
Virgin Mary (saint), Marian   34–35, 37–40, 43–44, 44*n*47, 54, 126–27, 130*n*49, 131, 168*n*38, 170, 192, 196–97, 200, 204–5, 205*n*55, 206, 212–15, 217–18, 218*n*88, 233, 233*n*8, 234, 248, 251, 255, 261, 272, 274, 276, 281–82
Visby   237–38
Vita S. Columbae   72–73, 89, 176
Vita S. Declani   93
Vita Edwardi Secundi   156–57, 159, 167*n*37
Vita S. Guthlaci   83
Vita S. Patricii. *See* Jocelin of Furness, hagiographer
Vukovich, Alexandra   10–11

Walachians   270
Wales   179*n*50
Walter Bower, chronicler   157, 162–63, 165–75, 177–81
Walter Espec, high sheriff of Yorkshire   101–4, 106
war, fighting (*also* ideology of)
  against Christian enemies   37, 134
  against pagans/unbelievers/heretics/schismatics/rebels/"bad Christians"   82, 123–25, 131, 161, 231, 237–39, 278, 282, 284
  as a holy vengeance   238
  as a medium of baptism and Christianization / missionary   232, 233, 244, 248, 251
  as God's judgement   155, 162
  holy war (*also* religious war and God's war), rhetoric and/or idea of   32, 35, 81, 98, 119–121, 144, 146, 190, 231–232, 234–237, 248, 255, 263, 279
    See also crusades
  just, just cause in, righteous, concepts of   31, 155, 161, 163
  sacralization / "religionization" of   262, 267, 269, 282, 284, 286
warrior-saints   43, 91, 122*n*17
Warsaw / Warszawa   268, 273
weapons/armor, clerical, spiritual, idea of   145, 147
Wenceslas (saint), prince of Bohemia (921–929)   12
Wenceslas IV, king of Bohemia (1378–1419), king of Germany (1376–1400)   281–82
Wends, Wendish   123, 125
  see also Slavs, Slavic
Wenta, Jarosław   8, 269

INDEX

Werner of Tettingen, marshal of the Teutonic Order   281
Western Europe, Latin West   5, 9–10, 15–16, 46, 74, 198, 204, 216, 235, 285
Wigand of Baldersheim, commander of Ragnit castle   261
Wigand of Marburg, Herald and chronicler   8*n*21, 205*n*55, 261, 267, 270, 274*n*58, 283, 285
Wilfrid of Ripon (saint)   98
Wilfrid of York (saint), bishop of York (664–678)   73
William (saint)   158
William of Newburgh, chronicler   128*n*41, 129
William of Tyre, chronicler   190*n*3, 199n34, 220
William Rishanger, annalist   156
William the Marshal, English knight   201–2
William I / the Conqueror, prince of Normandy (1035–1087), king of England (1066–1087)   7, 98
William I / the Lion, king of Scotland (1165–1214)   174–75
William I of Sicily / the Bad, king of Sicily (1154–1166)   43

Wilson, Jonathan   32, 48
Winrich of Kniprode, grand master of the Teutonic Order (1351–1382)   261, 284
Wisła / Vistula, river   208
Władysław Herman, Polish prince (1079–1102)   204
Władysław I / the Elbow (Łokietek), Polish prince and king of Poland (1320–1333)   206, 271
Władysław II Jagiełło / Jogaila, grand duke of Lithuania (1377–1381, 1382–1434), king of Poland (1386–1434)   264, 273
Wrocław   16, 210–11, 261
Wulfstan II of York, bishop of London (996–1002), bishop of Worcester (1002–1016), archbishop of York (1002–1023)   78
Wüst, Marcus   269

York   102

Zbigniew, prince of Poland (1102–1107)   191
Żmudzki, Paweł   17
Zonenberg, Sławomir   262*n*9
Zupka, Dušan   13, 44, 279

Printed in the United States
by Baker & Taylor Publisher Services